Nissan Rogue Automotive Repair Manual

by Jeff Killingsworth
and John H Haynes
Member of the Guild of Motoring Writers

Models covered:

Nissan Rogue - 2008 through 2020
Nissan Rogue Select - 2014 and 2015
Does not include information specific to Sport or hybrid models

Haynes Group Limited
Sparkford Nr Yeovil
Somerset BA22 7JJ England

(72042-2Y3)

ABCDE
FGHIJ
K

Haynes North America, Inc.
2801 Townsgate Road, Suite 340
Thousand Oaks, CA 91361 USA

www.haynes.com

Disclaimer

There are risks associated with automotive repairs. The ability to make repairs depends on the individual's skill, experience and proper tools. Individuals should act with due care and acknowledge and assume the risk of performing automotive repairs.

The purpose of this manual is to provide comprehensive, useful and accessible automotive repair information, to help you get the best value from your vehicle. However, this manual is not a substitute for a professional certified technician or mechanic.

This repair manual is produced by a third party and is not associated with an individual vehicle manufacturer. If there is any doubt or discrepancy between this manual and the owner's manual or the factory service manual, please refer to the factory service manual or seek assistance from a professional certified technician or mechanic.

Even though we have prepared this manual with extreme care and every attempt is made to ensure that the information in this manual is correct, neither the publisher nor the author can accept responsibility for loss, damage or injury caused by any errors in, or omissions from, the information given.

© Haynes North America, Inc. 2015, 2020
With permission from Haynes Group Limited

A book in the Haynes Automotive Repair Manual Series

Printed in India

All rights reserved. No part of this book may be reproduced or transmitted in any form or by any means, electronic or mechanical, including photocopying, recording or by any information storage or retrieval system, without permission in writing from the copyright holder.

ISBN-10: 1-62092-390-4
ISBN-13: 978-1-62092-390-0

Library of Congress Control Number: 2020934047

While every attempt is made to ensure that the information in this manual is correct, no liability can be accepted by the authors or publishers for loss, damage or injury caused by any errors in, or omissions from, the information given.

20-272

Contents

Haynes photographer and mechanic with a 2013 Nissan Rogue

About this manual

Its purpose

The purpose of this manual is to help you get the best value from your vehicle. It can do so in several ways. It can help you decide what work must be done, even if you choose to have it done by a dealer service department or a repair shop; it provides information and procedures for routine maintenance and servicing; and it offers diagnostic and repair procedures to follow when trouble occurs.

We hope you use the manual to tackle the work yourself. For many simpler jobs, doing it yourself may be quicker than arranging an appointment to get the vehicle into a shop and making the trips to leave it and pick it up. More importantly, a lot of money can be saved by avoiding the expense the shop must pass on to you to cover its labor and overhead costs. An added benefit is the sense of satisfaction and accomplishment that you feel after doing the job yourself.

Using the manual

The manual is divided into Chapters. Each Chapter is divided into numbered Sections, which are headed in bold type between horizontal lines. Each Section consists of consecutively numbered paragraphs.

The reference numbers used in illustration captions pinpoint the pertinent Section and the Step within that Section. That is, illustration 3.2 means the illustration refers to Section 3 and Step (or paragraph) 2 within that Section.

Procedures, once described in the text, are not normally repeated. When it's necessary to refer to another Chapter, the reference will be given as Chapter and Section number. Cross references given without use of the word "Chapter" apply to Sections and/or paragraphs in the same Chapter. For example, "see Section 8" means in the same Chapter.

References to the left or right side of the vehicle assume you are sitting in the driver's seat, facing forward.

Even though we have prepared this manual with extreme care, neither the publisher nor the author can accept responsibility for any errors in, or omissions from, the information given.

NOTE

A **Note** provides information necessary to properly complete a procedure or information which will make the procedure easier to understand.

CAUTION

A **Caution** provides a special procedure or special steps which must be taken while completing the procedure where the Caution is found. Not heeding a Caution can result in damage to the assembly being worked on.

WARNING

A **Warning** provides a special procedure or special steps which must be taken while completing the procedure where the Warning is found. Not heeding a Warning can result in personal injury.

Introduction

The Nissan Rogue is available as a four-door sport utility body style only.

The transversely mounted 2.5L four-cylinder engine used in these models is equipped with a sequential multi-port electronic fuel injection system.

The engine transmits power to the front wheels through a continuously variable automatic transaxle (CVT) via independent driveaxles.

On AWD models, the rear wheels are also propelled by way of a transfer case, driveshaft, rear differential and two rear driveaxles.

The Rogue has a steel uni-body structure and four-wheel independent suspension. The rack-and-pinion steering unit is mounted behind the engine. A small electric motor and control unit (EPS) is mounted to the steering column to provide the power assist as standard equipment.

All models are equipped with power assisted front and rear disc brakes. An anti-lock braking system is standard equipment on all models.

Vehicle identification numbers

Modifications are a continuing and unpublicized process in vehicle manufacturing. Since spare parts manuals and lists are compiled on a numerical basis, the individual vehicle numbers are essential to correctly identify the component required.

Vehicle Identification Number (VIN)

This very important identification number is located on a plate attached to the dashboard inside the windshield on the driver's side of the vehicle (see illustration) . The VIN also appears on the Vehicle Certificate of Title and Registration. It contains information such as where and when the vehicle was manufactured, the model year and the body style.

VIN engine and model year codes

Two particularly important pieces of information found in the VIN are the engine code and the model year code. Counting from the left, the engine code letter designation is the 4th character and the model year code designation is the 10th character.

On the models covered by this manual the engine code is

QR25DE 2.5L DOHC

On the models covered by this manual the model year codes are:

8 2008
9 2009
A 2010
B 2011
C 2012
D 2013
E 2014
F 2015
G 2016
H 2017
J 2018
K 2019
L 2020

Manufacturer's Certification Regulation label

The manufacturer's Certification Regulation label is attached to the driver's side door post (see illustration) . The label contains the name of the manufacturer, the month and year of production, the Gross Vehicle Weight Rating (GVWR), the Gross Axle Weight Rating (GAWR) and the certification statement.

Engine identification number

The engine code number can be found on a pad on the front (radiator) side of the cylinder block, near the transaxle (see illustration).

Transaxle identification number

The transaxle identification number is stamped on top of the bellhousing (see illustration).

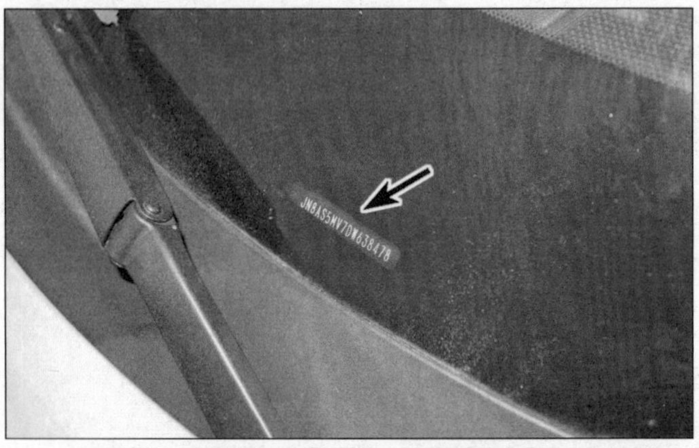

The Vehicle Identification Number (VIN) is visible through the driver's side of the windshield

The Manufacturer's Certification label is affixed to the driver's side door post

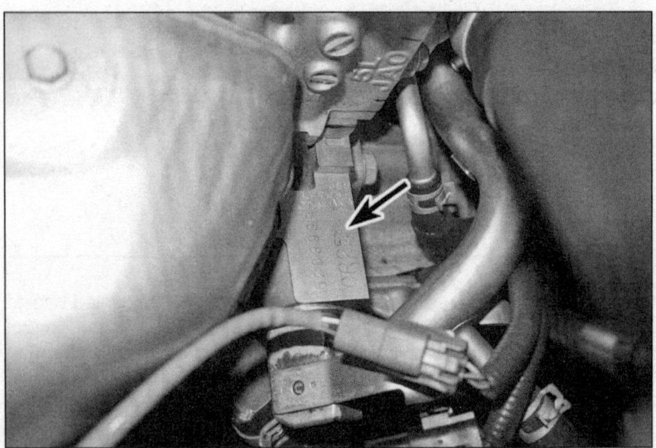

The Engine Identification Number is stamped on the front side of the engine block, near the transaxle

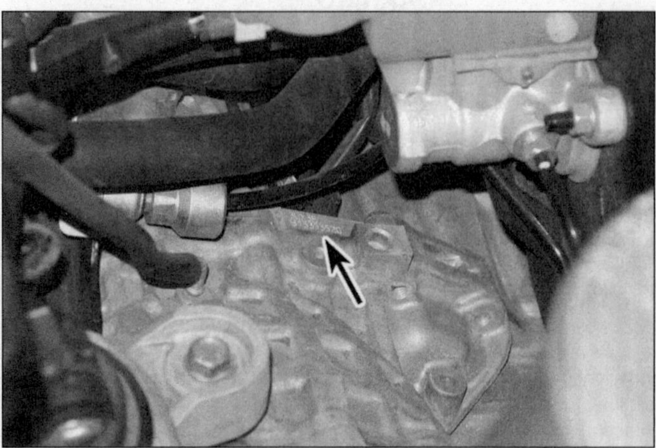

The CVT transaxle ID number is located on top of the transaxle bellhousing

Vehicle Emissions Control Information (VECI) label

The emissions control information label is found on the underside of the hood. This label contains information on the emissions control equipment installed on the vehicle (see illustration).

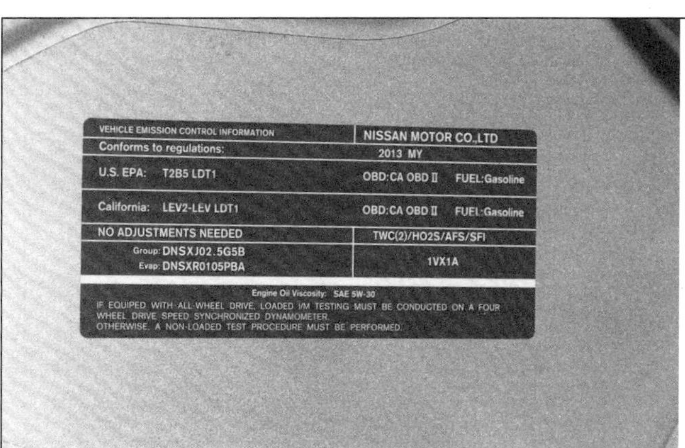

The Vehicle Emissions Control Information (VECI) label is located on the underside of the hood

Recall information

Vehicle recalls are carried out by the manufacturer in the rare event of a possible safety-related defect. The vehicle's registered owner is contacted at the address on file at the Department of Motor Vehicles and given the details of the recall. Remedial work is carried out free of charge at a dealer service department.

If you are the new owner of a used vehicle which was subject to a recall and you want to be sure that the work has been carried out, it's best to contact a dealer service department and ask about your individual vehicle - you'll need to furnish them your Vehicle Identification Number (VIN).

The table below is based on information provided by the National Highway Traffic Safety Administration (NHTSA), the body which oversees vehicle recalls in the United States. The recall database is updated constantly. For the latest information on vehicle recalls, check the NHTSA website at www.nhtsa.gov, www.safercar.gov, or call the NHTSA hotline at 1-888-327-4236.

Recall date	Recall campaign number	Model(s) affected	Concern
OCT 08, 2008	08V521000	2008 Rogue	On some models equipped with Continental Automotive Systems' Occupant Classification System (OCS) control units, a resistor in the OCS control unit located in the passenger seat cushion may have been manufactured out of specification. Under certain conditions, this could cause an interruption of signal between the OCS and the airbag control unit (ACU). This could result in the passenger airbag being suppressed which could fail to provide adequate protection in the event of a crash.
OCT 05, 2009	09V393000	2008, 2009, 2010 Rogue	On some models, the material in the nut used to secure the sensor-transmitter of the tire pressure monitoring system (TPMS) may corrode and potentially crack in areas with heavy concentrations of road salt. If this occurs, the nut may come out of the sensor-transmitter and the TPMS lamp will illuminate. If the TPMS lamp is disregarded and the vehicle continues to be driven in this condition, the tire will quickly lose air pressure at a consistent rate resulting in a flat tire, increasing the risk of a crash.

Recall date	Recall campaign number	Model(s) affected	Concern
OCT 19, 2009	09V411000	2008, 2009 Rogue	On some models, a screw in the steering gearhousing cover may loosen over time and could fall out. As it loosens, the steering response of the vehicle may be compromised but the driver will retain steering control. The screw may eventually come out of the steering gear cover.If large steering inputs are made with the cover screw missing, the pinion shaft may come out of the steering gear, resulting in a complete loss of steering control and increasing the risk of a crash.
SEPT 10, 2010	10V401000	2008, 2009, 2010 Rogue	On certain models equipped with a Garmin Nuvi model 750 navigation system, the batteries contained in the affected GPS units can overheat. Overheated batteries could result in a fire.
NOV 23, 2011	11V565000	2011 Rogue	On some models, the circuit board may not have been installed in the correct position on certain electric power steering (EPS) assist control units. This may cause additional stress on the solder of the terminal to the circuit board resulting in the solder cracking and separating completely from the circuit board. As the circuit board fails, the power steering assist feature will stop functioning, increasing the force needed to steer the vehicle and increasing the risk of a crash.
FEB 22, 2012	12V068000	2012 Rogue	On some models, the tire pressure monitoring system (TPMS) was not activated. A non-active TPMS cannot warn a driver that a tire is under-inflated. Underinflated tires can result in tire overloading and overheating, which could lead to a blowout and possible crash.
APR 28, 2014	14V218000	2014 Rogue	On some models, an incorrect bolt may have been used to connect the intermediate shaft to the steering column. The incorrect bolts could loosen and fall out resulting in a loss of vehicle control and increasing the risk of a crash.
MAY 02, 2014	14V229000	2014 Rogue	On some models, the right side wheels of the affected vehicles may have one lug nut each that was not properly tightened. If the lug nut becomes loose from not being properly tightened, it may fall off, allowing the other lug nuts to become loose, possibly resulting in a wheel separation, and increasing the risk of a crash.
JAN 14, 2015	15V012000	2014, 2015 Rogue	On some models, during the assembly process, the front wheel hub assembly fasteners may not have been properly torqued. The under-torqued fasteners may result in a brake caliper separating from the wheel assembly causing a reduction in braking performance or reduced steering control. These conditions increase the risk of a crash.

Recall date	Recall campaign number	Model(s) affected	Concern
JAN 26, 2015	15V032000	2008, 2009, 2010, 2011, 2012, 2013, 2014, 2015 Rogue	Some models may experience an electrical short in the harness connector due to a mixture of snow/water and salt seeping through the carpet on the driver side floor near the harness connector. An electrical short can cause a vehicle fire.
APR 03, 2015	15V197000	2014 Rogue	On some models, an improper nickel plating of components within the fuel pump may result in the fuel pump failing. If the fuel pump fails, the vehicle may stall, increasing the risk of a crash.
JUNE 12, 2015	15V368000	2015 Rogue	Some models have the incorrect tire size information on the tire labels. Installing tires of the incorrect size may increase the risk of a crash.
JULY 21, 2015	15V453000	2015 Rogue	On some models, the driver side front and rear doors may not fully latch. A door that does not fully latch may result in the door opening while the car is moving. The distraction may increase the risk of a crash and/or a vehicle occupant may fall out of the vehicle if they are not wearing a seatbelt, increasing their risk of injury.
NOV 20, 2015	15V775000	2014 Rogue	On some models, due to a problem with the shift selector knob, it may be possible to shift out of the "Park" position without depressing the brake pedal. If the shift selector can be moved out of the "Park" position while the brake pedal is not depressed, the vehicle may unexpectedly roll, increasing the risk of a crash.
MAR 11, 2016	16V149000	2014 Rogue	On some models, improper nickel plating of components within the fuel pump may result in the fuel pump failing. If the fuel pump fails, the vehicle may stall, increasing the risk of a crash.
APR 15, 2016	16V219000	2014, 2015, 2016 Rogue	On some models, the rear liftgate support stays may corrode due to insufficient anti-corrosion treatment. Corrosion of one or both of the rear lift gate support stays could cause a sudden release if pressure. If this occurs, the support stays may break off, increasing the risk of injury.
APR 26, 2016	16V244000	2014, 2015, 2016, 2017 Rogue	On some models, the front seat passenger Occupant Classification System (OCS) may incorrectly classify an adult passenger as a child or classify the seat as empty despite it being occupied. As a result, the passenger frontal airbag may be turned off and not deploy in the event of a crash. If the passenger frontal airbag does not deploy as intended in the event of a crash, the passenger is at an increased risk of injury.

Recall date	Recall campaign number	Model(s) affected	Concern
DEC 16, 2016	16V911000	2015, 2016 Rogue	On some models, an incorrect Occupant Classification System (OCS) Electronic Control Unit (ECU) may have been installed in the front passenger seat. The incorrect ECU and seat combination may misclassify the front passenger seat occupant. If the front passenger seat occupant is misclassified, the airbag may deploy incorrectly in the event of a crash, increasing the risk of injury
OCT 18, 2017	17V663000	2016, 2017 Rogue	On some models, the recliner joints on the lower seat frame for the rear seats may have improper welds. The insufficient welds can increase the risk of injury to the occupants in the event of a crash.
NOV 14, 2017	17V716000	2016 Rogue	On some models, the front passenger seat frames may be improperly welded. In the event of a crash, the improperly welded seat back frames may increase the risk of injury.
SEP 12, 2019	19V654000	2018, 2019 Rogue	On some models, the back-up camera and display settings can be adjusted such that the rear view image is no longer visible and the system will retain that setting the next time the vehicle is placed in Reverse. The lack of an image in the back-up camera display increases the risk of a crash.

Buying parts

Replacement parts are available from many sources, which generally fall into one of two categories - authorized dealer parts departments and independent retail auto parts stores. Our advice concerning these parts is as follows:

Retail auto parts stores: Good auto parts stores will stock frequently needed components which wear out relatively fast, such as clutch components, exhaust systems, brake parts, tune-up parts, etc. These stores often supply new or reconditioned parts on an exchange basis, which can save a considerable amount of money. Discount auto parts stores are often very good places to buy materials and parts needed for general vehicle maintenance such as oil, grease, filters, spark plugs, belts, touch-up paint, bulbs, etc. They also usually sell tools and general accessories, have convenient hours, charge lower prices and can often be found not far from home.

Authorized dealer parts department: This is the best source for parts which are unique to the vehicle and not generally available elsewhere (such as major engine parts, transmission parts, trim pieces, etc.).

Warranty information: If the vehicle is still covered under warranty, be sure that any replacement parts purchased - regardless of the source - do not invalidate the warranty!

To be sure of obtaining the correct parts, have engine and chassis numbers available and, if possible, take the old parts along for positive identification.

Maintenance techniques, tools and working facilities

Maintenance techniques

There are a number of techniques involved in maintenance and repair that will be referred to throughout this manual. Application of these techniques will enable the home mechanic to be more efficient, better organized and capable of performing the various tasks properly, which will ensure that the repair job is thorough and complete.

Fasteners

Fasteners are nuts, bolts, studs and screws used to hold two or more parts together. There are a few things to keep in mind when working with fasteners. Almost all of them use a locking device of some type, either a lockwasher, locknut, locking tab or thread adhesive. All threaded fasteners should be clean and straight, with undamaged threads and undamaged corners on the hex head where the wrench fits. Develop the habit of replacing all damaged nuts and bolts with new ones. Special locknuts with nylon or fiber inserts can only be used once. If they are removed, they lose their locking ability and must be replaced with new ones.

Rusted nuts and bolts should be treated with a penetrating fluid to ease removal and prevent breakage. Some mechanics use turpentine in a spout-type oil can, which works quite well. After applying the rust penetrant, let it work for a few minutes before trying to loosen the nut or bolt. Badly rusted fasteners may have to be chiseled or sawed off or removed with a special nut breaker, available at tool stores.

If a bolt or stud breaks off in an assembly, it can be drilled and removed with a special tool commonly available for this purpose. Most automotive machine shops can perform this task, as well as other repair procedures, such as the repair of threaded holes that have been stripped out.

Flat washers and lockwashers, when removed from an assembly, should always be replaced exactly as removed. Replace any damaged washers with new ones. Never use a lockwasher on any soft metal surface (such as aluminum), thin sheet metal or plastic.

Fastener sizes

For a number of reasons, automobile manufacturers are making wider and wider use of metric fasteners. Therefore, it is important to be able to tell the difference between standard (sometimes called U.S. or SAE) and metric hardware, since they cannot be interchanged.

All bolts, whether standard or metric, are sized according to diameter, thread pitch and length. For example, a standard 1/2 - 13 x 1 bolt is 1/2 inch in diameter, has 13 threads per inch and is 1 inch long. An M12 - 1.75 x 25 metric bolt is 12 mm in diameter, has a thread pitch of 1.75 mm (the distance between threads) and is 25 mm long. The two bolts are nearly identical, and easily confused, but they are not interchangeable.

In addition to the differences in diameter, thread pitch and length, metric and standard bolts can also be distinguished by examining the bolt heads. To begin with, the distance across the flats on a standard bolt head is measured in inches, while the same dimension on a metric bolt is sized in millimeters (the same is true for nuts). As a result, a standard wrench should not be used on a metric bolt and a metric wrench should not be used on a standard bolt. Also, most standard bolts have slashes radiating out from the center of the head to denote the grade or strength of the bolt, which is an indication of the amount of torque that can be applied to it. The greater the number of slashes, the greater the strength of the bolt. Grades 0 through 5 are commonly used on automobiles. Metric bolts have a property class (grade) number, rather than a slash, molded into their heads to indicate bolt strength. In this case, the higher the number, the stronger the bolt. Property class numbers 8.8, 9.8 and 10.9 are commonly used on automobiles.

Strength markings can also be used to distinguish standard hex nuts from metric hex nuts. Many standard nuts have dots stamped into one side, while metric nuts are marked with a number. The greater the number of dots, or the higher the number, the greater the strength of the nut.

Metric studs are also marked on their ends according to property class (grade). Larger studs are numbered (the same as metric bolts), while smaller studs carry a geometric code to denote grade.

It should be noted that many fasteners, especially Grades 0 through 2, have no distinguishing marks on them. When such is the case, the only way to determine whether it is standard or metric is to measure the thread pitch or compare it to a known fastener of the same size.

Standard fasteners are often referred to as SAE, as opposed to metric. However, it should be noted that SAE technically refers to a non-metric fine thread fastener only. Coarse thread non-metric fasteners are referred to as USS sizes.

Since fasteners of the same size (both standard and metric) may have different strength ratings, be sure to reinstall any bolts, studs or nuts removed from your vehicle in their original locations. Also, when replacing a fastener with a new one, make sure that the new one has a strength rating equal to or greater than the original.

Tightening sequences and procedures

Most threaded fasteners should be tightened to a specific torque value (torque is the twisting force applied to a threaded component such as a nut or bolt). Overtightening the fastener can weaken it and cause it to break, while undertightening can cause it to eventually come loose. Bolts, screws and studs, depending on the material they are made of and their thread diameters, have specific torque values, many of which are noted in the Specifications at the beginning of each Chapter. Be sure to follow the torque recommen-

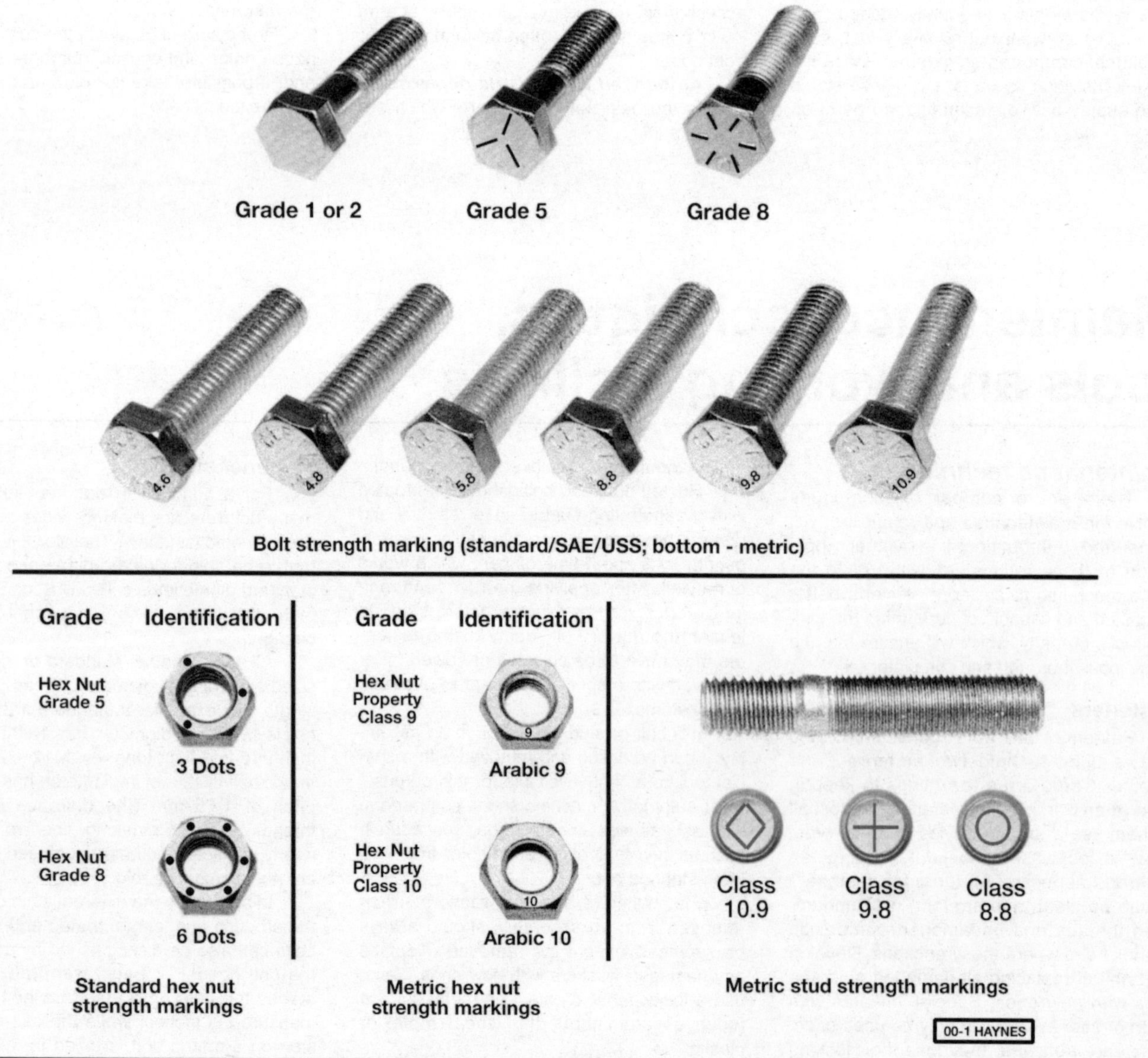

dations closely. For fasteners not assigned a specific torque, a general torque value chart is presented here as a guide. These torque values are for dry (unlubricated) fasteners threaded into steel or cast iron (not aluminum). As was previously mentioned, the size and grade of a fastener determine the amount of torque that can safely be applied to it. The figures listed here are approximate for Grade 2 and Grade 3 fasteners. Higher grades can tolerate higher torque values.

Fasteners laid out in a pattern, such as cylinder head bolts, oil pan bolts, differential cover bolts, etc., must be loosened or tightened in sequence to avoid warping the component. This sequence will normally be shown in the appropriate Chapter. If a specific pattern is not given, the following procedures can be used to prevent warping.

Initially, the bolts or nuts should be assembled finger-tight only. Next, they should be tightened one full turn each, in a criss-cross or diagonal pattern. After each one has been tightened one full turn, return to the first one and tighten them all one-half turn, following the same pattern. Finally, tighten each of them one-quarter turn at a time until each fastener has been tightened to the proper torque. To loosen and remove the fasteners, the procedure would be reversed.

Metric thread sizes	**Ft-lbs**	**Nm**
M-6	6 to 9	9 to 12
M-8	14 to 21	19 to 28
M-10	28 to 40	38 to 54
M-12	50 to 71	68 to 96
M-14	80 to 140	109 to 154
Pipe thread sizes		
1/8	5 to 8	7 to 10
1/4	12 to 18	17 to 24
3/8	22 to 33	30 to 44
1/2	25 to 35	34 to 47
U.S. thread sizes		
1/4 - 20	6 to 9	9 to 12
5/16 - 18	12 to 18	17 to 24
5/16 - 24	14 to 20	19 to 27
3/8 - 16	22 to 32	30 to 43
3/8 - 24	27 to 38	37 to 51
7/16 - 14	40 to 55	55 to 74
7/16 - 20	40 to 60	55 to 81
1/2 - 13	55 to 80	75 to 108

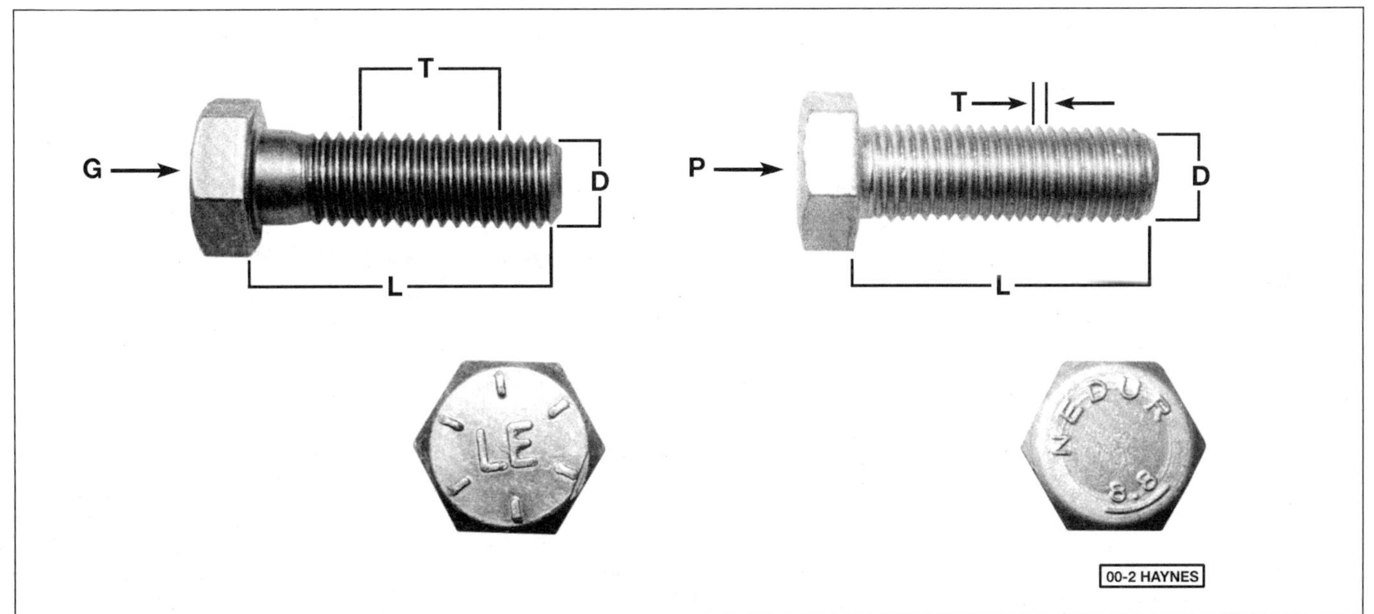

Standard (SAE and USS) bolt dimensions/grade marks

G *Grade marks (bolt strength)*
L *Length (in inches)*
T *Thread pitch (number of threads per inch)*
D *Nominal diameter (in inches)*

Metric bolt dimensions/grade marks

P *Property class (bolt strength)*
L *Length (in millimeters)*
T *Thread pitch (distance between threads in millimeters)*
D *Diameter*

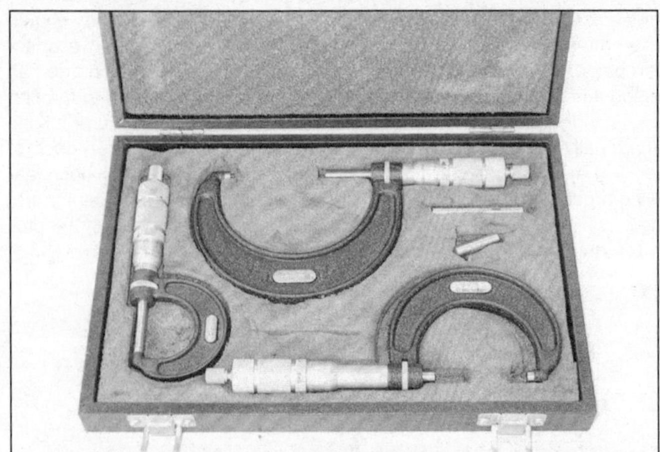

Micrometer set

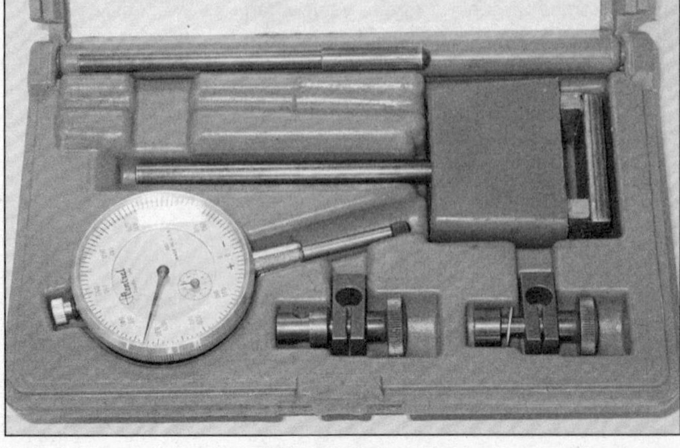

Dial indicator set

Component disassembly

Component disassembly should be done with care and purpose to help ensure that the parts go back together properly. Always keep track of the sequence in which parts are removed. Make note of special characteristics or marks on parts that can be installed more than one way, such as a grooved thrust washer on a shaft. It is a good idea to lay the disassembled parts out on a clean surface in the order that they were removed. It may also be helpful to make sketches or take instant photos of components before removal.

When removing fasteners from a component, keep track of their locations. Sometimes threading a bolt back in a part, or putting the washers and nut back on a stud, can prevent mix-ups later. If nuts and bolts cannot be returned to their original locations, they should be kept in a compartmented box or a series of small boxes. A cupcake or muffin tin is ideal for this purpose, since each cavity can hold the bolts and nuts from a particular area (i.e. oil pan bolts, valve cover bolts, engine mount bolts, etc.). A pan of this type is especially helpful when working on assemblies with very small parts, such as the carburetor, alternator, valve train or interior dash and trim pieces. The cavities can be marked with paint or tape to identify the contents.

Whenever wiring looms, harnesses or connectors are separated, it is a good idea to identify the two halves with numbered pieces of masking tape so they can be easily reconnected.

Gasket sealing surfaces

Throughout any vehicle, gaskets are used to seal the mating surfaces between two parts and keep lubricants, fluids, vacuum or pressure contained in an assembly.

Many times these gaskets are coated with a liquid or paste-type gasket sealing compound before assembly. Age, heat and pressure can sometimes cause the two parts to stick together so tightly that they are very difficult to separate. Often, the assembly can be loosened by striking it with a soft-face hammer near the mating surfaces. A regular hammer can be used if a block of wood is placed between the hammer and the part. Do not hammer on cast parts or parts that could be easily damaged. With any particularly stubborn part, always recheck to make sure that every fastener has been removed.

Avoid using a screwdriver or bar to pry apart an assembly, as they can easily mar the gasket sealing surfaces of the parts, which must remain smooth. If prying is absolutely necessary, use an old broom handle, but keep in mind that extra clean up will be necessary if the wood splinters.

After the parts are separated, the old gasket must be carefully scraped off and the gasket surfaces cleaned. Stubborn gasket material can be soaked with rust penetrant or treated with a special chemical to soften it so it can be easily scraped off. **Caution:** *Never use gasket removal solutions or caustic chemicals on plastic or other composite components.* A scraper can be fashioned from a piece of copper tubing by flattening and sharpening one end. Copper is recommended because it is usually softer than the surfaces to be scraped, which reduces the chance of gouging the part. Some gaskets can be removed with a wire brush, but regardless of the method used, the mating surfaces must be left clean and smooth. If for some reason the gasket surface is gouged, then a gasket sealer thick enough to fill scratches will have to be used during reassembly of the components. For most applications, a non-drying (or semi-drying) gasket sealer should be used.

Hose removal tips

Warning: *If the vehicle is equipped with air conditioning, do not disconnect any of the A/C hoses without first having the system depressurized by a dealer service department or a service station.*

Hose removal precautions closely parallel gasket removal precautions. Avoid scratching or gouging the surface that the hose mates against or the connection may leak. This is especially true for radiator hoses. Because of various chemical reactions, the rubber in hoses can bond itself to the metal spigot that the hose fits over. To remove a hose, first loosen the hose clamps that secure it to the spigot. Then, with slip-joint pliers, grab the hose at the clamp and rotate it around the spigot. Work it back and forth until it is completely free, then pull it off. Silicone or other lubricants will ease removal if they can be applied between the hose and the outside of the spigot. Apply the same lubricant to the inside of the hose and the outside of the spigot to simplify installation.

As a last resort (and if the hose is to be replaced with a new one anyway), the rubber can be slit with a knife and the hose peeled from the spigot. If this must be done, be careful that the metal connection is not damaged.

If a hose clamp is broken or damaged, do not reuse it. Wire-type clamps usually weaken with age, so it is a good idea to replace them with screw-type clamps whenever a hose is removed.

Tools

A selection of good tools is a basic requirement for anyone who plans to maintain and repair his or her own vehicle. For the owner who has few tools, the initial investment might seem high, but when compared to the spiraling costs of professional auto maintenance and repair, it is a wise one.

To help the owner decide which tools are needed to perform the tasks detailed in this manual, the following tool lists are offered: *Maintenance and minor repair, Repair/overhaul* and *Special.*

The newcomer to practical mechanics should start off with the *maintenance and minor repair* tool kit, which is adequate for the simpler jobs performed on a vehicle. Then, as confidence and experience grow, the owner can tackle more difficult tasks, buying additional tools as they are needed. Eventually the basic kit will be expanded into the *repair and overhaul* tool set. Over a period of time, the experienced do-it-yourselfer will assemble a tool set complete enough for most repair and overhaul procedures and will add tools from the special category when it is felt that the expense is justified by the frequency of use.

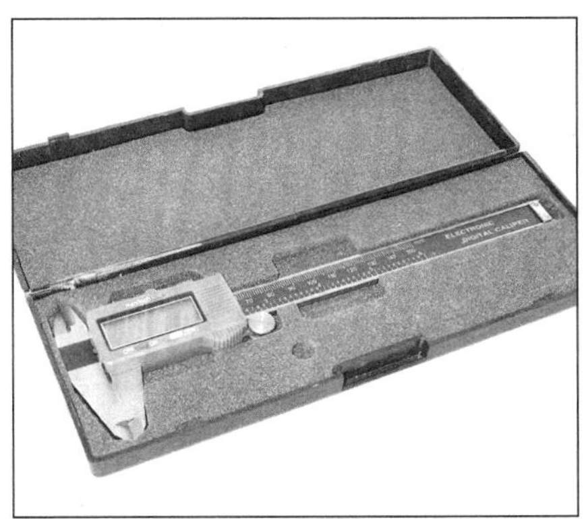

Dial caliper

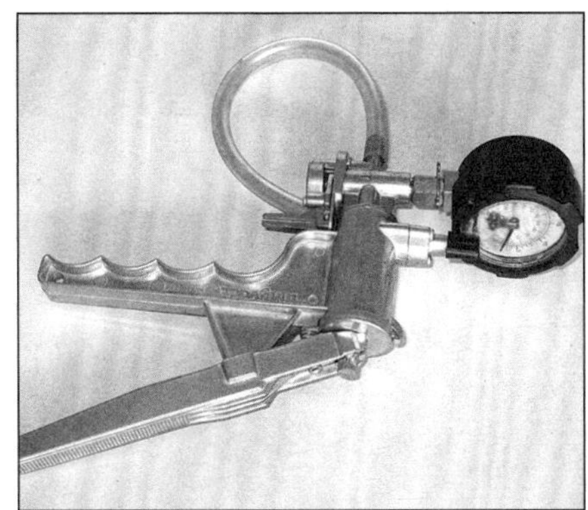

Hand-operated vacuum pump

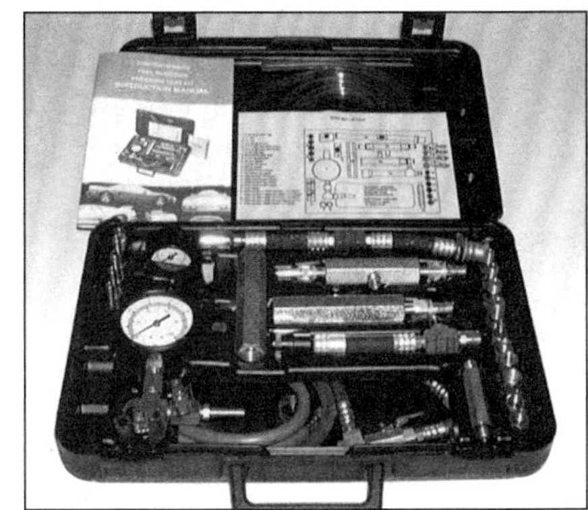

Fuel pressure gauge set

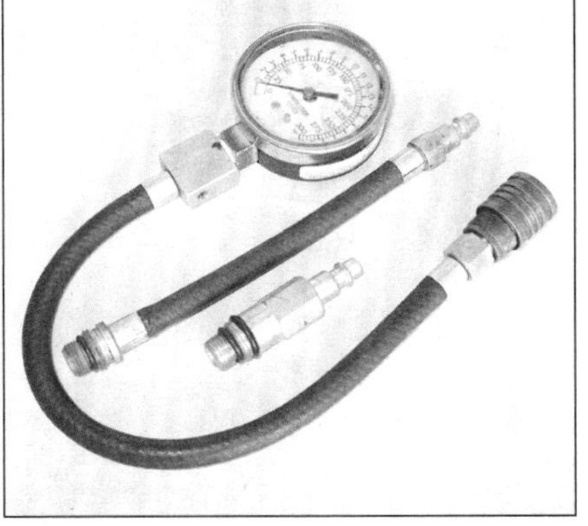

Compression gauge with spark plug hole adapter

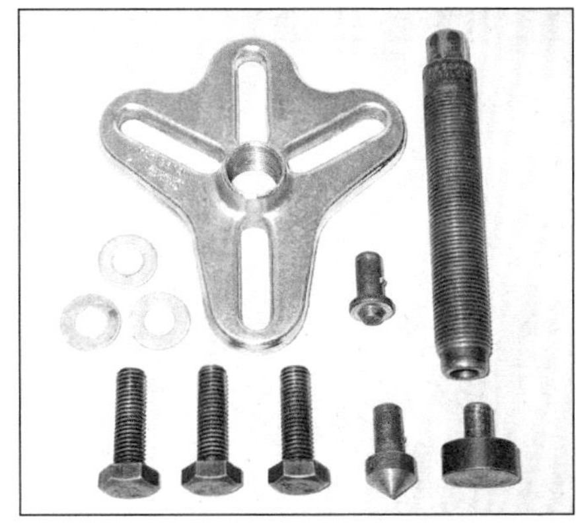

Damper/steering wheel puller

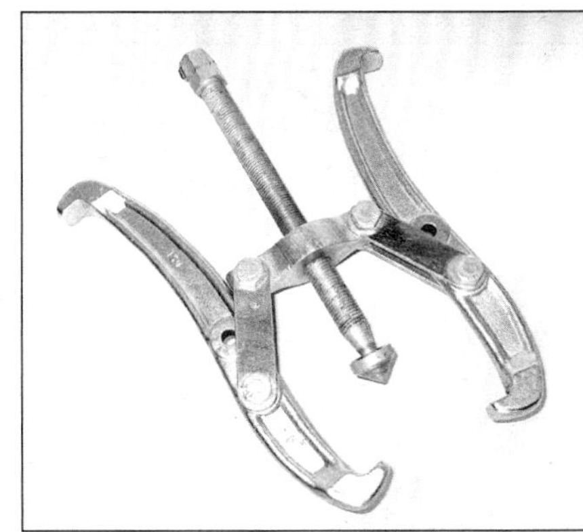

General purpose puller

Hydraulic lifter removal tool

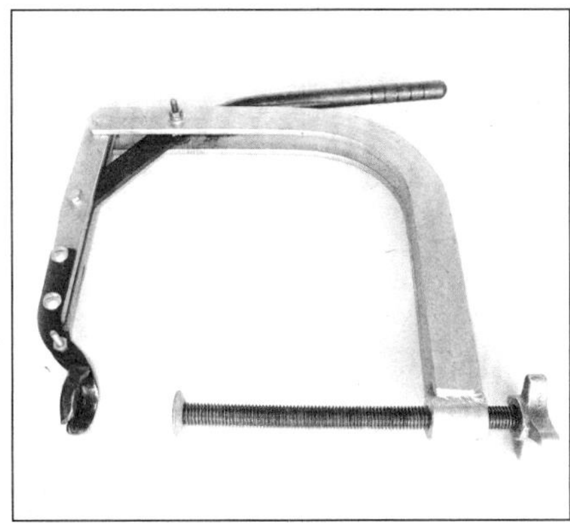

Valve spring compressor

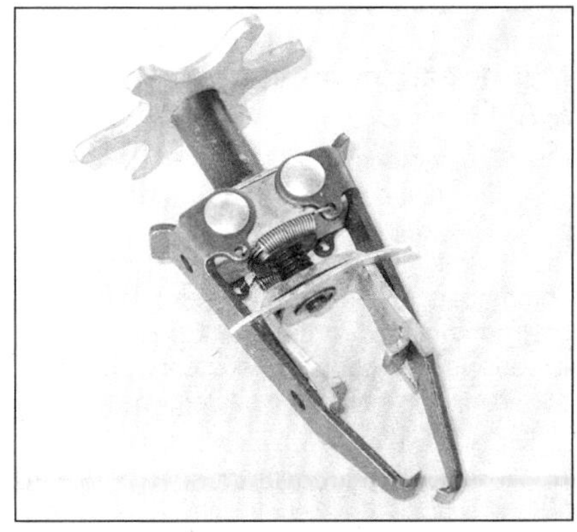

Valve spring compressor

Ridge reamer

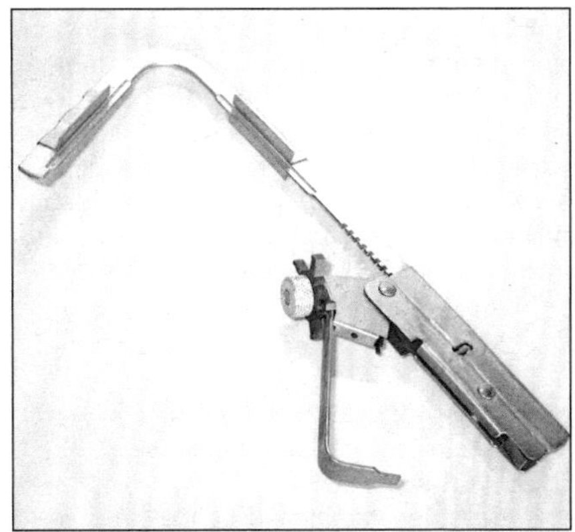

Piston ring groove cleaning tool

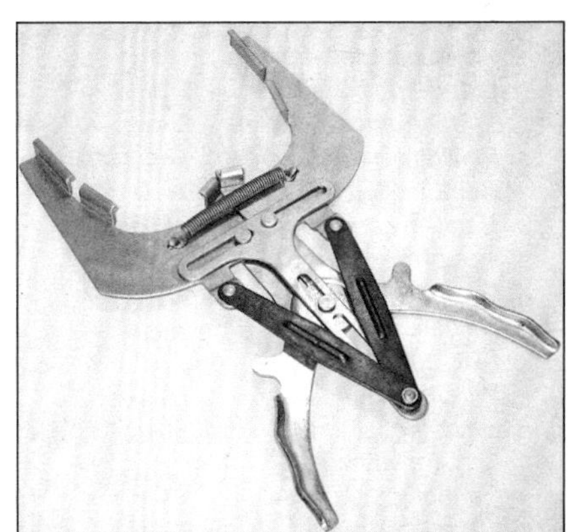

Ring removal/installation tool

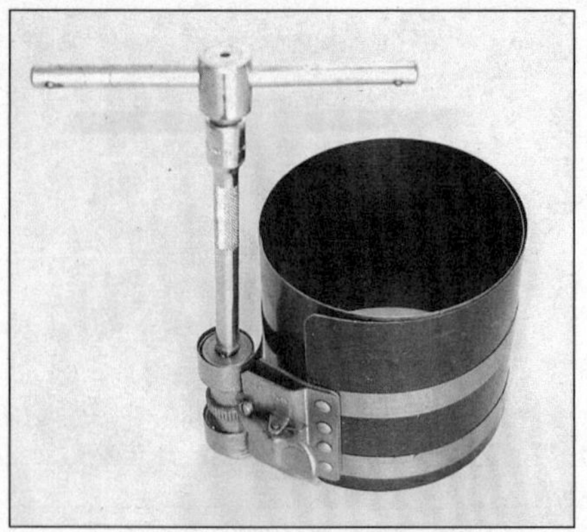
Ring compressor

Cylinder hone

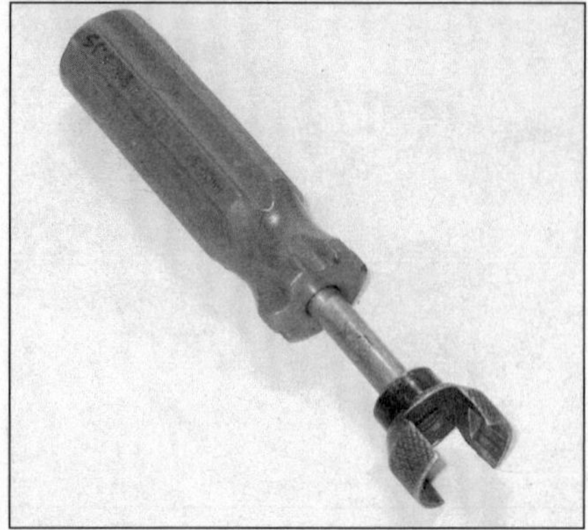
Brake hold-down spring tool

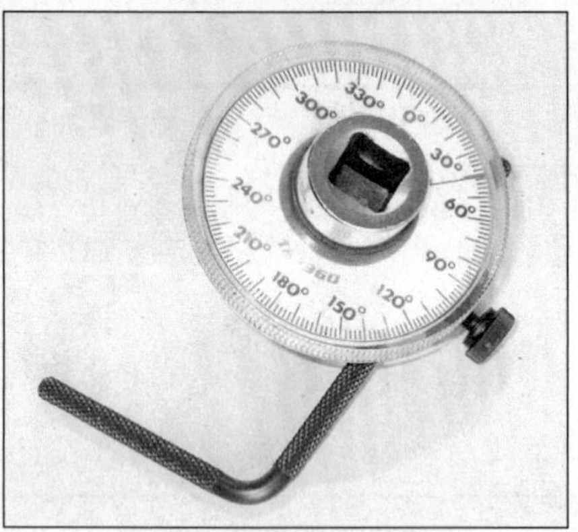

Torque angle gauge

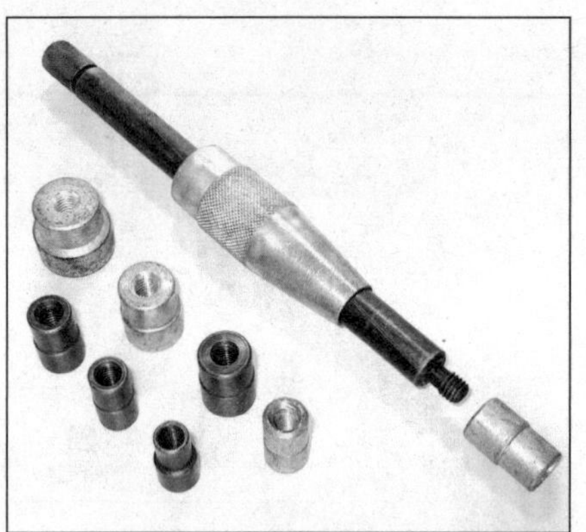
Clutch plate alignment tool

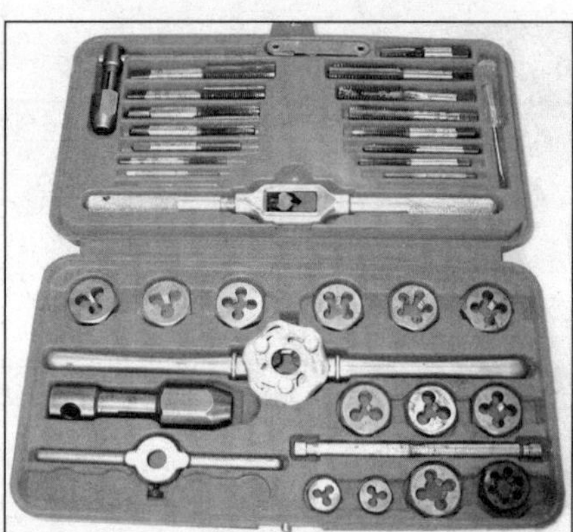
Tap and die set

Maintenance and minor repair tool kit

The tools in this list should be considered the minimum required for performance of routine maintenance, servicing and minor repair work. We recommend the purchase of combination wrenches (box-end and open-end combined in one wrench). While more expensive than open end wrenches, they offer the advantages of both types of wrench.

Combination wrench set (1/4-inch to 1 inch or 6 mm to 19 mm)
Adjustable wrench, 8 inch
Spark plug wrench with rubber insert
Spark plug gap adjusting tool
Feeler gauge set
Brake bleeder wrench
Standard screwdriver (5/16-inch x 6 inch)
Phillips screwdriver (No. 2 x 6 inch)
Combination pliers - 6 inch
Hacksaw and assortment of blades
Tire pressure gauge
Grease gun
Oil can
Fine emery cloth
Wire brush
Battery post and cable cleaning tool
Oil filter wrench
Funnel (medium size)
Safety goggles
Jackstands (2)
Drain pan

Note: *If basic tune-ups are going to be part of routine maintenance, it will be necessary to purchase a good quality stroboscopic timing light and combination tachometer/dwell meter. Although they are included in the list of special tools, it is mentioned here because they are absolutely necessary for tuning most vehicles properly.*

Repair and overhaul tool set

These tools are essential for anyone who plans to perform major repairs and are in addition to those in the maintenance and minor repair tool kit. Included is a comprehensive set of sockets which, though expensive, are invaluable because of their versatility, especially when various extensions and drives are available. We recommend the 1/2-inch drive over the 3/8-inch drive. Although the larger drive is bulky and more expensive, it has the capacity of accepting a very wide range of large sockets. Ideally, however, the mechanic should have a 3/8-inch drive set and a 1/2-inch drive set.

Socket set(s)
Reversible ratchet
Extension - 10 inch
Universal joint
Torque wrench (same size drive as sockets)
Ball peen hammer - 8 ounce
Soft-face hammer (plastic/rubber)
Standard screwdriver (1/4-inch x 6 inch)
Standard screwdriver (stubby - 5/16-inch)
Phillips screwdriver (No. 3 x 8 inch)
Phillips screwdriver (stubby - No. 2)
Pliers - vise grip
Pliers - lineman's
Pliers - needle nose
Pliers - snap-ring (internal and external)
Cold chisel - 1/2-inch
Scribe
Scraper (made from flattened copper tubing)
Centerpunch
Pin punches (1/16, 1/8, 3/16-inch)
Steel rule/straightedge - 12 inch
Allen wrench set (1/8 to 3/8-inch or 4 mm to 10 mm)
A selection of files
Wire brush (large)
Jackstands (second set)
Jack (scissor or hydraulic type)

Note: *Another tool which is often useful is an electric drill with a chuck capacity of 3/8-inch and a set of good quality drill bits.*

Special tools

The tools in this list include those which are not used regularly, are expensive to buy, or which need to be used in accordance with their manufacturer's instructions. Unless these tools will be used frequently, it is not very economical to purchase many of them. A consideration would be to split the cost and use between yourself and a friend or friends. In addition, most of these tools can be obtained from a tool rental shop on a temporary basis.

This list primarily contains only those tools and instruments widely available to the public, and not those special tools produced by the vehicle manufacturer for distribution to dealer service departments. Occasionally, references to the manufacturer's special tools are included in the text of this manual. Generally, an alternative method of doing the job without the special tool is offered. However, sometimes there is no alternative to their use. Where this is the case, and the tool cannot be purchased or borrowed, the work should be turned over to the dealer service department or an automotive repair shop.

Valve spring compressor
Piston ring groove cleaning tool
Piston ring compressor
Piston ring installation tool
Cylinder compression gauge
Cylinder ridge reamer
Cylinder surfacing hone
Cylinder bore gauge
Micrometers and/or dial calipers
Hydraulic lifter removal tool
Balljoint separator
Universal-type puller
Impact screwdriver
Dial indicator set
Stroboscopic timing light (inductivepick-up)
Hand operated vacuum/pressure pump
Tachometer/dwell meter
Universal electrical multimeter
Cable hoist
Brake spring removal and installation tools
Floor jack

Buying tools

For the do-it-yourselfer who is just starting to get involved in vehicle maintenance and repair, there are a number of options available when purchasing tools. If maintenance and minor repair is the extent of the work to be done, the purchase of individual tools is satisfactory. If, on the other hand, extensive work is planned, it would be a good idea to purchase a modest tool set from one of the large retail chain stores. A set can usually be bought at a substantial savings over the individual tool prices, and they often come with a tool box. As additional tools are needed, add-on sets, individual tools and a larger tool box can be purchased to expand the tool selection. Building a tool set gradually allows the cost of the tools to be spread over a longer period of time and gives the mechanic the freedom to choose only those tools that will actually be used.

Tool stores will often be the only source of some of the special tools that are needed, but regardless of where tools are bought, try to avoid cheap ones, especially when buying screwdrivers and sockets, because they won't last very long. The expense involved in replacing cheap tools will eventually be greater than the initial cost of quality tools.

Care and maintenance of tools

Good tools are expensive, so it makes sense to treat them with respect. Keep them clean and in usable condition and store them properly when not in use. Always wipe off any dirt, grease or metal chips before putting them away. Never leave tools lying around in the work area. Upon completion of a job, always check closely under the hood for tools that may have been left there so they won't get lost during a test drive.

Some tools, such as screwdrivers, pliers, wrenches and sockets, can be hung on a panel mounted on the garage or workshop wall, while others should be kept in a tool box or tray. Measuring instruments, gauges, meters, etc. must be carefully stored where they cannot be damaged by weather or impact from other tools.

When tools are used with care and stored properly, they will last a very long time. Even with the best of care, though, tools will wear out if used frequently. When a tool is damaged or worn out, replace it. Subsequent jobs will be safer and more enjoyable if you do.

How to repair damaged threads

Sometimes, the internal threads of a nut or bolt hole can become stripped, usually from overtightening. Stripping threads is an all-too-common occurrence, especially when working with aluminum parts, because aluminum is so soft that it easily strips out.

Usually, external or internal threads are only partially stripped. After they've been cleaned up with a tap or die, they'll still work. Sometimes, however, threads are badly damaged. When this happens, you've got three choices:

1) *Drill and tap the hole to the next suitable oversize and install a larger diameter bolt, screw or stud.*
2) *Drill and tap the hole to accept a threaded plug, then drill and tap the plug to the original screw size. You can also buy a plug already threaded to the original size. Then you simply drill a hole to the specified size, then run the threaded plug into the hole with a bolt and jam nut. Once the plug is fully seated, remove the jam nut and bolt.*
3) *The third method uses a patented thread repair kit like Heli-Coil or Slimsert. These easy-to-use kits are designed to repair damaged threads in straight-through holes and blind holes. Both are available as kits which can handle a variety of sizes and thread patterns. Drill the hole, then tap it with the special included tap. Install the Heli-Coil and the hole is back to its original diameter and thread pitch.*

Regardless of which method you use, be sure to proceed calmly and carefully. A little impatience or carelessness during one of these relatively simple procedures can ruin your whole day's work and cost you a bundle if you wreck an expensive part.

Working facilities

Not to be overlooked when discussing tools is the workshop. If anything more than routine maintenance is to be carried out, some sort of suitable work area is essential.

It is understood, and appreciated, that many home mechanics do not have a good workshop or garage available, and end up removing an engine or doing major repairs outside. It is recommended, however, that the overhaul or repair be completed under the cover of a roof.

A clean, flat workbench or table of comfortable working height is an absolute necessity. The workbench should be equipped with a vise that has a jaw opening of at least four inches.

As mentioned previously, some clean, dry storage space is also required for tools, as well as the lubricants, fluids, cleaning solvents, etc. which soon become necessary.

Sometimes waste oil and fluids, drained from the engine or cooling system during normal maintenance or repairs, present a disposal problem. To avoid pouring them on the ground or into a sewage system, pour the used fluids into large containers, seal them with caps and take them to an authorized disposal site or recycling center. Plastic jugs, such as old antifreeze containers, are ideal for this purpose.

Always keep a supply of old newspapers and clean rags available. Old towels are excellent for mopping up spills. Many mechanics use rolls of paper towels for most work because they are readily available and disposable. To help keep the area under the vehicle clean, a large cardboard box can be cut open and flattened to protect the garage or shop floor.

Whenever working over a painted surface, such as when leaning over a fender to service something under the hood, always cover it with an old blanket or bedspread to protect the finish. Vinyl covered pads, made especially for this purpose, are available at auto parts stores.

Jacking and towing

Jacking

Warning: *The jack supplied with the vehicle should only be used for changing a tire or placing jackstands under the frame. Never work under the vehicle or start the engine while this jack is being used as the only means of support.*

1 The vehicle should be on level ground. Place the shift lever in Park, if you have an automatic, or Reverse if you have a manual transaxle. Block the wheel diagonally opposite the wheel being changed. Set the parking brake.

2 Remove the spare tire and jack from stowage. Remove the wheel cover and trim ring (if so equipped) with the tapered end of the lug nut wrench by inserting and twisting the handle and then prying against the back of the wheel cover. Loosen the wheel lug nuts about 1/4 to 1/2 turn each.

3 Place the scissors-type jack under the side of the vehicle and adjust the jack height until it engages with the elongated tab that protrudes from the vertical rocker panel flange nearest the wheel to be changed. There is a front and rear jacking point on each side of the vehicle (see illustration).

4 Turn the jack handle clockwise until the tire clears the ground. Remove the lug nuts and pull the wheel off, then install the spare.

5 Install the lug nuts with the beveled edges facing in. Tighten them snugly. Don't attempt to tighten them completely until the vehicle is lowered or it could slip off the jack. Turn the jack handle counterclockwise to lower the vehicle. Remove the jack and tighten the lug nuts in a diagonal pattern to the torque listed in the Chapter 1 Specifications.

6 Install the cover (and trim ring, if used) and be sure it's snapped into place all the way around.

7 Stow the tire, jack and wrench. Unblock the wheels.

Towing

8 As a general rule, the vehicle should be towed with the front (drive) wheels off the ground. If they can't be raised, place them on a dolly. The intelligent key must be in its slot in the instrument panel and the starter button display must be in the ACC position to unlock the steering column lock.

9 Models with a manual transaxle can be towed with all four wheels on the ground (such as behind a motorhome) provided that every 500 miles the engine is started and allowed to idle for two minutes to circulate the transaxle lubricant.

10 Equipment specifically designed for towing should be used. It should be attached to the main structural members of the vehicle, not the bumpers or brackets.

11 Safety is a major consideration when towing and all applicable state and local laws must be obeyed. A safety chain system must be used at all times.

The jack fits over the rocker panel flange (there are two jacking points on each side of the vehicle, indicated by notches in the rocker panel flange)

Booster battery (jump) starting

1 Observe the following precautions when using a booster battery to start a vehicle:

a) *Before connecting the booster battery, make sure the ignition switch is in the Off position.*
b) *Turn off the lights, heater and other electrical loads.*
c) *Your eyes should be shielded. Safety goggles are a good idea.*
d) *Make sure the booster battery is the same voltage as the dead one in the vehicle.*
e) *The two vehicles MUST NOT TOUCH each other.*
f) *Make sure the transmission is in Park (automatic).*

2 Connect the red jumper cable to the positive (+) terminals of each battery.

3 Connect one end of the black cable to the negative (-) terminal of the booster battery. The other end of this cable should be connected to a good ground on the engine block **(see illustration)**. Make sure the cable will not come into contact with the fan, drivebelts or other moving parts of the engine.

4 Start the engine using the booster battery, then, with the engine running at idle speed, disconnect the jumper cables in the reverse order of connection.

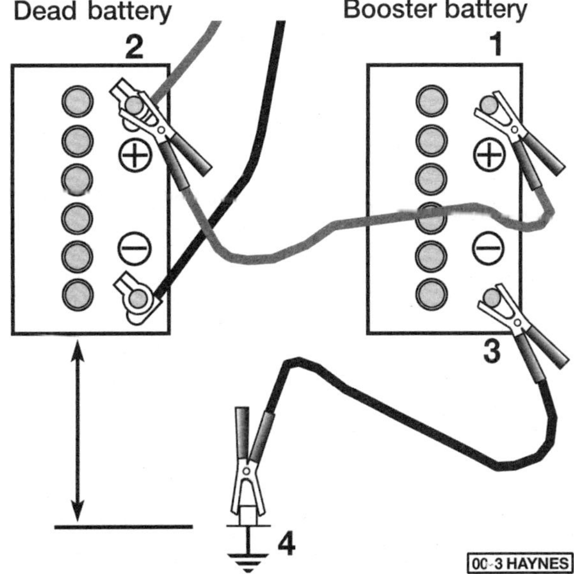

Make the booster battery cable connections in the numerical order shown (note that the negative cable of the booster battery is NOT attached to the negative terminal of the dead battery)

Automotive chemicals and lubricants

A number of automotive chemicals and lubricants are available for use during vehicle maintenance and repair. They include a wide variety of products ranging from cleaning solvents and degreasers to lubricants and protective sprays for rubber, plastic and vinyl.

Cleaners

Carburetor cleaner and choke cleaner is a strong solvent for gum, varnish and carbon. Most carburetor cleaners leave a dry-type lubricant film which will not harden or gum up. Because of this film it is not recommended for use on electrical components.

Brake system cleaner is used to remove brake dust, grease and brake fluid from the brake system, where clean surfaces are absolutely necessary. It leaves no residue and often eliminates brake squeal caused by contaminants.

Electrical cleaner removes oxidation, corrosion and carbon deposits from electrical contacts, restoring full current flow. It can also be used to clean spark plugs, carburetor jets, voltage regulators and other parts where an oil-free surface is desired.

Demoisturants remove water and moisture from electrical components such as alternators, voltage regulators, electrical connectors and fuse blocks. They are non-conductive and non-corrosive.

Degreasers are heavy-duty solvents used to remove grease from the outside of the engine and from chassis components. They can be sprayed or brushed on and, depending on the type, are rinsed off either with water or solvent.

Lubricants

Motor oil is the lubricant formulated for use in engines. It normally contains a wide variety of additives to prevent corrosion and reduce foaming and wear. Motor oil comes in various weights (viscosity ratings) from 0 to 50. The recommended weight of the oil depends on the season, temperature and the demands on the engine. Light oil is used in cold climates and under light load conditions. Heavy oil is used in hot climates and where high loads are encountered. Multi-viscosity oils are designed to have characteristics of both light and heavy oils and are available in a number of weights from 0W-20 to 20W-50.

Gear oil is designed to be used in differentials, manual transmissions and other areas where high-temperature lubrication is required.

Chassis and wheel bearing grease is a heavy grease used where increased loads and friction are encountered, such as for wheel bearings, balljoints, tie-rod ends and universal joints.

High-temperature wheel bearing grease is designed to withstand the extreme temperatures encountered by wheel bearings in disc brake equipped vehicles. It usually contains molybdenum disulfide (moly), which is a dry-type lubricant.

White grease is a heavy grease for metal-to-metal applications where water is a problem. White grease stays soft under both low and high temperatures (usually from -100 to +190-degrees F), and will not wash off or dilute in the presence of water.

Assembly lube is a special extreme pressure lubricant, usually containing moly, used to lubricate high-load parts (such as main and rod bearings and cam lobes) for initial start-up of a new engine. The assembly lube lubricates the parts without being squeezed out or washed away until the engine oiling system begins to function.

Silicone lubricants are used to protect rubber, plastic, vinyl and nylon parts.

Graphite lubricants are used where oils cannot be used due to contamination problems, such as in locks. The dry graphite will lubricate metal parts while remaining uncontaminated by dirt, water, oil or acids. It is electrically conductive and will not foul electrical contacts in locks such as the ignition switch.

Moly penetrants loosen and lubricate frozen, rusted and corroded fasteners and prevent future rusting or freezing.

Heat-sink grease is a special electrically non-conductive grease that is used for mounting electronic ignition modules where it is essential that heat is transferred away from the module.

Sealants

RTV sealant is one of the most widely used gasket compounds. Made from silicone, RTV is air curing, it seals, bonds, waterproofs, fills surface irregularities, remains flexible, doesn't shrink, is relatively easy to remove, and is used as a supplementary sealer with almost all low and medium temperature gaskets.

Anaerobic sealant is much like RTV in that it can be used either to seal gaskets or to form gaskets by itself. It remains flexible, is solvent resistant and fills surface imperfections. The difference between an anaerobic sealant and an RTV-type sealant is in the curing. RTV cures when exposed to air, while an anaerobic sealant cures only in the absence of air. This means that an anaerobic sealant cures only after the assembly of parts, sealing them together.

Thread and pipe sealant is used for sealing hydraulic and pneumatic fittings and vacuum lines. It is usually made from a Teflon compound, and comes in a spray, a paint-on liquid and as a wrap-around tape.

Chemicals

Anti-seize compound prevents seizing, galling, cold welding, rust and corrosion in fasteners. High-temperature anti-seize, usually made with copper and graphite lubricants, is used for exhaust system and exhaust manifold bolts.

Anaerobic locking compounds are used to keep fasteners from vibrating or working loose and cure only after installation, in the absence of air. Medium strength locking compound is used for small nuts, bolts and screws that may be removed later. High-strength locking compound is for large nuts, bolts and studs which aren't removed on a regular basis.

Oil additives range from viscosity index improvers to chemical treatments that claim to reduce internal engine friction. It should be noted that most oil manufacturers caution against using additives with their oils.

Gas additives perform several functions, depending on their chemical makeup. They usually contain solvents that help dissolve gum and varnish that build up on carburetor, fuel injection and intake parts. They also serve to break down carbon deposits that form on the inside surfaces of the combustion chambers. Some additives contain upper cylinder lubricants for valves and piston rings, and others contain chemicals to remove condensation from the gas tank.

Miscellaneous

Brake fluid is specially formulated hydraulic fluid that can withstand the heat and pressure encountered in brake systems. Care must be taken so this fluid does not come in contact with painted surfaces or plastics. An opened container should always be resealed to prevent contamination by water or dirt.

Weatherstrip adhesive is used to bond weatherstripping around doors, windows and trunk lids. It is sometimes used to attach trim pieces.

Undercoating is a petroleum-based, tar-like substance that is designed to protect metal surfaces on the underside of the vehicle from corrosion. It also acts as a sound-deadening agent by insulating the bottom of the vehicle.

Waxes and polishes are used to help protect painted and plated surfaces from the weather. Different types of paint may require the use of different types of wax and polish. Some polishes utilize a chemical or abrasive cleaner to help remove the top layer of oxidized (dull) paint on older vehicles. In recent years many non-wax polishes that contain a wide variety of chemicals such as polymers and silicones have been introduced. These non-wax polishes are usually easier to apply and last longer than conventional waxes and polishes.

Conversion factors

Length (distance)				
Inches (in)	X 25.4	= Millimeters (mm)	X 0.0394	= Inches (in)
Feet (ft)	X 0.305	= Meters (m)	X 3.281	= Feet (ft)
Miles	X 1.609	= Kilometers (km)	X 0.621	= Miles
Volume (capacity)				
Cubic inches (cu in; in^3)	X 16.387	= Cubic centimeters (cc; cm^3)	X 0.061	= Cubic inches (cu in; in^3)
Imperial pints (Imp pt)	X 0.568	= Liters (l)	X 1.76	= Imperial pints (Imp pt)
Imperial quarts (Imp qt)	X 1.137	= Liters (l)	X 0.88	= Imperial quarts (Imp qt)
Imperial quarts (Imp qt)	X 1.201	= US quarts (US qt)	X 0.833	= Imperial quarts (Imp qt)
US quarts (US qt)	X 0.946	= Liters (l)	X 1.057	= US quarts (US qt)
Imperial gallons (Imp gal)	X 4.546	= Liters (l)	X 0.22	= Imperial gallons (Imp gal)
Imperial gallons (Imp gal)	X 1.201	= US gallons (US gal)	X 0.833	= Imperial gallons (Imp gal)
US gallons (US gal)	X 3.785	= Liters (l)	X 0.264	= US gallons (US gal)
Mass (weight)				
Ounces (oz)	X 28.35	= Grams (g)	X 0.035	= Ounces (oz)
Pounds (lb)	X 0.454	= Kilograms (kg)	X 2.205	= Pounds (lb)
Force				
Ounces-force (ozf; oz)	X 0.278	= Newtons (N)	X 3.6	= Ounces-force (ozf; oz)
Pounds-force (lbf; lb)	X 4.448	= Newtons (N)	X 0.225	= Pounds-force (lbf; lb)
Newtons (N)	X 0.1	= Kilograms-force (kgf; kg)	X 9.81	= Newtons (N)
Pressure				
Pounds-force per square inch (psi; lbf/in^2; lb/in^2)	X 0.070	= Kilograms-force per square centimeter (kgf/cm^2; kg/cm^2)	X 14.223	= Pounds-force per square inch (psi; lbf/in^2; lb/in^2)
Pounds-force per square inch (psi; lbf/in^2; lb/in^2)	X 0.068	= Atmospheres (atm)	X 14.696	= Pounds-force per square inch (psi; lbf/in^2; lb/in^2)
Pounds-force per square inch (psi; lbf/in^2; lb/in^2)	X 0.069	= Bars	X 14.5	= Pounds-force per square inch (psi; lbf/in^2; lb/in^2)
Pounds-force per square inch (psi; lbf/in^2; lb/in^2)	X 6.895	= Kilopascals (kPa)	X 0.145	= Pounds-force per square inch (psi; lbf/in^2; lb/in^2)
Kilopascals (kPa)	X 0.01	= Kilograms-force per square centimeter (kgf/cm^2; kg/cm^2)	X 98.1	= Kilopascals (kPa)
Torque (moment of force)				
Pounds-force inches (lbf in; lb in)	X 1.152	= Kilograms-force centimeter (kgf cm; kg cm)	X 0.868	= Pounds-force inches (lbf in; lb in)
Pounds-force inches (lbf in; lb in)	X 0.113	= Newton meters (Nm)	X 8.85	= Pounds-force inches (lbf in; lb in)
Pounds-force inches (lbf in; lb in)	X 0.083	= Pounds-force feet (lbf ft; lb ft)	X 12	= Pounds-force inches (lbf in; lb in)
Pounds-force feet (lbf ft; lb ft)	X 0.138	= Kilograms-force meters (kgf m; kg m)	X 7.233	= Pounds-force feet (lbf ft; lb ft)
Pounds-force feet (lbf ft; lb ft)	X 1.356	= Newton meters (Nm)	X 0.738	= Pounds-force feet (lbf ft; lb ft)
Newton meters (Nm)	X 0.102	= Kilograms-force meters (kgf m; kg m)	X 9.804	= Newton meters (Nm)
Vacuum				
Inches mercury (in. Hg)	X 3.377	= Kilopascals (kPa)	X 0.2961	= Inches mercury
Inches mercury (in. Hg)	X 25.4	= Millimeters mercury (mm Hg)	X 0.0394	= Inches mercury
Power				
Horsepower (hp)	X 745.7	= Watts (W)	X 0.0013	= Horsepower (hp)
Velocity (speed)				
Miles per hour (miles/hr; mph)	X 1.609	= Kilometers per hour (km/hr; kph)	X 0.621	= Miles per hour (miles/hr; mph)
Fuel consumption*				
Miles per gallon, Imperial (mpg)	X 0.354	= Kilometers per liter (km/l)	X 2.825	= Miles per gallon, Imperial (mpg)
Miles per gallon, US (mpg)	X 0.425	= Kilometers per liter (km/l)	X 2.352	= Miles per gallon, US (mpg)

Temperature

Degrees Fahrenheit = (°C x 1.8) + 32   Degrees Celsius (Degrees Centigrade; °C) = (°F - 32) x 0.56

**It is common practice to convert from miles per gallon (mpg) to liters/100 kilometers (l/100km), where mpg (Imperial) x l/100 km = 282 and mpg (US) x l/100 km = 235*

DECIMALS to MILLIMETERS

Decimal	mm	Decimal	mm
0.001	0.0254	0.500	12.7000
0.002	0.0508	0.510	12.9540
0.003	0.0762	0.520	13.2080
0.004	0.1016	0.530	13.4620
0.005	0.1270	0.540	13.7160
0.006	0.1524	0.550	13.9700
0.007	0.1778	0.560	14.2240
0.008	0.2032	0.570	14.4780
0.009	0.2286	0.580	14.7320
0.010	0.2540	0.590	14.9860
0.020	0.5080		
0.030	0.7620		
0.040	1.0160	0.600	15.2400
0.050	1.2700	0.610	15.4940
0.060	1.5240	0.620	15.7480
0.070	1.7780	0.630	16.0020
0.080	2.0320	0.640	16.2560
0.090	2.2860	0.650	16.5100
		0.660	16.7640
0.100	2.5400	0.670	17.0180
0.110	2.7940	0.680	17.2720
0.120	3.0480	0.690	17.5260
0.130	3.3020		
0.140	3.5560		
0.150	3.8100		
0.160	4.0640	0.700	17.7800
0.170	4.3180	0.710	18.0340
0.180	4.5720	0.720	18.2880
0.190	4.8260	0.730	18.5420
		0.740	18.7960
0.200	5.0800	0.750	19.0500
0.210	5.3340	0.760	19.3040
0.220	5.5880	0.770	19.5580
0.230	5.8420	0.780	19.8120
0.240	6.0960	0.790	20.0660
0.250	6.3500		
0.260	6.6040		
0.270	6.8580	0.800	20.3200
0.280	7.1120	0.810	20.5740
0.290	7.3660	0.820	21.8280
		0.830	21.0820
0.300	7.6200	0.840	21.3360
0.310	7.8740	0.850	21.5900
0.320	8.1280	0.860	21.8440
0.330	8.3820	0.870	22.0980
0.340	8.6360	0.880	22.3520
0.350	8.8900	0.890	22.6060
0.360	9.1440		
0.370	9.3980		
0.380	9.6520		
0.390	9.9060		
		0.900	22.8600
0.400	10.1600	0.910	23.1140
0.410	10.4140	0.920	23.3680
0.420	10.6680	0.930	23.6220
0.430	10.9220	0.940	23.8760
0.440	11.1760	0.950	24.1300
0.450	11.4300	0.960	24.3840
0.460	11.6840	0.970	24.6380
0.470	11.9380	0.980	24.8920
0.480	12.1920	0.990	25.1460
0.490	12.4460	1.000	25.4000

FRACTIONS to DECIMALS to MILLIMETERS

Fraction	Decimal	mm	Fraction	Decimal	mm
1/64	0.0156	0.3969	33/64	0.5156	13.0969
1/32	0.0312	0.7938	17/32	0.5312	13.4938
3/64	0.0469	1.1906	35/64	0.5469	13.8906
1/16	0.0625	1.5875	9/16	0.5625	14.2875
5/64	0.0781	1.9844	37/64	0.5781	14.6844
3/32	0.0938	2.3812	19/32	0.5938	15.0812
7/64	0.1094	2.7781	39/64	0.6094	15.4781
1/8	0.1250	3.1750	5/8	0.6250	15.8750
9/64	0.1406	3.5719	41/64	0.6406	16.2719
5/32	0.1562	3.9688	21/32	0.6562	16.6688
11/64	0.1719	4.3656	43/64	0.6719	17.0656
3/16	0.1875	4.7625	11/16	0.6875	17.4625
13/64	0.2031	5.1594	45/64	0.7031	17.8594
7/32	0.2188	5.5562	23/32	0.7188	18.2562
15/64	0.2344	5.9531	47/64	0.7344	18.6531
1/4	0.2500	6.3500	3/4	0.7500	19.0500
17/64	0.2656	6.7469	49/64	0.7656	19.4469
9/32	0.2812	7.1438	25/32	0.7812	19.8438
19/64	0.2969	7.5406	51/64	0.7969	20.2406
5/16	0.3125	7.9375	13/16	0.8125	20.6375
21/64	0.3281	8.3344	53/64	0.8281	21.0344
11/32	0.3438	8.7312	27/32	0.8438	21.4312
23/64	0.3594	9.1281	55/64	0.8594	21.8281
3/8	0.3750	9.5250	7/8	0.8750	22.2250
25/64	0.3906	9.9219	57/64	0.8906	22.6219
13/32	0.4062	10.3188	29/32	0.9062	23.0188
27/64	0.4219	10.7156	59/64	0.9219	23.4156
7/16	0.4375	11.1125	15/16	0.9375	23.8125
29/64	0.4531	11.5094	61/64	0.9531	24.2094
15/32	0.4688	11.9062	31/32	0.9688	24.6062
31/64	0.4844	12.3031	63/64	0.9844	25.0031
1/2	0.5000	12.7000	1	1.0000	25.4000

Safety first!

Regardless of how enthusiastic you may be about getting on with the job at hand, take the time to ensure that your safety is not jeopardized. A moment's lack of attention can result in an accident, as can failure to observe certain simple safety precautions. The possibility of an accident will always exist, and the following points should not be considered a comprehensive list of all dangers. Rather, they are intended to make you aware of the risks and to encourage a safety conscious approach to all work you carry out on your vehicle.

Essential DOs and DON'Ts

DON'T rely on a jack when working under the vehicle. Always use approved jackstands to support the weight of the vehicle and place them under the recommended lift or support points.

DON'T attempt to loosen extremely tight fasteners (i.e. wheel lug nuts) while the vehicle is on a jack - it may fall.

DON'T start the engine without first making sure that the transmission is in Neutral (or Park where applicable) and the parking brake is set.

DON'T remove the radiator cap from a hot cooling system - let it cool or cover it with a cloth and release the pressure gradually.

DON'T attempt to drain the engine oil until you are sure it has cooled to the point that it will not burn you.

DON'T touch any part of the engine or exhaust system until it has cooled sufficiently to avoid burns.

DON'T siphon toxic liquids such as gasoline, antifreeze and brake fluid by mouth, or allow them to remain on your skin.

DON'T inhale brake lining dust - it is potentially hazardous (see *Asbestos* below).

DON'T allow spilled oil or grease to remain on the floor - wipe it up before someone slips on it.

DON'T use loose fitting wrenches or other tools which may slip and cause injury.

DON'T push on wrenches when loosening or tightening nuts or bolts. Always try to pull the wrench toward you. If the situation calls for pushing the wrench away, push with an open hand to avoid scraped knuckles if the wrench should slip.

DON'T attempt to lift a heavy component alone - get someone to help you.

DON'T rush or take unsafe shortcuts to finish a job.

DON'T allow children or animals in or around the vehicle while you are working on it.

DO wear eye protection when using power tools such as a drill, sander, bench grinder, etc. and when working under a vehicle.

DO keep loose clothing and long hair well out of the way of moving parts.

DO make sure that any hoist used has a safe working load rating adequate for the job.

DO get someone to check on you periodically when working alone on a vehicle.

DO carry out work in a logical sequence and make sure that everything is correctly assembled and tightened.

DO keep chemicals and fluids tightly capped and out of the reach of children and pets.

DO remember that your vehicle's safety affects that of yourself and others. If in doubt on any point, get professional advice.

Steering, suspension and brakes

These systems are essential to driving safety, so make sure you have a qualified shop or individual check your work. Also, compressed suspension springs can cause injury if released suddenly - be sure to use a spring compressor.

Airbags

Airbags are explosive devices that can **CAUSE** injury if they deploy while you're working on the vehicle. Follow the manufacturer's instructions to disable the airbag whenever you're working in the vicinity of airbag components.

Asbestos

Certain friction, insulating, sealing, and other products - such as brake linings, brake bands, clutch linings, torque converters, gaskets, etc. - may contain asbestos or other hazardous friction material. Extreme care must be taken to avoid inhalation of dust from such products, since it is hazardous to health. If in doubt, assume that they do contain asbestos.

Fire

Remember at all times that gasoline is highly flammable. Never smoke or have any kind of open flame around when working on a vehicle. But the risk does not end there. A spark caused by an electrical short circuit, by two metal surfaces contacting each other, or even by static electricity built up in your body under certain conditions, can ignite gasoline vapors, which in a confined space are highly explosive. Do not, under any circumstances, use gasoline for cleaning parts. Use an approved safety solvent.

Always disconnect the battery ground (-) cable at the battery before working on any part of the fuel system or electrical system. Never risk spilling fuel on a hot engine or exhaust component. It is strongly recommended that a fire extinguisher suitable for use on fuel and electrical fires be kept handy in the garage or workshop at all times. Never try to extinguish a fuel or electrical fire with water.

Fumes

Certain fumes are highly toxic and can quickly cause unconsciousness and even death if inhaled to any extent. Gasoline vapor falls into this category, as do the vapors from some cleaning solvents. Any draining or pouring of such volatile fluids should be done in a well ventilated area.

When using cleaning fluids and solvents, read the instructions on the container carefully. Never use materials from unmarked containers.

Never run the engine in an enclosed space, such as a garage. Exhaust fumes contain carbon monoxide, which is extremely poisonous. If you need to run the engine, always do so in the open air, or at least have the rear of the vehicle outside the work area.

The battery

Never create a spark or allow a bare light bulb near a battery. They normally give off a certain amount of hydrogen gas, which is highly explosive.

Always disconnect the battery ground (-) cable at the battery before working on the fuel or electrical systems.

If possible, loosen the filler caps or cover when charging the battery from an external source (this does not apply to sealed or maintenance-free batteries). Do not charge at an excessive rate or the battery may burst.

Take care when adding water to a non maintenance-free battery and when carrying a battery. The electrolyte, even when diluted, is very corrosive and should not be allowed to contact clothing or skin.

Always wear eye protection when cleaning the battery to prevent the caustic deposits from entering your eyes.

Household current

When using an electric power tool, inspection light, etc., which operates on household current, always make sure that the tool is correctly connected to its plug and that, where necessary, it is properly grounded. Do not use such items in damp conditions and, again, do not create a spark or apply excessive heat in the vicinity of fuel or fuel vapor.

Secondary ignition system voltage

A severe electric shock can result from touching certain parts of the ignition system (such as the spark plug wires) when the engine is running or being cranked, particularly if components are damp or the insulation is defective. In the case of an electronic ignition system, the secondary system voltage is much higher and could prove fatal.

Hydrofluoric acid

This extremely corrosive acid is formed when certain types of synthetic rubber, found in some O-rings, oil seals, fuel hoses, etc. are exposed to temperatures above 750-degrees F (400-degrees C). The rubber changes into a charred or sticky substance containing the acid. *Once formed, the acid remains dangerous for years. If it gets onto the skin, it may be necessary to amputate the limb concerned.*

When dealing with a vehicle which has suffered a fire, or with components salvaged from such a vehicle, wear protective gloves and discard them after use.

Troubleshooting

Contents

This section provides an easy reference guide to the more common problems which may occur during the operation of your vehicle. These problems and their possible causes are grouped under headings denoting various components or systems, such as Engine, Cooling system, etc. They also refer you to the chapter and/or section which deals with the problem.

Remember that successful troubleshooting is not a mysterious black art practiced only by professional mechanics. It is simply the result of the right knowledge combined with an intelligent, systematic approach to the problem. Always work by a process of elimination, starting with the simplest solution and working through to the most complex - and never overlook the obvious. Anyone can run the gas tank dry or leave the lights on overnight, so don't assume that you are exempt from such oversights.

Finally, always establish a clear idea of why a problem has occurred and take steps to ensure that it doesn't happen again. If the electrical system fails because of a poor connection, check the other connections in the system to make sure that they don't fail as well. If a particular fuse continues to blow, find out why - don't just replace one fuse after another. Remember, failure of a small component can often be indicative of potential failure or incorrect functioning of a more important component or system.

Engine

1 Engine will not rotate when attempting to start

1 Battery terminal connections loose or corroded (Chapter 1).
2 Battery discharged or faulty (Chapter 1).
3 Automatic transaxle not completely engaged in Park (Chapter 7).
4 Broken, loose or disconnected wiring in the starting circuit (Chapters 5 and 12).
5 Starter motor pinion jammed in flywheel ring gear (Chapter 5).
6 Starter solenoid faulty (Chapter 5).
7 Starter motor faulty (Chapter 5).
8 Ignition switch faulty (Chapter 12).
9 Starter pinion or flywheel teeth worn or broken (Chapter 5).
10 Faulty Body Control Module (BCM) or Intelligent Power Distribution Module (IPDM) (see Chapter 12).

2 Engine rotates but will not start

1 Fuel tank empty.
2 Battery discharged (engine rotates slowly) (Chapter 5).
3 Battery terminal connections loose or corroded (Chapter 1).
4 Leaking fuel injector(s), faulty fuel pump, pressure regulator, etc. (Chapter 4).
5 Broken timing chain (Chapter 2A).
6 Ignition system problem (Chapter 5).
7 Worn, faulty or incorrectly gapped spark plugs (Chapter 1).
8 Broken, loose or disconnected wiring in the starting circuit (Chapter 5).
9 Defective MAF sensor (see Chapter 6).

3 Engine hard to start when cold

1 Battery discharged or low (Chapter 1).
2 Malfunctioning fuel system (Chapter 4).
3 Faulty coolant temperature sensor or intake air temperature sensor (Chapter 6).
4 Injector(s) leaking (Chapter 4).
5 Faulty ignition system (Chapter 5).
6 Defective MAF sensor (see Chapter 6).

4 Engine hard to start when hot

1 Air filter clogged (Chapter 1).
2 Fuel not reaching the fuel injection system (Chapter 4).
3 Corroded battery connections, especially ground (Chapter 1).
4 Faulty coolant temperature sensor or intake air temperature sensor (Chapter 6).

5 Starter motor noisy or excessively rough in engagement

1 Pinion or flywheel gear teeth worn or broken (Chapter 5).
2 Starter motor mounting bolts loose or missing (Chapter 5).

6 Engine starts but stops immediately

1 Insufficient fuel reaching the fuel injector(s) (Chapter 4).
2 Vacuum leak at the gasket between the intake manifold/plenum and throttle body (Chapters 1 and 4).

7 Oil puddle under engine

1 Oil pan gasket and/or oil pan drain bolt washer leaking (Chapter 2A).
2 Oil pressure sending unit leaking (Chapter 2A).
3 Valve cover leaking (Chapter 2A).
4 Engine oil seals leaking (Chapter 2A).

8 Engine lopes while idling or idles erratically

1 Vacuum leakage (Chapters 2A and 4).
2 Air filter clogged (Chapter 1).
3 Fuel pump not delivering sufficient fuel to the fuel injection system (Chapter 4).
4 Leaking head gasket (Chapter 2A).
5 Timing chain and/or sprockets worn (Chapter 2A).
6 Camshaft lobes worn (Chapter 2A).

9 Engine misses at idle speed

1 Spark plugs worn or not gapped properly (Chapter 1).
2 Vacuum leaks (Chapters 2A and 4).
3 Uneven or low compression (Chapter 2A).
4 Problem with the fuel injection system (Chapter 4).
5 Faulty ignition coil(s) (Chapter 5).

10 Engine misses throughout driving speed range

1 Fuel filter clogged. The filter isn't replaceable; the fuel pump module must be replaced (Chapter 4).
2 Low fuel output at the fuel injector(s) (Chapter 4).
3 Faulty or incorrectly gapped spark plugs (Chapter 1).
4 Faulty ignition coils (Chapter 5).
5 Faulty emission system components (Chapter 6).
6 Low or uneven cylinder compression pressures (Chapter 2A).
7 Vacuum leak in fuel injection system, throttle body, intake manifold, IAC/AAC valve or vacuum hoses (Chapter 4).

11 Engine stumbles on acceleration

1 Spark plugs fouled (Chapter 1).
2 Problem with fuel injection system (Chapter 4).
3 Fuel filter clogged. The filter isn't replaceable; the fuel pump module must be replaced (Chapter 4).
4 Intake manifold air leak (Chapters 2A and 4).
5 EGR system malfunction (Chapter 6).

12 Engine surges while holding accelerator steady

1 Intake air leak (Chapter 4).
2 Fuel pump or fuel pressure regulator faulty (Chapter 4).
3 Problem with fuel injection system (Chapter 4).
4 Problem with the emissions control system (Chapter 6).

13 Engine stalls

1 Fuel filter clogged. The filter isn't replaceable; the fuel pump module must be replaced (Chapter 4).
2 Faulty emissions system components (Chapter 6).
3 Faulty or incorrectly gapped spark plugs (Chapter 1).
4 Vacuum leak in the fuel injection system, intake manifold or vacuum hoses (Chapters 2A and 4).
5 Valve clearances incorrectly set (Chapter 1).

14 Engine lacks power

1 Faulty or incorrectly gapped spark plugs (Chapter 1).
2 Problem with the fuel injection system (Chapter 4).
3 Plugged air filter (Chapter 1).
4 Brakes binding (Chapters 1 and 9).
5 Automatic transaxle fluid level incorrect (Chapter 1).
6 Clutch slipping (Chapter 8).
7 Fuel filter clogged. The filter isn't replaceable; the fuel pump module must be replaced (Chapter 4).

8 Emission control system not functioning properly (Chapter 6).
9 Low or uneven cylinder compression pressures (Chapter 2A).
10 Obstructed exhaust system (Chapters 2A and 4).

15 Engine backfires

1 Emission control system not functioning properly (Chapter 6).
2 Problem with the fuel injection system (Chapter 4).
3 Vacuum leak at fuel injector(s), intake manifold or vacuum hoses (Chapters 2A and 4).
4 Valve clearances incorrectly set and/or valves sticking (Chapter 1).

16 Pinging or knocking engine sounds during acceleration or uphill

1 Incorrect grade of fuel.
2 Fuel injection system faulty (Chapter 4).
3 Improper or damaged spark plugs (Chapter 1).
4 Malfunctioning knock sensor (Chapter 6).
5 Vacuum leak (Chapters 2A and 4).

17 Engine runs with oil pressure light on

1 Low oil level (Chapter 1).
2 Short in wiring circuit (Chapter 12).
3 Faulty oil pressure sender (Chapter 2B).
4 Worn engine bearings and/or oil pump (Chapter 2A).

18 Engine continues to run after switching off

Faulty ignition switch (Chapter 12), Powertrain Control Module (PCM) (Chapter 6), or Body Control Module (BCM).

Engine electrical system

19 Battery will not hold a charge

1 Alternator drivebelt defective or not adjusted properly (Chapter 1).
2 Battery electrolyte level low (Chapter 1).
3 Battery terminals loose or corroded (Chapter 1).
4 Alternator not charging properly (Chapter 5).
5 Loose, broken or faulty wiring in the charging circuit (Chapter 5).
6 Internally defective battery (Chapters 1 and 5).

20 Alternator light fails to go out

1 Faulty alternator or charging circuit (Chapter 5).
2 Alternator drivebelt defective or out of adjustment (Chapter 1).
3 Alternator voltage regulator inoperative (Chapter 5).

21 Alternator light fails to come on when key is turned on

1 Warning light bulb defective (Chapter 12).
2 Fault in the instrument cluster, dash wiring or bulb holder (Chapter 12).

Fuel system

22 Excessive fuel consumption

1 Dirty or clogged air filter element (Chapter 1).
2 Emissions/engine control system not functioning properly (Chapter 6).
3 Fuel injection system not functioning properly (Chapter 4).
4 Low tire pressure or incorrect tire size (Chapter 1).

23 Fuel leakage and/or fuel odor

1 Leaking fuel feed or return line (Chapters 1 and 4).
2 Tank overfilled.
3 Problem with fuel injection system (Chapter 4).

Cooling system

24 Overheating

1 Insufficient coolant in system (Chapter 1).
2 Drivebelt defective or out of adjustment (Chapter 1).
3 Radiator core blocked or grille restricted (Chapter 3).
4 Thermostat or water control valve faulty (Chapter 3).
5 Electric coolant fan inoperative or blades broken (Chapter 3).
6 Radiator cap not maintaining proper pressure (Chapter 3).

25 Overcooling

Faulty thermostat or water control valve (Chapter 3).

26 External coolant leakage

1 Deteriorated/damaged hoses; loose clamps (Chapters 1 and 3).
2 Water pump defective (Chapter 3).
3 Leakage from radiator core or coolant reservoir bottle (Chapter 3).
4 Engine drain or water jacket core plugs leaking.

27 Internal coolant leakage

1 Leaking cylinder head gasket (Chapter 2A).
2 Cracked cylinder bore or cylinder head (Chapter 2A).

28 Coolant loss

1 Too much coolant in system (Chapter 1).
2 Coolant boiling away because of overheating (Chapter 3).
3 Internal or external leakage (Chapter 3).
4 Faulty radiator cap (Chapter 3).

29 Poor coolant circulation

1 Inoperative water pump (Chapter 3).
2 Restriction in cooling system (Chapters 1 and 3).
3 Water pump drivebelt defective/out of adjustment (Chapter 1).
4 Thermostat or water control valve sticking (Chapter 3).

Automatic transaxle

30 Fluid leakage

1 On most models, automatic transaxle fluid is a deep red color. On CVT models it is a light green color. Fluid leaks should not be confused with engine oil, which can easily be blown onto the transaxle by air flow.
2 To pinpoint a leak, first remove all built-up dirt and grime from the transaxle housing with degreasing agents and/or steam cleaning. Then drive the vehicle at low speeds so air flow will not blow the leak far from its source. Raise the vehicle and determine where the leak is coming from. Common areas of leakage are:

a) PanDipstick tube
b) Transaxle oil lines
c) Speed sensor (Chapter 6)
d) Driveaxle oil seals (Chapter 8)

31 Transaxle fluid brown or has a burned smell

Transaxle fluid overheated (Chapter 1).

32 General shift mechanism problems

1 Chapter 7 deals with checking and adjusting the shift cable on automatic transaxles. Common problems which may be attributed to a poorly adjusted cable are:
Engine starting in gears other than Park or NeutralIndicator on shifter pointing to a gear other than the one actually being usedVehicle moves when in Park
2 Refer to Chapter 7 for the shift cable adjustment procedure.

33 Transaxle will not downshift with accelerator pedal pressed to the floor

The transaxle is electronically controlled. This type of problem - which is caused by a malfunction in the control unit, a sensor or solenoid, or the circuit itself - is beyond the scope of this book. Take the vehicle to a dealer service department or a competent automatic transmission shop.

34 Engine will start in gears other than Park or Neutral

Neutral start switch out of adjustment or malfunctioning (Chapter 7).

35 Transaxle slips, is noisy or has no drive in forward or reverse gears

There are many probable causes for the above problems, but the home mechanic should be concerned with only one possibility - fluid level. Before taking the vehicle to a repair shop, check the level and condition of the fluid as described in Chapter 1. Correct the fluid level as necessary or change the fluid if needed. If the problem persists, have a professional diagnose the cause.

Driveaxles

36 Clicking noise in turns

Worn or damaged outboard CV joint (Chapter 8).

37 Shudder or vibration during acceleration

1 Excessive toe-in (Chapter 10).
2 Worn or damaged inboard or outboard CV joints (Chapter 8).
3 Sticking inboard CV joint assembly (Chapter 8).

38 Vibration at highway speeds

1 Out of balance front wheels and/or tires.
2 Out of round front tires.
3 Worn CV joint(s) (Chapter 8).

Brakes

39 Vehicle pulls to one side during braking

1 Incorrect tire pressures (Chapter 1).
2 Front end out of alignment (have the front end aligned).
3 Front, or rear, tire sizes not matched to one another.
4 Restricted brake lines or hoses (Chapter 9).
5 Malfunctioning caliper assembly (Chapter 9).
6 Loose suspension parts (Chapter 10).
7 Excessive wear of brake pad material or disc on one side.

40 Noise (high-pitched squeal when the brakes are applied)

Front and/or rear disc brake pads/rear shoes worn out. Replace pads or shoes with new ones immediately (Chapter 9).

41 Brake roughness or chatter (pedal pulsates)

1 Excessive lateral runout (Chapter 9).
2 Uneven pad wear (Chapter 9).
3 Defective disc or drum (Chapter 9).

42 Excessive brake pedal effort required to stop vehicle

1 Malfunctioning power brake booster (Chapter 9).
2 Partial system failure (Chapter 9).
3 Excessively worn pads (Chapter 9).
4 Piston in caliper stuck or sluggish (Chapter 9).
5 Brake pads contaminated with brake fluid, oil or grease (Chapter 9).
6 Brake disc or drum grooved and/or glazed (Chapter 1).
7 New pads installed and not yet seated. It will take a while for the new material to seat against the disc.

43 Excessive brake pedal travel

1 Partial brake system failure (Chapter 9).
2 Insufficient fluid in master cylinder (Chapters 1 and 9).
3 Air trapped in system. Bleed the brakes (Chapter 9).

44 Dragging brakes

1 Master cylinder pistons not returning correctly (Chapter 9).
2 Restricted brakes lines or hoses (Chapter 10).
3 Incorrect parking brake adjustment (Chapter 9).

45 Grabbing or uneven braking action

Contaminated brake linings (Chapter 9).

46 Brake pedal feels spongy when depressed

1 Air in hydraulic lines. Bleed the system (Chapter 9).
2 Master cylinder defective (Chapter 9).

47 Brake pedal travels to the floor with little resistance

1 Leak in the brake system (Chapters 1 and 9).
2 Loose or damaged brake lines (Chapter 9).

48 Parking brake does not hold

Parking brake improperly adjusted (Chapter 9).

Suspension and steering systems

49 Vehicle pulls to one side

1 Mismatched or uneven tires.
2 Broken or sagging springs (Chapter 10).
3 Wheel alignment out of specifications.
4 Front brake dragging (Chapter 9).

50 Abnormal or excessive tire wear

1 Wheel alignment out of specifications (Chapter 10).
2 Sagging or broken springs (Chapter 10).
3 Tire out of balance.
4 Worn strut damper (Chapter 10).
5 Overloaded vehicle.
6 Tires not rotated regularly.

51 Wheel makes a thumping noise

1 Blister or bump on tire.
2 Improper strut damper action (Chapter 10).

52 Shimmy, shake or vibration

1 Tire or wheel out of balance or out of round.
2 Worn wheel bearings (Chapters 1, 8 and 10).
3 Worn tie-rod ends (Chapter 10).
4 Worn balljoints (Chapters 1 and 10).
5 Excessive wheel runout.
6 Blister or bump on tire.

53 Hard steering

1 Lack of lubrication at balljoints or tie-rod ends (Chapter 10).
2 Front wheel alignment out of specifications.
3 Low tire pressure(s) (Chapter 1).

54 Poor returnability of steering to center

1 Worn balljoints or tie-rod ends (Chapter 10).
2 Binding in balljoints (Chapter 10).
3 Binding in steering column (Chapter 10).
4 Worn steering gear assembly (Chapter 10).
5 Front wheel alignment out of specifications.

55 Abnormal noise at the front end

1 Worn balljoints or tie-rod ends (Chapter 10).
2 Damaged strut mounting (Chapter 10).
3 Worn control arm bushings or tie-rod ends (Chapter 10).
4 Loose stabilizer bar (Chapter 10).
5 Loose wheel nuts.
6 Loose suspension bolts (Chapter 10).

56 Wander or poor steering stability

1 Mismatched or uneven tires.
2 Worn balljoints or tie-rod ends (Chapter 10).
3 Worn strut assemblies (Chapter 10).
4 Loose stabilizer bar (Chapter 10).
5 Broken or sagging springs (Chapter 10).
6 Wheels out of alignment.

57 Erratic steering when braking

1 Wheel bearings worn (Chapter 10).
2 Broken or sagging springs (Chapter 10).
3 Leaking caliper (Chapter 9).
4 Warped brake discs (Chapter 9).

58 Excessive pitching and/or rolling around corners or during braking

1 Loose stabilizer bar (Chapter 10).
2 Worn strut dampers or mountings (Chapter 10).
3 Broken or sagging springs (Chapter 10).
4 Overloaded vehicle.

59 Suspension bottoms

1 Overloaded vehicle.
2 Worn strut dampers or springs (Chapter 10).

60 Cupped tires

1 Front wheel or rear wheel alignment out of specifications.
2 Worn strut dampers (Chapter 10).
3 Wheel bearings worn (Chapter 10).
4 Excessive tire or wheel runout.
5 Worn balljoints (Chapter 10).

61 Excessive tire wear on outside edge

1 Inflation pressures incorrect (Chapter 1).
2 Excessive speed in turns.
3 Front end alignment incorrect (excessive toe-in). Have professionally aligned.
4 Suspension arm bent (Chapter 10).

62 Excessive tire wear on inside edge

1 Inflation pressures incorrect (Chapter 1).
2 Front end alignment incorrect (toe-out). Have professionally aligned.
3 Loose or damaged steering components (Chapter 10).

63 Tire tread worn in one place

1 Tires out of balance.
2 Damaged wheel.
3 Defective tire (Chapter 1).

64 Excessive play or looseness in steering system

1 Wheel bearing(s) worn (Chapter 10).
2 Tie-rod end loose (Chapter 10).
3 Steering gear loose (Chapter 10).
4 Worn or loose steering intermediate shaft (Chapter 10).

65 Rattling or clicking noise in steering gear

1 Steering gear loose (Chapter 10).
2 Steering gear defective.

Chapter 1
Tune-up and routine maintenance

Contents

Specifications

Recommended lubricants and fluids

Note: *Listed here are manufacturer recommendations at the time this manual was written. Manufacturers occasionally upgrade their fluid and lubricant specifications, so check with your local auto parts store for current recommendations.*

Engine oil	
Type	API "certified for gasoline engines"
Viscosity	
2014 and earlier models	SAE 5W-30
2015 models	SAE 5W-30 or SAE 0W-20
2016 and later models	SAE 0W-20
Fuel	Unleaded gasoline, 87 octane or higher
CVT fluid	
2013 and earlier models	Nissan CVT fluid NS-2 only
2014 and later models	Nissan CVT fluid NS-3 only
Rear differential (AWD models)	API GL-5 80W-90 hypoid gear oil
Transfer case (AWD models)	API GL-5 80W-90 hypoid gear oil
Brake and clutch fluid	DOT 3 brake fluid or equivalent
Engine coolant	Pre-diluted Nissan Long Life antifreeze/coolant

Capacities*

Engine oil (including filter)	
2014 and earlier models	5-1/8 quarts
2015 and later models	4-7/8 quarts
Coolant (including reservoir tank)	
2014 and earlier models	7-3/4 quarts
2015 and later models	8-5/8 quarts
CVT transaxle	
2013 and earlier models	
2WD models	7-3/4 to 7-7/8 quarts
AWD models	8-7/8 to 9-1/8 quarts
2014 models	
2WD models	7-3/4 quarts
AWD models	8-3/4 quarts
2015 and later models (all)	8-3/8 quarts
2017 and later CVT transaxle fluid measurement	
VIN numbers beginning with 5N or JN	1.73 to 2.01 inches (44 to 51 mm)
VIN numbers beginning with KN	1.97 to 2.24 inches (50 to 57 mm)
Rear differential (AWD models)	1-1/8 pints
Transfer case (AWD models)	5/8 to 3/4 pint

Note: **All capacities approximate. Add as necessary to bring up to appropriate level.*
Note: ***The best way to determine the amount of fluid to add during a routine fluid change is to measure the amount drained.*

Ignition system

Spark plugs	
Type	
2013 and earlier models/2014 and later Rogue Select models	NGK DILKAR6A-11 or equivalent
2014 and later models (except Rogue Select models)	DENSO FXE20HE11C or equivalent
Gap	0.043 inch
Firing order	1-3-4-2

FRONT OF VEHICLE

1 2 3 4

Cylinder locations

Valve clearance (engine cold)

Intake valves	0.009 to 0.013 inch
Exhaust valves	0.010 to 0.013 inch

Cooling system

Thermostat starts to open	177 to 182-degrees F

Brakes

Disc brake lining thickness (minimum)	
Front pad	0.08 inch
Rear pad	0.06 inch
Brake pedal	See Chapter 9
Parking brake adjustment	See Chapter 9

Suspension and steering

Steering wheel freeplay limit	1-3/8 inches
Balljoint allowable movement	0 inch

Torque specifications

Note: *One foot-pound (ft-lb) of torque is equivalent to 12 inch-pounds (in-lbs) of torque. Torque values below approximately 15 ft-lbs are expressed in inch-pounds, because most foot-pound torque wrenches are not accurate at these smaller values.*

Torque specifications	Ft-lbs (unless otherwise indicated)
Engine oil drain plug	25
CVT transaxle drain plug	25
CVT transaxle overflow plug	89 in-lbs
Differential drain/fill plugs	26
Drivebelt tensioner bolt(s)	
2013 and earlier models/2014 and later Rogue Select models	18
2014 and later models (except Rogue Select models)	25
Spark plugs	168 in-lbs
Transfer case drain/fill plugs	25
Wheel lug nuts	
2013 and earlier models/2014 and later Rogue Select models	80
2014 and later models (except Rogue Select models)	83

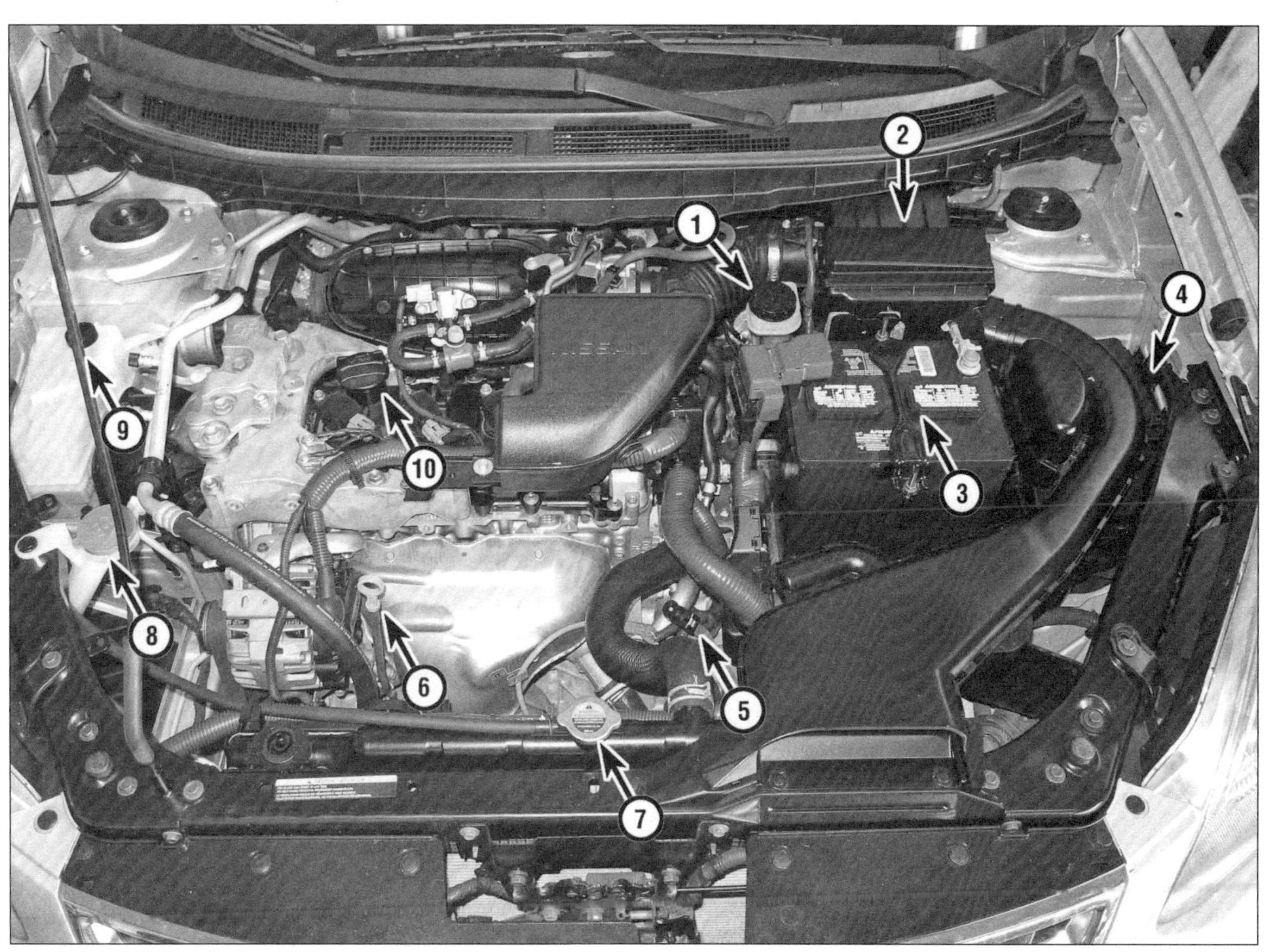

Typical engine compartment components

1. *Brake fluid reservoir*
2. *Air filter housing*
3. *Battery*
4. *Fuse/relay box*
5. *Automatic transaxle fluid dipstick*
6. *Engine oil dipstick*
7. *Radiator cap*
8. *Windshield washer fluid reservoir*
9. *Coolant reservoir*
10. *Engine oil filler cap*

Typical engine compartment underside components

1 *Engine oil drain plug*
2 *Driveaxle inner CV joint and boot*
3 *Tie-rod end*
4 *Balljoint*
5 *Control arm*
6 *Brake caliper*
7 *Exhaust pipe*
8 *Transaxle drain plug*
9 *Driveaxle outer CV joint and boot*

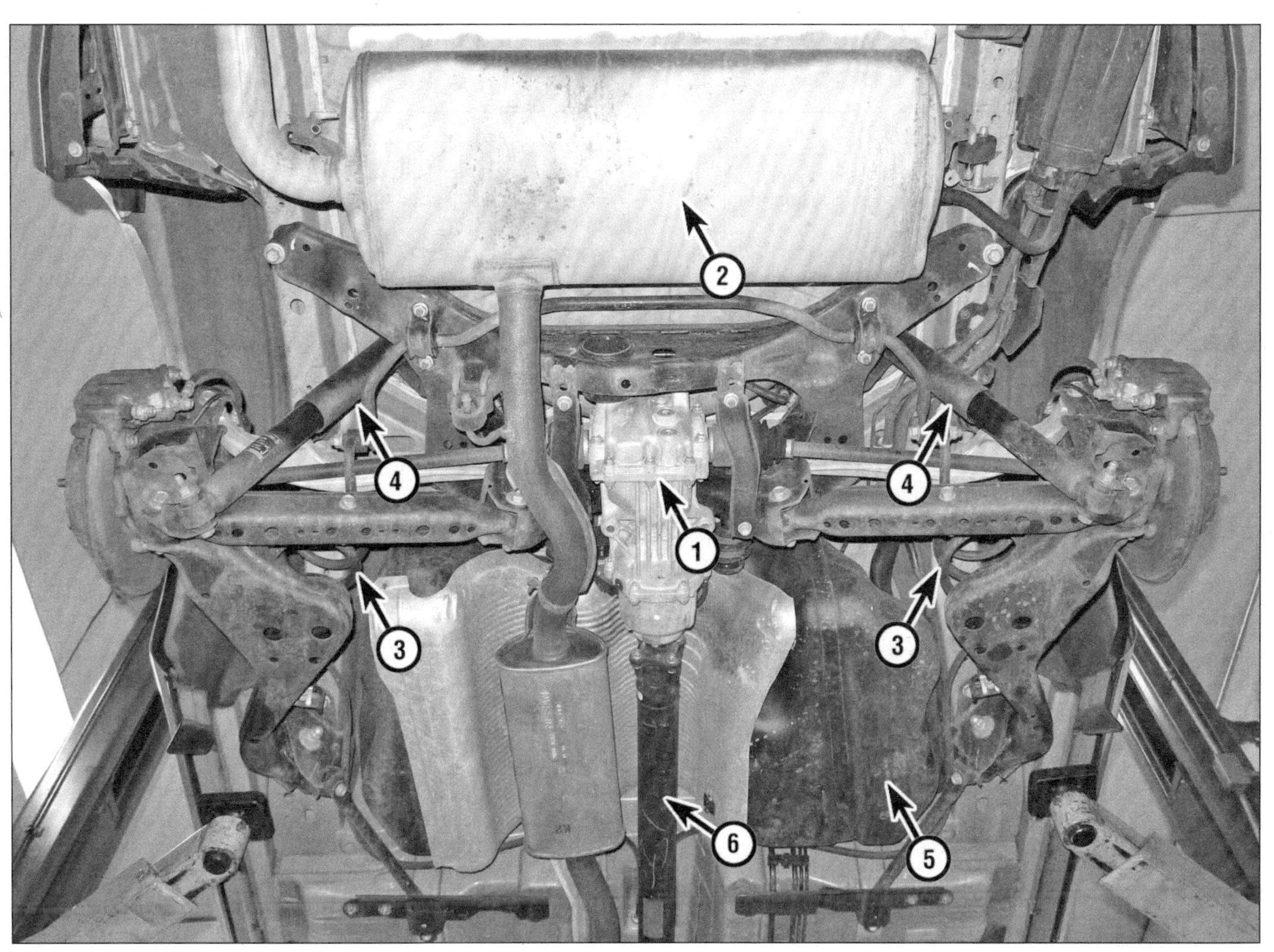

Typical rear underside components

1. *Rear differential (AWD) models only*
2. *Muffler*
3. *Coil spring*
4. *Shock absorber*
5. *Fuel tank*
6. *Driveshaft (AWD models only)*

1 Maintenance schedule

The maintenance intervals in this manual are provided with the assumption that you, not the dealer, will be doing the work. These are the minimum maintenance intervals recommended by the factory for vehicles that are driven daily. If you wish to keep your vehicle in peak condition at all times, you may wish to perform some of these procedures even more often. Because frequent maintenance enhances the efficiency, performance and resale value of your car, we encourage you to do so. If you drive in dusty areas, tow a trailer, idle or drive at low speeds for extended periods or drive for short distances (less than four miles) in below freezing temperatures, shorter intervals are also recommended.

When your vehicle is new, it should be serviced by a factory authorized dealer service department to protect the factory warranty. In many cases, the initial maintenance check is done at no cost to the owner.

Every 250 miles or weekly, whichever comes first

Check the engine oil level (Section 4)
Check the engine coolant level (Section 4)
Check the windshield washer fluid level (Section 4)
Check the battery electrolyte (Section 4)
Check the brake fluid level (Section 4)
Check the tires and tire pressures (Section 5)

Every 3000 miles or 3 months, whichever comes first

Note: *All items listed above plus:*
Check the automatic transaxle fluid level (2013 and earlier models) (Section 6)
Change the engine oil and oil filter (Section 7)

Every 7500 miles or 6 months, whichever comes first

Inspect and replace if necessary the windshield wiper blades (Section 8)
Check and service the battery (Section 9)
Check the engine drivebelt (Section 10)
Inspect and replace if necessary all underhood hoses (Section 11)
Check the cooling system (Section 12)
Rotate the tires (Section 13)

Every 10,000 miles

Check the automatic transaxle fluid level (2014 and later models) (Section 6)

Every 15,000 miles or 12 months, whichever comes first

Note: *All items listed above plus:*
Inspect the brake system (Section 16)*
Replace the cabin air filter (Section 17)
Inspect the fuel system (Section 19)
Inspect the suspension and steering components (Section 20)
Inspect the exhaust system (Section 21)
Check the driveaxle boots (Section 22)

Every 30,000 miles or 24 months, whichever comes first

Note: *All items listed above plus:*
Replace the air filter (Section 18)
Service the cooling system (drain, flush and refill) (Section 24)
Inspect the evaporative emissions control system (Section 25)
Check and replace if necessary the PCV valve (Section 27)

Every 60,000 miles or 48 months, whichever comes first

Change the automatic transaxle fluid (Section 26)**
Check (and adjust if noisy) the valve clearance (Section 30)

Every 105,000 miles or 72 months, whichever comes first

Replace the spark plugs (Section 23)

* *This item is affected by "severe" operating conditions as described below. If your vehicle is operated under "severe" conditions, perform all maintenance indicated with an asterisk (*) at half the indicated intervals. Severe conditions are indicated if you mainly operate your vehicle under one or more of the following conditions:*

a) Operating in dusty areas
b) Towing a trailer
c) Idling for extended periods and/or low speed operation
d) Operating when outside temperatures remain below freezing and when most trips are less than 4 miles

** *If operated under one or more of the following conditions, change the, manual or automatic transmission fluid and differential lubricant every 30,000 miles:*

a) In heavy city traffic where outside temperature regularly reaches 90-degrees F (32-degrees C) or higher
b) In hilly or mountainous terrain
c) Frequent trailer pulling

2 Introduction

1 This Chapter is designed to help the home mechanic maintain the Nissan Rogue for peak performance, economy, safety and long life.

2 Included in this Chapter is a master maintenance schedule, followed by Sections dealing specifically with each item on the schedule. Visual checks, adjustments, component replacement and other helpful items are included. Refer to the accompanying illustrations of the engine compartment and the underside of the vehicle for the location of various components.

3 Servicing your Rogue in accordance with the mileage/time maintenance schedule and the following Sections will provide it with a planned maintenance program that should result in a long and reliable service life. This is a comprehensive plan, so maintaining some items but not others at the specified service intervals will not produce the same results.

4 As you service your Rogue, you will discover that many of the procedures can, and should, be grouped together because of the nature of the particular procedure you're performing or because of the close proximity of two otherwise unrelated components to one another.

5 For example, if the vehicle is raised for any reason, you should inspect the exhaust, suspension, steering and fuel systems while you're under the vehicle. When you're rotating the tires, it makes good sense to check the brakes and wheel bearings since the wheels are already removed.

6 Finally, let's suppose you have to borrow or rent a torque wrench. Even if you only need to tighten the spark plugs, you might as well check the torque of as many critical fasteners as time allows.

7 The first step of this maintenance program is to prepare yourself before the actual work begins. Read through all Sections pertinent to the procedures you're planning to do, then make a list of and gather together all the parts and tools you will need to do the job. If it looks as if you might run into problems during a particular segment of some procedure, seek advice from your local auto parts stores or dealer service department.

3 Tune-up general information

1 The term tune-up is used in this manual to represent a combination of individual operations rather than one specific procedure.

2 If, from the time the vehicle is new, the routine maintenance schedule is followed closely and frequent checks are made of fluid levels and high wear items, as suggested throughout this manual, the engine will be kept in relatively good running condition and the need for additional work will be minimized.

3 More likely than not, however, there will be times when the engine is running poorly due to lack of regular maintenance. This is even more likely if a used vehicle, which has not received regular and frequent maintenance checks, is purchased. In such cases, an engine tune-up will be needed outside of the regular routine maintenance intervals.

4 The first step in any tune-up or engine diagnosis to help correct a poor running engine would be a cylinder compression check. A check of the engine compression (see Chapter 2B) will give valuable information regarding the overall performance of many internal components and should be used as a basis for tune-up and repair procedures. If, for instance, a compression check indicates serious internal engine wear, a conventional tune-up will not help the running condition of the engine and would be a waste of time and money.

5 The following series of operations are those most often needed to bring a generally poor running engine back into a proper state of tune.

Minor tune-up

Check all engine related fluids (Section 4)
Clean, inspect and test the battery (Section 9)
Check the drivebelt (Section 10)
Check all underhood hoses (Section 11)
Check the cooling system (Section 12)
Check the air filter (Section 18)

Major tune-up

Note: *All items listed under Minor tune-up, plus . . .*

Replace the air filter (Section 18)
Check the fuel system (Section 19)
Replace the spark plugs (Section 23)
Check the charging system (Chapter 5)
Check the ignition system (Chapter 5)

4 Fluid level checks (every 250 miles or weekly)

1 Fluids are an essential part of the lubrication, cooling, brake, clutch and other systems. Because these fluids gradually become depleted and/or contaminated during normal operation of the vehicle, they must be periodically replenished. See Recommended lubricants and fluids and Capacities in this Chapter's Specifications before adding fluid to any of the following components.

Note: *The vehicle must be on level ground before fluid levels can be checked.*

Engine oil

2 The engine oil level is checked with a dipstick located at the front of the engine (see illustration).

3 The oil level should be checked before the vehicle has been driven, or about 5 minutes after the engine has been shut off. If the oil is checked immediately after driving the vehicle, some of the oil will remain in the upper engine components, producing an inaccurate reading on the dipstick.

4 Pull the dipstick out and wipe all the oil from the end with a clean rag or paper towel. Insert the clean dipstick all the way back in and pull it out again. Observe the oil at the end of the dipstick; the level should be between the L and H marks (see illustration).

5 It takes about one quart of oil to raise the level from the L mark to the H mark on the dipstick. Do not allow the level to drop

4.2 Engine oil dipstick location

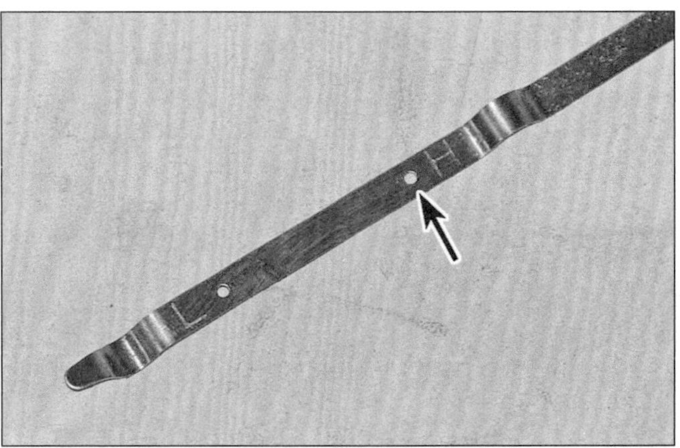

4.4 The oil level should be at or near the H mark - if it isn't, add enough oil to bring the level to near the H mark

4.6 Oil filler cap location

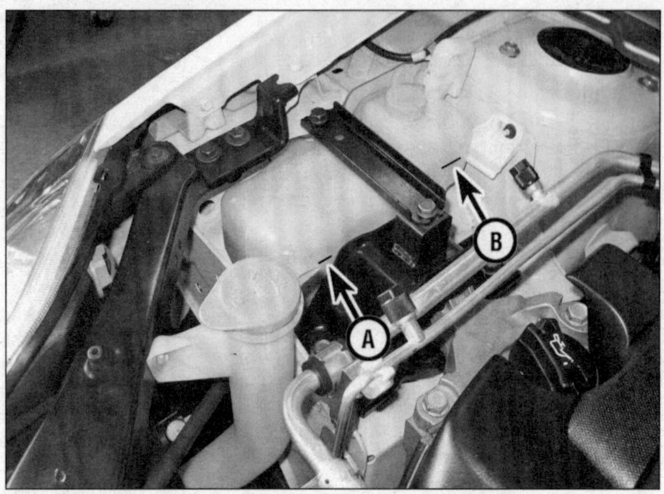

4.8 Location of the coolant reservoir

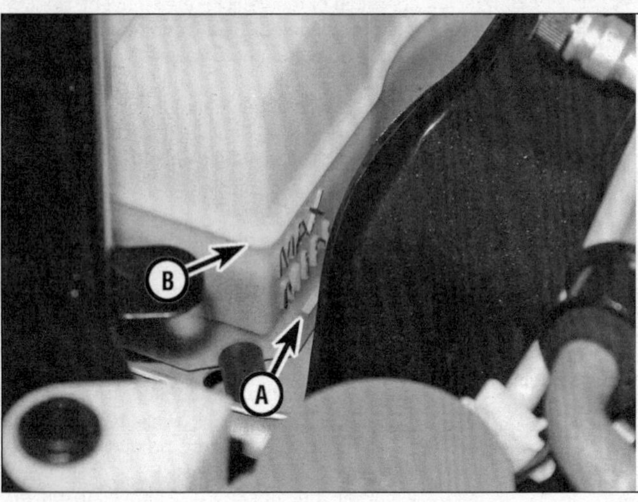

4.9 Coolant reservoir MIN (A) mark; add coolant to bring the level near the MAX (B) mark on the reservoir

below the L mark or oil starvation may cause engine damage. Conversely, overfilling the engine (adding oil above the H mark) may cause oil fouled spark plugs, oil leaks or oil seal failures.

6 Wipe the area around the filler cap, then remove the cap from the valve cover to add oil (see illustration). Use a funnel to prevent spills. After adding the oil, install the filler cap hand tight. Start the engine and look carefully for any small leaks around the oil filter or drain plug. Stop the engine and check the oil level again after it has had sufficient time to drain from the upper block and cylinder head galleys.

7 Checking the oil level is an important preventive maintenance step. A continually dropping oil level indicates oil leakage through damaged seals, from loose connections, or past worn rings or valve guides. If the oil looks milky in color or has water droplets in it, a cylinder head gasket may be leaking. The cylinder head should be checked immediately. The condition of the oil should also be checked. Each time you check the oil level, slide your thumb and index finger up the dipstick before wiping off the oil. If you see small dirt or metal particles clinging to the dipstick, the oil should be changed (see Section 7).

Engine coolant

Warning: *Do not allow antifreeze to come in contact with your skin or painted surfaces of the vehicle. Flush contaminated areas immediately with plenty of water. Don't store new coolant or leave old coolant lying around where it's accessible to children or pets - they're attracted by its sweet smell and may drink it. Ingestion of even a small amount of coolant can be fatal! Wipe up garage floor and drip pan spills immediately. Keep antifreeze containers covered and repair cooling system leaks as soon as they're noticed.*

8 All vehicles covered by this manual are equipped with a pressurized coolant recovery system. A white coolant reservoir located in the front of the engine compartment is connected by a hose to the base of the radiator cap (see illustration). If the coolant gets too hot during engine operation, coolant can escape through the relief valve in the radiator cap, then through a connecting hose into the reservoir. As the engine cools, the coolant is automatically drawn back into the cooling system to maintain the correct level.

9 The coolant level should be checked regularly. It must be between the Max and Min lines on the tank (see illustration). The level will vary with the temperature of the engine. When the engine is cold, the coolant level should be at or slightly above the Min mark on the tank. Once the engine has warmed up, the level should be at or near the Max mark. If it isn't, allow the fluid in the tank to cool, then remove the cap from the reservoir and add coolant to bring the level up to the Max line. Use only the specified type of coolant recommended by your owner's manual or in this Chapter's Specifications. Do not use supplemental inhibitor additives. If only a small amount of coolant is required to bring the system up to the proper level, water can be used. However, repeated additions of water will dilute the recommended antifreeze and water solution. In order to maintain the proper ratio of antifreeze and water, it is advisable to top up the coolant level with the correct mixture. Refer to your owner's manual for the recommended ratio.

10 If the coolant level drops within a short time after replenishment, there may be a leak in the system. Inspect the radiator, hoses, radiator cap, drain plugs and water pump. If no leak is evident, have the radiator cap pressure tested by your dealer.

Warning: *Never remove the radiator cap or the coolant recovery reservoir cap when the engine is running or has just been shut down, because the cooling system is hot. Escaping steam and scalding liquid could cause serious injury.*

11 If it is necessary to open the radiator cap, wait until the system has cooled completely, then wrap a thick cloth around the cap and slowly unscrew it. If any steam escapes, wait until the system has cooled further, then remove the cap.

12 When checking the coolant level, always note its condition. It should be relatively clear. If it is brown or rust colored, the system should be drained, flushed and refilled. Even

4.14 Windshield washer fluid reservoir location

4.15 Remove the cell caps to check the water level in the battery - if the level is low, add distilled water only

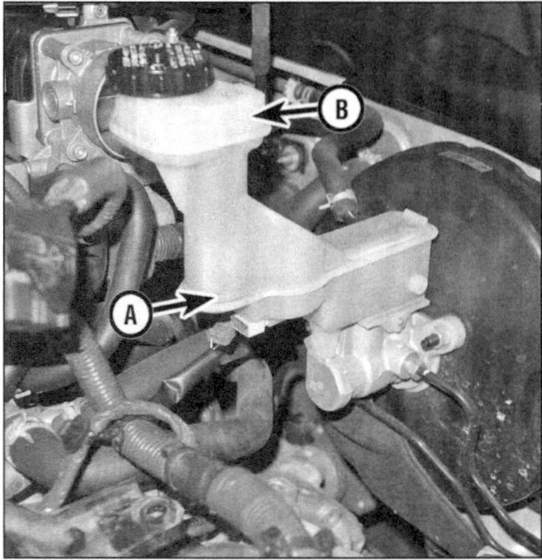

4.17 The brake fluid level should be kept between the MIN (A) and MAX (B) marks on the translucent plastic reservoir (the air filter housing has been removed for clarity)

if the coolant appears to be normal, the corrosion inhibitors wear out with use, so it must be replaced at the specified intervals.

13 Do not allow antifreeze to come in contact with your skin or painted surfaces of the vehicle. Flush contacted areas immediately with plenty of water.

Windshield washer fluid

14 Fluid for the windshield washer system is stored in a plastic reservoir which is located on the right side of the engine compartment just behind the headlight (see illustration). In milder climates, plain water can be used to top up the reservoir, but the reservoir should be kept no more than two-thirds full to allow for expansion should the water freeze. In colder climates, the use of a specially designed windshield washer fluid, available at your dealer and any auto parts store, will help lower the freezing point of the fluid. Mix the solution with water in accordance with the manufacturer's directions on the container. Do not use regular antifreeze. It will damage the vehicle's paint.

Battery electrolyte

15 On models not equipped with a sealed battery, check the electrolyte level (see illustration) of all six battery cells. It must be between the upper and lower levels. If the level is low, remove the filler/vent cap and add distilled water. Install and securely re-tighten the cap.

Caution: *Overfilling the cells may cause electrolyte to spill over during periods of heavy charging, causing corrosion or damage.*

Brake fluid

16 The brake master cylinder is mounted on the front of the power booster unit in the engine compartment.

17 To check the fluid level of the brake master cylinder, simply look at the marks on the reservoir (see illustration). The level should be between the MIN and MAX marks.

18 If the level is low, wipe the top of the reservoir and the cap with a clean rag to prevent contamination of the brake system before unscrewing the cover.

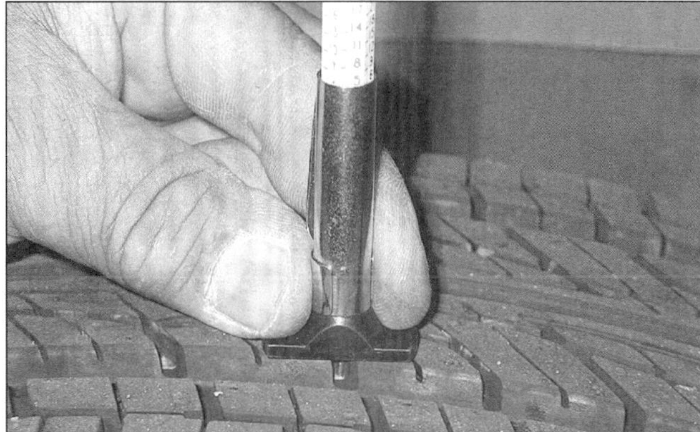
5.2 A tire tread depth indicator should be used to monitor tire wear - they are available at auto parts stores and service stations and cost very little

19 Add only the specified brake fluid to the brake reservoir (refer to Recommended lubricants and fluids in this Chapter's Specifications or your owner's manual). Mixing different types of brake fluid can damage the system. Fill the brake master cylinder reservoir only to the MAX line.

Warning: *Use caution when filling the reservoir - brake fluid can harm your eyes and damage painted surfaces. Do not use brake fluid that is more than one year old or has been left open. Brake fluid absorbs moisture from the air. Excess moisture can cause a dangerous loss of braking.*

20 While the reservoir cap is removed, inspect the master cylinder reservoir for contamination. If deposits, dirt particles or water droplets are present, the system should be drained and refilled.

21 After filling the reservoir to the proper level, make sure the cap is properly seated to prevent fluid leakage and/or system pressure loss.

22 The fluid in the brake master cylinder will drop slightly as the brake pads at each wheel wear down during normal operation. If the master cylinder requires repeated replenishing to keep it at the proper level, this is an indication of leakage in the brake system, which should be corrected immediately. If the brake system shows an indication of leakage, check all brake lines and connections, along with the calipers and booster (see Section 16 for more information).

23 If, upon checking the brake master cylinder fluid level, you discover the reservoir empty or nearly empty, the system should be bled (see Chapter 9).

5 Tire and tire pressure checks (every 250 miles or weekly)

1 Periodic inspection of the tires may spare you from the inconvenience of being stranded with a flat tire. It can also provide you with vital information regarding possible problems in the steering and suspension systems before major damage occurs.

2 Tires are equipped with 1/2-inch wide wear bands that will appear when tread depth reaches 1/16-inch, at which point the tires can be considered worn out. Tread wear can be monitored with a simple, inexpensive device known as a tread depth indicator (see illustration).

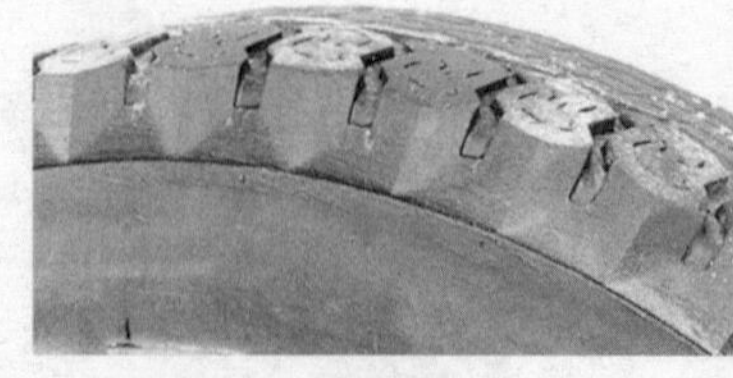

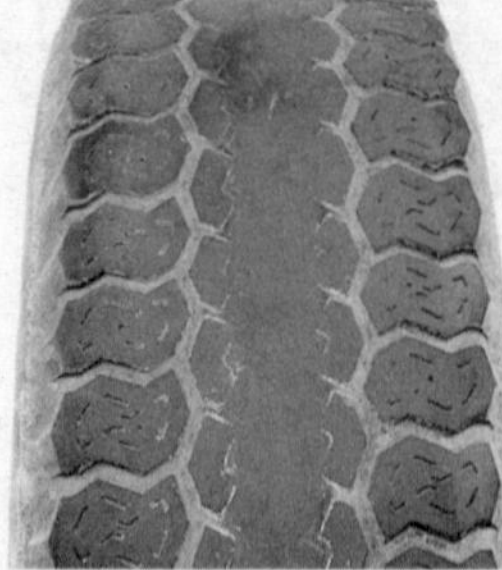

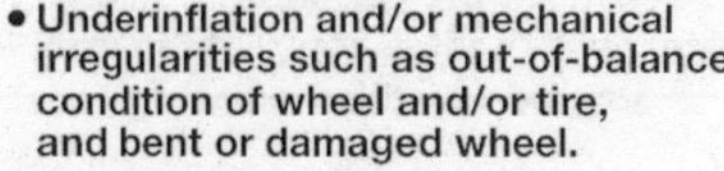

5.3 This chart will help you determine the condition of your tires, the probable cause(s) of abnormal wear and the corrective action necessary

3 Note any abnormal tread wear (see illustration). Tread pattern irregularities such as cupping, flat spots and more wear on one side than the other are indications of front end alignment and/or balance problems. If any of these conditions are noted, take the vehicle to a tire shop or service station to correct the problem.

4 Look closely for cuts, punctures and embedded nails or tacks. Sometimes a tire will hold its air pressure for a short time or leak down very slowly even after a nail has embedded itself into the tread. If a slow leak persists, check the valve stem core to make sure it is tight (see illustration). Examine the tread for an object that may have embedded itself into the tire or for a plug that may have begun to leak (radial tire punctures are repaired with a plug that is installed in a puncture). If a puncture is suspected, it can be easily verified by spraying a solution of soapy water onto the puncture area (see illustration). The soapy solution will bubble if there is a leak. Unless the puncture is inordinately large, a tire shop or gas station can usually repair the punctured tire.

5 Carefully inspect the inner sidewall of each tire for evidence of brake fluid leakage. If you see any, inspect the brakes immediately.

6 Correct tire air pressure adds miles to the lifespan of the tires, improves mileage and enhances overall ride quality. Tire pressure cannot be accurately estimated by looking at a tire, particularly if it is a radial. A tire pressure gauge is therefore essential. Keep an accurate gauge in the glove box. The pressure gauges fitted to the nozzles of air hoses at gas stations are often inaccurate.

5.4a If a tire loses air on a steady basis, check the valve core first to make sure it's snug (special inexpensive wrenches are commonly available at auto parts stores)

5.4b If the valve core is tight, raise the corner of the vehicle with the low tire and spray a soapy water solution onto the tread as the tire is turned slowly - slow leaks will cause small bubbles to appear

5.8 To extend the life of your tires, check the air pressure at least once a week with an accurate gauge (don't forget the spare!)

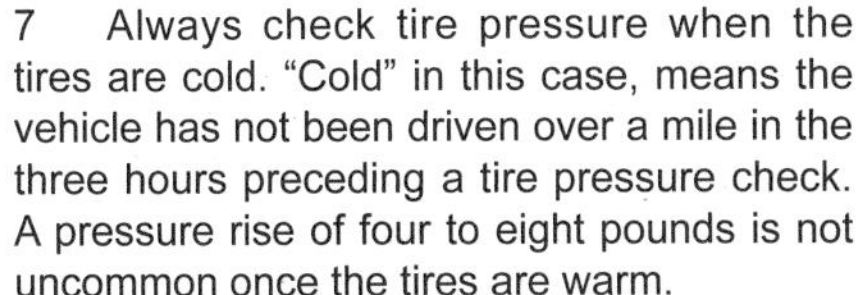

7 Always check tire pressure when the tires are cold. "Cold" in this case, means the vehicle has not been driven over a mile in the three hours preceding a tire pressure check. A pressure rise of four to eight pounds is not uncommon once the tires are warm.

8 Unscrew the valve cap protruding from the wheel or hubcap and push the gauge firmly onto the valve (see illustration). Note the reading on the gauge and compare this figure to the recommended tire pressure shown on the tire placard on the left door. Be sure to reinstall the valve cap to keep dirt and moisture out of the valve stem mechanism. Check all four tires and, if necessary, add enough air to bring them up to the recommended pressure levels.

9 Don't forget to keep the spare tire inflated to the specified pressure (consult your owner's manual). Note that the air pressure specified for the compact spare is significantly higher than the pressure of the regular tires.

6 Automatic CVT transaxle fluid level check (see Maintenance Schedule for service interval)

1 The level of the CVT transaxle fluid should be carefully maintained. Low fluid level can lead to slipping or loss of drive, while overfilling can cause foaming, loss of fluid and transaxle damage.

2 The transaxle fluid should only be checked when the transaxle is warm. On 2013 and earlier models the temperature of the fluid should be between 122 to 176-degrees F. On 2014 and later models, the fluid should be between 95 and 113-degrees F.

Caution: *If the vehicle has just been driven for a long time at high speed or in city traffic in hot weather, or if it has been pulling a trailer, an accurate fluid level reading cannot be obtained. Allow the fluid to cool down for about 30 minutes.*

3 If the vehicle has not been driven, park the vehicle on level ground, set the parking brake, then start the engine and bring it to operating temperature. While the engine is idling, depress the brake pedal and move the selector lever through all the gear ranges, beginning and ending in Park.

6.4 Press the tab on the dipstick to release the lock (2013 and earlier models)

2013 and earlier models

4 With the engine still idling, release and remove the dipstick from its tube (see illustration). Check the level of the fluid on the dipstick (see illustration 6.6) and note its condition.

5 Wipe the fluid from the dipstick with a clean rag and reinsert it back into the filler tube until the cap seats.

Note: *When inserting the dipstick, rotate it 1/2-turn so the tab on the cap doesn't lock into place when the dipstick is fully inserted.*

6 Pull the dipstick out again and note the fluid level (see illustration). If the level is at the low side of the range, add the specified automatic transaxle fluid through the dipstick tube with a funnel.

Caution: *This transaxle uses a special fluid designed specifically for Nissan CVT transaxles. Don't use another fluid or damage may occur. See this Chapter's Specifications.*

7 Add just enough of the recommended fluid to fill the transaxle to the proper level. It takes about one pint to raise the level from the low mark to the high mark when the fluid is hot, so add the fluid a little at a time and keep checking the level until it is correct. Once the fluid level is correct, reinstall the dipstick with the locking tab or looped stopper oriented correctly, making sure it locks into place.

2014 through 2016 models

8 Raise the front and rear of the vehicle and support it securely on jackstands.

Note: The vehicle must be supported in a level fashion for an accurate check.

9 Remove the overflow plug from the bottom of the converter housing area of the transaxle.

10 Thread special fluid charging fitting (Nissan tool no. KV311039S0 or equivalent) into the hole. Attach a hose and fluid pump to the fitting and add approximately ½ quart to the transaxle.

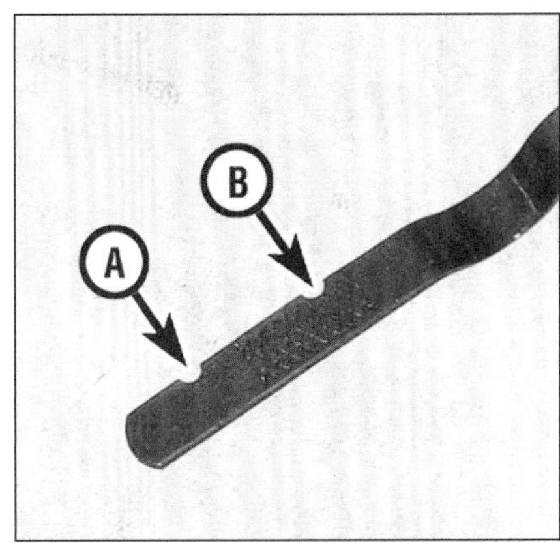

6.6 Check the CVT transaxle fluid with the engine idling at operating temperature and the gear selector in Park; if the fluid level is at the lower notch (A), add fluid to bring the level near the upper notch (B)

11 With the engine idling in Park, remove the hose and observe the fluid; some fluid should drain from the fitting. If it does not, add another ½ quart.

12 Remove the hose again and verify that the fluid drips out. If it does not, add some more until it does.

13 Remove the hose and allow the fluid to flow out until it slow to a drip, then remove the fitting and install the overflow plug, tightening it to the torque listed in this Chapter's Specifications.

14 Lower the vehicle.

2017 and later models

15 Verify the transaxle fluid is at normal operating temperature (170 to 180-degrees F).

16 Raise the vehicle and support it securely jackstands.

Caution: *Both ends of the vehicle must be raised and evenly supported on jackstands for and accurate check.*

17 Remove the cap from the oil filler tube using special tool #J-52611, or equivalent.

18 Using the dipstick special tool #J-51155, incort tho tool into tho CVT fluid fillor pipo.

Note: *The tool handle has two positions: one where the handle is up (blue position) and one where the handle is pushed down (red position). The handle must be in the up (blue) position for this check.*

19 Remove the dipstick tool and read the measurement of fluid on the tool and compare it to the specifications listed in this Chapter.

20 If fluid is needed, adjust the fluid level (see Steps 9 through 14).

All models

21 The condition of the fluid should also be checked along with the level. If the fluid at the end of the dipstick is black or a dark green color, or if it emits a burned smell, the fluid should be changed (see Section 26). If you are in doubt about the condition of the fluid, purchase some new fluid and compare the two for color and smell.

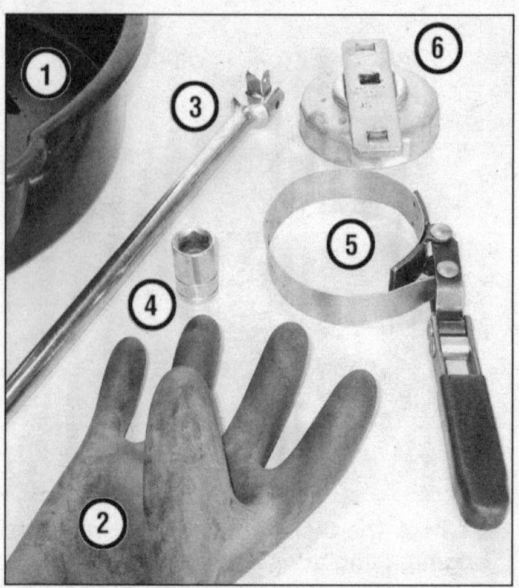

7.2 These tools are required when changing the engine oil and filter

1 *Drain pan - It should be fairly shallow in depth, but wide in order to prevent spills*
2 *Rubber gloves - When removing the drain plug and filter, it is inevitable that you will get oil on your hands (the gloves will prevent burns)*
3 *Breaker bar - Sometimes the oil drain plug is pretty tight and a long breaker bar is needed to loosen it*
4 *Socket - To be used with the breaker bar or a ratchet (must be the correct size to fit the drain plug)*
5 *Filter wrench - This is a metal band-type wrench, which requires clearance around the filter to be effective*
6 *Filter wrench - This type fits on the top of the filter and can be turned with a ratchet or breaker bar (different size wrenches are available for different types of filters)*

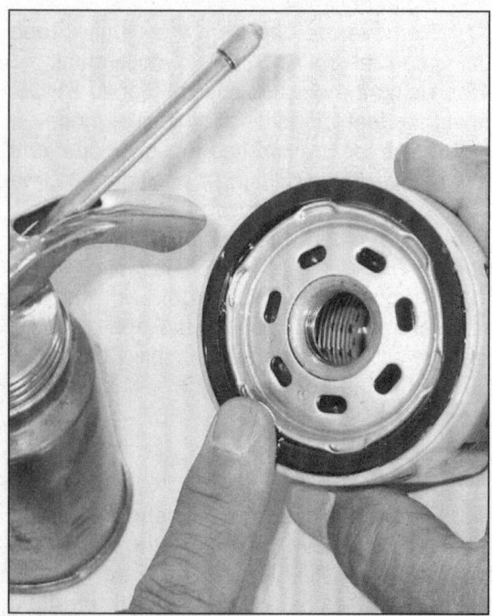
7.12 Lubricate the oil filter gasket with clean engine oil before installing the filter on the engine

7.5 Use a proper size box-end wrench or socket to remove the oil drain plug and avoid rounding it off

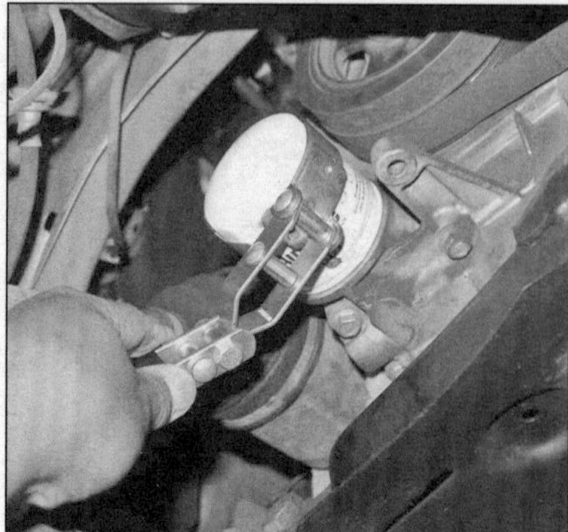
7.10 The oil filter is located on the right end of the engine. Use an oil filter wrench for removal; DO NOT use the wrench to tighten the new filter

7 Engine oil and oil filter change (every 3000 miles or 3 months)

1 Frequent oil changes are the best preventive maintenance the home mechanic can give the engine, because aging oil becomes diluted and contaminated, which leads to premature engine wear.

2 Make sure that you have all the necessary tools before you begin this procedure (see illustration). You should also have plenty of rags or newspapers handy for mopping up any spills.

3 Park the vehicle on a level spot. Start the engine and allow it to reach its normal operating temperature (the needle on the temperature gauge should be at least above the bottom mark). Warm oil and contaminates will flow out more easily. Turn off the engine when it's warmed up. Remove the filler cap in the valve cover.

4 Raise the vehicle and support it securely on jackstands.

Warning: *To avoid personal injury, never get beneath the vehicle when it is supported by only by a jack. The jack provided with your vehicle is designed solely for raising the vehicle to remove and replace the wheels. Always use jackstands to support the vehicle when it becomes necessary to place your body underneath the vehicle.*

5 Being careful not to touch the hot exhaust components, place the drain pan under the drain plug in the bottom of the pan and remove the plug (see illustration). You may want to wear gloves while unscrewing the plug the final few turns if the engine is really hot.

6 Allow the old oil to drain into the pan. It may be necessary to move the pan farther under the engine as the oil flow slows to a trickle. Inspect the old oil for the presence of metal shavings and chips.

7 After all the oil has drained, wipe off the drain plug with a clean rag. Even minute metal particles clinging to the plug would immediately contaminate the new oil.

8 Clean the area around the drain plug opening, reinstall the plug and tighten it to the torque listed in this Chapter's Specifications.

9 Move the drain pan into position under the oil filter.

10 Loosen the oil filter by turning it counterclockwise with the filter wrench (see illustration). Any standard filter wrench should work. Once the filter is loose, use your hands to unscrew it from the block. Just as the filter is detached from the block, immediately tilt the open end up to prevent the oil inside the filter from spilling out.

11 With a clean rag, wipe off the oil filter mounting surface. Make sure that none of the old gasket remains stuck to the mounting surface. It can be removed with a scraper if necessary.

12 Compare the old filter with the new one to make sure they are the same type. Smear some engine oil on the rubber gasket of the new filter and screw it into place (see illustration). Because over-tightening the filter will damage the gasket, do not use a filter wrench to tighten it. Tighten it by hand until the gasket contacts the seating surface, then seat the filter by giving it an additional 3/4- turn.

13 Remove all tools, rags, etc. from under the vehicle, being careful not to spill the oil in the drain pan, then lower the vehicle.

14 Remove the filler cap and add new oil to the engine. Use a spout or funnel to prevent oil from spilling onto the top of the engine. Pour four quarts of fresh oil into the engine. Wait a few minutes to allow the oil to drain into the pan, then check the level on the oil dipstick (see Section 4 if necessary). If the oil level is at or near the H mark, install the filler cap hand tight, start the engine and allow the new oil to circulate.

15 Allow the engine to run for about a minute. While the engine is running, look under the vehicle and check for leaks at the oil pan drain plug and around the oil filter. If either is leaking, stop the engine and tighten the plug or filter slightly.

8.3 Pry off the trim cap and check the tightness of the wiper arm retaining nut

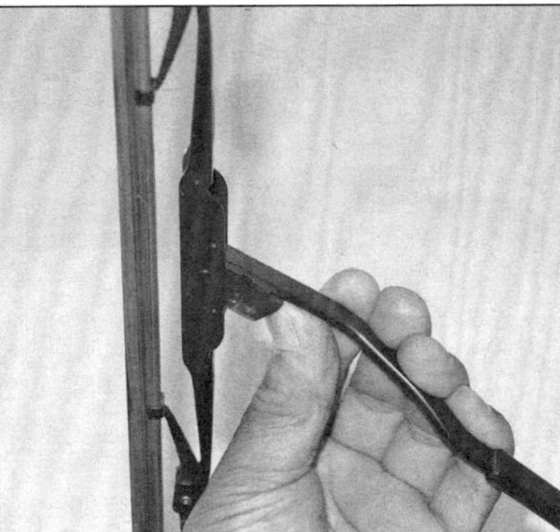

8.5 Press on the release tab and push the blade assembly down out of the hook in the arm

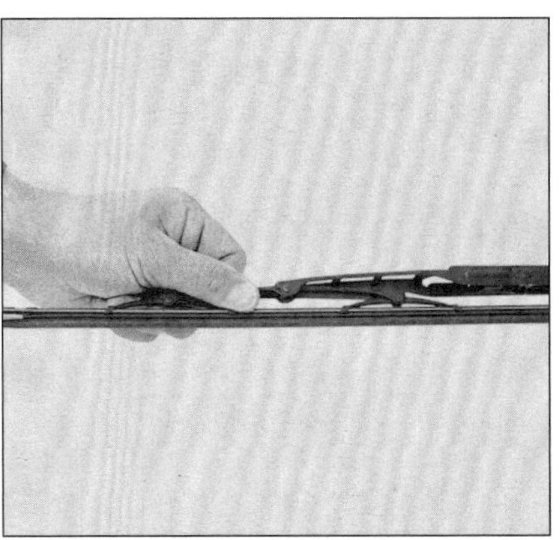

8.6 Use needle-nose pliers to compress the rubber element, then slide the element out - slide the new element in and lock the blade assembly fingers into the notches of the wiper element

16 Wait a few minutes to allow the oil to trickle down into the pan, then recheck the level on the dipstick and, if necessary, add enough oil to bring the level to the H mark.

17 During the first few trips after an oil change, make it a point to check frequently for leaks and proper oil level.

18 The old oil drained from the engine cannot be reused in its present state and should be disposed of. Check with your local auto parts store, disposal facility or environmental agency to see if they will accept the oil for recycling. After the oil has cooled it can be drained into a container (capped plastic jugs, topped bottles, milk cartons, etc.) for transport to one of these disposal sites. Don't dispose of the oil by pouring it on the ground or down a drain!

8 Windshield wiper blade inspection and replacement (every 7500 miles or 6 months)

1 The windshield wiper and blade assembly should be inspected periodically for damage, loose components and cracked or worn blade elements.

2 Road film can build up on the wiper blades and affect their efficiency, so they should be washed regularly with a mild detergent solution.

3 The action of the wiping mechanism can loosen the fasteners, so they should be checked and tightened, as necessary (see illustration), at the same time the wiper blades are checked.

4 If the wiper blade elements are cracked, worn or warped, or no longer clean adequately, they should be replaced with new ones.

5 Lift the arm assembly away from the glass for clearance, press on the release lever, then slide the wiper blade assembly out of the hook in the end of the arm (see illustration).

6 Use needle-nose pliers to compress the blade element, then slide the element out of the frame and discard it (see illustration).

7 Installation is the reverse of removal.

9 Battery check, maintenance and charging (every 7500 miles or 6 months)

Warning: *Certain precautions must be followed when checking and servicing the battery. Hydrogen gas, which is highly flammable, is always present in the battery cells, so keep lighted tobacco and all other open flames and sparks away from the battery. The electrolyte inside the battery is actually dilute sulfuric acid, which will cause injury if splashed on your skin or in your eyes. It will also ruin clothes and painted surfaces. When removing the battery cables, always detach the negative cable first and hook it up last!*

1 A routine preventive maintenance program for the battery in your vehicle is the only way to ensure quick and reliable starts. But before performing any battery maintenance, make sure that you have the proper equipment necessary to work safely around the battery (see illustration).

2 There are also several precautions that should be taken whenever battery maintenance is performed. Before servicing the battery, always turn the engine and all accessories off and disconnect the cable from the negative terminal of the battery.

3 The battery produces hydrogen gas, which is both flammable and explosive. Never create a spark, smoke or light a match around the battery. Always charge the battery in a ventilated area.

4 Electrolyte contains poisonous and corrosive sulfuric acid. Do not allow it to get in your eyes, on your skin or on your clothes. Never ingest it. Wear protective safety glasses when working near the battery. Keep children away from the battery.

5 Note the external condition of the battery. If the positive terminal and cable clamp on your vehicle's battery is equipped with a rubber protector, make sure it isn't torn or damaged. It should completely cover the terminal. Look for any corroded or loose connections, cracks in the case or cover or loose hold-down clamps. Also check the entire length of each cable for cracks and frayed conductors.

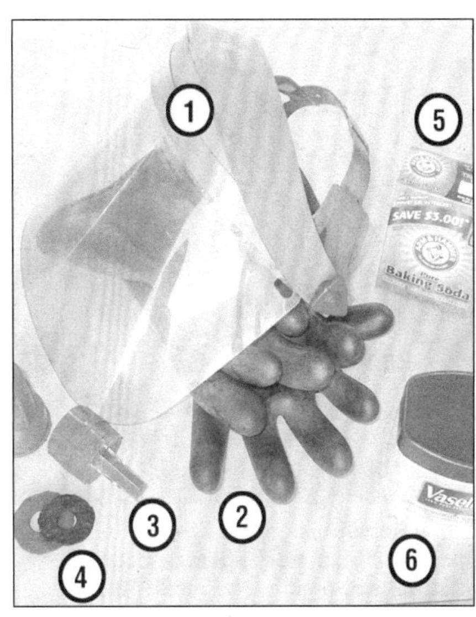

9.1 Tools and materials required for battery maintenance

1 *Face shield/safety goggles - When removing corrosion with a brush, the acidic particles can easily fly up into your eyes*

2 *Rubber gloves - Another safety item consider when servicing the battery; remember that's acid inside the battery*

3 *Battery post/cable cleaner - This wire brush cleaning tool will remove all traces of corrosion from the battery posts and cable clamps*

4 *Treated felt washers - Placing one of these on each post, directly under the cable clamps, will help prevent corrosion*

5 *Baking soda - A solution of baking soda and water can be used to neutralize corrosion*

6 *Petroleum jelly - A layer of this on the battery posts will help prevent corrosion*

9.6a Battery terminal corrosion usually appears as light, fluffy powder

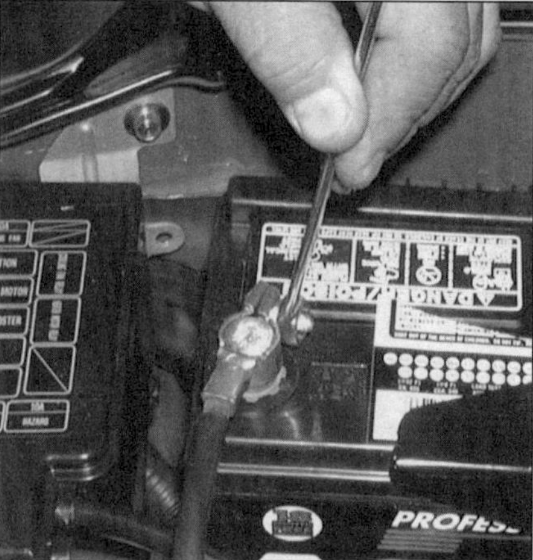

9.6b Removing a cable from the battery post with a wrench - sometimes special battery pliers are required for this procedure if corrosion has caused deterioration of the nut hex (always remove the ground cable first and hook it up last!)

9.7a When cleaning the cable clamps, all corrosion must be removed (the inside of the clamp is tapered to match the taper on the post, so don't remove too much material)

9.7b Regardless of the type of tool used to clean the battery posts, a clean, shiny surface should be the result 10.3 Here are some of the more common problems associated with drivebelts (check the belts very carefully to prevent an untimely breakdown)

6 If corrosion, which looks like white, fluffy deposits (see illustration) is evident, particularly around the terminals, the battery should be removed for cleaning. Loosen the cable clamp bolts with a wrench, being careful to remove the ground cable first, and slide them off the terminals (see illustration). Then disconnect the hold-down clamp bolt and nut, remove the clamp and lift the battery from the engine compartment.

7 Clean the cable clamps thoroughly with a battery brush or a terminal cleaner and a solution of warm water and baking soda (see illustration). Wash the terminals and the top of the battery case with the same solution but make sure that the solution doesn't get into the battery. When cleaning the cables, terminals and battery top, wear safety goggles and rubber gloves to prevent any solution from coming in contact with your eyes or hands. Wear old clothes too - even diluted, sulfuric acid splashed onto clothes will burn holes in them. If the terminals have been extensively corroded, clean them up with a terminal cleaner (see illustration). Thoroughly wash all cleaned areas with plain water.

8 Make sure the battery tray is in good condition and the hold-down clamp bolt or nut is tight. If the battery is removed from the tray, make sure no parts remain in the bottom of the tray when the battery is reinstalled. When reinstalling the hold-down clamp bolt or nut, do not over-tighten it.

9 Information on removing and installing the battery can be found in Chapter 5. Information on jump starting can be found at the front of this manual. For more detailed battery checking procedures, refer to the Haynes Automotive Electrical Manual.

Cleaning

10 Corrosion on the hold-down components, battery case and surrounding areas can be removed with a solution of water and baking soda. Thoroughly rinse all cleaned areas with plain water.

11 Any metal parts of the vehicle damaged by corrosion should be covered with a zinc-based primer, then painted.

Charging

Warning: *When batteries are being charged, hydrogen gas, which is very explosive and flammable, is produced. Do not smoke or allow open flames near a charging or a recently charged battery. Wear eye protection when near the battery during charging. Also, make sure the charger is unplugged before connecting or disconnecting the battery from the charger.*

12 Slow-rate charging is the best way to restore a battery that's discharged to the point where it will not start the engine. It's also a good way to maintain the battery charge in a vehicle that's only driven a few miles between starts. Maintaining the battery charge is particularly important in the winter when the battery must work harder to start the engine and electrical accessories that drain the battery are in greater use.

13 It's best to use a one or two-amp battery charger (sometimes called a "trickle" charger). They are the safest and put the least strain on the battery. They are also the least expensive. For a faster charge, you can use a higher amperage charger, but don't use one rated more than 1/10th the amp/hour rating of the battery. Rapid boost charges that claim to restore the power of the battery in one to two hours are hardest on the battery and can damage batteries not in good condition. This type of charging should only be used in emergency situations.

14 The average time necessary to charge a battery should be listed in the instructions that come with the charger. As a general rule, a trickle charger will charge a battery in 12 to 16 hours.

10 Drivebelt check (every 7500 miles or 6 months) and replacement

Check

1 These models use a serpentine drivebelt with an automatic adjuster tensioner. The good condition and proper tension of the belt is critical to the operation of the engine. Because of their composition and the high stresses to which they are subjected, drivebelts stretch and deteriorate as they get older. They must therefore be periodically inspected. The is no adjustment on these models.

2 The serpentine drivebelt transmits power to all the accessories.

3 With the engine off, open the hood and locate the drivebelt. With a flashlight, check each belt for separation of the adhesive rubber on both sides of the core, core separation

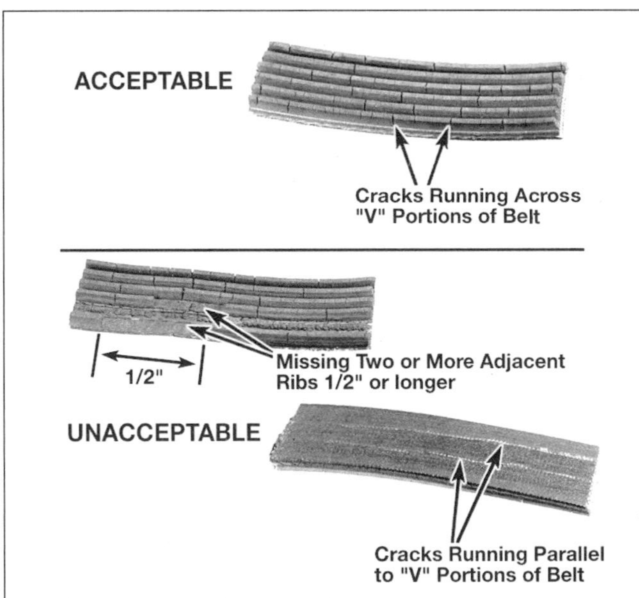

10.3 Here are some of the more common problems associated with drivebelts (check the belts very carefully to prevent an untimely breakdown)

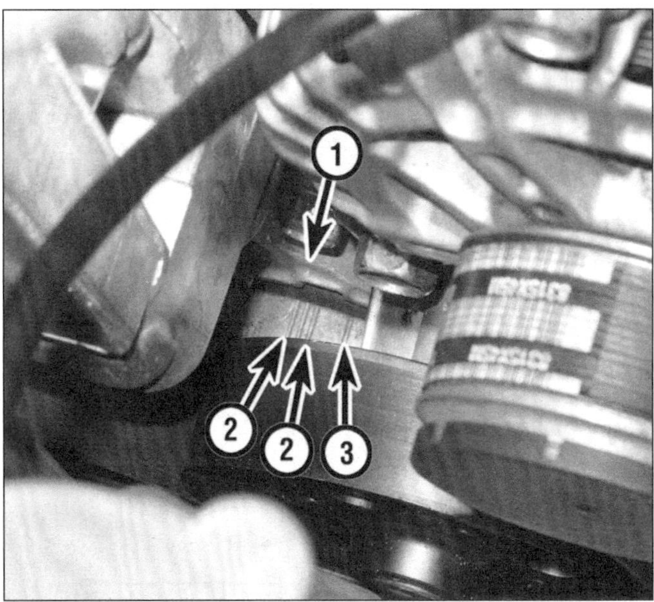

10.4 Drivebelt indicator markings (viewed from between the alternator and the cylinder head)

1 *Stationary mark*
2 *New belt range*
3 *Worn belt mark*

from the belt side, a severed core, separation of the ribs from the adhesive rubber, cracking or separation of the ribs, and torn or worn ribs or cracks in the inner ridges of the ribs (see illustration). Also check for fraying and glazing, which gives the belt a shiny appearance. Both sides of the belt should be inspected, which means you will have to twist the belt to check the underside. Use your fingers to feel the belt where you can't see it. If any of the above conditions are evident, replace the belt (see Steps 5 through 10).

4 Check the drivebelt indicator for excessive belt stretch (see illustration). If the drivebelt indicator is out of limit, replace the drivebelt (see Steps 5 through 10).

Drivebelt replacement

5 Disconnect the cable from the negative terminal of the battery (see Chapter 5).

6 Loosen the right front wheel lug nuts. Raise the vehicle and support it securely on jackstands. Remove the wheel and the inner fender splash shield (see Chapter 11).

7 Rotate the belt tensioner clockwise using a wrench on the pulley bolt to release tension on the drivebelt. The tensioner can be locked in position by inserting a drill bit or other metal rod into the lock holes (see illustration).

Caution: *Do not loosen the drivebelt tensioner pulley bolt or it will be necessary to replace the entire tensioner with a new one.*

8 Remove the drivebelt from the tensioner and all accessories.

9 Install the new drivebelt, making sure that it's properly routed (see illustrations).

10.7 Release the tension using a wrench, then insert an Allen wrench or rod into the hole to lock the tensioner in place

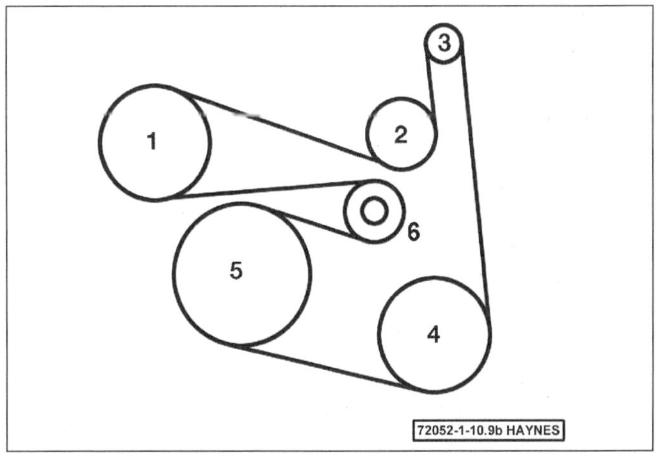

10.9a Drivebelt routing diagram - 2013 and earlier models/ 2014 and later Rogue Select models

1 *Idler pulley*
2 *Water pump pulley*
3 *Alternator*
4 *Air conditioning compressor*
5 *Crankshaft pulley*
6 *Automatic tensioner pulley*

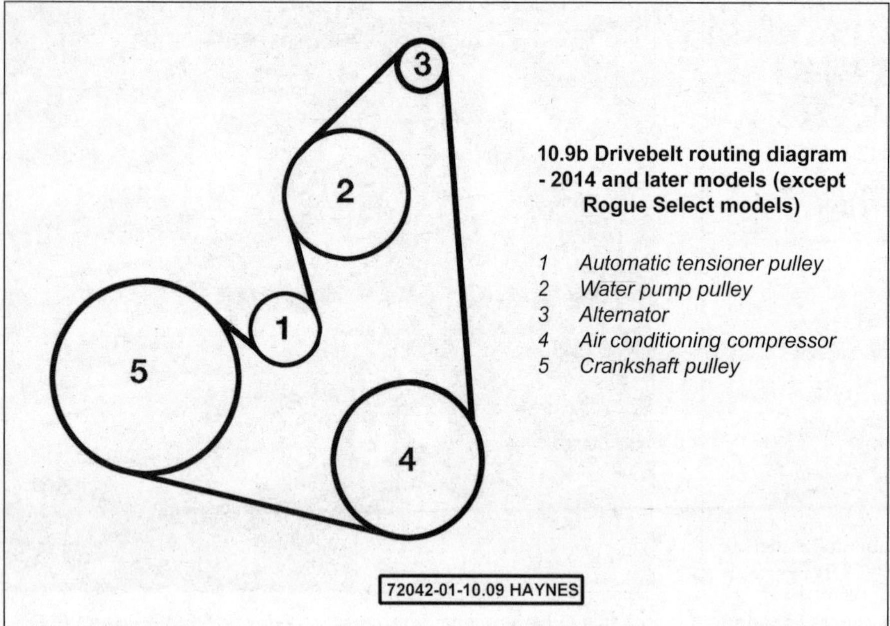

10.9b Drivebelt routing diagram - 2014 and later models (except Rogue Select models)

1 *Automatic tensioner pulley*
2 *Water pump pulley*
3 *Alternator*
4 *Air conditioning compressor*
5 *Crankshaft pulley*

10 Reconnect the battery and perform the necessary re-learn procedures (see Chapter 5).

Automatic tensioner replacement

11 Remove the drivebelt (see Steps 5 through 8).

12 Remove the drivebelt tensioner mounting bolts and remove the tensioner.

13 Installation is the reverse of removal. Tighten the tensioner mounting fasteners to the torque listed in this Chapter's Specifications.

11 Underhood hose check and replacement (every 7500 miles or 6 months)

Caution: *Replacement of air conditioning hoses must be left to a dealer service department or air conditioning shop that has the equipment to depressurize the system safely. Never remove air conditioning components or hoses until the system has been depressurized.*

General

1 High temperatures in the engine compartment can cause the deterioration of the rubber and plastic hoses used for engine, accessory and emission systems operation. Periodic inspection should be made for cracks, loose clamps, material hardening and leaks.

2 Information specific to the cooling system hoses can be found in Section 12.

3 Some, but not all, hoses are secured to the fittings with clamps. Where clamps are used, check to be sure they haven't lost their tension, allowing the hose to leak. If clamps aren't used, make sure the hose has not expanded and/or hardened where it slips over the fitting, allowing it to leak.

Vacuum hoses

4 It's quite common for vacuum hoses, especially those in the emissions system, to be color coded or identified by colored stripes molded into them. Various systems require hoses with different wall thickness, collapse resistance and temperature resistance. When replacing hoses, be sure the new ones are made of the same material.

5 Often the only effective way to check a hose is to remove it completely from the vehicle. If more than one hose is removed, be sure to label the hoses and fittings to ensure correct installation.

6 When checking vacuum hoses, be sure to include any plastic T-fittings in the check. Inspect the fittings for cracks and the hose where it fits over the fitting for distortion, which could cause leakage.

7 A small piece of vacuum hose (1/4-inch inside diameter) can be used as a stethoscope to detect vacuum leaks. Hold one end of the hose to your ear and probe around vacuum hoses and fittings, listening for the hissing sound characteristic of a vacuum leak.

Warning: *When probing with the vacuum hose stethoscope, be very careful not to come into contact with moving engine components such as the drivebelts, cooling fan, etc.*

Fuel hose

Warning: *There are certain precautions which must be taken when inspecting or servicing fuel system components. Work in a well ventilated area and do not allow open flames (cigarettes, appliance pilot lights, etc.) or bare light bulbs near the work area. Mop up any spills immediately and do not store fuel-soaked rags where they could ignite.*

8 Check all rubber fuel lines for deterioration and chafing. Check especially for cracks in areas where the hose bends and just before fittings, such as where a hose attaches to the fuel filter.

9 High quality fuel line, meeting the manufacturer's original specifications, should be used for fuel line replacement. Never, under any circumstances, use unreinforced vacuum line, clear plastic tubing or water hose for fuel lines.

10 Spring-type clamps are commonly used on fuel lines. These clamps often lose their tension over a period of time, and can be sprung during removal. Replace all spring-type clamps with screw clamps whenever a hose is replaced.

Metal lines

11 Sections of metal line are often used for fuel line between the fuel pump and carburetor or fuel injection unit. Check carefully to be sure the line has not been bent or crimped and that cracks have not started in the line.

12 If a section of metal fuel line must be replaced, only seamless steel tubing should be used, since copper and aluminum tubing don't have the strength necessary to withstand normal engine vibration.

13 Check the metal brake lines where they enter the master cylinder and brake proportioning unit (if used) for cracks in the lines or loose fittings. Any sign of brake fluid leakage calls for an immediate thorough inspection of the brake system.

12 Cooling system check (every 7500 miles or 6 months)

1 Many major engine failures can be attributed to a faulty cooling system. If the vehicle is equipped with an automatic transaxle, the cooling system also cools the transaxle fluid and thus plays an important role in prolonging transaxle life.

2 The cooling system should be checked with the engine cold. Do this before the vehicle is driven for the day or after the engine has been shut off for at least three hours.

3 Remove the radiator cap by turning it to the left until it reaches a stop. If you hear a hissing sound (indicating there is still pressure in the system), wait until it stops. Now press down on the cap with the palm of your hand and continue turning to the left until the cap can be removed. Thoroughly clean the cap, inside and out, with clean water. Also clean the filler neck on the radiator. All traces of corrosion should be removed. The coolant inside the radiator should be relatively transparent. If it's rust colored, the system should be drained and refilled (see Section 24). If the coolant level isn't up to the top, add additional antifreeze/coolant mixture (see Section 4).

4 Carefully check the large upper and lower radiator hoses along with the smaller diameter heater hoses which run from the engine to the firewall. Inspect each hose along its entire length, replacing any hose which is cracked, swollen or shows signs of deterioration. Cracks may become more apparent if the hose is squeezed (see

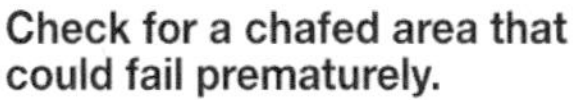

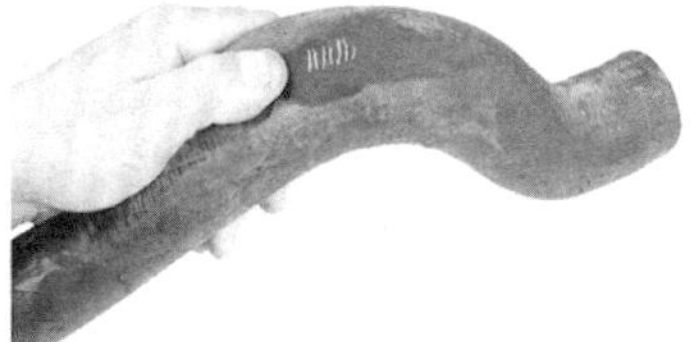

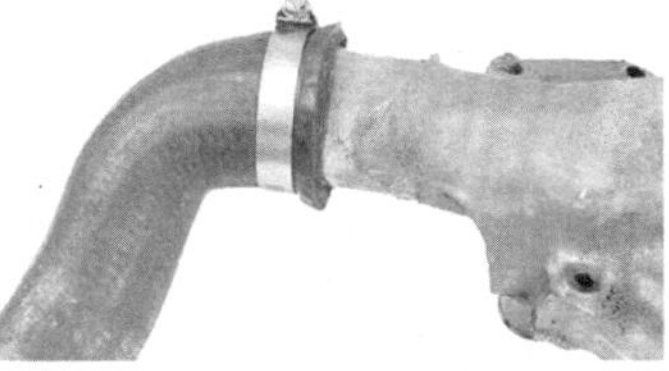

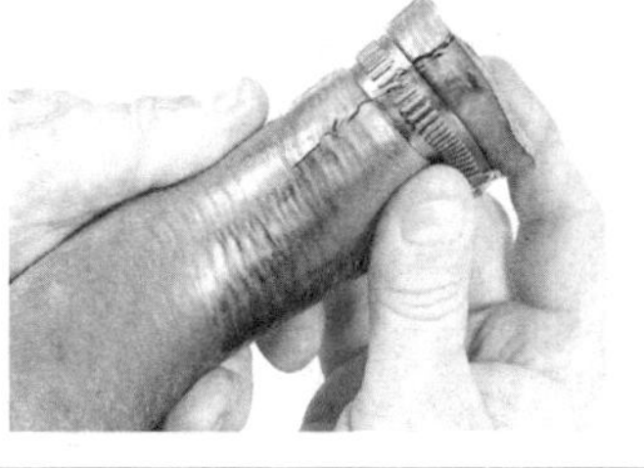

12.4 Hoses, like drivebelts, have a habit of failing at the worst possible time - to prevent the inconvenience of a blown radiator or heater hose, inspect them carefully as shown here

illustration). Regardless of condition, it's a good idea to replace hoses with new ones every two years.

5 Make sure that all hose connections are tight. A leak in the cooling system will usually show up as white or rust colored deposits on the areas adjoining the leak. If wire-type clamps are used at the ends of the hoses, it may be a good idea to replace them with more secure screw-type clamps.

6 Use compressed air or a soft brush to remove bugs, leaves, etc. from the front of the radiator or air conditioning condenser. Be careful not to damage the delicate cooling fins or cut yourself on them.

7 Every other inspection, or at the first indication of cooling system problems, have the cap and system pressure tested. If you don't have a pressure tester, most gas stations and repair shops will do this for a minimal charge.

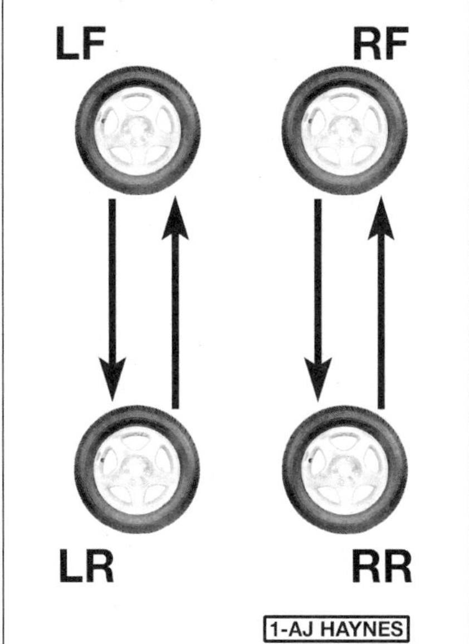

13.2 The recommended tire rotation pattern for these vehicles

15.2 Transfer case filler plug location (just to the rear of the right driveaxle intermediate shaft) - TY30A transfer case shown, TY21C similar

13 Tire rotation (every 7500 miles or 6 months)

1 The tires should be rotated at the specified intervals and whenever uneven wear is noticed. Since the vehicle will be raised and the tires removed anyway, check the brakes (see Section 16) at this time.

2 Radial tires must be rotated in a specific pattern (see illustration).

3 Refer to the information in *Jacking and towing* at the front of this manual, Section 8 for the proper procedures to follow when raising the vehicle and changing a tire. If the brakes are to be checked, do not apply the parking brake as stated.

4 Preferably, the entire vehicle should be raised at the same time. This can be done on a hoist or by jacking up each corner and then lowering the vehicle onto jackstands placed under the frame rails. Always use four jackstands and make sure the vehicle is firmly supported.

5 After rotation, check and adjust the tire pressures as necessary and be sure to check the lug nut tightness.

6 For further information on the wheels and tires, refer to Chapter 10.

14.2 Remove the filler plug from the rear cover

14 Differential lubricant level check (AWD models) (every 15,000 miles or 12 months)

1 Raise the vehicle and support it securely on jackstands. The vehicle should be as level as possible to ensure an accurate check.

2 Remove the plug from the filler hole (see illustration) in the differential.

3 The lubricant should be up to the bottom of the filler hole. If not, use a pump or squeeze bottle to add the specified lubricant until it just starts to run out of the hole.

4 Place a new sealing washer on the fill plug. Install the plug in the filler hole and tighten it to the torque listed in.

15 Transfer case lubricant level check (AWD models) (every 15,000 miles or 12 months)

1 Raise the vehicle and support it securely on jackstands. The vehicle should be as level as possible to ensure an accurate check.

2 Remove the plug from the filler hole in the transfer case (see illustration).

3 The lubricant should be up to the bottom of the filler hole. If not, use a pump or squeeze bottle to add the specified lubricant until it just starts to run out of the hole.

4 Place a new sealing washer on the fill plug. Install the plug in the filler hole and tighten it to the torque listed in Specifications.

16.6 You will find an inspection hole like this in each caliper - placing a ruler across the hole should enable you to determine the thickness of remaining pad material

16.11 Check along the brake hoses and at each fitting for deterioration and cracks

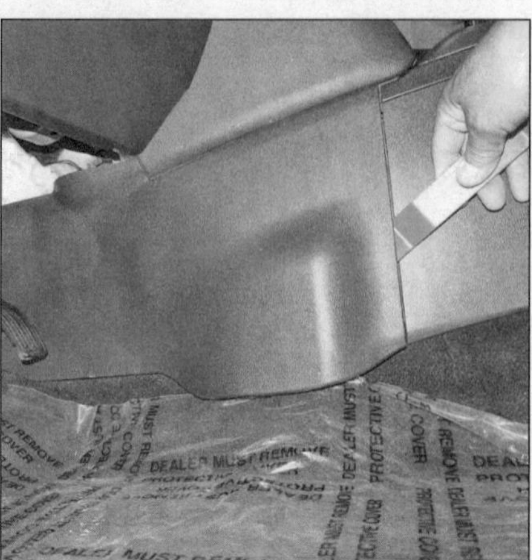

17.2 Carefully pry off this trim panel for access to the cabin air filter

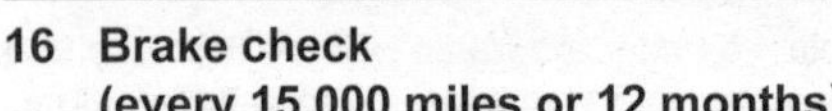

16 Brake check (every 15,000 miles or 12 months)

Warning: *The dust created by the brake system is harmful to your health. Never blow it out with compressed air and don't inhale any of it. An approved filtering mask should be worn when working on the brakes. Do not, under any circumstances, use petroleum-based solvents to clean brake parts. Use brake system cleaner only! Try to use non-asbestos replacement parts whenever possible.*

Note: *For detailed photographs of the brake system, refer to Chapter 9.*

1 In addition to the specified intervals, the brakes should be inspected every time the wheels are removed or whenever a defect is suspected. Any of the following symptoms could indicate a potential brake system defect: The vehicle pulls to one side when the brake pedal is depressed; the brakes make squealing or dragging noises when applied; brake pedal travel is excessive; the pedal pulsates; brake fluid leaks, usually onto the inside of the tire or wheel.

2 The disc brake pads have built-in wear indicators which should make a high pitched squealing or scraping noise when they are worn to the replacement point. When you hear this noise, replace the pads immediately or expensive damage to the discs can result.

3 Loosen the wheel lug nuts.

4 Raise the vehicle and support it securely on jackstands.

5 Remove the wheels (see *Jacking and towing* at the front of this manual, or your owner's manual, if necessary).

Disc brakes

6 There are two pads (an outer and an inner) in each caliper. The pads are visible through inspection holes in each caliper (see illustration), as well as from the top and bottom of each pad.

7 Check the pad thickness by looking at each end of the caliper and through the inspection hole in the caliper body. If the lining material is less than the thickness listed in this Chapter's Specifications , replace the pads.

Note: *Keep in mind that the lining material is riveted or bonded to a metal backing plate and the metal portion is not included in this measurement.*

8 If it is difficult to determine the exact thickness of the remaining pad material by the above method, or if you are at all concerned about the condition of the pads, remove the caliper(s), then remove the pads from the calipers for further inspection (see Chapter 9).

9 Once the pads are removed from the calipers, clean them with brake cleaner and re-measure them with a ruler or a vernier caliper.

10 Measure the disc thickness with a micrometer to make sure that it still has service life remaining. If any disc is thinner than the specified minimum thickness, replace it (see Chapter 9). Even if the disc has service life remaining, check its condition. Look for scoring, gouging and burned spots. If these conditions exist, remove the disc and have it resurfaced (see Chapter 9).

11 Before installing the wheels, check all brake lines and hoses for damage, wear, deformation, cracks, corrosion, leakage, bends and twists, particularly in the vicinity of the rubber hoses at the calipers (see illustration). Check the clamps for tightness and the connections for leakage. Make sure that all hoses and lines are clear of sharp edges, moving parts and the exhaust system. If any of the above conditions are noted, repair, reroute or replace the lines and/or hoses as necessary (see Chapter 9).

Brake booster check

12 Sit in the driver's seat and perform the following sequence of tests.

13 With the brake fully depressed, start the engine - the pedal should move down a little when the engine starts.

14 With the engine running, depress the brake pedal several times - the travel distance should not change.

15 Depress the brake, stop the engine and hold the pedal in for about 30 seconds - the pedal should neither sink nor rise.

16 Restart the engine, run it for about a minute and turn it off. Then firmly depress the brake several times - the pedal travel should decrease with each application.

17 If your brakes do not operate as described above when the preceding tests are performed, the brake booster is either in need of repair or has failed. Refer to Chapter 9 for the removal procedure.

Parking brake

18 Actuate the parking brake with a normal amount of force and count the number of clicks. The adjustment should be within the range listed in the Chapter 9 Specifications. If you hear more or fewer clicks, adjust the parking brake (see Chapter 9).

19 An alternative method of checking the parking brake is to park the vehicle on a steep hill with the parking brake set and the transaxle in Neutral (be sure to stay in the vehicle during this check!). If the parking brake cannot prevent the vehicle from rolling, it is in need of adjustment (see Chapter 9).

17 Cabin air filter replacement (every 15,000 miles or 12 months)

2013 and earlier Rogue models/ 2014 and 2015 Rogue Select models

1 The cabin air filter is under the center of the instrument panel, to the right of the accelerator pedal.

2 Remove the left instrument panel lower cover, forward of the console (see illustration).

3 Remove the accelerator pedal (see Chapter 6 Section 4).

4 Remove the cover from the side of the HVAC housing (see illustration).

5 Pull the cabin air filter out of the housing (see illustration).

17.4 Unclip the bottom of the filter cover, swing it out and unhook the top

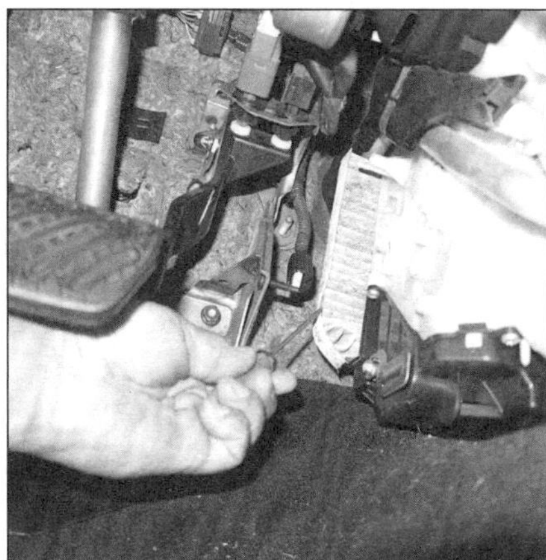

17.5 Pull the filter from the housing

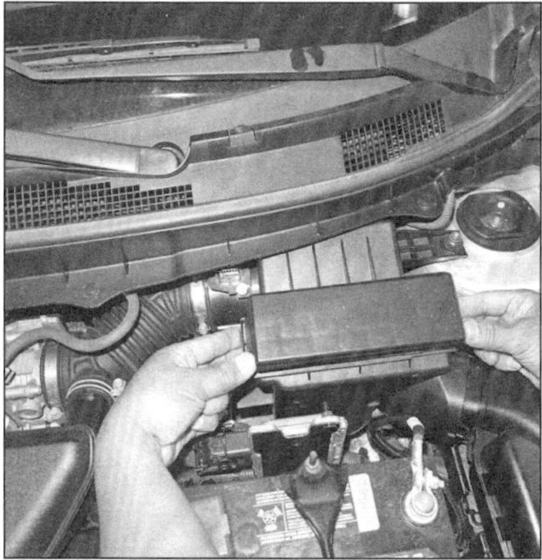

18.2a Release the locking clips on the sides of the cover . . .

18.2b . . . remove the cover . . .

18.2c . . . and pull out the filter element

6 Installation is the reverse of removal.

Note: *Make sure the arrow on the filter is pointing to the rear of the vehicle when installed.*

2014 and later Rogue models

Note: *The air cabin filter is located on the passenger's side of the center console.*

7 Remove the center console front corner trim panel (see Chapter 11).

8 Remove the filter cover retaining screw, then depress the tab on the cover and remove the cover.

9 Remove the filter from the housing, making a note on which way the airflow arrow on the filter is pointing.

10 Installation is the reverse of removal.

18 Air filter check and replacement (every 30,000 miles or 12 months)

1 The air filter is located inside the air filter housing at the left (driver's) side of the engine compartment.

2014 and earlier models

2 Release the two locking tabs at the sides of the top cover, then pull the air filter out of the housing (see illustrations).

Note: *On some models, the filter element might be contained in a filter element holder. If so, separate the element from the holder, install the new element into the holder, then install the holder and element assembly into the air filter housing.*

2015 and later models

3 Locate the locking tabs at the bottom of the air filter housing duct, then squeeze the tabs together and disconnect the duct.

4 Release the two locking clips on the sides of the housing.

5 Lift the housing and the housing duct assembly outwards until the both halves of the case can be separated.

6 Remove the filter from the case.

All models

7 Inspect the outer surface of the filter element. If it is dirty, replace it. If it is only moderately dusty, it can be reused by blowing it clean from the back to the front surface with compressed air. Because it is a pleated paper type filter, it cannot be washed or oiled. If it cannot be cleaned satisfactorily with compressed air, discard and replace it. While the cover is off, be careful not to drop anything down into the housing.

Caution: *Never drive the vehicle with the air filter removed. Excessive engine wear could result and backfiring could even cause a fire under the hood.*

8 Wipe out the inside of the air filter housing.

9 Place the new filter into the holder or housing, making sure it seats properly.

10 On 2014 and earlier models, slide the filter cover onto the housing until the tabs snap into place.

11 On 2015 and later models, place the housing assembly back into place and snap the clips into place to lock the housing assembly together and connect the tube at the bottom of the housing.

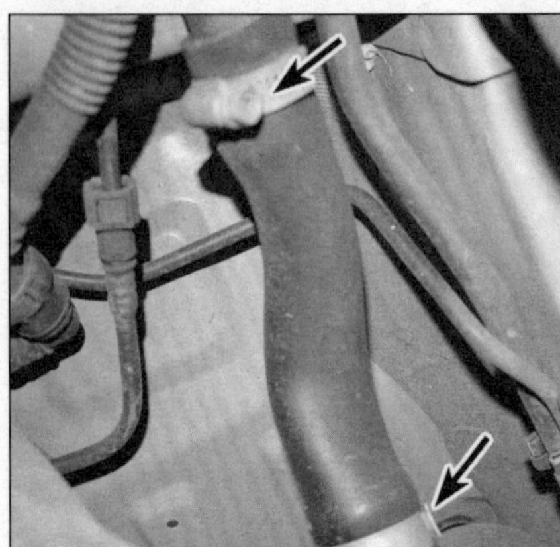

19.5 Inspect the fuel filler hoses for cracks and make sure the clamps are tight

20.1 Steering wheel freeplay is the amount of travel between an initial steering input and the point at which the front wheels begin to turn (indicated by a slight resistance)

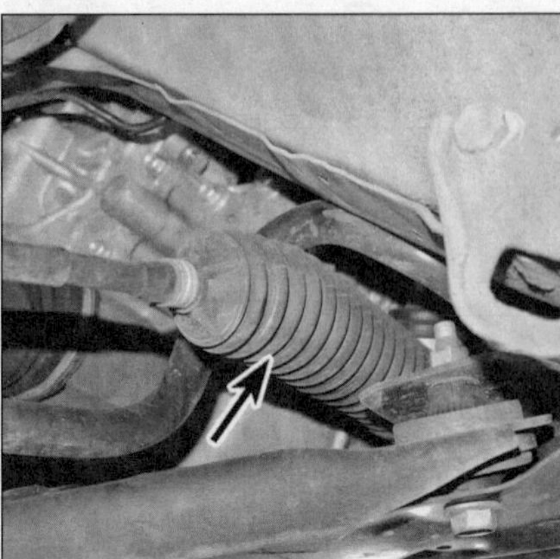

20.6a Check the steering gear boots for cracks or tears

20.6b Check the stabilizer bar bushings for deterioration at the front and the rear of the vehicle

19 Fuel system check (every 15,000 miles or 12 months)

Warning: *Gasoline is extremely flammable, so take extra precautions when you work on any part of the fuel system. Don't smoke or allow open flames or bare light bulbs near the work area, and don't work in a garage where a gas-type appliance (such as a water heater or clothes dryer) is present. Since gasoline is carcinogenic, wear fuel-resistant gloves when there's a possibility of being exposed to fuel, and, if you spill any fuel on your skin, rinse it off immediately with soap and water. Mop up any spills immediately and do not store fuel-soaked rags where they could ignite. The fuel system is under constant pressure, so, if any fuel lines are to be disconnected, the fuel pressure in the system must be relieved first (see Chapter 4 for more information). When you perform any kind of work on the fuel system, wear safety glasses and have a Class B type fire extinguisher on hand.*

1 If you smell gasoline while driving or after the vehicle has been sitting in the sun, inspect the fuel system immediately.

2 Remove the gas cap and inspect it for damage and corrosion. The gasket should have an unbroken sealing imprint. If the gasket is damaged or corroded, remove it and install a new one.

3 Inspect the fuel feed and return lines for cracks. Make sure the threaded flare nut type connectors (which secure the metal fuel lines to the fuel injection system) and the clamps (which secure the hoses to the in-line fuel filter) are tight.

4 Since some components of the fuel system - the fuel tank and part of the fuel feed and return lines, for example - are underneath the vehicle, they can be inspected more easily with the vehicle raised on a hoist. If that's not possible, raise the vehicle and support it securely on jackstands.

5 With the vehicle raised and safely supported, inspect the gas tank and filler neck for punctures, cracks and other damage. The connection between the filler neck and the tank is particularly critical. Sometimes a rubber filler neck will leak because of loose clamps or deteriorated rubber (see illustration). These are problems a home mechanic can usually rectify.

6 Carefully check all rubber hoses and metal lines leading away from the fuel tank. Check for loose connections, deteriorated hoses, crimped lines and other damage. Carefully inspect the lines from the tank to the fuel injection system. Repair or replace damaged sections as necessary (see Chapter 4).

20 Steering and suspension check (every 15,000 miles or 12 months)

Note: *For detailed illustrations of the steering and suspension components, refer to Chapter 10.*

With the wheels on the ground

1 With the vehicle stopped and the front wheels pointed straight ahead, rock the steering wheel gently back and forth. If freeplay (see illustration) is excessive, a front wheel bearing, main shaft yoke, intermediate shaft yoke, control arm balljoint or steering system joint is worn or the steering gear is worn. Refer to Chapter 10 for the appropriate repair procedure.

2 Other symptoms, such as excessive vehicle body movement over rough roads, swaying (leaning) around corners and binding as the steering wheel is turned, may indicate faulty steering and/or suspension components.

3 Check the shock absorbers by pushing down and releasing the vehicle several times at each corner. If the vehicle does not come back to a level position within one or two bounces, the shocks/struts are worn and must be replaced. When bouncing the vehicle up and down, listen for squeaks and noises from the suspension components.

Under the vehicle

4 Raise the vehicle with a floor jack and support it securely on jackstands.

5 Check the tires for irregular wear patterns and proper inflation. See Section 5 for information regarding tire wear.

6 Inspect the universal joint between the steering shaft and the steering gear housing. Check the steering gear housing for grease leakage. Make sure that the boots are not damaged and that the boot clamps are not loose (see illustration). Check the steering linkage for looseness or damage. Check the tie-rod ends for excessive play. Look for loose bolts, broken or disconnected parts and deteriorated rubber bushings on all suspension and steering components (see illustration). While an assistant turns the steering wheel from side to side, check the steering components for free movement, chafing and binding. If the steering components do not seem to be reacting with the movement of the steering wheel, try to determine where the slack is located.

7 Check the balljoints by moving each control arm up and down with a prybar to ensure that its balljoint has no play. If any balljoint does have play, replace it. See Chapter 10 for the front balljoint replacement procedure.

8 Inspect the balljoint boots for damage and leaking grease. Replace the balljoints with new ones if they are damaged (see Chapter 10).

21.2 Check the flange connections for exhaust leaks - also check that the retaining bolts or nuts are securely tightened

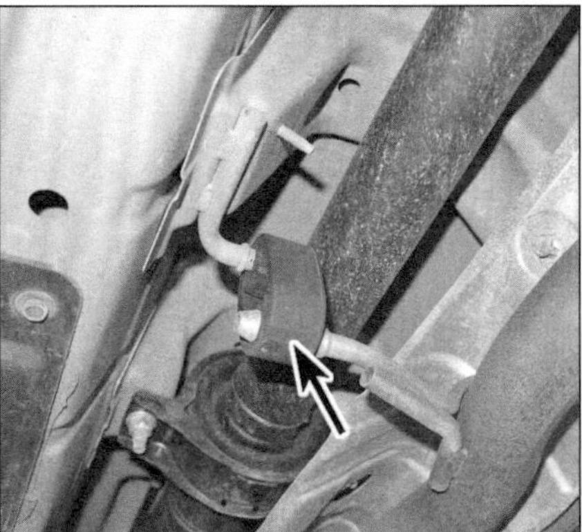

21.4 Check the exhaust system hangers for damage and cracks

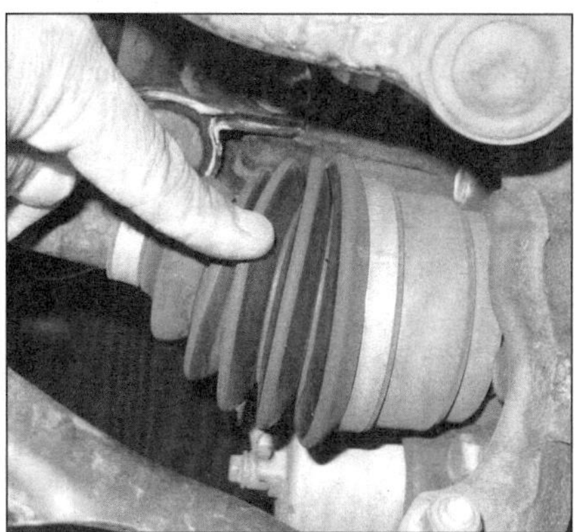

22.2 Check the driveaxle boot for cracks or leaking grease

21 Exhaust system check (every 15,000 miles or 12 months)

1 With the engine cold (at least three hours after the vehicle has been driven), check the complete exhaust system from its starting point at the engine to the end of the tailpipe. This should be done on a hoist where unrestricted access is available.

2 Check the pipes and connections for evidence of leaks (see illustration), severe corrosion or damage. Make sure that all brackets and hangers are in good condition and tight.

3 At the same time, inspect the underside of the body for holes, corrosion, open seams, etc. which may allow exhaust gases to enter the passenger compartment. Seal all body openings with silicone or body putty.

4 Rattles and other noises can often be traced to the exhaust system, especially the mounts and hangers (see illustration). Try to move the pipes, muffler and catalytic converter. If the components can come in contact with the body or suspension parts, secure the exhaust system with new mounts.

5 Check the running condition of the engine by inspecting inside the end of the tailpipe. The exhaust deposits here are an indication of engine state-of-tune. If the pipe is black and sooty or coated with white deposits, the engine is in need of a tune-up, including a thorough engine management and fuel system inspection.

22 Driveaxle boot check (every 15,000 miles or 12 months)

1 The driveaxle boots are very important because they prevent dirt, water and foreign material from entering and damaging the constant velocity (CV) joints.

2 Inspect the boots for tears and cracks as well as loose clamps (see illustration). If there is any evidence of cracks or leaking lubricant, they must be replaced (see Chapter 8).

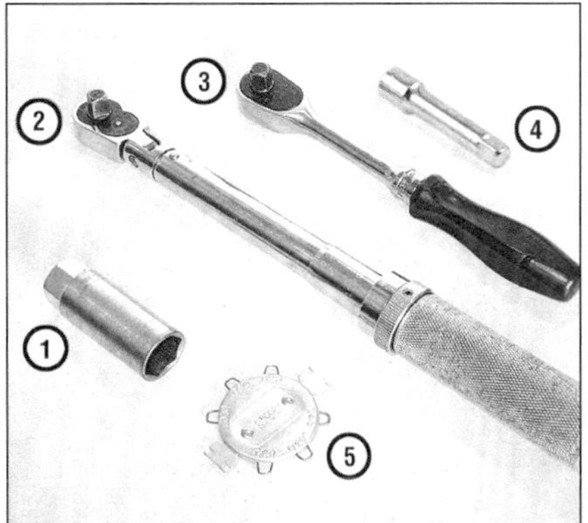

23.1 Tools required for changing spark plugs

1 ***Spark plug socket*** *- This will have special padding inside to protect the spark plug porcelain insulator*
2 ***Torque wrench*** *- Although not mandatory, use of this tool is the best way to ensure that the plugs are tightened properly*
3 ***Ratchet*** *- Standard hand tool to fit the plug socket*
4 ***Extension*** *- Depending on model and accessories, you may need special extensions and universal joints to reach one or more of the plugs*
5 ***Spark plug gap gauge*** *- This gauge for checking the gap comes in a variety of styles. Make sure the gap for your engine is included*

23 Spark plug check and replacement (every 105,000 miles or 72 months)

1 Spark plug replacement requires a spark plug socket and extension which fits onto a ratchet. This socket is lined with a rubber grommet to protect the porcelain insulator of the spark plug and to hold the plug while you remove it. You will also need a wire-type feeler gauge to check and adjust the spark plug gap and a torque wrench to tighten the new plugs to the specified torque (see illustration).

23.3 Spark plug manufacturers recommend using a wire-type gauge when checking the gap - if the wire does not slide between the electrodes with a slight drag, the spark plug will need to be replaced

2 Inspect each of the new plugs for defects. If there are any signs of cracks in the porcelain insulator of a plug, don't use it.

3 Check the electrode gaps of the new plugs. Check the gap by inserting the wire gauge of the proper thickness between the electrodes at the tip of the plug (see illustration). The gap between the electrodes should be identical to that listed in this Chapter's Specifications. If the gap is incorrect, the spark plug must be replaced.

Caution: *The gap can only be checked. Do not adjust the gap, the spark plug must be replaced if the gap is incorrect.*

4 If the side electrode is not exactly over the center electrode, the spark plug should be replaced.

Caution: *These spark plug tips are covered in iridium or platinum; do not use a wire brush or wheel to clean them.*

Removal

5 Remove the ignition coils (see Chapter 5).

23.7 Use a spark plug socket with a ratchet and an extension to remove the spark plugs

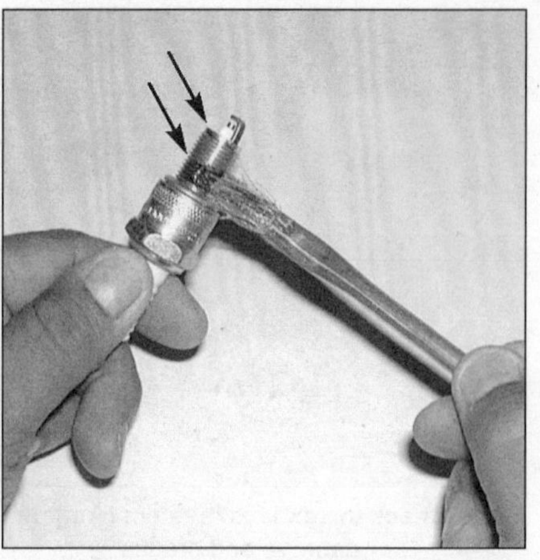

23.9a Apply a coat of anti-seize compound to the spark plug threads, being careful not to get any near the lower threads

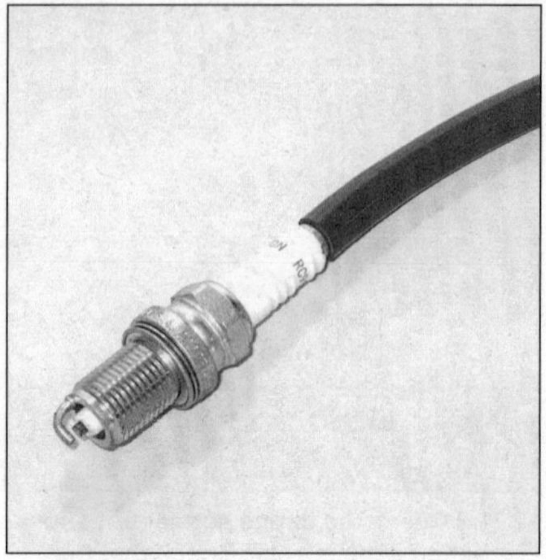

23.9b A length of snug-fitting rubber hose will save time and prevent damaged threads when installing the spark plugs

24.4 The radiator drain fitting is located at the bottom of the radiator

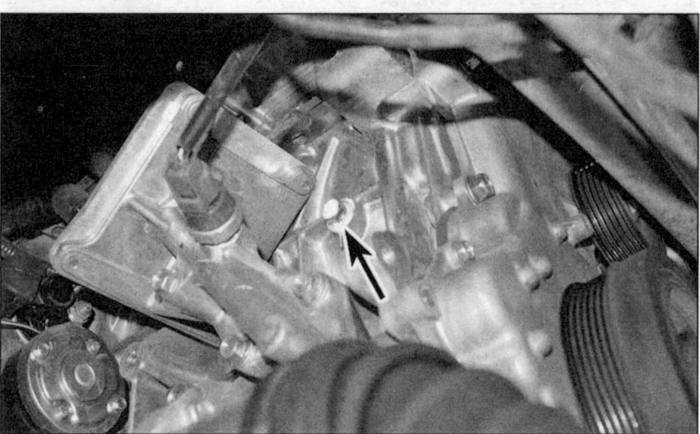

24.5 After draining the radiator, fully drain the cooling system by removing the engine block drain plug

6 If compressed air is available, blow any dirt or foreign material away from the spark plug area before proceeding (a common bicycle pump will also work).

7 Remove the spark plugs (see illustration).

8 Whether you are replacing the plugs at this time or intend to reuse the old plugs, compare each old spark plug with the chart shown on the inside back cover of this manual to determine the overall running condition of the engine.

Installation

9 Prior to installation, apply a coat of anti-seize compound to the plug threads (see illustration). It's often difficult to insert spark plugs into their holes without cross-threading them. To avoid this possibility, fit a short piece of snug-fitting rubber hose over the end of the spark plug (see illustration). The flexible hose acts as a universal joint to help align the plug with the plug hole. Should the plug begin to cross-thread, the hose will slip on the spark plug, preventing thread damage. Tighten the plug to the torque listed in this Chapter's Specifications.

10 Follow the above procedure for the remaining spark plugs.

11 After replacing all the plugs, install the ignition coils (see Chapter 5).

24 Cooling system servicing (draining, flushing and refilling) (every 30,000 miles or 24 months)

Warning: *Do not allow engine coolant (antifreeze) to come in contact with your skin or painted surfaces of the vehicle. Rinse off spills immediately with plenty of water. Antifreeze is highly toxic if ingested. Never leave antifreeze laying around in an open container or in puddles on the floor; children and pets are attracted by it's sweet smell and may drink it. Check with local authorities about disposing of used antifreeze. Many communities have collection centers which will see that antifreeze is disposed of safely.*

Warning: *The engine must be completely cool before beginning this procedure.*

1 Periodically, the cooling system should be drained, flushed and refilled to replenish the antifreeze mixture and prevent formation of rust and corrosion, which can impair the performance of the cooling system and cause engine damage. When the cooling system is serviced, all hoses and the radiator cap should be checked and replaced if necessary.

Draining

2 Apply the parking brake and block the wheels. If the vehicle has just been driven, wait several hours to allow the engine to cool down before beginning this procedure.

3 Raise the front of the vehicle and support it securely on jackstands. Remove the splash shield between the bumper cover and the subframe (see Chapter 11 Section 20).

4 Remove the radiator cap. Move a large container under the radiator drain to catch the coolant. Using a large screwdriver, open the radiator drain plug and direct the coolant into the container (see illustration).

5 After the coolant stops flowing out of the radiator, move the container under the engine block drain plug (see illustration). Remove the plug and allow the coolant in the block to drain. **Note:** *The engine block drain plug is located on the right end of the engine, on the firewall side.*

26.7 Automatic transaxle fluid drain plug

27.1 PCV valve location

6 While the coolant is draining, check the condition of the radiator hoses, heater hoses and clamps (refer to Section 11 if necessary).
7 Replace any damaged clamps or hoses (see Chapter 3).

Flushing

8 Once the system is completely drained, flush the radiator with fresh water from a garden hose until water runs clear at the drain. The flushing action of the water will remove sediments from the radiator but will not remove rust and scale from the engine and cooling tube surfaces.
9 These deposits can be removed by the chemical action of a cleaner. Follow the procedure outlined in the manufacturer's instructions. If the radiator is severely corroded, damaged or leaking, it should be removed (see Chapter 3) and taken to a radiator repair shop.
10 Remove the overflow hose from the coolant recovery reservoir. Drain the reservoir and flush it with clean water, then reconnect the hose.

Refilling

11 Close and tighten the radiator drain. Install and tighten the engine block drain plug.
12 Make sure the heater temperature control is in the maximum heat position.
13 Slowly refill the radiator with the specified coolant until coolant reaches the lip on the radiator filler neck. Add coolant to the reservoir up to the lower mark.
14 Install the radiator cap and run the engine in a well-ventilated area until the thermostat opens (coolant will begin flowing through the radiator and the upper radiator hose will become hot).
15 Rev the engine to approximately 2500 rpm for ten seconds, then let it idle; do this a few times.
16 Turn the engine off and let it cool. Add more coolant mixture to bring the level back up to the lip on the radiator filler neck.
17 Squeeze the upper radiator hose to expel air, then add more coolant mixture if necessary. Replace the radiator cap.
18 Start the engine, allow it to reach normal operating temperature and check for leaks.

25 Evaporative emissions control system check (every 30,000 miles or 24 months)

1 The function of the evaporative emissions control system is to draw fuel vapors from the gas tank and fuel system, store them in a charcoal canister, then burn them during normal engine operation.
2 The most common symptom of a fault in the evaporative emissions system is a strong fuel odor. If a fuel odor is detected, inspect the charcoal canister, located at the right rear corner of the vehicle, to the rear of the wheel. Check the canister and all hoses for damage and deterioration (see Chapter 6).

26 Automatic CVT transaxle fluid change (every 60,000 miles or 48 months)

Note: *Failure to use the correct fluid will damage the transaxle and void the warranty.*
1 At the specified time intervals, the CVT fluid should be drained and replaced.
2 Before beginning work, purchase the specified transaxle fluid (see Recommended fluids and lubricants and Capacities this Chapter's Specifications).
3 Other tools necessary for this job include jackstands to support the vehicle in a raised position, a wrench, a large drain pan, newspapers and clean rags.
4 The fluid should be drained after the vehicle has been driven and brought to operating temperature. Hot fluid is more effective than cold fluid at removing built up sediment.
Warning: *Fluid temperature can exceed 350-degrees F in a hot transaxle. Wear protective gloves.*
5 Raise the vehicle and support it securely on jackstands. Put the transaxle in Park and turn off the engine.
6 Move the necessary equipment under the vehicle, being careful not to touch any of the hot exhaust components.
7 Place the drain pan under the drain plug and remove the drain plug (see illustration). Be sure the drain pan is in position, as fluid will come out with some force. Once the fluid is drained, reinstall the drain plug and tighten it to the torque listed in this Chapter's Specifications.
8 Lower the vehicle.
9 With the engine off, add new fluid to the transaxle through the dipstick tube on 2013 and earlier models or through the special fluid charging fitting on 2014 and later models (see Section 6). Use a funnel to prevent spills. It is best to add a little fluid at a time, checking the level with the dipstick. Allow the fluid time to drain into the pan.
10 Start the engine and move the shift selector into all positions from Park through Low then shift into Park and apply the parking brake.
11 With the engine idling, check the fluid level (see Section 6).
Note: *After the fluid has been changed, the CVT fluid deterioration date must be changed using a factory CONSULT scanner; see your dealer service department or other properly equipped repair shop for this procedure.*

27 Positive Crankcase Ventilation (PCV) valve check and replacement (every 30,000 miles or 24 months)

1 Locate the PCV valve on the valve cover (see illustration).

27.2a Using a pair of pliers, disconnect the clamp and pull the hose off of the valve

27.2b Always replace the O-ring when the PCV valve is removed

28.3 Remove the fill plug (A) and the drain plug (B) and allow the lubricant to drain

29.3 Transfer case details

1 *Transfer case drain plug (TY30A transfer case shown, TY21C transfer case similar)*
2 *Tooth contact test plug (TY30A transfer case only)*

2 Disconnect the hose, then remove the PCV valve (see illustrations).

3 Reconnect the hose to the valve. With the engine idling at normal operating temperature, place your finger over the end of the valve. If there's no vacuum at the valve, check for a plugged hose or valve. Replace any plugged or deteriorated hoses.

4 When purchasing a replacement PCV valve, make sure it's for your particular vehicle and engine size. Compare the old valve with the new one to make sure they're the same.

5 Installation is the reverse of removal.

28 Differential lubricant change (AWD models) (every 60,000 miles or 48 months)

1 This procedure should be performed after the vehicle has been driven so the lubricant will be warm and therefore will flow out of the differential easily.

2 Raise the vehicle and support it securely on jackstands. Place a drain pan under the differential.

3 Remove the fill plug, then remove the drain plug (see illustration) and allow the lubricant to drain into the pan. Clean and reinstall the drain plug, using a new sealing washer. Tighten the plug to the torque listed in this Chapter's Specifications.

4 Using a hand pump, syringe or squeeze bottle, fill the differential housing with the specified lubricant until it's level with the bottom of the fill plug hole.

5 Clean and reinstall the fill plug, using a new sealing washer. Tighten the plug to the torque listed in this Chapter's Specifications.

6 Drive the vehicle a short distance and check for leaks.

29 Transfer case lubricant change (AWD models) (every 60,000 miles or 48 months)

1 This procedure should be performed after the vehicle has been driven so the lubricant will be warm and therefore will flow out of the transfer case easily.

2 Raise the vehicle and support it securely on jackstands. Position a drain pan, rags under the transaxle (the transfer case is the rear portion of the transaxle).

3 Remove the fill plug (see illustration 15.2), then remove the drain plug (see illustration) and allow the lubricant to drain into the pan. Clean and reinstall the drain plug, using a new sealing washer. Tighten the plug to the torque listed in this Chapter's Specifications.

Warning: *Never remove the tooth contact test plug - severe damage may occur.*

4 Using a hand pump, syringe or squeeze bottle, fill the transfer case with the specified lubricant until it's level with the bottom of the fill plug hole.

5 Clean and reinstall the fill plug, using a new sealing washer. Tighten the plug to the torque listed in this Chapter's Specifications.

6 Drive the vehicle a short distance and check for leaks.

30 Valve clearance check and adjustment (every 60,000 miles or 48 months)

Note: *The manufacturer recommends adjusting the valve clearance at the specified interval only if the valve train is making excessive noise.*

1 Disconnect the cable from the negative terminal of the battery (see Chapter 5).

2 Remove the spark plugs (see Section 23).

3 Remove the valve cover (see Chapter 2A).

4 Position the number 1 piston at TDC on the compression stroke (see Chapter 2A).

5 Measure the clearance of the indicated valves with a feeler gauge (see illustrations). Record each measurement and compare your measurements with the desired valve clearance found in this Chapter's Specifications. Note which are out of specification; this data will be used later to determine the required lifter.

6 Turn the crankshaft one complete revolution, realign the timing marks, and measure and record the clearances of the remaining valves (see illustration).

30.5a When the no. 1 piston is at TDC on the compression stroke, the valve clearance for the no. 1 and no. 3 cylinder exhaust valves and the no. 1 and no. 2 cylinder intake valves can be measured

30.5b You will feel drag as you pull the feeler gauge if the adjustment is correct

30.6 When the no. 4 piston is at TDC on the compression stroke, the valve clearances for the no. 2 and no. 4 cylinder exhaust valves and the no. 3 and no. 4 cylinder intake valves can be measured

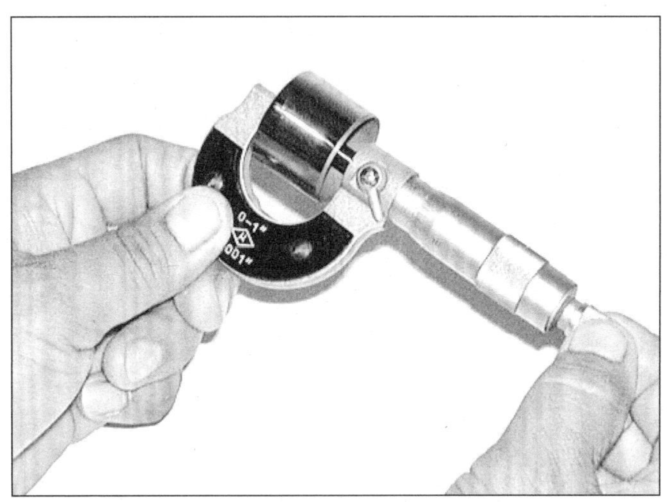

30.8 Measure the lifter thickness with a micrometer

7 These engines don't use valve adjusting shims. If a clearance is out of specification, the lifter must be replaced with a new lifter that has a different thickness head to correct the clearance. Remove the camshafts to access the lifters (see Chapter 2A).

8 Mark the lifters that are to be replaced, and record which valve they came from. Measure the thickness of the center of the lifter with a micrometer (see illustration).

9 To calculate the correct thickness of a replacement lifter that will place the valve clearance within the specified value, use the following formula:

$N = T + A - V$

N = thickness of the new lifter

T = thickness of the old lifter

A = valve clearance measured

V = desired valve clearance (see this Chapter's Specifications)

10 Select a lifter with a thickness as close as possible to the valve clearance calculated. Lifters are marked on the underside as to their size.

11 Mark the new lifters as to their destination, lubricate them with engine assembly lube and install them. After replacing the lifters, install the camshaft(s) (see Chapter 2A).

12 The remainder of installation is the reverse of removal. Reconnect the battery and perform the necessary re-learn procedures (see Chapter 5).

Notes

Chapter 2 Part A Engines

Contents

Specifications

General

Displacement	151.82 cu. in. (2.5 liters)
Designation	QR25DE
Cylinder numbers (timing chain end-to-transaxle end)	1-2-3-4
Firing order	1-3-4-2

Cylinder locations

Valve clearance (cold)

See Chapter 1

Warpage limits

Cylinder head-to-block surface	0.004 inch

Camshaft

Endplay	0.0045 to 0.0074 inch
Camshaft journal diameter	
No. 1	1.0998 to 1.1006 inches
No. 2 through 5	0.9226 to 0.9234 inch
Camshaft bearing inside diameter	
No. 1	1.1024 to 1.1032 inches
No. 2 through 5	0.9252 to 0.9260 inch
Bearing oil clearance	
Standard	0.0018 to 0.0034 inch
Service limit	0.0059 inch
Camshaft runout	0.0008 inch
Intake lobe height	
2013 and earlier models/2014 and later Rogue Select models	
California models	1.7677 to 1.7718 inhes
Non-California models	1.7722 to 1.7797 inches
2014 and later models (except Rogue Select models)	1.8057 to 1.8132 inches
Exhaust lobe height	
2013 and earlier models/2014 and later Rogue Select models	1.7313 to 1.7388 inches
2014 and later models (except Rogue Select models)	1.7392 to 1.7467 inches

Oil pump

Body-to-outer rotor clearance	0.0045 to 0.0070 inch
Inner rotor-to-outer rotor tip clearance	0.0067 to 0.0087 inch
Inner rotor-to-cover clearance	0.0014 to 0.0028 inch
Outer rotor-to-cover clearance	0.0024 to 0.0043 inch
Inner rotor-to-body clearance	
2013 and earlier models/2014 and later Rogue Select models	0.0018 to 0.0036 inch
2014 and later models (except Rogue Select models)	0.0014 to 0.0028 inch

Torque specifications

Ft-lbs (unless otherwise indicated)

Note: *One foot-pound (ft-lb) of torque is equivalent to 12 inch-pounds (in-lbs) of torque. Torque values below approximately 15 ft-lbs are expressed in inch-pounds, because most foot-pound torque wrenches are not accurate at these smaller values.*

Intake manifold bolts/nuts

2013 and earlier models/2014 and later Rogue Select models	168 in-lbs
2014 and later models (except Rogue Select models)	18
Exhaust manifold nuts	31
Crankshaft pulley bolt **	
Step 1	31
Step 2	
2013 and earlier models/2014 and later Rogue Select models	Tighten an additional 60-degrees
2014 and later models (except Rogue Select models)	Tighten an additional 66-degrees
Driveplate bolts	80
Balance shaft drive sprocket bolt**	48
Balance shaft assembly bolts *, **, ***	
2013 and earlier models/2014 and later Rogue Select models	
Step 1	
Bolts 1 through 5	31
Bolt 6	27
Step 2	
Bolts 1 through 5	Tighten an additional 120-degrees
Bolt 6	Tighten an additional 90-degrees
Step 3	Loosen all bolts completely in reverse sequence
Step 4	
Bolts 1 through 5	31
Bolt 6	27
Step 5	
Bolts 1 through 5	Tighten an additional 120-degrees
Bolt 6	Tighten an additional 90-degrees
2014 and later models (except Rogue Select)	
Step 1	
Bolts 1 through 5	31
Bolt 6	27
Step 2	
Bolts 1 through 5	Tighten an additional 125-degrees
Bolt 6	Tighten an additional 95-degrees
Step 3	Loosen all bolts completely in reverse sequence
Step 4	
Bolts 1 through 5	31
Bolt 6	27
Step 5	
Bolts 1 through 5	Tighten an additional 125-degrees
Bolt 6	Tighten an additional 90-degrees
Cylinder head bolts *, **, ***	
Step 1	37
Step 2	Tighten an additional 60-degrees
Step 3	Loosen all bolts completely in reverse sequence
Step 4	29
Step 5	Tighten an additional 75-degrees
Step 6	Tighten an additional 75-degrees

Note: ** Bolt(s) must be replaced with NEW ones*
Note: *** Lubricate fastener threads and heads with clean engine oil prior to installation*
Note: **** Tighten the fasteners in the correct sequence. See text for diagrams*

Torque specifications (continued) **Ft-lbs** (unless otherwise indicated)

Note: *One foot-pound (ft-lb) of torque is equivalent to 12 inch-pounds (in-lbs) of torque. Torque values below approximately 15 ft-lbs are expressed in inch-pounds, because most foot-pound torque wrenches are not accurate at these smaller values.*

Camshaft bearing cap bolts (all bolts) ***	
2013 and earlier models/2014 and later Rogue Select models	
Step 1 (bolts 9 through 11)	12 in-lbs
Step 2 (bolts 1 through 8)	12 in-lbs
Step 3 (bolts 9 through 11)	48 in-lbs
Step 4 (bolts 9 through 11)	96 in-lbs
2014 and later models (except Rogue Select models)	
Step 1 (bolts 9 through 11)	17 in-lbs
Step 2 (bolts 1 through 8)	17 in-lbs
Step 3 (bolts 1 through 11)	52 in-lbs
Step 4 (bolts 1 through 11)	96 in-lbs
Camshaft sprocket bolt **	
2013 and earlier models/2014 and later Rogue Select models	
Intake sprocket assembly	76
Exhaust sprocket	105
2014 and later models (except Rogue Select models)	76
Camshaft signal plate fastener	41
Engine mount bolts/nuts	
Upper (torque rod) mount bolts	
2013 and earlier models/2014 and later Rogue Select models	89
2014 and later models (except Rogue Select models)	63
Right (timing chain end) mount bolts	
2013 and earlier models/2014 and later Rogue Select models	41
2014 and later models (except Rogue Select models)	48
Right (timing chain end) mount bracket-to-engine bolts	
2013 and earlier models/2014 and later Rogue Select models	41
2014 and later models (except Rogue Select models)	36
Left (transaxle) insulator-to-transaxle bolts	37
Left (transaxle) insulator bracket-to-body bolts	59
Left (transaxle) support bracket nuts/bolts	89 in-lbs
Rear (torque rod) mount bolts	81
Rear (torque rod) support bracket bolts	81
Timing chain cover bolts ***	
Bolt A	36
Bolts B	108 in-lbs
Bolts C	108 in-lbs
Bolts D	36
IVT cover bolts	108 in-lbs
IVT solenoid mounting bolts	57 in-lbs
Timing chain components	
Timing chain slack guide bolts	144 in-lbs
Timing chain tension guide bolts	144 in-lbs
Timing chain tensioner bolts	62 in-lbs
Oil pump drive chain tensioner bolts	62 in-lbs
Oil pump fasteners	
Screws	61 in-lbs
Bolt	62 in-lbs
Oil pan	
Aluminum section-to-block ***	16
Aluminum section-to-transaxle ***	
Vertical bolts (2)	78 in-lbs
Horizontal bolts	
2013 and earlier models/2014 and later Rogue Select models (2)	31
2014 and later models (except Rogue Select models) (4)	37
Steel pan-to-aluminum section ***	61 in-lbs
Drain plug	25
Valve cover bolts ***	
Step 1	17 in-lbs
Step 2	73 in-lbs

Note: ** Bolt(s) must be replaced with NEW ones*
Note: *** Lubricate fastener threads and heads with clean engine oil prior to installation*
Note: **** Tighten the fasteners in the correct sequence. See text for diagrams*

1 General information

1 This Part of Chapter 2 is devoted to in-vehicle repair procedures for the engine. Information concerning engine removal and installation and engine overhaul can be found in Chapter 2B.

2 The following repair procedures are based on the assumption that the engine is installed in the vehicle. If the engine has been removed from the vehicle and mounted on a stand, many of the steps outlined in this Part of Chapter 2 will not apply.

2 Repair operations possible with the engine in the vehicle

Warning: *The models covered by this manual are equipped with a Supplemental Restraint System (SRS), more commonly known as airbags. Always disarm the airbag system before working in the vicinity of any airbag system component to avoid the possibility of accidental deployment of the airbag, which could cause personal injury (see Chapter 12). Do not use a memory saving device to preserve the PCM's memory when working on or near airbag system components.*

1 Many major repair operations can be accomplished without removing the engine from the vehicle.

2 Clean the engine compartment and the exterior of the engine with some type of degreaser before any work is done. It will make the job easier and help keep dirt out of the internal areas of the engine.

3 Depending on the components involved, it may be helpful to remove the hood to improve access to the engine as repairs are performed (refer to Chapter 11 if necessary). Cover the fenders to prevent damage to the paint. Special pads are available, but an old bedspread or blanket will also work.

4 If vacuum, exhaust, oil or coolant leaks develop, indicating a need for gasket or seal replacement, the repairs can generally be made with the engine in the vehicle. The intake and exhaust manifold gaskets, oil pan gasket, crankshaft oil seals and cylinder head gasket are all accessible with the engine in place.

5 Exterior engine components, such as the intake and exhaust manifolds, the oil pan, the oil pump, the water pump, the starter motor, the alternator, and the fuel system components can be removed for repair with the engine in place.

6 Since the cylinder head can be removed without pulling the engine, camshaft and valve component servicing can also be accomplished with the engine in the vehicle. Replacement of the timing chain and sprockets is also possible with the engine in the vehicle.

7 In extreme cases caused by a lack of necessary equipment, repair or replacement of piston rings, pistons, connecting rods and rod bearings is possible with the engine in the vehicle. However, this practice is not recommended because of the cleaning and preparation work that must be done to the components involved.

3 Top Dead Center (TDC) for number one piston - locating

1 Top Dead Center (TDC) is the highest point in the cylinder that each piston reaches as it travels up-and-down when the crankshaft turns. Each piston reaches TDC on the compression stroke and again on the exhaust stroke, but TDC generally refers to piston position on the compression stroke.

2 Positioning the number one piston at TDC is an essential part of certain procedures, such as camshaft and timing chain/sprocket removal.

3 Before beginning this procedure, place the transaxle in Park or Neutral and apply the parking brake or block the rear wheels. Disconnect the cable from the negative terminal of the battery (see Chapter 5).

4 In order to bring any piston to TDC, the crankshaft must be turned using a large breaker bar or ratchet and socket placed on the crankshaft pulley bolt. When looking at the front of the engine, normal crankshaft rotation is clockwise.

5 Disconnect the cable from the negative terminal of the battery (see Chapter 5), remove the spark plugs (see Chapter 1) and install a compression gauge in the number one spark plug hole. It should be a gauge with a screw-in fitting and a hose at least six inches long (see illustration 3.6 in Chapter 2B).

6 Remove the inner fender splash shield (see illustration). Rotate the crankshaft while observing for pressure on the compression gauge. The moment the gauge shows pressure indicates that the number one cylinder has begun the compression stroke.

7 Once the compression stroke has begun, TDC for the compression stroke is reached by bringing the piston to the top of the cylinder.

8 Continue turning the crankshaft until the TDC notch in the crankshaft damper is aligned with the pointer on the timing chain cover (see illustration). At this point, the number one cylinder is at TDC on the compression stroke. If the marks are aligned but there was no compression, the piston was on the exhaust stroke. Continue rotating the crankshaft 360-degrees (1-turn).

Note: *If a compression gauge is not available, you can simply place a blunt object (such as the end of a screwdriver handle) over the spark plug hole and listen for compression as the engine is rotated. Once compression at the No. 1 spark plug hole is noted, the remainder of the Step is the same.*

9 After the number one piston has been positioned at TDC on the compression stroke, TDC for any of the remaining cylinders can be located by turning the crankshaft 180-degrees and following the firing order (refer to this Chapter's Specifications). For example, rotating the engine 180-degrees past TDC 1 will put the engine at TDC compression for cylinder 3.

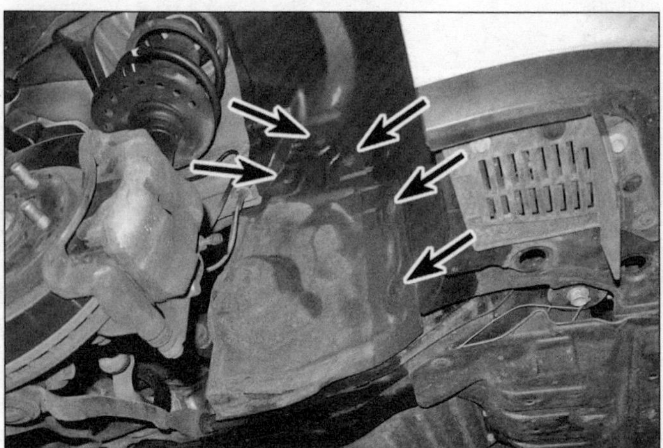

3.6 Remove the right inner fender splash shield retainers to access the crankshaft pulley

3.8 Top Dead Center (TDC) details

1 *Pointer on timing chain cover*
2 *TDC mark*

4.9 Remove the gasket from the cover

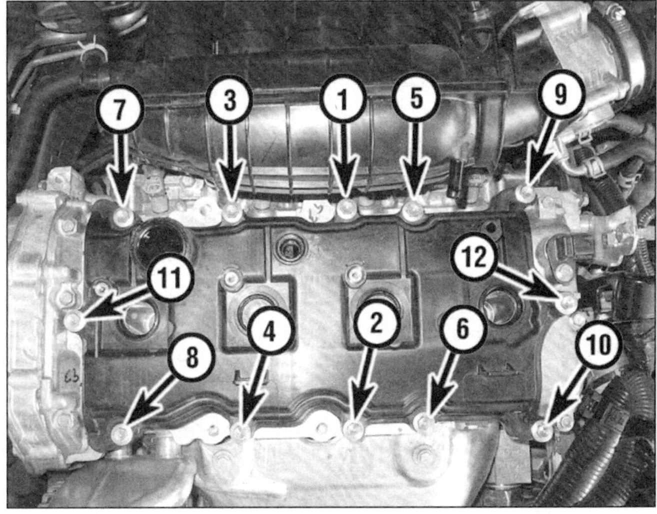

4.13a Valve cover bolt tightening sequence - Type 1 (used on 2011 and earlier models and some 2012 and 2013 models)

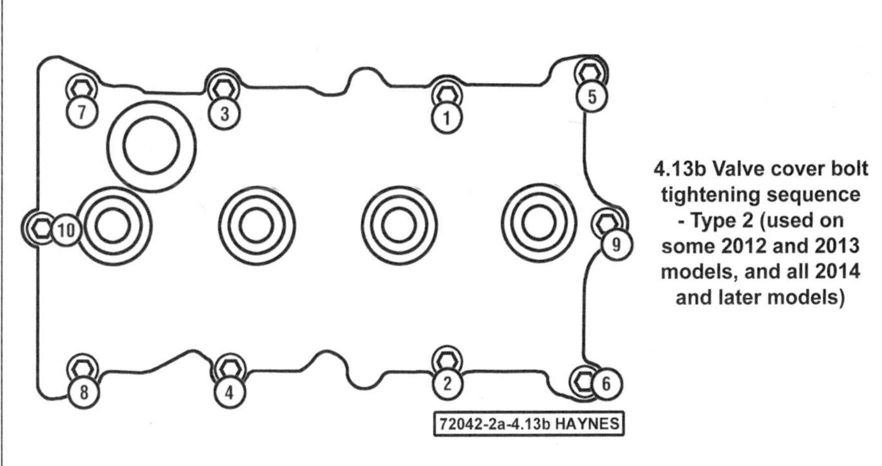

4.13b Valve cover bolt tightening sequence - Type 2 (used on some 2012 and 2013 models, and all 2014 and later models)

4 Valve cover - removal and installation

Removal

1 Disconnect the cable from the negative terminal of the battery (see Chapter 5).

2 Remove the upper air intake resonator (see Chapter 4).

3 Detach the fresh air hose from the left-rear corner of the cover.

4 Remove the ignition coils (see Chapter 5) and spark plugs (see Chapter 1).

5 Remove the intake manifold (see Section 5).

6 Support the engine from below using a block of wood on a floor jack or from above using an engine support fixture. Remove the right upper engine mount and mount bracket (see Section 16).

7 Disconnect the PCV hose.

8 Remove the bolts in the reverse of the tightening sequence (see Illustration 4.13a or 4.13b). Loosen the bolts starting at the ends and work toward the center. If the cover is stuck to the cylinder head, bump the end with a wood block and a hammer to jar it loose. If that doesn't work, try to slip a flexible putty knife between the cylinder head and cover to break the seal.

Caution: *Don't pry at the cover or housing-to-cylinder head joint or damage to the sealing surfaces may occur, leading to oil leaks after the cover is reinstalled.*

9 Remove the gasket from the valve cover (see illustration).

Installation

10 The mating surfaces of the valve cover and cylinder head must be clean when the cover is installed. Use a gasket scraper to remove all traces of sealant, then clean the mating surfaces with brake system cleaner. If there's residue or oil on the mating surfaces when the cover is installed, oil leaks may develop.

Caution: *Use care when scraping the soft aluminum of the cylinder head or the plastic valve cover. They are soft, and deep scratches may lead to oil leaks.*

11 Apply RTV sealant at the timing chain cover-to-cylinder head joints.

12 Install the valve cover and bolts.

13 Tighten the bolts in the indicated sequence (see illustrations) to the torque listed in this Chapter's Specifications.

14 The remainder of installation is the reverse of removal.

15 Reconnect the battery and perform the necessary re-learn procedures (see Chapter 5).

5 Intake manifold - removal and installation

Warning: *The engine must be completely cool before beginning this procedure.*

Removal

1 Relieve the fuel system pressure (see Chapter 4).

2 Remove the engine cover fasteners and remove the cover from the top of the engine, if equipped.

3 On 2013 and earlier models/2014 and later Rogue Select models, remove the cowl panel (see Chapter 11).

4 On 2014 and later models (except Rogue Select models), remove the air inlet duct from the throttle body and air filter housing (see Chapter 4).

5 On 2013 and earlier models/2014 and later Rogue Select models, remove the air filter housing and resonator assembly (see Chapter 4).

6 Disconnect the cable from the negative terminal of the battery (see Chapter 5).

7 Label and detach the PCV hose, brake booster hose, throttle control actuator, EVAP hose and the purge control solenoid.

8 Remove the throttle body and gasket (see Chapter 4) and position it aside. Do not disconnect the coolant hoses.

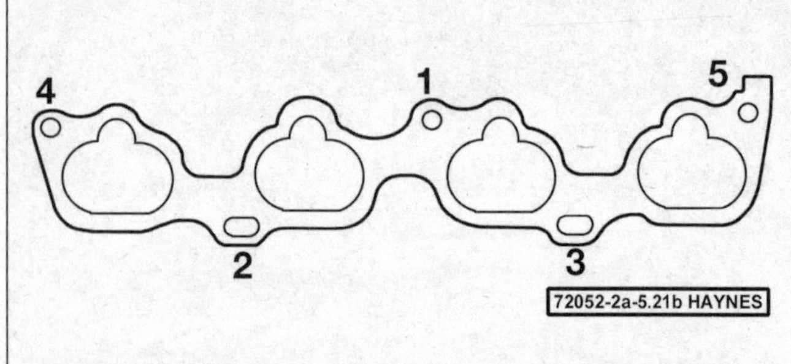

5.17a Intake manifold bolt tightening sequence - re-torque bolt 1 after finishing (2013 and earlier models/2014 and later Rogue Select models)

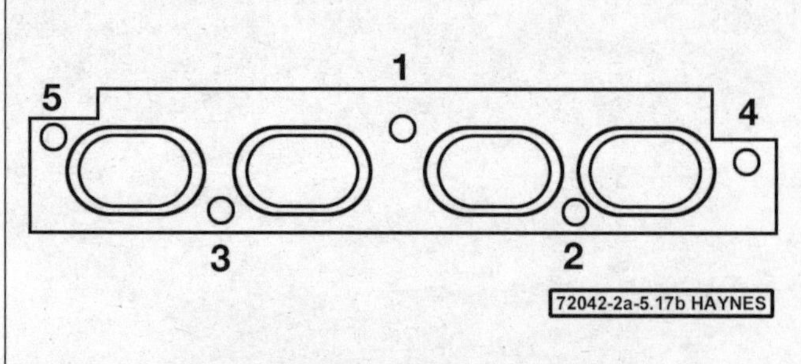

5.17b Intake manifold bolt tightening sequence - re-torque bolt 1 after finishing (2014 and later models, except Rogue Select models)

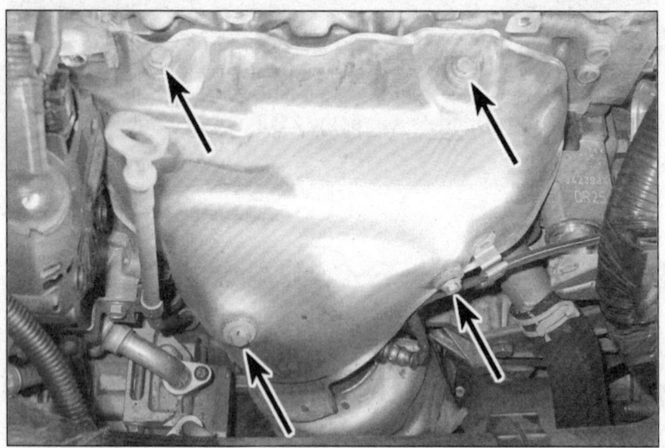

6.6 Remove the exhaust manifold heat shield bolts

6.13 Exhaust manifold nuts must be tightened twice in sequence

9 With the throttle body removed, remove the intake manifold support bracket fasteners and remove the bracket, if equipped.

10 Disconnect the fuel line from the fuel rail (see Chapter 4).

Note: *It may be necessary to remove the fuel injectors and fuel rail to gain access to the mounting bolts.*

11 On 2014 and later models, (except Rogue Select models), disconnect the front exhaust pipe then disconnect electrical connectors from intake manifold runner control valve position sensor and runner control valve.

12 Remove the intake manifold mounting nuts and bolts in the reverse of the tightening sequence (see illustration 5.21a or 5.21b).

13 Remove the intake manifold from the cylinder head.

Note: *On 2013 and earlier models/2014 and later Rogue Select models, remove the intake manifold adapter after removing the manifold.*

Installation

14 Use a scraper to remove all traces of old gasket material and sealant from the manifold and cylinder head, then clean the mating surfaces with brake system cleaner.

15 On 2013 and earlier models/2014 and later Rogue Select models, install a new gasket and position the intake manifold adapter on the cylinder head studs.

16 Install a new gasket, then position the intake manifold on the studs and install the nuts/bolts.

17 Tighten the nuts/bolts in sequence (see illustrations) to the torque listed in this Chapter's Specifications, then re-torque bolt number one.

18 The remainder of installation is the reverse of removal.

19 Reconnect the battery and perform the necessary re-learn procedures (see Chapter 5).

6 Exhaust manifold - removal and installation

Warning: *The engine must be completely cool before beginning this procedure.*

Note: *The primary catalytic converter is integrated into the exhaust manifold and cannot be serviced separately.*

Removal

1 Disconnect the cable from the negative terminal of the battery (see Chapter 5).

2 Block the rear wheels and set the parking brake. Loosen the right front wheel lug nuts. Raise the front of the vehicle and support it securely on jackstands. Remove the right front wheel.

3 Remove the engine splash shields.

4 Remove the right inner fender splash shield (see Chapter 11), then remove the drivebelt (see Chapter 1).

5 Disconnect the electrical connector from the oxygen sensor (see Chapter 6).

6 Remove the heat shield from the exhaust manifold (see illustration).

7 Disconnect the exhaust pipe from the catalytic converter.

Note: *Applying penetrating oil to the exhaust manifold fasteners may make removing the nuts/bolts easier.*

8 Unbolt the exhaust manifold brace.

9 Remove the exhaust manifold-to-cylinder head nuts, in the reverse order of the tightening sequence (see illustration 6.13), and detach the manifold and gasket.

Installation

10 Use a scraper to remove all traces of old gasket material and carbon deposits from the exhaust manifold and cylinder head mating surfaces.

11 Position the new exhaust manifold gasket over the cylinder head studs.

12 Install the manifold and thread the mounting nuts into place.

13 Working in the correct sequence (see illustration), tighten the nuts to the torque listed in this Chapter's Specifications.

7.4 Use a pin spanner to hold the pulley from turning, so the bolt can be loosened

7.5 Remove the pulley from the crankshaft using a puller

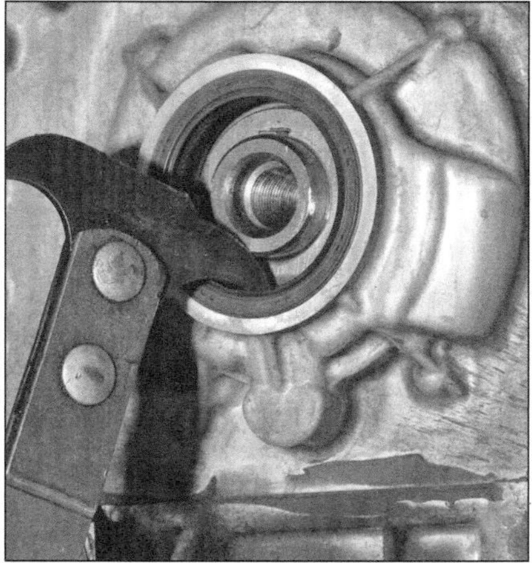
7.6 Use a seal puller, or screwdriver with the tip wrapped in tape, to pry the seal out of the timing chain cover

14 The remainder of installation is the reverse of removal. Use anti-seize lubricant on the exhaust pipe studs.
15 Reconnect the battery and perform the necessary re-learn procedures (see Chapter 5).

7 Crankshaft front oil seal - replacement

1 Loosen the right front wheel lug nuts. Raise the vehicle and support it securely on jackstands. Remove the right front wheel.
2 Remove the right inner fender splash shield (see Chapter 11).
3 Remove the drivebelt (see Chapter 1).
4 Using a pin spanner, hold the crankshaft pulley from turning and remove the crankshaft pulley bolt (see illustration).
5 Use a puller to remove the pulley from the crankshaft (see illustration).
Caution: *Use the proper adapter on the end of the crankshaft to prevent damage to the threads or end of the crankshaft. Also, the jaws of the puller must bolt to the hub of the pulley or grasp the hub of the pulley, not the outer diameter.*
6 Use a seal-puller tool, or wrap the tip of a screwdriver with tape, to pry out the seal, being careful not to damage the seal bore or scratch the surface of the crankshaft snout (see illustration).
7 Clean the bore in the timing chain cover and coat the outer edge of the new seal with engine oil or multi-purpose grease. Also lubricate the seal lips.
8 Using a seal driver or a socket with an outside diameter slightly smaller than the outside diameter of the seal, carefully drive the new seal into place (see illustration). Make sure it's installed squarely and driven in to the same depth as the original. Check the seal after installation to make sure the garter spring didn't pop out of place.
Caution: *The oil seal lip goes toward the engine, and the dust seal lip toward the pulley.*

7.8 Drive the new seal squarely into the timing chain cover with a seal driver or a large socket

9 Reinstall the crankshaft pulley (see illustration). Tighten the crankshaft pulley bolt to the torque listed in this Chapter's Specifications.
10 The remainder of installation is the reverse of removal.
11 Run the engine and check for oil leaks.

8 Timing chain/oil pump drive chain or balance shaft chain and sprockets - removal, inspection and installation

Warning: *The engine must be completely cool before beginning this procedure.*
Caution: *The timing system is complex. Severe engine damage will occur if you make any mistakes. Do not attempt this procedure unless you are highly experienced with this type of repair. If you are at all unsure of your abilities, consult an expert. Double-check all your work and be sure everything is correct before you attempt to start the engine.*

7.9 It's best to use a pulley installation tool to press the crankshaft pulley into place

Note: *On 2014 and later models (except Rogue Select models), the manufacturer recommends that the engine be removed for this procedure. This Section describes servicing the timing chain assembly with the engine in the vehicle, however it is usually easier to remove the engine first. See Chapter 2B for more information on engine removal. If you choose to remove the engine for this procedure, ignore the steps which don't apply.*
Note: *These models use a balance shaft drive chain and balance shaft assembly. The balance shaft unit cannot be disassembled.*

Removal

1 Position the engine at TDC for cylinder number one (see Section 3). Disconnect the cable from the negative terminal of the battery (see Chapter 5).
2 Loosen the right front wheel lug nuts. Raise the vehicle and support it securely on jackstands, then remove the right front wheel.
3 Remove the inner fenderwell splash shield (see Chapter 11).

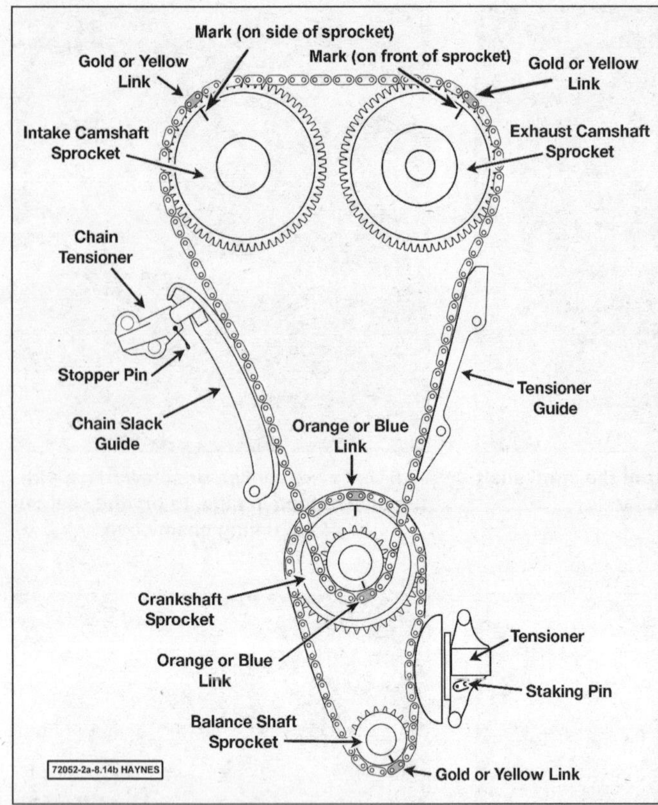

8.14a Timing chain details - with the engine set at TDC compression for cylinder number 1 (2013 and earlier models/ 2014 and later Rogue Select models)

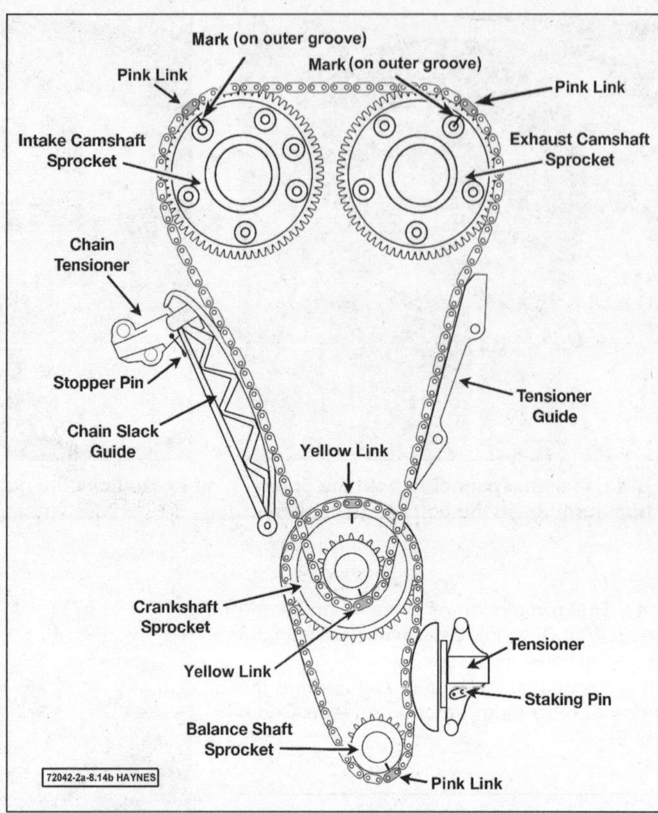

8.14b Timing chain details - with the engine set at TDC compression for cylinder number 1 (2014 and later models, except Rogue Select models)

4 Drain the engine oil (see Chapter 1).
5 Remove the coolant reservoir (see Chapter 3).
6 Remove the alternator and bracket (see Chapter 5).
7 Remove the valve cover (see Section 4) and intake manifold (see Section 5).
8 Support the engine from above with an engine hoist or engine support fixture.
9 Remove the oil pans (see Section 12).
10 On 2013 and earlier models/2014 and later Rogue Select models, disconnect the electrical connector for the Intake Valve Timing (IVT) control solenoid, then remove the mounting bolt and control solenoid from the timing chain cover.
11 On 2014 and later models (except Rogue Select models), disconnect the electrical connectors for the Intake Valve Timing (IVT) intermediate lock control solenoid valve, Intake Valve Timing control solenoid valve, Exhaust Valve Timing (EVT) control solenoid valve, then remove the mounting bolts and control solenoids from the timing chain cover.
12 Remove the bolts retaining the (VT) camshaft sprocket cover to the timing chain main cover. Remove the cover. Remove the bolts in the reverse of the tightening sequence (see illustration 8.34).

Note: *Use a sharp tool to cut the RTV sealant securing the cover.*

13 Remove the upper chain guide from between the two camshaft sprockets.
14 Check the positions of the camshaft sprockets. They should be aligned at TDC number 1 (see illustrations).
15 Remove the crankshaft pulley (see Section 7). Don't allow the crankshaft to turn while removing the bolt.
16 Remove the timing chain cover mounting bolts in the reverse of the tightening sequence (see illustration 8.33) and remove the cover.

Note: *Make notes on the timing chain cover bolt locations so they can be installed in their original locations.*

17 Using the tip of a screwdriver, push down on the tensioner plunger and insert a stopper pin of the correct diameter into the hole on the tensioner. Once the tensioner is locked in the retracted position, remove the bolts and the tensioner from the front of the engine.
18 Remove the timing chain.
19 Use an open-end wrench on the hex of the camshaft to hold it as you remove the camshaft sprocket bolts. If the chain is being removed only for removal of the camshafts or cylinder head, skip the remainder of this removal procedure.
20 Remove the balance shaft chain tensioner, locate the stop tab underneath the tensioner arm and press the stop tab away from the guide until a stopper pin of the correct diameter can be inserted into the hole on the tensioner. Once the tensioner is locked in the retracted position, the tensioner can be removed from the front of the engine.

Balance shaft chain and balance shaft assembly removal

21 Remove the balance shaft chain tensioner bolts, tensioner and tensioner guide.
22 Remove the balance shaft chain and crankshaft sprocket.
23 Remove the balance shaft unit mounting bolts following the reverse of the tightening sequence (see illustration 8.25).

Inspection

24 Inspect the camshaft, idler and crankshaft sprockets for wear of the teeth and keyways. Inspect the chains for cracks or excessive wear of the rollers. Inspect the facing of the chain guides for excessive wear.

Installation

25 Install the balance shaft unit using new bolts; tighten the bolts, in sequence (see illustration), to the torque listed in this Chapter's Specifications.
26 Install the crankshaft sprocket and the oil pump/balance shaft drive chain. Make sure the colored links on the oil pump or balance shaft chain align with the mating marks on the crankshaft sprocket and the oil pump or balance shaft sprocket (see illustration 8.14a or 8.14b).
27 Install the oil pump/balance shaft drive chain tensioner bolts and the tensioner. The

bolt hole positions may have changed since the tensioner was removed. The chain guide and the tensioner move freely with the staking pin as the pivot. Align and tighten the two chain tensioner bolts, then move the tensioner to match the bolt holes.

28 Double-check the drive chain alignment marks. Repeat the procedure if the alignment marks are incorrect. Release the staking pin from the tensioner to apply tension to the drive chain.

29 Install the timing chain, aligning the colored links with the mating marks on the camshaft and crankshaft sprockets (see illustration 8.14a or 8.14b).

30 Install the timing chain guide and chain slack guide. Tighten the bolts to the torque listed in this Chapter's Specifications.

31 Install the timing chain tensioner and release the stopper pin. Double-check the timing chain alignment marks; if they are incorrect, repeat the procedure. Tighten the sprocket bolts to the torque listed in this Chapter's Specifications.

32 Apply a bead of RTV sealant to the mating surfaces around the perimeter of the timing chain cover, as well as around the bolt hole in the center (bolt no. 11 in illustration 8.33).

33 Install the timing chain cover. Tighten the cover bolts in the correct sequence (see illustration), to the torque listed in this Chapter's Specifications.

34 Apply a bead of RTV sealant to the mating surfaces around the perimeter of the (VT) camshaft sprocket cover. Install the cover and tighten the bolts, in the correct sequence (see illustration), to the torque listed in this Chapter's Specifications.

35 The remainder of installation is the reverse of removal.

Caution: *Before starting the engine, carefully rotate the crankshaft by hand through at least two full revolutions (use a socket and breaker bar on the crankshaft pulley center bolt). If you feel any resistance, STOP! There is something wrong - most likely valves are contacting the pistons. You must find the problem before proceeding.*

36 Reconnect the battery and perform the necessary re-learn procedures (see Chapter 5).

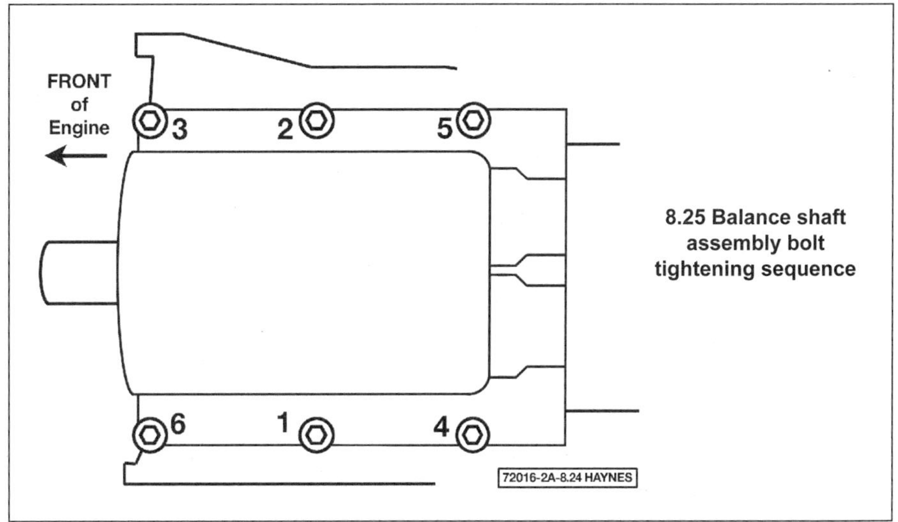

8.25 Balance shaft assembly bolt tightening sequence

9 Camshafts and lifters - removal, inspection and installation

Removal

1 Disconnect the cable from the negative terminal of the battery (see Chapter 5).

2 Remove the valve cover (see Section 4).

3 On 2013 and earlier models/2014 and later Rogue Select models, remove the intake manifold (see Section 5).

4 Check the valve clearances (see Chapter 1). Record the measurements; if any valves are out of specification, they can be corrected before reinstalling the camshafts.

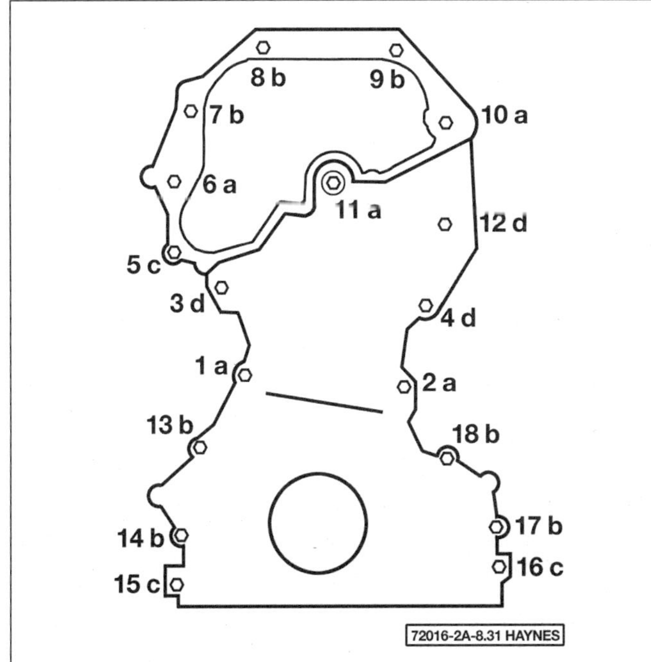

8.33 Timing chain main cover bolt tightening sequence; the letters refer to bolt lengths - bolts of different lengths have different torque values, as noted in this Chapter's Specifications - 2013 and earlier models shown, later models almost identical

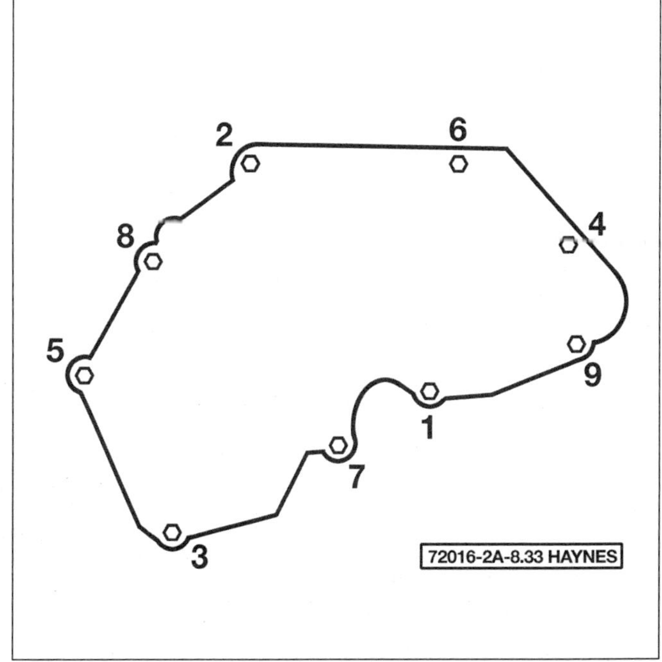

8.34 (VT) camshaft sprocket cover bolt tightening sequence

9.14 With a dial indicator in place, pry the camshaft forward and back to check the camshaft endplay

9.17a Pull the lifters straight up to remove them

9.17b The lifters can be stored in individually-marked plastic bags, or in a divided, marked box like this one

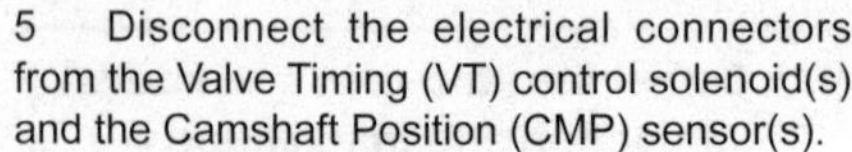

5 Disconnect the electrical connectors from the Valve Timing (VT) control solenoid(s) and the Camshaft Position (CMP) sensor(s).

6 Remove the (VT) camshaft sprocket cover bolts in the reverse of the tightening sequence (see illustrations 8.34). Remove the cover.

Note: *Use a sharp tool to cut the RTV sealant securing the cover.*

7 Remove the CMP sensor(s) and bracket (see Chapter 6).

Note: *2013 and earlier models/2014 and later Rogue Select models use an intake camshaft position sensor and 2014 and later models (except Rogue Select models) use an intake and exhaust camshaft position sensor.*

8 Loosen the right front wheel lug nuts. Raise the vehicle and support it securely on jackstands. Remove the right front wheel.

9 Remove the inner fender splash shield (see Chapter 11).

10 Position the engine at TDC on the compression stroke for number one cylinder (see Section 3). Using paint or an indelible marker, mark the links of the timing chain that correspond to the timing marks on the camshaft sprockets (see illustration 8.14a or 8.14b).

Caution: *Don't turn the camshaft(s) or the crankshaft after this has been done. The valves could contact the pistons and be damaged.*

11 Use a screwdriver to retract the plunger of the chain tensioner, then insert a drill bit or Allen wrench into the hole to secure the plunger in place. Remove the tensioner.

Note: *This procedure is done through the camshaft sprocket cover opening.*

12 Hold the hexagon part of the camshaft with a wrench, then remove the camshaft sprocket bolts. Remove the sprockets.

Note: *It isn't necessary to maintain tension on the timing chain; the timing chain won't separate from the crankshaft sprocket.*

13 Remove the upper timing chain guide through the timing chain cover.

14 Before removing the camshafts, use a dial indicator to check camshaft endplay (see illustration). Mount the dial indicator so the gauge tip can be placed at the end of the camshaft. Move the camshaft all the way to the rear and zero the dial indicator. Next, use a screwdriver to pry it all the way forward. If the endplay (the total amount of movement) exceeds the limit listed in this Chapter's Specifications, replace the camshaft and/or cylinder head.

9.19 Measure the lobe heights - if any lobe height is less than the minimum listed in this Chapter's Specifications, replace the camshaft

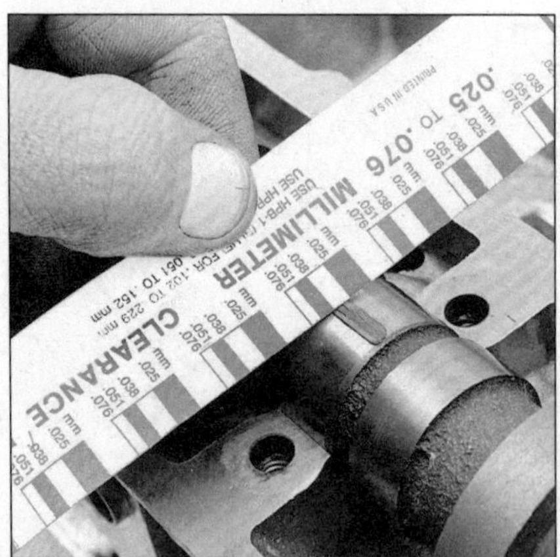

9.20b Compare the width of the crushed Plastigage to the scale on the envelope to determine the oil clearance

9.20a Place a strip of Plastigage under each camshaft bearing cap and tighten the caps to Specifications

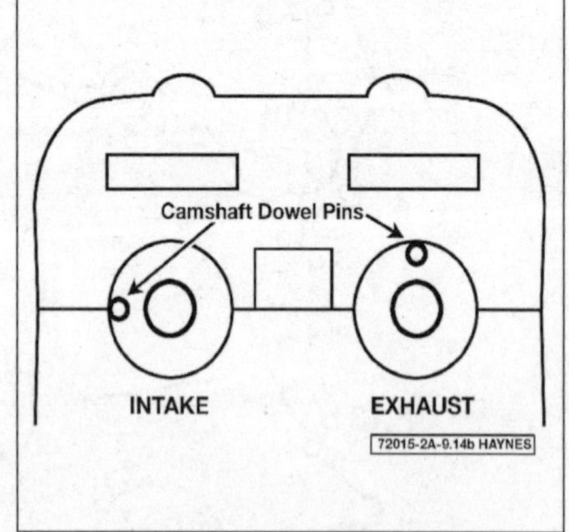

9.23 Correct positions of the dowel pins for camshaft installation

15 Loosen the camshaft bearing caps in the reverse of the tightening sequence (see illustration 9.24b).

Caution: *Keep the caps in order. They must be installed in their original locations.*

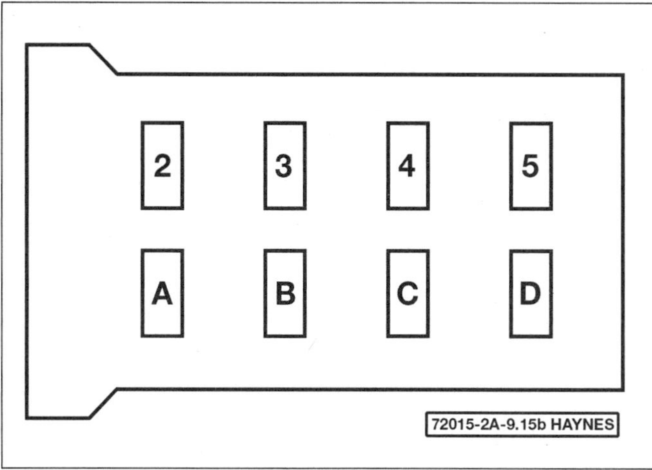

9.24a Camshaft bearing cap designations

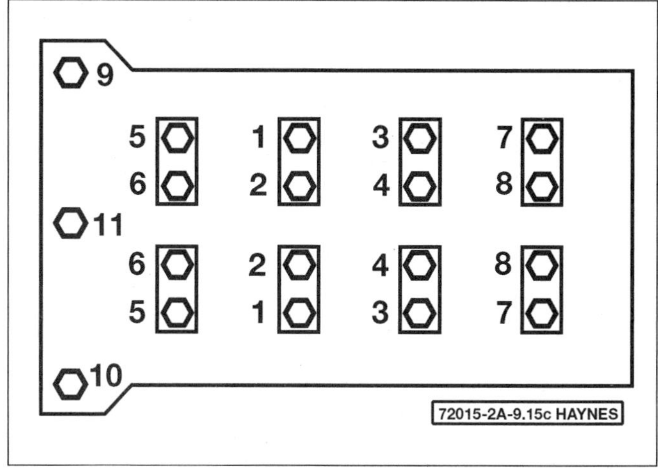

9.24b Camshaft bearing cap bolt tightening sequence - 2013 and earlier Rogue models/2014 and 2015 Rogue Select models

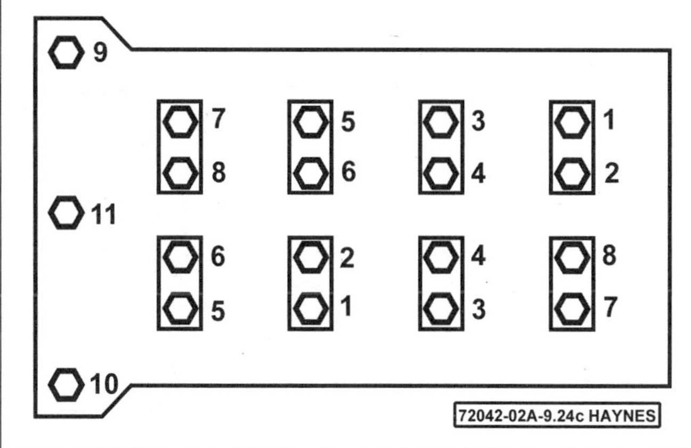

9.24c Camshaft bearing cap tightening sequence - 2014 through 2016 Rogue models

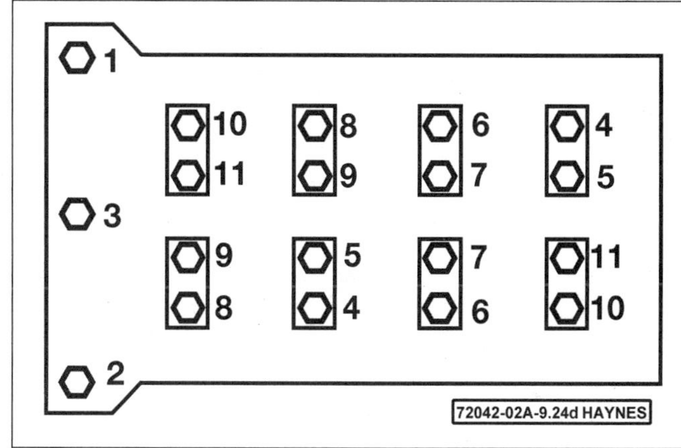

9.24d Camshaft bearing cap tightening sequence – 2017 and later models

16 Remove the bearing caps or bridge and lift the camshafts straight up and out.

17 Pull the lifters straight up and store them in numbered plastic bags or a marked box (see illustrations).

Inspection

18 Visually examine the camshaft lobes, journals, bearing caps and lifters. Check for score marks, pitting and evidence of overheating (blue, discolored areas). If wear is excessive or damage is evident, the component will have to be replaced.

19 Using a micrometer, measure camshaft journal diameter and lobe height (see illustration), and compare your measurements to this Chapter's Specifications. If the lobe height is less than the minimum allowable, the camshaft is worn and must be replaced.

20 Check the oil clearance for each camshaft journal as follows:

a) *Clean the bearing caps and the camshaft journals with brake system cleaner.*
b) *Carefully lay the camshafts in place in the cylinder head. DON'T use any lubrication.*
c) *Lay a strip of Plastigage on each journal.*
d) *Install the bearing caps with the arrows pointing toward the front (timing chain end) of the engine.*
e) *Tighten the bolts in sequence (see illustration 9.24b, 9.24c or 9.24d), to the torque listed in this Chapter's Specifications, in 1/4-turn increments.*

Caution: *Don't turn the camshaft while the Plastigage is in place.*

f) *Remove the bolts, in the proper sequence, and detach the bearing caps.*
g) *Compare the width of the crushed Plastigage (at its widest point) to the scale on the Plastigage envelope (see illustrations).*
h) *If the clearance is greater than specified, replace the camshaft and/or cylinder head.*

21 Scrape off the Plastigage with your fingernail or the edge of a credit card - don't scratch or nick the journals or bearing caps.

Installation

22 Apply moly-based engine assembly lubricant to the camshaft lobes and journals.

23 Install the camshafts in their original positions at TDC. The camshaft dowel pins must face the 12 o'clock position (exhaust camshaft) and the 9 o'clock position (intake camshaft) (see illustration).

24 Apply a 1/8-inch bead of RTV sealant to the mating surface of the timing chain cover. Install the bearing caps and bolts and tighten them in sequence (see illustrations) to the torque listed in this Chapter's Specifications.

Note: *When installing the no. 1 bearing cap (the one closest to the timing chain), be careful not to disturb the sealant while lowering it into place.*

25 Install the camshaft sprockets and timing chain (see Section 8). Align the marks on the timing chain (made in Step 10) with the timing marks on the camshaft spockets

26 The remainder of installation is the reverse of removal. If any part of the valve train was replaced, check and adjust the valve clearance (see Chapter 1).

27 Reconnect the battery and perform the necessary re-learn procedures (see Chapter 5).

10.2a Compress the valve spring and remove the keepers with needle-nose pliers or a magnet

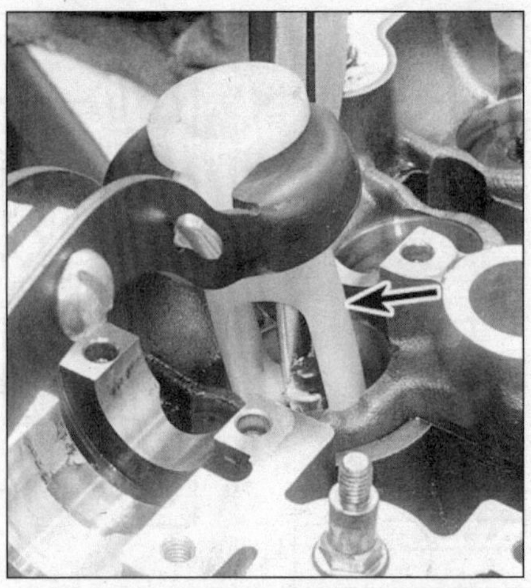
10.2b Because of the tight quarters, a spring compressor must be used with an adapter that has windows in the side to access the keepers

10.3 Remove the retainer and valve spring

10.4 Remove the valve stem seal with needle-nose pliers

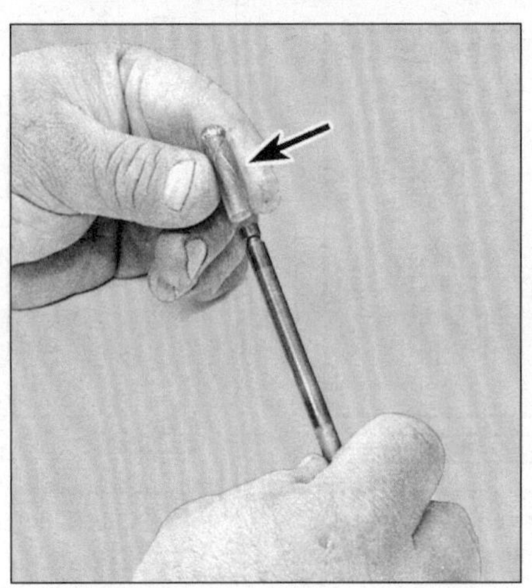
10.7 Slip a plastic sleeve over the valve stem to protect the new seal during installation

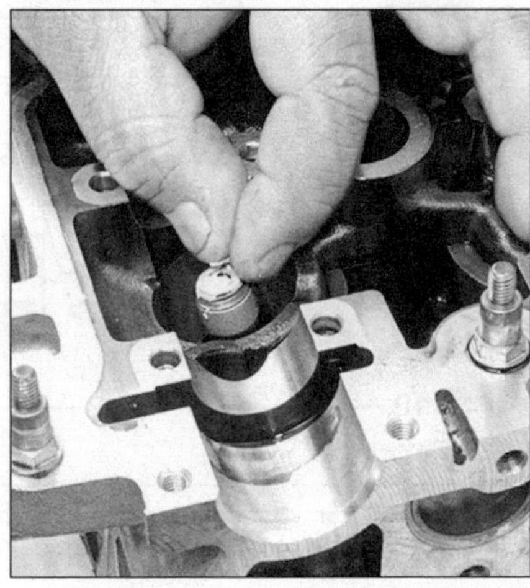
10.8 Lubricate the new seal and slip it onto the valve, past the protector

10.9 Tap the new seals down onto the valve guide with a deep socket

10 Valve springs, retainers and seals - replacement

1 Remove the cylinder head (see Section 11).

2 With the cylinder head on a sturdy workbench, use a large, clamp-type valve spring compressor and adapter to compress each valve spring (see illustrations). Make sure the bottom section of the tool is located under the valve of which spring is being removed, and compress the spring just enough to remove the keepers with a magnet or small pliers.

3 Pull the valve spring out with its retainer (see illustration).

4 Remove the old valve stem oil seal with pliers (see illustration).

5 Remove the valve and inspect the valve stem for damage. Rotate the valve in the guide and check the end for eccentric movement, which would indicate that the valve is bent.

6 Move the valve up-and-down in the guide and make sure it doesn't bind. If the valve stem binds, either the valve is bent or the guide is damaged. In either case, the cylinder head will require repair.

7 Lubricate the valve stem with engine oil and install it in the cylinder head. A plastic seal protector that slips over the valve stem is usually provided with the seals (see illustration). This protects the new seal from being torn as it passes over the keeper grooves in the valve. If you don't have the seal protector, apply a few wraps of cellulose tape around the valve stem instead.

8 Lubricate the new seal with multi-purpose grease and push it down over the valve stem by hand (see illustration). When it is down against the guide, remove the plastic protector or tape from the valve stem.

9 Use a deep socket of the appropriate size to lightly tap the new seal down against the top of the valve guide (see illustration).

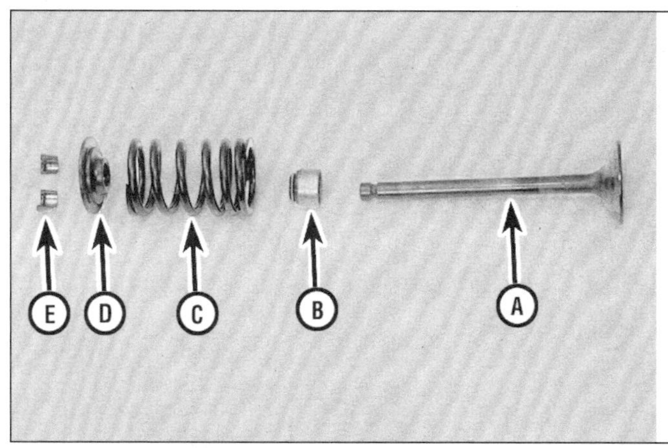

10.10 Arrangement of valve components

A Valve
B Valve stem seal
C Valve spring
D Retainer
E Keepers

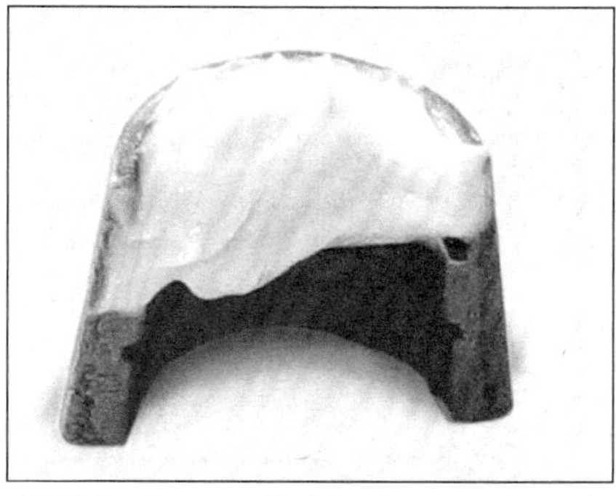

10.11 Apply a small dab of grease to each keeper before installation to retain them in place on the valve stem until the spring is released

11.9 Pry under the cylinder head under casting protrusions only - do not pry between mating surfaces

11.12 Remove all traces of old gasket material - the cylinder head and block mating surfaces must be perfectly clean to ensure a good gasket seal

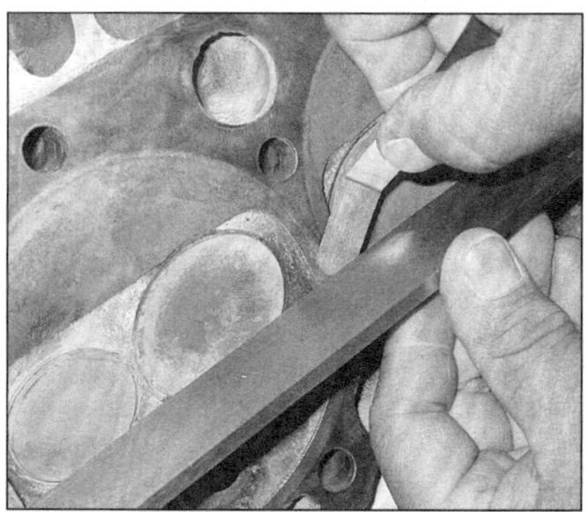

11.15 Check the cylinder head gasket surface for warpage by trying to insert a feeler gauge under the straightedge. See this Chapter's Specifications for the maximum warpage allowed and use a feeler gauge of that thickness

10 Install the spring in position over the valve, with the retainer in place (see illustration).
11 Compress the valve spring and retainer and carefully position the keepers in the groove. Apply a small dab of grease to the inside of each keeper to retain it in place if necessary (see illustration) and insert them with needle-nose pliers.
12 Remove the pressure from the spring tool and make sure the keepers are seated.
13 Reinstall the lifters and camshafts (see Section 9).
14 The remainder of installation is the reverse of removal.
15 Start the engine, then check for oil leaks and unusual sounds coming from the valve cover area.

11 Cylinder head - removal and installation

Warning: *The engine must be completely cool before beginning this procedure.*

Removal

1 Relieve the fuel system pressure (see Chapter 4). Disconnect the cable from the negative terminal of the battery (see Chapter 5), then position the engine at TDC compression for cylinder no. 1 (see Section 3).
2 Drain the coolant (see Chapter 1).
3 Remove the timing chain (see Section 8).
4 Remove the camshafts (see Section 9).
5 Remove the exhaust manifold (see Section 6)
6 Remove the intake manifold (see Section 5).
7 Label and remove any remaining items attached to the cylinder head, such as coolant fittings, tubes, cables, hoses or wiring harnesses.
8 Using a breaker bar and the appropriate-sized hex bit, loosen the cylinder head bolts in 1/4-turn increments until they can be removed by hand. Loosen the bolts in reverse of the tightening sequence (see illustration 11.19) to avoid warping or cracking the cylinder head.
9 Lift the cylinder head off the engine block. If it's stuck, very carefully pry up at the transaxle end, beyond the gasket surface, at a casting protrusion (see illustration).
10 Remove all external components from the cylinder head to allow for thorough cleaning and inspection.

Installation

11 The mating surfaces of the cylinder head and block must be perfectly clean when the cylinder head is installed.
12 Use a gasket scraper to remove all traces of carbon and old gasket material (see illustration), then clean the mating surfaces with lacquer thinner or acetone. If there's oil on the mating surfaces when the cylinder head is installed, the gasket may not seal correctly and leaks could develop. When working on the block, stuff the cylinders with clean shop rags to keep out debris. Use a vacuum cleaner to remove material that falls into the cylinders.
13 Check the block and cylinder head mating surfaces for nicks, deep scratches and other damage. If damage is slight, it can be removed with a fine file; if it's excessive, machining may be the only alternative.
14 Use a tap of the correct size to chase the threads in the cylinder head bolt holes, then clean the holes with compressed air - make sure that nothing remains in the holes.
Warning: *Wear eye protection when using compressed air!*
15 Once the cylinder head's gasket surface is clean, check the cylinder head for warpage (see illustration). Check the cylinder head gasket, intake and exhaust manifold surfaces.

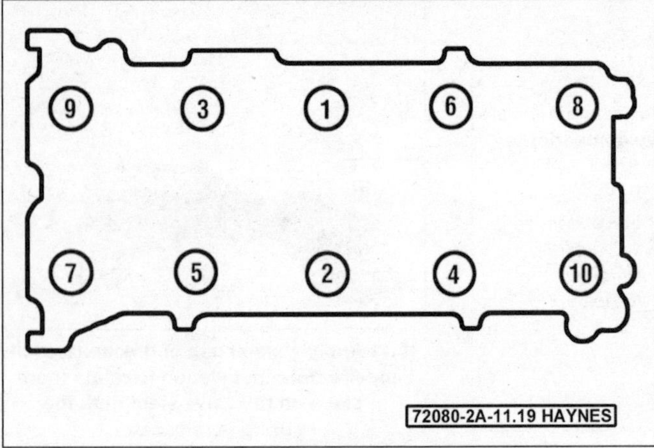

11.19 Cylinder head bolt TIGHTENING sequence

12.15 After cutting the pan seal with a putty knife, pry at the rear corners near the transaxle - do not pry in the gasket area

16 Install any components that were removed from the cylinder head.

17 Position the new cylinder head gasket over the dowel pins in the block and carefully set the cylinder head on the block without disturbing the gasket.

18 Before installing the new cylinder head bolts, apply a small amount of clean engine oil to the threads and hardened washers. The chamfered side of the washers must face the bolt heads, and the flat side of the washers must face the cylinder head.

19 Install the new cylinder head bolts and tighten them, following the recommended sequence (see illustration), to the torque listed in this Chapter's Specifications.

20 Install the lifters and camshafts (see Section 9).

21 Install the timing chain (see Section 8), then check the valve clearances (see Chapter 1).

22 The remainder of installation is the reverse of removal.

23 Refill the cooling system, install a new oil filter and add oil to the engine (see Chapter 1).

24 Reconnect the battery and perform the necessary re-learn procedures (see Chapter 5).

12 Oil pans - removal and installation

Note: *The following procedure describes removing the lower (steel) oil pan and the upper (aluminum) oil pan. If you're just removing the lower oil pan, many of the following steps are not necessary, as the pan is readily accessible.*

Removal

1 Disconnect the cable from the negative terminal of the battery (see Chapter 5).

2 Loosen the right front wheel lug nuts, raise the front of the vehicle and support it securely on jackstands, then remove the right front wheel.

3 Drain the engine oil and remove the filter (see Chapter 1).

4 Remove the engine oil dipstick tube fastener and remove the tube from the oil pan. Be sure to replace the O-ring.

5 Remove the front section of the exhaust pipe.

6 Remove the drivebelt (see Chapter 1).

7 Remove the right side driveaxle bearing bracket (see Chapter 8), then remove the air conditioning compressor (without disconnecting the lines) and secure it out of the way (see Chapter 3).

8 Remove the lower torque rod (see Section 16).

9 On AWD models, remove the transfer case (see Chapter 8, Section 10).

10 Remove the stabilizer bar link (see Chapter 10, Section 4).

11 Remove the front subframe (see Chapter 10, Section 14).

12 The oil pan is a two-piece design. A steel pan is attached to an aluminum section which is bolted to the engine block. Remove the oil pan bolts following the reverse of the recommended tightening sequence (see illustrations 12.22a or 12.22b). Separate the steel pan by inserting a thin putty knife between the steel and aluminum sections.

Caution: *Do not pry with a screwdriver between the steel pan and the aluminum flange or damage to the sealing surface may result.*

Note: *Mark each bolt to insure they are positioned in their original locations on reassembly.*

13 Remove the oil pump screen fasteners and remove the screen.

14 Remove the bolts attaching the aluminum section (upper oil pan) to the engine block, following the reverse of the tightening sequence (see illustration 12.21).

15 The sealant used to seal the aluminum section to the engine block can be very difficult to separate without damaging the aluminum section. Using a thin putty knife, work around the perimeter, cutting the pan free before prying the pan down at the transaxle end (see illustration).

Installation

16 Use a scraper to remove all traces of old gasket material and sealant from the block and oil pan. Clean the mating surfaces with brake system cleaner.

Caution: *Be careful not to scratch or gouge the gasket surface of the block or oil pan. A leak could develop after the repairs have been completed.*

17 Make sure the threaded bolt holes in the block are clean.

18 Check the steel pan flange for distortion, particularly around the bolt holes. If necessary, place the pan on a wood block and use a hammer to flatten and restore the gasket surface.

19 Apply a 3/16-inch wide bead of RTV sealant around the perimeter of the aluminum section (upper oil pan) (see illustration).

Note: *The oil pan must be installed within 15 minutes once the sealant has been applied.*

20 Install new O-rings into the upper oil pan, if equipped.

21 Carefully position the aluminum section on the engine block and install the bolts, tightening them hand-tight. Tighten the pan-to-transaxle bolts a little tighter than hand-tight, then tighten the oil pan-to-block fasteners in three or four steps, in the recommended sequence (see illustration 12.21), to the torque listed in this Chapter's Specifications. Tighten the pan-to-transaxle bolts (transaxle mounting bolts) to the torque listed in the Chapter 7 Specifications.

22 Apply a bead of RTV sealant around the perimeter of the steel pan and install it within 15 minutes of application. Tighten the bolts in sequence (see illustrations) to the torque listed in this Chapter's Specifications.

23 The remainder of installation is the reverse of removal. Install a new oil filter and wait at least thirty minutes for the RTV to setup before adding oil.

24 Reconnect the battery and perform the necessary re-learn procedures (see Chapter 5).

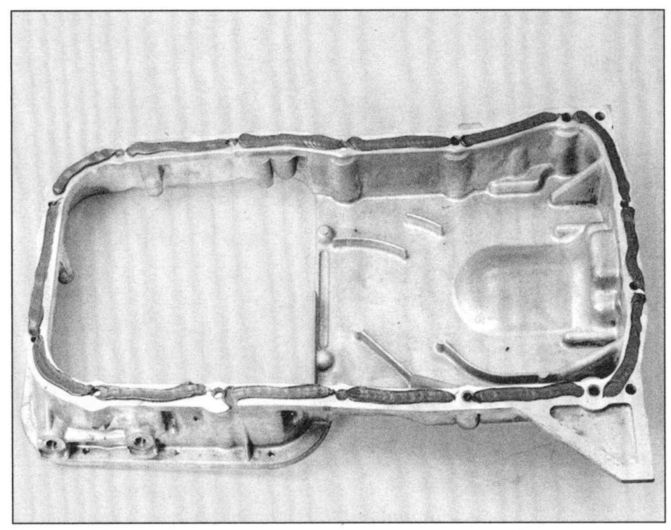

12.19 Apply a bead of RTV sealant around the perimeter of the aluminum section of the pan - typical bead shown

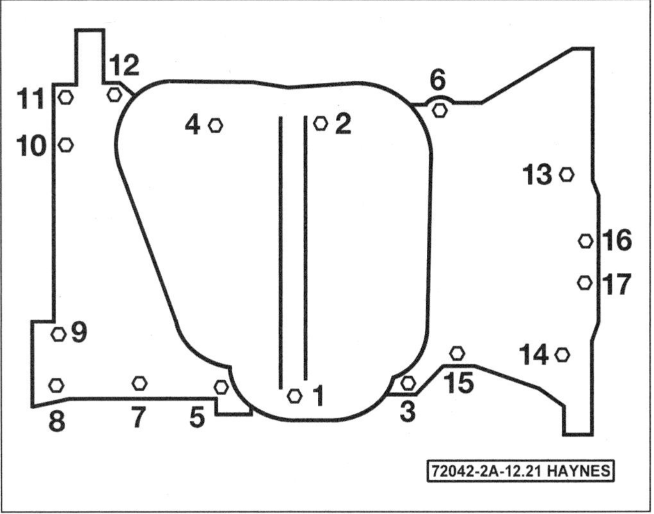

12.21 Bolt tightening sequence for the aluminum upper oil pan

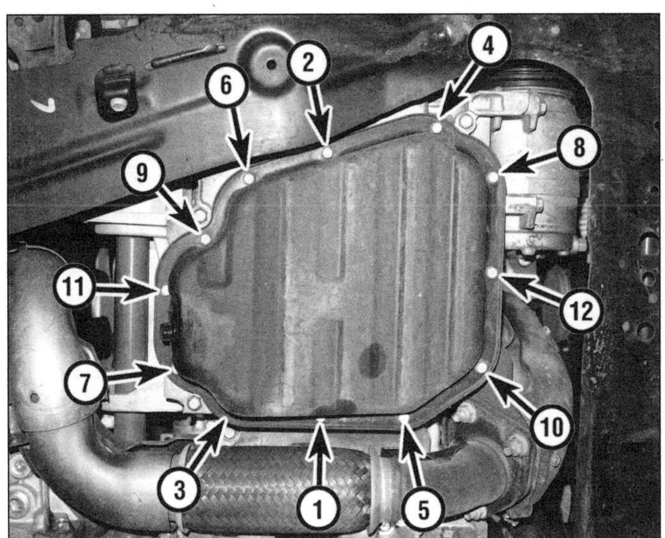

12.22a Bolt tightening sequence for the steel lower oil pan - 2013 and earlier models/2014 Rogue Select models

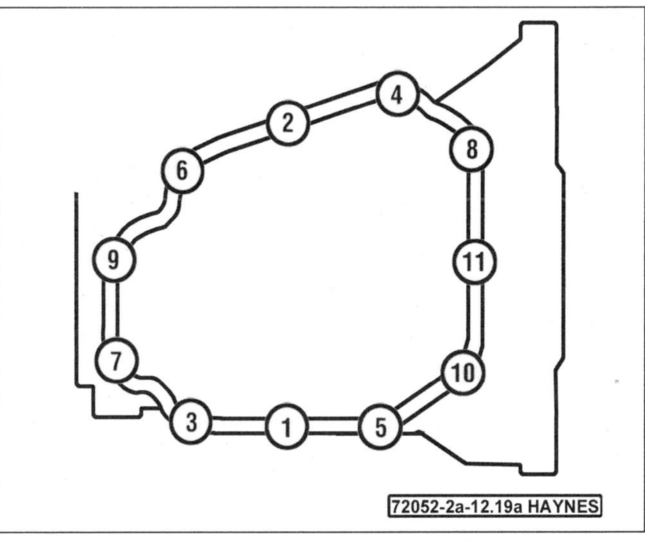

12.22b Bolt tightening sequence for the steel lower oil pan - 2014 and later models (except Rogue Select models)

13 Oil pump - removal, inspection and installation

Removal

1 The oil pump is located inside the timing chain cover and is driven by the crankshaft.

2 Remove the timing chain cover (see Section 8).

3 Remove the oil pump cover-to-oil pump body retaining fasteners (see illustration), then disassemble the inner and outer rotors.

Caution: *Be very careful with these components; the close tolerances are critical in creating the correct oil pressure. Any nicks or damage will require replacement of the complete pump/timing chain cover assembly.*

13.3 The oil pump is located inside the timing chain cover - remove the fasteners, then remove the oil pump cover

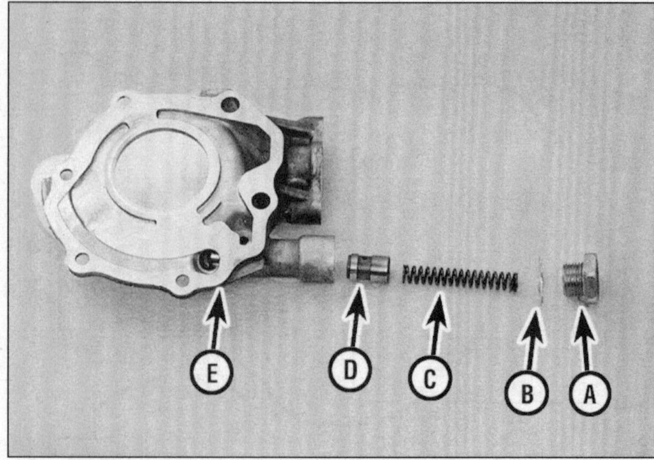

13.5 **Remove the oil pump pressure regulator valve assembly for cleaning and inspection**

A Cap
B Washer
C Spring
D Relief valve
E Oil pump cover

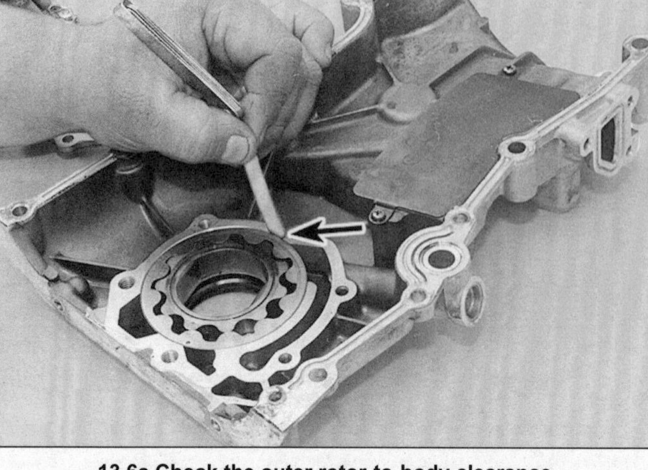

13.6a Check the outer rotor-to-body clearance with a feeler gauge as shown

13.6b Check the clearance between the inner and outer rotor tips

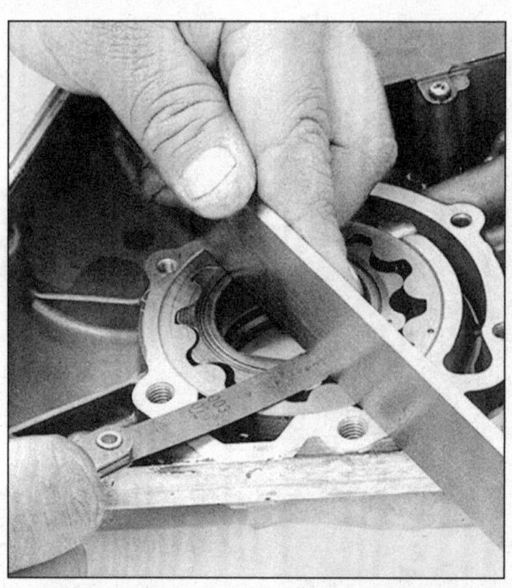

13.6c With a precision straightedge placed over the pump body and rotors, check the clearance between the inner and outer rotors and the pump body cover

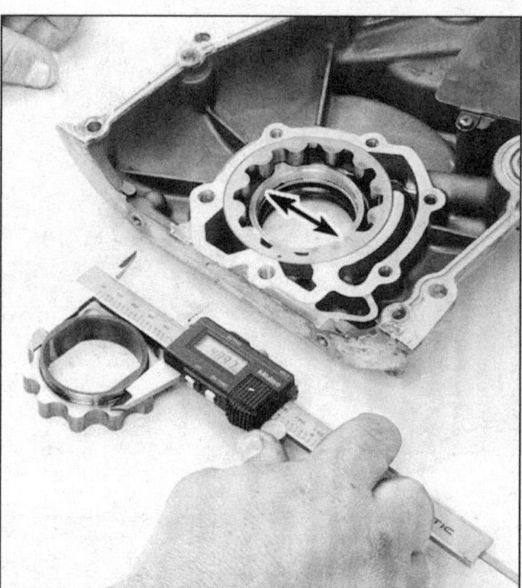

13.6d Measure the outer flanged surface of the inner rotor with a micrometer or precision calipers, then measure its bearing surface in the pump body - the difference is the inner rotor bearing clearance

Inspection

4 Clean all the components, including the timing chain cover and engine block gasket surfaces, with solvent, then inspect all surfaces for excessive wear and/or damage.

5 Disassemble the relief valve by removing the cap, washer, spring and regulator valve (see illustration). Check the oil pressure regulator valve sliding surface and valve spring. The regulator, when clean and oiled, should slide easily in the valve bore. If either the spring or the valve is damaged, they must be replaced as a set. If no damage is found, reassemble the relief valve parts, coating the parts with clean engine oil, and reinstall it in the oil pump cover.

6 Check the oil pump component clearance with a feeler gauge (see illustrations) and compare the results to this Chapter's Specifications. If any of the measurements are out of specification, replace both the timing chain cover and the oil pump components.

Installation

7 Assemble the oil pump components. There is a punch mark on each rotor; these marks must face away from the timing chain cover and toward the engine. Pour a generous amount of clean engine oil into the pump cavity and around the rotors. Install the cover to the pump body and tighten the fasteners to the torque listed in this Chapter's Specifications.

8 Install the timing chain cover, using a bead of RTV sealant on the cover-to-block surface (see Section 8).

Note: *Align the flats on the inner oil pump rotor with the crankshaft when installing the timing chain cover.*

9 Install the cylinder head and other components (see Section 9 and 11).

10 Install the oil pan (see Section 12). Install a new oil filter and add engine oil to the crankcase (see Chapter 1).

11 Start the engine and check for oil pressure and leaks.

12 Recheck the engine oil level.

14 Driveplate - removal and installation

Removal

1 Remove the engine/transaxle assembly (see Chapter 2B), then separate the transaxle from the engine (see Chapter 7).

2 If equipped with a manual transaxle, remove the pressure plate and clutch disc (see Chapter 8).

3 Use a center-punch or paint to make alignment marks on the flywheel/driveplate

14.3 Mark the driveplate and the crankshaft so they can be reassembled in their original positions

16.6 A long prybar can be used to check for relative movement in the engine mounts

and crankshaft to ensure correct alignment during installation (see illustration).

4 Remove the bolts that secure the flywheel/driveplate to the crankshaft.

5 Remove the flywheel/driveplate from the crankshaft.

Warning: *Since the flywheel is fairly heavy, be sure to support it while removing the last bolt. Flywheel teeth can be sharp; wear gloves or use rags to hold the flywheel.*

Installation

6 If equipped with a manual transaxle, clean the flywheel to remove grease and oil. Inspect the surface for cracks, rivet grooves, burned areas and score marks. Light scoring can be removed with emery cloth. Check for cracked and broken ring-gear teeth. Lay the flywheel on a flat surface and use a straightedge to check for warpage.

7 Clean and inspect the mating surfaces of the flywheel/driveplate and the crankshaft. If the crankshaft rear seal is leaking, replace it before reinstalling the flywheel/driveplate.

8 Position the flywheel/driveplate against the crankshaft. Install the spacer (if equipped) and align the marks made during removal. Some engines have an alignment dowel or staggered bolt holes to ensure correct installation. Before installing the bolts, apply thread-locking compound to the threads.

9 Wedge a screwdriver in the ring gear teeth to keep the flywheel/driveplate from turning as you tighten the bolts to the torque listed in this Chapter's Specifications. Follow a criss-cross pattern and work up to the final torque in three or four steps.

10 The remainder of installation is the reverse of removal.

11 Reconnect the battery and perform the necessary re-learn procedures (see Chapter 5).

15 Rear main oil seal - replacement

1 Remove the engine/transaxle assembly (see Chapter 2B), then separate the transaxle from the engine (see Chapter 7).

2 Remove the flywheel/driveplate (see Section 14).

3 Use a seal removal tool or a screwdriver wrapped with tape to pry out the seal, being careful not to gouge or nick the housing.

4 Lubricate the crankshaft seal journal and the lip of the new seal with multi-purpose grease.

5 Install the seal with the seal lip toward the engine and the dust seal toward the transaxle.

6 Tap the seal into place using a seal driver to make sure that it doesn't become tilted.

7 Install the seal so that its rear edge is flush with the face of the engine block, or up to 0.019 inch recessed.

8 The remainder of installation is the reverse of removal.

9 Reconnect the battery and perform the necessary re-learn procedures (see Chapter 5).

16 Engine mounts - check and replacement

1 Engine mounts seldom require attention, but broken or deteriorated mounts should be replaced immediately or the added strain placed on the driveline components may cause damage or wear.

Check

2 During the check, the engine must be raised slightly to remove the weight from the mounts.

3 Raise the vehicle and support it securely on jackstands and remove the splash shields.

4 Position a jack under the engine oil pan. Place a large wood block between the jack head and the oil pan, then carefully raise the engine just enough to take the weight off the mounts. Do not place the wood block under the oil pan drain plug.

Warning: *DO NOT place any part of your body under the engine when it's supported only by a jack!*

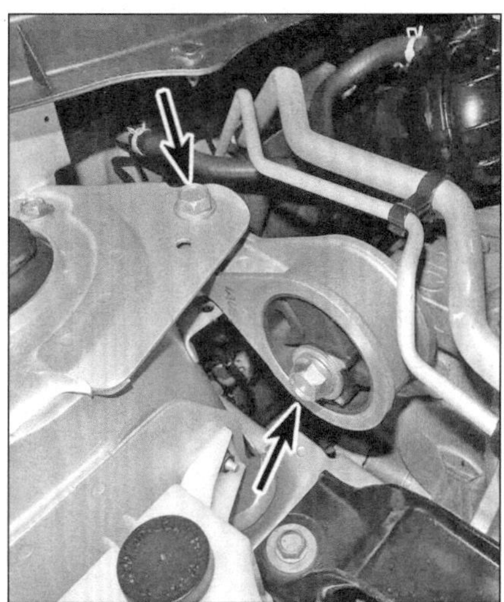
16.9 Upper torque rod mounting bolt locations

5 Check the mounts to see if the rubber is cracked, hardened or separated from the metal plates. Sometimes the rubber will split right down the center.

6 Check for relative movement between the mount plates and the engine or frame using a large screwdriver or prybar to attempt to move the mounts (see illustration). If movement is noted, lower the engine and tighten the mount fasteners.

7 Rubber preservative should be applied to the mounts to slow deterioration.

Replacement

8 Disconnect the cable from the negative terminal of the battery (see Chapter 5). Raise the vehicle and support it securely on jackstands. Support the engine as described in Step 4.

9 To remove the upper torque rod, remove the through-bolts and bracket bolts (see illustration).

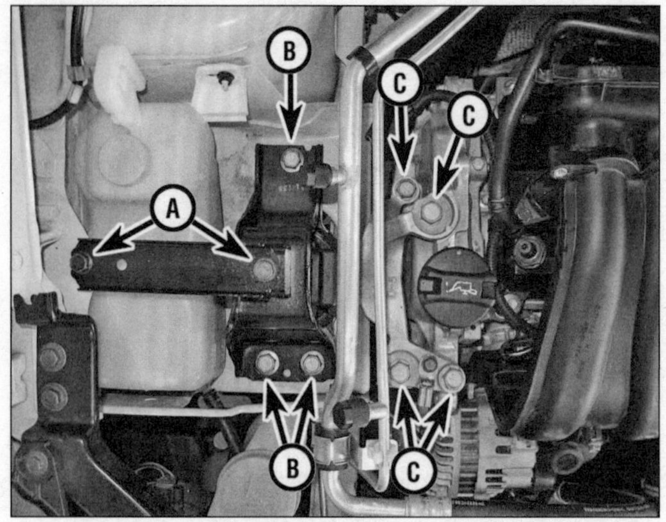

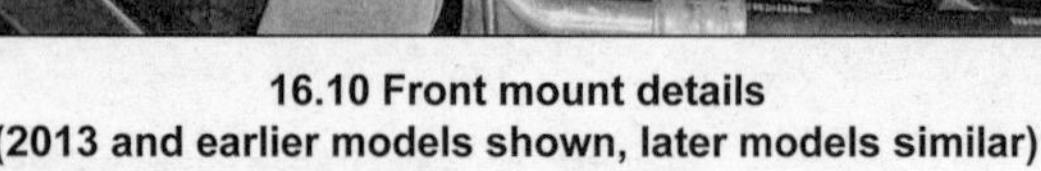

16.10 Front mount details
(2013 and earlier models shown, later models similar)

A Mount-to-body bolts *B Mount-to-engine bolts*

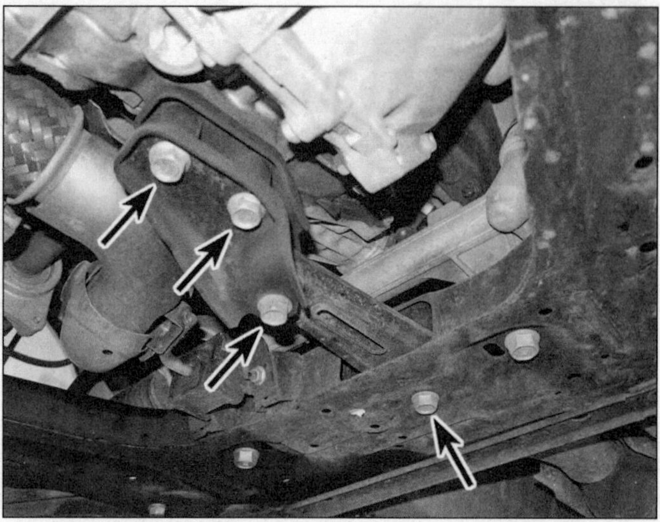

16.11 Lower torque rod mounting bolt locations

16.13a Remove the mount top bolts . . .

16.13b . . . and the side bolts through the wheel well

10 To remove the front engine mount, place a floor jack with a block of wood under the oil pan the remove the torque rod bracket, the engine mount to body bolts the engine mount-to-engine bolts and remove the mount (see illustration).

11 To remove the lower torque rod, remove the through-bolts and bracket bolts (see illustration).

12 To remove the left hand mount (transaxle end) remove the battery and battery tray (see Chapter 5) and air filter housing (see Chapter 4), then support the transaxle with a floor jack.

13 Remove the mount top bolts, then the side bolts (see illustrations) and remove the mount.

14 Installation is the reverse of removal. Use thread-locking compound on the mount bolts/nuts and tighten them securely.

Notes

Notes

Chapter 2 Part B
General engine overhaul procedures

Contents

Specifications

General

Engine designation	
2.5L engine	QR25DE
Displacement	151.82 cubic inches
Compression ratio	
2014 and earlier Rogue/2014 and 2015 Rogue Select models	9.6:1
2015 and later Rogue models	10:1
Cylinder compression pressure	
Standard	204.7 psi
Minimum	176.3 psi
Maximum variation between cylinders	14.5 to 15 psi
Oil pressure (minimum, warm engine)	
Idle	14 psi
2000 rpm	43 psi
6000 rpm	57 psi

Torque specifications

Ft-lbs (unless otherwise indicated)

Note: *One foot-pound (ft-lb) of torque is equivalent to 12 inch-pounds (in-lbs) of torque. Torque values below approximately 15 ft-lbs are expressed in inch-pounds, because most foot-pound torque wrenches are not accurate at these smaller values.*

Connecting rod cap bolts	
Step 1	20
Step 2	Loosen completely
Step 3	14
Step 4	Tighten an additional 90-degrees
Main bearing cap bolts	(see illustration 10.19)
Step 1, bolts 11 through 22	19
Step 2, bolts 1 through 10	29
Step 3, bolts 1 through 10	Tighten an additional 60-degrees
Crankshaft signal plate	16

Note: *Refer to Chapter 2A for additional torque specifications.*

1 General information - engine overhaul

1 Included in this portion of Chapter 2 are general information and diagnostic testing procedures for determining the overall mechanical condition of your engine.

2 The information ranges from advice concerning preparation for an overhaul and the purchase of replacement parts and/or components to detailed, step-by-step procedures covering removal and installation.

3 The following Sections have been written to help you determine whether your engine needs to be overhauled and how to remove and install it once you've determined it needs to be rebuilt. For information concerning in-vehicle engine repair, see Chapter 2A.

4 The Specifications included in this Part are general in nature and include only those necessary for testing the oil pressure and engine compression, and bottom-end torque specifications. Refer to Chapter 2A for additional engine Specifications.

5 It's not always easy to determine when, or if, an engine should be completely overhauled, because a number of factors must be considered.

6 High mileage is not necessarily an indication that an overhaul is needed, while low mileage doesn't preclude the need for an overhaul. Frequency of servicing is probably the most important consideration. An engine that's had regular and frequent oil and filter changes, as well as other required maintenance, will most likely give many thousands of miles of reliable service. Conversely, a neglected engine may require an overhaul very early in its service life.

7 Excessive oil consumption is an indication that piston rings, valve seals and/or valve guides are in need of attention. Make sure that oil leaks aren't responsible before deciding that the rings and/or guides are bad. Perform a cylinder compression check to determine the extent of the work required (see Section 3). Also, check the vacuum readings under various conditions (see Section 4).

8 Check the oil pressure with a gauge installed in place of the oil pressure sending unit (see Section 2) and compare it to this Chapter's Specifications. If it's extremely low, the bearings and/or oil pump are probably worn out.

9 Loss of power, rough running, knocking or metallic engine noises, excessive valve train noise and high fuel consumption rates may also point to the need for an overhaul, especially if they're all present at the same time. If a complete tune-up doesn't remedy the situation, major mechanical work is the only solution.

1.10a An engine block being bored. An engine rebuilder will use special machinery to recondition the cylinder bores

1.10b If the cylinders are bored, the machine shop will normally hone the engine on a machine like this

10 An engine overhaul involves restoring the internal parts to the specifications of a new engine. During an overhaul, the piston rings are replaced and the cylinder walls are reconditioned (rebored and/or honed) (see illustrations). If a rebore is done by an automotive machine shop, new oversize pistons will also be installed. The main bearings, connecting rod bearings and camshaft bearings are generally replaced with new ones and, if necessary, the crankshaft may be reground to restore the journals (see illustration). Generally, the valves are serviced as well, since they're usually in less-than-perfect condition at this point. While the engine is being overhauled, other components, such as the distributor, starter and alternator, can be rebuilt as well. The end result should be similar to a new engine that will give many trouble free miles.

Note: *Critical cooling system components such as the hoses, drivebelts, thermostat and water pump should be replaced with new parts when an engine is overhauled. The radiator should be checked carefully to ensure that it isn't clogged or leaking (see Chapter 3). If you purchase a rebuilt engine or short block, some rebuilders will not warranty their engines unless the radiator has been professionally flushed. Also, we don't recommend overhauling the oil pump - always install a new one when an engine is rebuilt.*

11 Overhauling the internal components on today's engines is a difficult and time-consuming task which requires a significant amount of specialty tools and is best left to a professional engine rebuilder (see illustrations). A competent engine rebuilder will handle the inspection of your old parts and offer advice concerning the reconditioning or replacement of the original engine, never purchase parts or have machine work done on other components until the block has been thoroughly inspected by a professional machine shop. As a general rule, time is the primary cost of an overhaul, especially since the vehicle may be tied up for a minimum of two weeks or more. Be aware that some engine builders only have the capability to rebuild the engine you bring them while other rebuilders have a large inventory of rebuilt exchange engines in stock. Also be aware that many machine shops could take as much as two weeks time to completely rebuild your engine depending on shop workload. Sometimes it makes more sense to simply exchange your engine for another engine that's already rebuilt to save time.

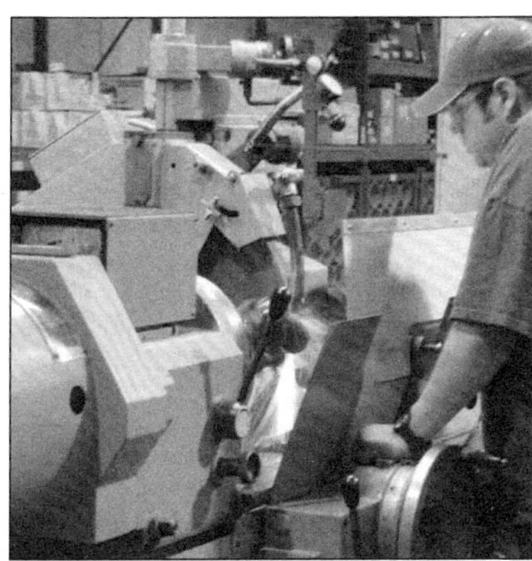

1.10c A crankshaft having a main bearing journal ground

1.11a A machinist checks for a bent connecting rod, using specialized equipment

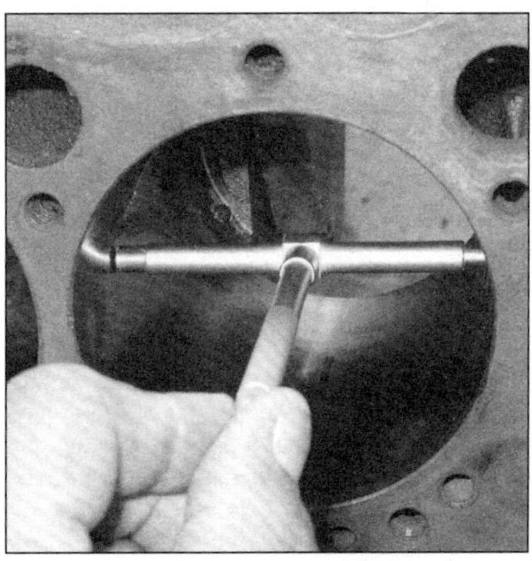

1.11b A bore gauge being used to check the main bearing bore

1.11c Uneven piston wear like this indicates a bent connecting rod

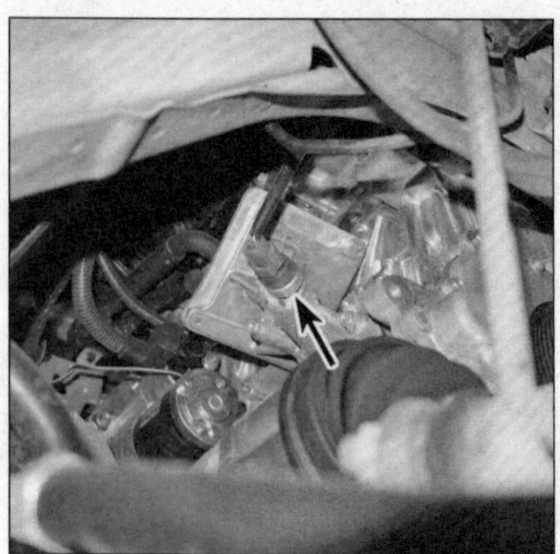

2.2 The oil pressure sending unit is located on the firewall side of the engine, just behind the timing chain cover (as seen from the right side wheel well)

3.6 Use a compression gauge with a threaded fitting for the spark plug hole, not the type that requires hand pressure to maintain the seal

4.4 A simple vacuum gauge can be handy in diagnosing engine condition and performance - be sure to connect it to intake manifold vacuum (not ported vacuum)

2 Oil pressure check

1 Low engine oil pressure can be a sign of an engine in need of rebuilding. A low oil pressure indicator (often called an "idiot light") is not a test of the oiling system. Such indicators only come on when the oil pressure is dangerously low. Even a factory oil pressure gauge in the instrument panel is only a relative indication, although much better for driver information than a warning light. A better test is with a mechanical (not electrical) oil pressure gauge.

2 The oil pressure sending unit is threaded into an adapter on the right end of the engine, firewall side, just behind the timing chain cover (see illustration).

3 Unscrew and remove the oil pressure sending unit and then screw in the hose for your oil pressure gauge. If necessary, install an adapter fitting. Use Teflon tape or thread sealant on the threads of the adapter and/or the fitting on the end of your gauge's hose.

4 Connect an accurate tachometer to the engine, according to the tachometer manufacturer's instructions.

5 Check the oil pressure with the engine running (normal operating temperature) at the specified engine speed, and compare it to this Chapter's Specifications. If it's extremely low, the bearings and/or oil pump are probably worn out.

3 Cylinder compression check

1 A compression check will tell you what mechanical condition the upper end of your engine (pistons, rings, valves, head gaskets) is in. Specifically, it can tell you if the compression is down due to leakage caused by worn piston rings, defective valves and seats or a blown head gasket.

Note: *The engine should be at normal operating temperature and the battery must be fully charged for this check.*

2 Begin by cleaning the area around the spark plugs before you remove them (compressed air should be used, if available). The idea is to prevent dirt from getting into the cylinders as the compression check is being done.

3 Remove the ignition coil assemblies (see Chapter 5). Also disable the fuel pump by removing the fuel pump fuse (see Chapter 4, Section 3).

4 Remove all of the spark plugs (see Chapter 1).

5 Block the throttle wide open.

6 Install a compression gauge in the spark plug hole (see illustration).

7 Crank the engine over at least seven compression strokes and watch the gauge. The compression should build up quickly in a healthy engine. Low compression on the first stroke, followed by gradually increasing pressure on successive strokes, indicates worn piston rings. A low compression reading on the first stroke, which doesn't build up during successive strokes, indicates leaking valves or a blown head gasket (a cracked head could also be the cause). Deposits on the undersides of the valve heads can also cause low compression. Record the highest gauge reading obtained.

8 Repeat the procedure for the remaining cylinders and compare the results to this Chapter's Specifications.

9 Add some engine oil (about three squirts from a plunger-type oil can) to each cylinder, through the spark plug hole, and repeat the test.

10 If the compression increases after the oil is added, the piston rings are definitely worn. If the compression doesn't increase significantly, the leakage is occurring at the valves or head gasket. Leakage past the valves may be caused by burned valve seats and/or faces or warped, cracked or bent valves.

11 If two adjacent cylinders have equally low compression, there's a strong possibility that the head gasket between them is blown. The appearance of coolant in the combustion chambers or the crankcase would verify this condition.

12 If one cylinder is slightly lower than the others, and the engine has a slightly rough idle, a worn lobe on the camshaft could be the cause.

13 If the compression is unusually high, the combustion chambers are probably coated with carbon deposits. If that's the case, the cylinder head(s) should be removed and decarbonized.

14 If compression is way down or varies greatly between cylinders, it would be a good idea to have a leak-down test performed by an automotive repair shop. This test will pinpoint exactly where the leakage is occurring and how severe it is.

4 Vacuum gauge diagnostic checks

1 A vacuum gauge provides inexpensive but valuable information about what is going on in the engine. You can check for worn rings or cylinder walls, leaking head or intake manifold gaskets, incorrect carburetor adjustments, restricted exhaust, stuck or burned valves, weak valve springs, improper ignition or valve timing and ignition problems.

2 Unfortunately, vacuum gauge readings are easy to misinterpret, so they should be used in conjunction with other tests to confirm the diagnosis.

3 Both the absolute readings and the rate of needle movement are important for accurate interpretation. Most gauges measure vacuum in inches of mercury (in-Hg). The following references to vacuum assume the diagnosis is being performed at sea level. As elevation increases (or atmospheric pressure decreases), the reading will decrease. For every 1,000 foot increase in elevation above approximately 2,000 feet, the gauge readings will decrease about one inch of mercury.

4 Connect the vacuum gauge directly to the intake manifold vacuum, not to ported (throttle body) vacuum (see illustration).

Some models are equipped with a vacuum fitting built into the brake booster vacuum hose grommet at the brake booster. Other models are equipped with a vacuum hose fitting on the intake manifold. Use a T-fitting to access the vacuum signal. Be sure no hoses are left disconnected during the test or false readings will result.

5 Before you begin the test, allow the engine to warm up completely. Block the wheels and set the parking brake. With the transaxle in Park, start the engine and allow it to run at normal idle speed.

Warning: *Keep your hands and the vacuum gauge clear of the fans.*

6 Read the vacuum gauge; an average, healthy engine should normally produce about 17 to 22 in-Hg with a fairly steady needle (see illustration). Refer to the following vacuum gauge readings and what they indicate about the engine's condition:

7 A low, steady reading usually indicates a leaking gasket between the intake manifold and cylinder head(s) or throttle body, a leaky vacuum hose, late ignition timing or incorrect camshaft timing. Check ignition timing with a timing light and eliminate all other possible causes, utilizing the tests provided in this Chapter before you remove the timing chain cover to check the timing marks.

8 If the reading is three to eight inches below normal and it fluctuates at that low reading, suspect an intake manifold gasket leak at an intake port or a faulty fuel injector.

9 If the needle has regular drops of about two-to-four inches at a steady rate, the valves are probably leaking. Perform a compression check or leak-down test to confirm this.

10 An irregular drop or down-flick of the needle can be caused by a sticking valve or an ignition misfire. Perform a compression check or leak-down test and read the spark plugs.

11 A rapid vibration of about four in-Hg vibration at idle combined with exhaust smoke indicates worn valve guides. Perform a leak-down test to confirm this. If the rapid vibration occurs with an increase in engine speed, check for a leaking intake manifold gasket or head gasket, weak valve springs, burned valves or ignition misfire.

12 A slight fluctuation, say one inch up and down, may mean ignition problems. Check all the usual tune-up items and, if necessary, run the engine on an ignition analyzer.

13 If there is a large fluctuation, perform a compression or leak-down test to look for a weak or dead cylinder or a blown head gasket.

14 If the needle moves slowly through a wide range, check for a clogged PCV system, incorrect idle fuel mixture, throttle body or intake manifold gasket leaks.

15 Check for a slow return after revving the engine by quickly snapping the throttle open until the engine reaches about 2,500 rpm and let it shut. Normally the reading should drop to near zero, rise above normal idle reading (about 5 in-Hg over) and then return to the previous idle reading. If the vacuum returns slowly and doesn't peak when the throttle is snapped shut, the rings may be worn. If there is a long delay, look for a restricted exhaust system (often the muffler or catalytic converter). An easy way to check this is to temporarily disconnect the exhaust ahead of the suspected part and redo the test.

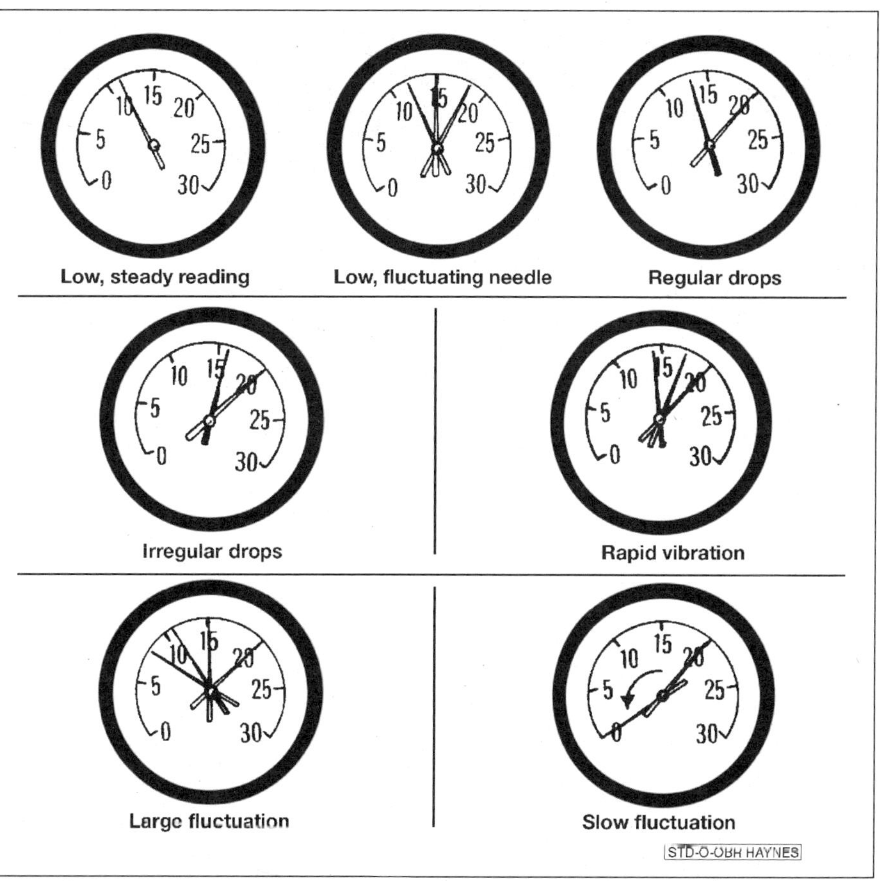

4.6 Typical vacuum gauge readings

5 Engine rebuilding alternatives

1 The do-it-yourselfer is faced with a number of options when purchasing a rebuilt engine. The major considerations are cost, warranty, parts availability and the time required for the rebuilder to complete the project. The decision to replace the engine block, piston/connecting rod assemblies and crankshaft depends on the final inspection results of your engine. Only then can you make a cost effective decision whether to have your engine overhauled or simply purchase an exchange engine for your vehicle.

2 Some of the rebuilding alternatives include:

3 **Individual parts** - If the inspection procedures reveal that the engine block and most engine components are in reusable condition, purchasing individual parts and having a rebuilder rebuild your engine may be the most economical alternative. The block, crankshaft and piston/connecting rod assemblies should all be inspected carefully by a machine shop first.

4 **Short block** - A short block consists of an engine block with a crankshaft and piston/connecting rod assemblies already installed. All new bearings are incorporated and all clearances will be correct. The existing camshafts, valve train components, cylinder head and external parts can be bolted to the short block with little or no machine shop work necessary.

5 **Long block** - A long block consists of a short block plus an oil pump, oil pan, cylinder head, valve cover, camshaft and valve train components, timing sprockets and chain or gears and timing cover. All components are installed with new bearings, seals and gaskets incorporated throughout. The installation of manifolds and external parts is all that's necessary.

6 **Low mileage used engines** - Some companies now offer low mileage used engines which is a very cost effective way to get your vehicle up and running again. These engines often come from vehicles which have been in totaled in accidents or come from other countries which have a higher vehicle turn over rate. A low mileage used engine also usually has a similar warranty like the newly remanufactured engines.

7 Give careful thought to which alternative is best for you and discuss the situation with local automotive machine shops, auto parts dealers and experienced rebuilders before ordering or purchasing replacement parts.

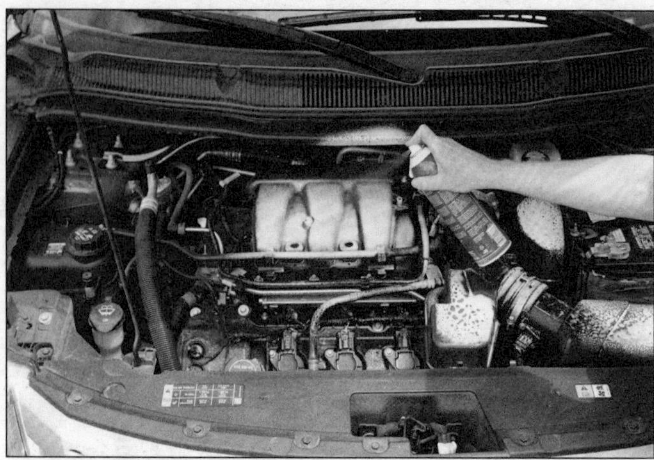

6.5a After tightly wrapping water-vulnerable components, use a spray cleaner on everything, with particular concentration on the greasiest areas, usually around the valve cover and lower edges of the block. If one section dries out, apply more cleaner

6.5b Depending on how dirty the engine is, let the cleaner soak in according to the directions and then hose off the grime and cleaner. Get the rinse water down into every area you can get at; then dry important components with a hair dryer or paper towels

6 Engine removal - methods and precautions

1 If you've decided that an engine must be removed for overhaul or major repair work, several preliminary steps should be taken. Read all removal and installation procedures carefully prior to committing to this job.

2 Locating a suitable place to work is extremely important. Adequate work space, along with storage space for the vehicle, will be needed. If a shop or garage isn't available, at the very least a flat, level, clean work surface made of concrete or asphalt is required.

3 These engines are removed by lowering the engine to the floor, along with the transaxle, and then raising the vehicle sufficiently to slide the assembly out; this will require a vehicle hoist.

4 An engine hoist will also be necessary. Make sure the hoist is rated in excess of the combined weight of the engine and transaxle. Safety is of primary importance, considering the potential hazards involved in removing the engine from the vehicle.

5 Cleaning the engine compartment and engine before beginning the removal procedure will help keep tools clean and organized (see illustrations).

6 If you're a novice at engine removal, get at least one helper. One person cannot easily do all the things you need to do to remove a big heavy engine and transaxle assembly from the engine compartment. Also helpful is to seek advice and assistance from someone who's experienced in engine removal.

7 Plan the operation ahead of time. Arrange for or obtain all of the tools and equipment you'll need prior to beginning the job (see illustration). Some of the equipment necessary to perform engine removal and installation safely and with relative ease are (in addition to a vehicle hoist and an engine hoist) a heavy duty floor jack (preferably fitted with a transmission jack head adapter), complete sets of wrenches and sockets as described in the front of this manual, wooden blocks, plenty of rags and cleaning solvent for mopping up spilled oil, coolant and gasoline.

8 Plan for the vehicle to be out of use for quite a while. A machine shop can do the work that is beyond the scope of the home mechanic. Machine shops often have a busy schedule, so before removing the engine, consult the shop for an estimate of how long it will take to rebuild or repair the components that may need work.

7 Engine - removal and installation

Warning: *Gasoline is extremely flammable, so take extra precautions when you work on any part of the fuel system. Don't smoke or allow open flames or bare light bulbs near the work area, and don't work in a garage where a gas-type appliance (such as a water heater or clothes dryer) is present. Since gasoline is carcinogenic, wear fuel-resistant gloves when there's a possibility of being exposed to fuel, and, if you spill any fuel on your skin, rinse it off immediately with soap and water. Mop up any spills immediately and do not store fuel-soaked rags where they could ignite. The fuel system is under constant pressure, so, if any fuel lines are to be disconnected, the fuel pressure in the system must be relieved first (see Chapter 4 for more information). When you perform any kind of work on the fuel system, wear safety glasses and have a Class B type fire extinguisher on hand.*

Warning: *The engine must be completely cool before beginning this procedure.*

Note: *Engine removal on these vehicles is a difficult job, especially for a do-it-yourselfer working at home. The manufacturer states that the engine and transaxle have to be removed as a unit from the bottom of the vehicle, not the top. With a floor jack and jackstands, it can't be raised high enough or supported safely enough for the engine/transaxle to slide out from underneath. The manufacturer recommends that removal of the engine/transaxle only be performed with a frame-contact type hoist.*

Note: *During this procedure you'll have to adjust the height of the vehicle with the vehicle hoist to perform certain operations.*

Removal

1 Park the car on a vehicle hoist, then raise the hoist arms to contact the jacking points on each side of the vehicle, but don't raise the vehicle yet.

2 Remove the engine cover, if equipped.

6.7 Get an engine stand sturdy enough to firmly support the engine while you're working on it. Stay away from three-wheeled models; they have a tendency to tip over more easily, so get a four-wheeled unit

3 Relieve the fuel system pressure (see Chapter 4), then remove the battery and battery tray (see Chapter 5).
4 Drain the engine coolant (see Chapter 1).
5 Loosen the front wheel lug nuts. Raise the vehicle on the hoist. Remove the front wheels and the splash shields under the vehicle.
6 Drain the transaxle fluid (see Chapter 1). Disconnect the coolant hoses from the CVT cooler.
7 Remove the air inlet duct and the air filter housing (see Chapter 4).
8 Remove the hood (see Chapter 11).
9 Remove the cowl cover and the lower cowl panel (see Chapter 11).
10 Remove the inner fender splash shields (see Chapter 11).
11 Remove the driveaxles (see Chapter 8).
12 Remove the heater and radiator hoses (see Chapter 3).
13 Disconnect the quick-disconnect connectors at the fuel rail and the feed hoses (see Chapter 4).
14 Disconnect the shift cable, wiring and any ground straps from the transaxle (see Chapter 7).
15 Disconnect all vacuum hoses between the engine and chassis.
16 Disconnect the EVAP hose from the purge control solenoid valve (see Chapter 6).
17 Unbolt the air conditioning compressor (see Chapter 3) and secure it out of the way without disconnecting the refrigerant lines.
18 Disconnect the ground straps from the engine, transaxle and alternator, if equipped.
19 Disconnect and remove the Intelligent Power Distribution Module (IPDM) (see Chapter 12), and the Transaxle Control Module (TCM) (see Chapter 6). Also remove the mounting brackets.
20 Disconnect the engine harness wiring, then remove it along with its bracket. Label and disconnect all interfering wiring (see illustration). Make sure that nothing will prevent the engine from being lowered.
21 Remove the front portion of the exhaust system.
22 Separate the steering shaft from the steering gear (see Chapter 10).
23 Disconnect the wiring from the PCM (see Chapter 6). Remove the PCM bracket.
24 Remove the drivebelt (see Chapter 1).
25 Remove the alternator (see Chapter 5).
26 Remove the starter (see Chapter 5).
27 Remove the cooling fan assembly (see Chapter 3).
28 Remove the rear (lower) torque rod (see Chapter 2A).
29 On AWD models, remove the driveshaft (see Chapter 8).
30 Remove the transaxle joint bolts that penetrate the oil pan on the lower rear side of the engine.
31 Remove the torque converter nuts (see Chapter 7).
32 Attach an engine hoist to the engine lifting brackets and raise it just enough to take weight off of the engine mounts. If no brackets are present, check with a Nissan dealer parts department to see if you can order them. Alternatively, attach the lifting chains or straps to substantial parts of the engine, such as threaded holes in the cylinder head and transaxle. Use washers under the bolt heads to prevent pull-through. The chains must be attached so they don't apply force to components that could be damaged.

Warning: *Don't put any part of your body under the engine or transaxle when it's supported only by a hoist or other lifting device.*

33 Take up the slack in the chain until there is slight tension on the hoist. Make sure it's connected so that the engine/transaxle is balanced.

Note: *The chain must be long enough to allow the hoist to lower the engine/transaxle assembly to the ground without letting the hoist arm contact the vehicle.*

34 Remove the front subframe (see Chapter 10).
35 Remove the right-side torque rod and engine mount, and the transaxle mount (see Chapter 2A).
36 Check that there is nothing connecting the engine/transaxle to the vehicle. Label and disconnect anything remaining.
37 Lower the engine/transaxle assembly slowly to the floor.
38 Disconnect the engine hoist after blocking the engine so it can't tip.
39 Raise the vehicle on the hoist.
40 Reconnect the chain of the engine hoist to the engine/transaxle to support it. The assembly can now be moved from under the vehicle to another work area.
41 Separate the transaxle from the engine. Be careful to support the engine and the transaxle securely so they can't fall.
42 Mount the engine on an engine stand using the hoist.

Installation

43 Installation is the reverse of removal noting these points:

a) *Check the engine and transaxle mounts. If they're worn or damaged, replace them.*
b) *Attach the transaxle to the engine (see Chapter 7).*
c) *Tighten the subframe mounting bolts to the torque listed in the Chapter 10 Specifications.*
d) *Tighten the wheel lug nuts to the torque listed in the Chapter 1 Specifications.*
e) *Tighten the driveaxle/hub nuts to the torque listed in the Chapter 8 Specifications.*
f) *Tighten the steering and suspension fasteners to the torque values listed in the Chapter 10 Specifications.*
g) *Refill the engine coolant, oil, power steering fluid, clutch fluid and transaxle fluid (see Chapter 1).*
h) *Recheck all fluid levels (see Chapter 1).*

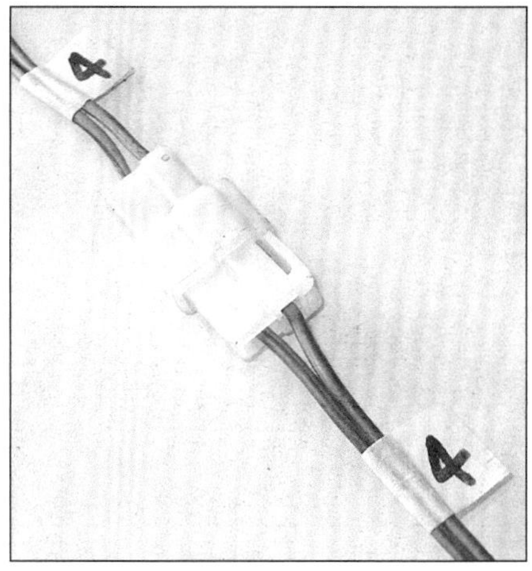

7.20 Label both ends of each wire or vacuum connection before disconnecting them

8 Engine overhaul - disassembly sequence

1 It's much easier to remove the external components if it's mounted on a portable engine stand. A stand can often be rented quite cheaply from an equipment rental yard. Before the engine is mounted on a stand, the flywheel/driveplate should be removed from the engine.
2 If a stand isn't available, it's possible to remove the external engine components with it blocked up on the floor. Be extra careful not to tip or drop the engine when working without a stand.
3 If you're going to obtain a rebuilt engine, all external components must come off first, to be transferred to the replacement engine. These components include:

- *Flywheel/driveplate*
- *Ignition coils and wiring harnesses*
- *Emissions-related components*
- *Engine mounts and mount brackets*
- *Intake/exhaust manifolds*
- *Fuel injection components*
- *Oil filter and oil cooler*
- *Spark plugs*
- *Thermostat and housing assembly*
- *Water pump*

Note: *When removing the external components from the engine, pay close attention to details that may be helpful or important during installation. Note the installed position of gaskets, seals, spacers, pins, brackets, washers, bolts and other small items.*

4 If you're going to obtain a short block (assembled engine block, crankshaft, pistons and connecting rods), then remove the timing chain, cylinder head, oil pan, oil pump pickup tube, oil pump and water pump from your engine so that you can turn in your old short block to the rebuilder as a core. See Section 5 for additional information regarding the different possibilities to be considered.

9.1 Before you try to remove the pistons, use a ridge reamer to remove the raised material (ridge) from the top of the cylinders

9.3 Checking the connecting rod endplay (side clearance)

9.4 If the connecting rods or caps are not marked, use permanent ink or paint to mark the caps to the rods by cylinder number (for example, this would be number 4 cylinder connecting rod)

9.13 Install the piston ring into the cylinder then push it down into position using a piston so the ring will be square in the cylinder

9 Pistons and connecting rods - removal and installation

Removal

Note: *Prior to removing the piston/connecting rod assemblies, remove the cylinder head, oil pans and oil pump (see Chapter 2A).*

1 Use your fingernail to feel if a ridge has formed at the upper limit of ring travel (about 1/4-inch down from the top of each cylinder). If carbon deposits or cylinder wear have produced ridges, they must be completely removed with a special tool (see illustration). Follow the manufacturer's instructions provided with the tool. Failure to remove the ridges before attempting to remove the piston/connecting rod assemblies may result in piston breakage.

2 After the cylinder ridges have been removed, turn the engine so the crankshaft is facing up.

3 Before the main bearing cap assembly and connecting rods are removed, check the connecting rod endplay with feeler gauges. Slide them between the first connecting rod and the crankshaft throw until the play is removed (see illustration). Repeat this procedure for each connecting rod. The endplay is equal to the thickness of the feeler gauge(s). Check with an automotive machine shop for the endplay service limit (a typical endplay should measure between 0.005 to 0.015 inch [0.127 to 0.381 mm]). If the play exceeds the service limit, new connecting rods will be required. If new rods (or a new crankshaft) are installed, the endplay may fall under the minimum allowable. If it does, the rods will have to be machined to restore it. If necessary, consult an automotive machine shop for advice.

4 Check the connecting rods and caps for identification marks. If they aren't plainly marked, use paint or marker (see illustration) to clearly identify each rod and cap (1, 2, 3, etc., depending on the cylinder they're associated with). Do not interchange the rod caps. Install the exact same rod cap onto the same connecting rod.

Caution: *Do not use a punch and hammer to mark the connecting rods or they may be damaged.*

5 Loosen each of the connecting rod cap bolts 1/2-turn at a time until they can be removed by hand.

Caution: *Obtain new connecting rod bolts; the old ones shouldn't be re-used.*

6 Remove the number one connecting rod cap and bearing insert. Don't drop the bearing insert out of the cap.

7 Remove the bearing insert and push the connecting rod/piston assembly out through the top of the engine. Use a wooden or plastic hammer handle to push on the upper bearing surface in the connecting rod. If resistance is felt, double-check to make sure that all of the ridge was removed from the cylinder.

8 Repeat the procedure for the remaining cylinders.

9 After removal, reassemble the connecting rod caps and bearing inserts in their respective connecting rods and install the cap bolts finger tight. Leaving the old bearing inserts in place until reassembly will help prevent the connecting rod bearing surfaces from being accidentally nicked or gouged.

10 The pistons and connecting rods are now ready for inspection and overhaul at an automotive machine shop.

Piston ring installation

11 Before installing the new piston rings, the ring end gaps must be checked. It's assumed that the piston ring side clearance has been checked and verified correct.

12 Lay out the piston/connecting rod assemblies and the new ring sets so the ring sets will be matched with the same piston and cylinder during the end gap measurement and engine assembly.

13 Insert the top (number one) ring into the first cylinder and square it up with the cylinder walls by pushing it in with the top of the piston (see illustration). The ring should be near the bottom of the cylinder, at the lower limit of ring travel.

14 To measure the end gap, slip feeler gauges between the ends of the ring until a gauge equal to the gap width is found (see illustration). The feeler gauge should slide between the ring ends with a slight amount of drag. A typical ring gap should fall between 0.010 and 0.020 inch (0.25 to 0.50 mm) for compression rings and up to 0.030 inch (0.76 mm) for the oil ring steel rails. If the gap is larger or smaller than specified, double-check to make sure you have the correct rings before proceeding.

15 If the gap is too small, it must be enlarged or the ring ends may come in contact with each other during engine operation, which can cause serious damage to the engine. If necessary, increase the end gaps

9.14 With the ring square in the cylinder, measure the ring end gap with a feeler gauge

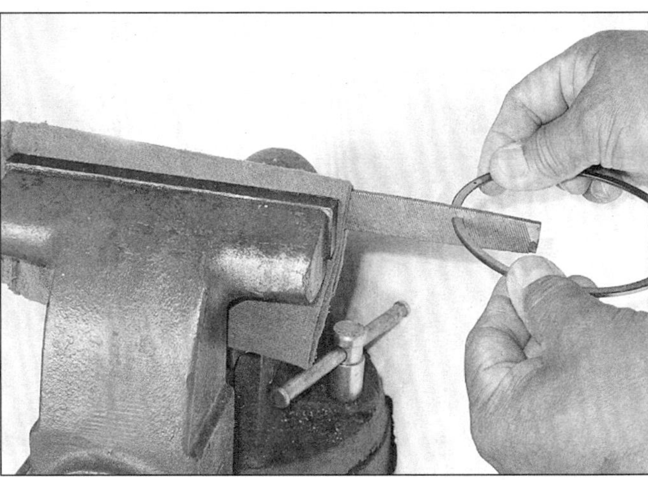

9.15 If the ring end gap is too small, clamp a file in a vise as shown and file the piston ring ends - be sure to remove all raised material

by filing the ring ends very carefully with a fine file. Mount the file in a vise equipped with soft jaws, slip the ring over the file with the ends contacting the file face and slowly move the ring to remove material from the ends. When performing this operation, file only by pushing the ring from the outside end of the file towards the vise (see illustration).

16 Excess end gap isn't critical unless it's greater than 0.040 inch (1.01 mm). Again, double-check to make sure you have the correct ring type.

17 Repeat the procedure for each ring that will be installed in the first cylinder and for each ring in the remaining cylinders. Remember to keep rings, pistons and cylinders matched up.

18 Once the ring end gaps have been checked/corrected, the rings can be installed on the pistons.

19 The oil control ring (lowest one on the piston) is usually installed first. It's composed of three separate components. Slip the spacer/expander into the groove (see illustration). If an anti-rotation tang is used, make sure it's inserted into the drilled hole in the ring groove. Next, install the lower side rail in the same manner (see illustration). Don't use a piston ring installation tool on the oil ring side rails, as they may be damaged. Instead, place one end of the side rail into the groove between the spacer/expander and the ring land, hold it firmly in place and slide a finger around the piston while pushing the rail into the groove. Finally, install the upper side rail.

20 After the three oil ring components have been installed, check to make sure that both the upper and lower side rails can be rotated smoothly inside the ring grooves.

21 The number two (middle) ring is installed next. It's usually stamped with a mark which must face up, toward the top of the piston. Do not mix up the top and middle rings, as they have different cross-sections.

Note: *Always follow the instructions printed on the ring package or box - different manufacturers may require different approaches.*

22 Use a piston ring installation tool and make sure the identification mark is facing the top of the piston, then slip the ring into the middle groove on the piston (see illustration). Don't expand the ring any more than necessary to slide it over the piston.

Note: *Be careful not to confuse the number one and number two rings.*

23 Install the number one (top) ring in the same manner.

24 Repeat the procedure for the remaining pistons and rings.

Installation

25 Before installing the piston/connecting rod assemblies, the cylinder walls must be perfectly clean, the top edge of each cylinder bore must be chamfered, and the crankshaft must be in place.

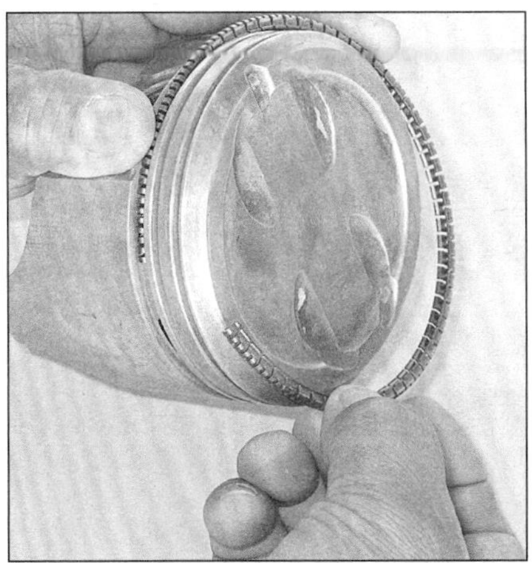

9.19a Installing the spacer/expander in the oil ring groove

9.19b DO NOT use a piston ring installation tool when installing the oil control side rails

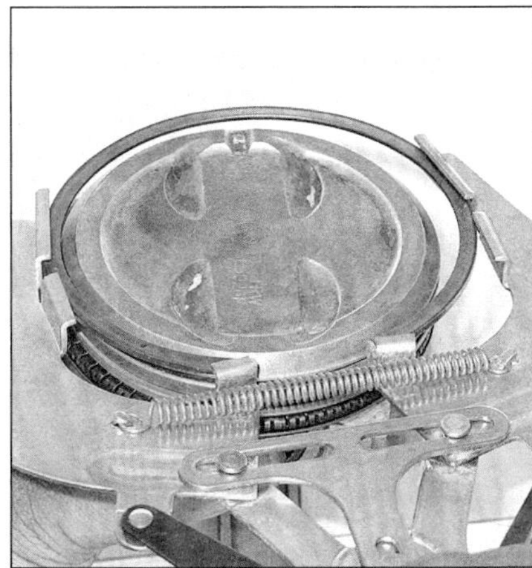

9.22 Use a piston ring installation tool to install the compression rings - on some engines the number two compression ring has a directional mark that must face toward the top of the piston

ENGINE BEARING ANALYSIS

Debris

Babbitt bearing embedded with debris from machinings

Microscopic detail of debris

Microscopic detail of gouges

Overplated copper alloy bearing gouged by cast iron debris

Aluminum bearing embedded with glass beads

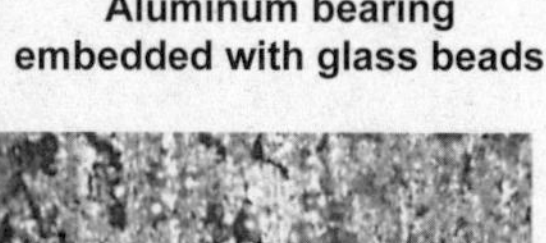

Microscopic detail of glass beads

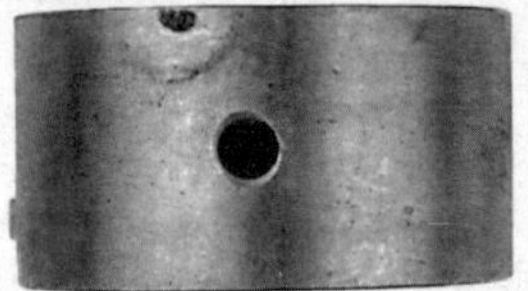

Damaged lining caused by dirt left on the bearing back

Misassembly

Result of a lower half assembled as an upper - blocking the oil flow

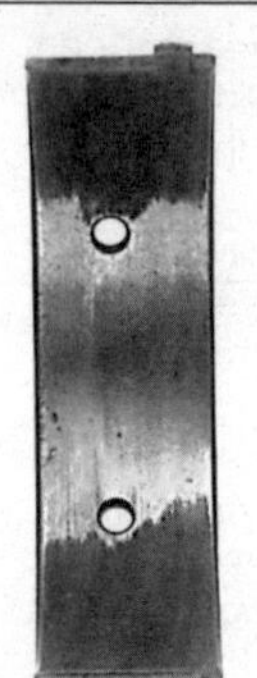

Excessive oil clearance is indicated by a short contact arc

Polished and oil-stained backs are a result of a poor fit in the housing bore

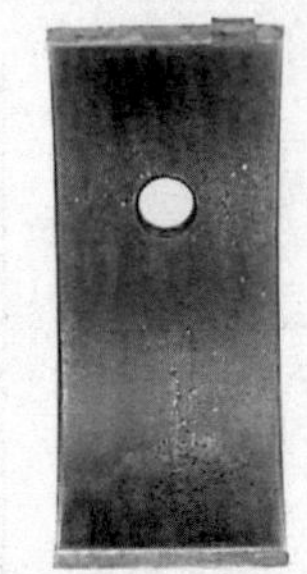

Result of a wrong, reversed, or shifted cap

Overloading

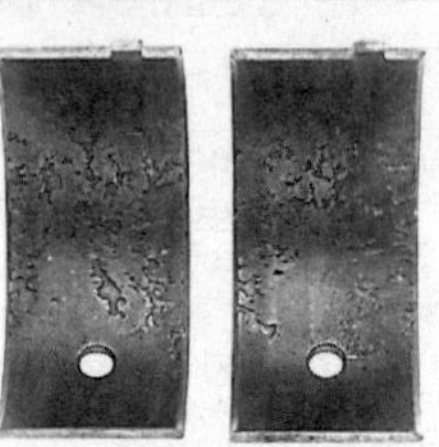

Damage from excessive idling which resulted in an oil film unable to support the load imposed

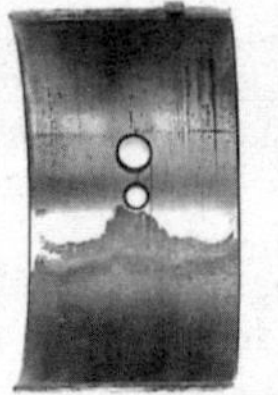

Damaged upper connecting rod bearings caused by engine lugging; the lower main bearings (not shown) were similarly affected

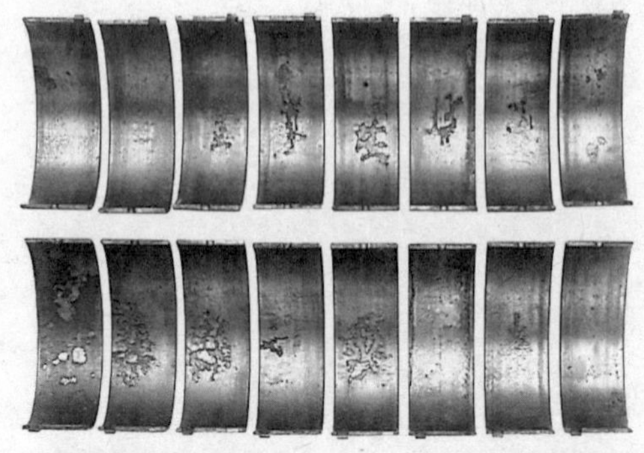

The damage shown in these upper and lower connecting rod bearings was caused by engine operation at a higher-than-rated speed under load

Misalignment

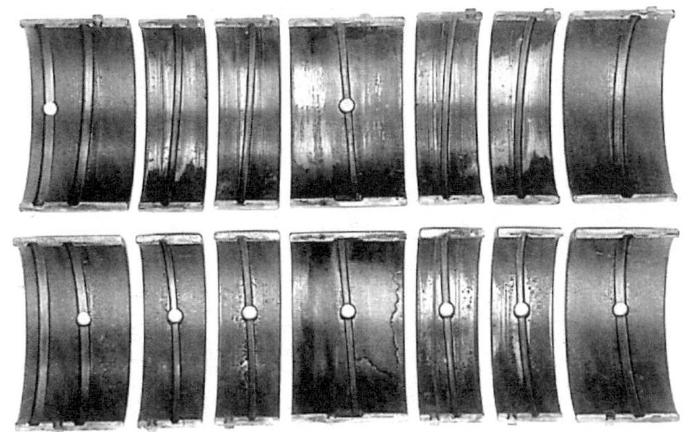
A warped crankshaft caused this pattern of severe wear in the center, diminishing toward the ends

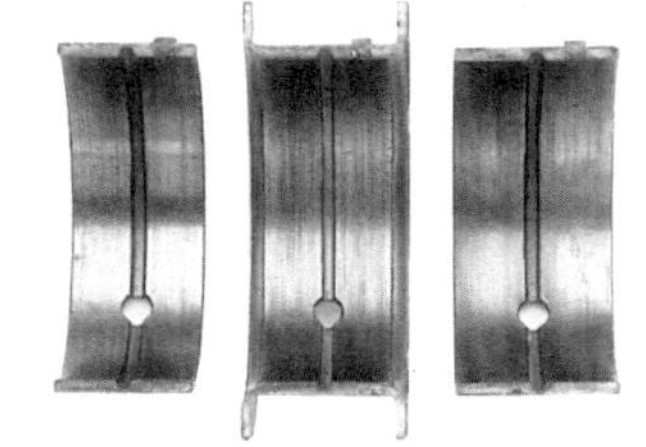
A poorly finished crankshaft caused the equally spaced scoring shown

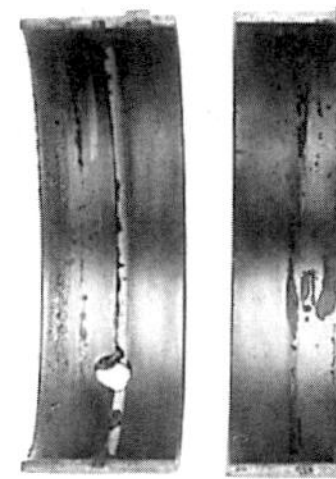
A tapered housing bore caused the damage along one edge of this pair

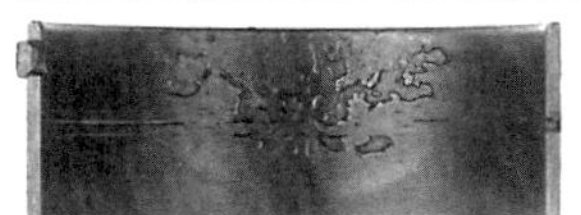
A bent connecting rod led to the damage in the "V" pattern

Lubrication

Result of dry start: The bearings on the left, farthest from the oil pump, show more damage

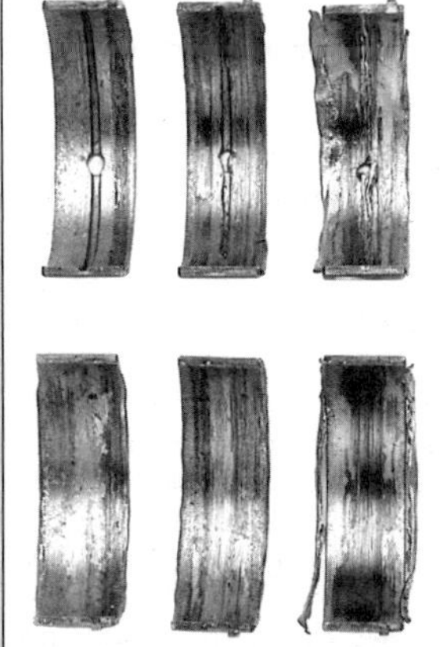
Result of a low oil supply or oil starvation

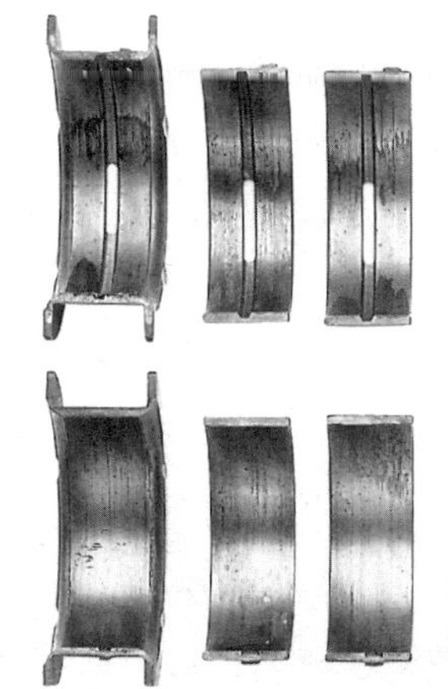
Severe wear as a result of inadequate oil clearance

Corrosion

Microscopic detail of corrosion

Corrosion is an acid attack on the bearing lining generally caused by inadequate maintenance, extremely hot or cold operation, or inferior oils or fuels

Microscopic detail of cavitation

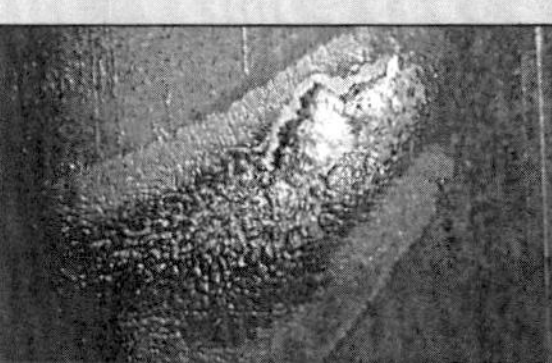

Example of cavitation - a surface erosion caused by pressure changes in the oil film

Damage from excessive thrust or insufficient axial clearance

Bearing affected by oil dilution caused by excessive blow-by or a rich mixture

© 1986 Federal-Mogul Corporation
Copy and photographs courtesy of Federal Mogul Corporation

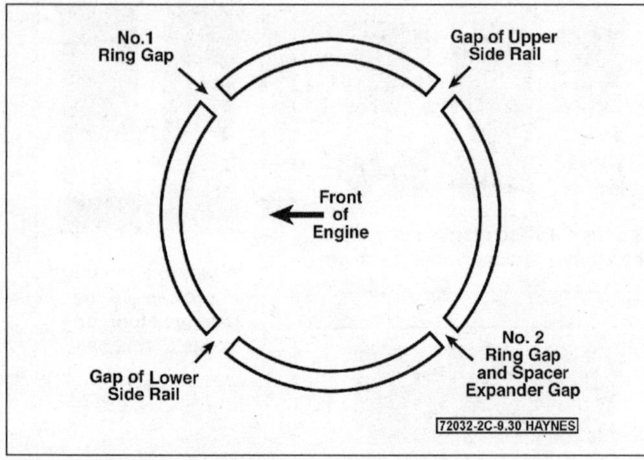

9.30 Position the piston ring end gaps as shown

9.35 Use a plastic or wooden hammer handle to push the piston into the cylinder

26 Remove the cap from the end of the number one connecting rod (refer to the marks made during removal). Remove the original bearing inserts and wipe the bearing surfaces of the connecting rod and cap with a clean, lint-free cloth. They must be kept spotlessly clean.

Connecting rod bearing oil clearance check

27 Clean the back side of the new upper bearing insert, then lay it in place in the connecting rod.

28 Make sure the tab on the bearing fits into the recess in the rod. Don't hammer the bearing insert into place and be very careful not to nick or gouge the bearing face. Don't lubricate the bearing at this time.

29 Clean the back side of the other bearing insert and install it in the rod cap. Again, make sure the tab on the bearing fits into the recess in the cap, and don't apply any lubricant. It's critically important that the mating surfaces of the bearing and connecting rod are perfectly clean and oil free when they're assembled.

30 Position the piston ring gaps at the intervals around the piston as shown (see illustration).

9.37 Place Plastigage on each connecting rod bearing journal parallel to the crankshaft centerline

31 Lubricate the piston and rings with clean engine oil and attach a piston ring compressor to the piston. Leave the skirt protruding about 1/4-inch to guide the piston into the cylinder. The rings must be compressed until they're flush with the piston.

32 Rotate the crankshaft until the number one connecting rod journal is at BDC (bottom dead center) and apply a liberal coat of engine oil to the cylinder walls.

33 With the "front" mark (dimples or dot) on the piston facing the front (timing chain end) of the engine, gently insert the piston/connecting rod assembly into the number one cylinder bore and rest the bottom edge of the ring compressor on the engine block.

Note: *Some engines have an arrow or dimples or groove on the top of the piston. All of these are marks that indicate the front of the piston.*

34 Tap the top edge of the ring compressor to make sure it's contacting the block around its entire circumference.

35 Gently tap on the top of the piston with the end of a wooden or plastic hammer handle (see illustration) while guiding the end of the connecting rod into place on the crankshaft journal. The piston rings may try to pop out of the ring compressor just before entering the cylinder bore, so keep some downward pressure on the ring compressor. Work slowly, and if any resistance is felt as the piston enters the cylinder, stop immediately. Find out what's hanging up and fix it before proceeding. Do not, for any reason, force the piston into the cylinder - you might break a ring and/or the piston.

9.41 Use the scale on the Plastigage package to determine the bearing oil clearance - be sure to measure the widest part of the Plastigage and use the correct scale; it comes with both standard and metric scales

36 Once the piston/connecting rod assembly is installed, the connecting rod bearing oil clearance must be checked before the rod cap is permanently installed.

37 Cut a piece of the appropriate size Plastigage slightly shorter than the width of the connecting rod bearing and lay it in place on the number one connecting rod journal, parallel with the journal axis (see illustration).

38 Clean the connecting rod cap bearing face and install the rod cap. Make sure the mating mark on the cap is on the same side as the mark on the connecting rod (see illustration 9.4).

39 Install the old rod bolts and tighten them to the torque listed in this Chapter's Specifications. DO NOT rotate the crankshaft at any time during this operation.

Note: *Use a thin-wall socket to avoid erroneous torque readings that can result if the socket is wedged between the rod cap and the bolt. If the socket tends to wedge itself between the fastener and the cap, lift up on it slightly until it no longer contacts the cap.*

40 Remove the fasteners and detach the rod cap, being careful not to disturb the Plastigage. If the connecting rod fasteners have any type of wear or distortion they cannot be reused.

41 Compare the width of the crushed Plastigage to the scale printed on the Plastigage envelope to obtain the oil clearance (see illustration). The connecting rod bearing oil clearance is usually about 0.001 to 0.002 inch. Consult an automotive machine shop for the clearance specified for the rod bearings on your engine.

10.1 Checking crankshaft endplay with a dial indicator

10.3 Checking crankshaft endplay with feeler gauges at the thrust bearing journal

42 If the clearance is not as specified, the bearing inserts may be the wrong size (which means different ones will be required). Before deciding that different inserts are needed, make sure that no dirt or oil was between the bearing inserts and the connecting rod or cap when the clearance was measured. Also, recheck the journal diameter. If the Plastigage was wider at one end than the other, the journal may be tapered. If the clearance still exceeds the limit specified, the bearing will have to be replaced with an undersize bearing.

Caution: *When installing a new crankshaft, always use a standard size bearing.*

Final installation

43 Carefully scrape all traces of the Plastigage material off the rod journal and/or bearing face. Be very careful not to scratch the bearing - use your fingernail or the edge of a plastic card.

44 Make sure the bearing faces are perfectly clean, then apply a uniform layer of clean moly-base grease or engine assembly lube to both of them. You'll have to push the piston into the cylinder to expose the face of the bearing insert in the connecting rod.

45 Slide the connecting rod back into place on the journal, install the rod cap, install the new bolts and tighten them to the torque listed in this Chapter's Specifications.

46 Repeat the entire procedure for the remaining pistons/connecting rods.

47 The important points to remember are:

a) *Keep the back sides of the bearing inserts and the insides of the connecting rods and caps perfecltly clean when assembling them.*
b) *Make sure you have the correct piston/rod assembly for each cyinder.*
c) *The mark on the piston must face the front (timing chain end) of he engine.*
d) *Lubricate the cylinder walls liberally with clean oil.*
e) *Lubricate the bearing faces when installing the old rod caps after the oil clearance has been checked.*

10 Crankshaft - removal and installation

Removal

Note: *The crankshaft can be removed only after the engine has been removed from the vehicle. It's assumed that the flywheel or driveplate, crankshaft pulley, timing chain, oil pan, oil pump, balance shaft, oil filter and piston/connecting rod assemblies have already been removed.*

1 Before the crankshaft is removed, measure the endplay. Mount a dial indicator with the indicator in line with the crankshaft and touching the end of the crankshaft (see illustration).

2 Pry the crankshaft all the way to the rear and zero the dial indicator. Next, pry the crankshaft to the front as far as possible and check the reading on the dial indicator. The distance traveled is the endplay. A typical crankshaft endplay will fall between 0.003 to 0.010 inch (0.076 to 0.254 mm). If it is greater than that, check the crankshaft thrust washer/bearing assembly surfaces for wear after it's removed. If no wear is evident, new main bearings should correct the endplay. Refer to Step 14 for the location of the thrust washer/bearing assembly on each engine.

3 If a dial indicator isn't available, feeler gauges can be used. Gently pry the crankshaft all the way to the front of the engine. Slip feeler gauges between the crankshaft and the front face of the thrust bearing or washer to determine the clearance (see illustration).

4 Loosen the main bearing cap/bedplate bolts 1/4-turn at a time each, until they can be removed by hand.

Caution: *Obtain new bolts - the old ones shouldn't be re-used.*

5 Gently tap the main bearing caps or bedplate assembly with a soft-face hammer around the perimeter of the assembly. Pull the main bearing cap/bedplate assembly straight up and off the cylinder block. Try not to drop the bearing inserts if they come out with the assembly.

Note: *The bedplate has built-in pry points; don't pry anywhere else or damage to the bedplate will occur.*

6 Carefully lift the crankshaft out of the engine. It may be a good idea to have an assistant available, since the crankshaft is quite heavy and awkward to handle. With the bearing inserts in place inside the engine block and main bearing caps, reinstall the main bearing cap assembly onto the engine block and tighten the bolts finger tight. Make sure you install the main bearing cap assembly with the arrow facing the front of the engine.

Installation

7 Crankshaft installation is the first step in engine reassembly. It's assumed at this point that the engine block and crankshaft have been cleaned, inspected and repaired or reconditioned.

8 Position the engine block with the bottom facing up.

9 Remove the mounting bolts and lift off the main bearing cap assembly.

10 If they're still in place, remove the original bearing inserts from the block and from the main bearing cap assembly. Wipe the bearing surfaces of the block and main bearing cap assembly with a clean, lint-free cloth. They must be kept spotlessly clean. This is critical for determining the correct bearing oil clearance.

Main bearing oil clearance check

11 Without mixing them up, clean the back sides of the new upper main bearing inserts (with grooves and oil holes) and lay one in each main bearing saddle in the block. Each upper bearing has an oil groove and oil hole in it. Clean the back sides of the lower main bearing inserts and lay them in the corresponding location in the main bearing cap. Make sure the tab on the bearing insert fits

10.14 Insert the thrust washer into the machined surface between the crankshaft and the upper bearing saddle, then rotate it down into the block until it's flush with the parting line on the main bearing saddle - make sure the oil grooves on the thrust washer face the crankshaft

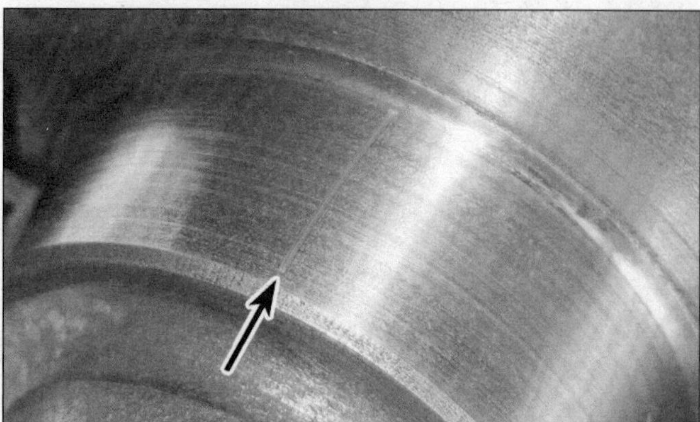
10.17 Place the Plastigage onto the crankshaft bearing journal as shown

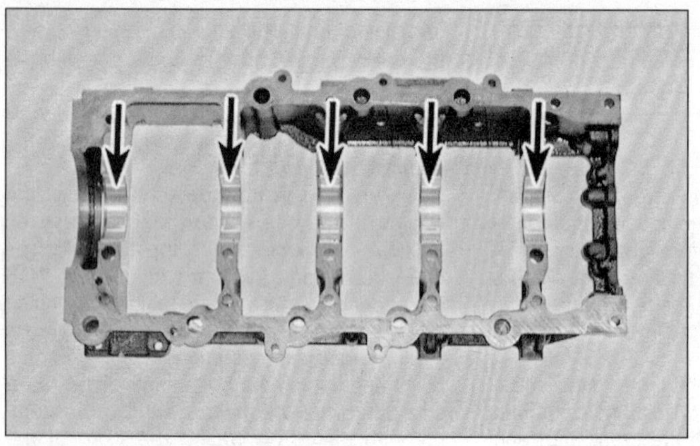
10.18a The bearings are installed into the corresponding saddles in the bedplate (typical view) . . .

10.18b . . . then the bedplate is set over the crankshaft onto the dowels on the engine block

into the recess in the block or main bearing cap. The upper bearings with the oil holes are installed into the engine block while the lower bearings without the oil holes are installed in the caps or bedplate.

Caution: *The oil holes in the block must line up with the oil holes in the upper bearing inserts. Do not hammer the bearing insert into place and don't nick or gouge the bearing faces. DO NOT apply any lubrication at this time.*

12 Clean the faces of the bearing inserts in the block and the crankshaft main bearing journals with a clean, lint-free cloth.

Note: *The backs of all bearings and the surfaces in which they are installed must be kept clean and free of oil at all times.*

13 Check or clean the oil holes in the crankshaft, as any dirt here can go only one way - straight through the new bearings.

14 Once you're certain the crankshaft is clean, carefully lay it in position in the block, which should be oriented on the engine stand to have the bottom side Up. Lube and insert the thrust washers on either side of journal 3 on all engines (see illustration). The thrust washers must be installed in the correct journal.

Note: *Install the thrust washers with the groove in the thrust washer facing the crankshaft with the smooth sides facing the main bearing saddle.*

15 Before the crankshaft can be permanently installed, the main bearing oil clearance must be checked.

16 Cut several strips of the appropriate size of Plastigage. They must be slightly shorter than the width of the main bearing journal.

17 Place one piece on each crankshaft main bearing journal, parallel with the journal axis as shown (see illustration).

18 Clean the faces of the bearing inserts in the main bearing caps or bedplate assembly (see illustrations). Hold the bearing inserts in place and install the assembly onto the crankshaft and cylinder block. DO NOT disturb the Plastigage. Make sure you install the main bearing cap assembly with the arrow facing the front (timing chain end) of the engine.

19 Apply clean engine oil to all bolt threads prior to installation, then install all bolts finger-tight. Tighten the main bearing caps/bedplate assembly bolts in the sequence shown (see illustration) progressing in steps, to the torque listed in this Chapter's Specifications. DO NOT rotate the crankshaft at any time during this operation.

Note: *Use the old bolts at this time.*

20 Remove the bolts in the reverse order of the tightening sequence and carefully lift the main bearing cap or bedplate assembly straight up and off the block. Do not disturb the Plastigage or rotate the crankshaft. If the main bearing cap or bedplate is difficult to remove, tap it gently from side-to-side with a soft-face hammer to loosen it.

21 Compare the width of the crushed Plastigage on each journal to the scale printed on the Plastigage envelope to determine the main bearing oil clearance (see illustration). A typical main bearing oil clearance should fall between 0.0015 and 0.0023-inch. Check with an automotive machine shop for the clearance specified for your engine.

22 If the clearance is not as specified, the bearing inserts may be the wrong size (which means different ones will be required). Before deciding if different inserts are needed, make sure that no dirt or oil was between the bearing inserts and the cap assembly or block when the clearance was measured. If the Plastigage was wider at one end than the other, the crankshaft journal

may be tapered. If the clearance still exceeds the limit specified, the bearing insert(s) will have to be replaced with an undersize bearing insert(s).

Caution: *When installing a new crankshaft, always install a standard bearing insert set.*

23 Carefully scrape all traces of the Plastigage material off the main bearing journals and/or the bearing insert faces. Be sure to remove all residue from the oil holes. Use your fingernail or the edge of a plastic card - don't nick or scratch the bearing faces.

Final installation

24 Carefully lift the crankshaft out of the cylinder block.

25 Clean the bearing insert faces in the cylinder block, then apply a thin, uniform layer of moly-base grease or engine assembly lube to each of the bearing surfaces that contact the crankshaft. Coat the thrust faces as well as the journal face of the thrust washers.

26 Make sure the crankshaft journals are clean, then lay the crankshaft back in place in the cylinder block.

27 Clean the bearing insert faces and then apply the same lubricant to them. Clean the engine block thoroughly. The surfaces must be free of oil residue. Install the thrust washers. The grooves on the thrust washers face outward, away from the bearing.

28 Apply a 5/32-inch (4 mm) continuous bead of RTV sealant to the bedplate sealing area on each side of the cylinder block.

29 Install the bedplate onto the crankshaft and cylinder block.

30 Prior to installation, apply clean engine oil to all bolt threads, wiping off any excess, then install all bolts finger-tight.

Note: *Install the new bolts at this time.*

31 Tighten the main bearing cap bolts in sequence (see illustration 10.19) to the torque listed in this Chapter's Specifications.

32 Recheck crankshaft endplay with a feeler gauge or a dial indicator. The endplay should be correct if the crankshaft thrust faces aren't worn or damaged and if new bearings have been installed.

33 Rotate the crankshaft a number of times by hand to check for any obvious binding. It should rotate with a running torque of 50 in-lbs or less. If the running torque is too high, identify and correct the problem at this time.

34 Install the new rear main oil seal (see Chapter 2A).

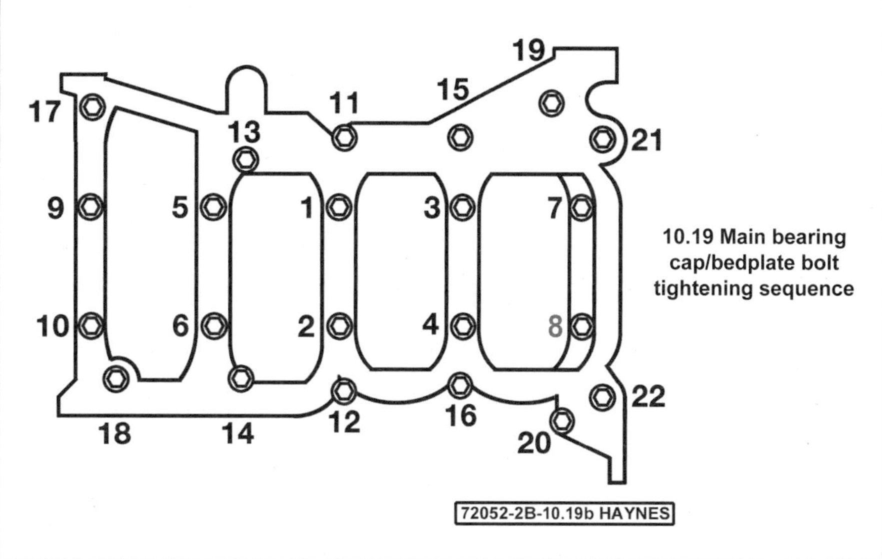

10.19 Main bearing cap/bedplate bolt tightening sequence

11 Engine overhaul - reassembly sequence

1 Before beginning engine reassembly, make sure you have all the necessary new parts, gaskets and seals as well as the following items on hand:

Common hand tools
A 1/2-inch drive torque wrench
New engine oil
Oil filter
Gasket sealant
Thread locking compound

2 If you obtained a short block it will be necessary to install the cylinder head, the oil pump and pick-up tube, the oil pan, the water pump, the timing chain and timing cover, and the valve cover (see Chapter 2A). In order to save time and avoid problems, the external components must be installed in the following general order:

Thermostat and housing cover
Water pump
Intake and exhaust manifolds
Fuel injection components
Emission control components
Spark plugs
Ignition coils
Oil filter and oil cooler
Engine mounts and mount brackets
Flywheel/driveplate

10.21 Use the scale on the Plastigage package to determine the bearing oil clearance - be sure to measure the widest part of the Plastigage and use the correct scale; it comes with both standard and metric scales

12 Initial start-up and break-in after overhaul

Warning: *Have a fire extinguisher handy when starting the engine for the first time.*

1 Once the engine has been installed in the vehicle, double-check the engine oil and coolant levels.

2 With the spark plugs out of the engine and the and the fuel pump disabled (see Chapter 4, Section 3), crank the engine until oil pressure registers on the gauge or the light goes out.

3 Install the spark plugs and ignition coils, and reinstall the fuel pump fuse.

4 Start the engine. It may take a few moments for the fuel system to build up pressure, but the engine should start without a great deal of effort.

5 After the engine starts, it should be allowed to warm up to normal operating temperature. While the engine is warming up, make a thorough check for fuel, oil and coolant leaks.

6 Shut the engine off and recheck the engine oil and coolant levels.

7 Drive the vehicle to an area with minimum traffic, accelerate from 30 to 50 mph, then allow the vehicle to slow to 30 mph with the throttle closed. Repeat the procedure 10 or 12 times. This will load the piston rings and cause them to seat properly against the cylinder walls. Check again for oil and coolant leaks.

8 Drive the vehicle gently for the first 500 miles (no sustained high speeds) and keep a constant check on the oil level. It is not unusual for an engine to use oil during the break-in period.

9 At approximately 500 to 600 miles, change the oil and filter.

10 For the next few hundred miles, drive the vehicle normally. Do not pamper it or abuse it.

11 After 2000 miles, change the oil and filter again and consider the engine broken in.

COMMON ENGINE OVERHAUL TERMS

B

Backlash - The amount of play between two parts. Usually refers to how much one gear can be moved back and forth without moving the gear with which it's meshed.

Bearing Caps - The caps held in place by nuts or bolts which, in turn, hold the bearing surface. This space is for lubricating oil to enter.

Bearing clearance - The amount of space left between shaft and bearing surface. This space is for lubricating oil to enter.

Bearing crush - The additional height which is purposely manufactured into each bearing half to ensure complete contact of the bearing back with the housing bore when the engine is assembled.

Bearing knock - The noise created by movement of a part in a loose or worn bearing.

Blueprinting - Dismantling an engine and reassembling it to EXACT specifications.

Bore - An engine cylinder, or any cylindrical hole; also used to describe the process of enlarging or accurately refinishing a hole with a cutting tool, as to bore an engine cylinder. The bore size is the diameter of the hole.

Boring - Renewing the cylinders by cutting them out to a specified size. A boring bar is used to make the cut.

Bottom end - A term which refers collectively to the engine block, crankshaft, main bearings and the big ends of the connecting rods.

Break-in - The period of operation between installation of new or rebuilt parts and time in which parts are worn to the correct fit. Driving at reduced and varying speed for a specified mileage to permit parts to wear to the correct fit.

Bushing - A one-piece sleeve placed in a bore to serve as a bearing surface for shaft, piston pin, etc. Usually replaceable.

C

Camshaft - The shaft in the engine, on which a series of lobes are located for operating the valve mechanisms. The camshaft is driven by gears or sprockets and a timing chain. Usually referred to simply as the cam.

Carbon - Hard, or soft, black deposits found in combustion chamber, on plugs, under rings, on and under valve heads.

Cast iron - An alloy of iron and more than two percent carbon, used for engine blocks and heads because it's relatively inexpensive and easy to mold into complex shapes.

Chamfer - To bevel across (or a bevel on) the sharp edge of an object.

Chase - To repair damaged threads with a tap or die.

Combustion chamber - The space between the piston and the cylinder head, with the piston at top dead center, in which air-fuel mixture is burned.

Compression ratio - The relationship between cylinder volume (clearance volume) when the piston is at top dead center and cylinder volume when the piston is at bottom dead center.

Connecting rod - The rod that connects the crank on the crankshaft with the piston. Sometimes called a con rod.

Connecting rod cap - The part of the connecting rod assembly that attaches the rod to the crankpin.

Core plug - Soft metal plug used to plug the casting holes for the coolant passages in the block.

Crankcase - The lower part of the engine in which the crankshaft rotates; includes the lower section of the cylinder block and the oil pan.

Crank kit - A reground or reconditioned crankshaft and new main and connecting rod bearings.

Crankpin - The part of a crankshaft to which a connecting rod is attached.

Crankshaft - The main rotating member, or shaft, running the length of the crankcase, with offset throws to which the connecting rods are attached; changes the reciprocating motion of the pistons into rotating motion.

Cylinder sleeve - A replaceable sleeve, or liner, pressed into the cylinder block to form the cylinder bore.

D

Deburring - Removing the burrs (rough edges or areas) from a bearing.

Deglazer - A tool, rotated by an electric motor, used to remove glaze from cylinder walls so a new set of rings will seat.

E

Endplay - The amount of lengthwise movement between two parts. As applied to a crankshaft, the distance that the crankshaft can move forward and back in the cylinder block.

F

Face - A machinist's term that refers to removing metal from the end of a shaft or the face of a larger part, such as a flywheel.

Fatigue - A breakdown of material through a large number of loading and unloading cycles. The first signs are cracks followed shortly by breaks.

Feeler gauge - A thin strip of hardened steel, ground to an exact thickness, used to check clearances between parts.

Free height - The unloaded length or height of a spring.

Freeplay - The looseness in a linkage, or an assembly of parts, between the initial application of force and actual movement. Usually perceived as slop or slight delay.

Freeze plug - See Core plug.

G

Gallery - A large passage in the block that forms a reservoir for engine oil pressure.

Glaze - The very smooth, glassy finish that develops on cylinder walls while an engine is in service.

H

Heli-Coil - A rethreading device used when threads are worn or damaged. The device is installed in a retapped hole to reduce the thread size to the original size.

I

Installed height - The spring's measured length or height, as installed on the cylinder head. Installed height is measured from the spring seat to the underside of the spring retainer.

J

Journal - The surface of a rotating shaft which turns in a bearing.

K

Keeper - The split lock that holds the valve spring retainer in position on the valve stem.

Key - A small piece of metal inserted into matching grooves machined into two parts fitted together - such as a gear pressed onto a shaft - which prevents slippage between the two parts.

Knock - The heavy metallic engine sound, produced in the combustion chamber as a result of abnormal combustion - usually detonation. Knock is usually caused by a loose or worn bearing. Also referred to as detonation, pinging and spark knock. Connecting rod or main bearing knocks are created by too much oil clearance or insufficient lubrication.

L

Lands - The portions of metal between the piston ring grooves.

Lapping the valves - Grinding a valve face and its seat together with lapping compound.

Lash - The amount of free motion in a gear train, between gears, or in a mechanical assembly, that occurs before movement can begin. Usually refers to the lash in a valve train.

Lifter - The part that rides against the cam to transfer motion to the rest of the valve train.

M

Machining - The process of using a machine to remove metal from a metal part.

Main bearings - The plain, or babbit, bearings that support the crankshaft.

Main bearing caps - The cast iron caps, bolted to the bottom of the block, that support the main bearings.

O

O.D. - Outside diameter.

Oil gallery - A pipe or drilled passageway in the engine used to carry engine oil from one area to another.

Oil ring - The lower ring, or rings, of a piston; designed to prevent excessive amounts of oil from working up the cylinder walls and into the combustion chamber. Also called an oil-control ring.

Oil seal - A seal which keeps oil from leaking out of a compartment. Usually refers to a dynamic seal around a rotating shaft or other moving part.

O-ring - A type of sealing ring made of a special rubberlike material; in use, the O-ring is compressed into a groove to provide the sealing action.

Overhaul - To completely disassemble a unit, clean and inspect all parts, reassemble it with the original or new parts and make all adjustments necessary for proper operation.

P

Pilot bearing - A small bearing installed in the center of the flywheel (or the rear end of the crankshaft) to support the front end of the input shaft of the transmission.

Pip mark - A little dot or indentation which indicates the top side of a compression ring.

Piston - The cylindrical part, attached to the connecting rod, that moves up and down in the cylinder as the crankshaft rotates. When the fuel charge is fired, the piston transfers the force of the explosion to the connecting rod, then to the crankshaft.

Piston pin (or wrist pin) - The cylindrical and usually hollow steel pin that passes through the piston. The piston pin fastens the piston to the upper end of the connecting rod.

Piston ring - The split ring fitted to the groove in a piston. The ring contacts the sides of the ring groove and also rubs against the cylinder wall, thus sealing space between piston and wall. There are two types of rings: Compression rings seal the compression pressure in the combustion chamber; oil rings scrape excessive oil off the cylinder wall.

Piston ring groove - The slots or grooves cut in piston heads to hold piston rings in position.

Piston skirt - The portion of the piston below the rings and the piston pin hole.

Plastigage - A thin strip of plastic thread, available in different sizes, used for measuring clearances. For example, a strip of plastigage is laid across a bearing journal and mashed as parts are assembled. Then parts are disassembled and the width of the strip is measured to determine clearance between journal and bearing. Commonly used to measure crankshaft main-bearing and connecting rod bearing clearances.

Press-fit - A tight fit between two parts that requires pressure to force the parts together. Also referred to as drive, or force, fit.

Prussian blue - A blue pigment; in solution, useful in determining the area of contact between two surfaces. Prussian blue is commonly used to determine the width and location of the contact area between the valve face and the valve seat.

R

Race (bearing) - The inner or outer ring that provides a contact surface for balls or rollers in bearing.

Ream - To size, enlarge or smooth a hole by using a round cutting tool with fluted edges.

Ring job - The process of reconditioning the cylinders and installing new rings.

Runout - Wobble. The amount a shaft rotates out-of-true.

S

Saddle - The upper main bearing seat.

Scored - Scratched or grooved, as a cylinder wall may be scored by abrasive particles moved up and down by the piston rings.

Scuffing - A type of wear in which there's a transfer of material between parts moving against each other; shows up as pits or grooves in the mating surfaces.

Seat - The surface upon which another part rests or seats. For example, the valve seat is the matched surface upon which the valve face rests. Also used to refer to wearing into a good fit; for example, piston rings seat after a few miles of driving.

Short block - An engine block complete with crankshaft and piston and, usually, camshaft assemblies.

Static balance - The balance of an object while it's stationary.

Step - The wear on the lower portion of a ring land caused by excessive side and back-clearance. The height of the step indicates the ring's extra side clearance and the length of the step projecting from the back wall of the groove represents the ring's back clearance.

Stroke - The distance the piston moves when traveling from top dead center to bottom dead center, or from bottom dead center to top dead center.

Stud - A metal rod with threads on both ends.

T

Tang - A lip on the end of a plain bearing used to align the bearing during assembly.

Tap - To cut threads in a hole. Also refers to the fluted tool used to cut threads.

Taper - A gradual reduction in the width of a shaft or hole; in an engine cylinder, taper usually takes the form of uneven wear, more pronounced at the top than at the bottom.

Throws - The offset portions of the crankshaft to which the connecting rods are affixed.

Thrust bearing - The main bearing that has thrust faces to prevent excessive endplay, or forward and backward movement of the crankshaft.

Thrust washer - A bronze or hardened steel washer placed between two moving parts. The washer prevents longitudinal movement and provides a bearing surface for thrust surfaces of parts.

Tolerance - The amount of variation permitted from an exact size of measurement. Actual amount from smallest acceptable dimension to largest acceptable dimension.

U

Umbrella - An oil deflector placed near the valve tip to throw oil from the valve stem area.

Undercut - A machined groove below the normal surface.

Undersize bearings - Smaller diameter bearings used with re-ground crankshaft journals.

V

Valve grinding - Refacing a valve in a valve-refacing machine.

Valve train - The valve-operating mechanism of an engine; includes all components from the camshaft to the valve.

Vibration damper - A cylindrical weight attached to the front of the crankshaft to minimize torsional vibration (the twist-untwist actions of the crankshaft caused by the cylinder firing impulses). Also called a harmonic balancer.

W

Water jacket - The spaces around the cylinders, between the inner and outer shells of the cylinder block or head, through which coolant circulates.

Web - A supporting structure across a cavity.

Woodruff key - A key with a radiused backside (viewed from the side).

Notes

Chapter 3
Cooling, heating and air conditioning systems

Contents

Specifications

General

Radiator cap pressure rating	Refer to pressure specification on cap
Cooling system capacity	See Chapter 1
Refrigerant type	R-134a
Refrigerant capacity	1.10 lbs

Torque specifications

Ft-lbs (unless otherwise indicated)

Note: *One foot-pound (ft-lb) of torque is equivalent to 12 inch-pounds (in-lbs) of torque. Torque values below approximately 15 ft-lbs are expressed in inch-pounds, because most foot-pound torque wrenches are not accurate at these smaller values.*

Thermostat water inlet bolts	16
Water outlet housing (water control valve) bolts	16
Cooling fan shroud mounting bolts	39 in-lbs
Cooling fan blade assembly-to-motor shaft nut	30 in-lbs
Cooling fan motor-to-shroud mounting bolts	39 in-lbs
Water pump mounting bolts	18
Water pump housing-to-block bolts	
2013 and earlier models/2014 and later Rogue Select models	16
2014 and later models (except Rogue Select models)	18
Air conditioning compressor mounting bolts	23
Expansion valve bolts	39 in-lbs

2.2 The cooling system pressure tester is connected in place of the pressure cap. then pumped up to pressurize the system

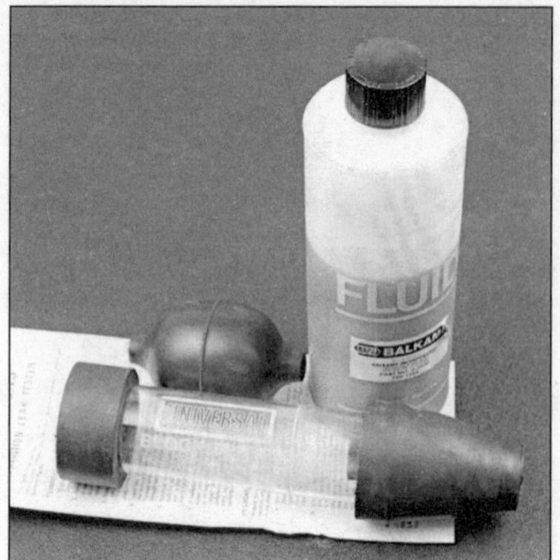

2.5a The combustion leak detector consists of a bulb, syringe and test fluid

2.5b Place the tester over the cooling system filler neck and use the bulb to draw a sample into the tester

1 General information

Warning: *Do not allow antifreeze to come in contact with your skin or painted surfaces of the vehicle. Rinse off spills immediately with plenty of water. Antifreeze is highly toxic if ingested. Never leave antifreeze lying around in an open container or in puddles on the floor; children and pets are attracted by it's sweet smell and may drink it. Check with local authorities about disposing of used antifreeze. Many communities have collection centers which will see that antifreeze is disposed of safely. Never dump used antifreeze on the ground or pour it into drains.*

Engine cooling system

1 All modern vehicles employ a pressurized engine cooling system with thermostatically controlled coolant circulation. The cooling system consists of a radiator, an expansion tank or coolant reservoir, a pressure cap (located on the expansion tank or radiator), a thermostat, a water control valve (2013 and earlier models/2014 and later Rogue Select models), a cooling fan, and a water pump.

2 The water pump circulates coolant through the engine. The coolant flows around each cylinder and around the intake and exhaust ports, near the spark plug areas and in close proximity to the exhaust valve guides.

3 A thermostat (and, on 2013 and earlier models/2014 and later Rogue Select models) controls engine coolant temperature. During warm up, the closed thermostat prevents coolant from circulating through the radiator. As the engine nears normal operating temperature, the thermostat opens and allows hot coolant to travel through the radiator, where it's cooled before returning to the engine.

Heating system

4 The heating system consists of a blower fan and heater core located in a housing under the dash, the hoses connecting the heater core to the engine cooling system and the heater/air conditioning control head on the dashboard. Hot engine coolant is circulated through the heater core. When the heater mode is activated, a flap door in the housing opens to expose the heater core to the passenger compartment through air ducts. A fan switch on the control head activates the blower motor, which forces air through the core, heating the air.

Air conditioning system

5 The air conditioning system consists of a condenser mounted in front of the radiator, an evaporator mounted adjacent to the heater core, a compressor mounted on the engine, a receiver-drier or accumulator and the plumbing connecting all of the above components.

6 A blower fan forces the warmer air of the passenger compartment through the evaporator core (sort of a radiator-in-reverse), transferring the heat from the air to the refrigerant. The liquid refrigerant boils off into low pressure vapor, taking the heat with it when it leaves the evaporator.

2 Troubleshooting

Coolant leaks

1 A coolant leak can develop anywhere in the cooling system, but the most common causes are:

a) A loose or weak hose clamp
b) A defective hose
c) A faulty pressure cap
d) A damaged radiator
e) A bad heater core
f) A faulty water pump
g) A leaking gasket at any joint that carries coolant

2 Coolant leaks aren't always easy to find. Sometimes they can only be detected when the cooling system is under pressure. Here's where a cooling system pressure tester comes in handy. After the engine has cooled completely, the tester is attached in place of the pressure cap, then pumped up to the pressure value equal to that of the pressure cap rating (see illustration). Now, leaks that only exist when the engine is fully warmed up will become apparent. The tester can be left connected to locate a nagging slow leak.

Coolant level drops, but no external leaks

3 If you find it necessary to keep adding coolant, but there are no external leaks, the probable causes include:

a) A blown head gasket
b) A leaking intake manifold gasket (only on engines that have coolant passages in the manifold)
c) A cracked cylinder head or cylinder block

4 Any of the above problems will also usually result in contamination of the engine oil, which will cause it to take on a milkshake-like appearance. A bad head gasket or cracked head or block can also result in engine oil contaminating the cooling system.

5 Combustion leak detectors (also known as block testers) are available at most auto parts stores. These work by detecting exhaust gases in the cooling system, which indicates a compression leak from a cylinder into the coolant. The tester consists of a large bulb-type syringe and bottle of test fluid (see illustration). A measured amount of the fluid is added to the syringe. The syringe is placed over the cooling system filler neck and, with the engine running, the bulb is squeezed and a sample of the gases present in the cooling system are drawn up through the test fluid (see illustration). If any combustion gases are present in the sample taken, the test fluid will change color.

6 If the test indicates combustion gas is present in the cooling system, you can be sure that the engine has a blown head gasket or a crack in the cylinder head or block, and will require disassembly to repair.

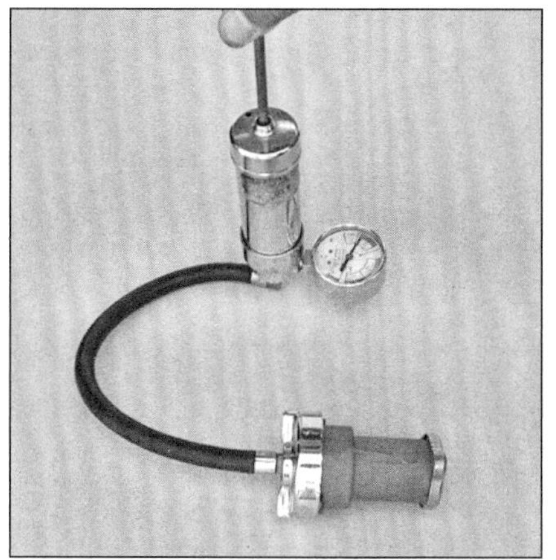

2.8 Checking the cooling system pressure cap with a cooling system pressure tester

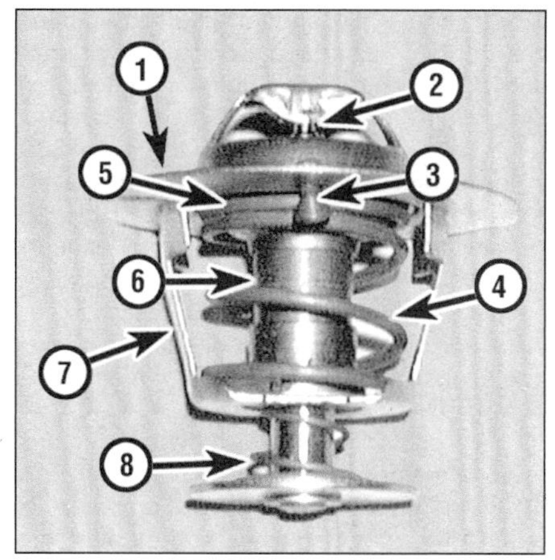

2.10 Typical thermostat:

1 Flange
2 Piston
3 Jiggle valve
4 Main coil spring
5 Valve seat
6 Valve
7 Frame
8 Secondary coil spring

2.28 The water pump weep hole is generally located on the underside of the pump

Pressure cap

Warning: *Wait until the engine is completely cool before beginning this check.*

7 The cooling system is sealed by a spring-loaded cap, which raises the boiling point of the coolant. If the cap's seal or spring are worn out, the coolant can boil and escape past the cap. With the engine completely cool, remove the cap and check the seal; if it's cracked, hardened or deteriorated in any way, replace it with a new one.

8 Even if the seal is good, the spring might not be; this can be checked with a cooling system pressure tester (see illustration). If the cap can't hold a pressure within approximately 1-1/2 lbs of its rated pressure (which is marked on the cap), replace it with a new one.

9 The cap is also equipped with a vacuum relief spring. When the engine cools off, a vacuum is created in the cooling system. The vacuum relief spring allows air back into the system, which will equalize the pressure and prevent damage to the radiator (the radiator tanks could collapse if the vacuum is great enough). If, after turning the engine off and allowing it to cool down you notice any of the cooling system hoses collapsing, replace the pressure cap with a new one.

Thermostat

10 Before assuming the thermostat or water control valve (see illustration) is responsible for a cooling system problem, check the coolant level (see Chapter 1), drivebelt tension (see Chapter 1) and temperature gauge (or light) operation.

11 If the engine takes a long time to warm up (as indicated by the temperature gauge or heater operation), the thermostat is probably stuck open. Replace the thermostat or water control valve with a new one.

12 If the engine runs hot or overheats, a thorough test of the thermostat should be performed.

13 Definitive testing of the thermostat or water control valve can only be made when it is removed from the vehicle. If the thermostat is stuck in the open position at room temperature, it is faulty and must be replaced.

Caution: *Do not drive the vehicle without a thermostat. The computer may stay in open loop and emissions and fuel economy will suffer.*

14 To test a thermostat, suspend the (closed) thermostat on a length of string or wire in a pot of cold water.

15 Heat the water on a stove while observing thermostat. The thermostat should fully open before the water boils.

16 If the thermostat doesn't open and close as specified, or sticks in any position, replace it.

Cooling fan

Electric cooling fan

17 If the engine is overheating and the cooling fan is not coming on when the engine temperature rises to an excessive level, unplug the fan motor electrical connector(s) and connect the motor directly to the battery with fused jumper wires. If the fan motor doesn't come on, replace the motor.

18 If the radiator fan motor is okay, but it isn't coming on when the engine gets hot, the fan relay might be defective. A relay is used to control a circuit by turning it on and off in response to a control decision by the Powertrain Control Module (PCM). These control circuits are fairly complex, and checking them should be left to a qualified automotive technician. Sometimes, the control system can be fixed by simply identifying and replacing a bad relay.

19 Locate the fan relays in the engine compartment fuse/relay box.

20 Test the relay (see Chapter 12).

21 If the relay is okay, check all wiring and connections to the fan motor. Refer to the wiring diagrams in Chapter 13. If no obvious problems are found, the problem could be the Engine Coolant Temperature (ECT) sensor or the Powertrain Control Module (PCM). Have the cooling fan system and circuit diagnosed by a dealer service department or repair shop with the proper diagnostic equipment.

Note: *These models are equipped with a cooling fan motor resistor. Have the resistor checked if the fan motor does not respond to the speed variations signaled by the PCM.*

Belt-driven cooling fan

22 Disconnect the cable from the negative terminal of the battery and rock the fan back and forth by hand to check for excessive bearing play.

23 With the engine cold (and not running), turn the fan blades by hand. The fan should turn freely.

24 Visually inspect for substantial fluid leakage from the clutch assembly. If problems are noted, replace the clutch assembly.

25 With the engine completely warmed up, turn off the ignition switch and disconnect the negative battery cable from the battery. Turn the fan by hand. Some drag should be evident. If the fan turns easily, replace the fan clutch.

Water pump

26 A failure in the water pump can cause serious engine damage due to overheating.

Drivebelt-driven water pump

27 There are two ways to check the operation of the water pump while it's installed on the engine. If the pump is found to be defective, it should be replaced with a new or rebuilt unit.

28 Water pumps are equipped with weep (or vent) holes (see illustration). If a failure occurs in the pump seal, coolant will leak from the hole.

29 If the water pump shaft bearings fail, there may be a howling sound at the pump while it's running. Shaft wear can be felt with the drivebelt removed if the water pump pulley is rocked up and down (with the engine off). Don't mistake drivebelt slippage, which causes a squealing sound, for water pump bearing failure.

Timing chain or timing belt-driven water pump

30 Water pumps driven by the timing chain or timing belt are located underneath the timing chain or timing belt cover.

31 Checking the water pump is limited because of where it is located. However, some basic checks can be made before deciding to remove the water pump. If the pump is found to be defective, it should be replaced with a new or rebuilt unit.

32 One sign that the water pump may be failing is that the heater (climate control) may not work well. Warm the engine to normal operating temperature, confirm that the coolant level is correct, then run the heater and check for hot air coming from the ducts.

33 Check for noises coming from the water pump area. If the water pump impeller shaft or bearings are failing, there may be a howling sound at the pump while the engine is running.

Note: *Be careful not to mistake drivebelt noise (squealing) for water pump bearing or shaft failure.*

34 It you suspect water pump failure due to noise, wear can be confirmed by feeling for play at the pump shaft. This can be done by rocking the drive sprocket on the pump shaft up and down. To do this you will need to remove the tension on the timing chain or belt as well as access the water pump.

All water pumps

35 In rare cases or on high-mileage vehicles, another sign of water pump failure may be the presence of coolant in the engine oil. This condition will adversely affect the engine in varying degrees.

Note: *Finding coolant in the engine oil could indicate other serious issues besides a failed water pump, such as a blown head gasket or a cracked cylinder head or block.*

36 Even a pump that exhibits no outward signs of a problem, such as noise or leakage, can still be due for replacement. Removal for close examination is the only sure way to tell. Sometimes the fins on the back of the impeller can corrode to the point that cooling efficiency is diminished significantly.

Heater system

37 Little can go wrong with a heater. If the fan motor will run at all speeds, the electrical part of the system is okay. The three basic heater problems fall into the following general categories:

a) *Not enough heat*
b) *Heat all the time*
c) *No heat*

38 If there's not enough heat, the control valve or door is stuck in a partially open position, the coolant coming from the engine isn't hot enough, or the heater core is restricted. If the coolant isn't hot enough, the thermostat in the engine cooling system is stuck open, allowing coolant to pass through the engine so rapidly that it doesn't heat up quickly enough. If the vehicle is equipped with a temperature gauge instead of a warning light, watch to see if the engine temperature rises to the normal operating range after driving for a reasonable distance.

39 If there's heat all the time, the control valve or the door is stuck wide open.

40 If there's no heat, coolant is probably not reaching the heater core, or the heater core is plugged. The likely cause is a collapsed or plugged hose, core, or a frozen heater control valve. If the heater is the type that flows coolant all the time, the cause is a stuck door or a broken or kinked control cable.

Air conditioning system

41 If the cool air output is inadequate:

a) *Inspect the condenser coils and fins to make sure they're clear*
b) *Check the compressor clutch for slippage*
c) *Check the blower motor for proper operation*
d) *Inspect the blower discharge passage for obstructions*
e) *Check the system air intake filter for clogging*

42 If the system provides intermittent cooling air:

a) *Check the circuit breaker, blower switch and blower motor for a malfunction*
b) *Make sure the compressor clutch isn't slipping*
c) *Inspect the plenum door to make sure it's operating properly*
d) *Inspect the evaporator to make sure it isn't clogged*
e) *If the unit is icing up, it may be caused by excessive moisture in the system, incorrect super heat switch adjustment or low thermostat adjustment*

43 If the system provides no cooling air:

a) *Inspect the compressor drivebelt; make sure it's not loose or broken*
b) *Make sure the compressor clutch engages; if it doesn't, check for a blown fuse*
c) *Inspect the wire harness for broken or disconnected wires*
d) *If the compressor clutch doesn't engage, bridge the terminals of the AC pressure switch(es) with a jumper wire; if the clutch now engages, and the system is properly charged, the pressure switch is bad*
e) *Make sure the blower motor is not disconnected or burned out*
f) *Make sure the compressor isn't partially or completely seized*
g) *Inspect the refrigerant lines for leaks*
h) *Check the components for leaks*
i) *Inspect the receiver-drier/accumulator or expansion valve/tube for clogged screens*

44 If the system is noisy:

a) *Look for loose panels in the passenger compartment*
b) *Inspect the compressor drivebelt; it may be loose or worn*
c) *Check the compressor mounting bolts; they should be tight*
d) *Listen carefully to the compressor; it may be worn out*
e) *Listen to the idler pulley and bearing, and the clutch; either may be defective*
f) *The winding in the compressor clutch coil or solenoid may be defective*
g) *The compressor oil level may be low*
h) *The blower motor fan bushing or the motor itself may be worn out*
i) *If there is an excessive charge in the system, you'll hear a rumbling noise in the high pressure line, a thumping noise in the compressor, or see bubbles or cloudiness in the sight glass*
j) *If there's a low charge in the system, you might hear hissing in the evaporator case at the expansion valve, or see bubbles or cloudiness in the sight glass*

3 Air conditioning and heating system - check and maintenance

Air conditioning system

Warning: *The air conditioning system is under high pressure. Do not loosen any hose fittings or remove any components until after the system has been discharged. Air conditioning refrigerant should be properly discharged into an EPA-approved recovery/recycling unit at a dealer service department or an automotive air conditioning repair facility. Always wear eye protection when disconnecting air conditioning system fittings.*

Caution: *All models covered by this manual use environmentally friendly R-134a. This refrigerant (and its appropriate refrigerant oils) are not compatible with R-12 refrigerant system components and must never be mixed or the components will be damaged.*

Caution: *When replacing entire components, additional refrigerant oil should be added equal to the amount that is removed with the component being replaced. Be sure to read the can before adding any oil to the system, to make sure it is compatible with the R-134a system.*

1 The following maintenance checks should be performed on a regular basis to ensure that the air conditioning continues to operate at peak efficiency.

a) *Inspect the condition of the compressor drivebelt. If it is worn or deteriorated, replace it (see Chapter 1).*
b) *Check the drivebelt tension (see Chapter 1).*

3.1 The evaporator drain hose extends through the floor to allow collected water to run out

3.9 Insert a thermometer in the center vent, turn on the air conditioning system and wait for it to cool down; depending on the humidity, the output air should be 30 to 40 degrees cooler than the ambient air temperature

- c) *Inspect the system hoses. Look for cracks, bubbles, hardening and deterioration. Inspect the hoses and all fittings for oil bubbles or seepage. If there is any evidence of wear, damage or leakage, replace the hose(s).*
- d) *Inspect the condenser fins for leaves, bugs and any other foreign material that may have become embedded in the fins. Use a fin comb or compressed air to remove debris from the condenser.*
- e) *Make sure the system has the correct refrigerant charge.*
- f) *If you hear water sloshing around in the dash area or have water dripping on the carpet, check the evaporator housing drain tube (see illustration) and insert a piece of wire into the opening to check for blockage.*

2 It's a good idea to operate the system for about ten minutes at least once a month. This is particularly important during the winter months because long term non-use can cause hardening, and subsequent failure, of the seals. Note that using the Defrost function operates the compressor.

3 If the air conditioning system is not working properly, proceed to Step 6 and perform the general checks outlined below.

4 Because of the complexity of the air conditioning system and the special equipment necessary to service it, in-depth troubleshooting and repairs beyond checking the refrigerant charge and the compressor clutch operation are not included in this manual. However, simple checks and component replacement procedures are provided in this Chapter. For more complete information on the air conditioning system, refer to the Haynes Automotive Heating and Air Conditioning Manual.

5 The most common cause of poor cooling is simply a low system refrigerant charge. If a noticeable drop in system cooling ability occurs, one of the following quick checks will help you determine if the refrigerant level is low.

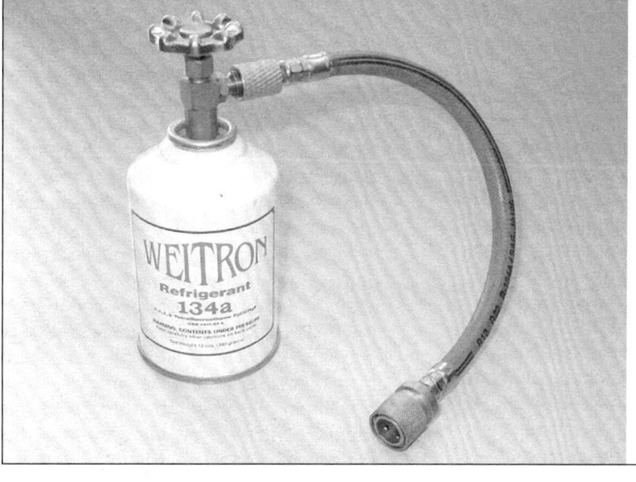

3.11 R-134a automotive air conditioning charging kit

Checking the refrigerant charge

6 Warm the engine up to normal operating temperature.

7 Place the air conditioning temperature selector at the coldest setting and put the blower at the highest setting.

8 After the system reaches operating temperature, feel the larger pipe exiting the evaporator at the firewall. The outlet pipe should be cold (the tubing that leads back to the compressor). If the evaporator outlet pipe is warm, the system probably needs a charge.

9 Insert a thermometer in the center air distribution duct (see illustration) while operating the air conditioning system at its maximum setting - the temperature of the output air should be 30 to 40 degrees F below the ambient air temperature (down to approximately 40 degrees F). If the ambient (outside) air temperature is very high, say 110 degrees F, the duct air temperature may be as high as 60 degrees F, but generally the air conditioning is 30 to 40 degrees F cooler than the ambient air.

10 Further inspection or testing of the system requires special tools and techniques and is beyond the scope of the home mechanic.

Adding refrigerant

Caution: *Make sure any refrigerant, refrigerant oil or replacement component you purchase is designated as compatible with R-134a systems.*

11 Purchase an R-134a automotive charging kit at an auto parts store (see illustration). A charging kit includes a can of refrigerant, a tap valve and a short section of hose that can be attached between the tap valve and the system low side service valve.

Caution: *Never add more than one can of refrigerant to the system. If more refrigerant than that is required, the system should be evacuated and leak tested.*

12 Back off the valve handle on the charging kit and screw the kit onto the refrigerant can, making sure first that the O-ring or rubber seal inside the threaded portion of the kit is in place.

Warning: *Wear protective eyewear when working with pressurized refrigerant cans.*

3.13 Location of the low-side charging port

13 Remove the dust cap from the low-side charging port and attach the hose's quick-connect fitting to the port (see illustration). The fittings on the charging kit are designed to fit only on the low side of the system.

Warning: *DO NOT hook the charging kit hose to the system high side!*

14 Warm up the engine and turn On the air conditioning. Keep the charging kit hose away from the fan and other moving parts.

Note: *The charging process requires the compressor to be running. If the clutch cycles off, you can put the air conditioning switch on High and leave the car doors open to keep the clutch on and compressor working.The compressor can be kept on during the charging by removing the connector from the pressure switch and bridging it with a paper clip or jumper wire during the procedure.*

15 Turn the valve handle on the kit until the stem pierces the can, then back the handle out to release the refrigerant. You should be able to hear the rush of gas. Keep the can upright at all times, but shake it occasionally. Allow stabilization time between each addition.

Note: *The charging process will go faster if you wrap the can with a hot-water-soaked rag to keep the can from freezing up.*

16 If you have an accurate thermometer, you can place it in the center air conditioning duct inside the vehicle and keep track of the output air temperature. A charged system that is working properly should cool down to approximately 40 degrees F. If the ambient (outside) air temperature is very high, say 110 degrees F, the duct air temperature may be as high as 60 degrees F, but generally the air conditioning is 30 to 40 degrees F cooler than the ambient air.

17 When the can is empty, turn the valve handle to the closed position and release the connection from the low-side port. Reinstall the dust cap.

18 Remove the charging kit from the can and store the kit for future use with the piercing valve in the UP position, to prevent inadvertently piercing the can on the next use.

Heating systems

19 If the carpet under the heater core is damp, or if antifreeze vapor or steam is coming through the vents, the heater core is leaking. Remove it (see Section 10) and install a new unit (most radiator shops will not repair a leaking heater core).

20 If the air coming out of the heater vents isn't hot, the problem could stem from any of the following causes:

a) *The thermostat is stuck open, preventing the engine coolant from warming up enough to carry heat to the heater core. Replace the thermostat (see Section 4).*
b) *There is a blockage in the system, preventing the flow of coolant through the heater core. Feel both heater hoses at the firewall. They should be hot. If one of them is cold, there is an obstruction in one of the hoses or in the heater core, or the heater control valve is shut. Detach the hoses and back flush the heater core with a water hose. If the heater core is clear but circulation is impeded, remove the two hoses and flush them out with a water hose.*
c) *If flushing fails to remove the blockage from the heater core, the core must be replaced (see Section 10).*

Eliminating air conditioning odors

21 Unpleasant odors that often develop in air conditioning systems are caused by the growth of a fungus, usually on the surface of the evaporator core. The warm, humid environment there is a perfect breeding ground for mildew to develop.

22 The evaporator core on most vehicles is difficult to access, and factory dealerships have a lengthy, expensive process for eliminating the fungus by opening up the evaporator case and using a powerful disinfectant and rinse on the core until the fungus is gone. You can service your own system at home, but it takes something much stronger than basic household germ-killers or deodorizers.

23 Aerosol disinfectants for automotive air conditioning systems are available in most auto parts stores, but remember when shopping for them that the most effective treatments are also the most expensive. The basic procedure for using these sprays is to start by running the system in the RECIRC mode for ten minutes with the blower on its highest speed. Use the highest heat mode to dry out the system and keep the compressor from engaging by disconnecting the wiring connector at the compressor.

24 The disinfectant can usually comes with a long spray hose. Insert the nozzle into an intake port inside the cabin, and spray according to the manufacturer's recommendations. Follow the manufacturer's recommendations for the length of spray and waiting time between applications.

25 Once the evaporator has been cleaned, the best way to prevent the mildew from coming back again is to make sure your evaporator housing drain tube is clear (see illustration 3.1).

Automatic heating and air conditioning systems

26 Some vehicles are equipped with an optional automatic climate control system. This system has its own computer that receives inputs from various sensors in the heating and air conditioning system. This computer, like the PCM, has self-diagnostic capabilities to help pinpoint problems or faults within the system. Vehicles equipped with automatic heating and air conditioning systems are very complex and considered beyond the scope of the home mechanic. Vehicles equipped with automatic heating and air conditioning systems should be taken to dealer service department or other qualified facility for repair.

4 Thermostat and water control valve - replacement

Warning: *See the antifreeze Warning in Section 1.*

Warning: *Wait until the engine is completely cool before beginning this procedure.*

Note: *These engines use a thermostat on the coolant inlet (located on the cylinder block), and on 2013 and earlier models, a water control valve on the coolant outlet (at the driver's end of the cylinder head). Although they have different names, these devices perform similar functions and are very similar in appearance. If you are experiencing an overheating condition attributed to a faulty thermostat or water control valve on a 2013 or earlier/2014 or later Rogue Select, it is recommended that both of them be replaced at the same time.*

1 Raise the front of the vehicle and support it securely on jackstands. Remove the splash guard between the bumper cover and the subframe.

2 Drain the cooling system (see Chapter 1). If the coolant is relatively new, or is in good condition (see Section 2), save it and reuse it. After the coolant has drained, lower the vehicle.

Thermostat

3 Remove the exhaust manifold heat shield (see Chapter 2A).

4 Loosen the clamps and remove the lower radiator hose and transaxle fluid cooler hose (if equipped) from the thermostat water inlet housing. If the hose is stuck, grasp it near the end with a pair of large adjustable pliers and twist it to break the seal, then pull it off. If the hose is old or deteriorated, cut it off and install a new one.

5 Unscrew the water inlet mounting bolts and remove the water inlet (see illustration). If the water inlet is stuck, tap it with a soft-face hammer to jar it loose. Be prepared for some coolant to spill as the gasket seal is broken.

6 Remove the thermostat. Clean the water inlet and engine block mating surfaces.

7 Install a new sealing ring onto the thermostat (see illustration), then insert the thermostat into the housing. Make sure that the air bleed valve (jiggle valve) faces up, and the spring end of the valve is directed toward the engine.

8 The remainder of installation is the reverse of removal. Tighten the fasteners to the torque values listed in this Chapter's Specifications

9 Refill the cooling system (see Chapter 1).

10 Start the engine and allow it to reach normal operating temperature, then check for leaks and proper thermostat operation.

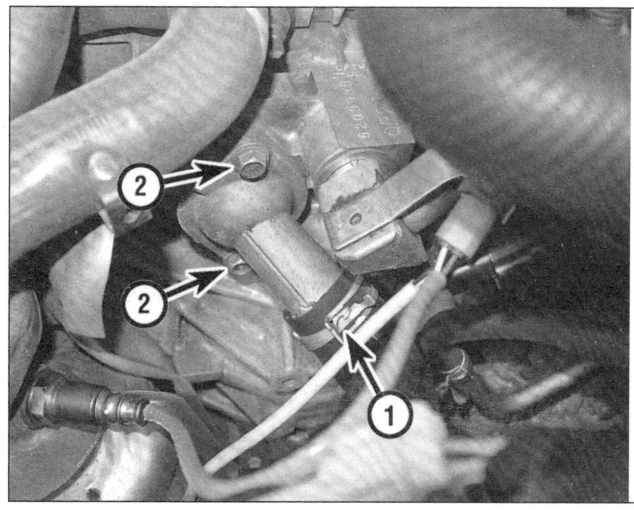

4.5 Water inlet housing location

1 *Lower radiator hose clamp*
2 *Water inlet housing mounting bolts*

Coolant outlet housing and water control valve

Note: *2013 and earlier models/2014 and later Rogue Select models are equipped with a water control valve in the control valve housing. 2014 and later non-Select models have a coolant outlet housing but do not use a water control valve.*

11 Remove the air inlet/resonator duct (see Chapter 4).

12 Disconnect the electrical connectors from the PCM and TCM and move the harness out of the way (see Chapter 6).

13 Remove the battery and battery tray (see Chapter 5).

14 Disconnect the hoses from the coolant outlet (see illustration). If a hose is stuck, grasp it near the end with a pair of large adjustable pliers and twist it to break the seal, then pull it off. If the hose is old or deteriorated, cut it off and install a new one.

15 Detach the hoses from the heater pipe, then unscrew the fastener and remove the heater pipe from the engine. Install a new O-ring on the end of the heater pipe where it mates with the engine.

16 Remove the fasteners and detach the water control valve housing. If it is stuck, tap it with a soft-face hammer to jar it loose. Be prepared for some coolant to spill as the gasket seal is broken.

17 Remove the water control valve, if equipped. Clean the mating surfaces of all gasket or sealant.

18 On models with a water control valve, install a new sealing ring onto the water control valve (see illustration 4.6), then insert the valve into the housing. Make sure the air bleed valve (jiggle valve) faces up and the spring end of the valve is directed toward the housing.

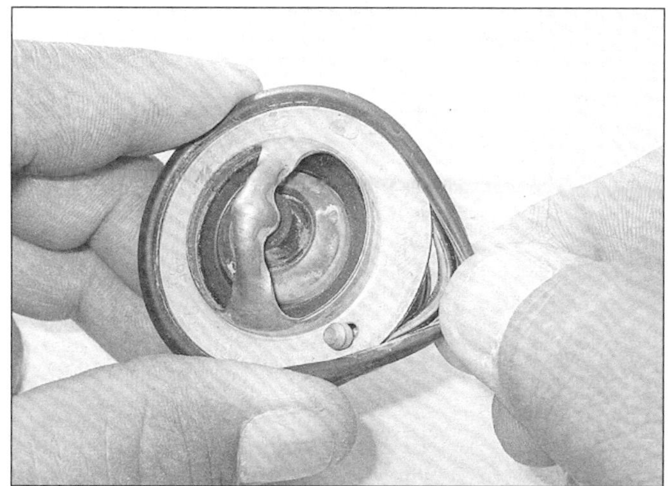

4.7 The thermostat (and water control valve on 2013 and earlier/2014 and later Rogue Select models) sealing ring fits around the edge of the flange

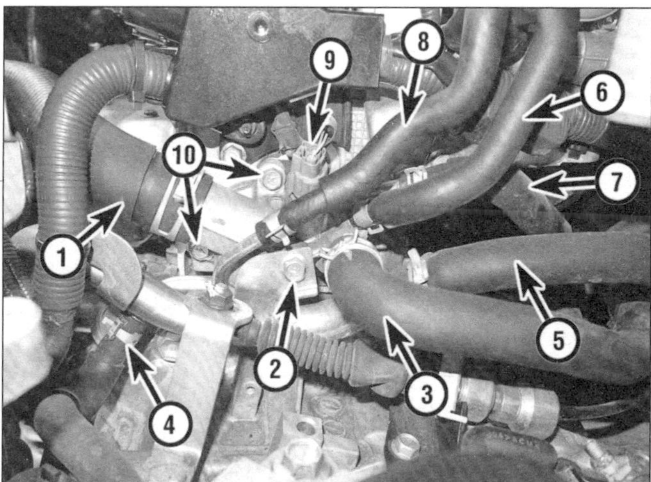

4.14 Water control valve details (2013 and earlier models/ 2014 and later Rogue Select models)

1 *Radiator hose*
2 *Heater pipe bolt*
3 *Heater hose*
4 *Hose to transaxle fluid cooler*
5 *Heater hose*
6 *Throttle body hose*
7 *Oil cooler hose*
8 *Throttle body hose*
9 *Engine Coolant Temperature (ECT) sensor*
10 *Water control valve mounting fastener (others not visible in this photo)*

5.5 Location of the cooling fan assembly mounting fasteners

5.12 Properly seated shroud mount

6.3 Disconnect the upper and lower radiator hoses (lower hose shown)

19 Install the housing (with a new gasket) and bolts. Tighten the bolts evenly to the torque listed in this Chapter's Specifications

20 The remainder of installation is the reverse of removal.

21 Refill the cooling system (see Chapter 1).

22 Start the engine and allow it to reach normal operating temperature, then check for leaks and proper thermostat/water valve operation.

5 Engine cooling fans - replacement

Warning: *The engine must be completely cool before beginning this procedure.*

Warning: *The models covered by this manual are equipped with a Supplemental Restraint System (SRS), more commonly known as airbags. Always disarm the airbag system before working in the vicinity of any airbag system component to avoid the possibility of accidental deployment of the airbag, which could cause personal injury (see Chapter 12). Do not use a memory saving device to preserve the PCM's memory when working on or near airbag system components.*

Warning: *See the antifreeze Warning in Section 1.*

1 Drain some coolant from the radiator to a level that's lower than the upper radiator hose (see Chapter 1).

2 Remove the fresh air intake duct (see Chapter 4).

3 Detach the upper radiator hose from the radiator and the coolant reservoir hose from the fan shroud.

4 Disconnect the electrical connectors from the fan motors. Also, detach the transaxle fluid cooler hoses from the fan shroud (where applicable).

5 Remove the cooling fan assembly-to-radiator fasteners (see illustration).

6 On 2014 and later models (except Rogue Select models), remove the radiator core support (see Section 6).

7 Remove the cooling fan assembly.

8 If necessary, remove the nuts for each fan blade assembly and remove them from their motor shafts.

9 Remove the fan motor-to-fan support retaining bolts, then remove the motor.

10 Installation is the reverse of removal.

11 Tighten all fasteners to the torque values listed in this Chapter's Specifications.

12 Be sure the cooling fan shroud mounts are seated properly at the base of the radiator (see illustration).

13 Refill the cooling system (see Chapter 1).

14 Reconnect the battery and perform the necessary re-learn procedures (see Chapter 5).

6 Radiator and coolant reservoir - removal and installation

Warning: *Wait until the engine is completely cool before beginning this procedure.*

Warning: *The models covered by this manual are equipped with a Supplemental Restraint System (SRS), more commonly known as airbags. Always disarm the airbag system before working in the vicinity of any airbag system component to avoid the possibility of accidental deployment of the airbag, which could cause personal injury (see Chapter 12). Do not use a memory saving device to preserve the PCM's memory when working on or near airbag system components.*

Warning: *See the antifreeze Warning in Section 1.*

Radiator

1 Drain the cooling system (see Chapter 1).

2013 and earlier models/2014 and later Rogue Select models)

2 Remove the fresh air intake duct (see Chapter 4).

3 Disconnect the upper and lower radiator hoses from the radiator (see illustration), and also the overflow hose from the radiator filler neck. If a hose is stuck, grasp it near the end with a pair of large adjustable pliers and twist it to break the seal, then pull it off. If the hose is old or deteriorated, cut it off and install a new one.

6.5 Pull the tabs on the radiator upper clips (A) outwards then side the clip (B) out from the radiator (left-side shown)

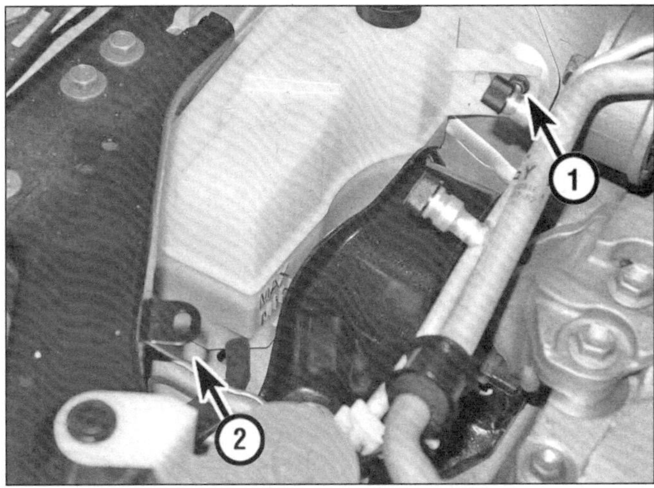

6.20 Coolant reservoir details

1 *Coolant reservoir mounting fastener*
2 *Mounting stud (underneath, plugs into grommet)*

4 Remove the cooling fan assembly from the vehicle (see Section 5).

5 Pull the tabs on the radiator upper clips outwards then side the clips out and remove the rubber mounts from the mounting pins (see illustration).

6 Tilt the radiator assembly toward the rear of the vehicle, then lift up to remove it.

Caution: *Avoid damaging the radiator or A/C condenser fins and tanks during radiator removal.*

2014 and later models (except Rogue Select models)

7 Remove the under-vehicle splash shield.

8 Remove the front air spoiler from under the radiator.

9 Remove the inner fender splash shield from both fenders (see Chapter 11, Section 19).

10 Remove the radiator core support.

Note: *It may be necessary to remove trim pieces from the fenders to allow the radiator support to be moved.*

11 Disconnect the upper and lower radiator hoses from the radiator, and also the overflow hose from the radiator filler neck. If a hose is stuck, grasp it near the end with a pair of large adjustable pliers and twist it to break the seal, then pull it off. If the hose is old or deteriorated, cut it off and install a new one.

Note: *The radiator hose clamps are glued in place from the factory. Use a heat gun to apply heat evenly around the clamps as you wiggle the clamp using a pair of adjustable pliers, until the clamps are free.*

12 Remove the condenser mounts (see Section 12) and move condenser forward.

13 Remove the cooling fans (see Section 5).

14 Tilt the radiator assembly toward the rear of the vehicle, then lift up to remove it.

All models

15 With the radiator removed, it can be inspected for leaks and damage. If it needs repair, have a radiator shop or dealer service department perform the work, as special techniques are required.

16 Bugs and dirt can be removed from the radiator with a soft brush, followed by forcing water from a garden hose through the core from the engine side. Don't bend the cooling fins as this is done.

Caution: *Avoid damaging the radiator or A/C condenser fins and tanks during radiator installation.*

17 Installation is the reverse of removal. Be sure the radiator mounting pads are seated properly at the base of the radiator. Refill the cooling system (see Chapter 1).

18 Reconnect the battery and perform the necessary re-learn procedures (see Chapter 5). Allow the engine to reach normal operating temperature, indicated by the upper radiator hose becoming hot. Recheck the coolant level and add more if required.

Coolant reservoir

19 Disconnect the overflow hose from the fitting by the radiator cap.

20 Remove the coolant reservoir mounting nut (see illustration).

21 Pull the coolant reservoir upwards to disengage the stud from its grommet, then remove the coolant reservoir from the vehicle.

22 Pour the coolant into a container. Wash out the reservoir, using soapy water and a long brush to make the coolant level easier to read. Inspect the reservoir for cracks and chafing. Replace it if any damage is found.

23 Installation is the reverse of removal. Add coolant to the reservoir up to the Min mark.

7 Water pump - replacement

Warning: *Wait until the engine is completely cool before beginning this procedure.*

Warning: *See the antifreeze Warning in Section 1.*

7.5 Remove the water pump bolts (2013 and earlier/2014 and later Rogue Select shown; 2014 and later non-Select models have four bolts)

1 Disconnect the cable from the negative terminal of the battery (see Chapter 5). Loosen the right front wheel lug nuts, raise the front of the vehicle and support it securely on jackstands. Remove the wheel.

2 Drain the cooling system (see Chapter 1). If the coolant is relatively new, or is in good condition, save it and re-use it.

3 On 2013 and earlier/2014 and later Rogue Select models, remove the drivebelt tensioner (see Chapter 1).

4 Remove the alternator (see Chapter 5).

5 Remove the water pump bolts and separate the pump from the pump housing (see illustration). If the pump is stuck, gently tap it with a soft faced hammer to break the gasket seal.

Caution: *When the pump is removed, be prepared for coolant spillage.*

Caution: *Avoid hitting or bumping the impeller against other parts during this procedure.*

8.8 Blower motor electrical connector (1) and mounting screw (2)

9.2 Pry up and remove the gear shift cover

6 Remove all old gasket material and clean the mating surfaces on the water pump and engine block.
7 Inspect the pump. Replace the unit if there is dirt or debris on the water pump impeller, the impeller turns smoothly by hand, the shaft is not loose, or the shaft has excessive play.
8 Tighten the pump-to-housing bolts to the torque values listed in this Chapter's Specifications.
9 The remainder of installation is the reverse of removal.
10 Refill the cooling system (see Chapter 1). Reconnect the battery and perform the necessary re-learn procedures (see Chapter 5).
11 Start the engine and check for any leaks. Re-check coolant fluid levels and add if necessary.

8 Blower motor - removal and installation

Warning: *The models covered by this manual are equipped with a Supplemental Restraint System (SRS), more commonly known as airbags. Always disarm the airbag system before working in the vicinity of any airbag system component to avoid the possibility of accidental deployment of the airbag, which could cause personal injury (see Chapter 12). Do not use a memory saving device to preserve the PCM's memory when working on or near airbag system components.*

Note: *If the blower motor is found to be faulty, replace the entire blower motor and fan. The blower motor unit is balanced at the factory; individual components cannot be replaced.*

1 Disconnect the cable from the negative terminal of the battery (see Chapter 5).

2013 and earlier models/2014 and later Rogue Select models

2 Remove the lower instrument panel cover (see Chapter 11 Section 26) and driver's side front floor duct.
3 Remove the instrument cluster (see Chapter 12).
4 Remove the knee bolster and the knee bolster support (see Chapter 11).
5 Unclip the front foot duct from the evaporator case.
6 Remove the mode door motor mounting screws and remove the mode door motor from the evaporator case.
7 Disconnect the brake pedal from the power brake booster (see Chapter 9) then remove the brake pedal assembly.
8 Disconnect the the electrical connector from the blower motor (see illustration).
9 Remove the blower motor mounting screw (see illustration 8.8).
10 Rotate the blower motor counterclockwise and remove it from the housing.
11 Installation is the reverse of removal.
12 Reconnect the battery and perform the necessary re-learn procedures (see Chapter 5).

2014 and later models (except for Rogue Select models)

13 Remove the glove box and housing (see Chapter 11).
14 Disconnect the the electrical connector from the blower motor.
15 Remove the blower motor mounting screw.
16 Pull the locking hook back on the housing then rotate the blower motor counterclockwise and remove it from the housing.
17 Installation is the reverse of removal.
18 Reconnect the battery and perform the necessary re-learn procedures (see Chapter 5).

9 Heater and air conditioning control assembly - removal and installation

Warning: *The models covered by this manual are equipped with a Supplemental Restraint System (SRS), more commonly known as airbags. Always disarm the airbag system before working in the vicinity of any airbag system component to avoid the possibility of accidental deployment of the airbag, which could cause personal injury (see Chapter 12). Do not use a memory saving device to preserve the PCM's memory when working on or near airbag system components.*

1 Disconnect the cable from the negative terminal of the battery (see Chapter 5).

2013 and earlier models/2014 and later Rogue Select models

2 Use a plastic trim tool or a screwdriver wrapped with tape to carefully pry up the gear shift cover. Remove the cover (see illustration).
3 Use a plastic trim tool or a screwdriver wrapped with tape to carefully pry out the heating and air conditioning control panel/cover assembly. Pull out the assembly and disconnect the electrical connectors (see illustrations).
4 Remove the heater and air conditioning control assembly-to-cover screws (see illustration) and separate the cover from the assembly.
5 Installation is the reverse of removal.
6 Reconnect the battery and perform the necessary re-learn procedures (see Chapter 5).

2014 and later models (except Rogue Select models)

Note: *The heating and air conditioning control assembly can't be separated from the panel. If*

9.3a Pry out and remove the heating and air conditioning control panel/cover assembly . . .

9.3b . . . then disconnect the electrical connectors from the assembly

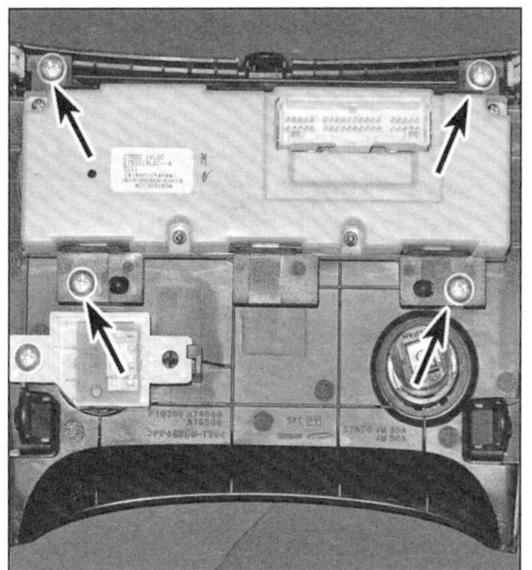

9.4 Remove the screws holding the cover to the heating and air conditioning control assembly

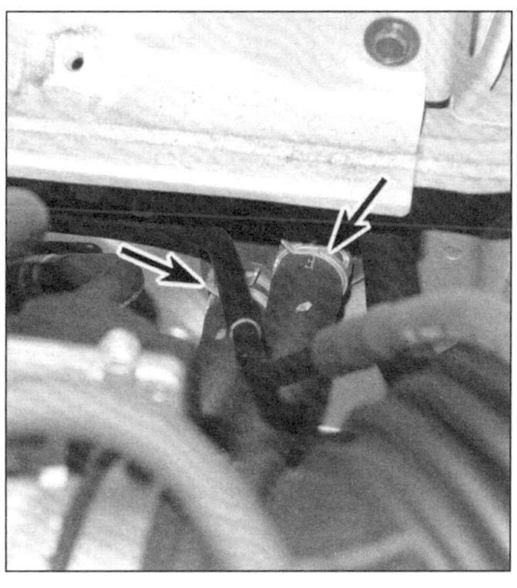

10.5 Location of the heater hoses at the firewall (to the right of the power brake booster)

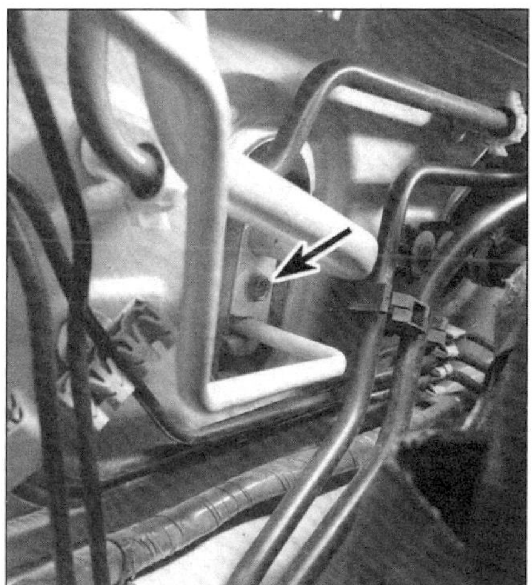

10.6 Evaporator line fitting bolt at the firewall

there is a problem with the control assembly, the panel and assembly is replaced as a unit.

7 Use a plastic trim tool or a screwdriver wrapped with tape to carefully pry out the heating and air conditioning control panel/cover assembly. Pull out the assembly and disconnect the electrical connectors.

8 Installation is the reverse of removal.

9 Reconnect the battery and perform the necessary re-learn procedures (see Chapter 5).

10 Heater core - removal and installation

Warning: *Wait until the engine is completely cool before beginning this procedure.*

Warning: *The models covered by this manual are equipped with a Supplemental Restraint System (SRS), more commonly known as airbags. Always disarm the airbag system before working in the vicinity of any airbag system component to avoid the possibility of accidental deployment of the airbag, which could cause personal injury (see Chapter 12). Do not use a memory saving device to preserve the PCM's memory when working on or near airbag system components.*

Note: *Replacement of the heater core is a difficult procedure for the home mechanic, involving removal of the entire dashboard, console, and many wiring connectors. If you attempt it at home, keep track of the assemblies by taking notes and keeping screws and other hardware in small, marked plastic bags for reassembly.*

1 Have the air conditioning system evacuated by a properly equipped shop.

2 Disconnect the cable from the negative terminal of the battery (see Chapter 5).

3 Drain the cooling system (see Chapter 1). If the coolant is relatively new, or is in good condition, save it and re-use it.

4 Move aside the lower dash insulation to access the heater core pipes.

5 Disconnect the heater hoses from the pipes protruding through the firewall (see illustration).

6 Disconnect the refrigerant lines from the evaporator (see illustration).

Note: *Plug all open fittings of disconnected lines to prevent entry of dirt and moisture into the lines.*

7 Remove the steering column (see Chapter 11).

10.14a Remove the heater core pipe bracket screws . . .

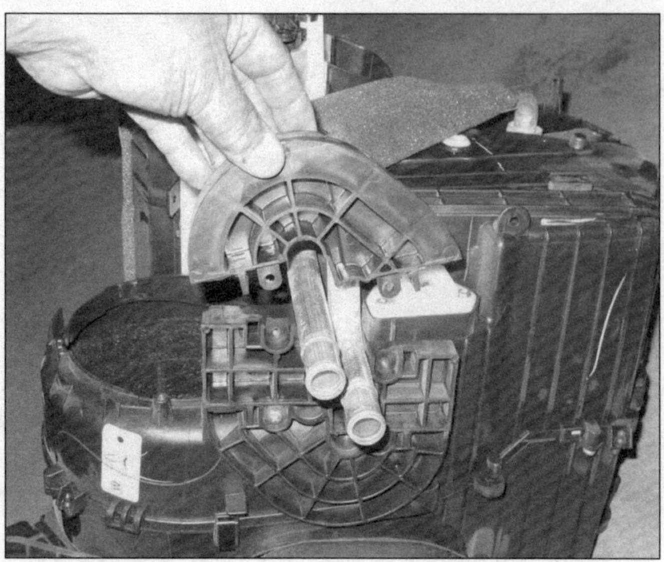

10.14b . . . and remove the heater core pipe bracket

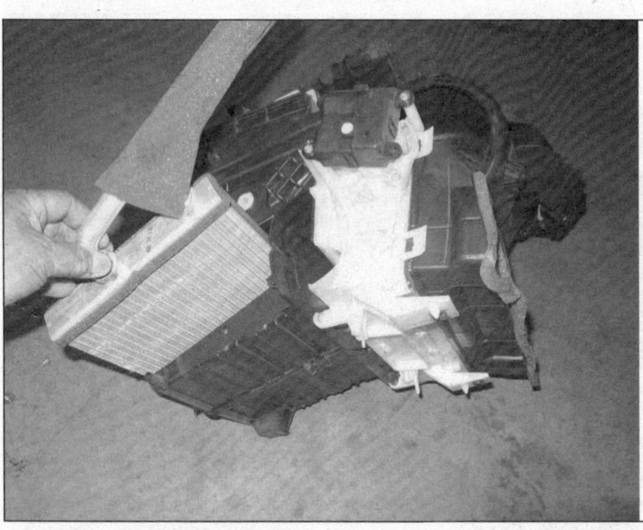

10.16 Slide out and remove the heater core

8 Remove the entire instrument panel assembly (see Chapter 11).

9 Disconnect the connectors for the following:

- a) *Shift lock cable*
- b) *Steering harness clips*
- c) *Super Multiple Junction (SMJ)*
- d) *Fuse box*
- e) *Door harness*
- f) *Front pillar harness*
- g) *Gear shift cable*
- h) *Air conditioning drain hose*
- i) *Airbag module control unit*

10 Disconnect the evaporator drain hose.

11 Remove the instrument panel support beam and the heating and air conditioning unit as a complete assembly, then place the assembly on a work bench.

Caution: *Handle the heating and air conditioning unit carefully during removal to avoid accidental damage to the interior.*

12 On 2014 and later models (except Rogue Select models), remove the front foot duct screws and separate the duct from the left side of the heating and air conditioning unit.

13 Remove the heater core insulation to expose the heater core pipe bracket screws.

14 Remove the heater core pipe bracket screws and remove the bracket (see illustrations), if equipped.

15 On 2014 and later models (except Rogue Select models), remove the heater core cover fasteners and cover.

16 Slide out the heater core and remove it from the HVAC housing (see illustration).

17 Installation is the reverse of removal, noting the following:

Note: *Do not use old O-rings for the refrigerant lines, replace with new ones and apply compressor oil to them before installation.*

18 Refill the cooling system (see Chapter 1). Reconnect the battery and perform the necessary re-learn procedures (see Chapter 5). Check for leaks and proper system operation. Check the operation of all electrical components of the steering column and dash.

19 Have the air conditioning system recharged by the shop that discharged it.

11 Air conditioning compressor - removal and installation

Warning: *The air conditioning system is under high pressure. Do not loosen any fittings or remove any components until after the system has been discharged. Air conditioning refrigerant should be properly discharged into an EPA-approved container at a dealer service department or an automotive air conditioning repair facility. Always wear eye protection when disconnecting air conditioning system fittings.*

Warning: *Wait until the engine is completely cool before beginning this procedure.*

1 Have the refrigerant discharged at a dealer service department or an automotive air conditioning repair facility.

Note: *If you are going to install a new compressor, inform the shop doing the work to record the amount of refrigerant oil recovered when the system is discharged (this measurement will be used when adding refrigerant oil to the system during installation.*

2 Disconnect the cable from the negative terminal of the battery (see Chapter 5).

3 Loosen the right front wheel lug nuts. Raise the vehicle and support it securely on jackstands. Remove the wheel and the inner fender splash shield (see Chapter 11).

4 Remove the splash guard underneath the engine.

5 Remove the fresh air intake duct (see Chapter 4).

6 Remove the drivebelt (see Chapter 1) and, on 2013 and earlier models/2014 and later Rogue Select models, remove the alternator (see Chapter 5).

11.8 Refrigerant line fitting fasteners

11.9 Remove the air conditioning compressor mounting bolts (lower bolt not shown)

7 Disconnect the electrical connector from the air conditioning compressor.

8 Remove the fasteners and disconnect the refrigerant lines from the compressor (see illustration).

Note: *Plug all open fittings to prevent entry of dirt and moisture into the lines.*

9 Remove the compressor mounting bolts and remove the compressor from the engine compartment (see illustration).

Note: *If a new compressor is being installed, the clutch assembly may have to be transferred to the new compressor. The removal of the clutch assembly will require the use of several special tools; this procedure should be performed by an air conditioning shop or dealer service department.*

10 If a new compressor is being installed, follow the directions with the compressor regarding the measuring and adding of oil prior to installation. Add to that the amount of oil measured during recovering of the refrigorant.

11 Installation is the reverse of removal. Tighten the compressor mounting bolts to the torque value listed in this Chapter's Specifications.

Note: *Do not use old O-rings for the refrigerant lines; replace them with new ones and apply compressor oil to them before installation.*

12 Reconnect the battery and perform the necessary re-learn procedures (see Chapter 5).

13 Have the system evacuated, charged and leak tested by the shop that discharged it.

12 Air conditioning condenser and liquid tank - removal and installation

12.6 Remove the hood latch support bolts, then rotate the support up and out of the way

Warning: *The models covered by this manual are equipped with a Supplemental Restraint System (SRS), more commonly known as airbags. Always disarm the airbag system before working in the vicinity of any airbag system component to avoid the possibility of accidental deployment of the airbag, which could cause personal injury (see Chapter 12). Do not use a memory saving device to preserve the PCM's memory when working on or near airbag system components.*

Warning: *The air conditioning system is under high pressure. Do not loosen any fittings or remove any components until after the system has been discharged. Air conditioning refrigerant should be properly discharged into an EPA-approved container at a dealer service department or an automotive air conditioning repair facility. Always wear eye protection when disconnecting air conditioning system fittings.*

Note: *The liquid tank is also known as the receiver-drier.*

1 On 2014 and later models (except Rogue Select models), the liquid tank is part of the condenser and is not serviceable.

2 Have the refrigerant discharged at a dealer service department or an automotive air conditioning repair facility.

3 Disconnect the cable from the negative terminal of the battery (see Chapter 5).

4 Remove air inlet duct (see Chapter 4).

5 Remove the bumper cover (see Chapter 11).

Note: *On 2014 and later models (except Rogue Select models), remove the right headlight housing (see Chapter 12).*

6 Remove the hood latch support bolts (see illustration), then rotate the support up and out of the way. It is not necessary to disconnect the electrical connectors or latch cable.

Warning: *The front crash zone sensor is mounted to the radiator support panel. Do not drop or hit the sensor when moving the radiator support panel.*

12.7a Disconnect the refrigerant line from the left-lower side of the condenser . . .

12.7b . . . and the right-upper side of the condenser

12.8 Disconnect the refrigerant pressure sensor electrical connector (1) and remove the pressure sensor (2) from the liquid tank (3)

7 Remove the refrigerant line fitting bolts and disconnect the lines from the condenser (see illustrations).

Note: *Plug all open fittings to prevent entry of dirt and moisture into the lines.*

8 Disconnect the electrical connector from the refrigerant pressure sensor (see illustration).

9 Remove the pressure sensor from the liquid tank attached to the condenser.

10 Remove the condenser-to-bracket fasteners and remove the condenser.

Caution: *Avoid damaging the condenser fins and tanks during removal.*

11 2013 and earlier models/2014 and later Rogue Select models: To detach the liquid tank from the condenser, remove the bolt at the bottom and the strap bolt mid-way up the tank, then detach the tank from the refrigerant line manifold at the bottom. If a new liquid tank is installed, add 0.4 ounce of refrigerant oil to the system.

12 Installation is the reverse of removal. If a new condenser was installed, add 1.2 ounces of refrigerant oil to the system.

Note: *Do not use old O-rings for the refrigerant lines; replace them with new ones and apply compressor oil to them before installation.*

13 Reconnect the battery and perform the necessary re-learn procedures (see Chapter 5).

14 Have the system evacuated, charged and leak tested by the shop that discharged it.

13 Expansion valve - removal and installation

Warning: *The air conditioning system is under high pressure. Do not loosen any fittings or remove any components until after the system has been discharged. Air conditioning refrigerant should be properly discharged into an EPA-approved container at a dealer service department or an automotive air conditioning repair facility. Always wear eye protection when disconnecting air conditioning system fittings.*

1 Have the refrigerant discharged at a dealer service department or an automotive air conditioning repair facility.

2 Move aside the lower dash insulation to access the expansion valve pipe.

3 Remove the cowl extension cover (see Chapter 11).

4 Remove the refrigerant line-to-expansion valve bolts and disconnect the refrigerant lines (see illustration 10.6).

5 Remove the expansion valve mounting bolts and remove the expansion valve.

6 Installation is the reverse of removal. Tighten the expansion valve bolts to the torque listed in this Chapter's Specifications.

Note: *Do not use old O-rings for the refrigerant lines; replace them with new ones and apply compressor oil to them before installation.*

7 Have the system evacuated, charged and leak tested by the shop that discharged it.

14 Evaporator - removal and installation

Warning: *The models covered by this manual are equipped with a Supplemental Restraint System (SRS), more commonly known as airbags. Always disarm the airbag system before working in the vicinity of any airbag system component to avoid the possibility of accidental deployment of the airbag, which could cause personal injury (see Chapter 12). Do not use a memory saving device to preserve the PCM's memory when working on or near airbag system components.*

Warning: *The air conditioning system is under high pressure. Do not loosen any fittings or remove any components until after the system has been discharged. Air conditioning refrigerant should be properly discharged into an EPA-approved container at a dealer service department or an automotive air conditioning repair facility. Always wear eye protection when disconnecting air conditioning system fittings.*

Note: *Replacement of the evaporator core is a difficult procedure for the home mechanic, involving removal of the entire dashboard, console, and many wiring connectors. If you attempt it at home, keep track of the assemblies by taking notes and keeping screws and other hardware in small, marked plastic bags for reassembly.*

1 Have the refrigerant discharged at a dealer service department or an automotive air conditioning repair facility.

2 Remove the expansion valve (see Section 13).

3 Drain the cooling system (see Chapter 1). If the coolant is relatively new, or is in good condition, save it and re-use it.

4 Move aside the lower dash insulation to access the heater core pipes.

5 Disconnect the heater hoses from the pipes protruding through the firewall (see illustration 10.5).

6 Disconnect the refrigerant lines from the evaporator.

Note: *Plug all open fittings of disconnected lines to prevent entry of dirt and moisture into the lines.*

7 Remove the steering column (see Chapter 11).

8 Remove the entire instrument panel assembly (see Chapter 11).

9 Disconnect the connectors for the following:

- *a) Shift lock cable*
- *b) Steering harness clips*
- *c) Super Multiple Junction (SMJ)*
- *d) Fuse box*
- *e) Door harness*
- *f) Front pillar harness*
- *g) Gear shift cable*
- *h) Air conditioning drain hose*
- *i) Airbag module control unit*

10 Disconnect the evaporator drain hose.

11 Remove the instrument panel support beam and the heating and air conditioning unit as a complete assembly, and place the assembly on a work bench.

Caution: *Handle the heating and air conditioning unit and steering member assembly carefully during removal to avoid accidental damage to the interior.*

2013 and earlier models/2014 and later Rogue Select models

12 Remove the evaporator lower case cover fasteners and side case cover fasteners then remove both covers.

13 Slide the evaporator out of the HVAC housing.

2014 and later models (except Rogue Select models)

14 Remove the heater core (see Section 10).

15 Remove the intake air door motor fasteners and motor.

16 Remove the mix air door motor fasteners and motor.

17 Separate the HVAC housing and remove the evaporator.

All models

18 Installation is the reverse of removal, noting the following:

- *a) Do not use old O-rings for the refrigerant lines, replace with new ones and apply compressor oil to them before installation.*
- *b) If a new evaporator was installed, add 2.5 ounces of refrigerant oil to the system.*
- *c) Tighten the expansion valve bolts to the torque listed in this Chapter's Specifications.*
- *d) Refill the cooling system (see Chapter 1). Reconnect the battery and perform the necessary re-learn procedures (see Chapter 5). Check for leaks and proper system operation. Check the operation of all electrical components of the steering column and dash.*

19 Have the air conditioning system recharged by the shop that discharged it.

Notes

Chapter 4
Fuel and exhaust systems

Contents

Specifications

Fuel system pressure, at idle (approximate) .... 51 psi

Torque specifications

Ft-lbs (unless otherwise indicated)

Note: *One foot-pound (ft-lb) of torque is equivalent to 12 inch-pounds (in-lbs) of torque. Torque values below approximately 15 ft-lbs are expressed in inch-pounds, because most foot-pound torque wrenches are not accurate at these smaller values.*

Fuel rail mounting bolts	
2013 and earlier models/2014 and later Rogue Select models	16
2014 and later models (except Rogue Select models)	18
Throttle body mounting fasteners	
2013 and earlier models/2014 and later Rogue Select models	74 in-lbs
2014 and later models (except Rogue Select models)	62 in-lbs

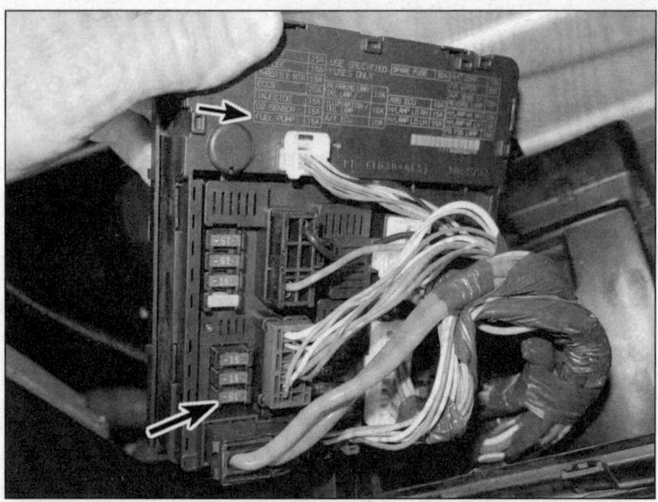

2.2 The fuel pump fuse is located in the engine compartment on the Intelligent Power Distribution Module (IPDM) (this is a 2013 model; be sure check the legend on the IPDM for the fuse location on your vehicle)

2.9 An automotive stethoscope is used to listen to the fuel injectors in operation

1 General information

Fuel system warnings

1 Gasoline is extremely flammable and repairing fuel system components can be dangerous. Consider your automotive repair knowledge and experience before attempting repairs which may be better suited for a professional mechanic.

a) *Don't smoke or allow open flames or bare light bulbs near the work area*
b) *Don't work in a garage with a gas-type appliance (water heater, clothes dryer)*
c) *Use fuel-resistant gloves. If any fuel spills on your skin, wash it off immediately with soap and water*
d) *Clean up spills immediately*
e) *Do not store fuel-soaked rags where they could ignite*
f) *Prior to disconnecting any fuel line, you must relieve the fuel pressure (see Section 3)*
g) *Wear safety glasses*
h) *Have a proper fire extinguisher on hand*

Fuel system

2 The fuel system consists of the fuel tank, electric fuel pump/fuel level sending unit (located in the fuel tank), fuel rail and fuel injectors. The fuel injection system is a multi-port system; multi-port fuel injection uses timed impulses to inject the fuel directly into the intake port of each cylinder. The Powertrain Control Module (PCM) controls the injectors. The PCM monitors various engine parameters and delivers the exact amount of fuel required into the intake ports.

3 Fuel is circulated from the fuel pump to the fuel rail through fuel lines running along the underside of the vehicle. Various sections of the fuel line are either rigid metal or nylon, or flexible fuel hose. The various sections of the fuel hose are connected either by quick-connect fittings or threaded metal fittings.

Exhaust system

4 The exhaust system consists of the exhaust manifold(s), catalytic converter(s), muffler(s), tailpipe and all connecting pipes, flanges and clamps. The catalytic converters are an emission control device added to the exhaust system to reduce pollutants.

2 Troubleshooting

Fuel pump

1 The fuel pump is located inside the fuel tank. Sit inside the vehicle with the windows closed, turn the ignition key to ON (not START) and listen for the sound of the fuel pump as it's briefly activated. You will only hear the sound for a second or two, but that sound tells you that the pump is working. Alternatively, have an assistant listen at the fuel filler cap.

2 If the pump does not come on, check the fuel pump fuse (see illustration). If the fuse is okay, check the wiring back to the fuel pump. If the fuse and wiring are okay, the pump might be defective. Other possibilities include a faulty fuel pump relay, which also part of the Intelligent Power Distribution Module (which is part of the underhood fuse/relay box), or a faulty Powertrain Control Module (PCM). If the pump runs continuously with the ignition key in the ON position, the Powertrain Control Module (PCM) is probably defective. Have the PCM checked by a professional mechanic.

Fuel injection system

Note: *The following procedure is based on the assumption that the fuel pump is working and the fuel pressure is adequate (see Section 4).*

3 Check all electrical connectors that are related to the system. Check the ground wire connections for tightness.

4 Verify that the battery is fully charged (see Chapter 5).

5 Inspect the air filter element (see Chapter 1).

6 Check all fuses related to the fuel system (see Chapter 12).

7 Check the air induction system between the throttle body and the intake manifold for air leaks. Also inspect the condition of all vacuum hoses connected to the intake manifold and to the throttle body.

8 Remove the air intake duct from the throttle body and look for dirt, carbon, varnish, or other residue in the throttle body, particularly around the throttle plate. If it's dirty, clean it with carb cleaner, a toothbrush and a clean shop towel.

9 With the engine running, place an automotive stethoscope against each injector, one at a time, and listen for a clicking sound that indicates operation (see illustration).

Warning: *Stay clear of the drivebelt and any rotating or hot components.*

10 If you can hear the injectors operating, but the engine is misfiring, the electrical circuits are functioning correctly, but the injectors might be dirty or clogged. Try a commercial injector cleaning product (available at auto parts stores). If cleaning the injectors doesn't help, replace the injectors.

11 If an injector is not operating (it makes no sound), disconnect the injector electrical connector and measure the resistance across the injector terminals with an ohmmeter. Compare this measurement to the other injectors. If the resistance of the non-operational injector is quite different from the other injectors, replace it.

12 If the injector is not operating, but the resistance reading is within the range of resistance of the other injectors, the PCM or the circuit between the PCM and the injector might be faulty.

4.1a Remove the safety cover from the quick disconnect fuel line connector

4.1b Insert the special fuel line disconnect tool into the fuel line

4.1c Using upward pressure, push the tool into the fuel line to unlock the fuel line connector

4.1d Remove the fuel line from the fuel rail

4.1e Use a fuel pressure gauge with hoses and fittings suitable for tee-ing into the fuel line at the fuel rail

3 Fuel pressure relief procedure

Warning: *Gasoline is extremely flammable. See* Fuel system warnings *in Section 1.*

Note: *After the fuel pressure has been relieved, it's a good idea to lay a shop towel over any fuel connection to be disassembled, to absorb the residual fuel that may leak out when servicing the fuel system.*

1 Remove the fuel pump fuse from the IPDM underhood fuse/relay box,located next to the battery (see illustration 2.2).

2 Start the engine and allow it to run until it stops. This should take only a few seconds. Disconnect the cable from the negative terminal of the battery before working on the fuel system (see Chapter 5).

3 The fuel system pressure is now relieved. It is a good idea to surround any fuel line that will be disconnected with a shop rag to catch fuel that might spill out.

4 When you're finished working on the fuel system, install the fuel pump fuse back into the fuse panel, connect the negative cable to the battery and perform the necessary relearn procedures (see Chapter 5).

4 Fuel pressure - check

Warning: *Gasoline is extremely flammable. See* Fuel system warnings *in Section 1.*

Note: *To perform the fuel pressure test, you will need to obtain a special fuel pressure gauge and adapter set (fuel line fittings).*

1 Relieve the fuel pressure (see Section 3). Disconnect the quick-connect fuel supply line fitting at the fuel rail (see illustrations). You must connect a special tee adapter in the line that incorporates a fuel pressure gauge. This special tee can be purchased or you can fabricate your own out of various fittings, hose and hose clamps (see illustration).

2 With the gauge connected and leak-tested, start the engine and allow it to idle. Note the gauge reading as soon as it stabilizes and compare it with the pressure listed inthis Chapter's Specifications.

3 If the fuel pressure is out of specification, check the following:

a) *If the pressure is lower than specified, check for a restriction in the fuel system (kinked fuel line, plugged fuel pump inlet strainer or clogged fuel filter). If no restrictions are found, replace the fuel pump module (seeSection 7).*

b) *If the fuel pressure is higher than specified, replace the fuel pump module (seeSection 7).*

4 Turn off the key. Fuel pressure should not fall more than 8 psi over five minutes. If it does, the problem could be a leaky fuel injector, fuel line leak, or faulty fuel pump module.

5 Disconnect the fuel pressure gauge. Wipe up any spilled gasoline.

Disconnecting Fuel Line Fittings

Two-tab type fitting; depress both tabs with your fingers, then pull the fuel line and the fitting apart

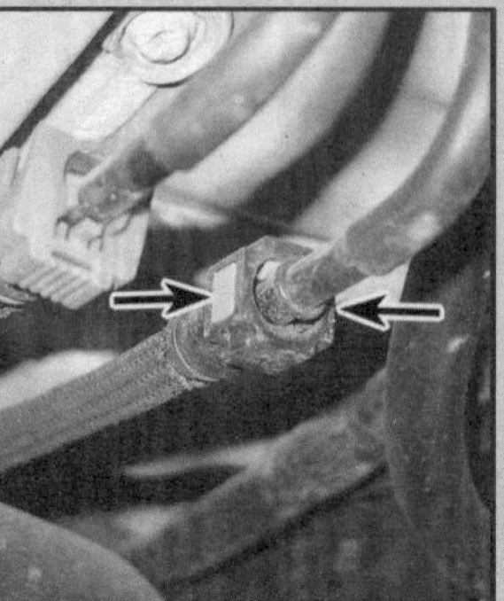

On this type of fitting, depress the two buttons on opposite sides of the fitting, then pull it off the fuel line

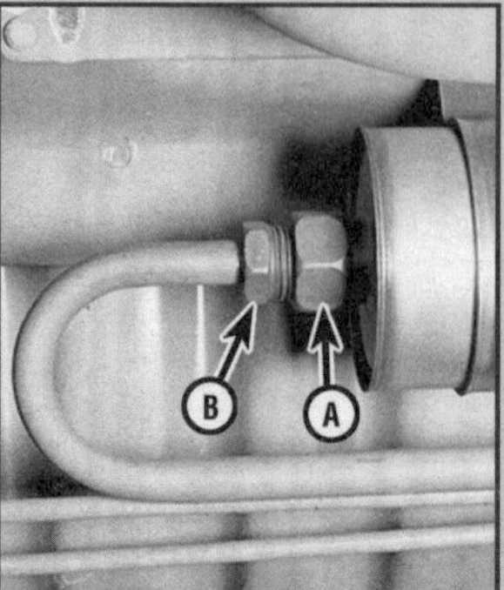

Threaded fuel line fitting; hold the stationary portion of the line or component (A) while loosening the tube nut (B) with a flare-nut wrench

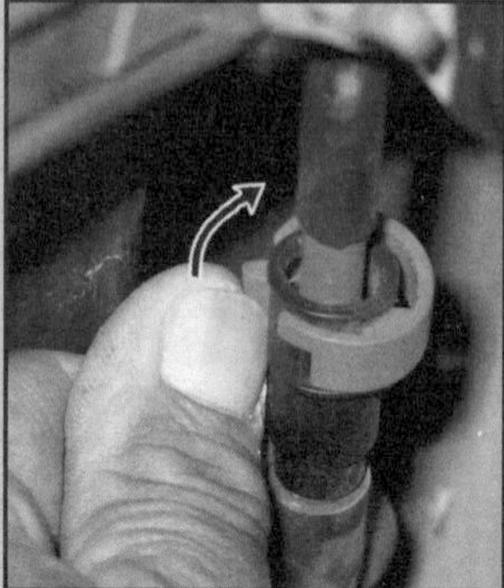

Plastic collar-type fitting; rotate the outer part of the fitting

Metal collar quick-connect fitting; pull the end of the retainer off the fuel line and disengage the other end from the female side of the fitting . . .

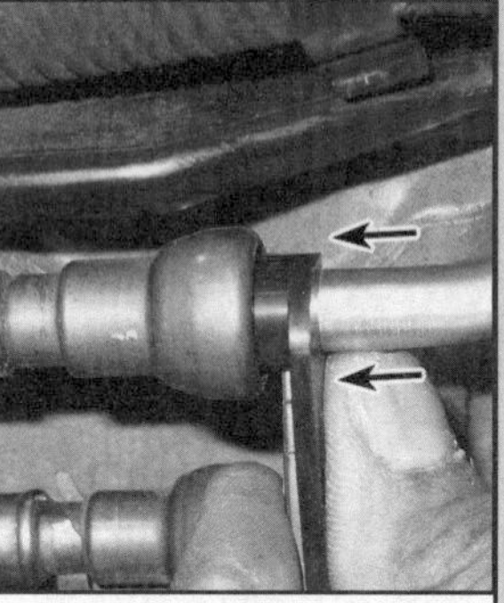

. . . insert a fuel line separator tool into the female side of the fitting, push it into the fitting and pull the fuel line off the pipe

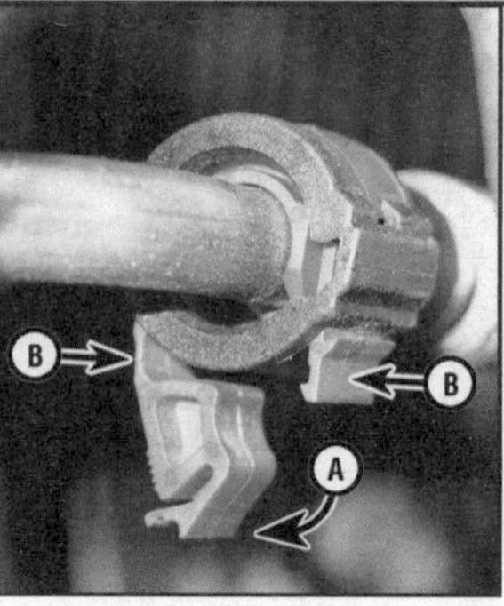

Some fittings are secured by lock tabs. Release the lock tab (A) and rotate it to the fully-opened position, squeeze the two smaller lock tabs (B) . . .

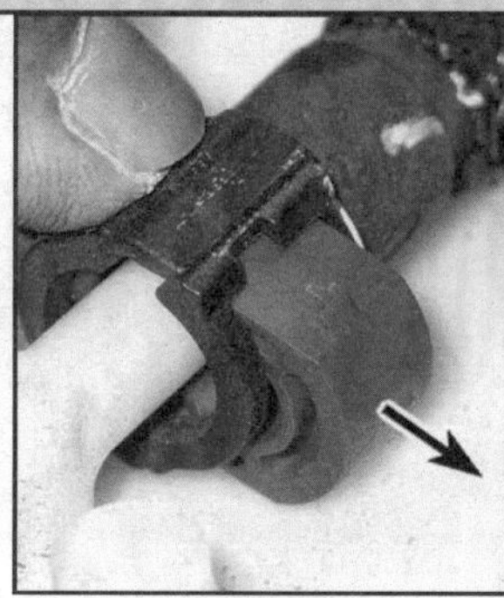

. . . then push the retainer out and pull the fuel line off the pipe

Spring-lock coupling; remove the safety cover, install a coupling release tool and close the tool around the coupling . . .

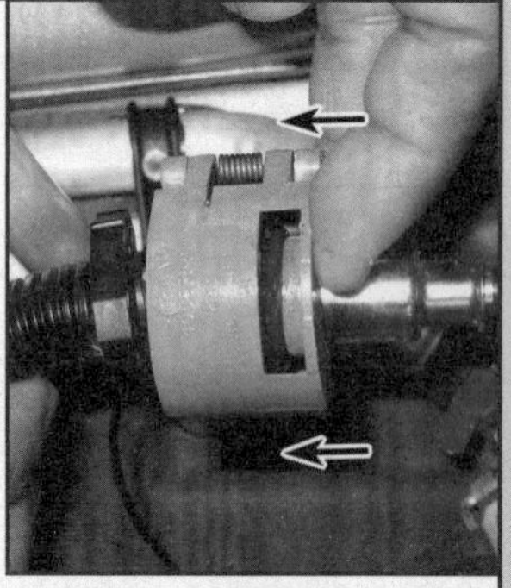

. . . push the tool into the fitting, then pull the two lines apart

Hairpin clip type fitting: push the legs of the retainer clip together, then push the clip down all the way until it stops and pull the fuel line off the pipe

5 Fuel lines and fittings - general information and disconnection

Warning: *Gasoline is extremely flammable. See* Fuel system warnings *in Section 1.*

1 Relieve the fuel pressure before servicing fuel lines or fittings (see Section 3), then disconnect the cable from the negative battery terminal (see Chapter 5) before proceeding.

2 The fuel supply line connects the fuel pump in the fuel tank to the fuel rail on the engine. The Evaporative Emission (EVAP) system lines connect the fuel tank to the EVAP canister and connect the canister to the intake manifold.

3 Whenever you're working under the vehicle, be sure to inspect all fuel and evaporative emission lines for leaks, kinks, dents and other damage. Always replace a damaged fuel or EVAP line immediately.

4 If you find signs of dirt in the lines during disassembly, disconnect all lines and blow them out with compressed air. Inspect the fuel strainer on the fuel pump pick-up unit for damage and deterioration.

Steel tubing

5 It is criticalthat the fuel lines be replaced with lines of equivalent type and specification.

6 Some steel fuel lines have threaded fittings. When loosening these fittings, hold the stationary fitting with a wrench while turning the tube nut.

Plastic tubing

7 When replacing fuel system plastic tubing, use only original equipment replacement plastic tubing.

Caution: *When removing or installing plastic fuel line tubing, be careful not to bend or twist it too much, which can damage it. Also, plastic fuel tubing is NOT heat resistant, so keep it away from excessive heat.*

Flexible hoses

8 When replacing fuel system flexible hoses, use only original equipment replacements.

9 Don't route fuel hoses (or metal lines) within four inches of the exhaust system or within ten inches of the catalytic converter. Make sure that no rubber hoses are installed directly against the vehicle, particularly in places where there is any vibration. If allowed to touch some vibrating part of the vehicle, a hose can easily become chafed and it might start leaking. A good rule of thumb is to maintain a minimum of 1/4-inch clearance around a hose (or metal line) to prevent contact with the vehicle underbody.

6 Exhaust system servicing - general information

Warning: *Allow exhaust system components to cool before inspection or repair. Also, when working under the vehicle, make sure it is securely supported on jackstands.*

1 The exhaust system consists of the exhaust manifolds, catalytic converter, muffler, tailpipe and all connecting pipes, flanges and clamps. The exhaust system is isolated from the vehicle body and from chassis components by a series of rubber hangers. Periodically inspect these hangers for cracks or other signs of deterioration, replacing them as necessary (see illustration).

2 Conduct regular inspections of the exhaust system to keep it safe and quiet. Look for any damaged or bent parts, open seams, holes, loose connections, excessive corrosion or other defects which could allow exhaust fumes to enter the vehicle. Do not repair deteriorated exhaust system components; replace them with new parts.

3 If the exhaust system components are extremely corroded, or rusted together, a cutting torch is the most convenient tool for removal. Consult a properly-equipped repair shop. If a cutting torch is not available, you can use a hacksaw, or if you have compressed air, there are special pneumatic cutting chisels that can also be used. Wear safety goggles to protect your eyes from metal chips and wear work gloves to protect your hands.

4 Here are some simple guidelines to follow when repairing the exhaust system:

- a) *Work from the back to the front when removing exhaust system components.*
- b) *Apply penetrating oil to the exhaust system component fasteners to make them easier to remove.*
- c) *Use new gaskets, hangers and clamps.*
- d) *Apply anti-seize compound to the threads of all exhaust system fasteners during reassembly.*
- e) *Allow sufficient clearance between newly installed parts and all points on the underbody to avoid overheating the floor pan and possibly damaging the interior carpet and insulation. Pay particularly close attention to the catalytic converter and heat shield.*

7 Fuel pump/fuel level sensor module - removal and installation

Warning: *Gasoline is extremely flammable. See* Fuel system warnings *in Section 1.*

Warning: *If the tank is more than 3/4 full, insert a hose into the fuel filler neck and draw-off at least four gallons of fuel using a siphoning kit (available at most auto parts stores) before beginning work.*

Note: *The fuel pump/fuel level sensor module is on the right side of the fuel tank; the sub fuel level sensor module is on the left side of the tank.*

Fuel pump/fuel level sensor module

Removal

1 Relieve the fuel pressure (see Section 3).

2 Disconnect the cable from the negative terminal of the battery (see Chapter 5).

3 Remove the rear seat cushion (see Chapter 11).

4 Remove the access cover for the fuel pump/fuel level sending unit assembly (see illustration).

6.1 Rear muffler uses rubber exhaust hangers for mounting

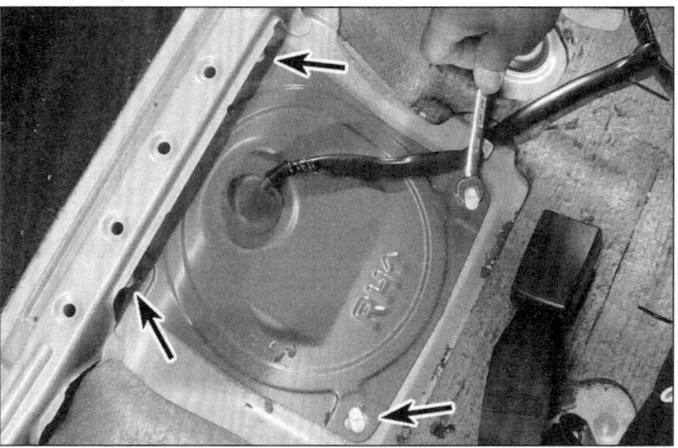

7.4 Turn the fuel pump/fuel level sensor access cover fasteners 90 degrees to remove the cover

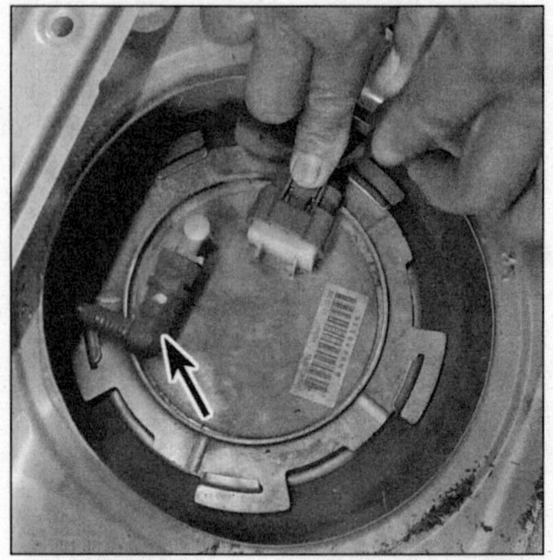
7.5 Depress the tab and disconnect the electrical connector, then detach the fuel feed hose

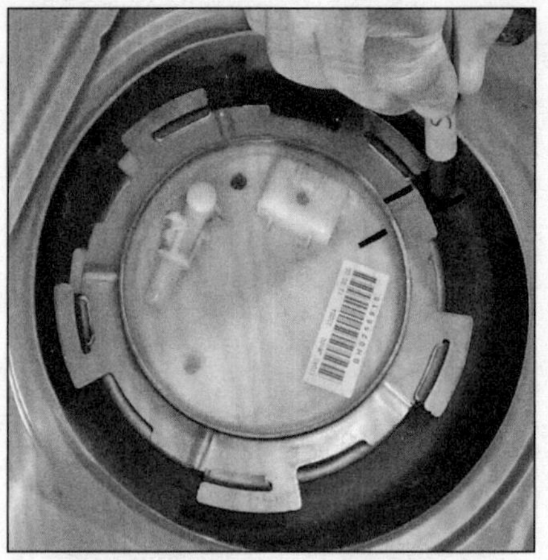
7.7 Make a set of matching marks for correct alignment of the locking ring on installation

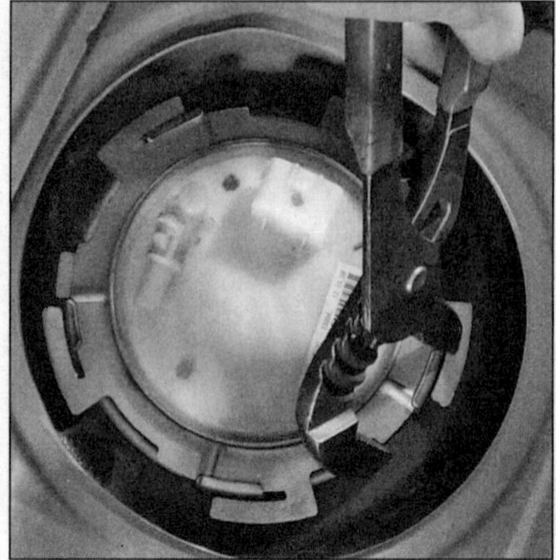
7.8a Some models have a metal lock ring; channel locking pliers can be used to turn it counterclockwise to remove it

7.8b On other models, the module is retained by a plastic lock ring; use a special lock ring removal tool (available at most auto parts stores) to unscrew it

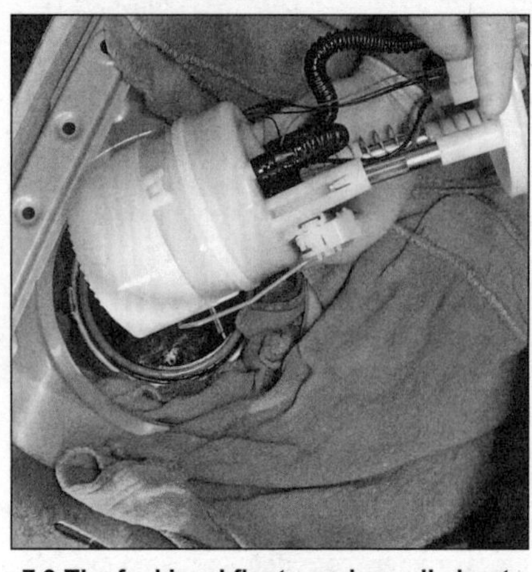
7.9 The fuel level float arm is easily bent, so proceed carefully when lifting the fuel pump module out

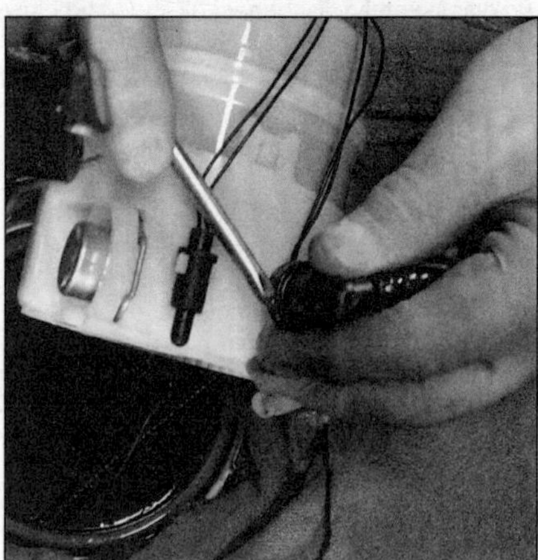
7.10 To remove the quick-connector, hold the sides of the connector, push in the tabs, and pull out the tube

5 Disconnect the electrical connector from the fuel pump/fuel level sending unit (see illustration).

6 Disconnect the fuel supply line from the fuel level sending unit/fuel pump assembly.

Note: *To remove the quick connector, hold the sides of the connector, push in the tabs, and pull off the tube.*

7 Make a mark across the top of the module, locking ring and the fuel tank (see illustration) to aid in correct alignment when the assembly is reinstalled.

8 Turn the fuel pump/fuel level sensor module lock ring counterclockwise (see illustrations), then remove it.

Caution: *The manufacturer recommends that the metal lock ring and the O-ring (on all models) be replaced with new ones.*

9 Lift the fuel pump module from the fuel tank. Manipulate it as you lift so you don't bend the float arm (see illustration).

10 If equipped, disconnect the fuel tube quick-connector at the bottom of the module (see illustration), then remove the module.

Note: *On AWD models and all 2014 and later models, disconnect the sub fuel level sensor module harness electrical connector.*

Fuel level sensor replacement

11 Squeeze the retaining tangs and remove the fuel level sensor from the module frame (see illustration). To install, slide the sensor onto the frame until the tangs click into place.

Installation

12 Replace the O-ring seal (see illustration).

13 Connect the fuel tube quick connector at the bottom of the module (see illustration 7.10), and sub fuel level sensor module harness electrical connectors, if equipped.

14 Carefully lower the fuel pump module into the fuel tank.

15 Position the assembly so the two plastic tangs are facing the front of the vehicle (see illustration).

16 Install and tighten the lock ring.

17 Reconnect the hoses and electrical connector, then reinstall the access cover.

18 Reinstall the rear seat cushion (see Chapter 11).

19 Reconnect the battery and perform the necessary re-learn procedures (see Chapter 5).

Sub fuel level sensor module

Note: *A second "sub" fuel level sensor module, located on the left side of the fuel tank, is used on AWD models and all 2014 and later models.*

Removal

20 Relieve the fuel pressure (see Section 3).

21 Disconnect the cable from the negative terminal of the battery (see Chapter 5).

22 Remove the rear seat cushion (see Chapter 11).

23 Remove the fuel pump/fuel level sensor module and disconnect the wiring harness and fuel tube (see Steps 4 through 10). Connect a length of fuel-resistant wire or rope to the fuel tube and wiring harness (this will be used to

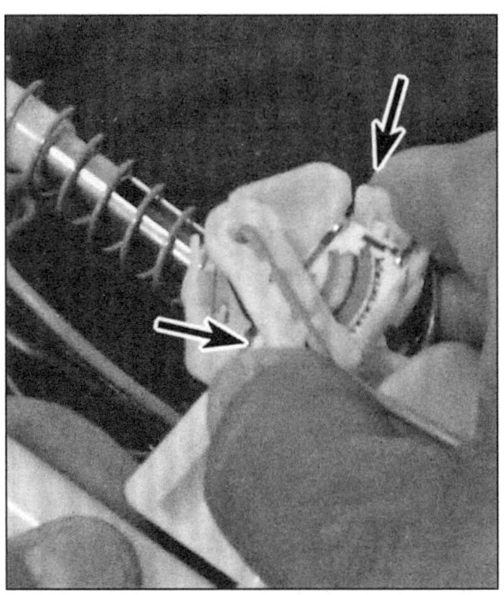

7.11 The fuel level sensor is secured with two retaining tangs; squeeze the tangs and slide the sensor off the module frame

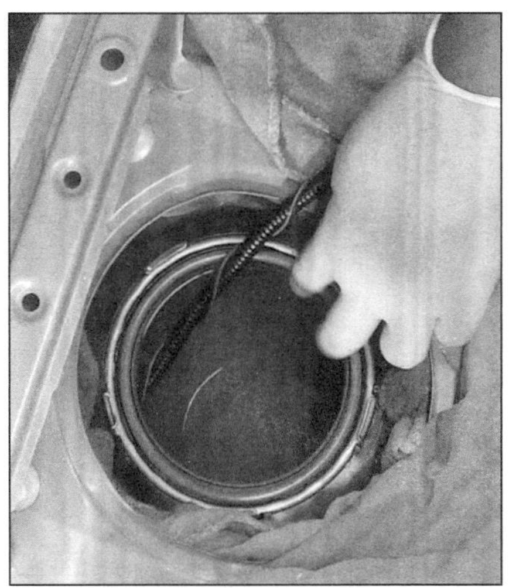

7.12 Install a new O-ring seal

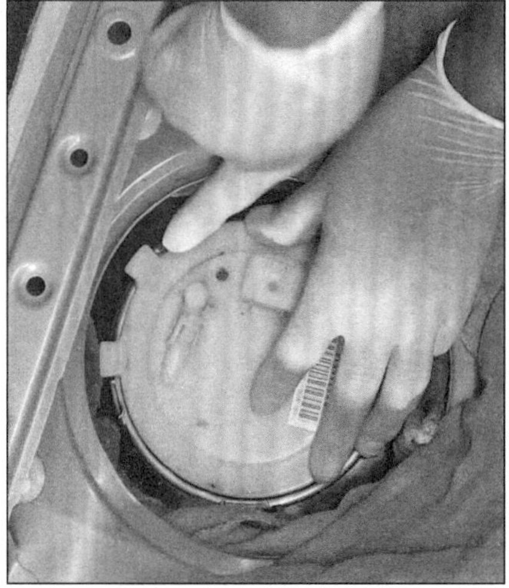

7.15 The fuel pump tangs must point to the front of the vehicle for correct alignment

pull the tube and harness back through the tank during installation).

24 Locate the inspection hole cover on the driver's side of the vehicle, then turn the cover fasteners 90 degrees and remove the access cover for the sub fuel level sensor assembly (see illustration 7.4).

25 Make a mark across the top of the module, locking ring and the fuel tank (see illustration 7.7) to aid in correct alignment when the assembly is reinstalled.

26 Remove the lock ring (see illustrations 7.8a and 7.8b).

Note: *The manufacturer recommends that the metal lock ring and the O-ring (on all models) be replaced with new ones.*

27 Lift the sub fuel level sensor module from the fuel tank. Manipulate it as you lift so you don't bend the float arm.

28 Remove the module until the wire or rope connected to the fuel tube is pulled out of the tank opening, then disconnect the wire or rope.

Caution: *The fuel tube is not removable from the sub fuel level sensor assembly, if the tube is damaged, the sub fuel level sensor assembly must be replaced.*

Installation

29 Replace the O-ring seal (see illustration 7.12).

30 Tie the wire or rope to the fuel tube and wiring harness, then carefully lower the sub fuel level sensor module into the fuel tank while pulling the rope or wire until the fuel tube reaches the fuel pump/level sensor module opening on the right side of the tank.

31 Rotate the assembly until the tabs are facing the front of the vehicle (see illustration 7.15).

32 Reconnect the fuel tube and electrical connector to the fuel pump/fuel level sensor module.

33 Install the lock ring.

34 Install the fuel pump/fuel level sensor module (see Steps 12 through 17).

35 Reinstall the access covers and the rear seat cushion (see Chapter 11).

36 Reconnect the battery and perform the necessary re-learn procedures (see Chapter 5).

8 Fuel tank - removal and installation

Warning: *Gasoline is extremely flammable. See Fuel system warnings in Section 1.*

Note: *The following procedure is much easier to perform if the fuel tank is empty. Drain the fuel into an approved fuel container using a commercially available siphoning kit (NEVER start the siphoning action by mouth) or wait until the fuel tank is nearly empty, if possible.*

1 Remove the fuel tank filler cap to relieve fuel tank pressure.

2 Relieve the fuel system pressure (see Section 3).

3 Disconnect the cable from the negative terminal of the battery (see Chapter 5).

4 Disconnect the lines and wiring from the fuel pump module at the top of the fuel tank. If desired, the fuel pump module can be removed at this time (see Section 7).

5 Raise the vehicle and place it securely on jackstands.

6 If there is still fuel in the tank, siphon it out from the fuel feed line. Remember - NEVER start the siphoning action by mouth! Use a siphoning kit, which can be purchased at most auto parts stores.

7 Remove the exhaust pipe and muffler assembly.

8 Remove the fuel tank heat shield mounting nuts and heat shield.

9 Disconnect the hoses and electrical connector from the fuel tank (see illustration 7.5).

10 On AWD models, remove the rear driveshaft (see Chapter 8).

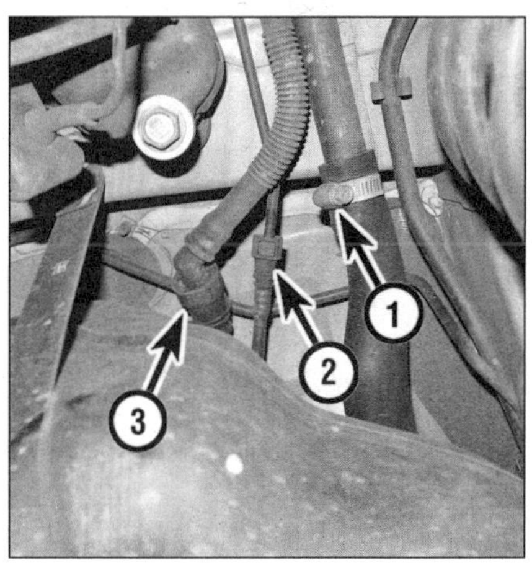

8.13 Disconnect the hoses near the right-rear corner of the fuel tank

1 *Fuel tank filler hose*
2 *Fuel line*
3 *EVAP canister vent hose*

11 On 2014 and earlier Rogue models/2014 and 2015 Rogue Select models, remove the rear subframe (see Chapter 10, Section14).

12 Disconnect the parking brake cables from their brackets. Move the cables aside and secure them in place with wire.

13 Loosen the fuel filler hose clamp and remove the fuel filler hose from the fuel tank (see illustration). Also disconnect the vent and EVAP hoses.

14 Support the fuel tank with a floor jack. Position a wood plank between the jack head and the fuel tank to protect the tank.

15 Remove the fuel tank strap bolts.

16 Remove the tank from the vehicle.

17 Installation is the reverse of removal.

18 Reconnect the battery and perform the necessary re-learn procedures (see Chapter 5).

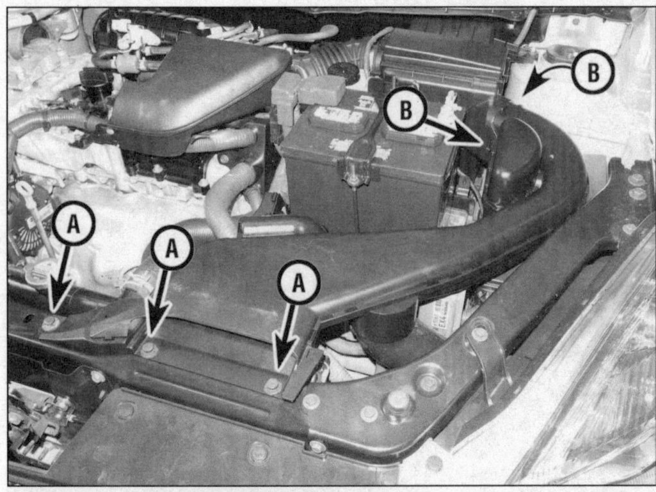

9.1 Remove the plastic fasteners (A) at the front of the air inlet duct, then free the rear of the duct from the clips on the air filter housing (B)

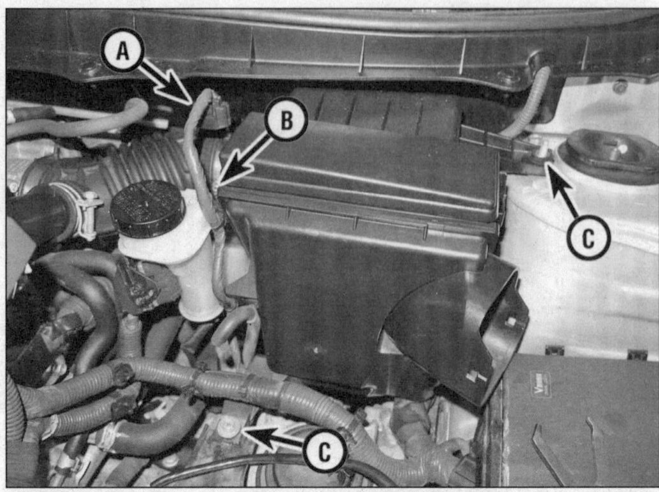

9.4a Disconnect the electrical connector from the MAF sensor (A), loosen the hose clamp (B) and remove the air filter housing fasteners (C) . . .

9.4b . . . then lift the air filter housing straight up and rotate it forward until it clears the cowl panel

9.13 Loosen the hose clamp at the air intake duct (A) and crankcase ventilation hose (B), then remove the resonator bolt (C)

9.18 Remove the air duct from the top of the resonator

9 Air filter housing and resonators - removal and installation

Air filter housing

2013 and earlier models/2014 and later Rogue Select models

1 Remove the air inlet duct (see illustration).

2 Remove the battery and battery tray (see Chapter 5).

3 Disconnect the electrical connector from the MAF sensor, then loosen the hose clamp on the duct at the air filter housing.

4 Remove the air filter housing fasteners (see illustrations).

5 Installation is the reverse of removal.

2014 and later Rogue models (except Rogue Select)

6 Remove the cowl cover (see Chapter 11).

7 Remove the resonator/air inlet duct assembly fasteners.

8 Release the filter housing clips and pull the air filter housing forward enough to unhook the resonator air inlet duct from the locking tab on the air filter housing.

9 Remove air inlet duct between the air filter housing and throttle body.

10 Disconnect the electrical connector from the MAF sensor.

11 Lift the air filter housing up and over the battery, and out of the vehicle.

12 Installation is the reverse of removal.

Resonator

Upper resonator

13 Loosen the clamp connecting the resonator to the air duct between the throttle body and air filter housing (see illustration).

14 Squeeze the hose clamp and slde it back on the crankcase ventilation hose, then disconnect the hose from the resonator.

15 Remove the resonator mounting bolt, then pull the resonator up and off of its grommet.

16 Installation is the reverse of removal.

Lower resonator

17 Remove the air inlet duct (see illustration 9.1).

18 Remove the air duct from the top of the resonator (see illustration).

9.20 Location of the resonator mounting fasteners - bumper cover removed for clarity

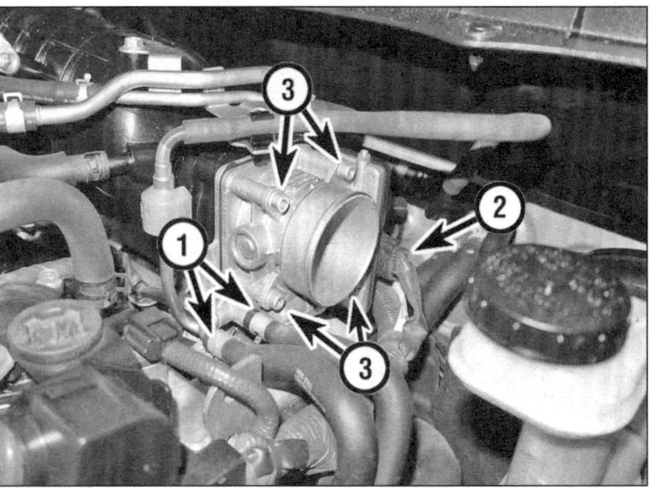

10.4 Throttle body details

1 Coolant hoses
2 Electrical connector
3 Mounting bolts (not all are visible in this photo)

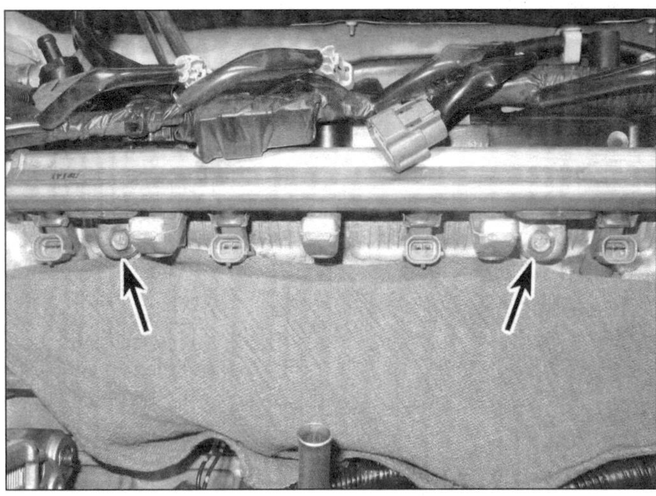

11.6 Fuel rail mounting bolts - 2013 and earlier models shown, later models similar

11.7 To free each injector from the fuel rail, pull off the retaining clip with a pair of pliers

19 Remove the inner fender splash shield (see Chapter11, Section 19).
20 Remove the resonator fasteners (see illustration), then remove the resonator through the wheel well opening.
21 Installation is the reverse of removal.

10 Throttle body - removal and installation

Warning: *The engine must be completely cool before beginning this procedure.*

1 Disconnect the cable from the negative terminal of the battery (see Chapter 5).
2 Remove the upper air intake resonator (see Section 9).
3 Remove the air duct between the throttle body and the air filter housing.
4 Clamp-off the coolant hoses to the throttle body, then disconnect them (see illustration).
5 Disconnect the electrical connector from the throttle body.
6 Loosen the throttle body mounting bolts a little at a time in a criss-cross pattern to prevent distortion.
7 Remove the throttle body.
8 Installation is the reverse of removal; use a new throttle body O-ring if the old one is not in perfect condition. Tighten the bolts a little at a time in a criss-cross pattern to the torque listed in this Chapter's Specifications.
9 Reconnect the battery and perform the necessary re-learn procedures (see Chapter 5).

11 Fuel rail and injectors - removal and installation

Warning: *Gasoline is extremely flammable. See Fuel system warnings in Section 1.*

1 Relieve the fuel system pressure (see Section 3).
2 Disconnect the cable from the negative terminal of the battery (see Chapter 5).
3 Disconnect the fuel supply line from the fuel rail (seeSection 4).
4 Remove the intake manifold (see Chapter 2A).
5 Disconnect the electrical connector from each fuel injector.
6 Remove the fuel rail mounting bolts (see illustration).
7 Remove the fuel injector retaining clips (see illustration).

11.8 Pull the injector straight out of its bore in the fuel rail

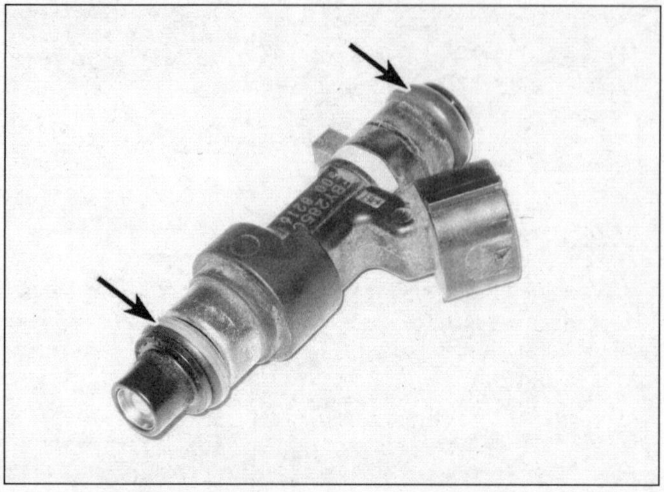

11.9 Whether you're installing new injectors or reusing the old ones, always remove the old O-rings and replace them with new ones

8 Remove the injectors from the fuel rail (see illustration), then remove and discard the O-rings.

9 Replace both O-rings of each fuel injector and lubricate them with clean engine oil prior to installation (see illustration).

Note: *There are two different O-rings used on each injector; they are color coded to make sure they are not installed improperly. On 2013 and earlier non-CA models, the upper O-ring (fuel rail side) is color coded blue and the lower O-ring (nozzle end) is color coded brown. On CA models and all 2014 and later models, the upper O-ring (fuel rail side) is color coded black and the lower O-ring (nozzle end) is color coded green.*

10 Install the injector retaining clips and insert each injector into its bore in the fuel rail until the retaining clip snaps into place (see illustration).

11 The remainder of installation is the reverse of removal.

12 Reconnect the battery and perform the necessary re-learn procedures (see Chapter 5).

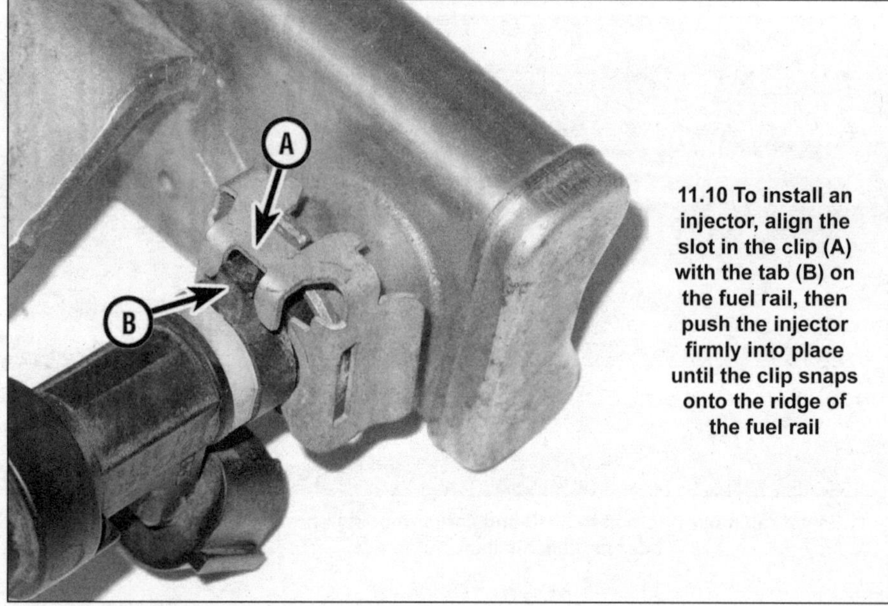

11.10 To install an injector, align the slot in the clip (A) with the tab (B) on the fuel rail, then push the injector firmly into place until the clip snaps onto the ridge of the fuel rail

Notes

Notes

Chapter 5
Engine electrical systems

Contents

Specifications

Charging voltage .... 13.5 to 14.5 volts

Torque specifications

Ft-lbs (unless otherwise indicated)

Note: *One foot-pound (ft-lb) of torque is equivalent to 12 inch-pounds (in-lbs) of torque. Torque values below approximately 15 ft-lbs are expressed in inch-pounds, because most foot-pound torque wrenches are not accurate at these smaller values.*

	Ft-lbs
Alternator bracket-to-cylinder bolts	48
Alternator mounting bolts	
2013 and earlier Rogue/2014 and 2015 Rogue Select models	48
2014 and later Rogue models	18
Starter mounting bolts	
2013 and earlier Rogue /2014 and 2015 Rogue Select models	37
2014 and later Rogue models	
Upper (long) bolt	50
Lower (short) bolt	33

1 General information and precautions

General information

Ignition system

1 The electronic ignition system consists of the Crankshaft Position (CKP) sensor, the Camshaft Position (CMP) sensor, the Knock Sensor (KS), the Powertrain Control Module (PCM), the ignition switch, the battery, the individual ignition coils or a coil pack, and the spark plugs. For more information on the CKP, CMP and KS sensors, as well as the PCM, refer to Chapter 6.

Charging system

2 The charging system includes the alternator (with an integral voltage regulator), the Powertrain Control Module (PCM), the Body Control Module (BCM), a charge indicator light on the dash, the battery, a fuse or fusible link and the wiring connecting all of these components. The charging system supplies electrical power for the ignition system, the lights, the radio, etc. The alternator is driven by a drivebelt.

Starting system

3 The starting system consists of the battery, the ignition switch, the starter relay, the Powertrain Control Module (PCM), the Body Control Module (BCM), the Transmission Range (TR) switch, the starter motor and solenoid assembly, and the wiring connecting all of the components.

Precautions

4 Always observe the following precautions when working on the electrical system:

a) *Be extremely careful when servicing engine electrical components. They are easily damaged if checked, connected or handled improperly.*
b) *Never leave the ignition switched on for long periods of time when the engine is not running.*
c) *Never disconnect the battery cables while the engine is running.*
d) *Maintain correct polarity when connecting battery cables from another vehicle during jump starting (see* Booster battery (jump) start starting *at the front of this manual, Section 7).*
e) *Always disconnect the cable from the negative battery terminal before working on the electrical system, but read the battery disconnection procedure first (see Section 3).*

5 It's also a good idea to review the safety-related information regarding the engine electrical systems located in electrical systems located in the *Safety first!* Section at the front of this manual before beginning any operation included in this Chapter.

2 Troubleshooting

Ignition system

1 If a malfunction occurs in the ignition system, do not immediately assume that any particular part is causing the problem. First, check the following items:

a) *Make sure that the cable clamps at the battery terminals are clean and tight.*
b) *Test the condition of the battery (see Steps 15 through 18). If it doesn't pass all the tests, replace it.*
c) *Check the ignition coil or coil pack connections.*
d) *Check any relevant fuses in the engine compartment fuse and relay box (see Chapter 12). If they're burned, determine the cause and repair the circuit.*

Check

Warning: *Because of the high voltage generated by the ignition system, use extreme care when performing a procedure involving ignition components.*

Note: *The ignition system components on these vehicles are difficult to diagnose. In the event of an ignition system failure that you can't diagnose, have the vehicle tested at a dealer service department or other qualified auto repair facility.*

Note: *You'll need a spark tester for the following test. Spark testers are available at most auto supply stores.*

2 If the engine turns over but won't start, verify that there is sufficient ignition voltage to fire the spark plugs as follows.

3 Remove a coil and install the tester between the boot at the lower end of the coil and the spark plug (see illustration).

4 Crank the engine and note whether or not the tester flashes.

Caution: *Do NOT crank the engine or allow it to run for more than five seconds; running the engine for more than five seconds may set a Diagnostic Trouble Code (DTC) for a cylinder misfire.*

5 If the tester flashes during cranking, the coil is delivering sufficient voltage to the spark plug to fire it. Repeat this test for each cylinder to verify that the other coils are OK.

6 If the tester doesn't flash, remove a coil from another cylinder and swap it for the one being tested. If the tester now flashes, you know that the original coil is bad. If the tester still doesn't flash, the PCM or wiring harness is probably defective. Have the PCM checked out by a dealer service department or other qualified repair shop (testing the PCM is beyond the scope of the do-it-yourselfer because it requires expensive special tools).

7 If the tester flashes during cranking but a misfire code (related to the cylinder being tested) has been stored, the spark plug could be fouled or defective.

Charging system

8 If a malfunction occurs in the charging system, do not automatically assume the alternator is causing the problem. First check the following items:

a) *Check the drivebelt tension and condition (see Chapter 1). Replace it if it's worn or deteriorated.*
b) *Make sure the alternator mounting bolts are tight.*
c) *Inspect the alternator wiring harness and the connectors at the alternator and voltage regulator. They must be in good condition, tight and have no corrosion.*
d) *Check the fusible link (if equipped) or main fuse in the underhood fuse/relay box. If it is burned, determine the cause, repair the circuit and replace the link or fuse (the vehicle will not start and/or the accessories will not work if the fusible link or main fuse is blown).*
e) *Start the engine and check the alternator for abnormal noises (a shrieking or squealing sound indicates a bad bearing).*
f) *Check the battery. Make sure it's fully charged and in good condition (one bad cell in a battery can cause overcharging by the alternator).*
g) *Disconnect the battery cables (negative first, then positive). Inspect the battery posts and the cable clamps for corrosion. Clean them thoroughly if necessary (see Chapter 1). Reconnect the cables (positive first, negative last).*

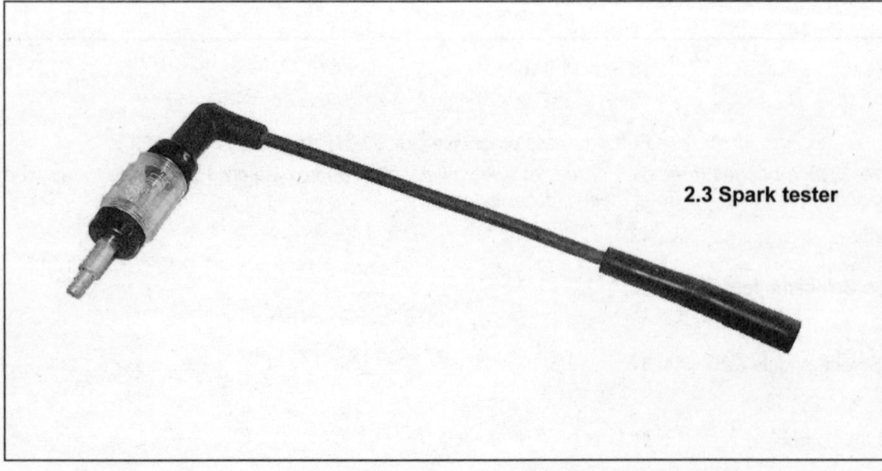

2.3 Spark tester

2.15 To test the open circuit voltage of the battery, touch the black probe of the voltmeter to the negative terminal and the red probe to the positive terminal of the battery; a fully charged battery should be at least 12.6 volts

2.17 Connect a battery load tester to the battery and check the battery condition under load following the tool manufacturer's instructions

Alternator - check

9 Use a voltmeter to check the battery voltage with the engine off. It should be at least 12.6 volts (see illustration 2.15).

10 Start the engine and check the battery voltage again. It should now be approximately 13.5 to 15 volts.

11 If the voltage reading is more or less than the specified charging voltage, the voltage regulator is probably defective, which will require replacement of the alternator (the voltage regulator is not replaceable separately). Remove the alternator and have it bench tested (most auto parts stores will do this for you).

12 The charging system (battery) light on the instrument cluster lights up when the ignition key is turned to ON, but it should go out when the engine starts.

13 If the charging system light stays on after the engine has been started, there is a problem with the charging system. Before replacing the alternator, check the battery condition, alternator belt tension and electrical cable connections.

14 If replacing the alternator doesn't restore voltage to the specified range, have the charging system tested by a dealer service department or other qualified repair shop.

Battery - check

Note: *The battery's surface charge must be removed before accurate voltage measurements can be made. Turn on the high beams for ten seconds, then turn them off and let the vehicle stand for two minutes.*

15 Check the battery state of charge. Visually inspect the indicator eye on the top of the battery (if equipped with one); if the indicator eye is black in color, charge the battery as described in Chapter 1. Next perform an open circuit voltage test using a digital voltmeter. With the engine and all accessories Off, touch the negative probe of the voltmeter to the negative terminal of the battery and the positive probe to the positive terminal of the battery (see illustration). The battery voltage should be 12.6 volts or slightly above. If the battery is less than the specified voltage, charge the battery before proceeding to the next test. Do not proceed with the battery load test unless the battery charge is correct.

16 Disconnect the negative battery cable, then the positive cable from the battery.

17 Perform a battery load test. An accurate check of the battery condition can only be performed with a load tester (see illustration). This test evaluates the ability of the battery to operate the starter and other accessories during periods of high current draw. Connect the load tester to the battery terminals. Load test the battery according to the tool manufacturer's instructions. This tool increases the load demand (current draw) on the battery.

18 Maintain the load on the battery for 15 seconds and observe that the battery voltage does not drop below 9.6 volts. If the battery condition is weak or defective, the tool will indicate this condition immediately.

Note: *Cold temperatures will cause the minimum voltage reading to drop slightly. Follow the chart given in the manufacturer's instructions to compensate for cold climates. Minimum load voltage for freezing temperatures (32 degrees F) should be approximately 9.1 volts.*

Starting system

The starter rotates, but the engine doesn't

19 Remove the starter (see Section 8). Check the overrunning clutch and bench test the starter to make sure the drive mechanism extends fully for proper engagement with the flywheel ring gear. If it doesn't, replace the starter.

20 Check the flywheel ring gear for missing teeth and other damage. With the ignition turned off, rotate the flywheel so you can check the entire ring gear.

The starter is noisy

21 If the solenoid is making a chattering noise, first check the battery (see Steps 15 through 18). If the battery is okay, check the cables and connections.

22 If you hear a grinding, crashing metallic sound when you turn the key to Start, check for loose starter mounting bolts. If they're tight, remove the starter and inspect the teeth on the starter pinion gear and flywheel ring gear. Look for missing or damaged teeth.

23 If the starter sounds fine when you first turn the key to Start, but then stops rotating the engine and emits a zinging sound, the problem is probably a defective starter drive that's not staying engaged with the ring gear. Replace the starter.

The starter rotates slowly

24 Check the battery (see Steps 15 through 18).

25 If the battery is okay, verify all connections (at the battery, the starter solenoid and motor) are clean, corrosion-free and tight. Make sure the cables aren't frayed or damaged.

26 Check that the starter mounting bolts are tight so it grounds properly. Also check the pinion gear and flywheel ring gear for evidence of a mechanical bind (galling, deformed gear teeth or other damage).

The starter does not rotate at all

27 Check the battery (see Steps 15 through 18).

28 If the battery is okay, verify all connections (at the battery, the starter solenoid and motor) are clean, corrosion-free and tight. Make sure the cables aren't frayed or damaged.

29 Check all of the fuses in the underhood fuse/relay box.

30 Check that the starter mounting bolts are tight so it grounds properly.

31 Check for voltage at the starter solenoid "S" terminal when the ignition key is turned to the start position. If voltage is present, replace the starter/solenoid assembly. If no voltage is present, the problem could be the starter relay, the Transmission Range (TR) switch (see Chapter 6) or clutch start switch (see Chapter 8), or with an electrical connector somewhere in the circuit (see the wiring diagrams at the end of Chapter 12). Also, on many modern vehicles, the Powertrain Control Module (PCM) and the Body Control Module (BCM) control the voltage signal to the starter solenoid; on such vehicles a special scan tool is required for diagnosis.

3 Battery - disconnection and reconnection

Caution: *Always disconnect the cable from the negative battery terminal FIRST and hook it up LAST or the battery may be shorted by the tool being used to loosen the cable clamps.*

1 Some systems on the vehicle require battery power to be available at all times, either to maintain continuous operation (alarm system, power door locks, etc.), or to maintain control unit memory (radio station presets, Powertrain Control Module and other control units). When the battery is disconnected, the power that maintains these systems is cut. So, before you disconnect the battery, please note that on a vehicle with power door locks, it's a wise precaution to remove the key or keyless entry fob, so that it does not get locked inside if the power door locks should engage accidentally when the battery is reconnected!

2 Devices known as "memory-savers" can be used to avoid some of these problems. Precise details vary according to the device used. The typical memory saver is plugged into the cigarette lighter and is connected to a spare battery. Then the vehicle battery can be disconnected from the electrical system. The memory saver will provide sufficient current to maintain audio unit security codes, PCM memory, etc. and will provide power to always hot circuits such as the clock and radio memory circuits.

Warning: *Some memory savers deliver a considerable amount of current in order to keep vehicle systems operational after the main battery is disconnected. If you're using a memory saver, make sure that the circuit concerned is actually open before servicing it.*

Warning: *If you're going to work near any of the airbag system components, the battery MUST be disconnected and a memory saver must NOT be used. If a memory saver is used, power will be supplied to the airbag, which means that it could accidentally deploy and cause serious personal injury.*

Disconnection

3 Install a memory saver device to avoid having to reprogram several of the vehicle's systems (see above).

Warning: *If you're working near any airbag system component, DO NOT use a memory saver.*

4 To disconnect the battery for service procedures requiring power to be cut from the vehicle, loosen the cable end bolt and disconnect the cable from the negative battery terminal. Isolate the cable end to prevent it from coming into accidental contact with the battery terminal.

Reconnection

5 Connect the positive battery cable first (if it was disconnected), followed by the negative cable.

6 After reconnecting the battery, several re-learn procedures must be performed. These include (and are specific to all model years unless otherwise noted):

a) *Steering angle sensor position learning*
b) *Idle air volume learning*
c) *Power window initialization and anti-pinch feature**
d) *Sunroof memory and anti-pinch feature**
e) *Radio presets**
f) *Navigation system adjustment**

* If a memory saver was used when the battery was disconnected, these functions won't have to be performed. Refer to your owner's manual for information on resetting the radio presets and navigation system adjustment.

Steering angle sensor position learning

7 This procedure MUST be performed by a qualified repair facility using specialized equipment.

Note: *It is possible that driving the vehicle on a long straight stretch of road may reset the sensor and turn the light off on the instrument cluster.*

Idle air volume learning

8 Ensure all of the following conditions are met. If any of the following conditions are not met, learning will be canceled.

a) *Battery voltage greater than 12.9 V at idle*
b) *Engine coolant at operating temperature (158 to 212°F [70 to 100°C])*
c) *Gearshift lever in P or N (automatic) or Neutral (manual)*
d) *All electrical loads are turned off (AC, headlights, etc.)*
e) *Steering wheel pointed in the straight ahead position*
f) *Vehicle stopped*
g) *Transaxle is at operating temperature (drive vehicle for 10 minutes to ensure operating temperature is reached)*

9 Perform the Accelerator pedal released position learning procedure (see Steps 21 through 26).

10 Perform the Throttle valve closed position learning procedure (see Steps 27 through 30).

11 Start the engine and confirm the above mentioned conditions have been met before continuing.

12 Turn the ignition off and wait a minimum of 10 seconds.

13 With your foot completely off the accelerator, and no objects resting on it (such as floor mats), turn the ignition to the ON position and wait for 3 seconds.

14 Fully press and release the accelerator pedal 5 times within 5 seconds of turning the ignition ON.

15 Wait 7 seconds, then press and hold the accelerator pedal to the floor for 20 seconds until the CHECK ENGINE (MIL) light stops blinking and lights up solidly.

16 Release the accelerator pedal within 3 seconds of the MIL lighting solidly.

17 Start the engine and allow it to idle for at least 20 seconds.

18 Rev the engine two or three times, then allow it to idle. Idle speed and ignition timing should be as follows:

a) *Automatic transaxle: 700 RPM +/- 50 RPM; timing 13 +/- 5 degrees BTDC in P or N position*
b) *Manual transaxle: 700 RPM +/- 50 RPM; timing 13 +/- 5 degrees BTDC in neutral position*

19 This completes the idle air volume learning procedure.

20 If the procedure cannot be completed successfully, check the following:

a) *Verify the throttle valve plate is fully closed*
b) *Check PCV operation*
c) *Check for vacuum leaks after the throttle body*
d) *If the engine stalls or the idle hunts, perform the procedure again*

Accelerator pedal released position learning procedure

21 Ensure your foot is completely off the accelerator, and no objects are resting on it (such as floor mats).

22 Turn the ignition switch to the ON position and wait 2 seconds.

23 Turn the ignition switch to the OFF position and wait at least 10 seconds.

24 Turn the ignition switch to the ON position and wait 2 seconds.

25 Turn the ignition switch to the OFF position and wait at least 10 seconds.

26 This completes the accelerator pedal released position learning procedure.

Throttle valve closed learning procedure

27 Ensure your foot is completely off and no objects resting on the accelerator (such as floor mats).

28 Turn the ignition to the ON position.

29 Turn the ignition to the OFF position for 10 seconds. Listen for the throttle valve to operate during the 10 seconds.

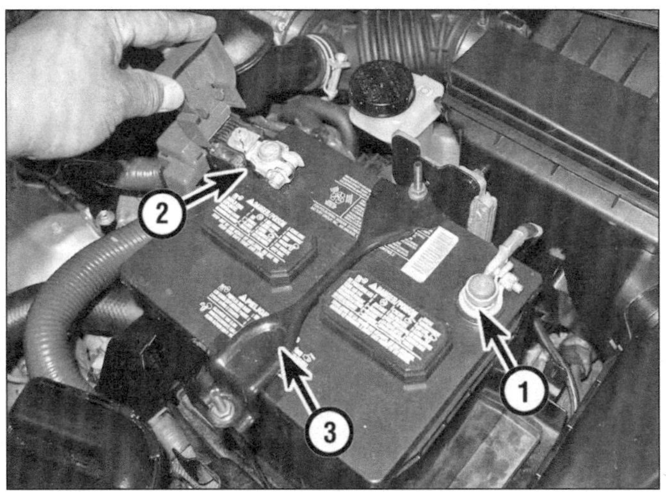

4.2 Battery details:

1 *Negative bvattery cable*
2 *Positive battery cable*
3 *Hold-down bracket*

4.10 Battery tray mounting bolts

30 This completes the throttle valve closed learning procedure.

Power window initialization and anti-pinch feature check

31 Close all doors.
32 Turn the ignition to the ON position.
33 Open the window completely (if it isn't already).
34 Pull the power window switch up to close the window, holding the switch in the Up position for at least four seconds after the glass has closed completely. Sometimes an audible click can be heard when the position sets.
35 Open the window completely, then place a piece of wood or other object near the top of the window frame.
Warning: *Do not use any part of your body for this check.*
36 Using the AUTO-UP feature, close the window; confirm that the window automatically reverses direction as soon as it contacts the object.

Sunroof initialization and anti-pinch feature check

37 Turn the ignition to the ON position.
38 Operate the sunroof switch in the tilt up position; hold it there until the sunroof has tilted up completely, then release the switch.
39 Within 5 seconds of releasing the switch, press and hold the switch in the tilt up position again. The sunroof should back up after a pause; release the switch.
Caution: *If the next step is not completed and the sunroof switch is released too early, repeat the entire procedure.*
40 Within five seconds, push the switch to the tilt up position again and hold it there; the sunroof should move from the tilt up position to the fully open position, then back to the fully closed position. Release the switch.
41 Open the sunroof completely, then place a piece of wood or other object near the front of the sunroof opening.
Warning: *Do not use any part of your body for this check.*
42 Operate the sunroof switch with the auto-close function and verify that the sunroof does not pinch the object.

4 Battery and battery tray - removal and installation

Battery

1 Install a memory saver device to avoid having to reprogram several of the vehicle's systems (see Section 3).
2 Disconnect the negative battery cable, then the positive battery cable, from the battery (see illustration).
Warning: *Always disconnect the negative cable first and hook it up last or the battery may be shorted by the tool being used to loosen the cable clamps.*
3 Remove the battery hold-down bracket on top of the battery.
4 Lift out the battery. Special battery removal and installation tools are available at auto parts stores; lifting and moving the battery is much easier if you use one.
5 Installation is the reverse of removal. Connect the positive cable first, then the negative cable. Refer to Section 3 and perform the necessary re-learn procedures.

Battery tray

6 Remove the battery (see Steps 1 through 5).
7 Remove the fresh air inlet duct.
8 Remove the battery tray liner.
9 Remove the fasteners and detach the PCM from the battery tray (see Chapter 6). Also detach the TCM from the battery tray (see Chapter 7).
10 Remove the battery tray mounting bolts (see illustration) and lift the tray out.
11 Installation is the reverse of removal. Connect the positive cable first, then the negative cable. Refer to Section 3 and perform the necessary re-learn procedures.

5 Battery cables - replacement

1 When removing the cables, always disconnect the cable from the negative battery terminal first and hook it up last, or you might accidentally short out the battery with the tool you're using to loosen the cable clamps. Even if you're only replacing the cable for the positive terminal, be sure to disconnect the negative cable from the battery first.
2 Disconnect the old cables from the battery, then trace each of them to their opposite ends and disconnect them. Note the routing of each cable before disconnecting it to ensure correct installation.
3 If you are replacing any of the old cables, take them with you when buying new cables. It is vitally important that you replace the cables with identical parts.
4 Clean the threads of the solenoid or ground connection with a wire brush to remove rust and corrosion. Apply a light coat of battery terminal corrosion inhibitor or petroleum jelly to the threads to prevent future corrosion.
5 Attach the cable to the solenoid or ground connection and tighten the mounting nut/bolt securely.
6 Before connecting a new cable to the battery, make sure that it reaches the battery post without having to be stretched.
7 Connect the cable to the positive battery terminal first, then connect the ground cable to the negative battery terminal.

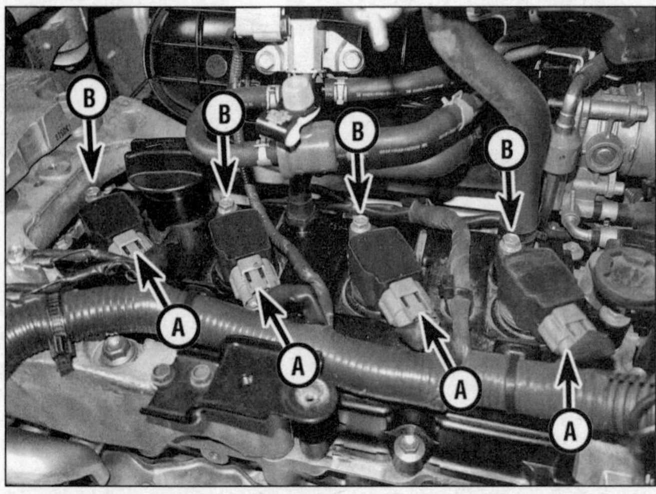

6.2 Coil electrical connectors (A) and mounting bolts (B)

7.3 Alternator electrical connector and battery cable

7.4 Alternator mounting bolts

8.5 Starter electrical connections "S" and "B" (A) and starter mounting bolts (B)

6 Ignition coil(s) - replacement

1 Remove the upper intake air resonator (see Chapter 4).
2 Disconnect the electrical connector(s) from the coil(s) (see illustration).
3 Remove the coil mounting bolt(s), then twist the coil slightly and pull it straight out.
4 Installation is the reverse of removal. Before installing the ignition coils, coat the interior of the boots with silicone dielectric compound.

7 Alternator - removal and installation

1 Disconnect the cable from the negative terminal of the battery (see Section 3).
2 Remove the drivebelt (see Chapter 1).
3 Disconnect the electrical harness connector and battery cable from the alternator (see illustration), then detach the cable clip from the bracket on top of the alternator.
4 On 2014 and later Rogue (not Rogue Select) models, remove the oil dipstick tube mounting bolt, then remove the oil dipstick tube from the upper oil pan. Take care not to damage the tube O-ring.
5 Remove the alternator mounting bolts. Separate and remove the alternator from the engine (see illustration).
6 Installation is the reverse of removal. Tighten the alternator mounting bolts to the torque listed in this Chapter's Specifications.
7 Reconnect the battery and perform the necessary re-learn procedures (see Section 3).

8 Starter motor - removal and installation

1 Disconnect the cable from the negative terminal of the battery (see Section 3).
2 If you're working on a 2013 or earlier/2014 or later Rogue Select AWD model, loosen the right-front wheel lug nuts.
3 If you're working on a 2014 or later model (except Rogue Select), remove the battery and battery tray (see Section 4).
4 If you're working on a 2013 or earlier model, 2014 or later Rogue Select model, raise the front of the vehicle and support it securely on jackstands. If you're working on an AWD model, remove the right-front wheel.
5 Disconnect the electrical connectors from the "S"and "B" terminals (see illustration).
6 Remove the starter mounting bolts and remove the starter.
7 Installation is the reverse of removal. Tighten the starter mounting bolts to the torque listed in this Chapter's Specifications.
8 Reconnect the battery and perform the necessary re-learn procedures (see Section 3).

Notes

Notes

Chapter 6
Emissions and engine control systems

Contents

General information

1 To prevent pollution of the atmosphere from incompletely burned and evaporating gases, and to maintain good driveability and fuel economy, a number of emission control systems are incorporated. They include the:

Catalytic converter

2 A catalytic converter is an emission control device in the exhaust system that reduces certain pollutants in the exhaust gas stream. There are two types of converters: oxidation converters and reduction converters.

3 Oxidation converters contain a monolithic substrate (a ceramic honeycomb) coated with the semi-precious metals platinum and palladium. An oxidation catalyst reduces unburned hydrocarbons (HC) and carbon monoxide (CO) by adding oxygen to the exhaust stream as it passes through the substrate, which, in the presence of high temperature and the catalyst materials, converts the HC and CO to water vapor (H2O) and carbon dioxide (CO2).

4 Reduction converters contain a monolithic substrate coated with platinum and rhodium. A reduction catalyst reduces oxides of nitrogen (NOx) by removing oxygen, which in the presence of high temperature and the catalyst material produces nitrogen (N) and carbon dioxide (CO2).

5 Catalytic converters that combine both types of catalysts in one assembly are known as "three-way catalysts" or TWCs. A TWC can reduce all three pollutants.

Evaporative Emissions Control (EVAP) system

6 The Evaporative Emissions Control (EVAP) system prevents fuel system vapors (which contain unburned hydrocarbons) from escaping into the atmosphere. On warm days, vapors trapped inside the fuel tank expand until the pressure reaches a certain threshold. Then the fuel vapors are routed from the fuel tank through the fuel vapor vent valve and the fuel vapor control valve to the EVAP canister, where they're stored temporarily until the next time the vehicle is operated. When the conditions are right (engine warmed up, vehicle up to speed, moderate or heavy load on the engine, etc.) the PCM opens the canister purge valve, which allows fuel vapors to be drawn from the canister into the intake manifold. Once in the intake manifold, the fuel vapors mix with incoming air before being drawn through the intake ports into the combustion chambers where they're burned up with the rest of the air/fuel mixture. The EVAP system is complex and virtually impossible to troubleshoot without the right tools and training.

Exhaust Gas Recirculation (EGR) system

7 The EGR system reduces oxides of nitrogen by recirculating exhaust gases from the exhaust manifold, through the EGR valve and intake manifold, then back to the combustion chambers, where it mixes with the incoming air/fuel mixture before being consumed. These recirculated exhaust gases dilute the incoming air/fuel mixture, which cools the combustion chambers, thereby reducing NOx emissions.

8 The EGR system consists of the Powertrain Control Module (PCM), the EGR valve, the EGR valve position sensor and various other information sensors that the PCM uses to determine when to open the EGR valve. The degree to which the EGR valve is opened is referred to as "EGR valve lift." The PCM is programmed to produce the ideal EGR valve lift for varying operating conditions. The EGR valve position sensor, which is an integral part of the EGR valve, detects the amount of EGR valve lift and sends this information to the PCM. The PCM then compares it with the appropriate EGR valve lift for the operating conditions. The PCM increases current flow to the EGR valve to increase valve lift and reduces the current to reduce the amount of lift. If EGR flow is inappropriate to the operating conditions (idle, cold engine, etc.) the PCM simply cuts the current to the EGR valve and the valve closes.

Secondary Air Injection (AIR) system

9 Some vehicles are equipped with a secondary air injection (AIR) system. The secondary air injection system is used to reduce tailpipe emissions on initial engine start-up. The system uses an electric motor/pump assembly, relay, vacuum valve/solenoid, air shut-off valve, check valves and tubing to inject fresh air directly into the exhaust

2.4a Simple code readers are an economical way to extract trouble codes when the CHECK ENGINE light comes on

2.4b Hand-held scan tools like these can extract computer codes and also perform diagnostics

manifolds. The fresh air (oxygen) reacts with the exhaust gas in the catalytic converter to reduce HC and CO levels. The air pump and solenoid are controlled by the PCM through the AIR relay. During initial start-up, the PCM energizes the AIR relay, the relay supplies battery voltage to the air pump and the vacuum valve/solenoid, engine vacuum is applied to the air shut-off valve which opens and allows air to flow through the tubing into the exhaust manifolds. The PCM will operate the air pump until closed loop operation is reached (approximately four minutes). During normal operation, the check valves prevent exhaust backflow into the system.

Powertrain Control Module (PCM)

10 The Powertrain Control Module (PCM) is the brain of the engine management system. It also controls a wide variety of other vehicle systems. In order to program the new PCM, the dealer needs the vehicle as well as the new PCM. If you're planning to replace the PCM with a new one, there is no point in trying to do so at home because you won't be able to program it yourself.

Positive Crankcase Ventilation (PCV) system

11 The Positive Crankcase Ventilation (PCV) system reduces hydrocarbon emissions by scavenging crankcase vapors, which are rich in unburned hydrocarbons. A PCV valve or orifice regulates the flow of gases into the intake manifold in proportion to the amount of intake vacuum available.

12 The PCV system generally consists of the fresh air inlet hose, the PCV valve or orifice and the crankcase ventilation hose (or PCV hose). The fresh air inlet hose connects the air intake duct to a pipe on the valve cover. The crankcase ventilation hose (or PCV hose) connects the PCV valve or orifice in the valve cover to the intake manifold.

2 On Board Diagnosis (OBD) system

General description

1 All models are equipped with the second generation OBD-II system. This system consists of an on-board computer known as the Powertrain Control Module (PCM), and information sensors, which monitor various functions of the engine and send data to the PCM. This system incorporates a series of diagnostic monitors that detect and identify fuel injection and emissions control system faults and store the information in the computer memory. This system also tests sensors and output actuators, diagnoses drive cycles, freezes data and clears codes.

2 The PCM is the brain of the electronically controlled fuel and emissions system. It receives data from a number of sensors and other electronic components (switches, relays, etc.). Based on the information it receives, the PCM generates output signals to control various relays, solenoids (fuel injectors) and other actuators. The PCM is specifically calibrated to optimize the emissions, fuel economy and driveability of the vehicle.

3 It isn't a good idea to attempt diagnosis or replacement of the PCM or emission control components at home while the vehicle is under warranty. Because of a federally-mandated warranty which covers the emissions system components and because any owner-induced damage to the PCM, the sensors and/or the control devices may void this warranty, take the vehicle to a dealer service department if the PCM or a system component malfunctions.

Scan tool information

4 Because extracting the Diagnostic Trouble Codes (DTCs) from an engine management system is now the first step in troubleshooting many computer-controlled systems and components, a code reader, at the very least, will be required (see illustration). More powerful scan tools can also perform many of the diagnostics once associated with expensive factory scan tools (see illustration). If you're planning to obtain a generic scan tool for your vehicle, make sure that it's compatible with OBD-II systems. If you don't plan to purchase a code reader or scan tool and don't have access to one, you can have the codes extracted by a dealer service department or an independent repair shop.

Note: *Some auto parts stores even provide this service.*

3 Obtaining and clearing Diagnostic Trouble Codes (DTCs)

1 All models covered by this manual are equipped with on-board diagnostics. When the PCM recognizes a malfunction in a monitored emission or engine control system, component or circuit, it turns on the Malfunction Indicator Light (MIL) on the dash. The PCM will continue to display the MIL until the problem is fixed and the Diagnostic Trouble Code (DTC) is cleared from the PCM's memory. You'll need a scan tool to access any DTCs stored in the PCM.

2 Before outputting any DTCs stored in the PCM, thoroughly inspect ALL electrical connectors and hoses. Make sure that all electrical connections are tight, clean and free of corrosion. And make sure that all hoses are correctly connected, fit tightly and are in good condition (no cracks or tears).

Information Sensors

Accelerator Pedal Position (APP) sensor - as you press the accelerator pedal, the APP sensor alters its voltage signal to the PCM in proportion to the angle of the pedal, and the PCM commands a motor inside the throttle body to open or close the throttle plate accordingly

Camshaft Position (CMP) sensor - produces a signal that the PCM uses to identify the number 1 cylinder and to time the firing sequence of the fuel injectors

Crankshaft Position (CKP) sensor - produces a signal that the PCM uses to calculate engine speed and crankshaft position, which enables it to synchronize ignition timing with fuel injector timing, and to detect misfires

Engine Coolant Temperature (ECT) sensor - a thermistor (temperature-sensitive variable resistor) that sends a voltage signal to the PCM, which uses this data to determine the temperature of the engine coolant

Fuel tank pressure sensor - measures the fuel tank pressure and controls fuel tank pressure by signaling the EVAP system to purge the fuel tank vapors when the pressure becomes excessive

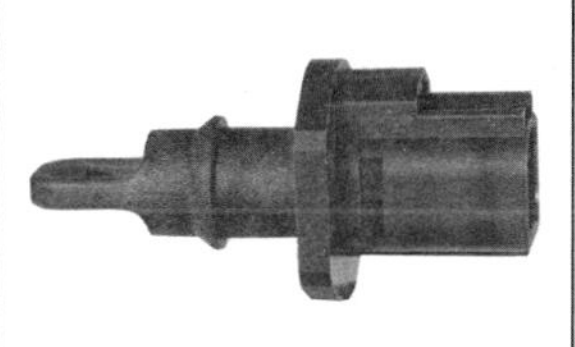

Intake Air Temperature (IAT) sensor - monitors the temperature of the air entering the engine and sends a signal to the PCM to determine injector pulse-width (the duration of each injector's on-time) and to adjust spark timing (to prevent spark knock)

Knock sensor - a piezoelectric crystal that oscillates in proportion to engine vibration which produces a voltage output that is monitored by the PCM. This retards the ignition timing when the oscillation exceeds a certain threshold

Manifold Absolute Pressure (MAP) sensor - monitors the pressure or vacuum inside the intake manifold. The PCM uses this data to determine engine load so that it can alter the ignition advance and fuel enrichment

Mass Air Flow (MAF) sensor - measures the amount of intake air drawn into the engine. It uses a hot-wire sensing element to measure the amount of air entering the engine

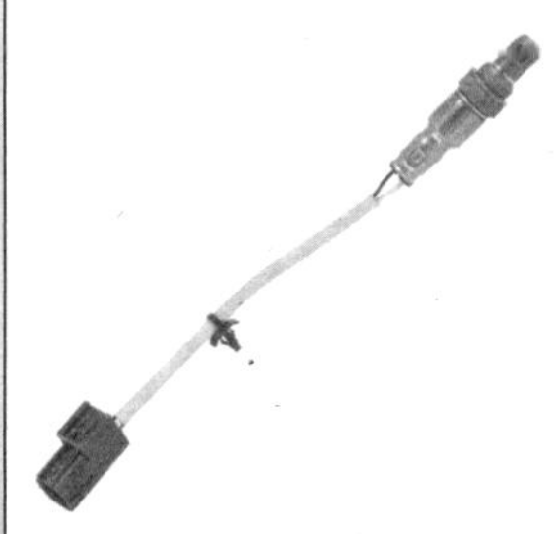

Oxygen sensors - generates a small variable voltage signal in proportion to the difference between the oxygen content in the exhaust stream and the oxygen content in the ambient air. The PCM uses this information to maintain the proper air/fuel ratio. A second oxygen sensor monitors the efficiency of the catalytic converter

Throttle Position (TP) sensor - a potentiometer that generates a voltage signal that varies in relation to the opening angle of the throttle plate inside the throttle body. Works with the PCM and other sensors to calculate injector pulse width (the duration of each injector's on-time)

Photos courtesy of Wells Manufacturing, except APP and MAF sensors.

Accessing the DTCs

3 The Diagnostic Trouble Codes (DTCs) can only be accessed with a code reader or scan tool. Professional scan tools are expensive, but relatively inexpensive generic code readers or scan tools (see illustrations 2.4a and 2.4b) are available at most auto parts stores. Simply plug the connector of the scan tool into the diagnostic connector (see illustration). Then follow the instructions included with the scan tool to extract the DTCs.

4 Once you have outputted all of the stored DTCs, look them up on the accompanying DTC chart.

5 After troubleshooting the source of each DTC, make any necessaryrepairs or replace the defective component(s).

Clearing the DTCs

6 Clear the DTCs with the code reader or scan tool in accordance with the instructions provided by the tool's manufacturer.

Diagnostic Trouble Codes

7 The accompanying tables are a list of the Diagnostic Trouble Codes (DTCs) that can be accessed by a do-it-yourselfer working at home (there are many, many more DTCs available to professional mechanics with proprietary scan tools and software, but those codes cannot be accessed by a generic scan tool). If, after you have checked and repaired the connectors, wire harness and vacuum hoses (if applicable) for an emission-related system, component or circuit, the problem persists, have the vehicle checked by a dealer service department or other qualified repair shop.

3.3 The Data Link Connector (DLC) is located under the lower edge of the dash, to the left of the steering column

Trouble codes

Code	Proable cause
P0011	Intake valve timing control solenoid performance problem
P0014	Exhaust valve timing control solenoid performance problem
P0030	Air fuel ratio (A/F) sensor 1, bank 1 heater performance problem
P0031	Upstream oxygen sensor heater control circuit low voltage signal
P0032	Upstream oxygen sensor heater control circuit high voltage signal
P0037	Downstream oxygen sensor heater control circuit low voltage signal
P0038	Downstream oxygen sensor heater control circuit high voltage signal
P0053	Heater oxygen sensor (HO2S), bank 1, sensor 1 resistance problem
P0057	Downstream oxygen sensor heater control circuit low voltage signal (Bank 2)
P0058	Downstream oxygen sensor heater control circuit high voltage signal (Bank 2)
P0075	Intake valve control solenoid, bank 1 circuit problem
P0078	Exhaust valve control solenoid, bank 1 circuit problem
P0101	Mass Air Flow sensor circuit range or performance fault
P0102	Mass Air Flow sensor circuit low input
P0103	Mass Air Flow sensor circuit high input
P0111	Intake Air sensor sensor circuit range/performance problem
P0112	Intake Air Temperature sensor circuit low input
P0113	Intake Air Temperature sensor circuit high input
P0116	Engine coolant temperature circuit range/performance problem
P0117	Engine coolant temperature circuit, low input

Code	Proable cause
P0118	Engine Coolant Temperature sensor circuit high input
P0122	Throttle Position Sensor circuit low input
P0123	Throttle Position Sensor circuit high input
P0125	Engine Coolant Temperature sensor or circuit fault
P0127	Intake Air Temperature too high
P0128	Thermostat function - engine coolant does not reach correct temperature after warm-up
P0130	Upstream oxygen sensor or circuit fault
P0131	Upstream oxygen sensor lean shift monitor fault
P0132	Upstream oxygen sensor rich shift monitor fault
P0136	Heater oxygen sensor (HO2S), bank 1, sensor 2 high voltage response
P0137	Downstream oxygen sensor minimum voltage monitor fault
P0138	Downstream oxygen sensor maximum voltage monitor fault
P0139	Downstream oxygen sensor circuit slow response fault
P014C	Oxygen sensor 1 problem
P014D	Oxygen sensor 1 problem
P015A	Oxygen sensor 1 problem
P015B	Oxygen sensor 1 problem
P0171	Fuel injection system lean
P0172	Fuel injection system rich
P0174	System too lean
P0175	System too rich
P0181	Fuel Tank Temperature sensor circuit range or performance
P0182	Fuel Tank Temperature sensor circuit low input
P0183	Fuel Tank Temperature sensor circuit high input
P0196	Fuel rail pressure sensor circuit, range or performance problem
P0197	Fuel rail pressure sensor circuit, low input
P0198	Fuel rail pressure sensor circuit, high input
P0222	Throttle Position Sensor circuit low input
P0223	Throttle Position Sensor circuit high input
P0300	Multiple cylinder misfire detected
P0301	Cylinder no. 1 misfire detected

Trouble codes (continued)

Code	Proable cause
P0302	Cylinder no. 2 misfire detected
P0303	Cylinder no. 3 misfire detected
P0304	Cylinder no. 4 misfire detected
P0327	Knock Sensor circuit low input
P0328	Knock Sensor circuit high input
P0322	Crankshaft Position (CKP) sensor/engine speed (RPM) sensor - no signal
P0323	Crankshaft Position (CKP) sensor/engine speed (RPM) sensor - circuit intermittent
P0340	Camshaft Position sensor or circuit fault
P0345	Camshaft Position sensor or circuit fault (Bank 2)
P0420	Catalyst system defective (Bank 1)
P0441	EVAP control system incorrect purge flow
P0442	EVAP system small leak (negative pressure check)
P0443	EVAP canister purge control valve circuit fault
P0444	EVAP canister purge control valve circuit open
P0445	EVAP canister purge control valve circuit shorted
P0447	EVAP canister vent control valve circuit open
P0448	EVAP canister vent control valve remains closed under certain driving conditions
P0451	EVAP system pressure sensor or circuit fault
P0452	EVAP system pressure sensor low input voltage signal
P0453	EVAP system pressure sensor high input
P0455	EVAP system gross leak
P0456	EVAP system very small leak (negative pressure check)
P0460	Fuel level sensor or circuit fault
P0461	Fuel level sensor or circuit fault
P0462	Fuel level sensor circuit low input
P0463	Fuel level sensor circuit high input
P0500	Vehicle Speed Sensor or circuit fault
P0506	Idle Air Control system signal low
P0507	Idle Air Control system signal high
P050A	Cold start control problem
P050B	Cold start control problem

Code	Proable cause
P050E	Cold start control problem
P0520	Engine Oil Pressure (EOP) switch circuit problem
P0524	Engine oil pressure too low
P0603	PCM back-up RAM does not function properly
P062F	Internal control module EEPROM error
P0604	Internal control module random access memory (RAM) error
P0605	PCM or EEPROM fault
P0606	Control Module processor problem
P0607	Control module performance
P060A	Internal control module monitoring processor performance problem
P060B	Internal control module monitoring A/D processing performance problem
P0643	PCM detects sensor power supply low or high voltage
P0850	Park/Neutral position switch circuit fault in Drive and Park
P1148	Closed loop control fault
P1211	Traction Control System (TCS), problem with ABS control unit
P1217	Engine overheating
P1225	Closed throttle position learning value low
P1226	Closed throttle position learning performance fault
P1550	Battery current sensor problem
P1551	Battery current sensor problem
P1552	Battery current sensor problem
P1553	Battery current sensor problem
P1554	Battery current sensor problem
P1564	ACSD steering switch problem
P1572	ASCD brake switch or circuit fault
P1574	ASCD speed sensor signal performance fault
P1700	Automatic transmission control system problem
P1715	Input speed sensor problem
P1720	Vehicle speed sensor problem
P1800	VIAS control solenoid valve circuit performance fault
P1805	Brake switch or circuit fault
P2A00	Oxygen sensor 1

Trouble codes (continued)

Code	Proable cause
P2A03	Oxygen sensor 1
P2004	Tumble control valve problem
P2014	Tumble control valve position sensor problem
P2100	Throttle Control motor voltage signal is open or low voltage
P2103	Throttle Control motor relay voltage signal is shorted (ON)
P2101	Electric throttle control function problem
P2118	Throttle Control motor performance fault in circuit and/or throttle control motor
P2119	Throttle Control motor defective or stuck in position
P2122	Accelerator Pedal Position sensor 1 circuit low
P2123	Accelerator Pedal Position sensor 1 circuit high
P2127	Accelerator Pedal Position sensor 2 circuit low
P2128	Accelerator Pedal Position sensor 2 circuit high
P2135	Throttle Position Sensor circuit range or performance
P2138	Accelerator Pedal Position sensor or circuit range or performance
P2237	O2 sensor bank1, sensor 1 positive control circuit/open
P2238	O2 sensor bank1, sensor 1 positive control circuit low
P2239	O2 sensor bank1, sensor 1 positive control circuit high
P2251	O2 sensor bank1, sensor 1 negative control circuit/open
P2252	O2 sensor bank1, sensor 1 negative control circuit low
P2253	O2 sensor bank1, sensor 1 negative control circuit high
P2270	O2 sensor bank1, sensor 2 signal biased/stuck lean
P2271	O2 sensor bank1, sensor 2 signal biased/stuck rich
P2423	HC absorption catalyst function

4.2 Disconnect the electrical connector to the Accelerator Pedal Position (APP) sensor

4 Accelerator Pedal Position (APP) sensor - replacement

1 Disconnect the cable from the negative terminal of the battery (see Chapter 5).
2 Disconnect the wiring from the sensor/pedal assembly (see illustration).
3 Unscrew the nuts and remove the pedal.
4 Installation is the reverse of removal.
5 Reconnect the battery and perform the necessary re-learn procedures (see Chapter 5).

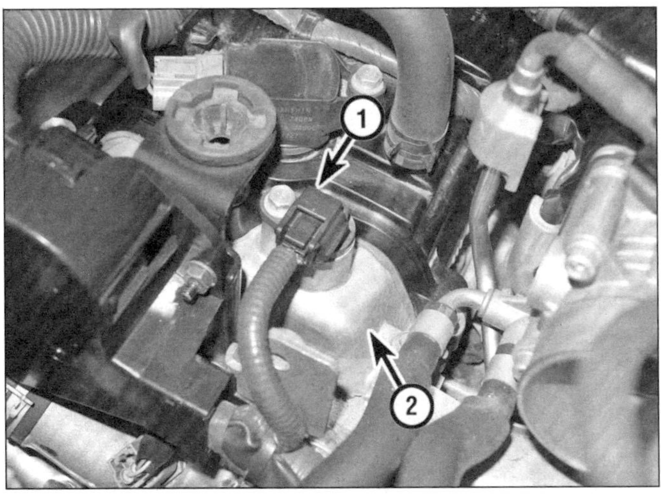

5.1 The Camshaft Position (CMP) sensor(s) is located at the driver's side of the engine (2013 and earlier models/2014 and later model Rogue Select models shown)

1 Camshaft position sensor (CMP)
2 Camshaft position sensor bracket

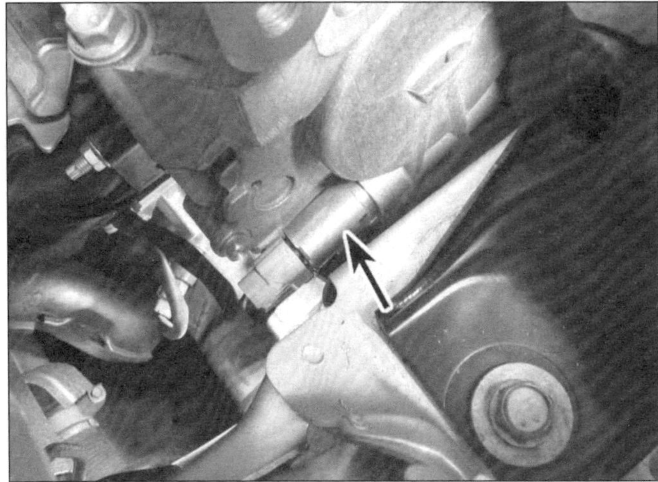

6.2 The IVT control solenoid valve is located on the control cover, on the front of the timing chain cover (EVT control solenoid similar)

5 Camshaft Position (CMP) sensor - replacement

Note: *On 2013 and earlier models/2014 and later model Rogue Select models, a camshaft position (CMP) sensor is only used on the intake camshaft. On 2014 and later models (except Rogue Select models) two CMP sensors are used (one for each camshaft).*

1 The CMP sensor(s) is mounted on the camshaft position sensor bracket at the driver's side of the cylinder head (see illustration).

2Remove the upper intake air resonator (see Chapter 4 Section 9).

3 Disconnect the electrical connector from the sensor.

4 Remove the mounting bolt and pull out the sensor.

5 Installation is the reverse of removal. Be sure to use a new O-ring.

6 Intake Valve Timing (IVT) and Exhaust Valve Timing (EVT) control solenoid(s) - replacement

1 2013 and earlier models/2014 and later Rogue Select models use an intake valve timing (IVT) solenoid. 2014 and later models (except Rogue Select models) use an intake valve timing intermediate lock control solenoid, an intake valve timing (IVT) control solenoid valve and an exhaust valve timing (EVT) solenoid. All the solenoid(s) are located on the upper part of the timing chain cover on the control cover (bolted to the timing chain cover). The solenoid valves direct oil to the intake camshaft actuator or exhaust camshaft actuator to vary the intake or exhaust camshaft timing.

2 Remove the mounting bolt, then pull out the solenoid valve (see illustration).

7.4 CKP sensor mounting bolt

3 Installation is the reverse of removal. Replace the O-ring with a new one, if necessary.

7 Crankshaft Position (CKP) sensor - replacement

1 The CKP sensor is mounted on the back side of the cylinder block near the transaxle end of the engine, just below the starter.

2 If equipped, remove the CKP sensor heat shield attaching bolt and remove the shield.

3 Disconnect the electrical connector from the CKP sensor.

4 Remove the mounting bolt from the CKP sensor and extract the sensor from the engine block (see illustration).

5 Before installation, check the O-ring for cracks or tears and replace it if necessary.

6 Installation is the reverse of removal.

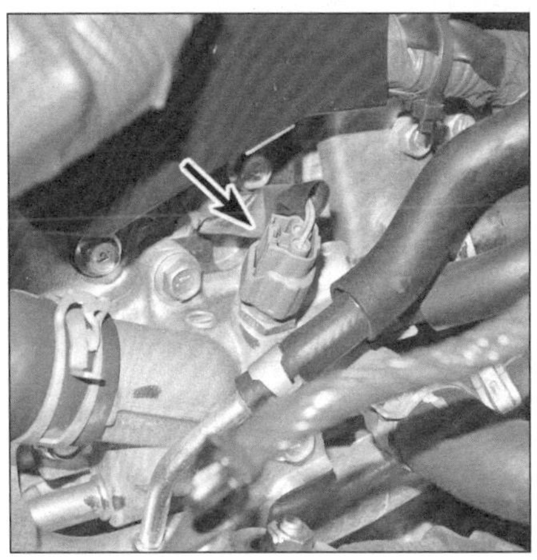

8.1 The Engine Coolant Temperature (ECT) sensor is located in the water outlet at the left (driver's) side of the engine.

8 Engine Coolant Temperature (ECT) sensor - replacement

Warning: *Wait until the engine has completely cooled before beginning this procedure.*

1 The ECT sensor is mounted in the water outlet, where the upper radiator hoses is connected to the engine, at the left (driver's) side of the engine (see illustration).

2 Drain some engine coolant (see Chapter 1) to minimize coolant spillage.

3 Disconnect the electrical connector from the ECT sensor.

4 Unscrew the sensor from the engine and discard the sealing washer (a new one should be used).

5 Installation is the reverse of removal. Refill the cooling system (see Chapter 1).

9.1 The Mass Air Flow/Intake Air Temperature (MAF/IAT) sensor is installed in the air filter housing and is retained by two screws - 2013 model shown all other models similar

10.1 The knock sensor is located on the back side of the engine block, below the intake manifold

9 Mass Air Flow/Intake Air Temperature (MAF/IAT) sensor - replacement

Note: *2013 and earlier models/2014 and later Rogue Select models are equipped with a (MAF/IAT) 2014 and later models (except Rogue Select models) are equipped with (MAF) sensor.*

1 The MAF/IAT sensor is mounted on the air filter housing, near the air duct going to the throttle body (see illustration).

2 Disconnect the electrical connector from the MAF/IAT sensor.

3 Remove the screws and remove the sensor from the air filter housing.

4 Installation is the reverse of removal.

10 Knock sensor - replacement

1 The knock sensor is mounted on the firewall side of the engine block (see illustration).

2 Disconnect the electrical connector from the knock sensor.

3 Remove the sensor mounting bolt, then remove the sensor.

4 Installation is the reverse of removal. Tighten the mounting bolt to 16 ft-lbs.

11 Oxygen sensors - replacement

Note: *Because it is installed in the exhaust system, which contracts when cool, an oxygen sensor can be very difficult to loosen when the engine is cold. Rather than risking damage to the sensor or its mounting threads, run the engine for a minute or two, then shut it off. Be careful to avoid burns during this procedure.*

1 Be very careful when servicing an oxygen sensor:

a) The oxygen sensor has a permanently attached pigtail and electrical connector which should not be removed from the sensor. Damage or removal of the pigtail or electrical connector can adversely affect operation of the sensor.

b) Grease, dirt and other contaminants should be kept away from the electrical connector and the louvered end of the sensor.

c) Do not use cleaning solvents of any kind on the oxygen sensor.

d) Do not drop or roughly handle the sensor.

e) The silicone boot must be installed in the correct position to prevent the boot from being melted and to allow the sensor to operate properly.

Replacement

Upstream oxygen sensor

2 Locate the upstream oxygen sensor electrical connector and disconnect it (see illustration). Detach the sensor wiring harness from any clips.

3 Unscrew the sensor with an oxygen sensor socket if one is available. You may have to raise the vehicle and support it securely on jackstands to reach it.

4 If you're going to install the old sensor, apply anti-seize compound to the threads to ease future removal. If you're installing a new sensor, the threads will already have anti-seize on them.

5 Installation is the reverse of removal. Tighten the sensor securely.

Downstream oxygen sensor

6 Raise the vehicle and support it securely on jackstands.

7 Disconnect the wiring harness from the pigtail of the sensor (see illustration).

Note: *On 2014 and later models (except Rogue Select models), the downstream oxygen sensor is located in the front exhaust pipe.*

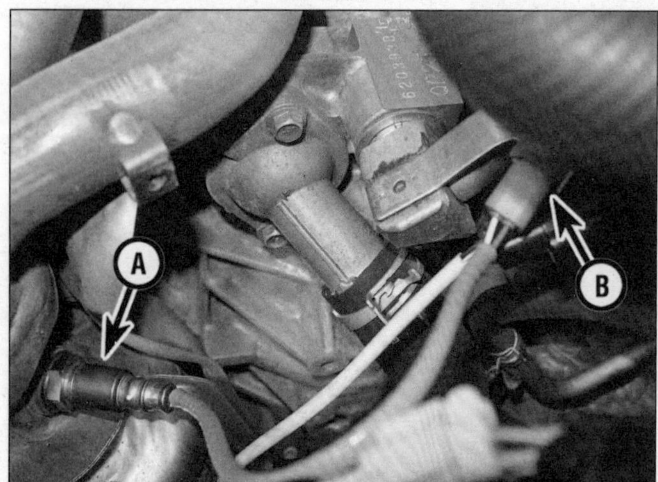

11.2 The upstream oxygen sensor (A), installed in the exhaust manifold just before the catalytic converter, and its electrical connector (B)

11.7 The downstream oxygen sensor is installed in the outlet side of the catalytic converter - 2013 and earlier models/2014 and later Rogue Select models shown

8 Unscrew the sensor using an oxygen sensor socket if one is available.
9 If you're going to install the old sensor, apply anti-seize compound to the threads to ease future removal. If you're installing a new sensor, the threads will already have anti-seize on them.
10 Installation is the reverse of removal. Tighten the sensor securely.

12 Transmission range switch - replacement and adjustment

Replacement

1 The transmission range switch is mounted on the top of the transaxle (see illustration).
2 Remove the battery and the battery tray (see Chapter 5).
3 Remove the shift cable from the manual shaft.
4 Disconnect the electrical connector from the switch.
5 Unscrew the mounting bolts and remove the switch.
6 Installation is the reverse of removal. Adjust the switch.
7 Verify that the engine will start only in Park or Neutral. Verify that the back-up lights come on only in Reverse. Adjust the range switch as necessary to ensure that these conditions are met.

Adjustment

8 Set the parking brake.
9 Move the shifter to the "N" position.
10 Loosen the control cable-to-manual lever nut.
11 Loosen the range switch mounting bolts (see illustration).
12 Rotate the switch and insert a drill bit (4 mm) into the adjusting holes (see illustration) on both the switch and manual lever.
13 Tighten the mounting bolts.
14 Tighten the control cable-to-manual lever nut.

13 Transmission speed sensors - replacement

Note: *On 2013 and earlier models/2014 and later Rogue Select models, the transaxle uses two speed sensors: primary and secondary.*
Note: *On 2014 and later models (except Rogue Select models), the transaxle uses three speed sensors: input speed, primary speed and output speed sensor.*

2013 and earlier models/2014 and later Rogue Select models

1 The primary sensor is located on the front side of the transaxle, facing the radiator. The secondary sensor is located on the left end of the transaxle case.
2 If you're replacing the primary speed sensor, remove the left inner fender splash shield (see Chapter 11). If you're removing the secondary speed sensor, remove the battery (see Chapter 5) and the air filter housing (see Chapter 4).
3 Disconnect the electrical connector from the speed sensor (see illustrations).
4 Remove the mounting bolt and remove the sensor. Discard the O-ring.
5 Apply some transmission fluid to the new O-ring and install it on the sensor.
6 Installation is the reverse of removal.

2014 and later models (except Rogue Select models)

7 The input sensor is located on the front side of the transaxle facing the radiator. The

12.1 Transmission range switch location

12.11 Transmission range switch mounting bolts

12.12 Insert a 4 mm drill bit through the hole in the manual lever and into the hole in the switch body to align it

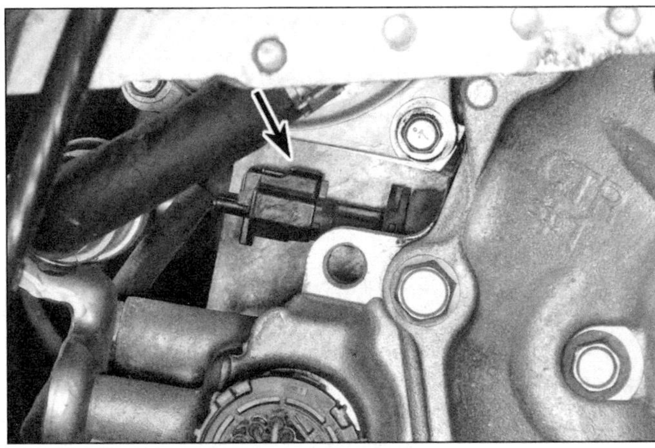

13.3a Primary transmission speed sensor

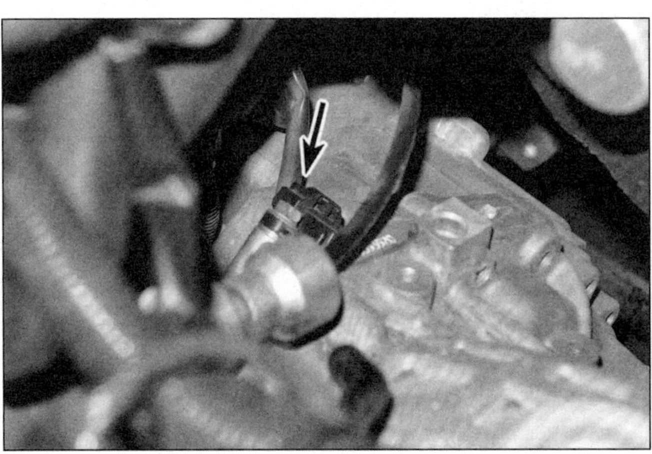

13.3b Secondary transmission speed sensor

14.3 Rotate the connector lock upward to disconnect the connector

primary speed sensor in located on the end of the transaxle facing the left wheel. The output speed sensor is located just above the left driveaxle.

Input speed sensor

8 Remove the battery and battery tray (see Chapter 5).
9 Remove the starter motor (see Chapter 5).
10 Disconnect the electrical connector from the speed sensor.
11 Remove the mounting bolt and remove the sensor. Discard the O-ring.
12 Apply some transmission fluid to the new O-ring and install it on the sensor.
13 Installation is the reverse of removal.

Primary speed sensor and ouput speed sensor

14 Loosen the left front wheel lug nuts, raise the vehicle and support it securely on jackstands. Remove the left front wheel.

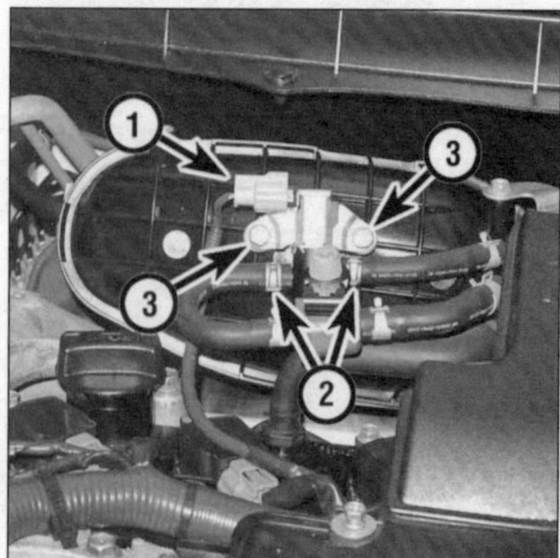

16.1 Canister purge control solenoid valve details - 2013 model shown other models similar

1 *Electrical connector*
2 *Hoses*
3 *Mounting bolts*

14.4 PCM mounting fasteners

15 Remove the left inner fender splash shield.
16 Disconnect the electrical connector from the speed sensor.
17 Remove the mounting bolt and remove the sensor. Discard the O-ring.
18 Apply some transmission fluid to the new O-ring and install it on the sensor.
19 Installation is the reverse of removal.

14 Powertrain Control Module (PCM) - removal and installation

Note: *The Powertrain Control Module (PCM) cannot be replaced at home because the new unit must be programmed with the Vehicle Identification Number (VIN) and other data. Doing so is impossible without a factory scan tool. This Section only shows PCM removal to gain access to other components.*
1 The PCM is located on a bracket mounted to the battery tray.
2 Remove the air inlet duct and the tube to the lower resonator (see Chapter 4).
3 Starting with the top connector, push in on the tang in the center of the PCM connector lock, then rotate the connector lock upward. Pull the connector away from the PCM to disconnect it. Repeat the procedure on the other two connectors (see illustration).
4 Remove the two mounting fasteners and remove the PCM (see illustration).
5 Installation is the reverse of removal.

16.10 Canister mounting bolt

15 Catalytic converter - replacement

Primary catalytic converter

1 The primary catalytic converter is an integral part of the exhaust manifold (see Chapter 2A).

Secondary catalytic converter

2 Raise the vehicle and support it securely on jackstands.
3 Spray a liberal amount of penetrating oil onto the threads of all fasteners to be removed.
4 Unscrew the two nuts that fasten the center exhaust pipe (catalytic converter) to the front exhaust pipe.
5 Unscrew the two nuts that fasten the center exhaust pipe (catalytic converter) to the rear pipe.
6 Remove the exhaust pipe (catalytic converter) and discard the front and rear gaskets.
7 Installation is the reverse of removal. Use new exhaust gaskets. Use anti-seize compound on all fasteners.

16 Evaporative Emissions Control (EVAP) system - component replacement

Purge control solenoid valve

1 Disconnect the hoses from the valve (see illustration).
2 Disconnect the electrical connector from the valve.
3 Remove the mounting bolts and detach the valve from the intake manifold.
4 Installation is the reverse of removal.

EVAP canister

Note: *The EVAP canister is located under the vehicle, to the rear of the right-rear wheel.*
5 Raise the rear of the vehicle and support it securely on jackstands.
6 Disconnect the electrical connectors from the control pressure sensor and the vent control valve.
7 Disconnect the canister purge hose from the canister.
8 Disconnect the fuel tank EVAP breather hose.
9 Disconnect the vent control valve hose.
10 Remove the canister retaining bolt (see illustration).
11 Remove the EVAP canister.
12 Installation is the reverse of removal.

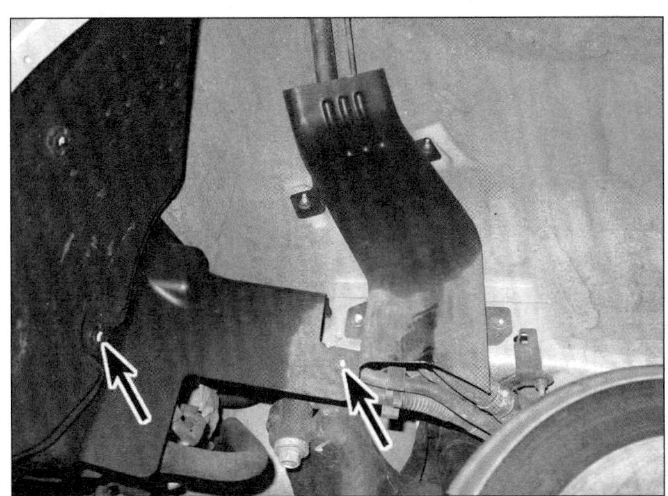

16.13 EVAP canister splash shield fasteners

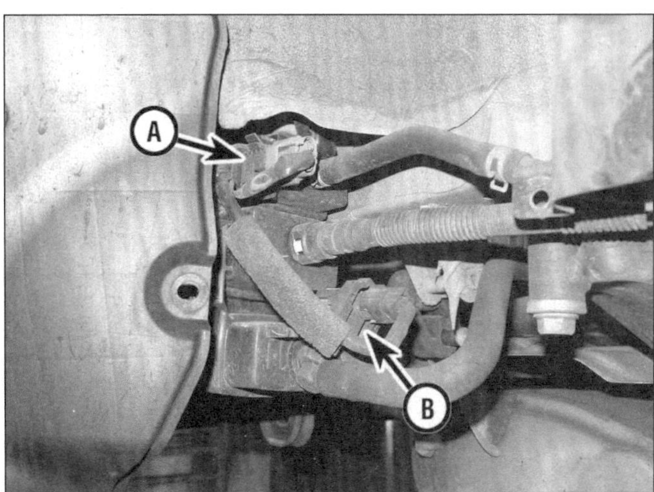

16.14 EVAP canister vent control valve (A) and pressure sensor (B)

EVAP pressure sensor and vent control valve

Note: *The EVAP canister vent control valve and EVAP canister system pressure sensor can be removed without removing the EVAP canister.*

13 Remove the EVAP canister splash shield (see illustration).

14 Remove the pressure sensor by pulling it straight out of the canister (see illustration).

15 To remove the vent control valve, turn it counterclockwise to unlock it, then pull it out of the canister.

16 Inspect the O-ring for cracks or tears and replace if necessary.

17 Installation is the reverse of removal.

17 Positive Crankcase Ventilation (PCV) valve - replacement

1 Refer to Chapter 1, Section 27 for information on the PCV system.

18 Throttle Position (TP) sensor - replacement

1 The Throttle Position sensor on these vehicles is an integral part of the throttle body and is not serviceable separately. Refer to Chapter 4 for the throttle body replacement procedure.

19 Engine Oil Temperature Sensor - replacement

Note: *Only 2014 and later models (except Rogue Select) are equipped with an oil temperature sensor.*

1 The engine oil temperature sensor is mounted on the firewall side of the engine block, near the oil cooler.

2 Disconnect the electrical connector from the engine oil temperature sensor.

3 Unscrew the sensor from the engine block.

4 Installation is the reverse of removal.

Notes

Chapter 7
Automatic transaxle

Contents

Specifications

Torque specifications

Ft-lbs (unless otherwise indicated)

Note: *One foot-pound (ft-lb) of torque is equivalent to 12 inch-pounds (in-lbs) of torque. Torque values below approximately 15 ft-lbs are expressed in inch-pounds, because most foot-pound torque wrenches are not accurate at these smaller values.*

Driveplate-to-torque converter nuts	38
Shift cable nut at transaxle	120 in-lbs
Transaxle-to-engine mounting bolts	
2013 and earlier models/2014 and later Rogue Select models	
Bolt 1	26
Bolts 2 and 5	55
Bolts 3 and 4	31
Bolts 6	37
2014 and later models (except Rogue Select models)	
Bolt 1	55
Bolts 2	37
Bolt 3	35
Bolt 4	55
Bolts 5, 6	37

1 General information

1 The vehicles covered by this manual are equipped with an automatic, Continuously Variable-ratio Transaxle (CVT). 2013 and earlier Rogue models and 2014/2015 Rogue Select models use a RE0F10A CVT, and 2014 and later Rogue models use a RE0F10D CVT. Both transaxles are very similar to each other.

2 Because of the complexity of the automatic transaxle and the specialized equipment needed to service it, this Chapter contains only those procedures related to general diagnosis, routine maintenance, adjustment, and removal and installation.

3 If the transaxle requires major repair work, it should be taken to a dealer service department or an automotive or transmission repair shop. You can, however, save money by removing and installing the transaxle yourself, even if the repair work is done by a shop.

2 Diagnosis - general

Note: *Automatic transaxle malfunctions may be caused by five general conditions: poor engine performance, improper adjustments, hydraulic malfunctions, mechanical malfunctions or malfunctions in the computer or its signal network. Diagnosis of these problems should always begin with a check of the easily repaired items: fluid level and condition (see Chapter 1), shift cable adjustment and throttle linkage adjustment. Next, perform a road test to determine if the problem has been corrected or if more diagnosis is necessary. If the problem persists after the preliminary tests and corrections are completed, additional diagnosis should be done by a dealer service department or transmission repair shop. Refer to the* Troubleshooting *section at the front of this manual for information on symptoms of transaxle problems.*

Preliminary checks

1 Drive the vehicle to warm the transaxle to normal operating temperature.

2 Check the fluid level as described in Chapter 1 :

a) *If the fluid level is unusually low, add enough fluid to bring the level within the designated area of the dipstick, then check for external leaks (see below).*

b) *If the fluid level is abnormally high, drain off the excess, then check the drained fluid for contamination by coolant. The presence of engine coolant in the automatic transmission fluid indicates that a failure has occurred in the internal radiator walls that separate the coolant from the transmission fluid (see Chapter 3).*

c) *If the fluid is foaming, drain it and refill the transaxle, then check for coolant in the fluid, or a high fluid level.*

3 Check for the presence of any stored diagnostic trouble codes (see Chapter 6). There are many potential transaxle-specific trouble codes that could be set, but certain engine-related problems can also affect transaxle operation.

4 Inspect the shift cable (see Section 5). Make sure that it's properly adjusted and operates smoothly.

Fluid leak diagnosis

5 Most fluid leaks are easy to locate visually. Repair usually consists of replacing a seal or gasket. If a leak is difficult to find, the following procedure may help.

6 Identify the fluid. Make sure it's transmission fluid and not engine oil or brake fluid (the fluid used in these transaxles is a light green color).

7 Try to pinpoint the source of the leak. Drive the vehicle several miles, then park it over a large sheet of cardboard. After a minute or two, you should be able to locate the leak by determining the source of the fluid dripping onto the cardboard.

8 Make a careful visual inspection of the suspected component and the area immediately around it. Pay particular attention to gasket mating surfaces. A mirror is often helpful for finding leaks in areas that are hard to see.

9 If the leak still cannot be found, clean the suspected area thoroughly with a degreaser or solvent, then dry it.

10 Drive the vehicle for several miles at normal operating temperature and varying speeds. After driving the vehicle, visually inspect the suspected component again.

11 Once the leak has been located, the cause must be determined before it can be properly repaired. If a gasket is replaced but the sealing flange is bent, the new gasket will not stop the leak. The bent flange must be straightened.

12 Before attempting to repair a leak, check to make sure that the following conditions are corrected or they may cause another leak.

Note: *Some of the following conditions cannot be fixed without highly specialized tools and expertise. Such problems must be referred to a transmission shop or a dealer service department.*

Gasket leaks

13 Check the pan periodically. Make sure the bolts are tight, no bolts are missing, the gasket is in good condition and the pan is flat (dents in the pan may indicate damage to the valve body inside).

14 If the pan gasket is leaking, the fluid level or the fluid pressure may be too high, the vent may be plugged, the pan bolts may be too tight, the pan sealing flange may be warped, the sealing surface of the transaxle housing may be damaged, the gasket may be damaged or the transaxle casting may be cracked or porous. If sealant instead of gasket material has been used to form a seal between the pan and the transaxle housing, it may be the wrong sealant.

Seal leaks

15 If a transaxle seal is leaking, the fluid level or pressure may be too high, the vent may be plugged, the seal bore may be damaged, the seal itself may be damaged or improperly installed, the surface of the shaft protruding through the seal may be damaged or a loose bearing may be causing excessive shaft movement.

16 Make sure the dipstick tube seal is in good condition and the tube is properly seated. Periodically check the area around the speedometer gear or sensor for leakage. If transmission fluid is evident, check the O-ring for damage.

Case leaks

17 If the case itself appears to be leaking, the casting is porous and will have to be repaired or replaced.

18 Make sure the oil cooler hose fittings are tight and in good condition.

Fluid comes out vent pipe or fill tube

19 If this condition occurs, the transaxle is overfilled, there is coolant in the fluid, the case is porous, the dipstick is incorrect, the vent is plugged or the drain-back holes are plugged.

3 Shift knob - removal and installation

Warning: *The models covered by this manual are equipped with Supplemental Restraint Systems (SRS), more commonly known as airbags. Always disable the airbag system before working in the vicinity of any airbag system components to avoid the possibility of accidental deployment of the airbags, which could cause personal injury (see Chapter 12).*

1 Move the shifter to the Neutral position. If necessary, push the shift interlock release with a screwdriver to allow shifting (see illustration).

2 Slide down the lower shift knob cover.

3 Using a small screwdriver or similar tool, remove the spring clip at the front of the shift knob (see illustration).

4 Remove the shift knob from the shifter.

5 Installation is reverse of removal.

4 Shifter assembly - removal and installation

Warning: *The models covered by this manual are equipped with Supplemental Restraint Systems (SRS), more commonly known as airbags. Always disable the airbag system before working in the vicinity of any airbag system components to avoid the possibility of accidental deployment of the airbags, which could cause personal injury (see Chapter 12).*

1 Remove the center console (see Chapter 11).

2 Disconnect the shifter assembly wiring harness (see illustration).

3 Disconnect the shift lock solenoid electrical connector (see illustration) then remove the solenoid by inserting a feeler gauge under the solenoid to release the locking tab and remove the solenoid.

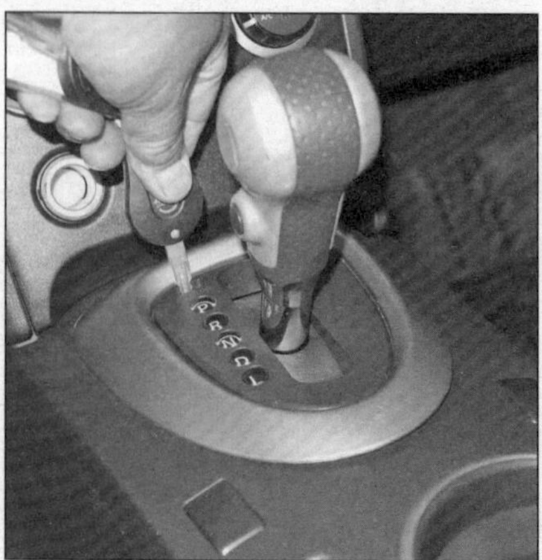

3.1 Push down on the manual shift release using the key to allow shifting to neutral

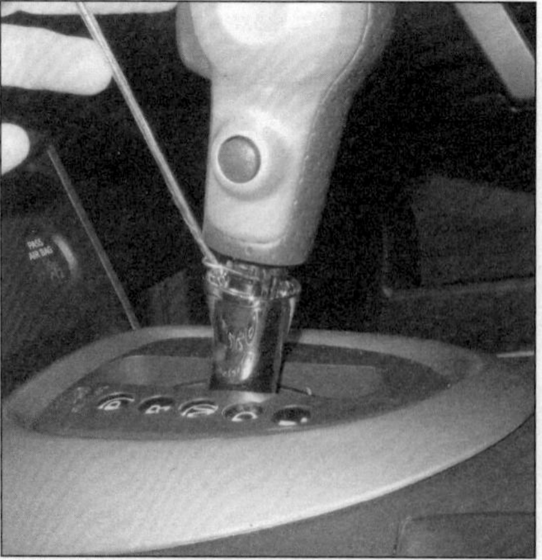

3.3 After sliding the cover down, pry out the spring clip

4.2 Disconnect the shifter electrical connector

4 Remove the shift interlock cable from the shifter assembly (see Section 8).

5 Remove the shift cable from the shifter assembly (see Section 5).

6 Remove the shifter assembly mounting bolts (see illustration) and remove the assembly.

7 Installation is the reverse of removal. Adjust the shift cable (see Section 5) and the shift interlock cable (see Section 8).

5 Shift cable - replacement and adjustment

Replacement

Warning: *The models covered by this manual are equipped with Supplemental Restraint*

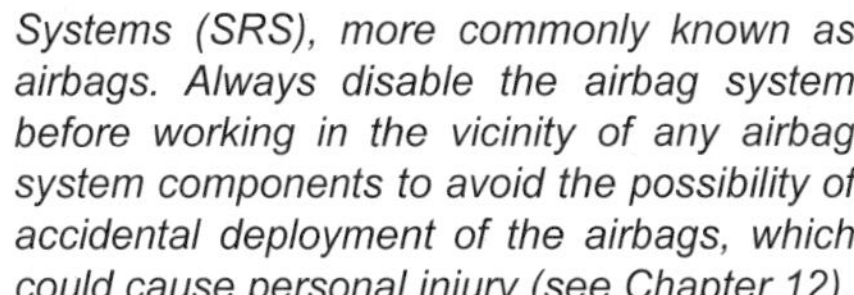

Systems (SRS), more commonly known as airbags. Always disable the airbag system before working in the vicinity of any airbag system components to avoid the possibility of accidental deployment of the airbags, which could cause personal injury (see Chapter 12).

1 Place the shifter in Park.

2 Detach the shift cable from the shifter assembly (see illustrations).

3 Remove the battery and battery tray (see Chapter 5). Once the tray is removed, remove the bracket mounting bolts and bracket (see illustration).

4 Remove the air filter housing (see Chapter 4).

5 Detach the cable from the shift lever and bracket on the transaxle (see illustration).

6 Raise the vehicle and support it securely on jackstands.

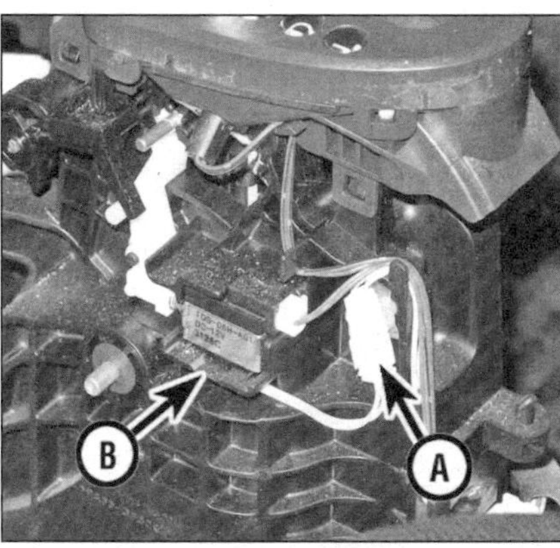

4.3 Disconnect the shift lock solenoid electrical connector (A), then insert a feeler gauge under the solenoid (B) to release the locking tab

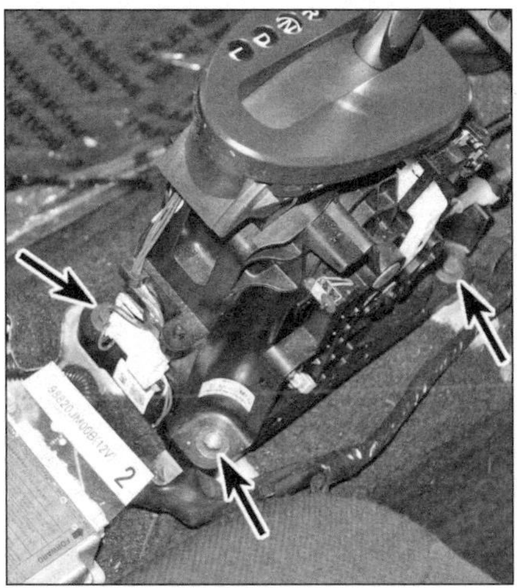

4.6 Remove the shifter assembly mounting bolts - three of four bolts shown

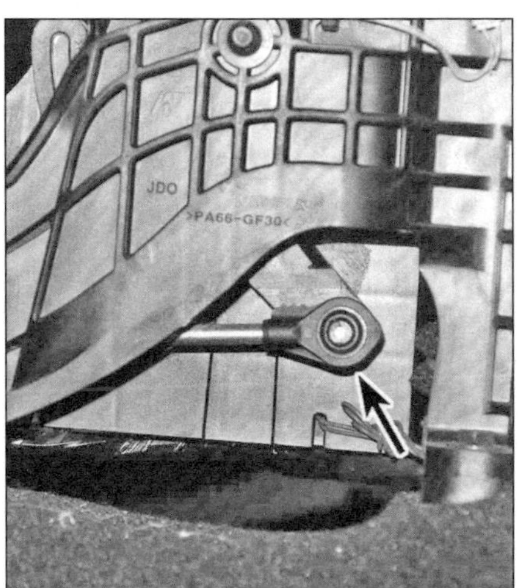

5.2a Pry the shifter cable from the pivot

5.2b Slide the cable up to disconnect it from the bracket

5.3 Remove the battery tray bracket fasteners

5.5 Shift cable details at the transaxle

1 Cable-to-manual lever locknut
2 Cable-to-bracket retaining clip

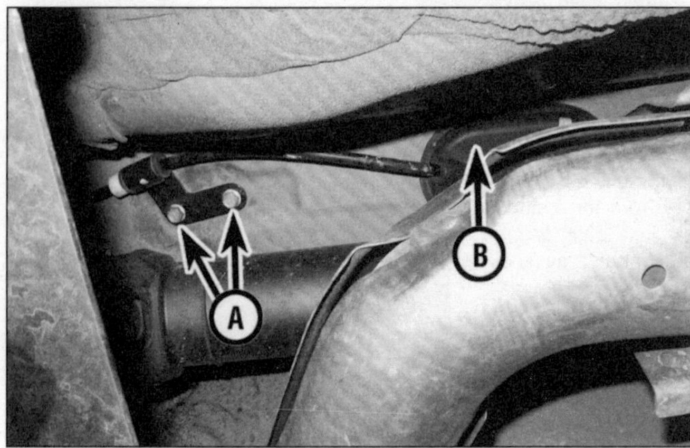

5.7 Shift cable support bracket bolts (A) and cable grommet (B)

7.3 Rotate the connector lock away from the TCM to disconnect the connector

8.5 Shift interlock cable details:

1 *Casing cap*
2 *Slider*
3 *Slider tangs*
4 *Adjuster holder (lock)*
5 *Interlock rod*

8.9 Remove the clip from the holder and remove the cable

1 *Clip*
2 *Holder*
3 *Interlock cable*

7 Unbolt the cable support bracket from the floorpan (see illustration).

8 Dislodge the grommet from the floorpan and remove the cable.

9 Installation is the reverse of removal, making sure the grommet seats properly in the floorpan. Adjust the cable (see Steps 101 through 15).

Adjustment

10 Remove the battery and battery tray (see Chapter 5) and the air filter housing (see Chapter 4).

11 Place the shift lever in the "P" position.

12 Loosen the shift cable-to-manual lever locknut (see illustration 5.5) and place the transaxle manual shift lever fully in the Park position.

13 Holding the manual lever in position, tighten the locknut.

14 Move the shift lever from "P" to "1." Make sure that it moves smoothly and that the shift indicator on the cluster matches the actual positions of the shift lever.

15 Verify the engine can be started only in Park and Neutral.

6 Transmission range switch - replacement and adjustment

1 Refer to Chapter 6 for this procedure.

7 Transmission Control Module (TCM) - removal and installtion

Note: *The Transaxle Control Module (TCM) cannot be replaced at home because the new unit must be programmed with the Vehicle Identification Number (VIN) and other data. Doing so is impossible without a factory scan tool. This Section only shows TCM removal to gain access to other components.*

1 Disconnect the cable from the negative terminal of the battery (see Chapter 5).

2 The TCM is mounted to a bracket on the battery tray.

3 Push in on the tang in the center of the TCM connector lock, rotate the lock lever back, then unplug the connector (see illustration).

4 Remove the TCM mounting nut and bolt and remove the TCM from the bracket.

5 Installation is the reverse of removal.

8 Shift interlock cable - replacement and adjustment

Replacement

1 Move the shift lever to the Neutral position.

2 Remove the shift knob (see Section 3).

3 Remove the center console (see Chapter 11).

4 Move the shift lever to the Park position.

5 Disconnect the shift interlock cable from the interlock rod by pressing in on the slider tangs (see illustration), and sliding slider away from the adjuster holder.

6 Pry the shift interlock cable from the shifter assembly bracket.

7 Remove the lower steering column trim panel (see Chapter 11).

8 Remove the steering column covers (see Chapter 11).

9 At the lock cylinder, remove the clip from the holder then remove the cable by pulling it from the lock cylinder (see illustration).

9.3 Carefully pry out the driveaxle oil seal with a seal removal tool or alarge screwdriver; make sure you don't damage the seal bore or the new seal may leak

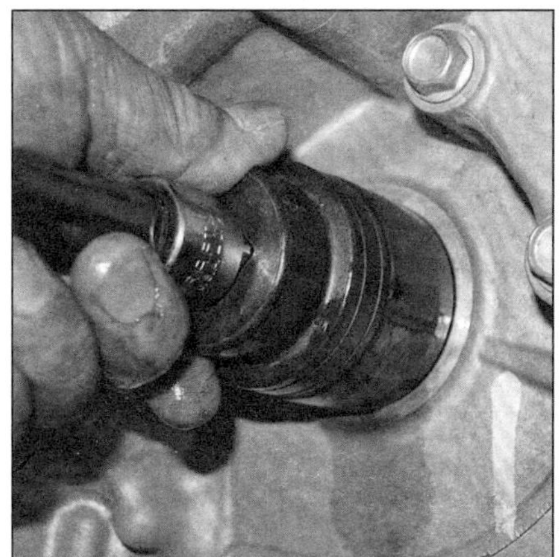

9.4 Use a seal installer or a large socket to install the new seal

10.14a Remove the inspection cover fasteners

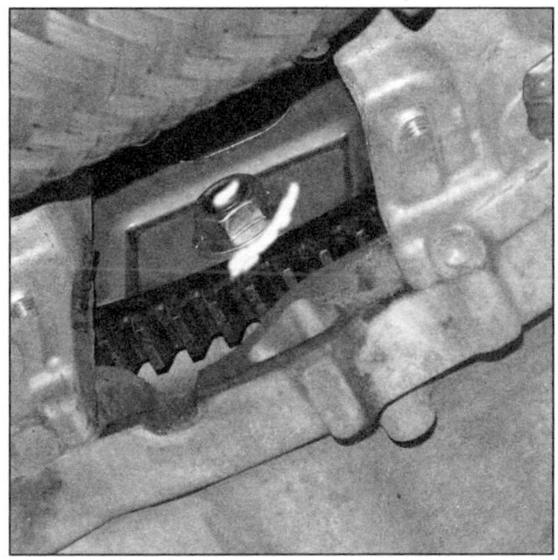

10.14b Mark the position of a torque converter stud to the driveplate, then remove the torque converter nuts by turning the crankshaft to bring each nut into the opening

10 Remove the cable from the vehicle.

11 Installation is the reverse of removal, noting the following:

a) *Ensure the shift lever is in the Park position*
b) *Turn the ignition switch to ACC or ON when installing the lock plate and cable into the ignition switch. After installing, turn the ignition switch to LOCK.*

Adjustment

12 Adjustment is not possible on the shift interlock cable. If the key cannot be removed when in Park, check the shift cable adjustment (see Section 5).

9 Driveaxle oil seal - replacement

1 The driveaxle oil seals are located on the sides of the transaxle, where the inner ends of the driveaxles are splined into the differential side gears. If you suspect that a driveaxle oil seal is leaking, raise the vehicle and support it securely on jackstands. If the seal is leaking, you'll see lubricant on the side of the transaxle, below the seal.

2 Remove the driveaxle (left side) or driveaxle and intermediate shaft (right side) (see Chapter 8).

3 Using a screwdriver or seal removal tool, carefully pry the seal out of the transaxle bore (see illustration).

4 Using a seal driver or a large deep socket as a drift, install the new oil seal. Drive it into the bore squarely and make sure it's fully seated (see illustration). Lubricate the lip of the new seal with multi-purpose grease.

5 Install the driveaxle (or driveaxle and extension shaft). Be careful not to damage the lip(s) of the new seal(s). Check the transaxle fluid level and add some, if necessary, to bring it up to the required level (see Chapter 1).

10 Automatic transaxle - removal and installation

Warning: *Wait until the engine is completely cool before beginning this procedure.*

Removal

1 Drain the transaxle fluid (see Chapter 1).

2013 and earlier models/2014 and later Rogue Select models

2 Remove the battery, battery tray (see Chapter 5) and the battery tray bracket (see illustration 5.3).

3 Remove the air inlet ducts and air filter housing (see Chapter 4).

4 Loosen the front wheel lug nuts and the driveaxle/hub nuts. Raise the vehicle and support it securely on jackstands.

5 Drain the engine coolant (see Chapter 1), then remove the engine splash shield.

6 Remove the transaxle dipstick tube fastener and tube. Be sure to replace the O-ring on the tube.

7 On models equipped with a transaxle cooler, disconnect the lines and plug the lines and openings.

8 Disconnect the electrical connectors from the transaxle then release the harness retaining clips and place the harness out of the way.

9 Disconnect the coolant hoses from the transaxle.

10 Remove the front section of the exhaust system.

11 Remove the drivaxles and, on AWD models, remove the driveshaft (see Chapter 8).

12 Remove the shift cable (see Section 5).

13 Remove the starter motor (see Chapter 5).

14 Remove the inspection cover fasteners and cover (see illustration), then paint match marks on the torque converter and driveplate so they can be assembled in the same position, then remove the torque converter nuts through the starter opening (see illustration).

15 Support the engine securely from above with a fixture that mounts between the fenders. These can be rented at most equipment rental yards.

16 Remove the transaxle upper mounting bolts.

17 Make sure that the engine is solidly supported by the fixture. Remove the subframe (see Chapter 10, Section 14).

18 Put a transmission jack (or a floor jack with an appropriate saddle) under the transaxle. Safety chains will help steady the transaxle on the jack.

19 Remove the remaining transaxle-to-engine bolts. Check to make certain that all connections between the transaxle and the vehicle are disconnected.

20 Move the transaxle to the rear to disengage it from the engine block dowel pins; make sure the torque converter is detached from the driveplate. Lower the transaxle with the jack. Clamp a pair of locking pliers on the

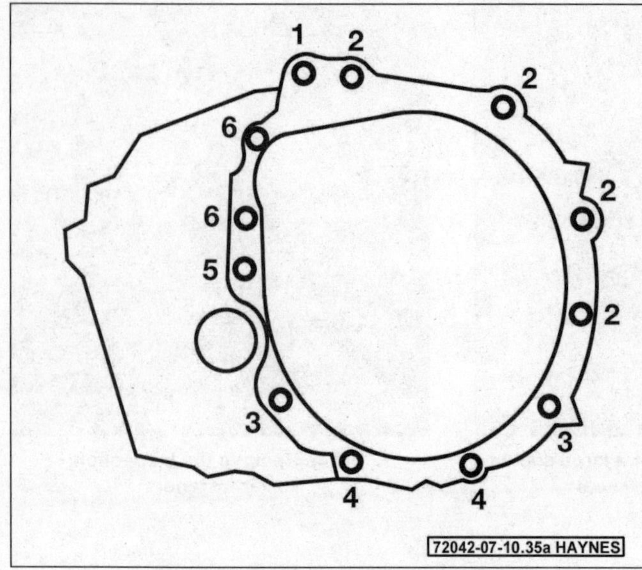

10.35a Transaxle mounting bolt length chart (2013 and earlier models/2014 and later Rogue Select models)

1, 2, 3 and 5: 1.77 inches
4: 1.38 inches
6: 2.36 inches

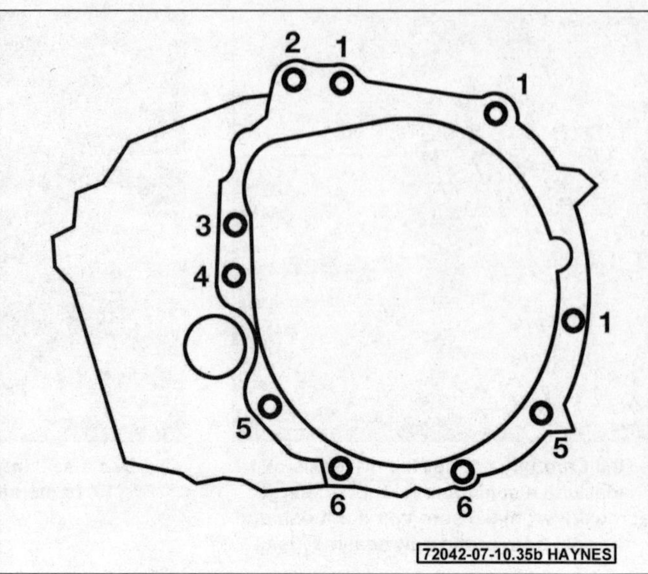

10.35b Transaxle mounting bolt length chart (2014 and later models, except Rogue Select models)

1, 2, 3, 4, 5: 1.77 inches
6: 1.38 inches

bellhousing case. The pliers will prevent the torque converter from falling out while you're removing the transaxle.

21 Pull the transaxle out from beneath the vehicle, remove it from the jack and set it where it can't roll over and become damaged.

2014 and later models (except Rogue Select models)

22 Remove the engine and transaxle assembly from the vehicle (see Chapter 2B).

23 Disconnect the component connectors and any harness brackets and remove the wiring harness from the transaxle.

24 Remove the starter (if not already done).

25 Remove the inspection cover fasteners and cover (see illustration 10.14a). Paint match marks on the torque converter and driveplate so they can be assembled in the same position, then remove the torque converter nuts through the starter opening (see illustration 10.14b).

26 Support the transaxle with a floor jack (preferably equipped with a transmission adapter). Remove the engine-to-transaxle bolts. Keep them organized so they can be installed in the same positions.

27 Separate the transaxle from the engine and slide it away.

28 If necessary, remove any external transaxle components.

29 Seal any openings to prevent contamination while removed.

Installation

Caution: *Use new O-rings and copper washers during installation; DO NOT reuse any of these.*

30 Flush the transaxle cooler and the cooler hoses and lines with solvent whenever the transaxle is removed from the vehicle. Flush the lines and fluid cooler thoroughly and make sure no solvent remains in the lines or cooler after flushing. It's a good idea to repeat the flushing procedure with clean automatic transmission fluid to ensure that no solvent remains in the lines or cooler.

31 Prior to installation, make sure that the torque converter hub is securely engaged in the pump. The front face of the torque converter must be 1/2-inch or more behind the front edge of the transaxle housing to be fully seated. Use a straight-edge and ruler to measure this distance so as to not damage the transaxle after installation.

32 Maneuver the transaxle to the rear of the engine.

33 Turn the torque converter to line it up with the driveplate. The marks you made on the torque converter and the driveplate must line up.

34 Move the transaxle forward carefully until the dowel pins and the torque converter are engaged.

35 Install the transaxle mounting bolts. Make sure the bolts are installed in the proper locations (see illustrations).

Caution: *Don't use the bolts to force the transaxle and engine together. If the transaxle doesn't slide easily up against the engine, find out why before you tighten the bolts.*

36 Tighten the bolts to the torque values listed in this Chapter's Specifications.

37 Install the torque converter bolts and tighten them to the torque listed in this Chapter's Specifications.

38 The remainder of installation is the reverse of removal.

39 Refill the cooling system (see Chapter 1).

40 Refill the transaxle with fluid to the specified level (see Chapter 1). Note that the transaxle may require more fluid than in a normal fluid and filter change, since the torque converter may be empty (the converter is not drained during a fluid change).

41 Start the engine, set the parking brake and shift the transaxle through all gears three times. Make sure the shift cable is working properly (see Section 5).

42 Allow the engine to reach its proper operating temperature with the transaxle in Park or Neutral, then turn it off and check the fluid level.

43 Road test the vehicle and check for fluid leaks.

Notes

Notes

Chapter 8
Clutch and driveaxles

Contents

Specifications

Driveaxles

Driveaxle CV joint length
- Front
  - Outer joint
    - 2013 and earlier models/2014 and later Rogue Select models... 5.26 inches
    - 2014 and later models (except Rogue Select models)........... 5.57 inches
  - Inner joint
    - 2013 and earlier models/2014 and later Rogue Select models... 6.52 inches
    - 2014 and later models (except Rogue Select models)........... 6.96 inches
- Rear
  - Outer joint
    - 2013 and earlier models/2014 and later Rogue Select models... 3.551 to 3.630 inches
    - 2014 and later models (except Rogue Select models)........... 3.75 inches
  - Inner joint
    - 2013 and earlier models/2014 and later Rogue Select models... 5.97 to 6.05 inches
    - 2014 and later models (except Rogue Select models)........... Not available

Torque specifications — **Ft-lbs** (unless otherwise indicated)

Note: *One foot-pound (ft-lb) of torque is equivalent to 12 inch-pounds (in-lbs) of torque. Torque values below approximately 15 ft-lbs are expressed in inch-pounds, because most foot-pound torque wrenches are not accurate at these smaller values.*

Item	Ft-lbs
Driveaxle/hub nut	
Front	
2013 and earlier models/2014 and later Rogue Select models	133 to 136
2014 and later models (except Rogue Select models)	188
Rear	92
Driveaxle support bearing retainer plate bolts	18
Driveaxle support bearing bracket-to-engine block bolts	
Step 1	35
Step 2	35
Driveshaft	
Driveshaft flange-to-differential flange bolt/nuts	
2013 and earlier models/2014 and later Rogue Select models	37
2014 and later models (except Rogue Select models)	48
Driveshaft flange-to-transfer case flange bolts	36
Driveshaft center bearing bracket nuts	33
Electric Controlled Coupling (ECC) bolts	144 in-lbs
Rear differential pinion flange nut (2013 and earlier models/2014 and later Rogue Select models)	103
Transfer case bolts	
2013 and earlier models/2014 and later Rogue Select models	32
2014 and later models (except Rogue Select models)	33

1 General information

1 The information in this Chapter deals with the driveaxles, and on AWD models the driveshaft, rear driveaxles, rear differential and transfer case components, from the rear of the engine to the front wheels, except for the transaxle, which is dealt with in Chapter 7.

2 Since nearly all the procedures covered in this Chapter involve working under the vehicle, make sure it's securely supported on sturdy jackstands or a hoist where the vehicle can be easily raised and lowered.

2 Driveaxles - general information

1 Power is transmitted from the transaxle to the wheels through a pair of driveaxles. The inner end of each driveaxle is splined into the differential side gears. The outer ends of the driveaxles are splined to the axle hubs and locked in place by a large nut.

2 The inner ends of the driveaxle are equipped with tripod-type constant velocity joints which are capable of both angular and axial motion. The right-side driveaxle is equipped with a solid intermediate shaft, which allows the use of equal-length driveaxles on each side.

3 The outer CV joints are the ball-and-cage type.

4 The boots should be inspected periodically for damage and leaking lubricant. Torn CV joint boots must be replaced as soon as possible or the joints can be damaged. Boot replacement involves removal of the driveaxle (see Section 4). The most common symptom of worn or damaged CV joints, besides lubricant leaks, is a clicking noise in turns, a clunk when accelerating after coasting and vibration at highway speeds. To check for wear in the CV joints and driveaxle shafts, grasp each axle (one at a time) and rotate it in both directions while holding the CV joint housings, feeling for play indicating worn splines or sloppy CV joints.

3 Driveaxles - removal and installation

Front

Removal

1 Loosen the front wheel lug nuts, raise the vehicle and support it securely on jackstands. Remove the wheel.

Note: *As an alternative you can leave the vehicle on the ground, remove the hubcap or center cap, remove the cotter pin and loosen the driveaxle nut.*

2 Remove the cotter pin and nut lock (if equipped) and unscrew the driveaxle/hub nut (see illustration).

3 Remove the lock nut and washer from the end of the driveaxle.

4 Remove the ABS wheel speed sensor from the steering knuckle (see Chapter 9, Section 3).

5 Remove the control arm balljoint-to-steering knuckle pinch bolt (see illustration).

6 Pry downward on the control arm to separate the balljoint from the steering knuckle (see illustration).

7 Push the driveaxle out of the hub while pulling outward on the steering knuckle and hub assembly. If the driveaxle splines are frozen, free them by tapping the end of the driveaxle with a soft-faced hammer or a hammer and a brass punch, or use a puller to push the driveaxle from the hub. Use a puller if necessary.

8 Place a drain pan underneath the transaxle to catch any lubricant that may spill out when the driveaxles are removed.

9 For the left driveaxle, use a prybar to carefully pry the inner CV joint out of the transaxle, and remove the driveaxle (see illustration).

10 The inner CV joint housing on the right (passenger's side) driveaxle terminates at a support bracket. To detach the right driveaxle assembly from the bracket, remove the retainer-to-bracket bolts (see illustration), mark the relationship of the bearing to the support bracket and pull out the driveaxle assembly. Do not try to separate the bearing from the inner CV joint until you have the entire assembly on the bench.

11 Install a new driveaxle oil seal on the transaxle case (see Chapter 7).

3.2 Place a prybar between two wheel studs while you loosen the driveaxle nut

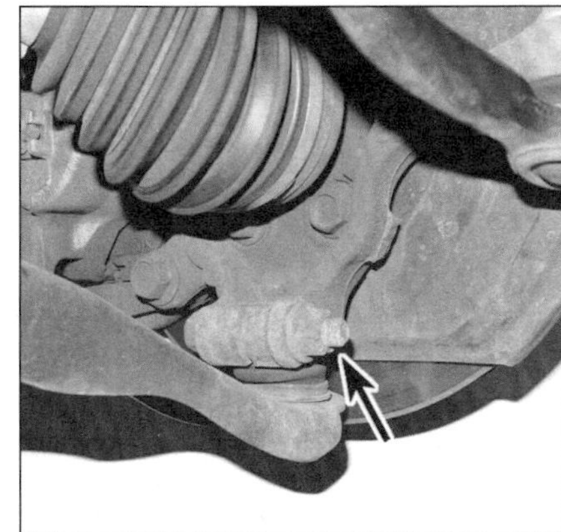

3.5 Remove the pinch-bolt

3.6 Pry downward to remove the balljoint from the knuckle

3.9 If you're removing the left driveaxle, carefully pry the inner CV joint out of the transaxle

3.10 Remove the retainer plate-to-bracket bolts

Installation

12 Installation is the reverse of removal, noting the following:

13 If reusing the old axle, install a new retaining clip on the axle end before installation (see illustration).

14 When installing the right driveaxle, tighten the retainer plate-to-bracket bolts in two steps to the torque listed in this Chapter's Specifications.

a) *When installing the left driveaxle, push the driveaxle in sharply to seat the retaining ring on the inner CV joint into its groove in the differential side gear. To ease insertion and seating of the retaining ring, position the gap in the ring at the bottom.*
b) *Tighten the control arm balljoint-to-steering knuckle pinch bolt to the torque listed in the Chapter 10 Specifications.*
c) *Tighten the driveaxle/hub nut to the torque listed in this Chapter's Specifications , then install a new cotter pin.*
d) *Install the wheel and lug nuts, lower the vehicle and tighten the lug nuts to the torque listed in the Chapter 1 Specifications.*
e) *Check the transaxle lubricant and add, if necessary, to bring it to the proper level (see Chapter 1).*

Rear

Removal

15 Loosen the rear wheel lug nuts, raise the vehicle and support it securely on jackstands. Remove the wheel(s).

Note: *As an alternative you can leave the vehicle on the ground, remove the hubcap or center cap, remove the cotter pin and loosen the driveaxle nut.*

16 Remove the cotter pin, then place a prybar between two wheel studs while you loosen the driveaxle nut (see illustration 3.2). Unscrew the driveaxle/hub nut until it is flush with the end of the axle.

17 To loosen the driveaxle from the hub splines, place a block of wood between the nut and driveaxle end and strike it with a hammer, or use a hammer and brass punch to tap the end of the driveaxle in. If the driveaxle is stuck in the hub splines and won't move, it may be necessary to push the driveaxle with a suitable puller.

18 Once the axle is free, remove the nut from the end of the driveaxle.

19 Remove the wheel speed sensor from the trailing arm (see Chapter 9).

20 Remove the rear brake disc (see Chapter 9).

21 Unbolt the rear stabilizer bar link from the lower suspension arm (see Chapter 10).

22 Place a floor jack under the coil spring pocket of the trailing arm and raise it slightly.

Warning: *The jack must stay in this position throughout the procedure.*

23 Unbolt the lower end of the shock absorber from the trailing arm (see Chapter 10).

24 Unbolt the upper and lower control arms from the trailing arm (see Chapter 10).

25 Push the driveaxle out of the hub while pulling outward on the trailing arm assembly. Adjust the height of the jack as necessary.

26 Place a drain pan underneath the rear differential to catch any lubricant that may spill out when the driveaxles are removed.

27 Use a prybar to carefully pry the inner CV joint out of the rear differential, and remove the driveaxle.

28 If necessary, install a new driveaxle oil seal on the rear differential housing (see Section 8).

Installation

29 Installation is the reverse of removal, noting the following:

30 If reusing the old axle, install a new retaining clip on the axle end before installation.

a) *When installing the driveaxle, push the driveaxle in sharply to seat the retaining ring on the inner CV joint into its groove in the differential side gear. To ease insertion and seating of the retaining ring, position the gap in the ring at the bottom.*
b) *Tighten the control arms bolts to the torque listed in the Chapter 10 Specifications.*
c) *Tighten the driveaxle/hub nut to the torque listed in this Chapter's Specifications , then install a new cotter pin.*
d) *Install the wheel and lug nuts, lower the vehicle and tighten the lug nuts to the torque listed in the Chapter 1 Specifications.*
e) *Check the differential lubricant and add, if necessary, to bring it to the proper level (see Chapter 1).*

4 Driveaxle boot - replacement

Note: *If the CV joints must be overhauled (usually due to torn boots), explore all options before beginning the job. Complete rebuilt driveaxles are available on an exchange basis, which eliminates much time and work. Whichever route you choose to take, check on the cost and availability of parts before disassembling the vehicle.*

Inner CV joint

Disassembly

Note: *Because the manufacturer does not give an inner CV joint length dimension for 2014 and later models (except Rogue Select models), be sure to measure the length of the joint prior to disassembly (see illustration 4.11a).*

1 Remove the driveaxle (see Section 3).

2 Remove the boot clamps (see illustrations).

3 Pull the boot back from the inner CV joint, remove the retaining ring, then slide off the joint housing (see illustration).

Note: *Not all models are equipped with a retaining ring.*

4 Mark the tripod and axleshaft to ensure that they are reassembled properly (see illustration).

5 Remove the snap-ring from the end of the axleshaft with a pair of snap-ring pliers (see illustration).

3.13 Install a new retaining clip if reusing the old driveaxle

4.2a Pry up the retaining tabs on the boot clamps . . .

4.2b . . . then open the clamps and remove them from the boot

6 Use a hammer and a brass punch to drive the tripod joint from the driveaxle (see illustration). Some driveaxles are equipped with a rubber dynamic balancer that is retained by clamps. If it is necessary to remove the balancer, be sure to first mark the location of the balancer and clamps so they can be reinstalled in the same location.

Check

7 Clean all components with solvent to remove the grease, and check for cracks, pitting, scoring and other signs of wear.

Reassembly

8 Slide the clamps and boot onto the axleshaft. It's a good idea to wrap the axleshaft splines with tape to prevent damaging the boot (see illustration). Remove the tape, place the tripod on the shaft (see illustration) and install the snap-ring. Apply grease to the tripod assembly, the inside of the joint housing and the inside of the boot.

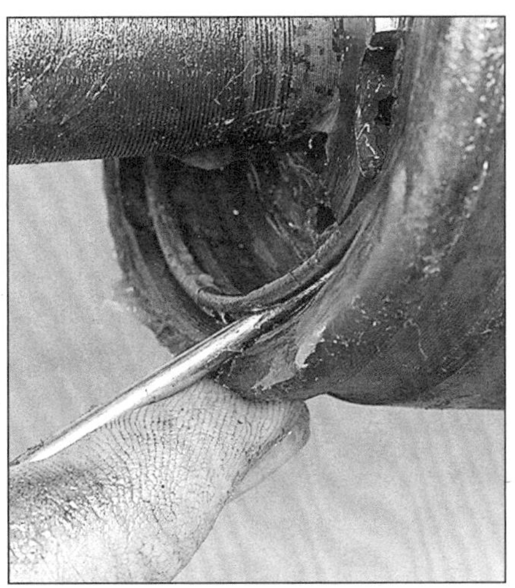

4.3 Pull the boot back, then pry the retaining ring from its groove

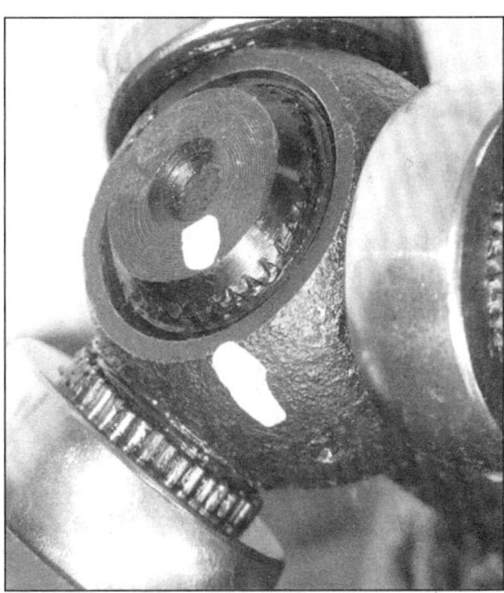

4.4 Use paint or a center punch to place marks on the tripod and the driveaxle to ensure that they're properly reassembled

4.5 Remove the snap-ring from the groove in the end of the axleshaft

4.6 Drive the tripod joint from the axleshaft with a brass punch and hammer - make sure you don't damage the bearing surfaces or the splines on the shaft

4.8a Wrap the splined area of the axleshaft with tape to prevent damage to the boots when installing them

4.8b Install the tripod with the chamfered (tapered) ends of the splines facing toward the axleshaft

9 Install the housing on the joint, then install the retaining ring, if equipped, making sure it seats in its groove in the housing.

10 Slide the boot into place, making sure both ends seat in their grooves.

11 Adjust the length of the joint (see illustration), equalize the pressure in the boot (see illustration), then tighten and secure the boot clamps (see illustrations).

12 Install a new circlip on the inner CV joint stub axle.

13 Install the driveaxle (see Section 3).

Outer CV joint

14 Remove the driveaxle (see Section 3), then remove the boot clamps (see illustrations 4.2a and 4.2b).

15 Refer to the accompanying illustrations and perform the outer CV joint boot replacement procedure (see illustrations).

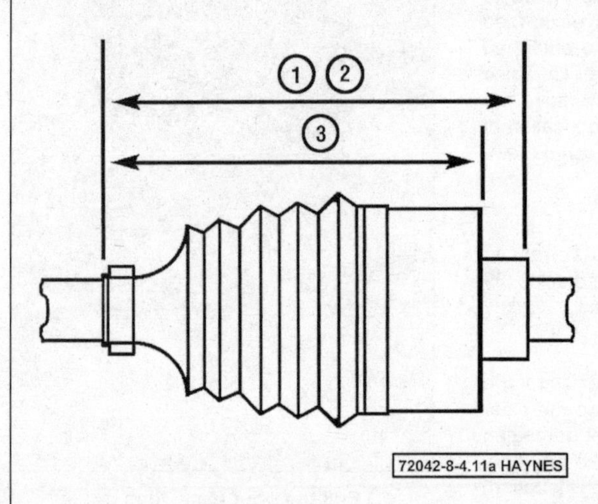

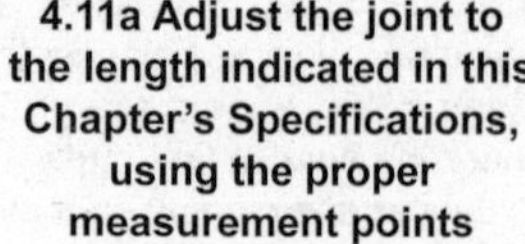

4.11a Adjust the joint to the length indicated in this Chapter's Specifications, using the proper measurement points

1 *Rear driveaxle - 2013 and earlier models/2014 and later Rogue Select models*
2 *Front driveaxle - all models*
3 *Rear driveaxle - 2014 and later models (except Rogue Select models)*

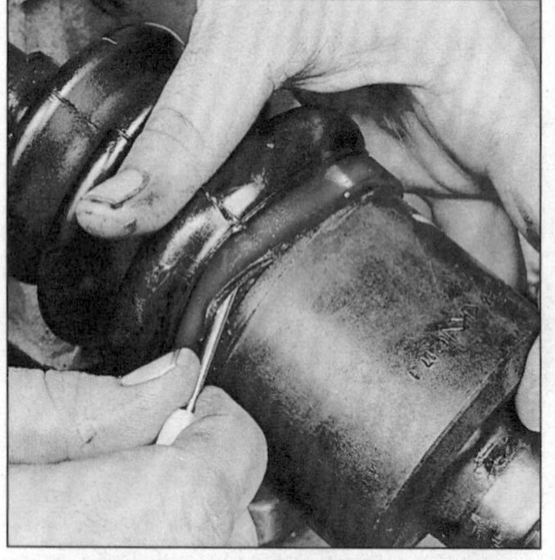

4.11b Equalize the pressure inside the boot by inserting a small, DULL screwdriver between the boot and the CV joint housing

4.11c To install the new clamps, bend the tang down . . .

4.11d . . . and tap the tabs down to hold it in place

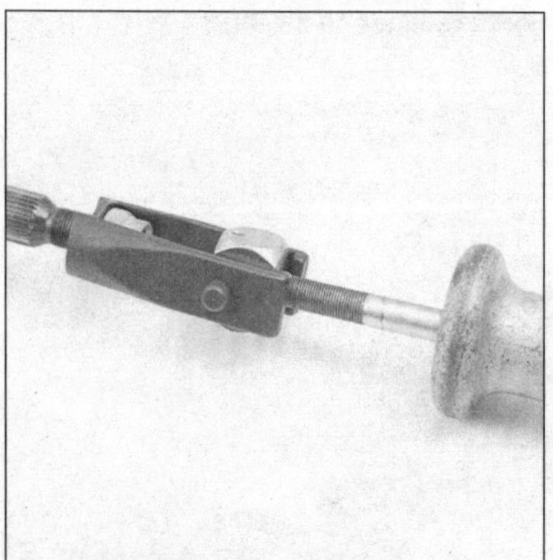

4.15a Outer CV joints can be removed with a slide hammer; you'll need an adapter and a slide hammer setup such as the one shown here

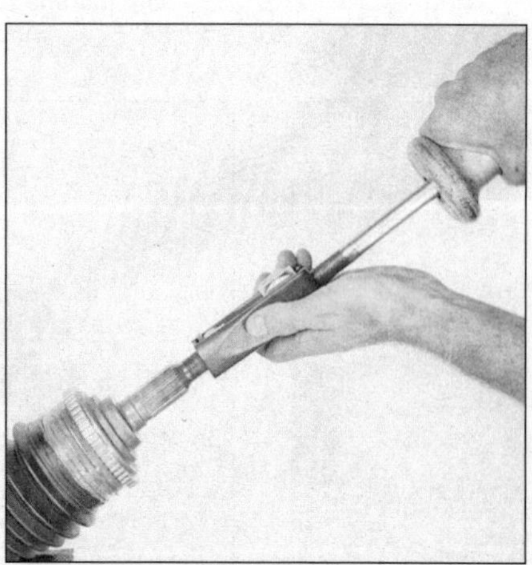

4.15b With the axleshaft firmly clamped down in a bench vise and the adapter gripping the driveaxle/hub nut, carefully extract the outer CV joint from the axleshaft. If it won't come off after five or six attempts, replace the driveaxle assembly

4.15c After the old grease has been rinsed away, move the inner race through its full range of motion and inspect the bearing surfaces for wear or damage

4.15d Apply CV joint grease through the splined hole, then insert a wooden dowel (slightly smaller in diameter than the hole) into the hole and push down - the dowel will force the grease into the joint. Repeat this until the joint is packed

4.15e Wrap the splined area of the axleshaft with tape to prevent damage to the boot when installing it

4.15f Install the small clamp and the boot on the driveaxle and apply grease to the inside of the axle boot . . .

4.15g . . . until the level is up to the end of the axle

4.15h Install a new circlip into the groove at the end of the driveaxle. Position the CV joint assembly on the driveaxle, aligning the splines . . .

4.15i . . . then use a hammer and brass punch to carefully drive the joint onto the driveaxle

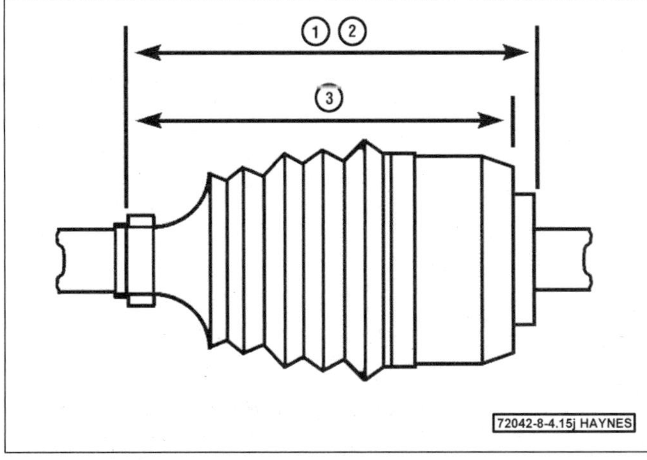

4.15j Adjust the joint to the length indicated in this Chapter's Specifications, using the proper measurement points . . .

1 Front driveaxle - all models
2 Rear driveaxle - 2014 and later models (except Rogue Select models)
3 Rear driveaxle - 2013 and earlier models/2014 and later Rogue Select models

4.15k . . . then equalize the pressure inside the boot by inserting a small, dull screwdriver between the boot and the outer race, then tighten the clamps (see illustrations 4.11c and 4.11d)

5.3 Mark the relationship of the driveshaft to the differential (shown) and transfer case flanges

5.4 Driveshaft center support bearing bracket nuts

5 Driveshaft (AWD models) - removal and installation

1 Raise the rear of the vehicle and support it securely on jackstands. Block the front wheels to prevent the vehicle from rolling.

Note: *If you're concerned about a possibly bent driveshaft causing a vibration, mount a dial indicator to the floor of the vehicle and check the driveshaft runout in the middle of the front and rear sections.*

2 Turn the key On, then shift the transaxle into Neutral. Turn the key Off. Release the parking brake.

3 Mark the relationship of the driveshaft flanges to the differential and transfer case flanges (see illustration).

4 Loosen (but don't remove) the nuts of the center bearing brackets (see illustration).

5 Remove the flange bolts from each end of the driveshaft. You'll have to insert a tool into the u-joint to keep the driveshaft from turning as you break the nuts and bolts loose.

6 Remove the center support bearing nuts and remove the driveshaft.

7 Remove the center bearing bracket from the driveshaft.

8 Installation is the reverse of removal. Attach the center bearing bracket so that the arrow on it is facing forward. Align the match marks you made previously as you attach each end of the driveshaft. Tighten the nuts and bolts to the torque values listed in this Chapter's Specifications.

6 Driveshaft and universal joints (AWD models) - general information and inspection

General information

1 The driveshaft used on these vehicles is a pair of tubes that transmit power between the transfer case and the rear differential. There are universal joints at each end of the driveshaft and a constant velocity joint in the center, supported by a bearing.

2 The driveshaft assembly requires very little service. The universal joints are lubricated for life; if any part of the driveshaft develops a problem, the manufacturer states that the entire driveshaft must be replaced. Some driveline specialty shops are capable of rebuilding these assemblies, though. It's a good idea to call around to see if this is a viable option before purchasing a new driveshaft.

3 Since the driveshaft is a balanced unit, it's important that no undercoating or mud be allowed to stay on it. When the vehicle is raised for service, it's a good idea to clean the driveshaft and inspect it for obvious damage. Make sure that the small weights welded on to balance the driveshaft haven't been knocked off. Whenever it's removed, the driveshaft must be installed in the same position relative to the flanges on the transfer case and the differential in order to maintain the balance.

4 Problems with the driveshaft are usually indicated by a noise or vibration. A road test should verify if the problem is the driveshaft or another component. Refer to the Troubleshooting Section at the front of this manual.

Inspection

5 Raise the vehicle and support it securely on jackstands. Block the wheels at the opposite end to keep it from rolling off the stands. Release the parking brake and place the transaxle in Neutral.

6 Visually inspect the driveshaft as you turn it by hand. Look for dents and cracks. If any are found, replace the driveshaft.

7 Check for leakage at the front and rear. Oil leakage here means a defective transfer case or differential seal. Also check for looseness of the joints of the rear driveaxles. Grease leakage at the CV joint boots indicates a damaged rubber boot.

8 Rotate the driveshaft and make sure the universal joints are operating properly with no binding, noise or looseness. Listen for noise from the center bearing; this indicates wear or damage.

9 Grip each joint and try to twist it and wiggle it up and down. Any movement at all in the joint is a sign of considerable wear.

10 Check the driveshaft mounting bolts and nuts at each end to be sure they're tight. Finally, check the center bearing for looseness or rubber deterioration and be sure that the bearing bracket isn't bent.

7 Differential oil seals (rear, AWD models) - replacement

Driveaxle oil seals

1 Loosen the wheel lug nuts, raise the rear of the vehicle and support it securely on jackstands. Chock the front wheels to prevent the vehicle from rolling. Remove the wheel.

2 Remove the driveaxle (see Section 3).

3 The side oil seals in the rear differential can be pried out with a large screwdriver or seal removal tool.

4 The new seal should be driven in with a seal installer. If you don't have a seal installer, a large socket with an outside diameter just slightly smaller than that of the seal can be used as a driver.

5 Install the driveaxle (see Section 3).

Caution: *Take care not to cut or scratch the new seal with the splines of the driveaxles during installation.*

6 The remainder of installation is the reverse of removal. Check the differential lubricant level and add some, if necessary (see Chapter 1).

7 Install the wheel and lug nuts. Lower the vehicle and tighten the lug nuts to the torque listed in the Chapter 1 Specifications.

8.5 Remove the differential mounting nut from the rear of the subframe

8.6 Remove the differential mounting bracket-to-subframe nuts and through-bolts

Pinion shaft oil seal

8 Raise the rear of the vehicle and support it securely on jackstands.

9 Remove the driveshaft (see Section 5).

2013 and earlier models/2014 and later Rogue Select models

10 Make match marks on the pinion flange and the pinion shaft.

11 Unscrew the pinion flange nut while holding the flange from turning with a flange holding tool, pin spanner or chain wrench. Remove the flange from the shaft.

12 Using a seal removal tool, pry the seal from the Electric Controlled Coupling.

13 Using a seal driver, install the new seal until it is flush with the Electric Controlled Coupling.

14 Lubricate the seal lips with multi-purpose grease, then install the pinion flange, lining up the previously made matchmarks.

15 Install the nut, tightening it to the torque listed in this Chapter's Specifications.

16 Install the driveshaft (see Section 5).

17 Check the rear differential lubricant level (see Chapter 1).

2014 and later models (except Rogue Select models)

18 Remove the Electric Controlled Coupling (see Section 9).

19 Using a seal removal tool, pry the seal from the differential housing.

20 Using a seal driver, install the new seal until it 0.031 to 0.047-inch below the surface of the differential housing.

21 Install the Electric Controlled Coupling (see Section 9).

22 Install the driveshaft (see Section 5).

23 Check the rear differential lubricant level (see Chapter 1).

8 Rear differential (AWD models) - removal and installation

1 Disconnect the driveshaft from the differential (see Section 5). Use wire to hang the rear of the driveshaft out of the way.

2 Remove the rear driveaxles (see Section 3).

3 Note the routing of the wiring, then disconnect the wiring from the differential. Note the routing of the breather hoses, then detach them.

4 Place a floor jack under the differential and adjust it so it supports the weight of the differential.

5 Remove the differential mounting nut from the rear of the subframe (see illustration).

6 Make sure that the jack is properly seated under the differential, then remove the differential mounting bracket-to-subframe nuts and through-bolts (see illustration).

7 Carefully lower the differential with the jack until it can be slid from under the vehicle.

8 Installation is the reverse of removal. Route the vent hoses and wiring as they were originally and align the driveshaft flange mark with the mark on the differential flange.

9 Tighten the mounting fasteners to the torques listed in this Chapter's Specifications. Check the lubricant level and add some if necessary (see Chapter 1 Specifications).

9.4 Disconnect the electrical connector from the ECC - 2013 and earlier models/2014 and later Rogue Select models shown,other models similar

9 Electric Controlled Coupling (ECC) - removal and installation

1 Raise the vehicle and support it securely on jackstands.

2 Remove rear driveshaft (see Section 5).

3 Drain the rear differential lubricant (see Chapter 1).

4 Disconnect the electrical connectors from the Electric Controlled Coupling (ECC) magnetic clutch (see illustration).

5 Remove the ECC mounting bolt/nuts, then use a flat-blade screwdriver to separate the coupling from the differential.

6 Clean the sealing surfaces, making sure all the sealant is removed, then spray the mating surfaces with brake cleaner to remove all oil residue.

7 Apply a continuous bead of sealant, approximately 1/8-inch (3 mm) wide, around the coupling mating surface. If the sealant is not in a continuous bead, overlap any breaks in the bead by 1/8-inch (3 mm).

8 Align the coupling with the differential, place the coupling onto the differential and install the bolts. Tighten the bolts to the torque listed in this Chapter's Specifications.

9 The remainder of installation is the reverse of removal.

10 Transfer case (AWD models) - removal and installation

1 Remove the front section of the exhaust pipe nuts and remove the exhaust pipe.

Note: *On 2013 and earlier models/2014 and later Rogue Select models, it may be necessary to remove the center section of the exhaust pipe.*

2 Remove the driveshaft (see Section 5).

3 Remove the right-side driveaxle (see Section 3).

4 Remove the front subframe (see Chapter 10, Section 14).

5 Support the transaxle with a floor jack. Place a piece of wood between the jack head and the transaxle to protect the aluminum housing.

Caution: *Make sure that the jack doesn't contact the drain plug.*

6 Remove the transfer case mounting bolts, making note of their locations (the bolts are different lengths and must be installed in their original positions).

7 Remove the transfer case.

Note: *The manufacturer recommends always replacing the transaxle oil seal when the transfer case is removed (see Chapter 7).*

8 Installation is the reverse of removal.

9 Check the transaxle lubricant and transfer case lubricant and add, if necessary, to bring it to the proper level (see Chapter 1).

Chapter 9
Brakes

Contents

Specifications

General

Brake fluid type .... See Chapter 1

Disc brakes

Minimum pad thickness .... See Chapter 1
Brake disc minimum thickness .... Cast into disc
Maximum disc runout
 Front .... 0.0014 inch
 Rear .... 0.0028 inch
Maximum disc thickness variation
 Front .... 0.0008 inch
 Rear .... 0.0006 inch

Power brake booster

Booster-to-clevis hole center dimension
 2013 and earlier models/2014 and later Rogue Select models .... 6.03 to 6.07 inches
 2014 and later models (except Rogue Select models) .... Not adjustable

Brake pedal dimensions

Free height from steel floor to top of pedal
 2013 and earlier models/2014 and later Rogue Select models .... 7.23 to 7.63 inches
 2014 and later models (except Rogue Select models) .... 9.63 to 7.32 inches

Parking brake

Parking brake adjustment (pedal-operated parking brake) .... 6 to 7 clicks

Brake light and brake pedal position switches

Clearance between pedal stopper bracket and switch contact end
 2013 and earlier models/2014 and later Rogue Select models .... 0.0039 to 0.0772 inch
 2014 and later models (except Rogue Select models) .... 0.0079 to 0.0772 inch

Torque specifications

Ft-lbs (unless otherwise indicated)

Note: *One foot-pound (ft-lb) of torque is equivalent to 12 inch-pounds (in-lbs) of torque. Torque values below approximately 15 ft-lbs are expressed in inch-pounds, because most foot-pound torque wrenches are not accurate at these smaller values.*

Brake caliper

Caliper mounting bolts	
Front	25
Rear	32
Caliper mounting bracket bolts	
Front	122
Rear	62
Brake hose-to-caliper banjo bolt	156 in-lbs
Master cylinder-to-brake booster retaining nuts	
2013 and earlier models/2014 and later Rogue Select models	156 in-lbs
2014 and later models (except Rogue Select models)	96 in-lbs
Power brake booster mounting nuts	
2013 and earlier models/2014 and later Rogue Select models	108 in-lbs
2014 and later models (except Rogue Select models)	96 in-lbs
ABS wheel speed sensor	
Front	84 in-lbs
Rear	84 in-lbs

1 General information

1 The vehicles covered by this manual are equipped with hydraulically operated front and rear brake systems. The front and rear brakes are self-adjusting disc-type brakes.

Hydraulic system

2 The hydraulic system consists of two separate circuits. The master cylinder has separate reservoirs for the two circuits, and, in the event of a leak or failure in one hydraulic circuit, the other circuit will remain operative and a warning indicator will light up on the instrument panel when a substantial amount of brake fluid is lost, showing that a failure has occurred.

Power brake booster

3 The power brake booster uses engine manifold vacuum to provide assistance to the brakes. It is mounted on the firewall in the engine compartment, directly behind the master cylinder.

Parking brake

4 The parking brake actuates a pair of parking brake shoes mounted inside a drum (hub) portion of each rear brake disc. The parking brake cables and shoes are adjustable.

Service

5 After completing any operation involving disassembly of any part of the brake system, always test drive the vehicle to check for proper braking performance before resuming normal driving. When testing the brakes, perform the tests on a clean, dry, flat surface. Conditions other than these can lead to inaccurate test results.

6 Test the brakes at various speeds with both light and heavy pedal pressure. The vehicle should stop evenly without pulling to one side or the other. Under hard braking, the ABS system may engage, resulting in brake pedal pulsation. This is considered normal operation.

7 Tires, vehicle load and wheel alignment are factors which also affect braking performance.

Precautions

8 There are some general cautions and warnings involving the brake system on this vehicle:

a) *Use only brake fluid conforming to DOT 3 specifications.*
b) *The brake pads and linings contain fibers which are hazardous to your health if inhaled. Whenever you work on brake system components, clean all parts with brake system cleaner. Do not allow the fine dust to become airborne. Also, wear an approved filtering mask.*
c) *Safety should be paramount whenever any servicing of the brake components is performed. Do not use parts or fasteners which are not in perfect condition, and be sure that all clearances and torque specifications are adhered to. If you are at all unsure about a certain procedure, seek professional advice. Upon completion of any brake system work, test the brakes carefully in a controlled area before putting the vehicle into normal service. If a problem is suspected in the brake system, don't drive the vehicle until it's fixed.*
d) *Used brake fluid is considered a hazardous waste and it must be disposed of in accordance with federal, state and local laws. DO NOT pour it down the sink, into septic tanks or storm drains, or on the ground.*
e) *Clean up any spilled brake fluid immediately and then wash the area with large amounts of water. This is especially true for any finished or painted surfaces.*

2 Troubleshooting

PROBABLE CAUSE	CORRECTIVE ACTION
No brakes - pedal travels to floor	
1 Low fluid level 2 Air in system	1 and 2 Low fluid level and air in the system are symptoms of another problem a leak somewhere in the hydraulic system. Locate and repair the leak
3 Defective seals in master cylinder	3 Replace master cylinder
4 Fluid overheated and vaporized due to heavy braking	4 Bleed hydraulic system (temporary fix). Replace brake fluid (proper fix)
Brake pedal slowly travels to floor under braking or at a stop	
1 Defective seals in master cylinder	1 Replace master cylinder
2 Leak in a hose, line, caliper or wheel cylinder	2 Locate and repair leak
3 Air in hydraulic system	3 Bleed the system, inspect system for a leak
Brake pedal feels spongy when depressed	
1 Air in hydraulic system	1 Bleed the system, inspect system for a leak
2 Master cylinder or power booster loose	2 Tighten fasteners
3 Brake fluid overheated (beginning to boil)	3 Bleed the system (temporary fix). Replace the brake fluid (proper fix)
4 Deteriorated brake hoses (ballooning under pressure)	4 Inspect hoses, replace as necessary (it's a good idea to replace all of them if one hose shows signs of deterioration)

Troubleshooting (continued)

Brake pedal feels hard when depressed and/or excessive effort required to stop vehicle

PROBABLE CAUSE	CORRECTIVE ACTION
1 Power booster faulty	1 Replace booster
2 Engine not producing sufficient vacuum, or hose to booster clogged, collapsed or cracked	2 Check vacuum to booster with a vacuum gauge. Replace hose if cracked or clogged, repair engine if vacuum is extremely low
3 Brake linings contaminated by grease or brake fluid	3 Locate and repair source of contamination, replace brake pads or shoes
4 Brake linings glazed	4 Replace brake pads or shoes, check discs and drums for glazing, service as necessary
5 Caliper piston(s) or wheel cylinder(s) binding or frozen	5 Replace calipers or wheel cylinders
6 Brakes wet	6 Apply pedal to boil-off water (this should only be a momentary problem)
7 Kinked, clogged or internally split brake hose or line	7 Inspect lines and hoses, replace as necessary

Excessive brake pedal travel (but will pump up)

PROBABLE CAUSE	CORRECTIVE ACTION
1 Drum brakes out of adjustment	1 Adjust brakes
2 Air in hydraulic system	2 Bleed system, inspect system for a leak

Excessive brake pedal travel (but will not pump up)

PROBABLE CAUSE	CORRECTIVE ACTION
1 Master cylinder pushrod misadjusted	1 Adjust pushrod
2 Master cylinder seals defective	2 Replace master cylinder
3 Brake linings worn out	3 Inspect brakes, replace pads and/or shoes
4 Hydraulic system leak	4 Locate and repair leak

Brake pedal doesn't return

PROBABLE CAUSE	CORRECTIVE ACTION
1 Brake pedal binding	1 Inspect pivot bushing and pushrod, repair or lubricate
2 Defective master cylinder	2 Replace master cylinder

Brake pedal pulsates during brake application

PROBABLE CAUSE	CORRECTIVE ACTION
1 Brake drums out-of-round	1 Have drums machined by an automotive machine shop
2 Excessive brake disc runout or disc surfaces out-of-parallel	2 Have discs machined by an automotive machine shop
3 Loose or worn wheel bearings	3 Adjust or replace wheel bearings
4 Loose lug nuts	4 Tighten lug nuts

Brakes slow to release

PROBABLE CAUSE	CORRECTIVE ACTION
1 Malfunctioning power booster	1 Replace booster
2 Pedal linkage binding	2 Inspect pedal pivot bushing and pushrod, repair/lubricate
3 Malfunctioning proportioning valve	3 Replace proportioning valve
4 Sticking caliper or wheel cylinder	4 Repair or replace calipers or wheel cylinders
5 Kinked or internally split brake hose	5 Locate and replace faulty brake hose

Brakes grab (one or more wheels)

PROBABLE CAUSE	CORRECTIVE ACTION
1 Grease or brake fluid on brake lining	1 Locate and repair cause of contamination, replace lining
2 Brake lining glazed	2 Replace lining, deglaze disc or drum

PROBABLE CAUSE	CORRECTIVE ACTION

Vehicle pulls to one side during braking

PROBABLE CAUSE	CORRECTIVE ACTION
1 Grease or brake fluid on brake lining	1 Locate and repair cause of contamination, replace lining
2 Brake lining glazed	2 Deglaze or replace lining, deglaze disc or drum
3 Restricted brake line or hose	3 Repair line or replace hose
4 Tire pressures incorrect	4 Adjust tire pressures
5 Caliper or wheel cylinder sticking	5 Repair or replace calipers or wheel cylinders
6 Wheels out of alignment	6 Have wheels aligned
7 Weak suspension spring	7 Replace springs
8 Weak or broken shock absorber	8 Replace shock absorbers

Brakes drag (indicated by sluggish engine performance or wheels being very hot after driving)

PROBABLE CAUSE	CORRECTIVE ACTION
1 Brake pedal pushrod incorrectly adjusted	1 Adjust pushrod
2 Master cylinder pushrod (between booster and master cylinder)	2 Adjust pushrod incorrectly adjusted
3 Obstructed compensating port in master cylinder	3 Replace master cylinder
4 Master cylinder piston seized in bore	4 Replace master cylinder
5 Contaminated fluid causing swollen seals throughout system	5 Flush system, replace all hydraulic components
6 Clogged brake lines or internally split brake hose(s)	6 Flush hydraulic system, replace defective hose(s)
7 Sticking caliper(s) or wheel cylinder(s)	7 Replace calipers or wheel cylinders
8 Parking brake not releasing	8 Inspect parking brake linkage and parking brake mechanism, repair as required
9 Improper shoe-to-drum clearance	9 Adjust brake shoes
10 Faulty proportioning valve	10 Replace proportioning valve

Brakes fade (due to excessive heat)

PROBABLE CAUSE	CORRECTIVE ACTION
1 Brake linings excessively worn or glazed	1 Deglaze or replace brake pads and/or shoes
2 Excessive use of brakes	2 Downshift into a lower gear, maintain a constant slower speed (going down hills)
3 Vehicle overloaded	3 Reduce load
4 Brake drums or discs worn too thin	4 Measure drum diameter and disc thickness, replace drums or discs as required
5 Contaminated brake fluid	5 Flush system, replace fluid
6 Brakes drag	6 Repair cause of dragging brakes
7 Driver resting left foot on brake pedal	7 Don't ride the brakes

Brakes noisy (high-pitched squeal)

PROBABLE CAUSE	CORRECTIVE ACTION
1 Glazed lining	1 Deglaze or replace lining
2 Contaminated lining (brake fluid, grease, etc.)	2 Repair source of contamination, replace linings
3 Weak or broken brake shoe hold-down or return spring	3 Replace springs
4 Rivets securing lining to shoe or backing plate loose	4 Replace shoes or pads
5 Excessive dust buildup on brake linings	5 Wash brakes off with brake system cleaner
6 Brake drums worn too thin	6 Measure diameter of drums, replace if necessary
7 Wear indicator on disc brake pads contacting disc	7 Replace brake pads
8 Anti-squeal shims missing or installed improperly	8 Install shims correctly

Troubleshooting (continued)

PROBABLE CAUSE	CORRECTIVE ACTION

Brakes noisy (scraping sound)

1 Brake pads or shoes worn out; rivets, backing plate or brake	1 Replace linings, have discs and/or drums machined (or replace) shoe metal contacting disc or drum

Brakes chatter

1 Worn brake lining	1 Inspect brakes, replace shoes or pads as necessary
2 Glazed or scored discs or drums	2 Deglaze discs or drums with sandpaper (if glazing is severe, machining will be required)
3 Drums or discs heat checked	3 Check discs and/or drums for hard spots, heat checking, etc. Have discs/drums machined or replace them
4 Disc runout or drum out-of-round excessive	4 Measure disc runout and/or drum out-of-round, have discs or drums machined or replace them
5 Loose or worn wheel bearings	5 Adjust or replace wheel bearings
6 Loose or bent brake backing plate (drum brakes)	6 Tighten or replace backing plate
7 Grooves worn in discs or drums	7 Have discs or drums machined, if within limits (if not, replace them)
8 Brake linings contaminated (brake fluid, grease, etc.)	8 Locate and repair source of contamination, replace pads or shoes
9 Excessive dust buildup on linings	9 Wash brakes with brake system cleaner
10 Surface finish on discs or drums too rough after machining	10 Have discs or drums properly machined (especially on vehicles with sliding calipers)
11 Brake pads or shoes glazed	11 Deglaze or replace brake pads or shoes

Brake pads or shoes click

1 Shoe support pads on brake backing plate grooved or	1 Replace brake backing plate excessively worn
2 Brake pads loose in caliper	2 Loose pad retainers or anti-rattle clips
3 Also see items listed under Brakes chatter	

Brakes make groaning noise at end of stop

1 Brake pads and/or shoes worn out	1 Replace pads and/or shoes
2 Brake linings contaminated (brake fluid, grease, etc.)	2 Locate and repair cause of contamination, replace brake pads or shoes
3 Brake linings glazed	3 Deglaze or replace brake pads or shoes
4 Excessive dust buildup on linings	4 Wash brakes with brake system cleaner
5 Scored or heat-checked discs or drums	5 Inspect discs/drums, have machined if within limits (if not, replace discs or drums)
6 Broken or missing brake shoe attaching hardware	6 Inspect drum brakes, replace missing hardware

Rear brakes lock up under light brake application

1 Tire pressures too high	1 Adjust tire pressures
2 Tires excessively worn	2 Replace tires
3 Defective proportioning valve	3 Replace proportioning valve

Brake warning light on instrument panel comes on (or stays on)

1 Low fluid level in master cylinder reservoir (reservoirs with fluid level sensor)	1 Add fluid, inspect system for leak, check the thickness of the brake pads and shoes
2 Failure in one half of the hydraulic system	2 Inspect hydraulic system for a leak
3 Piston in pressure differential warning valve not centered	3 Center piston by bleeding one circuit or the other (close bleeder valve as soon as the light goes out)

PROBABLE CAUSE	CORRECTIVE ACTION
Brake warning light on instrument panel comes on (or stays on) (continued)	
4 Defective pressure differential valve or warning switch	4 Replace valve or switch
5 Air in the hydraulic system	5 Bleed the system, check for leaks
6 Brake pads worn out (vehicles with electric wear sensors - small probes that fit into the brake pads and ground out on the disc when the pads get thin)	6 Replace brake pads (and sensors)
Brakes do not self adjust	
Disc brakes	
1 Defective caliper piston seals	1 Replace calipers. Also, possible contaminated fluid causing soft or swollen seals (flush system and fill with new fluid if in doubt)
2 Corroded caliper piston(s)	2 Same as above
Drum brakes	
1 Adjuster screw frozen	1 Remove adjuster, disassemble, clean and lubricate with high-temperature grease
2 Adjuster lever does not contact star wheel or is binding	2 Inspect drum brakes, assemble correctly or clean or replace parts as required
3 Adjusters mixed up (installed on wrong wheels after brake job)	3 Reassemble correctly
4 Adjuster cable broken or installed incorrectly (cable-type adjusters)	4 Install new cable or assemble correctly
Rapid brake lining wear	
1 Driver resting left foot on brake pedal	1 Don't ride the brakes
2 Surface finish on discs or drums too rough	2 Have discs or drums properly machined
3 Also see Brakes drag	

3 Anti-lock Brake System (ABS) - general information

1 The Anti-lock Brake System (ABS) is designed to maintain vehicle steerability, directional stability and optimum deceleration under severe braking conditions and on most road surfaces. It does so by monitoring the rotational speed of each wheel and controlling the brake line pressure to each wheel during braking. This prevents the wheels from locking up.

Components

Actuator assembly

2 The actuator assembly consists of an electric hydraulic pump and a pair of solenoid valves for each wheel. It's located at the right rear corner of the engine compartment, behind the lower cowl panel (see illustration). The electric pump provides hydraulic pressure to charge the reservoirs in the actuator, which supplies pressure to the braking system during ABS operation. The solenoid valves modulate brake line pressure during ABS operation. The body contains four valves - one for each wheel. The pump, the reservoirs and the solenoid valves are all housed in the actuator assembly.

3.2 ABS actuator

3.3a Location of the front wheel speed sensor

3.3b Location of the rear wheel speed sensor

4.5 On all calipers except rear calipers with an Electric Parking Brake, use a C-clamp to depress the piston into the caliper before removing the caliper and pads

Speed sensors

3 The speed sensors, which are located at each wheel, generate a sine wave current when the sensor rotors are turning (see illustrations). This analog voltage signal is monitored by the ABS control unit, which converts it to a digital signal from which it can determine wheel rotational speed.

ABS computer

4 The ABS control unit is the brain of the ABS system and is part of the ABS actuator. The function of the control unit is to monitor and process information received from the wheel speed sensors to control the hydraulic line pressure, avoiding wheel lock up. The control unit also monitors the system for malfunctions, even when the ABS system is inactive during normal driving conditions.

5 Each time you start the engine, the system turns on the ABS warning light on the instrument cluster for about a second. As soon as the engine is running, the light should go off. The system then performs a self-test the first time the vehicle speed exceeds four mph. You may hear a mechanical noise during the test; this is normal. If the system detects a problem, the ABS light will come on and remain on. A diagnostic code will also be stored in the control unit, which indicates the problem area or component.

4 Disc brake pads - replacement

Warning: *Disc brake pads must be replaced on both front wheels at the same time - never replace the pads on only one wheel. Also, the dust created by the brake system is harmful to your health. Never blow it out with compressed air and don't inhale any of it. An approved filtering mask should be worn when working on the brakes. Do not, under any circumstances, use petroleum-based solvents to clean brake parts. Use brake system cleaner only!*

Caution: *Some 2018 and later models are equipped with an Electric Parking Brake (EBP). The system must be deactivated (put into service mode) before any work is performed on the rear brakes. The Nissan "CONSULT" scan tool or equivalent must be used to do this (see Section 15, Step 3).*

Note: *On 2014 and later models (except for Rogue Select models) two types of front calipers are used: Type 1 is a single-piston caliper and Type 2 is a dual-piston caliper. All other components are identical.*

Note: *This procedure applies to front and rear disc brakes.*

1 Remove the cap from the brake fluid reservoir.

2 Loosen the front or rear wheel lug nuts, raise the front or rear of the vehicle and support it securely on jackstands. Block the wheels at the opposite end.

3 Remove the wheels. Work on one brake assembly at a time, using the assembled brake for reference if necessary.

4 Inspect the brake disc carefully (see Section 6). If machining is necessary, follow the information in that Section to remove the disc.

5 On all calipers except rear calipers with an Electric Parking Brake, push the piston back into its bore to provide room for the new brake pads. A C-clamp can be used to accomplish this (see illustration). As the piston is depressed to the bottom of the caliper bore, the fluid in the master cylinder will rise. Make sure that it doesn't overflow. If necessary, siphon off some of the fluid.

6 Follow the accompanying photos (see illustrations) for the front or rear pad replacement procedure. Be sure to stay in order and read the caption under each illustration.

Note: *The illustrations show a Type 1 caliper front brake pad replacement, but the Type 2 caliper and the rear brakes are almost identical.*

4.6a Before disassembling the brake, wash it thoroughly with brake system cleaner and allow it to dry - position a drain pan under the brake to catch the residue - DO NOT use compressed air to blow off brake dust!

4.6b Remove the caliper lower mounting bolt (A); don't remove the brake hose banjo bolt (B) unless the caliper or hose requires service . . .

4.6c . . . then pivot the caliper up and secure it in that position with a piece of wire

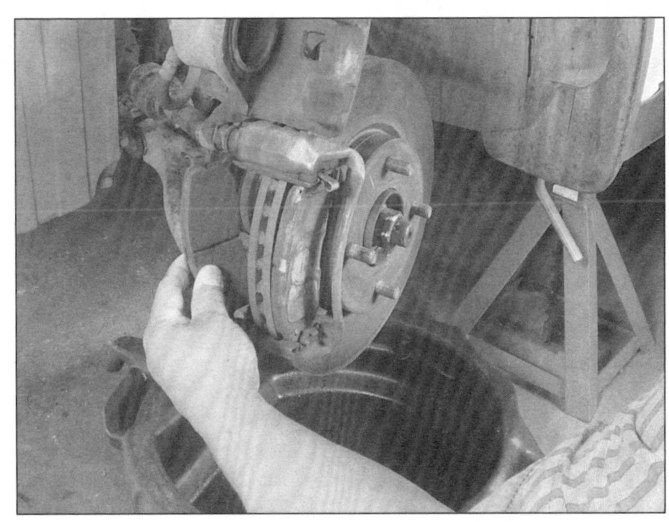

4.6d Remove the inner brake pad

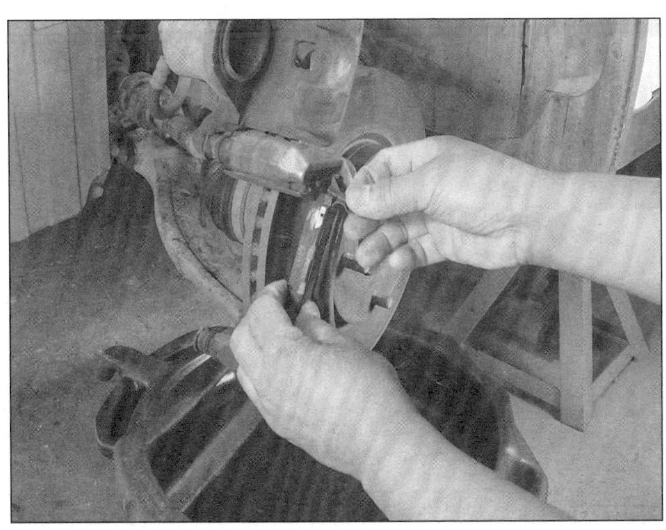

4.6e Remove the outer brake pad

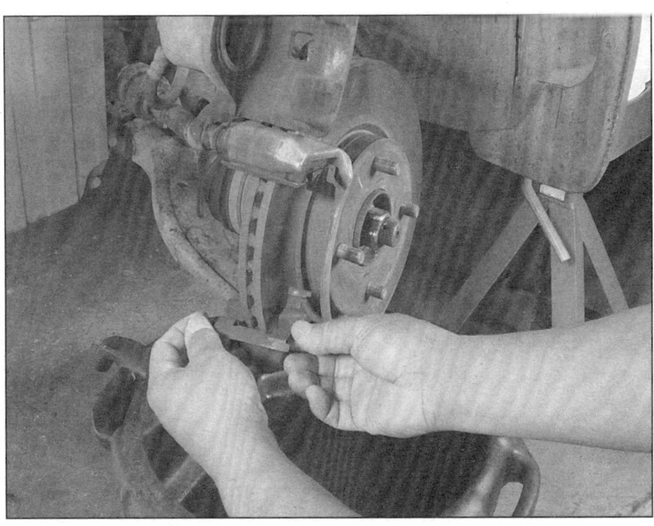

4.6f Remove the lower pad retainer

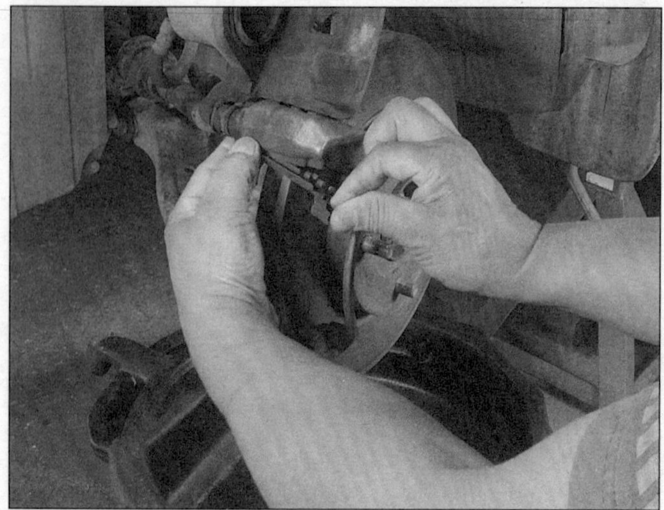
4.6g Remove the upper pad retainer

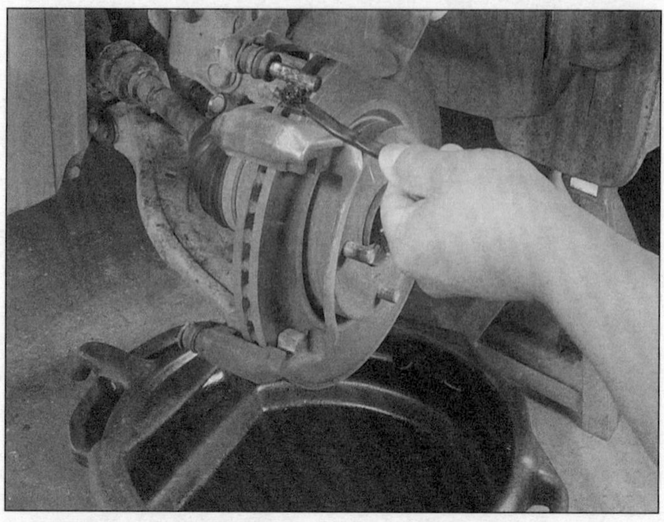
4.6h Pull the caliper upper slide pin out of the mounting bracket, then clean it and lubricate it with high-temperature brake grease

4.6i Also remove the lower slide pin, clean it, lubricate it with high-temperature brake grease, then reinstall it

4.6j Install the pad retainers

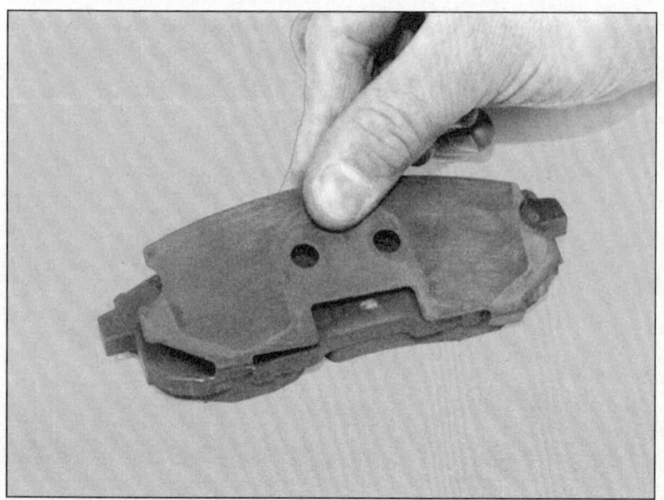
4.6k Install the shim (or shim and shim cover) on the pads

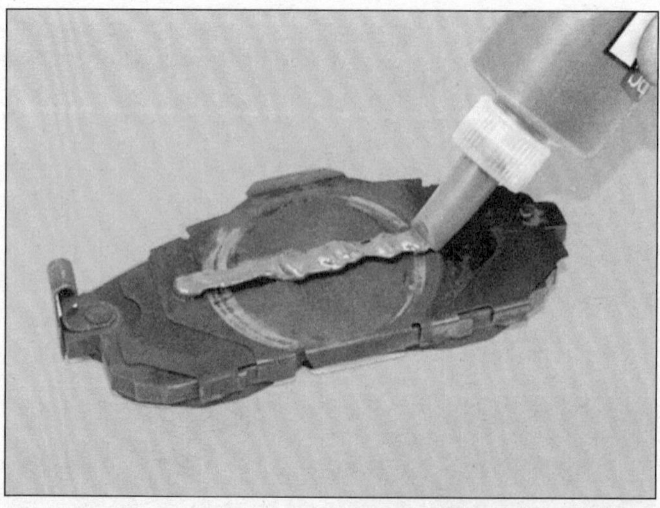
4.6l Apply anti-squeal compound to the back of both pads (let the compound set-up for a few minutes before installing them)

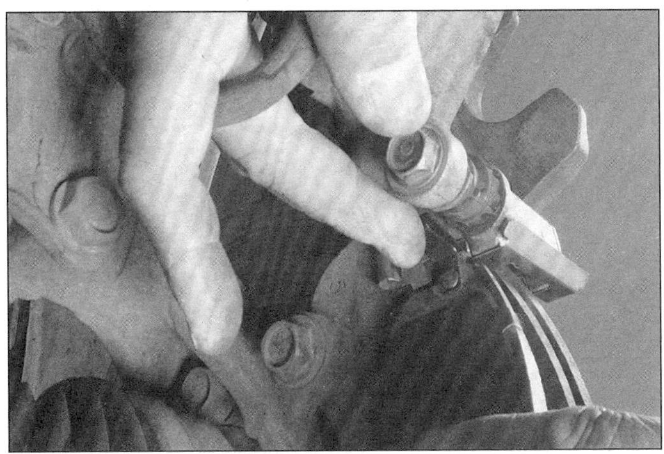

4.6m Install the inner brake pad and shim, making sure the wear indicator is positioned correctly

4.6n Install the outer brake pad. Note how the wear indicator and spring are oriented

4.6o Swing the caliper down, install the caliper mounting bolt and tighten it to the torque listed in this Chapter's Specifications.

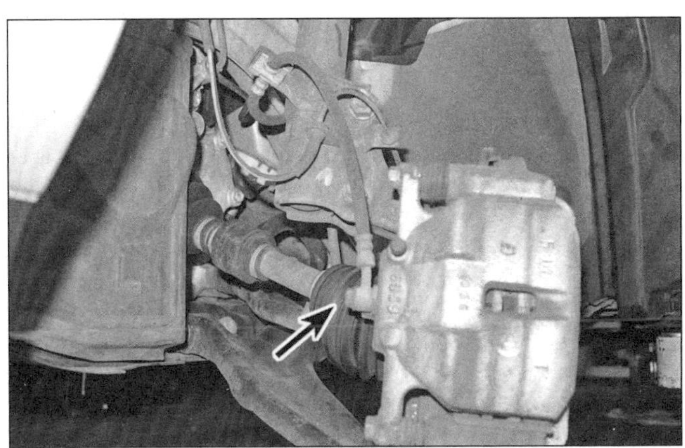

5.2a Remove the banjo bolt (arrow) - front caliper shown rear caliper similar

7 When reinstalling the caliper, tighten the mounting bolts to the torque listed in this Chapter's Specifications. Tighten the wheel lug nuts to the torque listed in the Chapter 1 Specifications.

8 After the job has been completed, firmly depress the brake pedal a few times to bring the pads into contact with the disc. Check the level of the brake fluid, adding some if necessary. Check the operation of the brakes carefully before placing the vehicle into normal service.

Caution: *Some 2018 and later models are equipped with an Electric Parking Brake (EBP). The system must be initialized and self-adjusted after any work is performed on the rear brakes. The Nissan "CONSULT" scan tool or equivalent must be used to do this (see Section 15, Step 4).*

5 Disc brake caliper - removal and installation

Warning: *The dust created by the brake system is harmful to your health. Never blow it out with compressed air and don't inhale any of it. An approved filtering mask should be worn when working on the brakes. Do not, under any circumstances, use petroleum-based solvents to clean brake parts. Use brake system cleaner only!*

Caution: *Some 2018 and later models are equipped with an Electric Parking Brake (EBP). The system must be deactivated (put into service mode) before any work is performed on the rear brakes. The Nissan "CONSULT" scan tool or equivalent must be used to do this (see Section 15, Step 3).*

Note: *If replacement is indicated (usually because of fluid leakage), it is recommended that the calipers be replaced, not overhauled. New and factory rebuilt units are available on an exchange basis, which makes this job quite easy. Always replace the calipers in pairs - never replace just one of them.*

Removal

1 Loosen the front or rear wheel lug nuts, raise the front or rear of the vehicle and place it securely on jackstands. Block the wheels at the opposite end. Remove the front or rear wheel.

2 Remove the banjo bolt (see illustration). Disconnect the brake hose from the caliper and discard the sealing washers (new ones should be used on installation). Plug the brake hose to keep contaminants out of the brake system and to prevent losing any more brake fluid than is necessary (see illustration).

Note: *If the caliper is only being removed to allow access to another component, do not disconnect the brake hose.*

3 Remove the caliper mounting bolts and lift the caliper from its bracket.

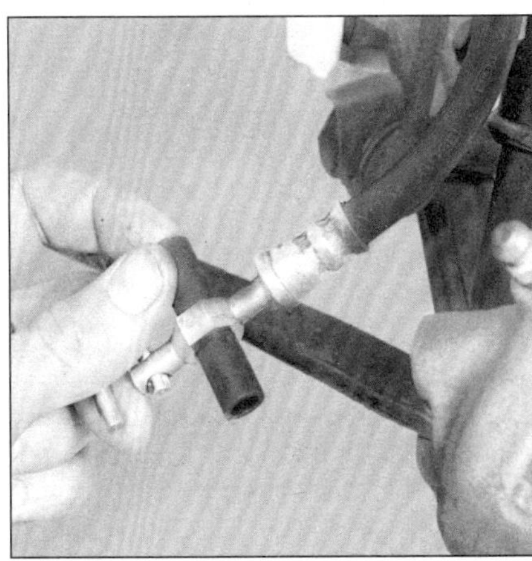

5.2b Using a piece of rubber hose of the appropriate size, plug the brake line

6.3 The brake pads on this vehicle were obviously neglected, as they wore down completely and cut deep grooves into the disc - wear this severe means the disc must be replaced

6.4a To check disc runout, mount a dial indicator as shown and rotate the disc

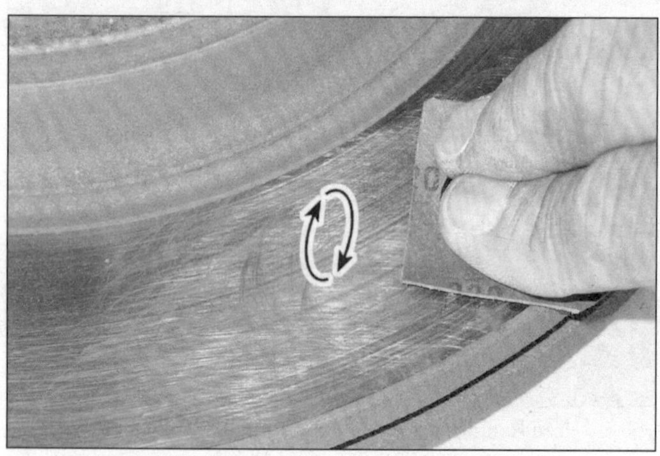
6.4b Using a swirling motion, remove the glaze from the disc surface with sandpaper or emery cloth

6.5 Use a micrometer to measure disc thickness

Installation

Caution: *Some 2018 and later models are equipped with an Electric Parking Brake (EBP). The system must be initialized and self-adjusted after any work is performed on the rear brakes. The Nissan "CONSULT" scan tool or equivalent must be used to do this (see Section 15, Step 4).*

4 Installation is the reverse of removal. Tighten the caliper mounting bolt to the torque listed in this Chapter's Specifications and the wheel lug nuts to the torque in the Chapter 1 Specifications. Use new sealing washers for the brake hose-to-caliper banjo bolt.

5 Bleed the brake system (see Section 9). Make sure there are no leaks from the hose connections. Test the brakes carefully before returning the vehicle to normal service.

6 Brake disc - inspection, removal and installation

Inspection

1 Loosen the wheel lug nuts, raise the vehicle and support it securely on jackstands. Remove the wheel and install the lug nuts to hold the disc in place.

Note: *If the lug nuts don't contact the disc when screwed on all the way, install washers under them.*

2 Remove the brake caliper (see Section 5). It isn't necessary to disconnect the brake hose. After removing the caliper bolts, suspend the caliper out of the way with a piece of wire.

3 Visually inspect the disc surface for score marks and other damage. Light scratches and shallow grooves are normal after use and may not always be detrimental to brake operation, but deep scoring - over 0.039-inch (1.0 mm) - requires disc removal and refinishing by an automotive machine shop. Be sure to check both sides of the disc (see illustration). If pulsating has been noticed during application of the brakes, suspect disc runout.

4 To check disc runout, place a dial indicator at a point about 1/2-inch from the outer edge of the disc (see illustrations). Set the indicator to zero and turn the disc. The indicator reading should not exceed the specified allowable runout limit. If it does, the disc should be refinished by an automotive machine shop.

Note: *When replacing the brake pads, it's a good idea to resurface the discs regardless of the dial indicator reading, as this will impart a smooth finish and ensure a perfectly flat surface, eliminating any brake pedal pulsation or other undesirable symptoms related to questionable discs. At the very least, if you elect not to have the discs resurfaced, remove the glaze from the surface with emery cloth using a swirling motion (see illustration).*

5 It's absolutely critical that the disc not be machined to a thickness under the specified minimum allowable disc refinish thickness. The minimum wear (or discard) thickness is cast into the disc. The disc thickness can be checked with a micrometer (see illustration).

Removal

6 Remove the two caliper mounting bracket bolts (see illustrations) and detach the caliper mounting bracket.

7 Remove the lug nuts which you installed to hold the disc in place and remove the disc from the hub.

6.6a To remove the front caliper mounting bracket, remove these bolts

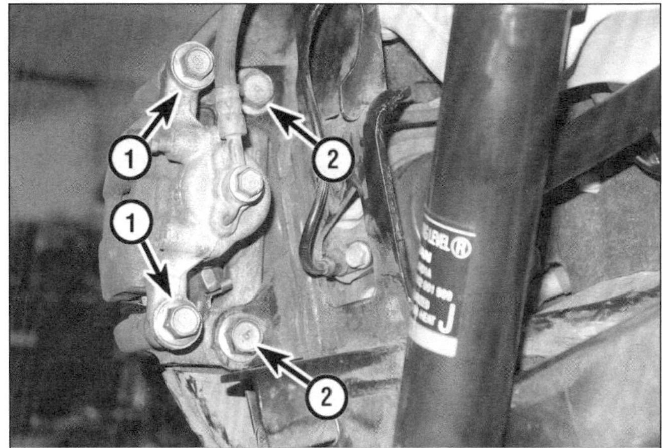

6.6b Remove the rear caliper mounting bracket bolts

1 *Caliper mounting bolts*
2 *Caliper bracket mounting bolts*

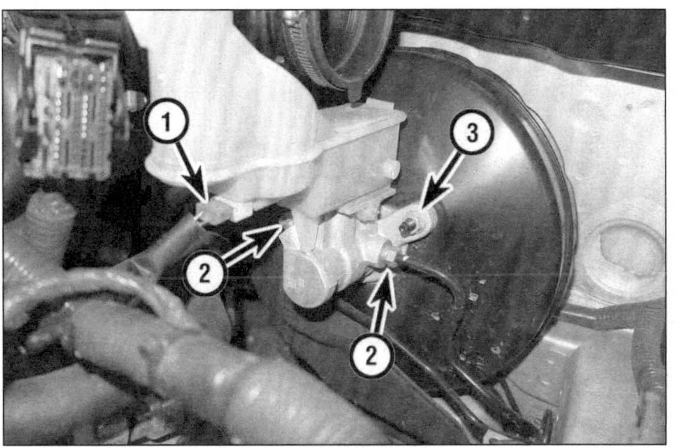

7.2 Master cylinder details

1 *Electrical connector*
2 *Fluid line fittings*
3 *Mounting nut (other nut not visible)*

7.8 The best way to bleed the master cylinder before installing it is with a pair of bleeder tubes

Note: *If a rear disc won't come off, remove the rubber plug from the parking brake adjuster hole. Use a small screwdriver to turn the star wheel and retract the parking brake shoes (see Section 11).*

Installation

8 Place the disc in position over the threaded studs.

9 Install the caliper mounting bracket over the disc and tighten the bolts to the torque listed in this Chapter's Specifications.

10 Install the caliper and tighten the bolts to the torque listed in this Chapter's Specifications.

11 Install the wheel, then lower the vehicle to the ground. Tighten the lug nuts to the torque listed in the Chapter 1 Specifications. Depress the brake pedal a few times to bring the brake pads into contact with the disc. Bleeding won't be necessary unless the brake hose was disconnected from the caliper. Check the operation of the brakes carefully before driving the vehicle.

7 Master cylinder - removal and installation

Removal

1 Remove the battery (see Chapter 5). Also remove the air filter housing and the intake duct to the throttle body (see Chapter 4).

2 Unplug the electrical connector for the fluid level warning switch (see illustration).

3 Remove as much fluid as possible from the reservoir with a syringe.

Caution: *Brake fluid will damage paint. Cover all body parts and be careful not to spill fluid during this procedure.*

4 Place rags under the fittings and prepare caps or plastic bags to cover the ends of the lines once they're disconnected. Loosen the fittings at the ends of the brake lines where they enter the master cylinder. To prevent rounding off the flats, use a flare-nut wrench, which wraps around the fitting hex.

5 Pull the brake lines away from the master cylinder and plug the ends to prevent contamination.

6 Remove the nuts attaching the master cylinder to the power booster. Pull the master cylinder off the studs to remove it. Again, be careful not to spill any remaining fluid as this is done.

Installation

7 Bench bleed the new master cylinder before installing it. Mount the master cylinder in a vise, with the jaws of the vise clamping on the mounting flange.

8 Attach a pair of master cylinder bleeder tubes to the outlet ports of the master cylinder (see illustration).

9 Fill the reservoir with brake fluid of the recommended type (see Chapter 1).

10 Slowly push the pistons into the master cylinder (a large Phillips screwdriver can be used for this) - air will be expelled from the pressure chambers and into the reservoir. Because the tubes are submerged in fluid, air

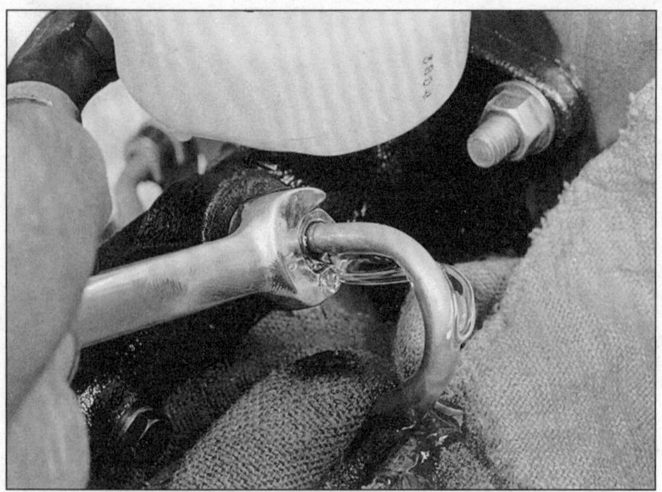

7.16 Have an assistant depress the brake pedal and hold it down, then loosen the fitting nut, allowing the air and fluid to escape; repeat this procedure on both fittings until the fluid is clear of air bubbles

8.3a If you're removing a hose, loosen the threaded fitting on the brake line (use a flare-nut wrench to protect the corners of the nut) . . .

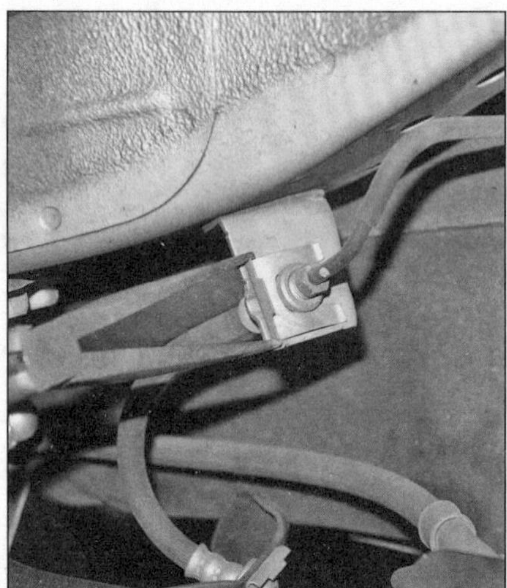

8.3b . . . then remove the u-clip

can't be drawn back into the master cylinder when you release the pistons. Repeat the procedure until no more air bubbles are present.

11 Remove the bleed tubes, one at a time, and install plugs in the open ports to prevent fluid leakage and air from entering. Install the reservoir cap.

12 Install a new O-ring seal in the groove on the end of the master cylinder and coat it with silicone grease. Also coat the bore of the power brake booster.

13 Install the master cylinder over the studs on the power brake booster and tighten the nuts only finger-tight at this time.

14 Thread the brake line fittings into the master cylinder. Since the master cylinder is still a bit loose, it can be moved slightly so the fittings thread in easily. Don't strip the threads as the fittings are tightened.

15 Tighten the mounting nuts to the torque listed in this Chapter's Specifications. Tighten the brake line fittings securely.

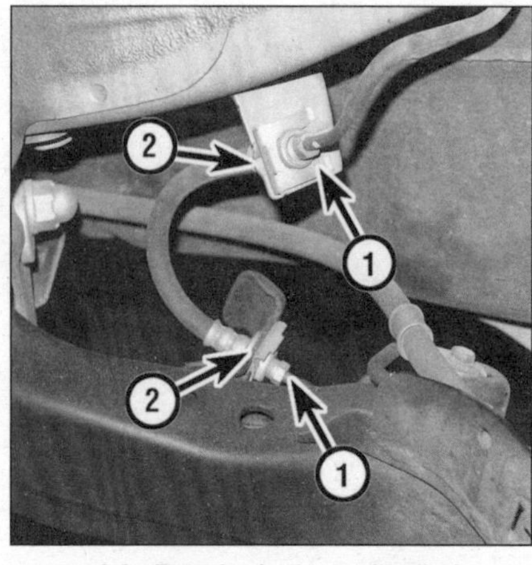

8.3c Rear brake hose details

1 Brake line fittings
2 U-clips

16 Fill the master cylinder reservoir with fluid, then bleed the lines at the master cylinder, followed by bleeding the remainder of the brake system (see Section 9). To bleed the lines at the master cylinder, have an assistant depress the brake pedal and hold it down. Loosen the fitting to allow air and fluid to escape (see illustration). Tighten the fitting, then allow your assistant to return the pedal to its rest position. Repeat this procedure on both fittings until the fluid is free of air bubbles, then bleed the rest of the system. Check the operation of the brake system carefully before driving the vehicle.

Warning: *If you do not have a firm brake pedal at the end of the bleeding procedure, or have any doubts as to the effectiveness of the brake system, DO NOT drive the vehicle. Have it towed to a dealer service department or other qualified repair shop for diagnosis.*

17 The remainder of installation is the reverse of removal. Reconnect the battery and perform the necessary re-learn procedures (see Chapter 1).

8 Brake hoses and lines - inspection and replacement

Inspection

1 About every six months, with the vehicle raised and supported securely on jackstands, the flexible hoses which connect the steel brake lines with the front and rear brake assemblies should be inspected for cracks, chafing of the outer cover, leaks, blisters and other damage. These are important and vulnerable parts of the brake system and inspection should be complete. A light and mirror will be helpful for a thorough check. If a hose exhibits any of the above conditions, replace it with a new one.

Replacement

Brake hoses

2 Loosen the wheel lug nuts, raise the vehicle and support it securely on jackstands. Remove the wheel.

Note: *If you're replacing a rear brake hose, it isn't necessary to remove the wheels.*

3 At the bracket, unscrew the brake line fitting from the hose (see illustrations). Use a flare-nut wrench to prevent rounding off the corners.

4 Remove the U-clip from the female fitting at the bracket with a pair of pliers, then pass the hose through the bracket.

5 At the caliper end of the hose, remove the banjo bolt (see illustration 4.6b), then separate the hose from the caliper. Note that there are two sealing washers on either side of the banjo fitting - they should be replaced with new ones during installation.

6 If you're replacing a front brake hose,

remove the U-clip from the strut bracket, then detach the hose from the bracket.

7 To install the hose, pass the caliper fitting end through the strut bracket (front hose only), then connect the fitting to the caliper with the banjo bolt and new sealing washers.

8 Make sure the hose isn't twisted between the caliper and the strut bracket (or the chassis on rear brake hoses).

9 Route the hose into the frame bracket, again making sure it isn't twisted, then connect the brake line fitting, starting the threads by hand. Install the U-clip, then tighten the fitting securely.

10 Bleed the caliper (see Section 9).

11 Install the wheel and lug nuts, lower the vehicle and tighten the lug nuts to the torque listed in the Chapter 1 Specifications.

Metal brake lines

12 When replacing brake lines, be sure to use the correct parts. Don't use copper tubing for any brake system components. Purchase steel brake lines from a dealer or auto parts store.

13 Prefabricated brake line, with the tube ends already flared and fittings installed, is available at auto parts stores and dealer parts departments.

14 When installing the new line, make sure it's securely supported in the brackets and has plenty of clearance between moving or hot components.

15 After installation, check the master cylinder fluid level and add fluid as necessary. Bleed the brake system (see Section 9) and test the brakes carefully before driving the vehicle in traffic.

9 Brake hydraulic system - bleeding

Warning: *Wear eye protection when bleeding the brake system. If the fluid comes in contact with your eyes, immediately rinse them with water and seek medical attention.*

Caution: *Before bleeding the system, disconnect the ABS actuator and control unit electrical connectors or disconnect the cable from the negative terminal of the battery (see Chapter 5).*

Note: *Bleeding the hydraulic system is necessary to remove any air that manages to find its way into the system when it's been opened during removal and installation of a hose, line, caliper or master cylinder.*

1 You'll probably have to bleed the system at all four brakes if air has entered it due to low fluid level, or if the brake lines have been disconnected at the master cylinder.

2 If a brake line was disconnected only at a wheel, then only that caliper or wheel cylinder must be bled.

3 If a brake line is disconnected at a fitting located between the master cylinder and any of the brakes, that part of the system served by the disconnected line must be bled.

4 Remove any residual vacuum from the brake power booster by applying the brake several times with the engine off.

5 Remove the master cylinder reservoir cover and fill the reservoir with brake fluid. Reinstall the cover. Check the fluid level often during the bleeding operation and add fluid as necessary to prevent the fluid level from falling low enough to allow air bubbles into the master cylinder.

Caution: *Turn the ignition switch off and disconnect the electrical connectors for the ABS actuator or detach the battery negative cable.*

6 Have an assistant on hand, as well as a supply of new brake fluid, a clear plastic container partially filled with clean brake fluid, a length of 3/16-inch plastic, rubber or vinyl tubing to fit over the bleeder valve and a wrench to open and close the bleeder valve.

7 Beginning at the right rear wheel (2013 and earlier models/2014 and later Rogue Select models) or right front wheel (2014 and later models [except Rogue Select]), loosen the bleeder valve slightly, then tighten it to a point where it's snug but can still be loosened quickly and easily.

8 Place one end of the tubing over the bleeder valve and submerge the other end in brake fluid in the container (see illustration).

9 Have the assistant pump the brakes slowly a few times to get pressure in the system, then hold the pedal down firmly.

10 While the pedal is held down, open the bleeder valve just enough to allow a flow of fluid to leave the valve. Watch for air bubbles to exit the submerged end of the tube. When the fluid flow slows after a couple of seconds, close the valve and have your assistant release the pedal.

11 Repeat Steps 9 and 10 until no more air is seen leaving the tube, then tighten the bleeder valve and proceed to the other wheels in the following order, performing the same procedure:

2013 and earlier models/2014 and later Rogue Select models

a) Left front
b) Left rear
c) Right front

2014 and later models (except Rogue Select)

a) Left front
b) Right rear
c) Left rear

12 Never use old brake fluid. It contains moisture which will deteriorate the brake system components and could cause the fluid to boil, which could render the brake system inoperative.

13 Refill the master cylinder with fluid at the end of the operation. On models with ABS, reconnect the electrical connectors to the ABS actuator, or reconnect the battery.

14 Check the operation of the brakes. The pedal should feel solid when depressed, with no sponginess. If necessary, repeat the entire process.

Warning: *Do not operate the vehicle if you're in doubt about the effectiveness of the brake system.*

10 Power brake booster - check, replacement and adjustment

Check

Operating check

1 Depress the brake pedal several times with the engine off and make sure there's no change in the pedal reserve distance.

2 Depress the pedal and start the engine. If the pedal goes down slightly, operation is normal.

Airtightness check

3 Start the engine and turn it off after one or two minutes. Depress the brake pedal slowly several times. If the pedal depresses less each time, the booster is airtight.

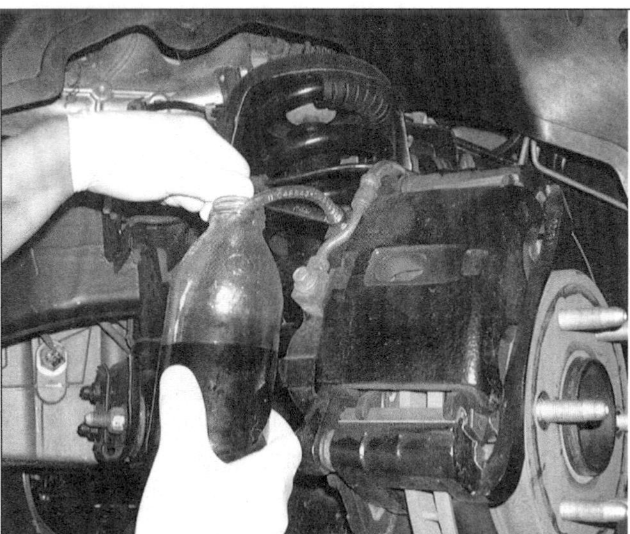

9.8 When bleeding the brakes, a hose is connected to the bleed screw at the caliper or wheel cylinder and then submerged in brake fluid - air will be seen as bubbles in the tube and container (all air must be expelled before moving to the next wheel)

10.10a Remove the knee bolster support bracket nuts . . .

10.10b . . . then maneuver the bracket out from under the instrument panel

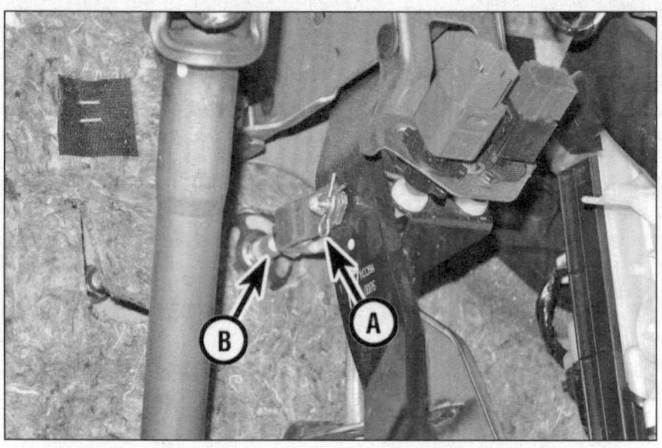

10.11 Brake booster retaining clip (A) and clevis lock nut (B)

10.12 Disconnect the electrical connectors from the brake pedal switches

4 Depress the brake pedal while the engine is running, then stop the engine with the pedal depressed. If there's no change in the pedal reserve travel after holding the pedal for 30 seconds, the booster is airtight.

Replacement

Note: *Power brake booster units shouldn't be disassembled. They require special tools not normally found in most automotive repair stations or shops. They're fairly complex and, because of their critical relationship to brake performance, should be replaced with a new or rebuilt one.*

5 Remove the battery (see Chapter 5).

6 Remove the air filter housing and intake duct (see Chapter 4).

7 Disconnect the vacuum hose from the booster.

8 Remove the master cylinder (see Section 7).

9 Remove the driver's side knee bolster and support (see Chapter 11).

10 Remove the knee bolster support bracket nuts and remove the support bracket (see illustrations).

11 Pull out the safety clip, then remove the pin from the clevis to detach it from the brake pedal (see illustration).

12 Disconnect the electrical connectors to the brake pedal switches (see illustration).

13 Remove the brake pedal assembly mounting nuts and remove the pedal assembly (see illustration).

Note: *On 2014 and later models (except Rogue Select models), it isn't necessary to remove the brake pedal assembly. Once the mounting nuts are removed, the pedal assembly can stay in place.*

14 On 2013 and earlier models/2014 and later Rogue Select models, remove the remaining brake booster mounting nut (see

10.13 Pedal assembly mounting nuts

10.14 Booster mounting nut

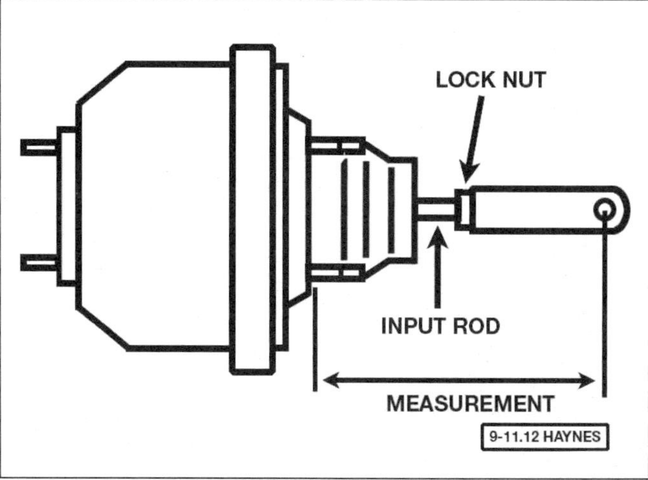

10.17 Measure the distance between the power brake booster and the hole in the clevis and compare your measurement to the dimension listed in this Chapter's Specifications; if necessary, adjust the clevis before installing the power brake booster

illustration) then remove the booster from the engine compartment and separate the spacer from the booster.

15 On 2013 and earlier models/2014 and later Rogue Select models, before installing the new booster, measure the booster input rod length and adjust it if necessary (see Step 17).

16 Installation is the reverse of removal. Use a new gasket between the booster and the firewall.

Adjustment (2013 and earlier models/2014 and later Rogue Select models only)

17 Measure the distance between the power brake booster and the hole in the input rod clevis (see illustration) and compare it to the dimension listed in this Chapter's Specifications. If necessary, loosen the adjusting nut and turn the clevis in or out to the specified length, then install the booster, connect the clevis to the brake pedal, and tighten the nut securely.

11 Parking brake (models with a parking brake pedal) - check and adjustment

Check

1 The parking brake pedal, when properly adjusted, should travel the correct number of clicks when a 45 pound force is applied - see this Chapter's Specifications.

2 If the parking brake pedal travels less than the specified minimum number of clicks, it might not be releasing completely and the shoes could even be dragging against the drum. If it moves more than the specified maximum number of clicks, the parking brake may not hold adequately on an incline, allowing the car to roll.

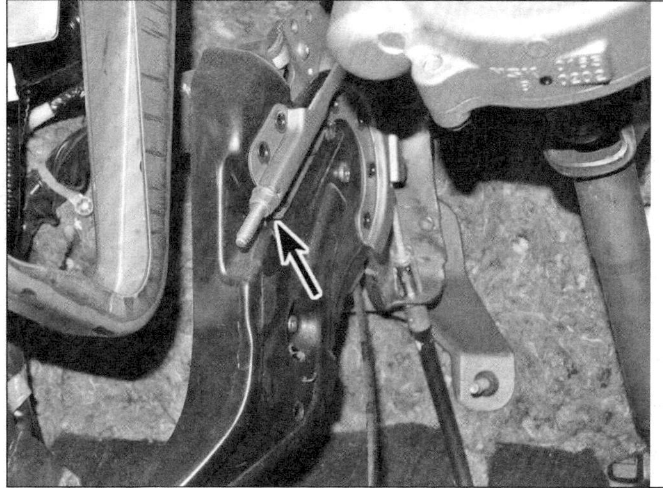

11.4 The parking brake adjustment nut is located at the top of the parking brake pedal - knee bolster panel removed for clarity

Adjustment

3 Loosen the rear wheel lug nuts. Raise the vehicle and support it securely on jackstands. Remove the rear wheels.

4 Working under the driver's side of the instrument panel, locate the adjustment cable nut on the top of the parking brake pedal (see illustration), then loosen the cable adjusting nut. Release the parking brake.

5 Install the lug nuts snugly to each rear brake disc to support it against the hub flange.

6 Remove the rubber adjuster hole plugs from the rear brake discs (see illustration 12.4a).

7 Turn the star wheel until it locks the disc, then back it off five or six notches.

8 Turn the disc and make sure there is no drag. Readjust it if necessary to obtain a close adjustment with zero drag. Reinstall the hole plugs.

9 Tighten the adjusting nut (see Step 4) so you get the proper number of clicks when you apply a 45 pound force to the pedal.

10 Release the parking brake and turn the rear discs again to verify that there is no drag. If drag exists, go over the adjustment procedure until it's correct.

11 Reinstall the wheels, lower the vehicle and tighten the lug nuts to the torque listed in the Chapter 1 Specifications.

12 Parking brake shoes (models with a parking brake pedal) - replacement

1 Loosen the rear wheel lug nuts. Raise the vehicle and support it securely on jackstands. Remove the rear wheels.

2 Release the parking brake. Remove the discs (see Section 6).

3 Inspect the parking brake surfaces of each disc for wear or damage. Replace the discs if necessary.

4 Follow the accompanying photos (see illustrations 12.4a through 12.4t) for the actual parking brake shoe replacement procedure. Be sure to stay in order and read the caption under each illustration. Work on only one side at a time to avoid confusion.

5 Adjust the shoes (see Section 11).

6 When reinstalling the calipers, be sure to tighten the mounting bolts to the torque listed in this Chapter's Specifications.

7 The remainder of installation is the reverse of removal.

8 The parking brake pedal may require adjustment in a few weeks after the parking brake shoes become seated.

12.4a If the disc can't be removed when the parking brake is fully released, you'll have to remove this rubber plug and use a screwdriver to turn the star wheel to retract the parking brake shoes

12.4b Wash the assembly with brake system cleaner; DO NOT blow off the brake dust with compressed air

12.4c Remove the lower spring . . .

12.4d . . . then take out the adjuster

12.4e Use a screwdriver to remove the upper front retractor spring . . .

12.4f . . . then remove the upper rear retractor spring

12.4g Depress the spring and turn the shoe hold-down spring pin to release the spring . . .

12.4h . . . then lift the shoe off

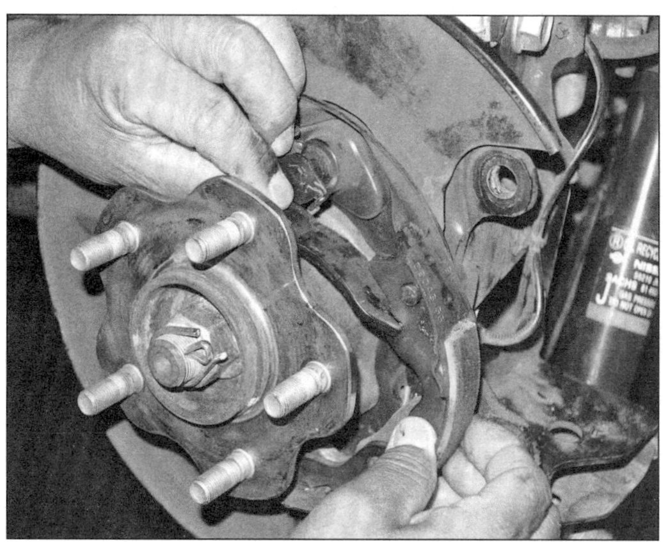

12.4i Remove the brake strut

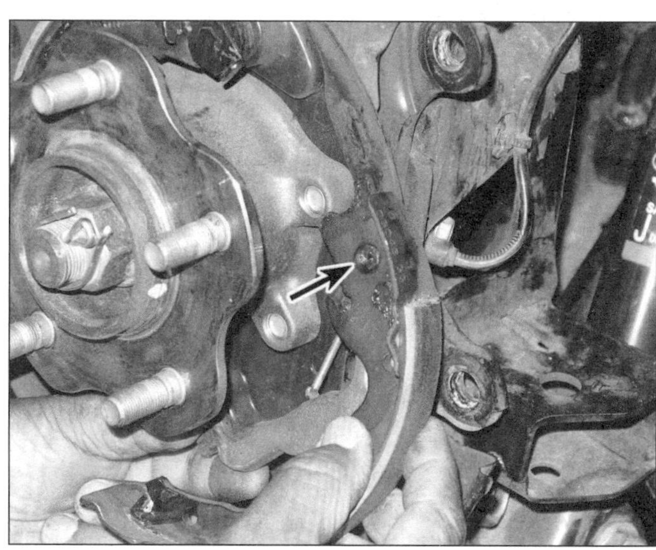

12.4j Separate the actuator lever pin from the rear shoe

12.4k Do the same to the remaining shoe

12.4l After cleaning the backing plates, apply brake grease to the raised contact surfaces around the perimeter

12.4m Install pin on the actuator lever (A) into the hole (B) in the new rear parking brake shoe . . .

12.4n . . . then slide the brake strut into place on the shoe . . .

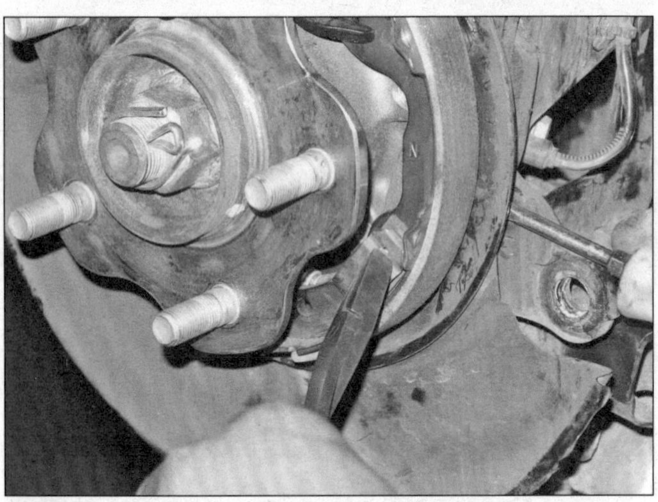
12.4o . . . and secure the shoe with a hold-down spring and pin

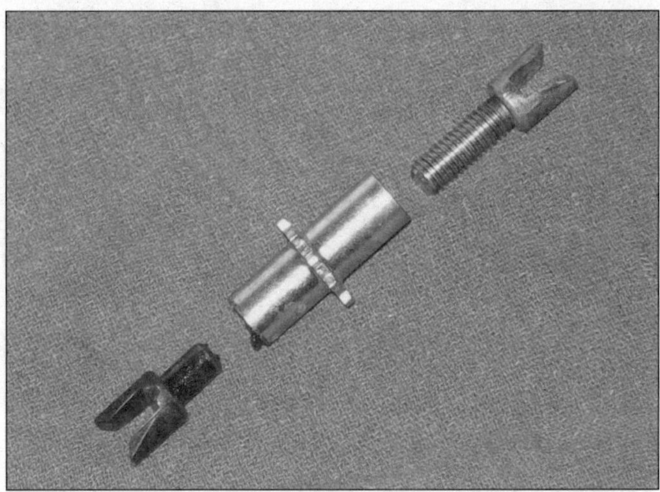
12.4p Disassemble the adjuster, clean it and lightly lubricate the threads with high-temperature brake grease

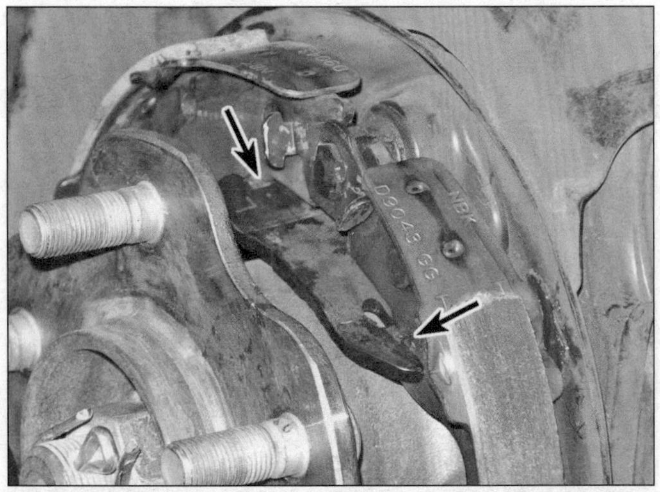
12.4q Install the front shoe, making sure the brake strut is seated correctly into the shoe, then secure the shoe with a hold-down spring

12.4r Place the adjuster between the shoes; the threaded end must face the rear of the vehicle

12.4s Install the lower spring, making sure the spring is hooked into the correct locations on the shoes and the coils rest on top of the star wheel

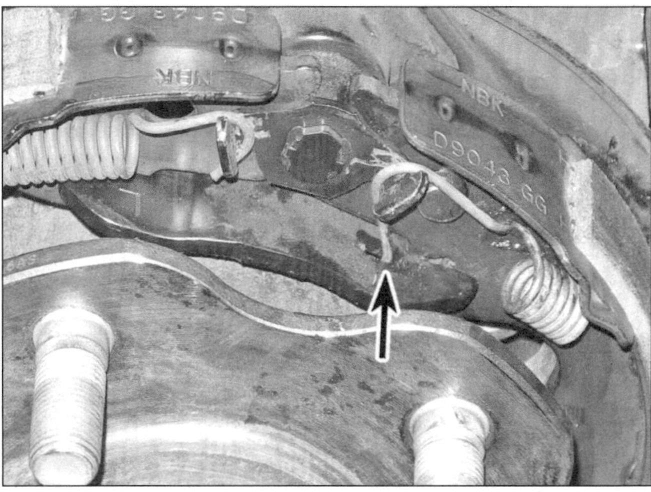

12.4t Attach the upper springs, making sure the end of the rear spring locks into the brake strut, then reinstall the disc

13 Brake pedal - adjustment

1 With the brake pedal fully released, measure the distance from the top of the pad to the floor with the carpet and padding removed. Measure at a right angle to the floor.

2 If the height is not as listed in this Chapter's Specifications, it must be adjusted.

3 Release the brake light and cruise control cancel switches by turning them counterclockwise 45 degrees.

4 Loosen the lock nut just in front of the power brake booster clevis (see illustration 10.10).

5 Turn the booster input rod until the pedal height is correct.

6 Tighten the lock nut.

7 With the threaded portion of the brake light and cruise control cancel switches contacting the bracket, turn the switches 45 degrees clockwise to lock them in place.

8 Adjust the brake light and cruise control switches if necessary (see Section 14).

14 Brake light switch, cruise control cancel switch and brake pedal position sensor - adjustment and replacement

Note: *On 2013 and earlier models/2014 and later Rogue Select models, the cruise control cancel switch is also known as the ASCD (Automatic Speed Control Device) switch, and on 2014 and later models (except Rogue Select models) the switch has been replaced by the brake pedal position sensor.*

Adjustment

1 The brake light switch and cruise control cancel switch or brake pedal position sensor are located on a bracket near the top of the brake pedal. The switches activate the brake lights at the rear of the vehicle when the pedal is depressed and cancel the cruise control operation.

14.6 The clearance between the body of the switch and the pedal bracket must be as shown in the Specifications

2 To check the brake light switch, simply note whether the brake lights come on when the pedal is depressed and go off when the pedal is released.

3 If the brake lights don't come on or the cruise control doesn't cancel when the brake pedal is depressed, make sure the brake pedal is correctly adjusted (see Section 13), then try adjusting the switch as follows.

4 Release the switch by turning it counterclockwise 45-degrees.

5 Pull the brake pedal back and hold it there, then push the switch into its bracket until the body of the switch (threaded portion) touches its stop.

6 Turn the switch 45-degrees clockwise to lock it in place. The distance from the pedal and the body of the switch should be as listed in this Chapter's Specifications (see illustration).

Replacement

7 Unplug the electrical connector from the switch.

8 Turn the switch 45-degrees counterclockwise, pull the switch to the rear and remove it.

9 Installation is the reverse of removal.

10 Adjust the brake pedal height (see Section 13), then adjust the switch (see Steps 4 through 6).

15 Electric Parking Brake (EPB) - general information, troubleshooting, deactivation/activation and component replacement

Caution: *Dust created by the brake system is harmful to your health. Never blow it out with compressed air and don't inhale any of it. An approved filtering mask should be worn when working on the brakes. Do not, under any circumstances, use petroleum-based solvents to clean brake parts. Use brake system cleaner only.*

Caution: *Do NOT perform any repairs to the rear braking system on a vehicle equipped with Electric Parking Brake (EPB) unless a Nissan "CONSULT" scan tool or equivalent has been used to place the system into "work procedure" mode.*

General information

1 The Electric Parking Brake (EPB) system utilizes an actuator mounted on each rear brake caliper. The EPB control module monitors the functions of the actuators for the engagement and release and is integrated into the ABS control module (see Section 3). The control module also stores any trouble codes related to the EPB system. If a malfunction occurs in the EPB system, the controller will turn on the parking brake warning light in the instrument panel.

2 The brake system warning light (yellow) which has the exclamation point in a circle is for hydraulic issues; the parking brake warning light is a P in a circle and is for issues with the EPB system. In some cases, both the warning lights can come on, informing you of a problem with the EPB system. The parking brake warning light will also come on when the EPB system is in the service mode.

Troubleshooting

SYSTEM FAULT	***SERVICE PRODCEDURE***
Red warning light is on, never comes on, or is flashing	Low on brake fluid, wiring, connections, faulty brake fluid level sensor, parking brake is on, brake booster vacuum sensor, EPB, IPC, or ABS concerns
Yellow warning light is on or never comes on	Faulty parking brake switch, connections, wiring, EPB module concerns
Message center displays parking brake malfunction or "Service Parking Brake System Now"	Have system checked for codes
Message center displays "Maintenance Mode"	System is in the service mode
Rear brakes are dragging	Service the rear brake system
Parking brake system does not release or fails to engage	Check for codes and have the system checked for network communication concerns

Before starting any work on the EPB system

Caution: *Once the parking brake system is being serviced, NEVER operate the electric parking brake switch or depress the brake pedal.*

3 Connect the CONSULT scan tool to the Data Link connector under the instrument panel (see Chapter 6).

a) *Turn the ignition switch to the ON position.* **Caution:** *Do not start the engine.*
b) *Select the "EHS/PKB" then the "WORK SUPPORT" and then "START BRAKE PAD REPLACEMENT" in this order and touch the "START" menu. After the actuators have retracted, the system can be worked on.*

After completing any work on the EPB system

Caution: *Once the parking brake system is being serviced, NEVER operate the electric parking brake switch or depress the brake pedal.*

4 Connect the CONSULT scan tool to the Data Link connector under the instrument panel (see Chapter 6).

a) *Turn the ignition switch to the ON position.* **Caution:** *Do not start the engine.*
b) *Select the "EHS/PKB" then the "WORK SUPPORT" and "INITIALIZATION POSITION ADJUSTMENT" in this order, then touch the "START" menu.*
c) *Select the "EHS/PKB" then the "WORK SUPPORT" and "BRAKE OPERATION" in this order, then touch the "START" menu.*
b) *Select the "EHS/PKB" then the "WORK SUPPORT" and "BRAKE RELEASE" in this order, then touch the "START" menu.*
d) *With the CONSULT scan tool connected, pull the electric parking brake switch to activate the electric parking brake.*
e) *With the CONSULT scan tool connected, push the electric parking brake switch to release the electric parking brake.*
f) *Select the "EHS/PKB" self-diagnosis and touch the "START" menu. If no Diagnostic codes are detected, go to the next Step. If codes are detected, follow the menu for the code diagnosis.*
g) *Select the "EHS/PKB" then the "DATA MONITOR", "BR FORCE EST (LH)" and "BR FORCE EST (RH)" in this order. If the test result is normal proceed to the next Step. If they are not, restart this from Step a).*
h) *Turn the ignition switch to the OFF position, wait 10 seconds, then turn the switch to the ON position and select the "EHS/PKB" to erase self-diagnosis results. The memory should be erased if there are no problems and the system is now active.*

Component replacement

EPB control module

4 Turn the ignition off, then disconnect the cable from the negative terminal of the battery (see Chapter 5).

5 Remove the center console cup holder (see Chapter 11).

6 Disconnect the electrical harness retainers, then remove the rear section of the center console (see Chapter 11).

7 *Remove the EPB control module fasteners and lift the module out of the console, then disconnect the electrical connector from the module. Caution: Do not drop the EPB module. If it is dropped it must be replaced.*

8 Installation is the reverse of removal.

9 If a new module is installed, follow the menu on the CONSULT scan tool to ID and configure the new module.

10 If the module was removed for some other work, see Step 4.

EPB actuator

11 The EPB actuator can't be replaced - it is an integral component of the rear brake caliper. To replace the caliper, see Section 5, then see Step 3 in this Section.

12 Installation is the reverse of removal.

EPB control switch

13 Turn the ignition off, then disconnect the cable from the negative terminal of the battery (see Chapter 5).

14 Remove the center console shift panel (see Chapter 11).

15 Disconnect the electrical connector from the EPB switch.

16 Push the EPB switch out from the backside of the center console shift panel.

17 Installation is the reverse of removal.

Chapter 10
Suspension and steering

Contents

Specifications

Torque specifications

Ft-lbs (unless otherwise indicated)

Note: *One foot-pound (ft-lb) of torque is equivalent to 12 inch-pounds (in-lbs) of torque. Torque values below approximately 15 ft-lbs are expressed in inch-pounds, because most foot-pound torque wrenches are not accurate at these smaller values.*

Front suspension

Strut/coil spring assembly	
Strut upper mounting fasteners	168 in-lbs
Strut piston rod nut	58
Strut-to-knuckle bolt/nuts	
2013 and earlier models/2014 and later Rogue Select models)	104
2014 and later models (except Rogue Select)	66
Stabilizer bar	
Rogue (except Rogue Select)	
2011 and earlier models	25
2012 and later models (in stages)	24
Rogue Select	
2014 models	21
2015 models	27
Stabilizer bar link nuts	
2013 and earlier models/2014 and later Rogue Select models	62
2014 and later models (except Rogue Select)	
Link-to-stabilizer bar	55
Link-to-strut	72
Control arm	
Control arm-to-subframe fasteners	
Rear bushing bolt/nut	
2013 and earlier models/2014 and later Rogue Select models	104
2016 and earlier models	91
2017 and later models	85
Front pivot shaft bolts	126
Balljoint pinch bolt/nut	
2013 and earlier models/2014 and later Rogue Select models	46
2014 and later models (except Rogue Select)	76
Hub and bearing assembly bolts	65
Subframe	
Subframe stay mounting bolts	
2013 and earlier models/2014 and later Rogue Select models	53
2014 and later models (except Rogue Select)	56
Subframe mounting bolts	
2013 and earlier models/2014 and later Rogue Select models	69
2014 and later models (except Rogue Select)	64
Wheel lug nuts	See Chapter 1

Torque specifications

Ft-lbs (unless otherwise indicated)

Note: *One foot-pound (ft-lb) of torque is equivalent to 12 inch-pounds (in-lbs) of torque. Torque values below approximately 15 ft-lbs are expressed in inch-pounds, because most foot-pound torque wrenches are not accurate at these smaller values.*

Rear suspension

Shock absorber bolts/nuts*	
2013 and earlier models/2014 and 2015 Rogue Select models	89
2014 through 2017 models (exc. Rogue Select)	76
2018 and later models	64
Upper control arm*	
2013 and earlier models/2014 and later Rogue Select models	
Control arm inner end-to-rear subframe bolt/nut	96
Control arm outer end-to-trailing arm bolt/nut	111
2014 and later models (except Rogue Select)	111
Lower control arm*	
2013 and earlier models/2014 and later Rogue Select models	
Control arm inner end-to-rear subframe bolt/nut	96
Control arm outer end-to-trailing arm bolt/nut	111
2014 and later models (except Rogue Select)	
Control arm inner end-to-rear subframe bolt/nut	122
Control arm outer end-to-trailing arm bolt/nut	111
Trailing arms*	
Trailing arm-to-body bracket bolt/nut	111
Trailing arm body bracket-to-body bolts	96
Hub and bearing assembly bolts	65
Rear stabilizer bar	
Stabilizer bar bushing clamp nuts/bolts	
2013 and earlier models/2014 and later Rogue Select models	26
2014 and later models (except Rogue Select)	28
Stabilizer bar link nuts	
2013 and earlier models/2014 and later Rogue Select models	81
2014 and later models (except Rogue Select)	82
Rear subframe	
Subframe mounting bolts	96
Subframe support bracket bolts/nuts	37
Rubber bound bumper bolts	18

** Nuts(s) must be replaced with NEW ones*

Steering

Airbag module bolts	96 in-lbs
Steering gear-to-subframe mounting bolts/nuts	109
Steering wheel nut/bolt	
2013 and earlier models/2014 and later Rogue Select models	25
2014 and later models (except Rogue Select)	32
Steering intermediate shaft pinch bolts	
Upper bolt (2013 and earlier models/2014 and later Rogue Select models)	23
Lower bolt/nut	
2013 and earlier models/2014 and later Rogue Select models	27
2014 and later models (except Rogue Select)	37
Steering column mounting fasteners	144 in-lbs
Tie-rod end-to-knuckle nuts	25
Wheel lug nuts	See Chapter 1

1 General information

1 The front suspension system is fully independent with (see illustration) a strut/coil spring design. The upper end of each strut is attached to the vehicle body. The lower end of the strut is connected to the upper end of the steering knuckle. The steering knuckle is attached to a balljoint mounted on the outer end of the control arm. The balljoint is an integral part of the control arm; if the balljoint is worn, the control arm must be replaced. A stabilizer bar is used on all models. The bar is attached to the subframe with a pair of clamps and to the struts with link rods.

2 The rear suspension is also fully independent (see illustration). It consists of separate shock absorbers, trailing arms, upper and lower control arms, and a stabilizer bar. The upper end of each shock is attached to the body and the lower end is bolted to the trailing arm. The "knuckle" is incorporated into the trailing arm. The inner ends of the control arms are bolted to the subframe; the outer ends of the control arms are bolted to the trailing arm. The front ends of the trailing arms are bolted to the body. The stabilizer bar is attached to the subframe by a pair of clamps and is connected to the lower arms by links.

3 The rack-and-pinion steering gear is bolted to the subframe. The steering gear actuates the tie-rods, which are attached to the steering knuckles. The inner ends of the tie-rods are protected by rubber boots which should be inspected periodically for secure attachment, tears and leaking lubricant (which would indicate failed rack seals).

4 The power assist system consists of an electric motor mounted on the steering column.

5 The steering wheel operates the steering shaft, which actuates the steering gear through universal joints. Looseness in the steering can be caused by wear in the steering shaft universal joints, the steering gear, or the tie-rod ends, as well as loose retaining bolts.

6 Frequently, when working on the suspension or steering system components, you may come across fasteners which seem impossible to loosen. These fasteners on the underside of the vehicle are continually subjected to water, road grime, mud, etc.,

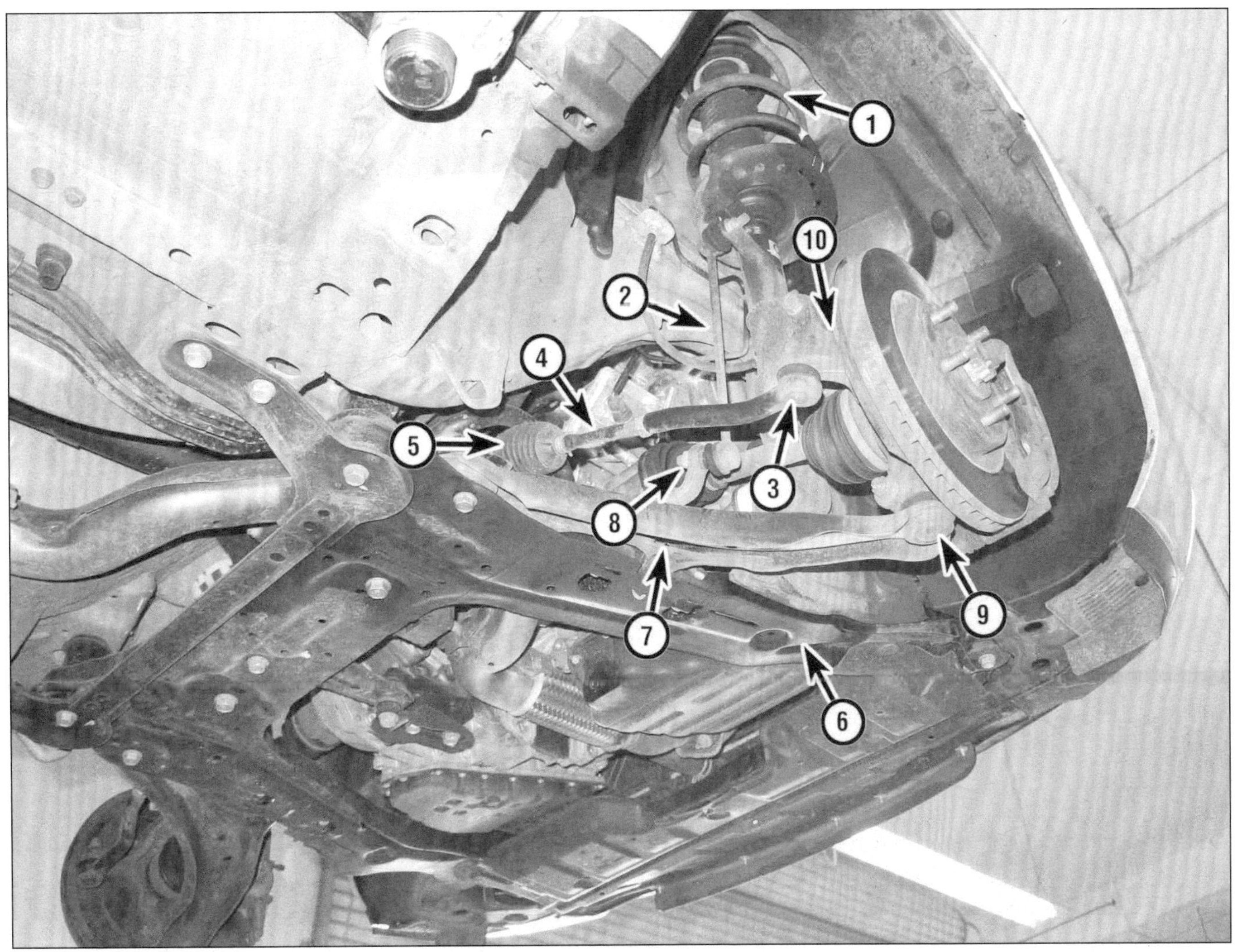

1.1 Front suspension components

1 Strut/coil spring assembly
2 Stabilizer bar link
3 Tie-rod end
4 Tie-rod
5 Steering gear boot
6 Subframe
7 Control arm
8 Stabilizer bar
9 Balljoint
10 Steering knuckle

and can become rusted or frozen, making them extremely difficult to remove. In order to unscrew these stubborn fasteners without damaging them (or other components), be sure to use lots of penetrating oil and allow it to soak in for a while. Using a wire brush to clean exposed threads will also ease removal of the nut or bolt and prevent damage to the threads. Sometimes a sharp blow with a hammer and punch will break the bond between a nut and bolt threads, but care must be taken to prevent the punch from slipping off the fastener and ruining the threads. Heating the stuck fastener and surrounding area with a torch sometimes helps too, but isn't recommended because of the obvious dangers associated with fire. Long breaker bars and extension, or cheater, pipes will increase leverage, but never use an extension pipe on a ratchet - the ratcheting mechanism could be damaged. Sometimes tightening the nut or bolt first will help to break it loose. Fasteners that require drastic measures to remove should always be replaced with new ones.

7 Since most of the procedures dealt with in this Chapter involve jacking up the vehicle and working underneath it, a good pair of jackstands will be needed. A hydraulic floor jack is the preferred type of jack to lift the vehicle, and it can also be used to support certain components during various operations.

Warning: *Never, under any circumstances, rely on a jack to support the vehicle while working on it. Whenever any of the suspension or steering fasteners are loosened or removed they must be inspected and, if necessary, replaced with new ones of the same part number or of original equipment quality and design. Torque specifications must be followed for proper reassembly and component retention. Never attempt to heat or straighten any suspension or steering components. Instead, replace any bent or damaged part with a new one.*

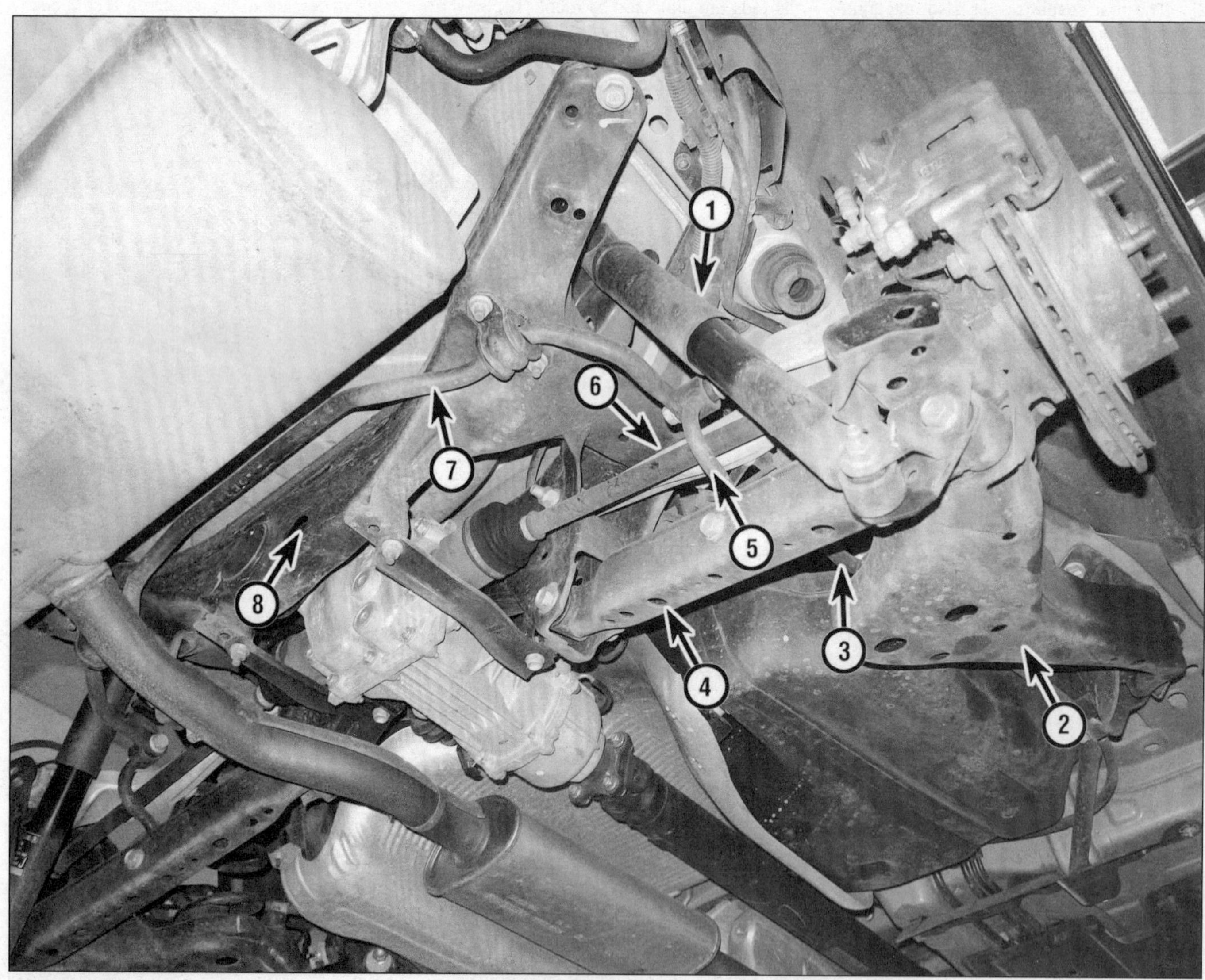

1.2 Typical rear suspension components

1 *Shock absorber*
2 *Trailing arm*
3 *Coil spring*
4 *Lower control arm*
5 *Stabilizer link*
6 *Upper control arm*
7 *Stabilizer bar*
8 *Rear subframe*

2 Strut/coil spring assembly (front) - removal, inspection and installation

Removal

1 Loosen the front wheel lug nuts, raise the front of the vehicle and support it securely on jackstands. Remove the wheels.

2 Remove the cowl cover (see Chapter 11).

Note: *There is an access plug on each side of the cowl cover to access the rearmost strut upper mounting bolt, but in most cases it is easier to remove the cowl cover. If you decide to leave the cover in place, you'll need a magnet or magnetic socket insert, or for bolt installation, a piece of tape can be used to hold the bolt to the socket.*

3 Disconnect the wheel speed sensor wiring harness from the strut (see illustration).

4 Remove the brake hose-to-strut retaining clip and detach the hose from the bracket.

5 Disconnect the stabilizer bar link from the strut (see illustration).

6 On 2013 and earlier models, remove the strut-to-knuckle nuts and knock the bolts out with a hammer and punch.

7 On 2014 and later models, remove the strut-to-knuckle pinch bolt/nut.

8 Separate the strut from the steering knuckle.

9 Support the strut and spring assembly with one hand and remove the three strut upper mounting bolts (see illustration). Remove the assembly from the fenderwell.

Warning: *Don't unscrew the piston rod nut (the nut in the center of the strut tower).*

Inspection

10 Check the strut body for leaking fluid, dents, cracks and other obvious damage which would warrant repair or replacement.

11 Check the coil spring for chips or cracks in the spring coating (this will cause premature spring failure due to corrosion). Inspect the spring seat for cuts, hardness and general deterioration.

12 If any undesirable conditions exist, proceed to the strut disassembly procedure (see Section 3).

Installation

13 Guide the strut assembly up into the fenderwell and install the upper mounting bolts, tightening them to the torque listed in this Chapter's Specifications. This is most easily accomplished with the help of an assistant, as the strut is quite heavy and awkward.

14 Connect the steering knuckle to the strut and insert the bolt(s). Install the nut(s) and tighten to the torque listed in this Chapter's Specifications.

15 The remainder of installation is the reverse of removal. Tighten the stabilizer bar link nut to the torque listed in this Chapter's Specifications. Tighten the wheel lug nuts to the torque listed in the Chapter 1 Specifications.

16 Have the front end alignment checked and, if necessary, adjusted.

3 Strut/coil spring assembly (front) - component replacement

Warning: *Always replace the struts or coil springs in pairs - never replace just one of them.*

1 If the struts or coil springs exhibit the telltale signs of wear (leaking fluid, loss of damping capability, chipped, sagging or cracked coil springs) explore all options before beginning any work. The strut/shock absorber assemblies are not serviceable and must be replaced if a problem develops. However, strut assemblies complete with springs may be available on an exchange basis, which eliminates much time and work. Whichever route you choose to take, check on the cost and availability of parts before disassembling your vehicle.

Warning: *Disassembling a strut is a potentially dangerous undertaking and utmost attention must be directed to the job, or serious injury may result. Use only a high-quality spring compressor and carefully follow the manufacturer's instructions furnished with the tool. After removing the coil spring from the strut assembly, set it aside in a safe, isolated area.*

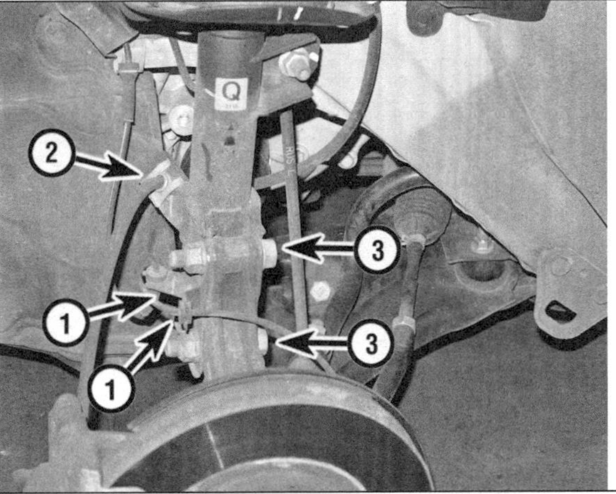

2.3 Strut lower mounting details - 2013 and earlier models/2014 and later Rogue Select models shown

1 *Wheel speed sensor harness bracket*
2 *Brake hose retaining clip*
3 *Strut-to-steering knuckle nuts/bolts*

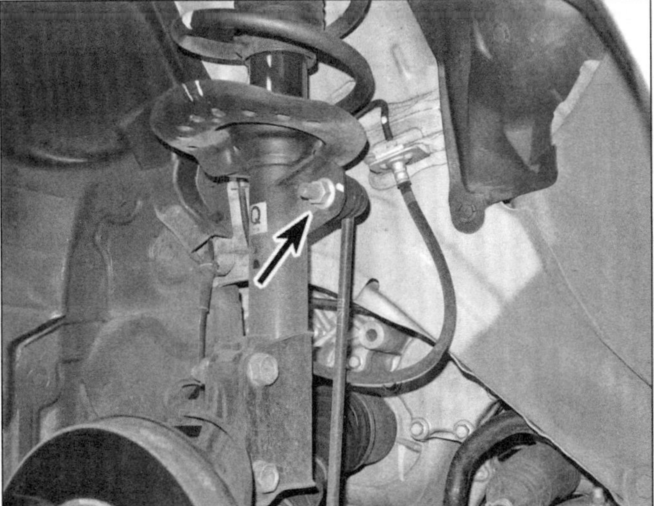

2.5 Stabilizer bar link-to-strut nut

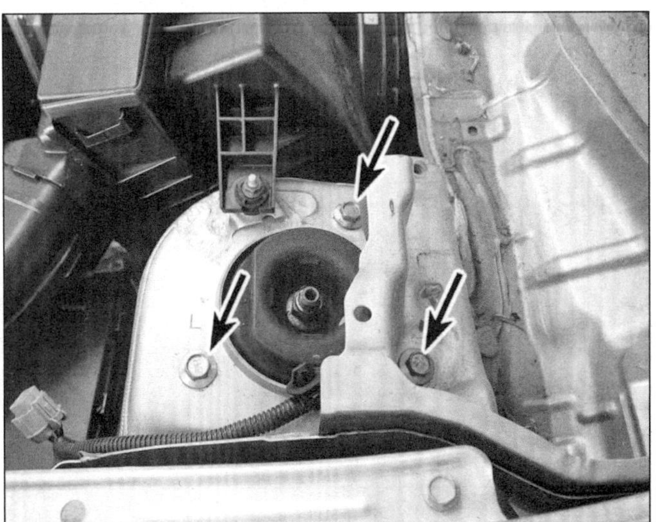

2.9 Strut upper mounting bolts

Disassembly

2 Remove the strut and spring assembly (see Section 2). Mount the strut assembly in a vise. Line the vise jaws with wood or rags to prevent damage to the unit and don't tighten the vise excessively.

3 Following the tool manufacturer's instructions, install the spring compressor (which can be obtained at most auto parts stores or equipment yards on a daily rental basis) on the spring and compress it sufficiently to relieve all pressure from the upper spring seat (see illustration). This can be verified by wiggling the spring.

4 Remove the piston rod nut (see illustration).

5 Remove the upper suspension support (see illustration). Inspect the bearing in the suspension support for smooth operation. If it does not turn smoothly, replace the suspension support. Check the rubber portion of the suspension support for cracking and general deterioration. If there is any separation of the rubber, replace it.

6 Lift the spring seat and upper insulator from the piston rod. Check the rubber spring seat for cracking and hardness, replacing it if necessary.

7 Carefully lift the compressed spring from the assembly (see illustration) and set it in a safe place.

Warning: *Carry the spring carefully and never place any part of your body near the end of the spring!*

8 Slide the dust boot off the piston rod.

9 Check the lower insulator (if equipped) for wear, cracking and hardness and replace it if necessary.

Reassembly

10 If the lower insulator is being replaced, set it into position with the dropped portion seated in the lowest part of the seat. Extend the damper rod to its full length and install the dust boot.

11 Place the coil spring onto the lower insulator, with the end of the spring resting in the lowest part of the insulator (see illustration).

12 Install the upper insulator and the spring seat. Make sure the marks or arrow on the spring seat and mount insulator are facing out (away from the vehicle), in line with the strut-to-knuckle flange.

13 Install the dust seal and suspension support to the piston rod.

14 Install the nut and tighten it to the torque listed in this Chapter's Specifications.

15 Install the strut/shock absorber and coil spring assembly (see Section 2).

4 Stabilizer bar (front) - removal and installation

1 Loosen the front wheel lug nuts, raise the front of the vehicle, support it securely on jackstands and remove the wheels.

2 Separate the intermediate shaft from the steering gear shaft (see Section 18).

3 Detach the stabilizer bar links from the strut. (see illustration 2.5).

4 Disconnect the tie-rod ends from the steering knuckles (see Section 16).

3.3 Install the spring compressor according to the tool manufacturer's instructions and compress the spring until all pressure is relieved from the upper spring seat

3.4 Hold the piston rod with an Allen wrench, then unscrew the nut

3.5 Remove the upper suspension support mount and spring seat

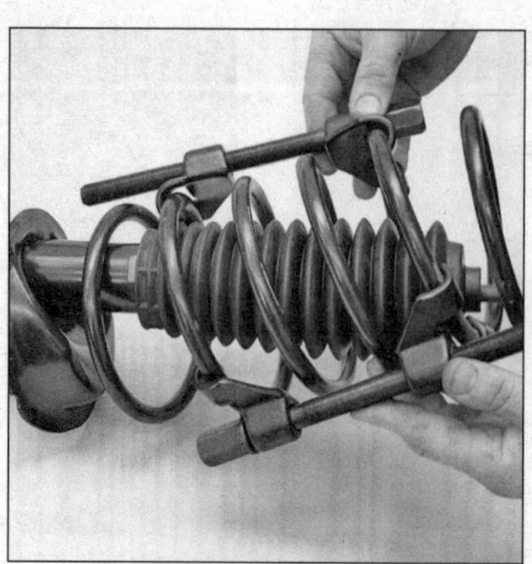

3.7 Remove the compressed spring assembly

3.11 When installing the spring, make sure the end fits into the recessed portion of the lower seat

5 If you're working on a 2014 or later model (except Rogue Select models), remove front exhaust mount and the exhaust manifold/catalytic converter assembly (see Chapter 2A).

6 Remove the torque rod (see Chapter 2A, Section 16).

7 Support the rear of the subframe with a floor jack. Remove the subframe stay bolts, remove the stay, loosen the subframe mounting bolts (see Section 14) and slowly lower the jack just enough to access the stabilizer bar bracket bolts towards the rear of the subframe.

8 Remove the the stabilizer bar clamps and bushings (see illustration).

9 Remove the stabilizer bar.

10 Inspect the clamp bushings and the link bushings. If they're cracked or torn, replace them.

Note: *When installing new bushings, the slit in the bushing should face the front of the vehicle. Install the clamps in their original positions.*

11 Installation is the reverse of removal. Tighten all suspension and steering fasteners to the torque values listed in this Chapter's Specifications. Tighten the wheel lug nuts to the torque listed in the Chapter 1 Specifications.

5 Control arm - removal, inspection and installation

Removal

1 Loosen the front wheel lug nuts, raise the front of the vehicle, support it securely on jackstands and remove the wheel.

2 On 2013 and earlier models/2014 and later Rogue Select models, detach the stabilizer bar links from the stabilizer bar, then swing the ends of the stabilizer bar upward.

Note: *This step is only necessary IF the rear bolt of the front pivot shaft will not clear the stabilizer bar.*

3 Separate the control arm balljoint from the steering knuckle (see illustrations).

4 Remove the control arm fasteners and remove the arm from the subframe (see illustration).

Inspection

5 Inspect the front and rear bushings for cracks and tears. If either bushing is damaged or worn, replace the control arm; the bushings are not replaceable.

6 Inspect the control arm for straightness. If it's bent, replace it. Do not attempt to straighten a bent control arm.

Installation

Note: *When installing the control arm, loosely tighten all the bolts, move the suspension to its normal ride-height angle and position (a floor jack can be used to do this), then fully tighten the bolts.*

7 Installation is the reverse of removal. Tighten all of the fasteners to the torque values listed in this Chapter's Specifications.

8 Install the wheel and lug nuts, lower the vehicle and tighten the lug nuts to the torque listed in the Chapter 1 Specifications.

9 It's a good idea to have the front wheel alignment checked and, if necessary, adjusted.

6 Balljoints - replacement

1 The balljoint is an integral part of the control arm. If it's worn or damaged, the control arm must be replaced (see Section 5).

7 Steering knuckle - removal and installation

Warning: *Dust created by the brake system is harmful to your health. Never blow it out with compressed air and don't inhale any of it. Do not, under any circumstances, use petroleum-based solvents to clean brake parts. Use brake system cleaner only.*

Removal

1 Loosen the wheel lug nuts, raise the vehicle and support it securely on jackstands. Remove the wheel.

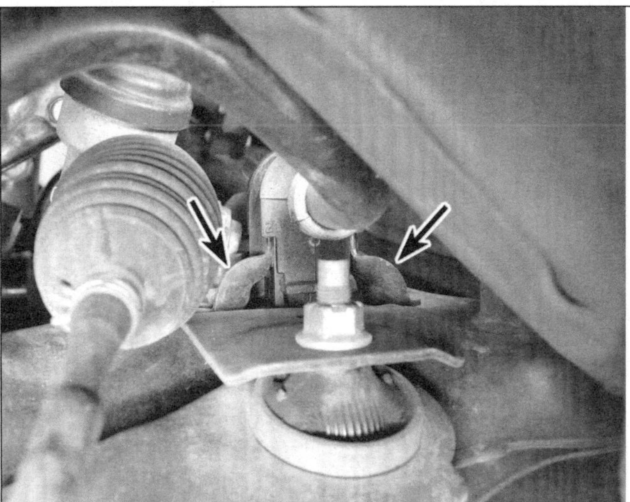

4.8 Stabilizer bar bushing clamp bolts

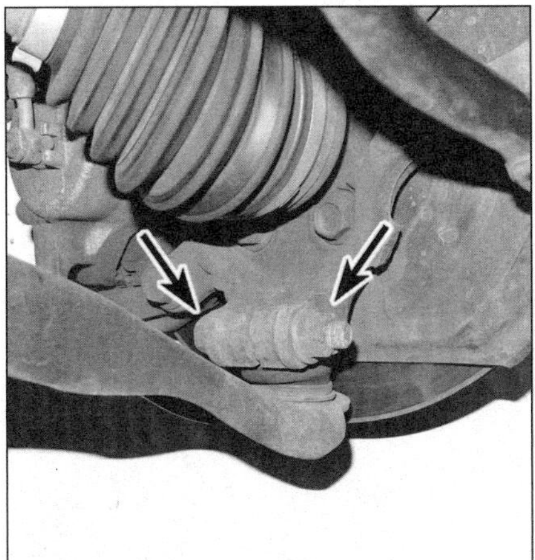

5.3a Remove the balljoint-to steering knuckle pinch bolt/nut

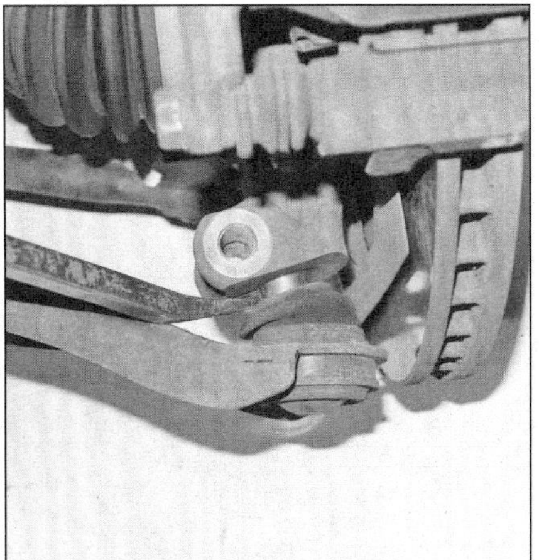

5.3b Pry the balljoint stud out of the steering knuckle, taking care not to damage the boot

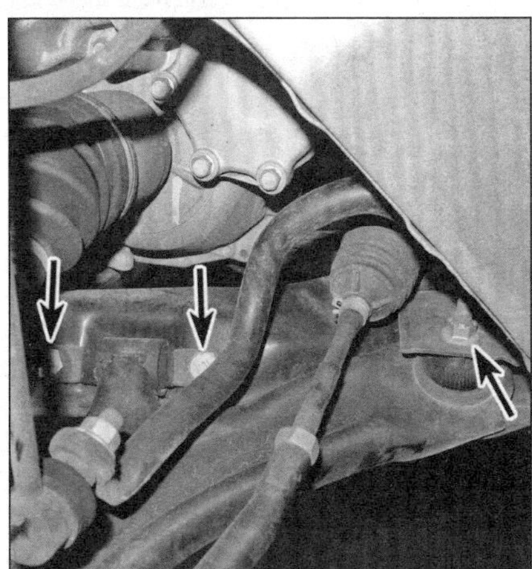

5.4 Control arm fastener locations

2 Remove the driveaxle/hub nut (see Chapter 8).

3 Remove the brake disc (see Chapter 9).

4 Remove the ABS wheel speed sensor from the steering knuckle (see Chapter 9).

5 Separate the tie-rod end from the steering knuckle (see Section 16).

6 On 2013 and earlier models/2014 and later Rogue Select models, remove the strut-to-steering knuckle nuts, but don't remove the bolts yet (see Section 2). On 2014 and later models (except Rogue Select), remove the strut-to-steering knuckle pinch bolt and nut.

7 Separate the control arm balljoint from the steering knuckle (see Section 5).

8 Separate the driveaxle from the steering knuckle (see Chapter 8). Support the end of the driveaxle with a length of wire so the CV joints aren't overextended.

9 Remove the strut-to-knuckle bolts and separate the knuckle from the strut.

Installation

10 Lubricate the splines of the driveaxle with multi-purpose grease. Guide the knuckle and hub assembly into position, inserting the driveaxle into the hub.

11 On 2013 and earlier models/2014 and later Rogue Select models, push the knuckle into the strut flange and install the bolts and nuts, but don't tighten them yet.

12 On 2014 and later models (except Rogue Select), insert the end of the strut into the top of the knuckle until the the pinch bolt can be inserted, but don't tighten the bolt/nut yet.

13 Attach the control arm balljoint to the steering knuckle (see Section 5).

14 Attach the tie-rod end to the steering knuckle arm (see Section 16). Tighten the tie-rod end nut and the strut-to-knuckle nuts to the torque listed in this Chapter's Specifications. On 2014 and later models (except Rogue Select), install a new cotter pin through the tie-rod end ballstud.

15 Place the brake disc on the hub, then install the caliper (see Chapter 9).

16 Install the driveaxle/hub nut and tighten it to the torque listed in the Chapter 8 Specifications.

17 Install the wheel and lug nuts. Lower the vehicle and tighten the lug nuts to the torque listed in the Chapter 1 Specifications.

8 Hub and bearing assembly - removal and installation

Front

1 Loosen the driveaxle/hub nut (see Chapter 8).

2 Loosen the front wheel lug nuts, raise the front of the vehicle and support it securely on jackstands. Remove the wheel.

3 Remove the brake disc (see Chapter 9).

4 Remove the driveaxle/hub nut.

5 Separate the control arm balljoint from the steering knuckle (see Section 5). Also detach the tie-rod end from the steering knuckle (see Section 16).

6 Pull the steering knuckle outward and detach the driveaxle from the hub. Once the driveaxle has been freed from the hub, support it with a length of wire to prevent overextension of the inner CV joint.

7 Remove the hub/bearing assembly mounting bolts from the rear of the steering knuckle (see illustration).

8 Remove the hub/bearing assembly from the steering knuckle.

Note: *If the driveaxle splines stick in the hub, push the driveaxle out of the hub with a two-jaw puller.*

9 Installation is the reverse of removal. Tighten all fasteners to the proper torque values.

Rear

10 Loosen the rear wheel lug nuts. Raise the rear of the vehicle and support it securely on jackstands. Remove the wheel.

11 Remove the wheel speed sensor (see Chapter 9).

12 Remove the brake disc (see Chapter 9).

13 On AWD models, loosen the rear driveaxle hub nut (see Chapter 8).

14 Remove the hub and bearing assembly mounting bolts (see illustration).

15 Remove the hub and bearing assembly. If you're working on an AWD model and the driveaxle splines stick in the hub, use a puller to push the driveaxle from the hub as the hub and bearing assembly is removed from the trailing arm.

16 Installation is the reverse of removal. Tighten all fasteners to the proper torque values.

9 Shock absorbers (rear) - removal and installation

Warning: *Always replace the shock absorbers in pairs - never replace just one of them.*

1 Loosen the rear wheel lug nuts. Raise the rear of the vehicle and support it securely on jackstands. Block the front wheels to prevent the vehicle from rolling. Remove the wheel.

2 Support the lower rear control arm with a floor jack placed under the coil spring pocket.

Warning: *The jack must remain in this position until the shock absorber is reinstalled.*

3 Remove the shock absorber upper mounting nut and bolt (see illustration).

4 Remove the shock absorber lower mounting nut and bolt and remove the shock absorber (see illustration).

5 Installation is the reverse of removal, noting the following points:

6 Raise the control arm with the jack to simulate normal ride height, then tighten the mounting fasteners to the torque listed in this Chapter's Specifications.

7 Install the wheel and lug nuts. Lower the vehicle and tighten the lug nuts to the torque listed in the Chapter 1 Specifications.

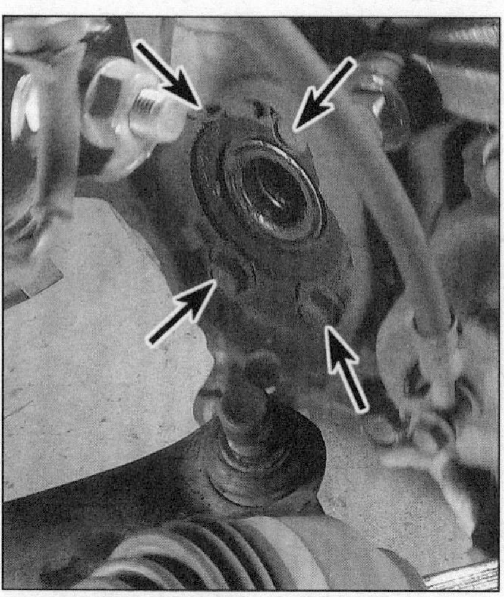

8.7 Front hub and bearing mounting bolts

8.14 Rear hub and bearing mounting bolts

9.3 Shock absorber upper mounting bolt

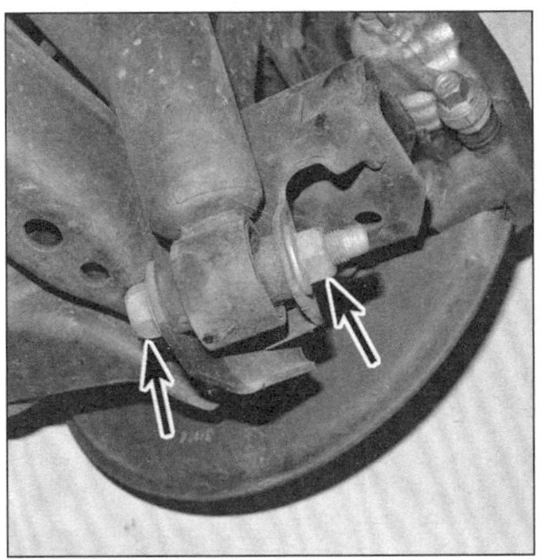
9.4 Shock absorber lower mounting bolt/nut

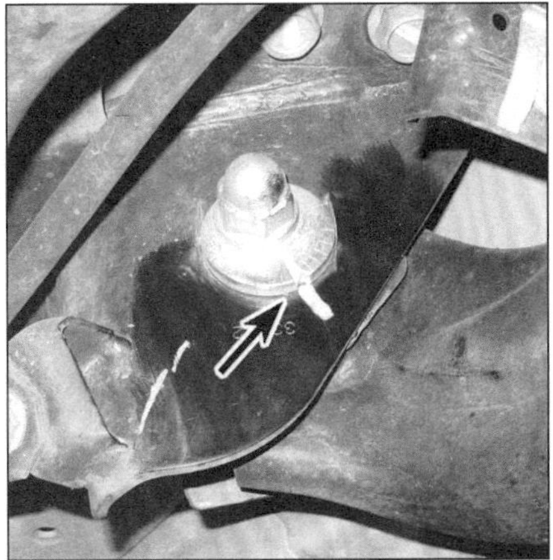
11.3 Mark the adjuster cam to the body bracket

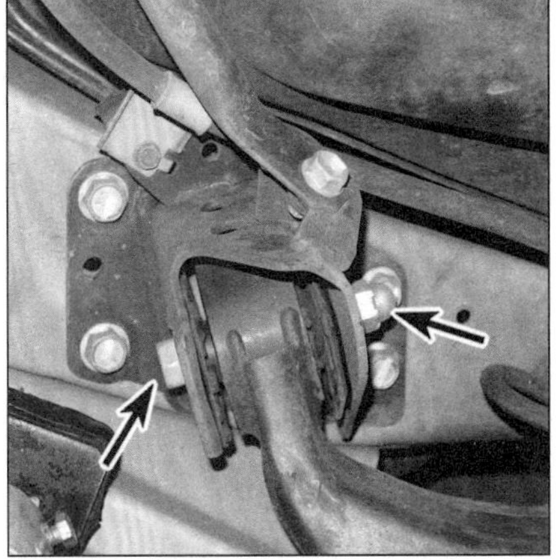
11.4 Trailing arm-to-bracket mounting bolt

10 Coil springs (rear) - removal and installation

Warning: *Always replace the coil springs in pairs - never replace just one of them.*

1 Loosen the rear wheel lug nuts, raise the rear of the vehicle, support it securely on jackstands and remove the wheel.

2 Position a floor jack under the coil spring seat portion of the trailing arm, then raise the jack slightly.

3 Remove the brake caliper, caliper mounting bracket and brake disc (see Chapter 9).

4 Remove the ABS wheel speed sensor (see Chapter 9).

5 Unbolt the upper and lower control arms from the trailing arm (see Section 11).

6 Detach the stabilizer bar link from the lower control arm (see Section 12).

7 Separate the parking brake cable and brake pipe from the trailing arm. Also disconnect the height sensor, if equipped.

8 Remove both shock absorber lower mounting bolts (see Section 9).

9 On AWD models, remove the driveaxle (see Chapter 8).

10 Carefully lower the suspension arm using the floor jack until the coil spring is fully extended.

11 Remove the coil spring, the rubber mount and the rubber seat.

12 Installation is the reverse of removal, noting the following points:

a) *Raise the trailing arm with a floor jack until it is at normal ride height, then tighten the suspension component bolt/nuts to the torque listed in this Chapter's Specifications.*
b) *Tighten the brake fasteners to the torque listed in the Chapter 9 Specifications.*
c) *On AWD models, tighten the driveaxle/hub nut to the torque listed in the Chapter 8 Specifications.*
d) *Tighten the wheel lug nuts to the torque listed in the Chapter 1 Specifications.*

Note: *It's possible that, when raising the trailing arm to connect the upper and lower control arms, the coil spring might force the trailing arm outwards. In the event that you have trouble aligning the upper and lower control arm bolt holes with the holes in the trailing arm, you can use a come-along connected to the trailing arm and the trailing arm on the other side. Tighten the come-along and use a long drift punch to align the bolt holes so the bolts can be inserted.*

11.8 Mark the adjuster cam to the subframe

11 Rear suspension arms and rear subframe - removal and installation

1 Loosen the rear wheel lug nuts. Raise the rear of the vehicle and support it securely on jackstands. Remove the wheel.

Trailing arm

2 Remove the coil spring (see Section 10).

3 Mark the position of the adjuster cams on the pivot bolt to the trailing arm bracket (see illustration).

4 Remove the trailing arm-to-body bracket mounting bolt/nut (see illustration).

5 Remove the trailing arm from the vehicle.

Note: *When the trailing arm is removed, the two rubber washers on either side of the pivot bushing will fall out. Be sure to reinstall them.*

6 Installation is the reverse of removal, noting the following points:

a) *Replace the pivot bolt nut with a new one.*
b) *Align the previously made matchmarks on the adjuster cam and the body bracket.*
c) *Raise the trailing arm with a floor jack until it is at normal ride height, then tighten the trailing arm bolt/nuts to the torque listed this Chapter's Specifications.*
d) *Bleed the brake system (see Chapter 9).*
e) *Tighten the wheel lug nuts to the torque listed in Chapter's 1, Specifications.*
f) *Have the wheel alignment checked and, if necessary adjusted.*

Lower control arm

7 Remove the stabilizer bar link from the lower control arm (see Section 12).

8 Mark the position of the adjuster cams on the inner pivot bolt to the subframe (see illustration).

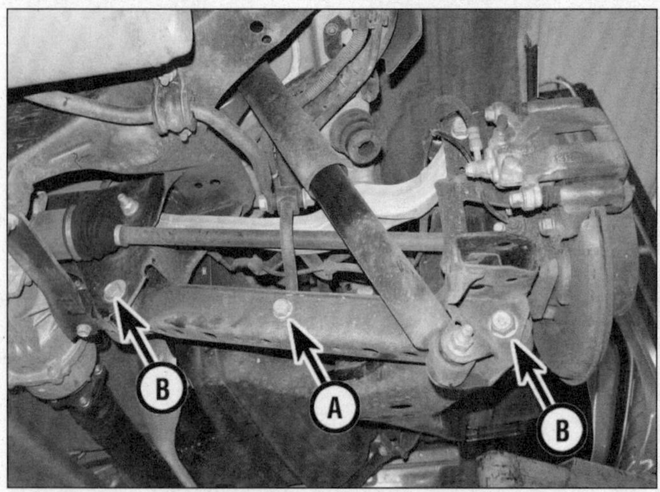

11.10 Remove the stabilizer link bolt (A) then the lower control arm fasteners (B)

11.15 Remove the wheel sensor harness fastener from the upper control arm

11.16 Remove the upper control arm fasteners from each end of the arm

11.28 Location of the rear subframe mounting points

9 Support the trailing arm with a floor jack placed under the coil spring pocket.

Warning: *The jack must remain in this position until the arm is reinstalled.*

10 Remove the lower control arm-to-subframe and trailing arm pivot bolts/nuts (see illustration).

11 Remove the arm from the vehicle.

12 Installation is the reverse of removal, noting the following points:

13 Replace the pivot bolt nuts with a new ones.

- a) *Raise the trailing arm with a floor jack until it is at normal ride height, then tighten the control arm bolt/nuts to the torque listed in this Chapter's Specifications. Be sure to align the marks on the adjusting cam and the subframe before tightening the bolt/nut.*
- b) *Tighten the wheel lug nuts to the torque listed in Chapter 1, Specifications.*
- c) *Have the wheel alignment checked and, if necessary adjusted.*

Upper control arm

14 Support the trailing arm with a floor jack placed under the coil spring pocket.

Warning: *The jack must remain in this position until the arm is reinstalled.*

15 Remove the ABS wheel speed sensor harness mounting bolt (see illustration) from the arm and move the harness out of the way.

16 Remove the upper control arm-to-subframe and trailing arm pivot bolts/nuts (see illustration).

17 Remove the arm from the vehicle.

18 Installation is the reverse of removal, noting the following points:

- a) *Raise the trailing arm with a floor jack until it is at normal ride height, then tighten the control arm bolt/nuts to the torque listed in this Chapter's Specifications.*
- b) *Tighten the wheel lug nuts to the torque listed in Chapter 1, Specifications.*

Rear subframe

19 Raise the vehicle and support it securely on jackstands.

20 Remove the coil springs (see Section 10).

21 Remove the rear section of the exhaust system (see Chapter 4).

22 On AWD models, remove the rear differential (see Chapter 8).

23 Remove the shock absorbers (see Section 9).

24 Remove the upper and lower control arms as described earlier in this Secion.

25 Remove the stabilizer bar (see Section 12).

26 Disconnect the wiring harness from the rear subframe.

27 Place two floor jacks under the rear subframe so it is securely supported.

28 Remove the subframe mounting bolts, then carefully lower the rear subframe a little at a time until it is clear of the body of the vehicle (see illustration).

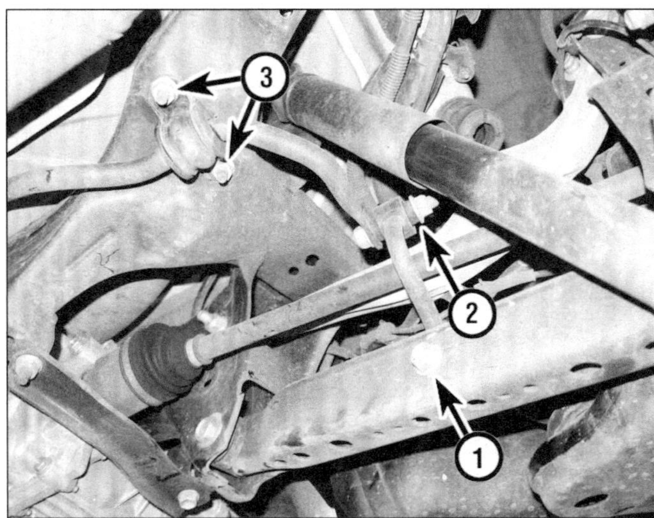

12.2 Stabilizer bar mounting details

1 Stabilizer link-to-lower suspension arm mounting bolt/nut
2 Stabilizer link-to-stabilizer bar mounting bolt/nut
3 Stabilizer bar clamp mounting bolt/nuts

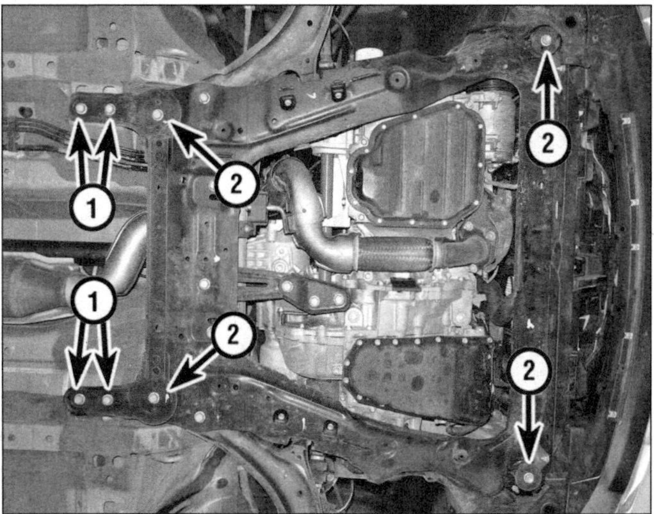

14.11 Subframe mounting details

1 Subframe stay bolts
2 Subframe mounting bolts

29 Installation is the reverse of removal. Tighten all subframe and suspension fasteners to the torque values listed in this Chapter's Specifications. Tighten the wheel lug nuts to the torque listed in the Chapter 1 Specifications.

Note: *Before tightening the suspension fasteners, raise the trailing arm with a floor jack until it is at normal ride height.*

12 Stabilizer bar (rear) - removal and installation

1 Loosen the rear wheel lug nuts, raise the rear of the vehicle, support it securely on jackstands and remove the wheels.
2 Detach the stabilizer bar link-to-lower suspension arm bolt/nut (see illustration).
3 Detach the stabilizer bar link-to-stabilizer bar bolt/nut.
4 Remove the the stabilizer bar clamps and bushings.

Note: *On some models, it may be necessary to remove the muffler to access the stabilizer bar clamp bolts.*

5 Remove the stabilizer bar.
6 Inspect the clamp bushings and the link bushings. If they're cracked or torn, replace them.

Note: *When installing new bushings, the slit in the bushing should face the rear of the vehicle. Install the clamps in their original positions.*

7 Installation is the reverse of removal. Tighten the fasteners to the torque values listed in this Chapter's Specifications. Tighten the wheel lug nuts to the torque listed in the Chapter 1 Specifications.

Note: *Before tightening the stabilizer bar link-to-lower arm fasteners, raise the trailing arm with a floor jack until it is at normal ride height.*

13 Steering column - removal and installation

Warning: *The models covered by this manual are equipped with Supplemental Restraint Systems (SRS), more commonly known as airbags. Always disarm the airbag system before working in the vicinity of any airbag system component to avoid the possibility of accidental deployment of the airbag, which could cause personal injury (see Chapter 12). Do not use a memory saving device to preserve the PCM's memory when working on or near airbag system components.*

1 Disconnect the cable from the negative terminal of the battery (see Chapter 5).
2 Set the wheels in the straight ahead position.
3 Remove the steering wheel (see Section 15).
4 Remove the upper and lower steering column covers (see Chapter 11).
5 Disconnect and remove the combination switch and the spiral cable (see Chapter 12).
6 Remove the driver's knee bolster (see Chapter 11).
7 Detach each of the switch connectors that are installed on the steering column.
8 Disconnect the steering column wiring harness.
9 On 2013 and earlier models/2014 and later Rogue Select models, remove the upper intermediate shaft bolt and detach the intermediate shaft from the column.
10 On 2014 and later models (except Rogue Select models), remove the lower intermediate shaft bolt and separate the shaft from the steering gear (see Section 18).
11 Remove the steering column mounting fateners and remove the steering column.
12 Installation is the reverse of removal. Tighten all fasteners to the torques listed in this Chapter's Specifications. Refer to Section 15 for spiral cable and steering wheel installation.
13 Reconnect the battery and perform the necessary relearn procedures (see Chapter 5).

14 Subframe (front) - removal and installation

1 Loosen the front wheel lug nuts. Raise the front of the vehicle and support it securely on jackstands, then remove the wheels.
2 Disconnect the cable from the negative terminal of the battery (see Chapter 5).
3 Separate the intermediate shaft from the steering gear pinion shaft.
4 Remove the ABS wheel speed sensors from the steering knuckles (if equipped) (see Chapter 9).
5 Detach the stabilizer bar links from the stabilizer bar.
6 Detach the tie-rod ends from the steering knuckles (see Section 16).
7 Remove the rear engine mount torque rod (see Chapter 2A).
8 Remove the oxygen sensor bracket bolt from the subframe.
9 Separate the control arms from the steering knuckles (see Section 5).
10 Support the subframe with two floor jacks (one on each side).
11 Remove the subframe stay and the subframe mounting bolts (see illustration). Slowly lower the jack, making sure nothing is still connected, until the subframe clears the rest of the vehicle, then remove it.
12 Installation is the reverse of removal. Tighten the subframe, suspension and steer-

15.3a Pry off the covers to access the bolts - 2013 and earlier Rogue models/2014 and 2015 Rogue Select models

15.3b Remove the bolts on each side of the steering wheel - 2013 and earlier Rogue models/2014 and 2015 Rogue Select models

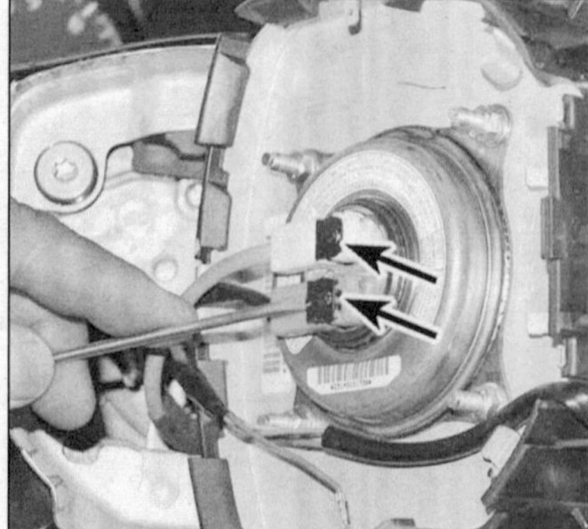
15.3c Pry up the locking tabs on the two connectors, then unplug them

15.5a Remove the nut or bolt

15.5b Note the alignment marks on the wheel and shaft (if there are no marks, make your own)

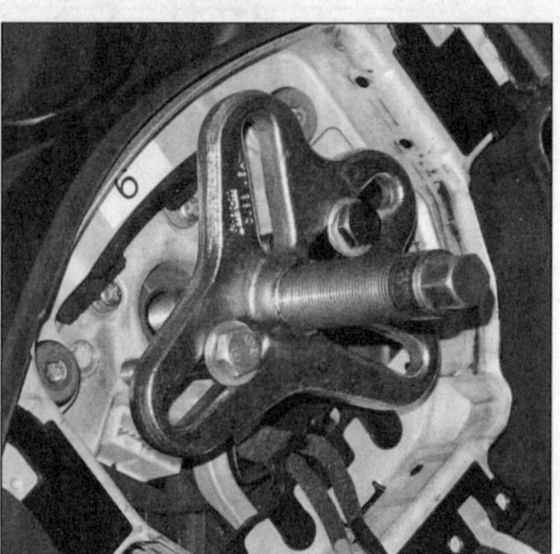
15.6 Use a steering wheel puller threaded into the holes in the steering wheel

ing fasteners to the torque values listed in this Chapter's Specifications. Tighten the wheel lug nuts to the torque listed in the Chapter 1 Specifications.

13 Reconnect the battery and perform the necessary re-learn procedures (see Chapter 5).

15.7 Spiral cable details

1 *Mounting screws*
2 *Retaining tab*

14 Have the front wheel alignment checked, and, if necessary, adjusted.

15 Steering wheel - removal and installation

Warning: *The models covered by this manual are equipped with Supplemental Restraint Systems (SRS), more commonly known as airbags. Always disarm the airbag system before working in the vicinity of any airbag system component to avoid the possibility of accidental deployment of the airbag, which could cause personal injury (see Chapter 12). Do not use a memory saving device to preserve the PCM's memory when working on or near airbag system components.*

Removal

1 Set the wheels in the straight ahead position. Disconnect the cable from the negative terminal of the battery (see Chapter 5).

2 On 2013 and earlier Rogue models and 2014 and 2015 Rogue Select models, remove the airbag module (see illustrations).

3 On 2014 through 2016 Rogue models (except Rogue Select), insert a punch into one of the two holes on the bottom side of the steering wheel until the punch contacts the spring then push the spring inwards and press the upper side of the airbag module in at the same time to release the spring. Lift the airbag module up and disconnect the electrical connectors (see illustration 15.3c).

4 On 2017 and later models, insert a punch into one of the three openings on the back side of the steering wheel (one at a time) and push the bottom of the locking tab in, then tilt the punch up to prevent the locking tab from re-engaging. Repeat this to the remaining locking tabs. Lift the airbag module up and disconnect the electrical connectors (see illustration 15.3c).

5 Lock the steering wheel in the straight ahead position and remove the nut or bolt, as applicable (see illustrations).

6 Remove the steering wheel from the shaft. If it won't slide off the shaft splines, use a steering wheel puller to remove it (see illustration).

Caution: *Do not hammer on the steering wheel or shaft to break it loose*

7 If it's necessary to remove the airbag spiral cable, remove the steering column

15.8 These two marks (A) on the surface of the spiral cable housing will be aligned when it's centered, and the locating pin (B) will be at the top (and must engage with the hole in the steering wheel).

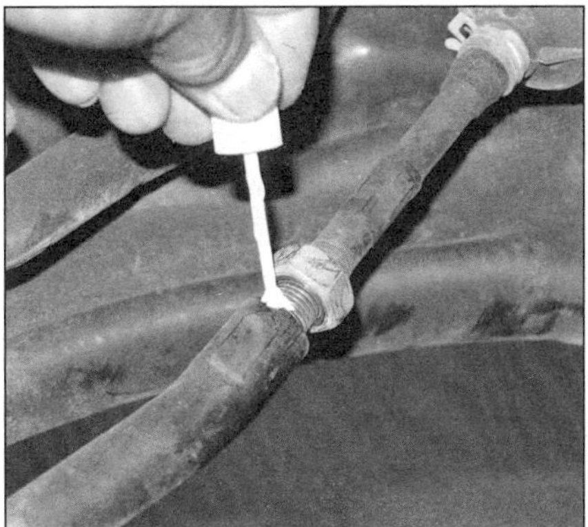
16.2 Loosen the jam nut, then mark the position of the tie-rod end on the threaded part of the tie-rod

16.3 Hold the ballstud from turning using a Torx bit while loosening the nut

16.4 Use a puller to detach the tie-rod end

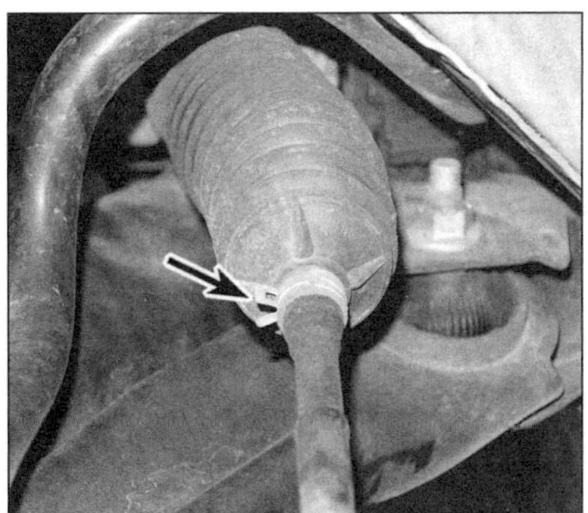
17.3a The outer end of the boot is secured by a spring clamp that can be slid off by pinching the ends together

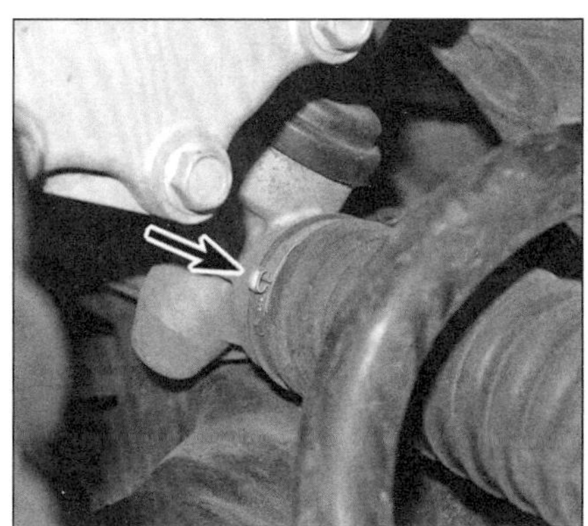
17.3b The inner end of the boot is retained by a clamp that must be cut off and discarded

covers (see Chapter 11), remove the wiper/washer switch and the turn signal switch (see Chapter 12), then remove the screws and release the tab at the top to remove the spiral cable (see illustration).

Installation

8 Verify that the front wheels are pointing straight ahead. If the spiral cable for the airbag has been removed and/or its center position lost, turn the spiral cable clockwise by hand until it becomes hard to turn (don't apply too much force), then rotate it about 2-1/2 turns counterclockwise until the marks align and the location pin is straight up at the 12 o'clock position (see illustration).

9 Feed the airbag spiral cable harness through the hub in the steering wheel, then slip the wheel onto the shaft, making sure the marks are aligned. Make sure the spiral cable pin is properly engaged with the corresponding hole in the back of the steering wheel.

10 Install the steering wheel retaining nut or bolt and tighten it to the torque listed in this Chapter's Specifications.

11 Install the airbag module, tightening the bolts to the torque listed in this Chapter's Specifications. Install the covers.

12 Reconnect the battery and, with your body out of the path of the airbag, verify that the airbag circuit is operational by turning the ignition key to the On or Start position. The "AIR BAG" warning light should illuminate for a few seconds, then turn off.

13 Perform the necessary re-learn procedures (see Chapter 5).

16 Tie-rod ends - removal and installation

Removal

1 Loosen the front wheel lug nuts. Raise the front of the vehicle, support it securely on jackstands, then remove the wheel.

2 Loosen the jam nut enough to mark the position of the tie-rod end in relation to the threads (see illustration).

3 Loosen, but don't remove, the nut on the tie-rod end ballstud (see illustration).

4 Disconnect the tie-rod end from the steering knuckle arm with a puller (see illustration).

5 Remove the nut and separate the tie-rod end from the steering knuckle.

6 Unscrew the tie-rod end from the tie-rod.

Installation

7 Thread the tie-rod end on to the marked position and insert the tie-rod stud into the steering knuckle arm. Tighten the jam nut securely.

8 Install the nut on the ballstud and tighten it to the torque listed in this Chapter's Specifications.

9 Install the wheel and lug nuts. Lower the vehicle and tighten the lug nuts to the torque listed in the Chapter 1 Specifications.

10 Have the wheel alignment checked and, if necessary, adjusted.

17 Steering gear boots - replacement

1 Loosen the lug nuts, raise the vehicle and support it securely on jackstands. Remove the wheel.

2 Remove the tie-rod end and jam nut (see Section 16).

3 Remove the outer steering gear boot clamp (see illustration) with a pair of pliers. Cut off the inner boot clamp (see illustration) with a pair of diagonal cutters. Slide the boot off.

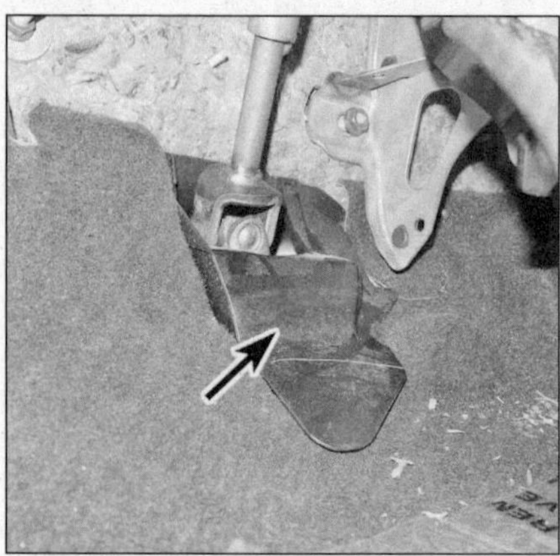
18.2 Pry the cover up to acces the lower intermediate shaft bolt

18.3 Intermediate shaft pinch bolt

4 Before installing the new boot, wrap the threads on the end of the steering rod with a layer of tape so the small end of the new boot isn't damaged.
5 Slide the new boot into position on the steering gear until it seats in the groove in the steering rod and install new clamps.
6 Remove the tape and install the tie-rod end (see Section 16).
7 Install the wheel and lug nuts. Lower the vehicle and tighten the lug nuts to the torque listed in the Chapter 1 Specifications.
8 Have the wheel alignment checked and, if necessary, adjusted.

18 Steering gear - removal and installation

Warning: *The models covered by this manual are equipped with Supplemental Restraint Systems (SRS), more commonly known as airbags. Always disarm the airbag system before working in the vicinity of any airbag system component to avoid the possibility of accidental deployment of the airbag, which could cause personal injury (see Chapter 12). Do not use a memory saving device to preserve the PCM's memory when working on or near airbag system components.*

Removal

Warning: *Do not turn the steering wheel while the steering gear is removed. If the steering wheel is inadvertently turned, remove the steering wheel and center the spiral cable (see Section 15). To prevent the steering wheel from turning, loop the seat belt through the steering wheel and fasten it into its latch.*
1 Set the wheels in the straight ahead position.
2 Remove the lower intermediate shaft joint cover (see illustration).
3 Remove the lower intermediate shaft bolt and remove the intermediate shaft from the steering gear (see illustration).
4 Loosen the front wheel lug nuts. Raise the vehicle and support it securely on jackstands. Block the rear wheels.
5 Remove the wheels
6 Remove the subframe (see Section 14).
7 Remove the steering gear mounting nuts/bolts.

Installation

Note: *Make sure the steering gear is centered from side to side before installing it. Ensure the mounting surface on the body side of the firewall seal is clean and free from damage.*
8 Place the gear on the subframe, install the bolts and tighten them to the torque listed in this Chapter's Specifications.
9 Install the subframe (see Section 14)
10 Install the wheels and lug nuts, then lower the vehicle and tighten the lug nuts to the torque listed in the Chapter 1 Specifications.
11 Have the wheel alignment checked and, if necessary, adjusted.

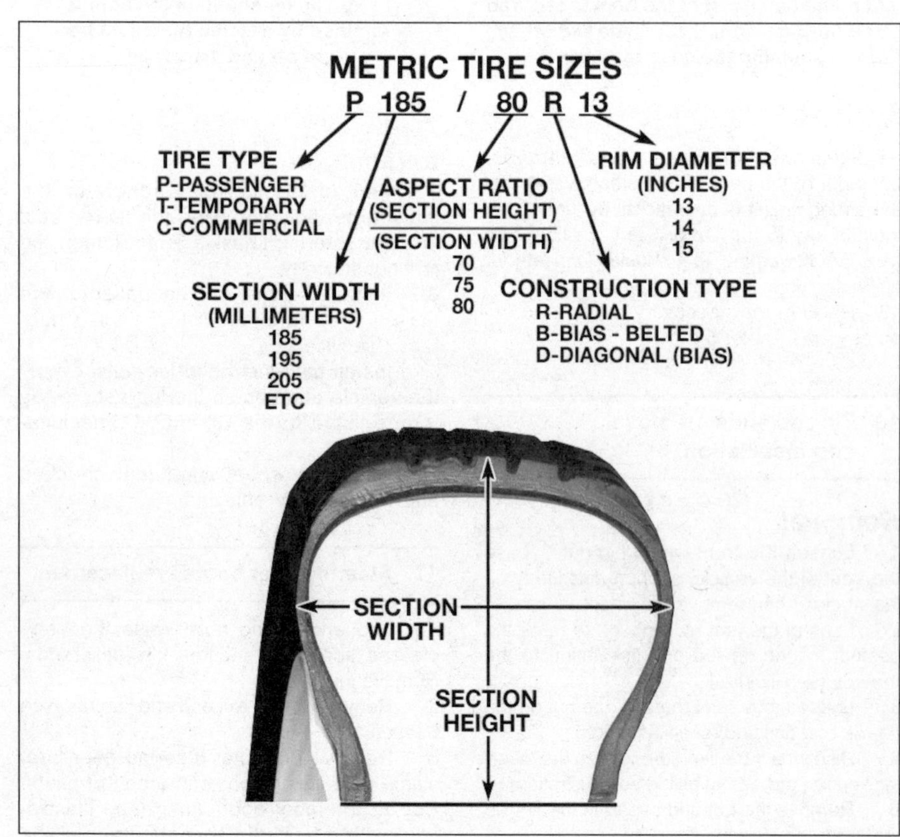

19.1 Metric tire size code

19 Wheels and tires - general information

1 All vehicles covered by this manual are equipped with metric-sized steel belted radial tires (see illustration). Use of other size or type of tires may affect the ride and handling of the vehicle. Don't mix different types of tires, such as radials and bias belted, on the same vehicle as handling may be seriously affected. It's recommended that tires be replaced in pairs on the same axle, but if only one tire is being replaced, be sure it's the same size, structure and tread design as the other.
2 Because tire pressure has a substantial effect on handling and wear, the pressure on all tires should be checked at least once a month or before any extended trips (see Chapter 1).
3 Wheels must be replaced if they are bent, dented, leak air, have elongated bolt holes, are heavily rusted, out of vertical symmetry or if the lug nuts won't stay tight. Wheel repairs that use welding or peening are not recommended.
4 Tire and wheel balance is important in the overall handling, braking and performance of the vehicle. Unbalanced wheels can adversely affect handling and ride characteristics as well as tire life. Whenever

a tire is installed on a wheel, the tire and wheel should be balanced by a shop with the proper equipment.

20 Wheel alignment - general information

1 A wheel alignment refers to the adjustments made to the wheels so they are in proper angular relationship to the suspension and the ground. Wheels that are out of proper alignment not only affect vehicle control, but also increase tire wear. The front end angles normally measured are camber, caster and toe-in (see illustration). On the front end, camber and caster are preset at the factory; toe-in is the only adjustable angle (however, camber and caster are usually measured to check for bent or worn suspension parts). Toe-in and camber are both adjustable at the rear.

2 Getting the proper wheel alignment is an exacting process, one in which complicated and expensive machines are necessary to perform the job properly. Because of this, you should have a technician with the proper equipment perform these tasks. We will, however, use this space to give you a basic idea of what is involved with a wheel alignment so you can better understand the process and deal intelligently with the shop that does the work.

3 Toe-in is the turning in of the wheels. The purpose of a toe specification is to ensure parallel rolling of the wheels. In a vehicle with zero toe-in, the distance between the front edges of the wheels will be the same as the distance between the rear edges of the wheels. The actual amount of toe-in is normally only a fraction of an inch. Incorrect toe-in will cause the tires to wear improperly by making them scrub against the road surface.

4 Camber is the tilting of the wheels from vertical when viewed from one end of the vehicle. When the wheels tilt out at the top, the camber is said to be positive (+). When the wheels tilt in at the top the camber is negative (-). The amount of tilt is measured in degrees from vertical and this measurement is called the camber angle. This angle affects the amount of tire tread which contacts the road and compensates for changes in the suspension geometry when the vehicle is cornering or traveling over an undulating surface.

5 Caster is the tilting of the front steering axis from the vertical. A tilt toward the rear is positive caster and a tilt toward the front is negative caster.

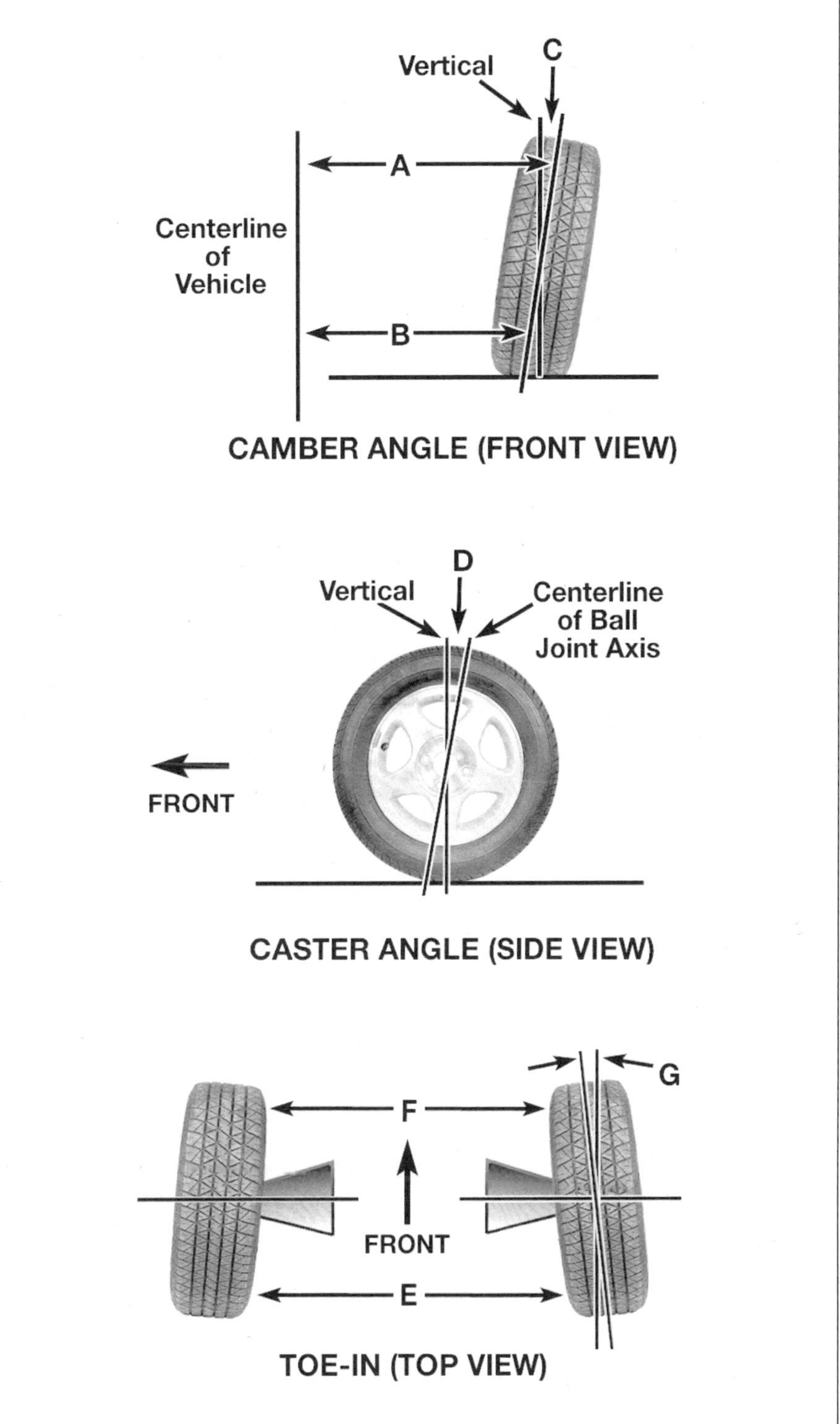

20.1 Camber, caster and toe-in angles

A minus B = C (degrees camber)
D = degrees caster
E minus F = toe-in (measured in inches)
G = toe-in (expressed in degrees)

Notes

Chapter 11
Body

Contents

1 General information

Warning: *The models covered by this manual are equipped with Supplemental Restraint Systems (SRS), more commonly known as airbags. Always disable the airbag system before working in the vicinity of any airbag system components to avoid the possibility of accidental deployment of the airbags, which could cause personal injury (see Chapter 12).*

1 Certain body components are particularly vulnerable to accident damage and can be unbolted and repaired or replaced. Among these parts are the hood, doors, tailgate, liftgate, bumpers and front fenders.

2 Only general body maintenance practices and body panel repair procedures within the scope of the do-it-yourselfer are included in this Chapter.

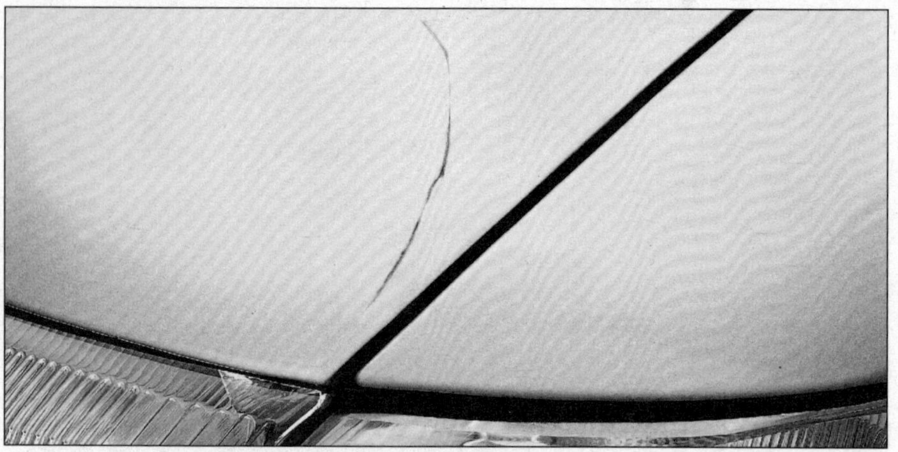

2.1a Make sure the damaged area is perfectly clean and rust free. If the touch-up kit has a wire brush, use it to clean the scratch or chip. Or use fine steel wool wrapped around the end of a pencil. Clean the scratched or chipped surface only, not the good paint surrounding it. Rinse the area with water and allow it to dry thoroughly

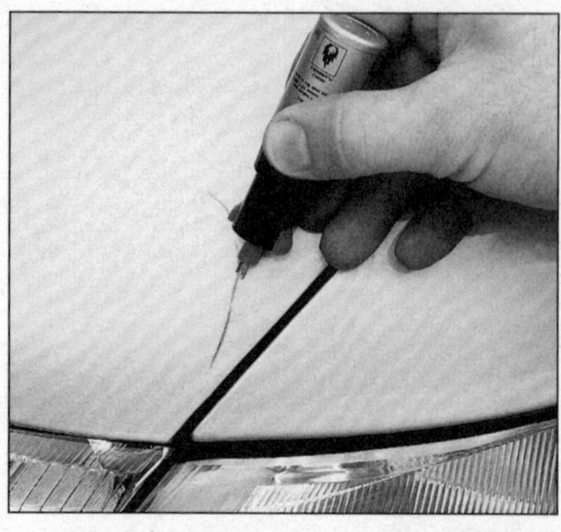

2.1b Thoroughly mix the paint, then apply a small amount with the touch-up kit brush or a very fine artist's brush. Brush in one direction as you fill the scratch area. Do not build up the paint higher than the surrounding paint

2 Repairing minor paint scratches

1 No matter how hard you try to keep your vehicle looking like new, it will inevitably be scratched, chipped or dented at some point. If the metal is actually dented, seek the advice of a professional. But you can fix minor scratches and chips yourself (see illustrations). Buy a touch-up paint kit from a dealer service department or an auto parts store. To ensure that you get the right color, you'll need to have the specific make, model and year of your vehicle and, ideally, the paint code, which is located on a special metal plate under the hood or in the door jamb.

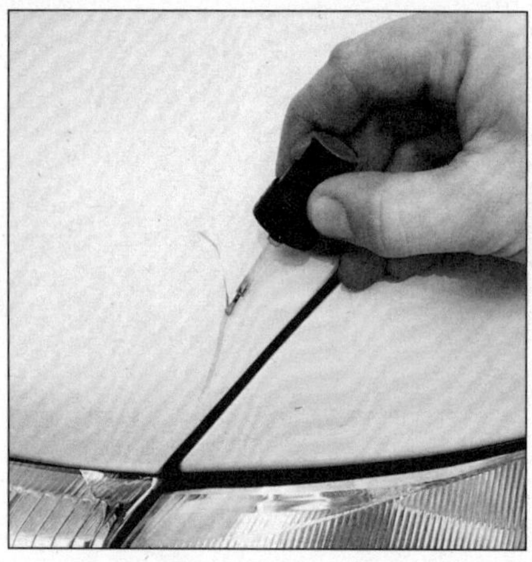

2.1c If the vehicle has a two-coat finish, apply the clear coat after the color coat has dried

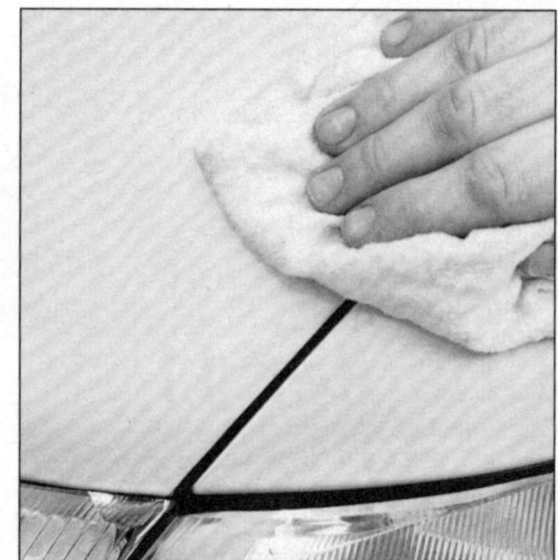

2.1d Wait a few days for the paint to dry thoroughly, then rub out the repainted area with a polishing compound to blend the new paint with the surrounding area. When you're happy with your work, wash and polish the area

3 Body repair - minor damage

Plastic body panels

1 The following repair procedures are for minor scratches and gouges. Repair of more serious damage should be left to a dealer service department or qualified auto body shop. Below is a list of the equipment and materials necessary to perform the following repair procedures on plastic body panels.

Wax, grease and silicone removing solvent
Cloth-backed body tape
Sanding discs
Drill motor with three-inch disc holder
Hand sanding block
Rubber squeegees
Sandpaper
Non-porous mixing palette
Wood paddle or putty knife
Curved-tooth body file
Flexible parts repair material

Flexible panels (bumper trim)

2 Remove the damaged panel, if necessary or desirable. In most cases, repairs can be carried out with the panel installed.

3 Clean the area(s) to be repaired with a wax, grease and silicone removing solvent applied with a water-dampened cloth.

4 If the damage is structural, that is, if it extends through the panel, clean the backside of the panel area to be repaired as well. Wipe dry.

5 Sand the rear surface about 1-1/2 inches beyond the break.

6 Cut two pieces of fiberglass cloth large enough to overlap the break by about 1-1/2 inches. Cut only to the required length.

7 Mix the adhesive from the repair kit according to the instructions included with the kit, and apply a layer of the mixture approximately 1/8-inch thick on the backside of the panel. Overlap the break by at least 1-1/2 inches.

8 Apply one piece of fiberglass cloth to the adhesive and cover the cloth with additional adhesive. Apply a second piece of fiberglass cloth to the adhesive and immediately cover the cloth with additional adhesive in sufficient quantity to fill the weave.

9 Allow the repair to cure for 20 to 30 minutes at 60-degrees to 80-degrees F.

10 If necessary, trim the excess repair material at the edge.

11 Remove all of the paint film over and around the area(s) to be repaired. The repair material should not overlap the painted surface.

12 With a drill motor and a sanding disc (or a rotary file), cut a "V" along the break line approximately 1/2-inch wide. Remove all dust and loose particles from the repair area.

13 Mix and apply the repair material. Apply a light coat first over the damaged area; then continue applying material until it reaches a level slightly higher than the surrounding finish.

14 Cure the mixture for 20 to 30 minutes at 60-degrees to 80-degrees F.

15 Roughly establish the contour of the area being repaired with a body file. If low

areas or pits remain, mix and apply additional adhesive.

16 Block sand the damaged area with sandpaper to establish the actual contour of the surrounding surface.

17 If desired, the repaired area can be temporarily protected with several light coats of primer. Because of the special paints and techniques required for flexible body panels, it is recommended that the vehicle be taken to a paint shop for completion of the body repair.

Steel body panels

See photo sequence.

Repair of dents

18 When repairing dents, the first job is to pull the dent out until the affected area is as close as possible to its original shape. There is no point in trying to restore the original shape completely as the metal in the damaged area will have stretched on impact and cannot be restored to its original contours. It is better to bring the level of the dent up to a point that is about 1/8-inch below the level of the surrounding metal. In cases where the dent is very shallow, it is not worth trying to pull it out at all.

19 If the backside of the dent is accessible, it can be hammered out gently from behind using a soft-face hammer. While doing this, hold a block of wood firmly against the opposite side of the metal to absorb the hammer blows and prevent the metal from being stretched.

20 If the dent is in a section of the body which has double layers, or some other factor makes it inaccessible from behind, a different technique is required. Drill several small holes through the metal inside the damaged area, particularly in the deeper sections. Screw long, self-tapping screws into the holes just enough for them to get a good grip in the metal. Now pulling on the protruding heads of the screws with locking pliers can pull out the dent.

21 The next stage of repair is the removal of paint from the damaged area and from an inch or so of the surrounding metal. This is easily done with a wire brush or sanding disk in a drill motor, although it can be done just as effectively by hand with sandpaper. To complete the preparation for filling, score the surface of the bare metal with a screwdriver or the tang of a file or drill small holes in the affected area. This will provide a good grip for the filler material. To complete the repair, see the Section on filling and painting.

Repair of rust holes or gashes

22 Remove all paint from the affected area and from an inch or so of the surrounding metal using a sanding disk or wire brush mounted in a drill motor. If these are not available, a few sheets of sandpaper will do the job just as effectively.

23 With the paint removed, you will be able to determine the severity of the corrosion and decide whether to replace the whole panel, if possible, or repair the affected area. New body panels are not as expensive as most people think and it is often quicker to install a new panel than to repair large areas of rust.

24 Remove all trim pieces from the affected area except those which will act as a guide to the original shape of the damaged body, such as headlight shells, etc. Using metal snips or a hacksaw blade, remove all loose metal and any other metal that is badly affected by rust. Hammer the edges of the hole in to create a slight depression for the filler material.

25 Wire-brush the affected area to remove the powdery rust from the surface of the metal. If the back of the rusted area is accessible, treat it with rust inhibiting paint.

26 Before filling is done, block the hole in some way. This can be done with sheet metal riveted or screwed into place, or by stuffing the hole with wire mesh.

27 Once the hole is blocked off, the affected area can be filled and painted. See the following subsection on filling and painting.

Filling and painting

28 Many types of body fillers are available, but generally speaking, body repair kits which contain filler paste and a tube of resin hardener are best for this type of repair work. A wide, flexible plastic or nylon applicator will be necessary for imparting a smooth and contoured finish to the surface of the filler material. Mix up a small amount of filler on a clean piece of wood or cardboard (use the hardener sparingly). Follow the manufacturer's instructions on the package, otherwise the filler will set incorrectly.

29 Using the applicator, apply the filler paste to the prepared area. Draw the applicator across the surface of the filler to achieve the desired contour and to level the filler surface. As soon as a contour that approximates the original one is achieved, stop working the paste. If you continue, the paste will begin to stick to the applicator. Continue to add thin layers of paste at 20-minute intervals until the level of the filler is just above the surrounding metal.

30 Once the filler has hardened, the excess can be removed with a body file. From then on, progressively finer grades of sandpaper should be used, starting with a 180-grit paper and finishing with 600-grit wet-or-dry paper. Always wrap the sandpaper around a flat rubber or wooden block, otherwise the surface of the filler will not be completely flat. During the sanding of the filler surface, the wet-or-dry paper should be periodically rinsed in water. This will ensure that a very smooth finish is produced in the final stage.

31 At this point, the repair area should be surrounded by a ring of bare metal, which in turn should be encircled by the finely feathered edge of good paint. Rinse the repair area with clean water until all of the dust produced by the sanding operation is gone.

32 Spray the entire area with a light coat of primer. This will reveal any imperfections in the surface of the filler. Repair the imperfections with fresh filler paste or glaze filler and once more smooth the surface with sandpaper. Repeat this spray-and-repair procedure until you are satisfied that the surface of the filler and the feathered edge of the paint are perfect. Rinse the area with clean water and allow it to dry completely.

33 The repair area is now ready for painting. Spray painting must be carried out in a warm, dry, windless and dust free atmosphere. These conditions can be created if you have access to a large indoor work area, but if you are forced to work in the open, you will have to pick the day very carefully. If you are working indoors, dousing the floor in the work area with water will help settle the dust that would otherwise be in the air. If the repair area is confined to one body panel, mask off the surrounding panels. This will help minimize the effects of a slight mismatch in paint color. Trim pieces such as chrome strips, door handles, etc., will also need to be masked off or removed. Use masking tape and several thickness of newspaper for the masking operations.

34 Before spraying, shake the paint can thoroughly, then spray a test area until the spray painting technique is mastered. Cover the repair area with a thick coat of primer. The thickness should be built up using several thin layers of primer rather than one thick one. Using 600-grit wet-or-dry sandpaper, rub down the surface of the primer until it is very smooth. While doing this, the work area should be thoroughly rinsed with water and the wet-or-dry sandpaper periodically rinsed as well. Allow the primer to dry before spraying additional coats.

35 Spray on the top coat, again building up the thickness by using several thin layers of paint. Begin spraying in the center of the repair area and then, using a circular motion, work out until the whole repair area and about two inches of the surrounding original paint is covered. Remove all masking material 10 to 15 minutes after spraying on the final coat of paint. Allow the new paint at least two weeks to harden, then use a very fine rubbing compound to blend the edges of the new paint into the existing paint. Finally, apply a coat of wax

4 Body repair - major damage

1 Major damage must be repaired by an auto body shop specifically equipped to perform body and frame repairs. These shops have the specialized equipment required to do the job properly.

2 If the damage is extensive, the frame must be checked for proper alignment or the vehicle's handling characteristics may be adversely affected and other components may wear at an accelerated rate.

3 Due to the fact that all of the major body components (hood, fenders, etc.) are separate and replaceable units, any seriously damaged components should be replaced rather than repaired. Sometimes the components can be found in a wrecking yard that specializes in used vehicle components, often at considerable savings over the cost of new parts.

These photos illustrate a method of repairing simple dents. They are intended to supplement *Body repair - minor damage* in this Chapter and should not be used as the sole instructions for body repair on these vehicles.

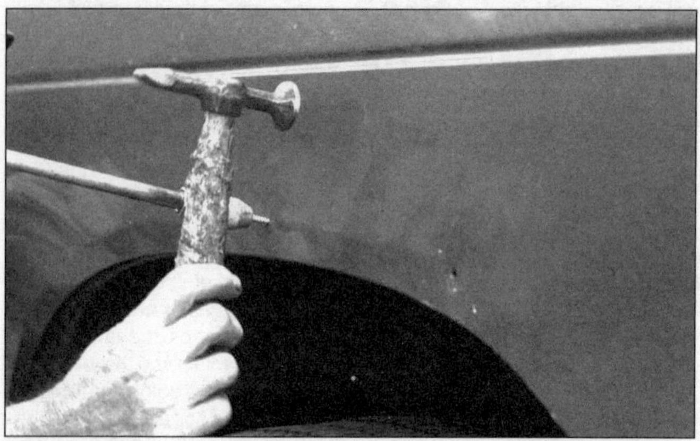

1 If you can't access the backside of the body panel to hammer out the dent, pull it out with a slide-hammer-type dent puller. Tap with a hammer near the edge of the dent to help 'pop' the metal back to its original shape, about 1/8-inch below the surface of the surrounding metal

2 Using coarse-grit sandpaper, remove the paint down to the bare metal. Clean the repair area with wax/silicone remover.

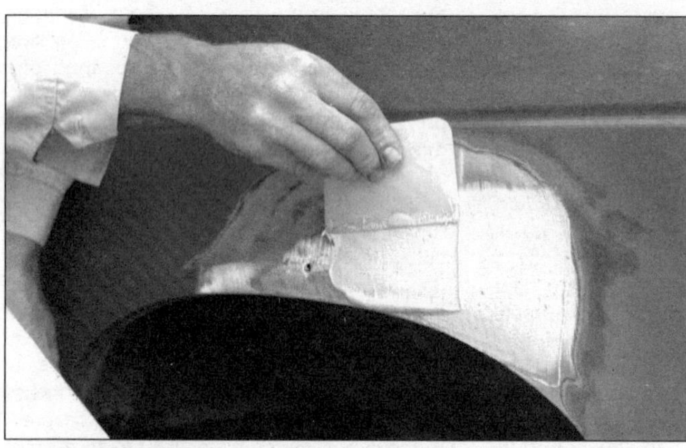

3 Following label instructions, mix up a batch of plastic filler and hardener, then quickly press it into the metal with a plastic applicator. Work the filler until it matches the original contour and is slightly above the surrounding metal

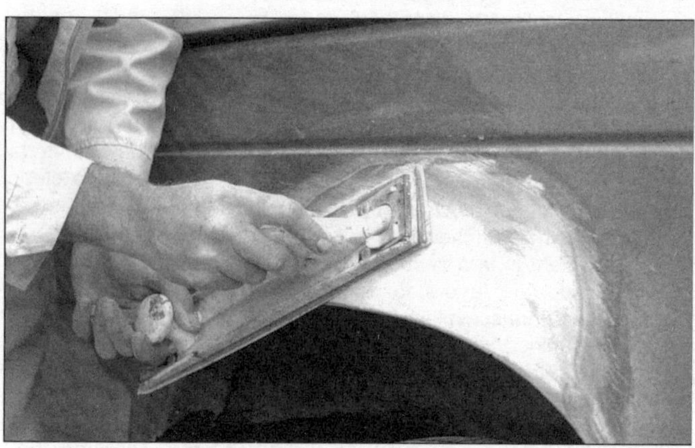

4 Let the filler harden until you can just dent it with your fingernail. File, then sand the filler down until it's smooth and even. Work down to finer grits of sandpaper - always using a board or block - ending up with 360 or 400 grit

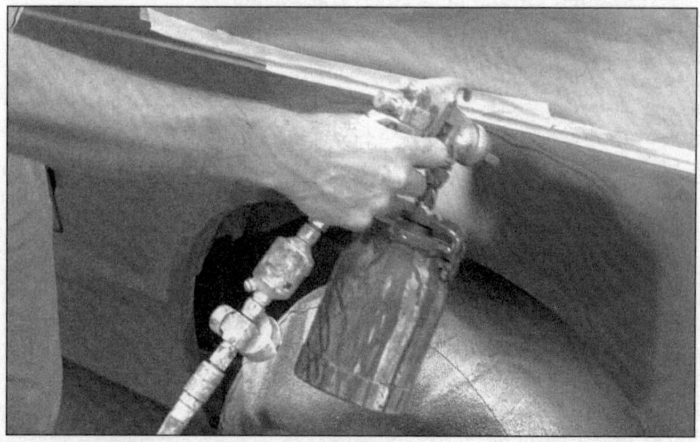

5 When the area is smooth to the touch, clean the area and mask around it. Apply several layers of primer to the area. A professional-type spray gun is being used here, but aerosol spray primer works fine

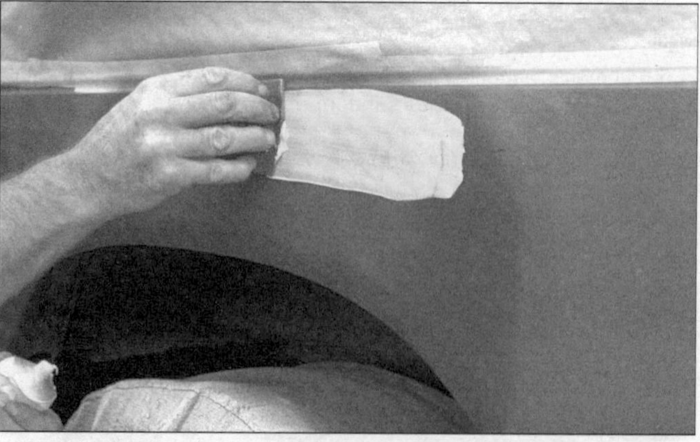

6 Fill imperfections or scratches with glazing compound. Sand with 360 or 400-grit and re-spray. Finish sand the primer with 600 grit, clean thoroughly, then apply the finish coat. Don't attempt to rub out or wax the repair area until the paint has dried completely (at least two weeks)

5 Fastener and trim removal

1 There is a variety of plastic fasteners used to hold trim panels, splash shields and other parts in place in addition to typical screws, nuts and bolts. Once you are familiar with them, they can usually be removed without too much difficulty.

2 The proper tools and approach can prevent added time and expense to a project by minimizing the number of broken fasteners and/or parts.

3 The following illustration shows various types of fasteners that are typically used on most vehicles and how to remove and install them (see illustration). Replacement fasteners are commonly found at most auto parts stores, if necessary.

4 Trim panels are typically made of plastic and their flexibility can help during removal. The key to their removal is to use a tool to pry the panel near its retainers to release it without damaging surrounding areas or breaking-off any retainers. The retainers will usually snap out of their designated slot or hole after force is applied to them. Stiff plastic tools designed for prying on trim panels are available at most auto parts stores (see illustration). Tools that are tapered and wrapped in protective tape, such as a screwdriver or small pry tool, are also very effective when used with care.

6 Upholstery, carpets and vinyl trim - maintenance

Upholstery and carpets

1 Every three months remove the floormats and clean the interior of the vehicle (more frequently if necessary). Use a stiff whiskbroom to brush the carpeting and loosen dirt and dust, then vacuum the upholstery and carpets thoroughly, especially along seams and crevices.

2 Dirt and stains can be removed from carpeting with basic household or automotive carpet shampoos available in spray cans. Follow the directions and vacuum again, then use a stiff brush to bring back the nap of the carpet.

3 Most interiors have cloth or vinyl upholstery, either of which can be cleaned and maintained with a number of material-specific

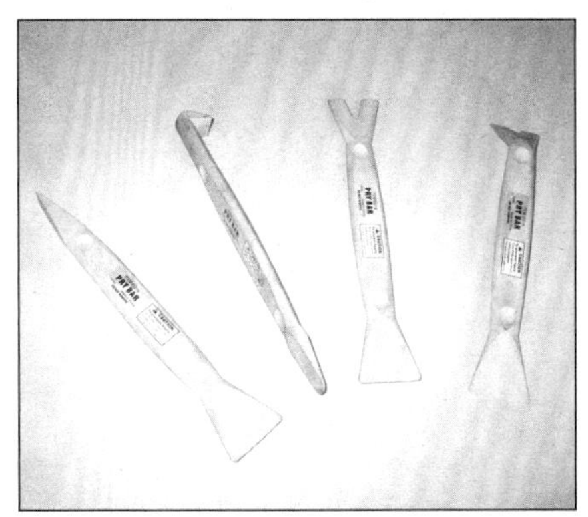

5.4 These small plastic pry tools are ideal for prying off trim panels

Fasteners

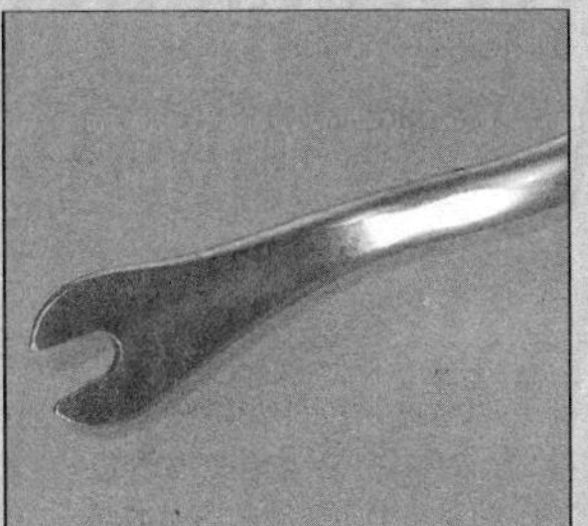

This tool is designed to remove special fasteners. A small pry tool used for removing nails will also work well in place of this tool

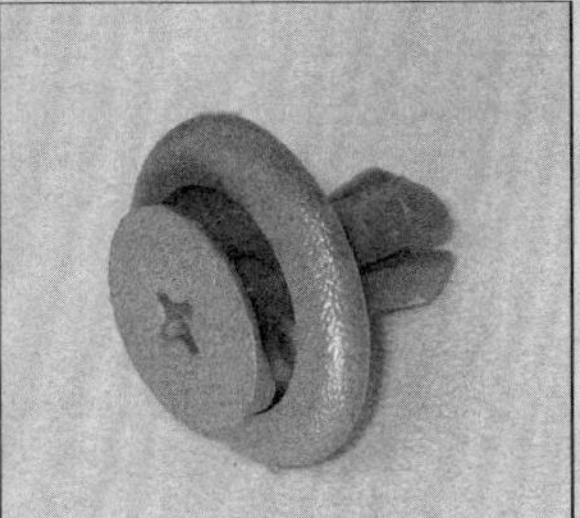

A Phillips head screwdriver can be used to release the center portion, but light pressure must be used because the plastic is easily damaged. Once the center is up, the fastener can easily be pried from its hole

Here is a view with the center portion fully released. Install the fastener as shown, then press the center in to set it

This fastener is used for exterior panels and shields. The center portion must be pried up to release the fastener. Install the fastener with the center up, then press the center in to set it

This type of fastener is used commonly for interior panels. Use a small blunt tool to press the small pin at the center in to release it . . .

. . . the pin will stay with the fastener in the released position

Reset the fastener for installation by moving the pin out. Install the fastener, then press the pin flush with the fastener to set it

This fastener is used for exterior and interior panels. It has no moving parts. Simply pry the fastener from its hole like the claw of a hammer removes a nail. Without a tool that can get under the top of the fastener, it can be very difficult to remove

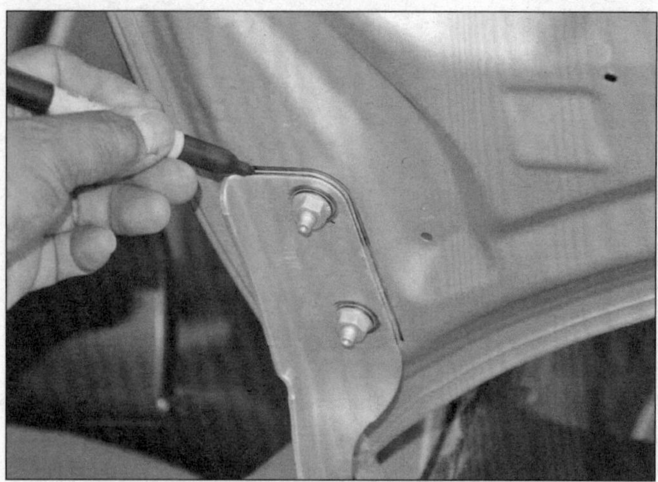

9.2 Before removing the hood, draw a mark around the hinge plate

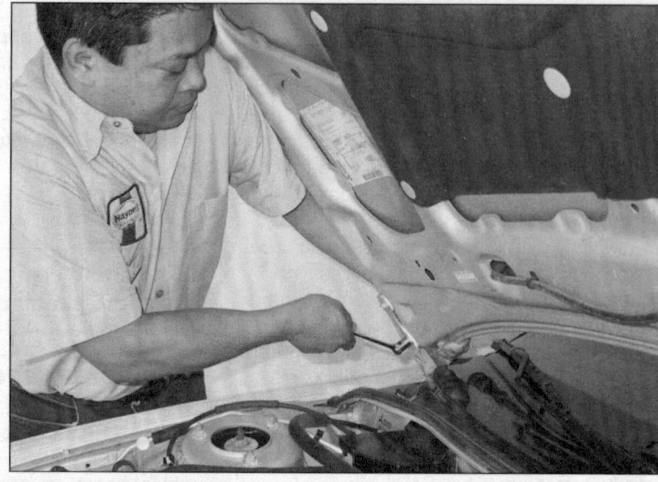

9.4 Support the hood with your shoulder while removing the hood nuts

cleaners or shampoos available in auto supply stores. Follow the directions on the product for usage, and always spot-test any upholstery cleaner on an inconspicuous area (bottom edge of a backseat cushion) to ensure that it doesn't cause a color shift in the material.

4 After cleaning, vinyl upholstery should be treated with a protectant.

Note: *Make sure the protectant container indicates the product can be used on seats - some products may make a seat too slippery.*

Caution: *Do not use protectant on vinyl-covered steering wheels.*

5 Leather upholstery requires special care. It should be cleaned regularly with saddlesoap or leather cleaner. Never use alcohol, gasoline, nail polish remover or thinner to clean leather upholstery.

6 After cleaning, regularly treat leather upholstery with a leather conditioner, rubbed in with a soft cotton cloth. Never use car wax on leather upholstery.

7 In areas where the interior of the vehicle is subject to bright sunlight, cover leather seating areas of the seats with a sheet if the vehicle is to be left out for any length of time.

Vinyl trim

8 Don't clean vinyl trim with detergents, caustic soap or petroleum-based cleaners. Plain soap and water works just fine, with a soft brush to clean dirt that may be ingrained. Wash the vinyl as frequently as the rest of the vehicle.

9 After cleaning, application of a high-quality rubber and vinyl protectant will help prevent oxidation and cracks. The protectant can also be applied to weather-stripping, vacuum lines and rubber hoses, which often fail as a result of chemical degradation, and to the tires.

7 Hinges and locks - maintenance

1 Once every 3000 miles, or every three months, the hinges and latch assemblies on the doors, hood and trunk should be given a few drops of light oil or lock lubricant. The door latch strikers should also be lubricated with a thin coat of grease to reduce wear and ensure free movement. Lubricate the door and trunk locks with spray-on graphite lubricant.

8 Windshield and fixed glass - replacement

1 Replacement of the windshield and fixed glass requires the use of special fast-setting adhesive/caulk materials and some specialized tools. It is recommended that these operations be left to a dealer or a shop specializing in glass work.

9 Hood - removal, installation and adjustment

Note: *The hood is heavy and somewhat awkward to remove and install - at least two people should perform this procedure.*

Removal and installation

1 Use blankets or pads to cover the cowl area of the body and fenders. This will protect the body and paint as the hood is lifted off.

2 Make marks or scribe a line around the hood hinge to ensure proper alignment during installation (see illustration).

3 Disconnect any cables or wires that will interfere with removal.

4 Have an assistant support one side of the hood while you support the other. Remove the hinge-to-hood nuts (see illustration).

5 Lift off the hood.

6 Installation is the reverse of removal.

Adjustment

7 Fore-and-aft and side-to-side adjustment of the hood is done by moving the hinge plate slot after loosening the bolts or nuts.

8 Scribe a line around the entire hinge plate so you can determine the amount of movement (see illustration 9.2).

9 Loosen the bolts or nuts and move the hood into correct alignment. Move it only a little at a time. Tighten the hinge bolts and carefully lower the hood to check the position.

10 If necessary after installation, the entire hood latch assembly can be adjusted up-and-down as well as from side-to-side on the radiator support so the hood closes securely and flush with the fenders. To make the adjustment, scribe a line or mark around the hood latch mounting bolts to provide a reference point, then loosen them and reposition the latch assembly, as necessary (see illustration). Following adjustment, retighten the mounting bolts.

11 Finally, adjust the hood bumpers on the ends of the radiator support, so when closed, is flush with the fenders (see illustration).

12 The hood latch assembly, as well as the hinges, should be periodically lubricated with white, lithium-base grease to prevent binding and wear.

10 Hood release latch and cable - removal and installation

Warning: *The models covered by this manual are equipped with a Supplemental Restraint System (SRS), more commonly known as airbags. Always disarm the airbag system before working in the vicinity of any airbag system component to avoid the possibility of accidental deployment of the airbag, which could cause personal injury (see Chapter 12). Do not use a memory saving device to preserve the PCM's memory when working on or near airbag system components.*

Latch

1 Remove the radiator grille (see Section 11).

9.10 To adjust the hood latch, loosen the retaining bolts, move the latch and retighten the bolts, then close the hood to check the fit

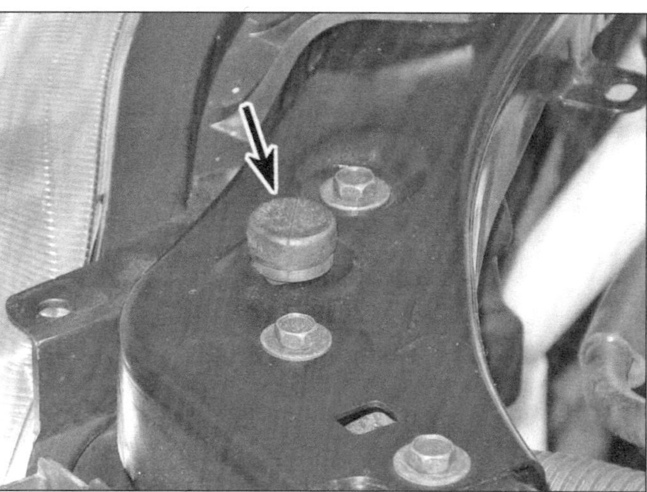
9.11 Adjust the hood closing height by turning the hood bumpers in or out

10.3 Pry out the cable retainer from the rear of the hood latch assembly, then disengage the cable end

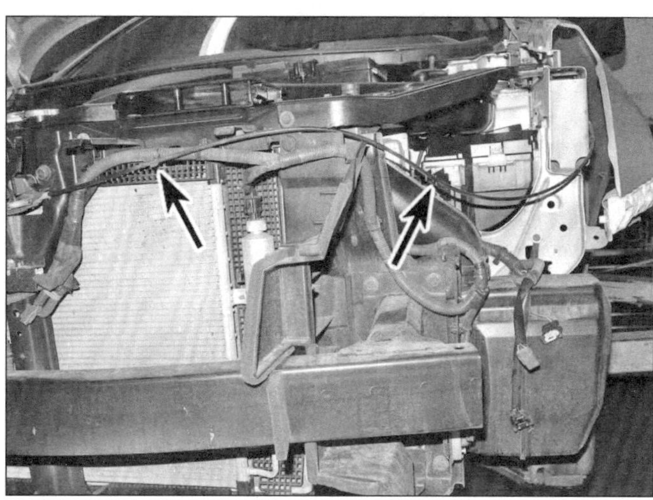
10.7 The hood release cable is secured along its length with clips (bumper cover removed for clarity)

2 Scribe a line around the latch to aid alignment when installing, then remove the latch retaining bolts (see illustration 9.10) and remove the latch.

3 Disconnect the hood release cable by disengaging the cable from the latch assembly (see illustration).

4 Installation is the reverse of removal. **Note:** *Adjust the latch so the hood engages securely when closed and the hood bumpers are slightly compressed.*

Cable

5 Disconnect the hood release cable from the latch assembly (see Step 3).

6 Remove the radiator grille (see Section 11) and the left inner fender liner (see Section 19).

7 Detach the cable from the clips along its length (see illustration).

8 Detach the cable from the hood release handle (see illustration).

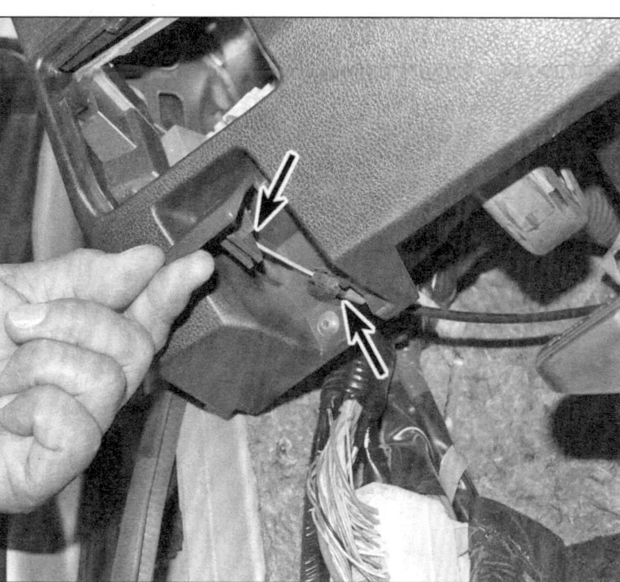
10.8 Release the end of the cable from the handle, then snap the cable housing from its retainer

11.2 Radiator grille upper fasteners

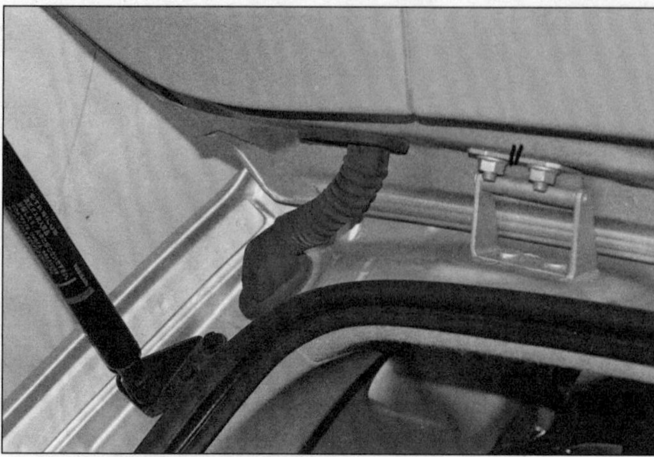
12.7 Mark around the liftgate hinges so it can be installed in the same position

9 Pull the cable grommet into the passenger compartment, then pull the cable through the hole.

Note: *Be careful not to kink the cable during handling.*

10 Installation is the reverse of the removal.

Note: *Push on the grommet with your fingers from the passenger compartment to seat the grommet in the firewall correctly; use sealant around the grommet.*

11 Radiator grille - removal and installation

Warning: *The models covered by this manual are equipped with a Supplemental Restraint System (SRS), more commonly known as airbags. Always disarm the airbag system before working in the vicinity of any airbag system component to avoid the possibility of accidental deployment of the airbag, which could cause personal injury (see Chapter 12). Do not use a memory saving device to preserve the PCM's memory when working on or near airbag system components.*

1 Open the hood.

2 Remove the center of the push-pin plastic fasteners (on top on of the grille on 2014 and earlier models and a few inches below the top on 2015 and later models), then pull out the fasteners (see illustration). Pull the grille outwards to release the lower clips from the bumper cover.

3 On models equipped with a front camera, disconnect the electrical connector from the camera on the backside of the grille.

4 Installation is the reverse of removal.

12 Liftgate - removal, installation and adjustment

Note: *The liftgate is heavy and somewhat awkward to remove and install - at least two people should perform this procedure.*

Removal and installation

1 Disconnect the cable from the negative battery terminal (see Chapter 5, Section 3).

2 Open the liftgate all the way.

3 Remove the liftgate trim panel (see Section 14).

4 Disconnect all electrical connections, ground wires and harness retaining clips from the liftgate.

Note: *It is a good idea to label all connections to aid the reassembly process.*

5 Detach the rubber conduit between the body and the liftgate. Pull the wiring harness through the conduit hole and remove it from the liftgate.

6 Detach the liftgate support struts (see Section 13) and have an assistant hold the weight of the liftgate.

7 Mark around the liftgate hinges with a pen or a scribe to facilitate realignment during reassembly (see illustration).

8 With the assistant still holding the liftgate, unscrew the hinge-to-liftgate nuts and remove the liftgate.

9 Installation is the reverse of removal.

Adjustment

10 Having proper liftgate-to-body alignment is a critical part of a well-functioning liftgate assembly. First check the liftgate hinge pins for excessive play. Fully open the liftgate and lift up and down on the liftgate without lifting the body. If a liftgate has 1/16-inch or more excessive play, the hinges should be replaced.

11 Liftgate-to-body alignment adjustments are made by loosening the hinge-to-body nuts or hinge-to-liftgate nuts and moving the liftgate. Proper body alignment is achieved when the top of the liftgate is parallel with the roof section, the sides of the liftgate are flush with the rear quarter panels, and the bottom of the liftgate is aligned with the lower liftgate sill. If these goals can't be reached by adjusting the hinge-to-body or hinge-to-liftgate nuts, body alignment shims may have to be purchased and inserted behind the hinges to achieve correctalignment.

12 To adjust the liftgate-closed position, scribe a line or mark around the striker plate to provide a reference point, then check that the liftgate latch is contacting the center of the latch striker. If not, adjust the up and down position first.

13 Finally adjust the latch striker fore-and-aft position, so that the liftgate panel is flush with the rear quarter panel and provides positive engagement with the latch mechanism.

13 Liftgate latch, opening switch and support struts - removal and installation

Liftgate latch

1 Disconnect the cable from the negative battery terminal (see Chapter 5).

2 Open the liftgate and remove the trim panel and watershield (see Section 14).

3 Disconnect the electrical connector for the latch through the opening (see illustration).

4 Remove the fasteners securing the latch to the liftgate (see illustration). Remove the latch assembly.

5 Installation is the reverse of removal.

Opening switch

6 Open the liftgate and remove the trim panel and watershield (see Section 14).

7 Disconnect the electrical connector to the liftgate opening switch and rear view camera, if equipped.

8 Remove the liftgate opening switch trim panel mounting nuts and pull the trim panel off of the liftgate.

9 Remove the liftate opening switch fasteners and separate the switch from the panel.

10 Installation is the reverse of removal.

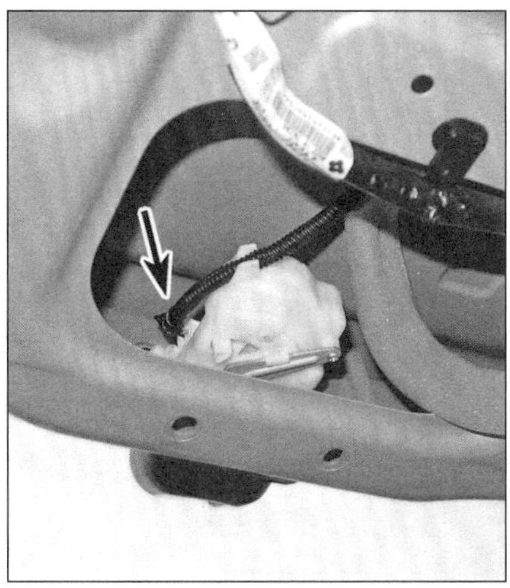

13.3 Disconnect the electrical connector

13.4 Liftgate latch fasteners

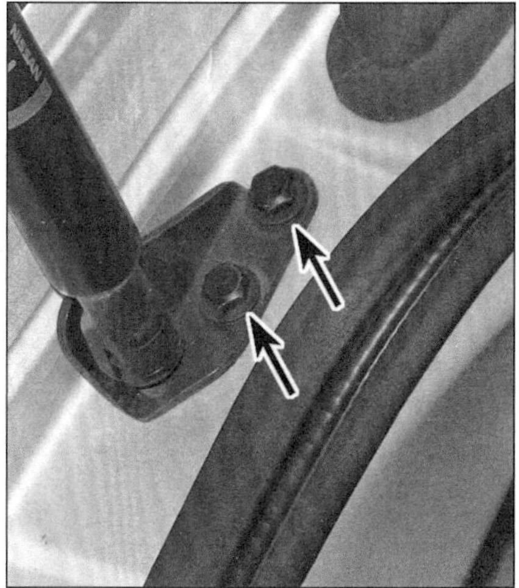

13.11a Remove the lifgate support strut-to-body bolts . . .

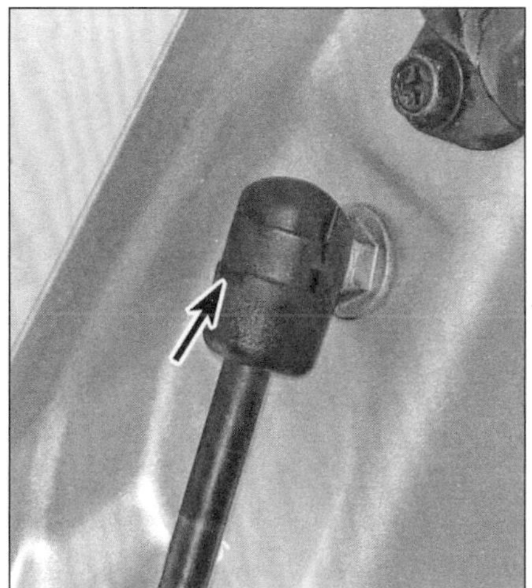

13.11b . . . or insert a small screwdriver under the locking clip and pry it up, then separate the ball socket connection

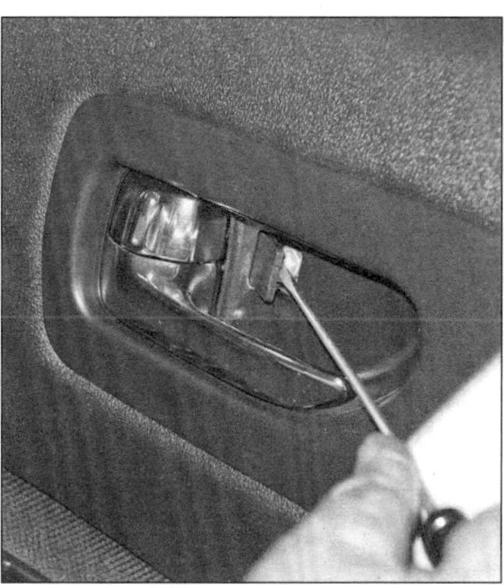

14.2 Use a pry tool to remove the door handle trim to gain access to the mounting screw

14.3 Using a plastic tool, start at the rear of the power window switch panel and pry upwards

Liftgate support struts or spindles

Note: *2014 and later models have an automatic open-and-close option for the liftgate. These models use powered spindles instead of support struts.*

11 On models without automatic open-and-close option, detach the liftgate support struts by either unbolting them at the top or using a small screwdriver to separate the ball socket connection (see illustrations). Have an assistant hold the weight of the liftgate.

12 On models with automatic open-and-close option, disconnect the spindle electrical connectors, then unbolt the spindles from the liftgate and body. Have an assistant hold the weight of the liftgate while the spindles are being unbolted.

13 Installation is the reverse of removal.

14 Door trim panels - removal and installation

Caution: *Plastic trim tools should be used on all operations in this Section to avoid damage to the soft plastic interior parts (see Section 6).*

Doors

Note: *The procedure is the same for the front or rear doors.*

1 Open the door and lower the window.

2 On 2015 and earlier models, pry off the inside handle screw cover, then remove the mounting screw (see illustration). On 2016 and later models, pry the finish trim off from around the inside door handle.

3 Insert a plastic trim tool into the back edge of the door power window switch, prying upwards to release the clips, and remove the power switch panel (see illustration).

4 Disconnect the switch electrical connectors (see illustration)

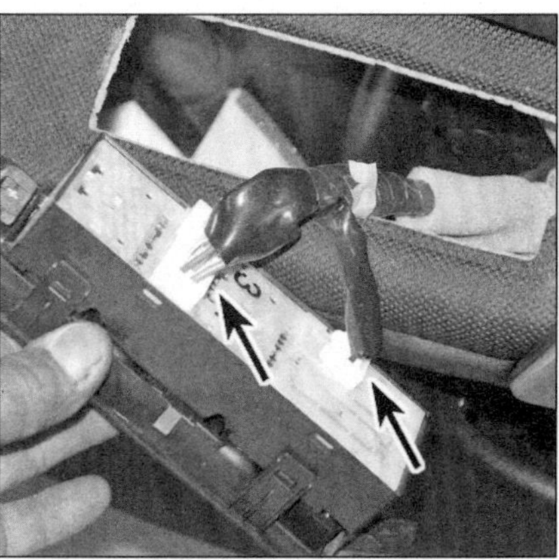

14.4 Disconnect the electrical connectors from the power window switch and door lock assembly

14.5a Pry off the pull handle trim, then . . .

14.5b . . . remove the mounting screws

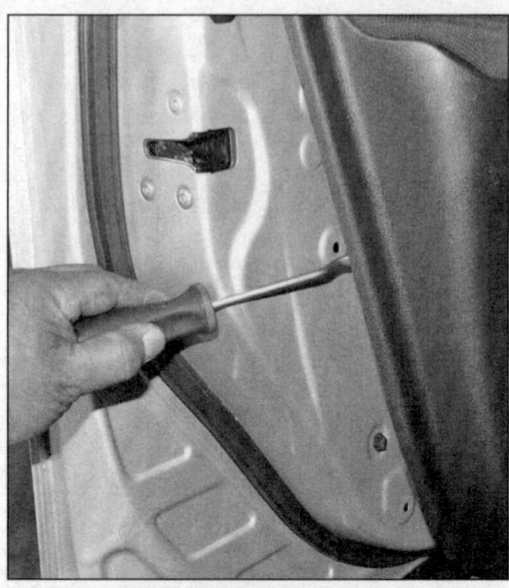

14.7 Use a pry tool to release the clips on the door panel

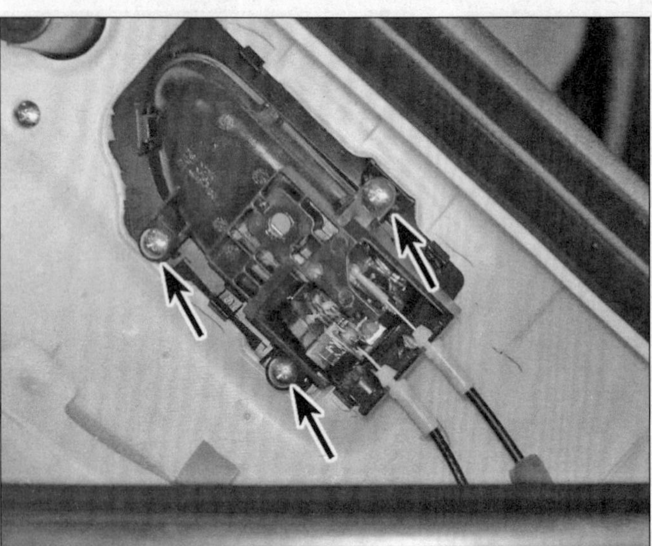

14.9 Remove the inside handle mounting screws

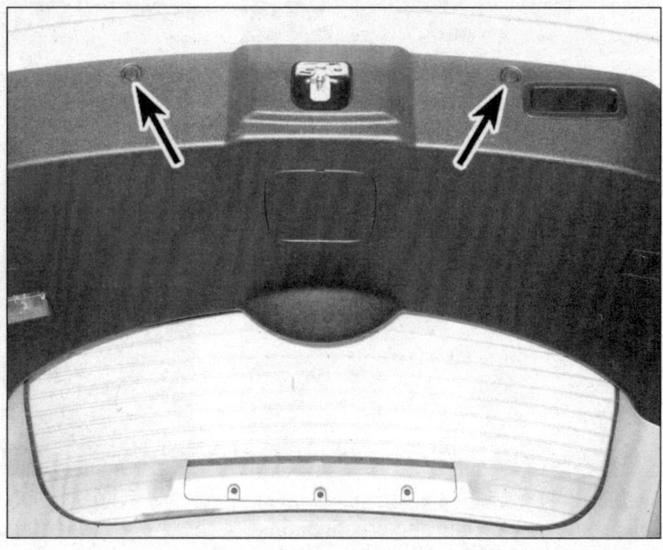

14.12 Plastic trim panel fastener locations

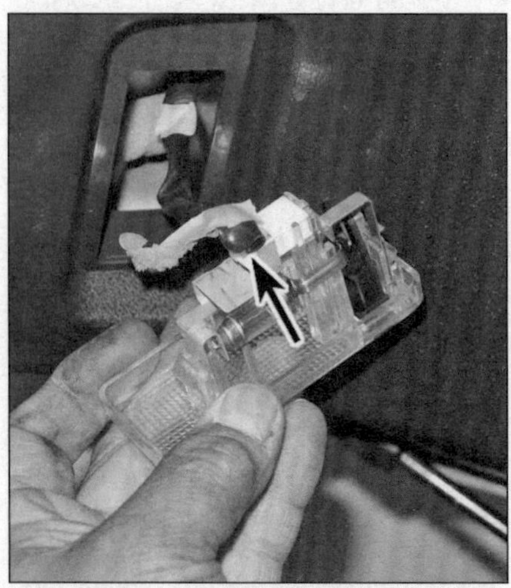

14.13 Disconnect the electrical connector to the liftgate light

5 Pry off the pull handle trim, then remove the mounting screws (see illustrations).

6 Insert a plastic trim tool into the back edge of the door power window switch, prying upwards to release the clips, and remove the power switch panel.

7 Using a pry tool, carefully release the clips around the perimeter of the door trim panel (see illustration).

8 Lift the door trim panel upwards from the door to remove it.

9 Remove the inside handle fasteners and separate the handle from the door panel (see illustration).

10 Installation is the reverse of removal.

Liftgate

11 Open the liftgate.

12 Push the center of the plastic trim fastener in, then pry the fasteners out (see illustration).

13 Pry the liftgate light out of the trim panel (see illustration) and disconnect the electrical connector.

14 Pry the liftgate the pull handle out (see illustration).

15 Pry out the trim panel screw covers (see illustration), then remove the mounting screws (see illustration).

16 Carefully pry the trim panel from the liftgate (see illustration) by working slowly around the outer edge of the trim panel until it's free. Unplug any wiring harness connectors and remove the panel.

17 Using a trim tool, start with the top center liftgate window trim panel and pry it off, then pry the two remaining panels off.

18 For access to other components inside the liftgate, carefully peel back the plastic watershield, if equipped.

19 Installation is the reverse of removal.

14.14 The screws for the pull handle are located under the plastic covers

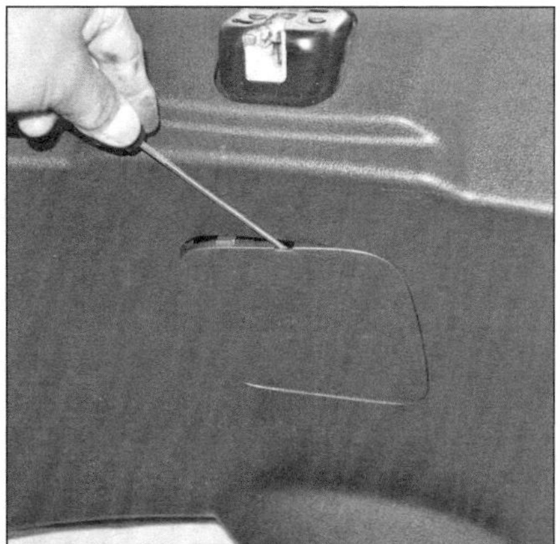

14.15a Pry out the trim panel screw covers (one of three shown) . . .

14.15b . . . then remove the mounting screws

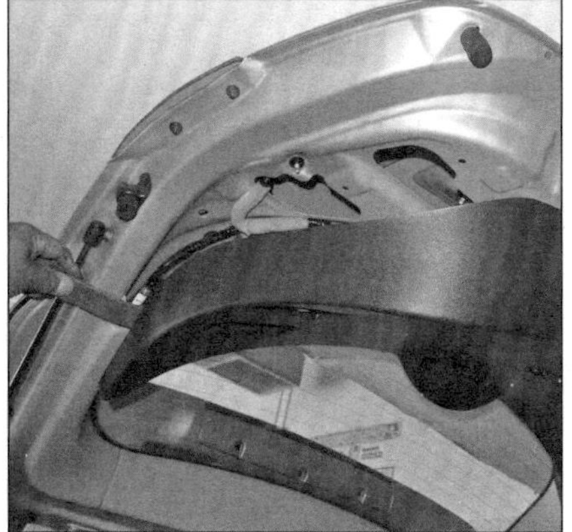

14.16 Use a trim tool to pry off the panel

15.4 Door stop strut bolt

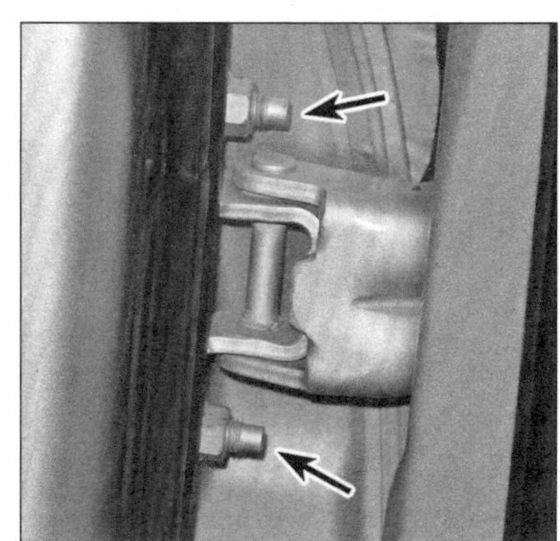

15.6 Unbolt the lower hinge first and allow the door to rest on its support while removing the upper nuts

15 Door - removal, installation and adjustment

Note: *The door is heavy and somewhat awkward to remove and install - at least two people should perform this procedure.*

Removal and installation

1 Lower the window completely in the door.

2 Open the door all the way and support it on jacks or blocks covered with rags to prevent damaging the paint.

3 Remove the kick panel underneath the instrument panel (if removing a front door) or the center pillar trim panel (if removing a rear door), then unplug the door wiring harness electrical connectors. Push the rubber conduit out of the door pillar and pull the wiring harness through.

4 Unbolt the door stop strut (see illustration).

5 Mark around the door hinges with a pen or a scribe to facilitate realignment during reassembly.

6 With an assistant holding the door, remove the upper and lower hinge-to-door nuts (see illustration) and lift the door off.

7 Installation is the reverse of removal.

Adjustment

8 Having proper door-to-body alignment is a critical part of a well-functioning door assembly. First check the door hinge pins for excessive play. Fully open the door and lift up and down on the door without lifting the body. If a door has 1/16-inch or more excessive play, the hinges should be replaced.

9 Door-to-body alignment adjustments are made by loosening the hinge-to-body bolts or hinge-to-door bolts and moving the door. Proper body alignment is achieved when the top of the doors are parallel with the roof section, the front door is flush with the fender, the rear door is flush with the rear quarter panel and the bottom of the doors are aligned with the lower rocker panel. If these goals can't be reached by adjusting the hinge-to-body or hinge-to-door fasteners, body alignment shims may have to be purchased and inserted behind the hinges to achieve correct alignment.

10 To adjust the door closed position, scribe a line or mark around the striker plate to provide a reference point, then check that the door latch is contacting the center of the latch striker. If not, adjust the up and down position first.

11 Finally, adjust the latch striker sideways position, so that the door panel is flush with the center pillar or rear quarter panel and provides positive engagement with the latch mechanism (see illustration).

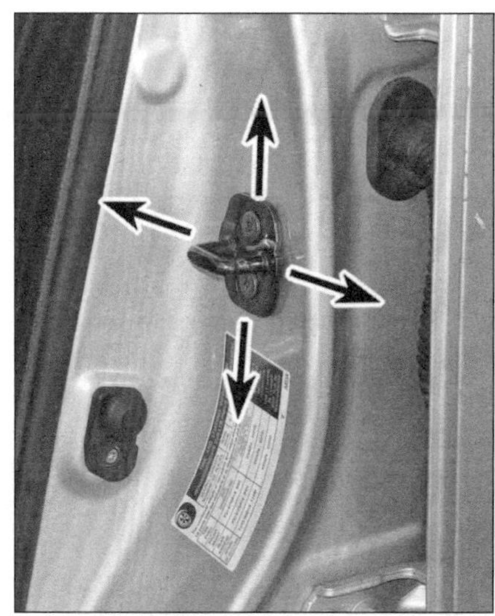

15.11 Adjust the door lock striker by loosening the mounting screws and gently tapping the striker in the desired direction

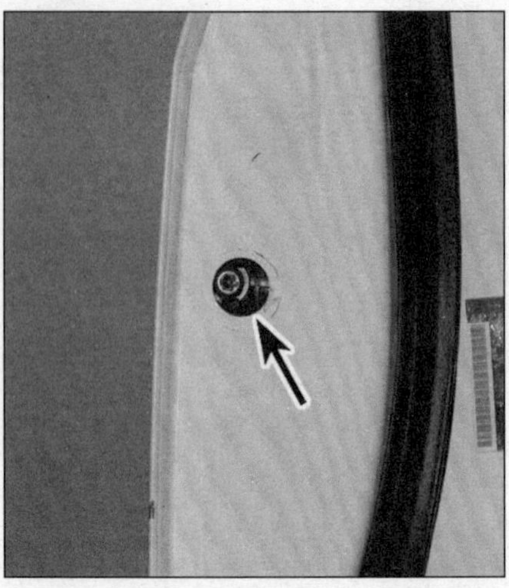
16.5 Pry out the grommet for access to the bolt underneath

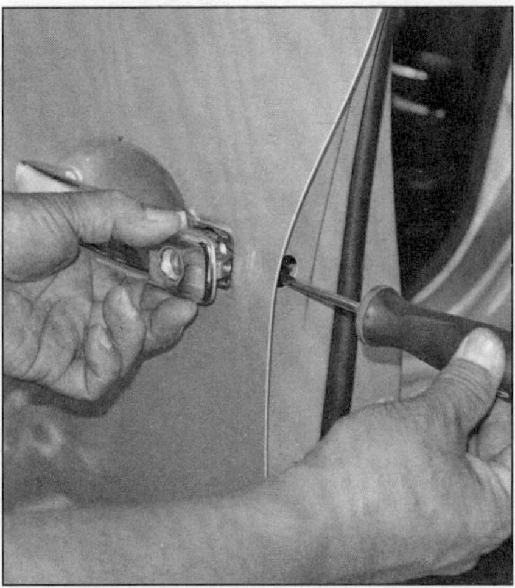
16.7a Pull the door lock cylinder away from the door

16.7b Use a small screwdriver to release the key rod clip and remove the key cylinder

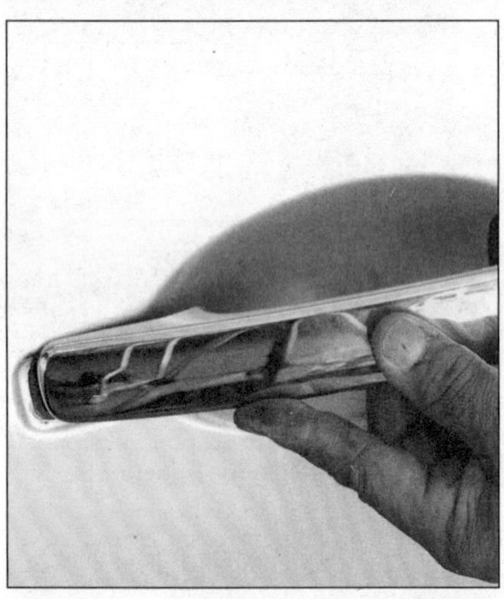
16.8a Slide the door handle toward the rear of the vehicle

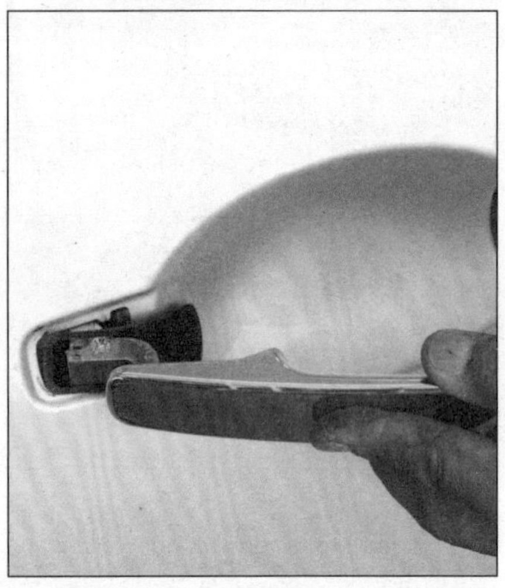
16.8b Pull the rear of the door handle away from the door

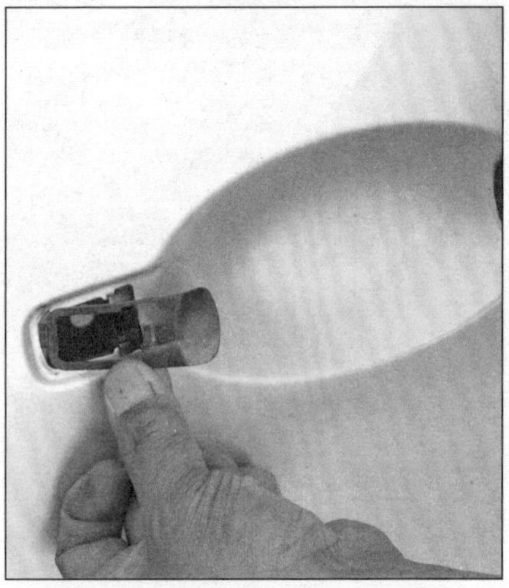
16.9 Carefully remove the front and rear gaskets

16 Door lock, cylinder and handles - removal and installation

Note: *This Section applies to both front and rear doors.*

1 Remove the power window switch.

2 Remove the door trim panel and watershield (see Section 14).

3 Remove the door window module (see Section 18).

4 On models equipped with "Intelligent Key system" disconnect the electrical connectors to the door antenna and door request switch, then remove the harness retaining clip from the door outside handle bracket.

5 Remove the door side grommet, and the door key cylinder trim panel bolt (see illustration).

6 Disconnect the key lock rod from the lock cylinder from inside the door.

7 Remove the door lock cylinder and cover assembly while pulling the outside handle forward (see illustration). If the key lock rod couldn't be disconnected from the inside, pull the door lock cylinder out enough to disconnect the key cylinder connection rod (see illustration) then remove the door lock cylinder.

8 Pull out the outside door handle and slide it towards the rear of the vehicle to remove it (see illustrations).

9 Remove the front and rear gaskets (see illustration).

10 Remove the door lock assembly mounting bolts.

11 Slide the outside handle bracket towards the rear of the vehicle and remove the assembly.

12 If equipped, disconnect the door lock assembly electrical connector.

13 Separate the outside handle cable from the outside handle bracket.

14 Installation is the reverse of removal.

17 Door window glass - removal and installation

Front door

1 Remove the door trim panel and the plastic watershield (see Section 14).

2 Remove the access hole plugs (see illustration).

3 Reconnect the power window switch and raise/lower the window until the glass bolts can be seen in the access holes.

4 Remove the glass mounting bolts (see illustration).

5 While holding the window, raise it at the rear to pull the glass out of the sash toward the inside of the door.

6 Remove the door glass run from the door panel.

7 Installation is the reverse of removal.

17.2 Access hole plug locations

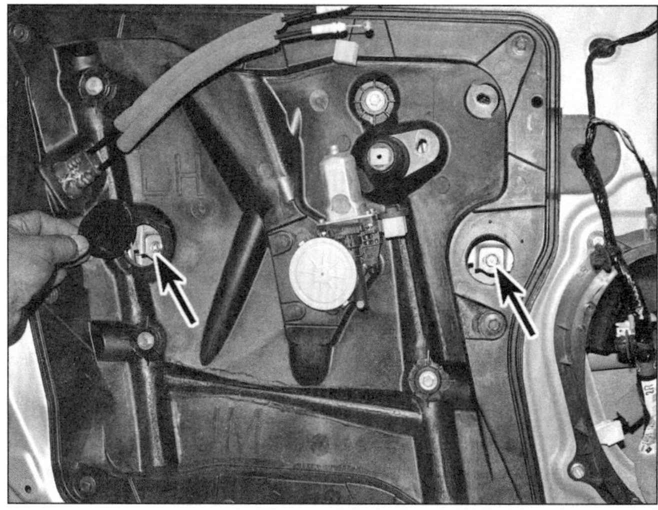
17.4 Window glass-to-regulator bolts (front door shown, rear door similar)

18.4 Typical glass holding tools

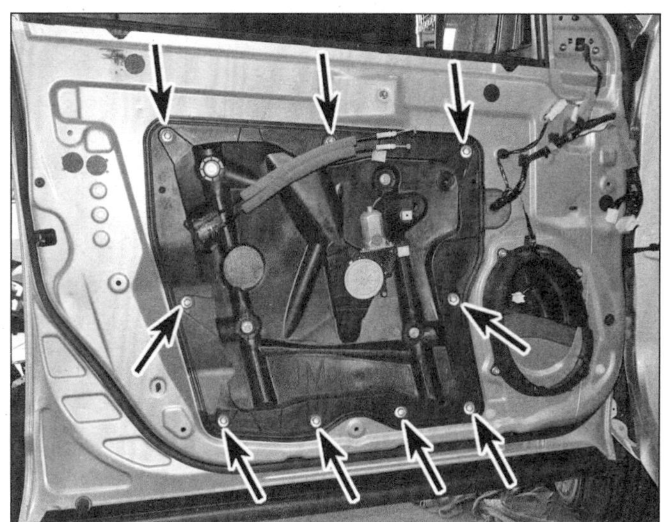
18.6 Door module mounting bolt locations

Rear door

8 Remove the door trim panel and the plastic watershield (see Section 14).

9 Remove partition sash bolt and screw, pull partition sash downward and tilt the upper end of the sash forward to pull the sash upwards, and out.

10 Pull the partition glass toward the front of the vehicle.

11 If equipped, reconnect the power window switch and raise/lower the window until the glass bolts can be seen.

12 Remove the glass bolts.

13 Pull the glass toward the outside of the vehicle to remove it.

14 Installation is the reverse of removal.

Initialization of the system

Note: *This procedure must be done whenever any window component has been removed or when an electrical component of the system has been removed or disconnected. These parts include the battery, switches, glass, regulator, power window switch, door glass, etc.*

15 Close all doors.

16 Turn ignition switch on.

17 Open the window completely.

18 Select Auto Up (front window) and hold the switch for at least 4 seconds after the window has stopped in the fully up position.

19 Confirm normal window operation.

Installed glass inspection

20 Make sure the glass is securely set into the glass run groove.

21 Lower the glass about 1/2 inch and check to see if the glass clearance to the sash is parallel.

22 If the clearance between the glass and sash is not parallel, loosen the guide rail bolts to correct the glass position.

23 Check the window by raising/lowering the glass.

18 Door module and window glass regulator - removal and installation

Note: *The following procedure applies to both front and rear window glass regulators.*

1 Remove the door trim panel and the plastic watershield (see Section 14).

2 Connect the window switch temporarily and adjust the window so the bolts can be reached through the access holes.

3 Remove the door glass bolts.

4 Raise the window and hold it up with tape or glass holding tools (see illustration).

5 Disconnect the wiring harness connector (if equipped) from the power window motor.

6 Remove the door module assembly bolts, then remove the module (see illustration).

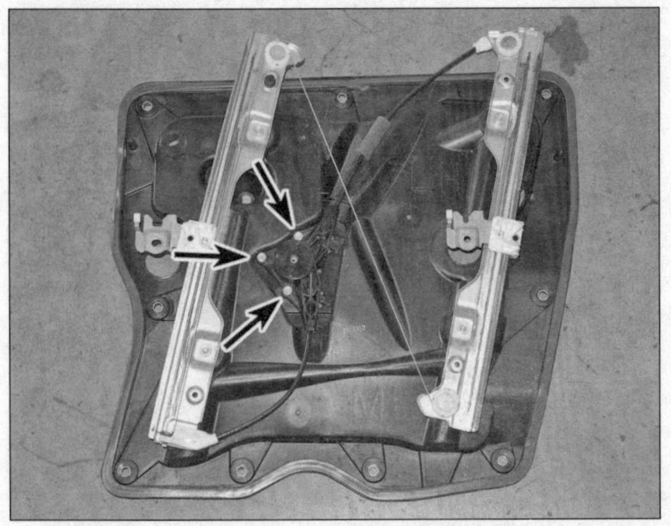
18.7a Remove the power window motor fasteners . . .

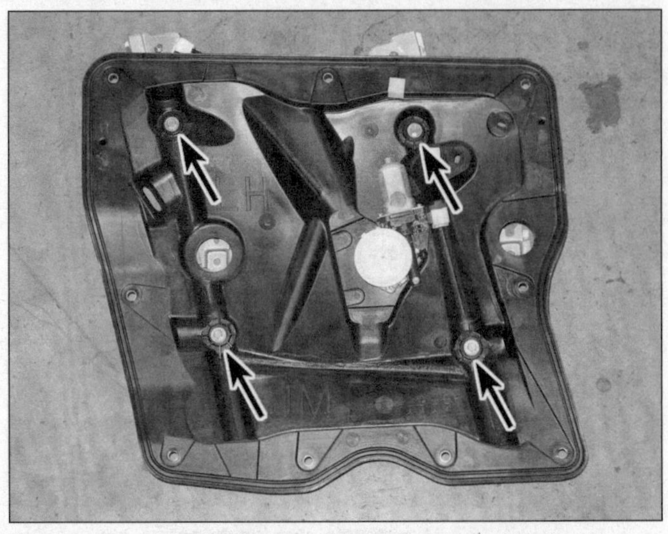
18.7b . . . then the window regulator mounting fasteners

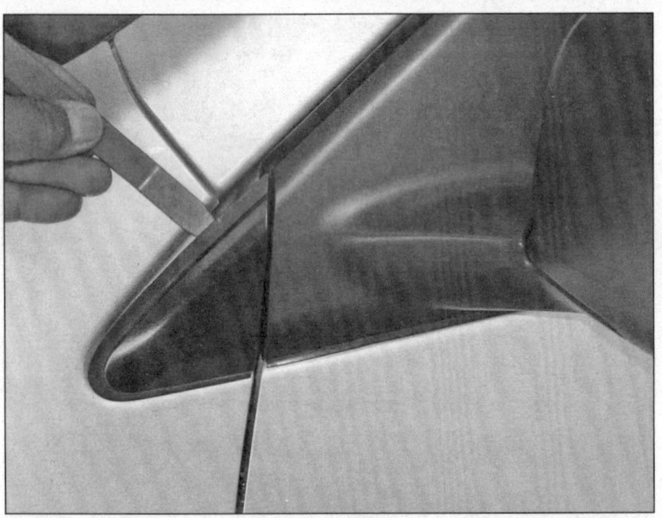
19.4a Pry the trim panel from the top corner of the fender, then . . .

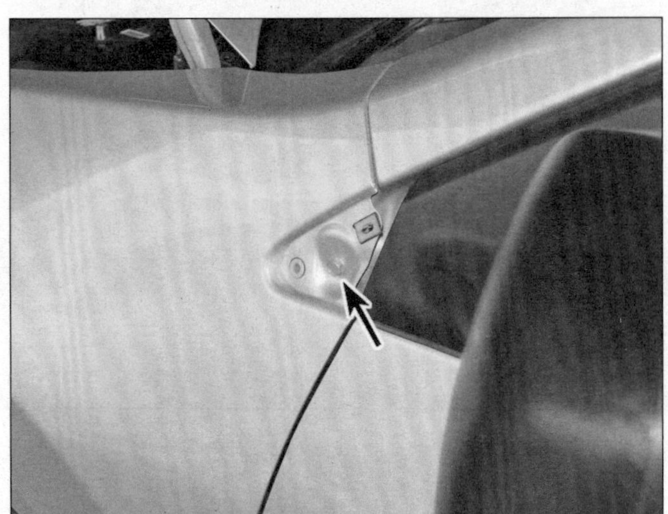
19.4b . . . remove the mounting bolt

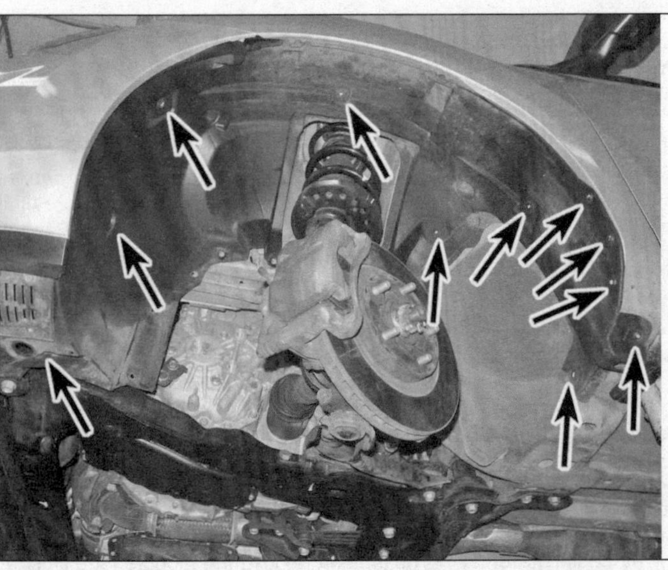
19.5 Inner fender splash shield fasteners

7 Remove the power window motor mounting fasteners from the back side of the door module (see illustration), then the regulator fasteners from the front side of the module (see illustration) and remove the regulator.

8 Installation is in the reverse of removal. Apply grease to all moving parts.

19 Fender (front) - removal and installation

1 Remove the bumper cover (see Section 20).

2 Remove the cowl top cover fasteners (see Section 27).

3 Remove the front fender protector (mud guard) fasteners from the lower corners of the fenders, if equipped.

4 Pry the fender trim panel out then remove the fender mounting bolt (see illustrations).

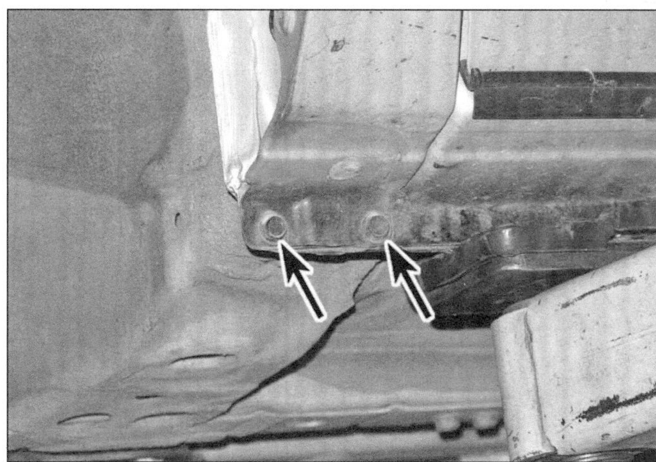

19.6a Fender lower mounting bolts

19.6b Fender inner mounting bolt

5 Remove the inner fender splash shield (see illustration).
6 Remove the fender mounting bolts (see illustrations).
7 Carefully remove the front fender.
8 Installation is the reverse of removal.

19.6c Front mounting bolt

20 Bumper covers - removal and installation

Warning: *The models covered by this manual are equipped with a Supplemental Restraint System (SRS), more commonly known as airbags. Always disarm the airbag system before working in the vicinity of any airbag system component to avoid the possibility of accidental deployment of the airbag, which could cause personal injury (see Chapter 12). Do not use a memory saving device to preserve the PCM's memory when working on or near airbag system components.*

Front bumper cover

1 Raise the vehicle and support it securely on jackstands.
2 Remove the fasteners along the the top edge of the grille and bumper cover (see illustration).

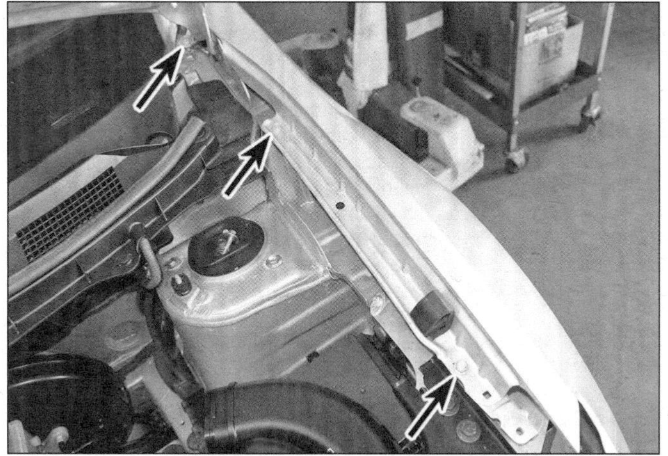

19.6d Fender upper mounting bolts

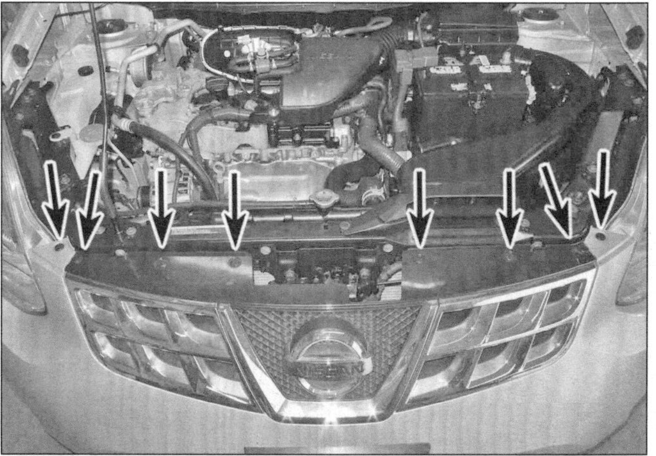

20.2 Remove the top edge fasteners - typical early models shown

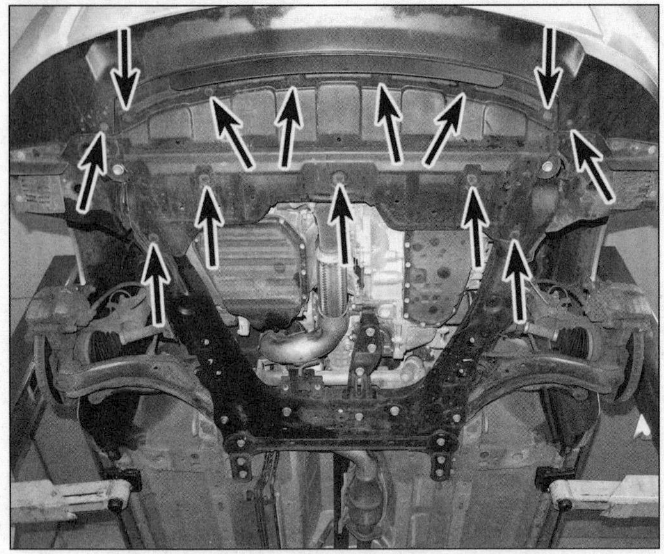
20.4 Remove the engine undercover fasteners

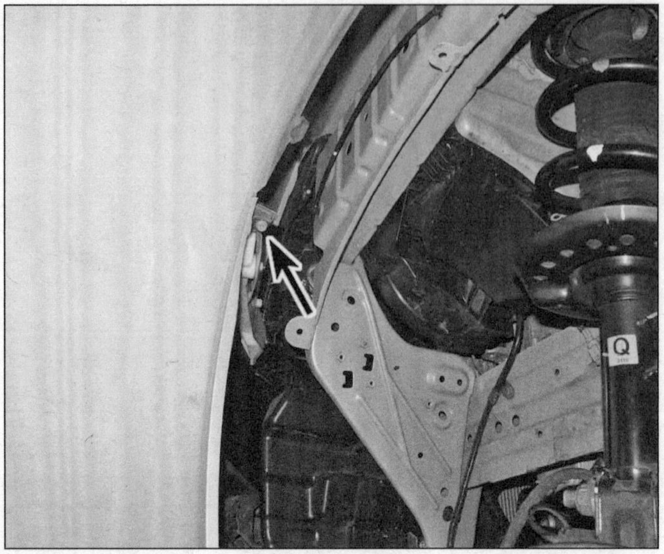
20.5 Remove the fastener at the upper corner on each side

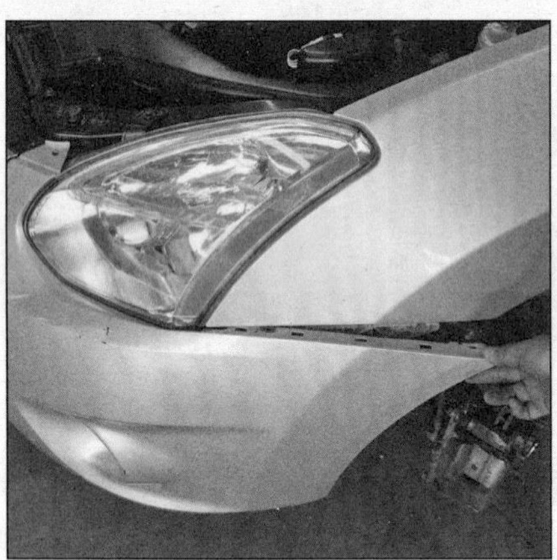
20.6 Carefully disengage the front bumper fascia from under the headlight housing

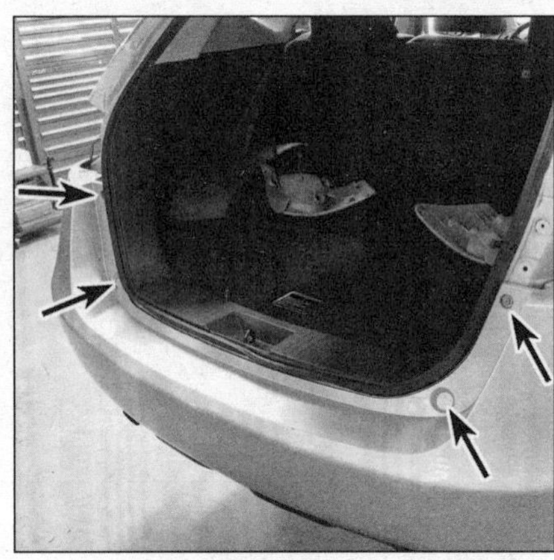
20.18 Remove the bumper cover fasteners from both sides

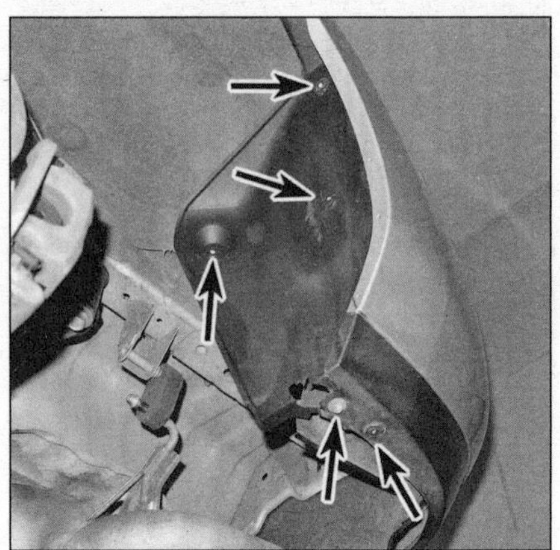
20.20 Remove the rear splash shield fasteners

3 Remove the screws at the front edge of the inner fender splash shield (see Section 19).

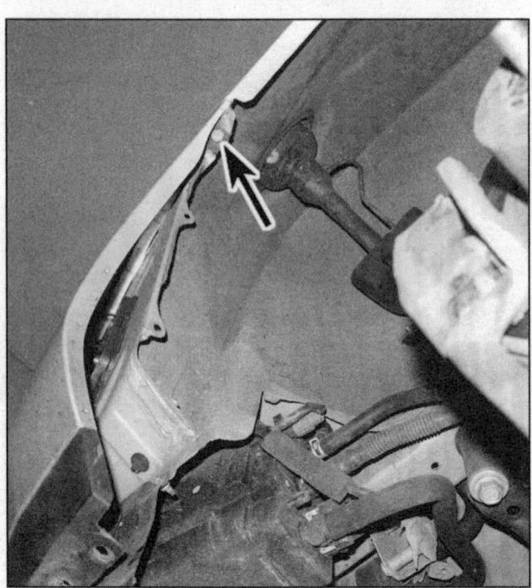
20.21 Remove the fastener from each corner

4 Remove the fasteners and remove the engine undercover (see illustration).

5 Remove the upper screws (both sides) from the front bumper cover at the front fender (see illustration).

6 Pull the outboard edge of the front bumper fascia away from the vehicle to disengage it from the bumper side retainer (see illustration).

7 Disconnect the fog light harness connector, if equipped (see Chapter 12).

8 Remove the front bumper cover.

9 Remove the fog light assembly, if equipped (see Chapter 12).

10 Disengage the clips and remove the bumper energy absorber.

11 Disengage the clips and remove the radiator air guides.

12 Remove the retaining pins at the lower edge, remove the bolts, and remove the bumper reinforcement.

13 Remove the bumper side retainers from the front fender.

14 Installation is the reverse of removal.

Rear bumper cover

15 Open the liftgate.

16 Remove the taillight housings (see Chapter 12).

17 Disengage the clips, then remove the rear fender protector, if equipped.

18 Remove the rear bumper cover upper fasteners (see illustration).

19 Raise the vehicle and support it securely on jackstands.

20 Remove the rear splash shield fasteners and splash shield from the corner of the wheel opening (see illustration).

21 Remove the rear bumper upper corner fasteners (see illustration).

22 Remove the rear bumper cover lower fasteners (see illustration).

23 Pull the rear bumper cover rearward, away from the vehicle (see illustration) and remove the bumper cover.

24 Remove the energy absorbing plastic from the rear bumper reinforcement.

25 Remove the bolts and remove the rear bumper reinforcement.

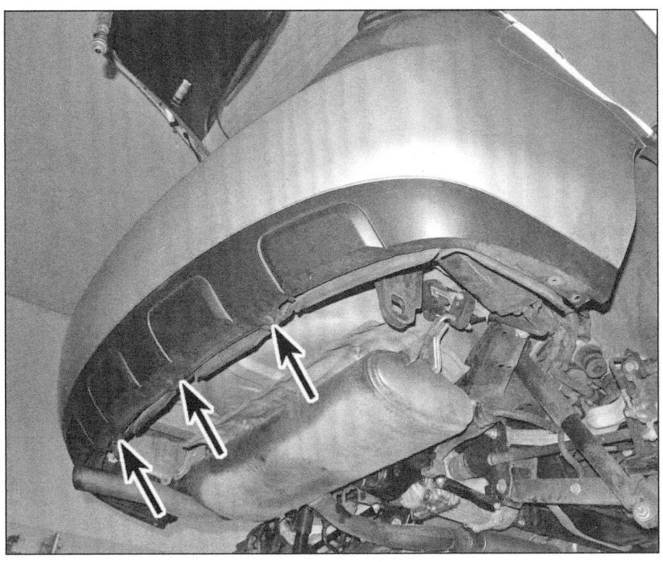

20.22 Remove the lower bumper cover fasteners

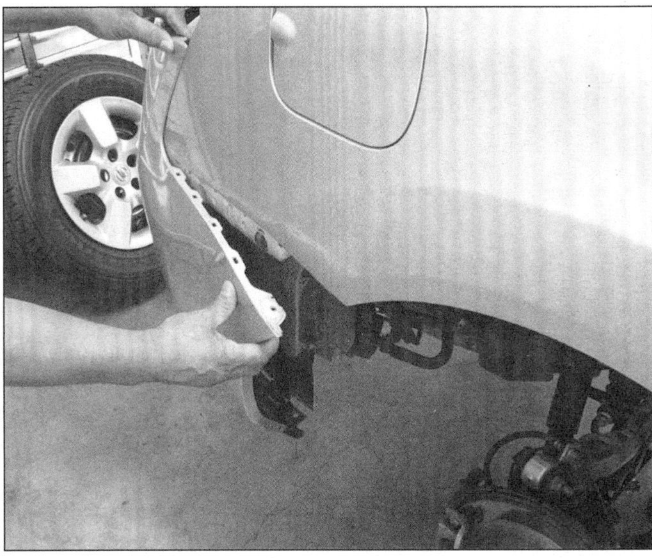

20.23 Carefully disengage the rear bumper fascia

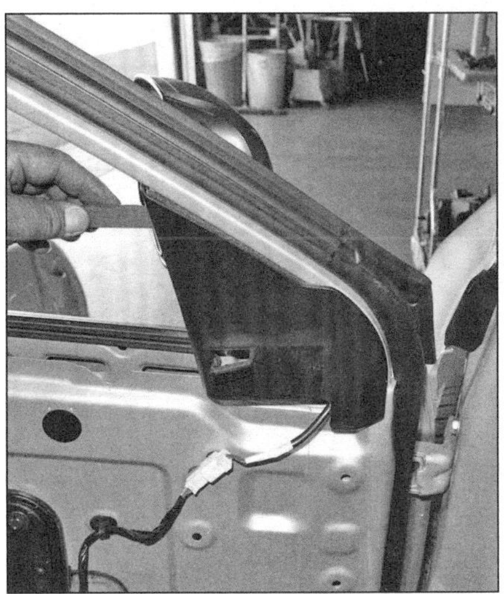

21.2 Use a plastic trim tool to pry the mirror trim panel from the door frame

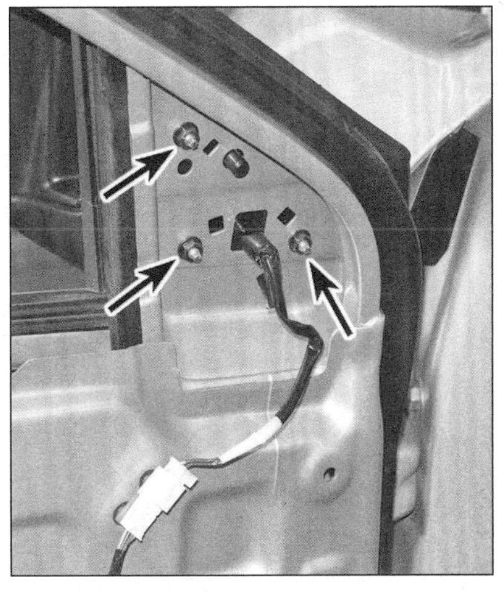

21.4 Remove the mirror mounting nuts

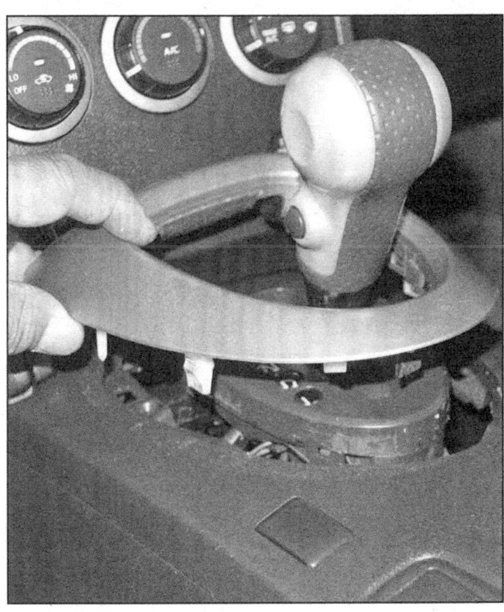

22.3 Pry up the shifter trim plate

26 Release the pawls and remove the rear bumper side retainer from both sides.

27 Installation is the reverse of removal.

Active grille shutter

28 Remove the front bumper cover (see Steps 1 through 8).

29 Disconnect the electrical connectors from the active shutter grill module.

30 Use a trim tool and disengage the retaining clip for the ambient temperature sensor, then move the harness and sensor out of the way.

31 Remove the active grill mounting bolts along the bottom of the grille and remove the assembly.

33 Installation is the reverse of removal.

21 Outside mirrors - removal and installation

1 Remove the door trim panel (see Section 14).

2 Remove the mirror trim panel (see illustration).

3 Disconnect the electrical connector from the mirror.

4 Remove the mirror mounting nuts, then remove the mirror assembly from the door (see illustration).

5 Installation is the reverse of removal.

22 Center console - removal and installation

Warning: *The models covered by this manual are equipped with a Supplemental Restraint System (SRS), more commonly known as airbags. Always disarm the airbag system before working in the vicinity of any airbag system component to avoid the possibility of accidental deployment of the airbag, which could cause personal injury (see Chapter 12). Do not use a memory saving device to preserve the PCM's memory when working on or near airbag system components.*

1 Disconnect the cable from the negative terminal of the battery (see Chapter 5).

2 Place the shifter in NEUTRAL.

3 Use a plastic trim tool or a screwdriver wrapped with tape to carefully pry up the gear shift cover. Remove the cover (see illustration).

4 Use a plastic trim tool or a screwdriver wrapped with tape to carefully pry out the heating and air conditioning control panel/cover assembly. Pull out the assembly and disconnect the electrical connectors (see Chapter 3, Section 9).

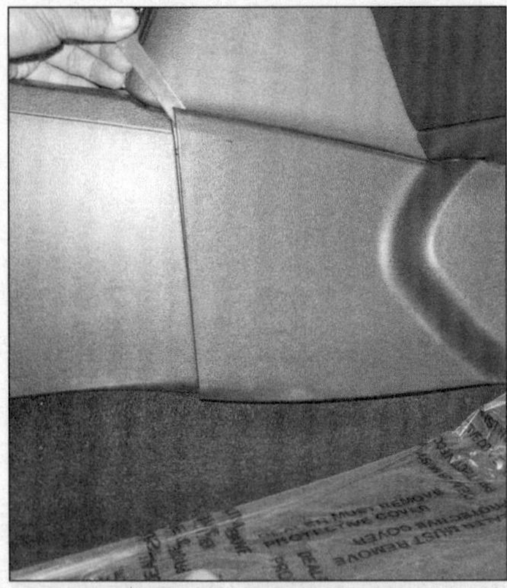

22.5 Pry up the trim panel, starting from the rear then along the top edge to disengage the clips

22.6 Disconnect the electrical connectors from the right side of the console

22.7 Remove the fasteners from the sides of the lower console trim

22.8 Remove the fasteners from the top of the console

22.9 Remove the fasteners from the rear of the console - right side shown left side identical

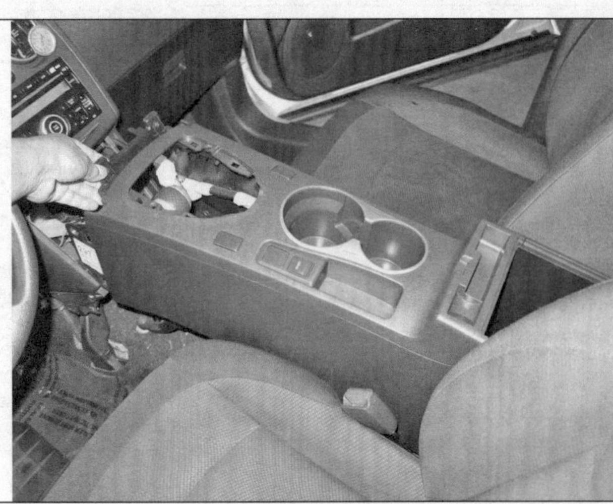

22.10 On 2013 and earlier models/2014 and later Rogue Select models, lift the console assembly out starting from the front. On 2014 and later non-Select models, start from the rear

5 Working at the front of the console pry out the side trim panels from both sides of the console (see illustration).

6 On the right side once the trim panel is removed, disconnect the electrical connectors (see illustration).

7 Remove the fasteners from each side of the console (see illustration).

8 Remove the screws from the front, top portion of the console (see illustration).

9 Slide the front seats forward. On 2015 and earlier models remove the fasteners from the rear sides of the trim panel (see illustration), and on 2016 and later models, carefully pry out the rear trim panel/vent assembly from the end of the console to access the rear mounting bolts.

10 Lift the console out of the vehicle (see illustration).

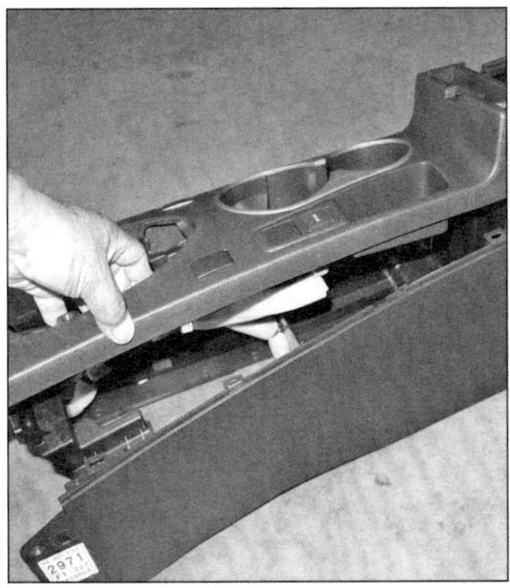
22.11a Carefully separate the top of the console from the lower half . . .

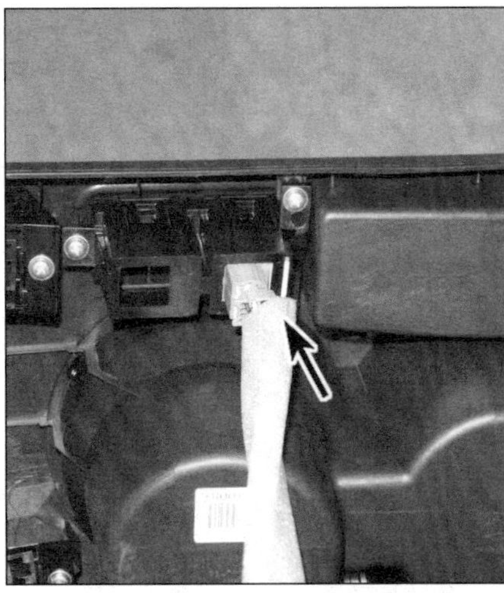
22.11b . . . then disconnect the electrical connector(s)

23.2a Pry the switch panel out . . .

23.2b . . . and disconnect the electrical connectors

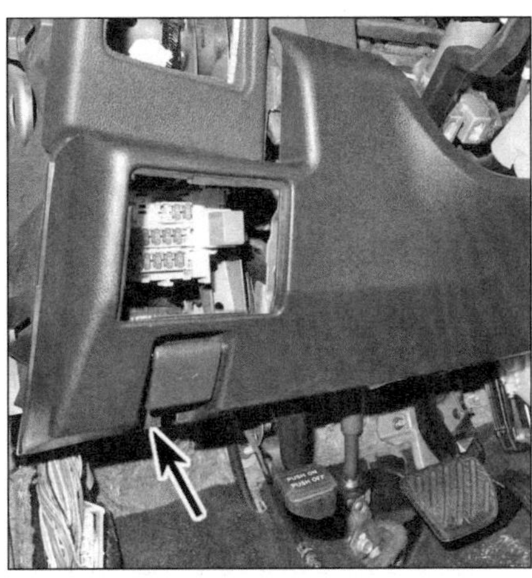
23.3a Remove the knee bolster screw . . .

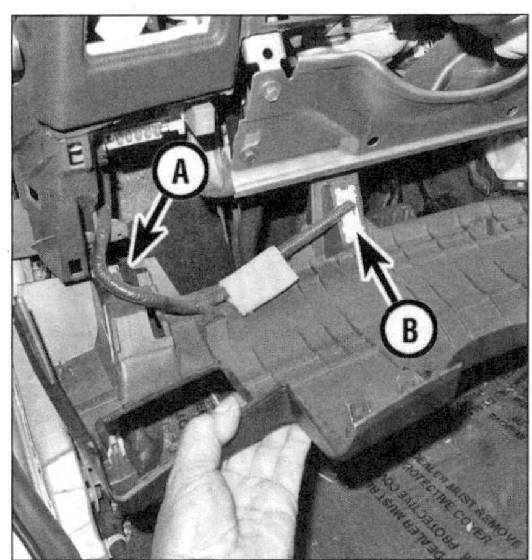

23.3b . . . then disconnect the hood release cable (A) and diagnostic connector (B)

11 On 2013 and earlier models/2014 and later Rogue Select models, once the console is removed, the console top can be separated and the electrical connectors disconnected from the top of the cover (see illustrations). To replace a console switch, remove the mounting screws and switch from the console top.

12 On 2014 and later models (except Rogue Select models), pry the cup holder from trim panel and disconnect the electrical connectors to the switches. To replace the seat heater switches, push the switch out from the back side.

13 Installation is the reverse of removal.

23 Dashboard trim panels - removal and installation

Warning: *The models covered by this manual are equipped with a Supplemental Restraint System (SRS), more commonly known as airbags. Always disarm the airbag system before working in the vicinity of any airbag system component to avoid the possibility of accidental deployment of the airbag, which could cause personal injury (see Chapter 12). Do not use a memory saving device to preserve the PCM's memory when working on or near airbag system components.*

Caution: *Plastic trim tools must be used on all operations in this Section to avoid damage to the soft plastic interior parts (see Section 6).*

1 Disconnect the cable from the negative terminal of the battery (see Chapter 5).

Knee bolster

2 Pry out the mirror switch and AWD switch panel (see illustrations).

3 Remove the lower knee bolster screw, then disconnect the diagnostic connector and hood release cable (see illustrations).

4 Remove the knee bolster support bolts and support (see illustration).

5 Installation is the reverse of removal.

23.4 Knee support bolt locations

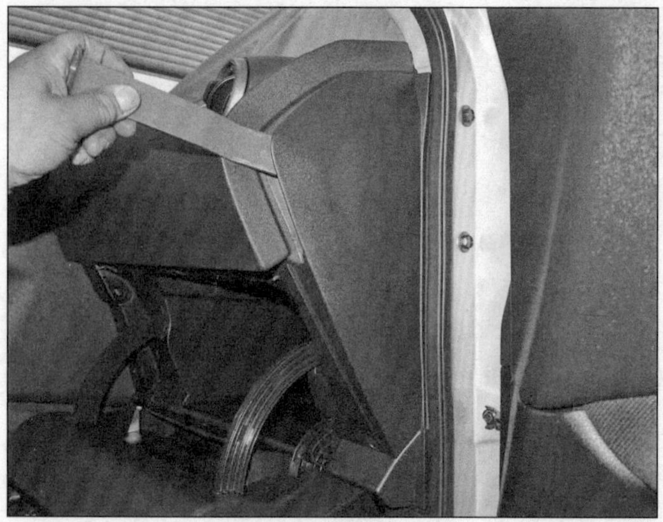
23.6 Pry off the end caps

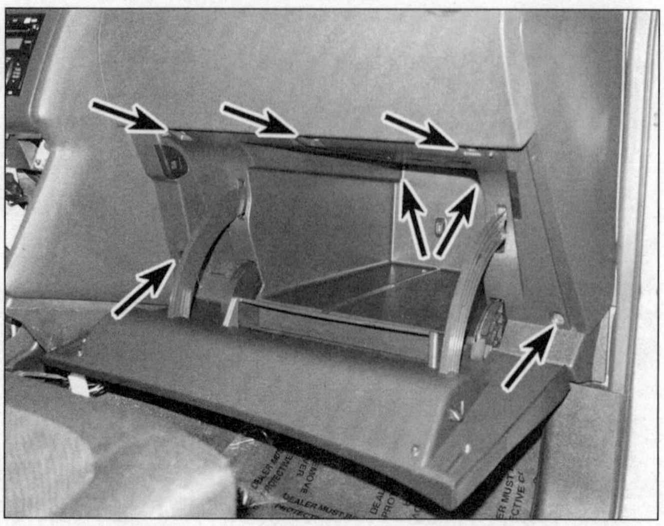
23.8 Remove the glove box mounting screws

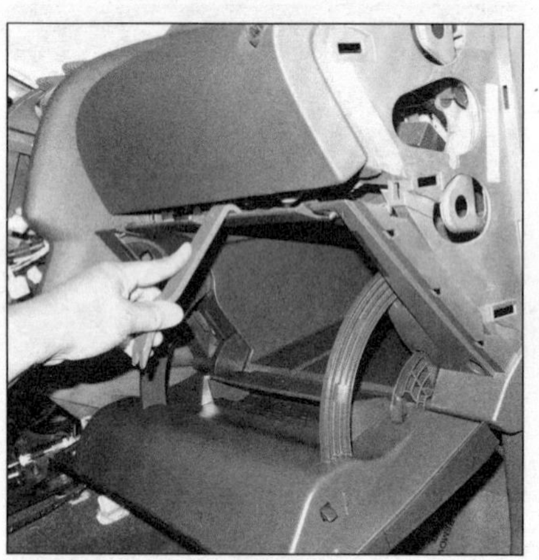
23.10a Pry the glove box from the dash panel . . .

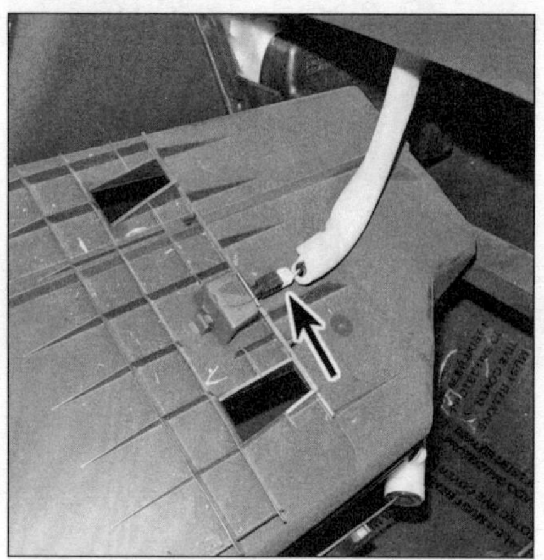
23.10b . . . then disconnect the electrical connector and remove the glove box

23.14 Carefully pry the vent trim panel from the instrument panel

23.15 Disconnect the electrical connector from the hazard switch

Instrument panel end caps

6 Use a plastic trim tool or a screwdriver wrapped with tape to pry off the end caps (see illustration).

7 Installation is the reverse of removal.

Glove box

8 Open the glove box and remove the glove box panel screws (see illustration).

9 Remove the right side instrument panel trim (see illustration 23.6).

10 Use a plastic trim tool to pry the glove box away from the dash panel (see illustrations).

11 Remove the glove box assembly.

12 Installation is the reverse of removal.

Center trim panel

13 Remove the heater and air conditioning control assembly (see Chapter 3).

14 Carefully pry the vent trim panel (see illustration) out of the center of the instrument panel.

15 Disconnect the electrical connector from the hazard switch (see illustration).

23.16 Remove the hazard switch fasteners

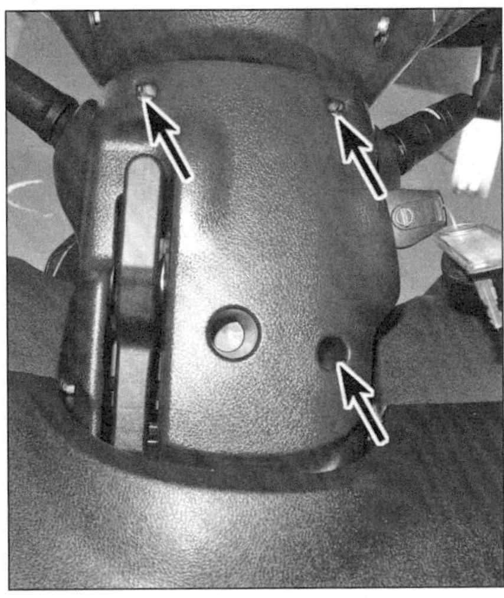
24.2 Lower steering column cover screws

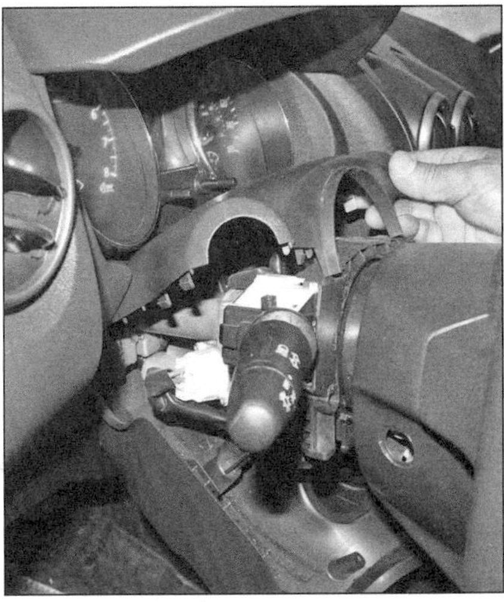
24.3 Remove the upper steering column cover

25.2a Use a plastic trim tool to disengage the fasteners, then . . .

25.2b . . . pull the instrument cluster hood out and off

16 If the hazard switch needs to be replaced, remove the mounting screws and switch from the panel (see illustration).
17 Installation is the reverse of removal.

Glove box trim panel (2016 and later models)

Note: *2015 and earlier models, the glove box trim panel and instrument panel are combined into one assembly.*
18 Remove the glove box (see 8 through 10).
19 Remove the right-side center trim panel above the glove box opening using a trim stick.
20 Remove the radio (see Chapter 12).
21 If not already done, remove the heater and air conditioning control assembly (see Chapter 3).
22 Remove the glove box panel fasteners.
23 Use a trim tool along the edges of the panel and remove the glove box trim panel from the instrument panel.
24 Installation is the reverse of removal.

24 Steering column covers - removal and installation

1 Remove steering lock trim panel.
2 Remove the steering column lower cover screws (see illustration).
3 Remove the steering column upper and lower covers (see illustration).
4 Installation is the reverse of removal.

25 Instrument cluster hood or bezel - removal and installation

1 Remove the steering column covers (see Section 24).

Instrument cluster hood - 2013 and earlier models/2014 and later Rogue Select models

2 Carefully pull off the instrument cluster hood (see illustrations).
3 Installation is the reverse of removal.

Instrument cluster bezel - 2014 and later models (except Rogue Select models)

4 Remove the knee bolster (see Section 23).
5 Remove the drivers's side upper trim panel (see Section 23).
6 Use a plastic trim tool to pry the instrument cluster trim bezel away from the dash panel.
7 Installation is the reverse of removal.

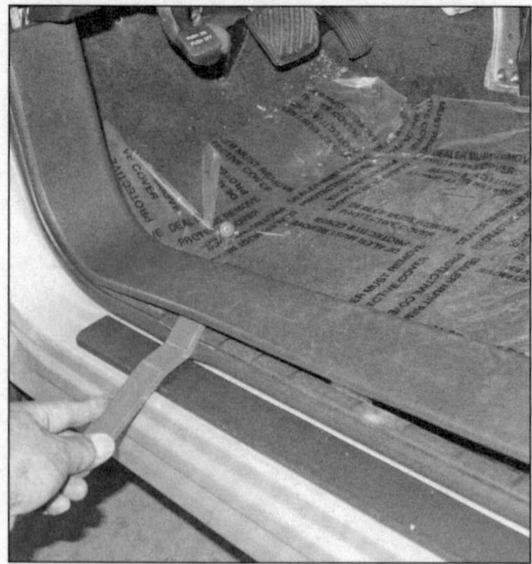

26.6a Remove the door opening trim panel

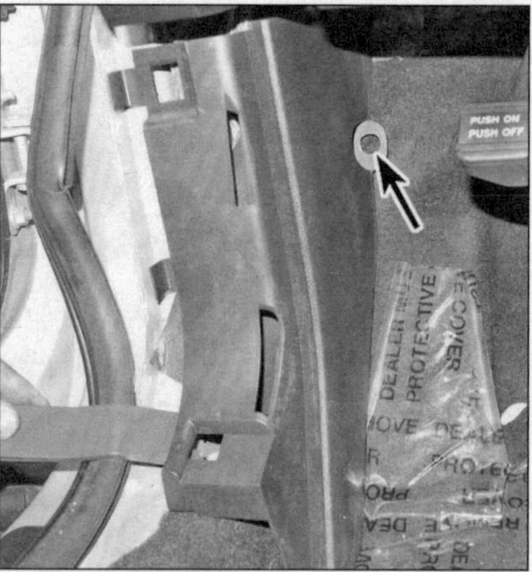

26.6b Remove hte kick panel mounting screw then remove kick panel

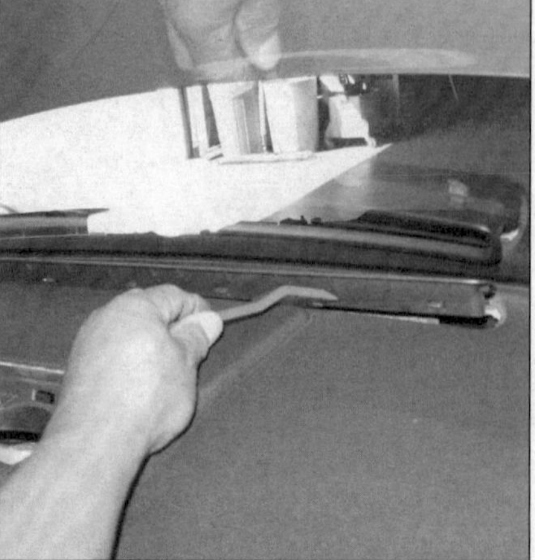

26.8 Carefully the pry out the defrost vent

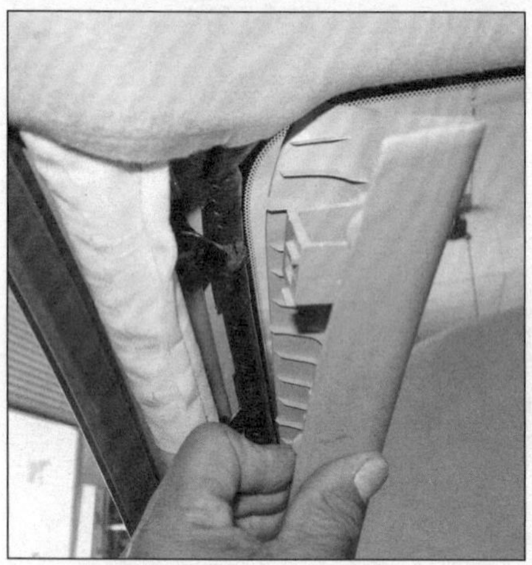

26.13a Pry the trim covers back . . .

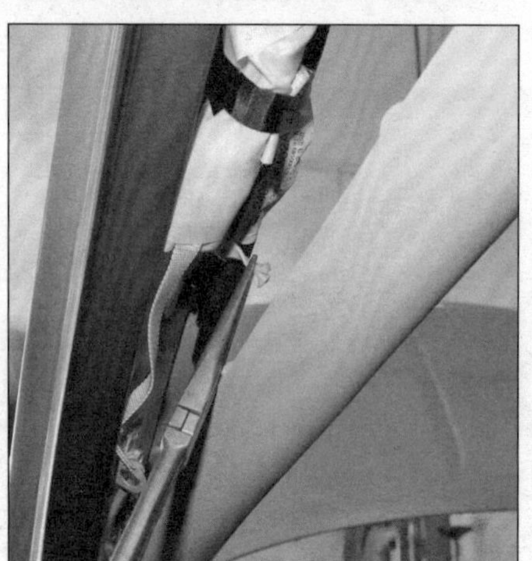

26.13b . . . then disconnect clip anchors

26.15 Pry up the locking tabs on the two connectors, then unplug them

26 Instrument panel - removal and installation

Warning: *The models covered by this manual are equipped with a Supplemental Restraint System (SRS), more commonly known as airbags. Always disarm the airbag system before working in the vicinity of any airbag system component to avoid the possibility of accidental deployment of the airbag, which could cause personal injury (see Chapter 12). Do not use a memory saving device to preserve the PCM's memory when working on or near airbag system components.*

1 Disconnect the cable from the negative terminal of the battery (see Chapter 5).

2 Remove the center console (see Section 22).

3 Remove the steering wheel (see Chapter 10).

4 Remove the dashboard trim panels (see Section 23).

5 Remove the steering column covers (see Section 24).

6 Remove the door opening panel and kick panels (see illustrations).

7 Remove the speaker grilles (see Chapter 12, Section 11).

8 Carefully pry the defrost vent out of the instrument panel (see illustration).

9 Remove screws on the front air control panel and remove the panel.

10 Remove the glove box assembly (see Section 23).

11 Unbolt the steering column from the instrument panel support brace.

12 Remove the instrument cluster (see Chapter 12).

13 Remove the front pillar trim covers (see illustrations).

14 Remove the front speakers (left, right and center) if equipped.

15 Disconnect the passenger air bag module connectors (see illustration).

16 Remove the passenger's airbag module bolt from the steering brace.

17 Remove the instrument panel fasteners (see illustrations).

18 Disconnect the radio antenna (see Chapter 12).

19 Remove the suport fasteners and lift out the instrument panel assembly.

20 Installation is the reverse of removal.

27 Cowl cover - removal and installation

1 Pry off the plastic trim cap on the windshield wiper arms, then detach the wiper arms retaining nuts and remove the wiper arms (see Chapter 12).

2 Disconnect the windshield washer tube.

3 Disengage the cowl extension panels from each corner of the windshield (see illustration).

4 Remove the cowl top cover fasteners (see illustration) then pull the panel forward and up to lift the panel out of the vehicle.

5 Disconnect and remove the front wiper motor and linkage assembly (see Chapter 12).

6 Remove the bolts and remove the cowl extension panel (see illustration).

7 Installation is the reverse of removal.

Note: *Always replace the sealant and double-faced adhesive tape when installing cowl top cover.*

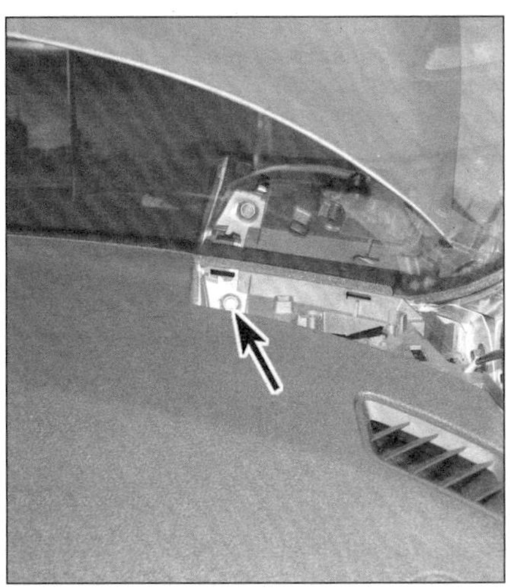
26.17a Remove the fasteners from the speaker grille openings . . .

26.17b . . . the top center . . .

26.17c . . . the left side of the instrument panel . . .

26.17d . . . and the right side of the instrument panel

27.3 Disengage the cowl extension panels

27.4 Use a trim tool to pry out the cowl seal clips

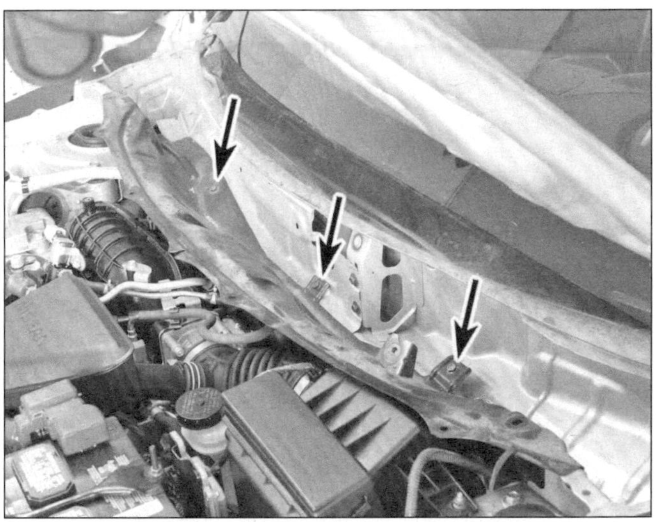
27.6 Remove the cowl extension panel bolts - 2013 and earlier models/2014 and later Rogue Select models shown; 2014 and later non-Select models have more fasteners

28 Seats - removal and installation

Warning: *The models covered by this manual are equipped with a Supplemental Restraint System (SRS), more commonly known as airbags. Always disarm the airbag system before working in the vicinity of any airbag system component to avoid the possibility of accidental deployment of the airbag, which could cause personal injury (see Chapter 12). Do not use a memory saving device to preserve the PCM's memory when working on or near airbag system components.*

Front seat

1 Disconnect the cable from the negative terminal of the battery (see Chapter 5).

2 Remove the headrest.

3 Disconnect the side airbag module connector.

4 Position the seat to the fully forward position and remove the two rear seat Torx bolt caps and bolts (see illustration).

5 Position the seat to its fully backward position and remove the two front seat bolts (see illustration).

6 Tilt the seat back and disconnect any wiring attached to the seat (see illustration).

7 Installation is the reverse of removal. Reconnect the battery and perform the necessary re-learn procedures (see Chapter 5).

Second row seats

2013 and earlier models/2014 and later Rogue Select models

8 Lift corners of the rear seat cushion up to disengage the fasteners (see illustration).

9 Remove the seat bolt trim covers then remove the seat fasteners and seats (see illustrations).

10 Remove the seat cushions.

11 Installation is the reverse of removal.

2014 and later models (except Rogue Select models)

12 Remove the headrest.

13 Position the seat to the fully forward position and remove the trim covers and two rear seat bolts.

14 Position the seat to its fully backward position and remove the trim cover and two front seat bolts.

15 Remove the seat.

16 Installation is the reverse of removal. Reconnect the battery and perform the necessary re-learn procedures (see Chapter 5).

28.4 With the seat moved forward, the rear Torx mounting bolt caps are exposed

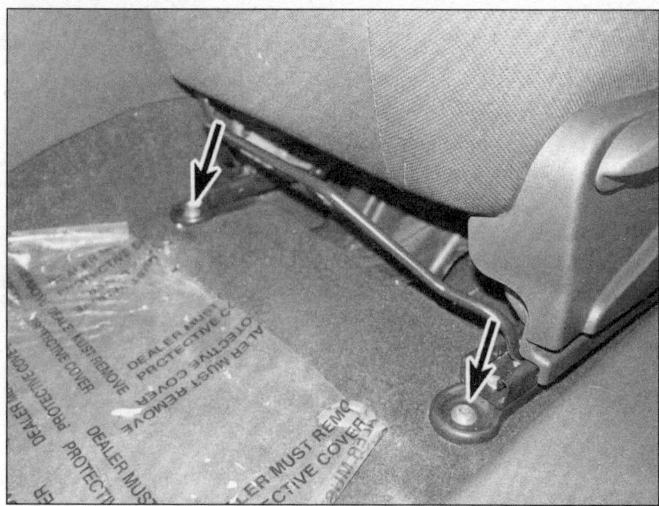

28.5 Move the seat rearward to gain access to the mounting bolts

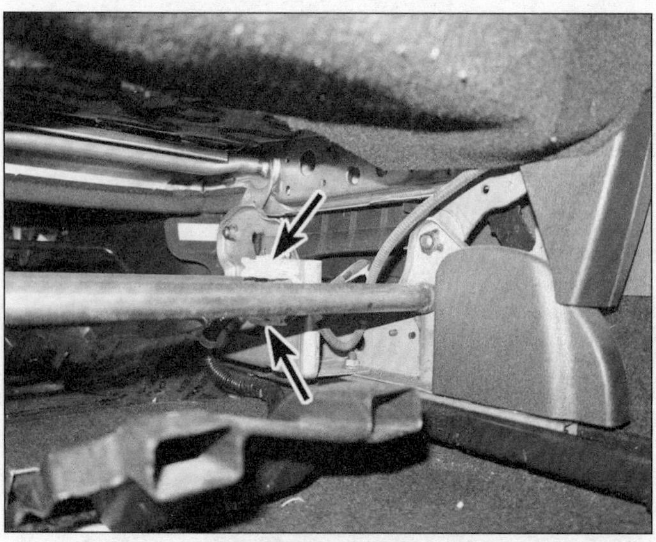

28.6 Disconnect any electrical connectors before removing the seat

28.8 Rear seat cushion lifted up showing seat mounting hook and lock (left side shown)

Third row seats - 2014 and later models (except Rogue Select models)

17 Using a trim removal tools remove the seat bolt trim covers from the front side of the seats.

18 Insert a screwdriver, or equivalent through each of the U-wires on the third row seat legs.

Warning: *Do not remove seat front bolts until the screwdrivers, or equivalent, have been inserted through both U-wires to prevent the gas struts from expanding rapidly, springing the seat frame open, which can cause severe personal injury.*

19 Remove the seat, front bolts.

20 Fold the seatback down to the flat position then pull on the release straps to to disengage the seat locks from the strikers.

21 Open the liftgate and remove the seats through the rear of the vehicle.

22 Installation is the reverse of removal.

28.9a Carefully remove seat back fastener trim covers

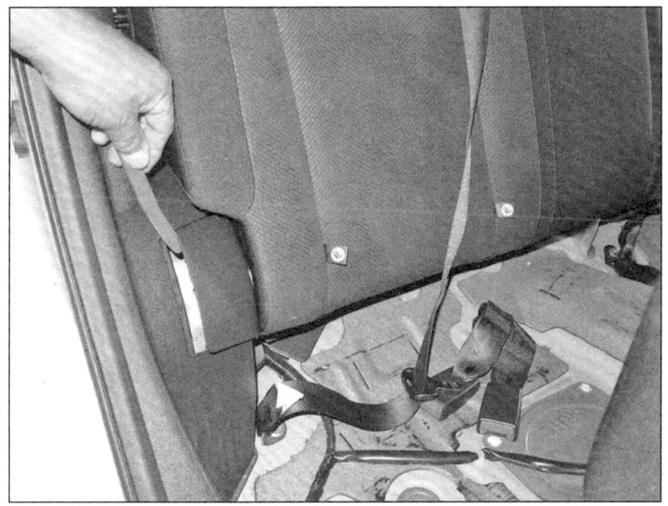

28.9b Right side seat mounting fastener locations

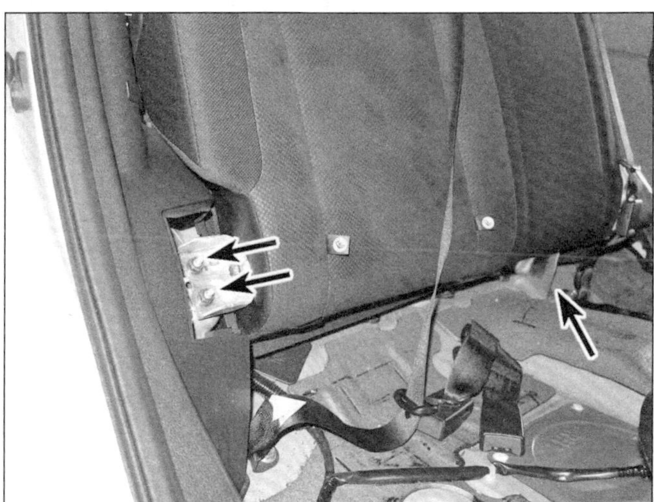

28.9c Left side seat mounting fastener locations

Notes

Chapter 12
Chassis electrical system

Contents

1 General information

1 The electrical system is a 12-volt, negative ground type. Power for the lights and all electrical accessories is supplied by a lead/acid-type battery that is charged by the alternator.

2 This Chapter covers repair and service procedures for the various electrical components not associated with the engine. Information on the battery, alternator, ignition system and starter motor can be found in Chapter 5.

3 It should be noted that when portions of the electrical system are serviced, the negative cable should be disconnected from the battery to prevent electrical shorts and/or fires.

2 Electrical troubleshooting - general information

1 A typical electrical circuit consists of an electrical component, any switches, relays, motors, fuses, fusible links or circuit breakers related to that component and the wiring and connectors that link the component to both the battery and the chassis. To help you pinpoint an electrical circuit problem, wiring diagrams are included at the end of this Chapter.

2 Before tackling any troublesome electrical circuit, first study the appropriate wiring diagrams to get a complete understanding of what makes up that individual circuit. Trouble spots, for instance, can often be narrowed down by noting if other components related to the circuit are operating properly. If several components or circuits fail at one time, chances are the problem is in a fuse or ground connection, because several circuits are often routed through the same fuse and ground connections.

3 Electrical problems usually stem from simple causes, such as loose or corroded connections, a blown fuse, a melted fusible link or a failed relay. Visually inspect the condition of all fuses, wires and connections in a problem circuit before troubleshooting the circuit.

4 If test equipment and instruments are going to be utilized, use the diagrams to plan ahead of time where you will make the necessary connections in order to accurately pinpoint the trouble spot.

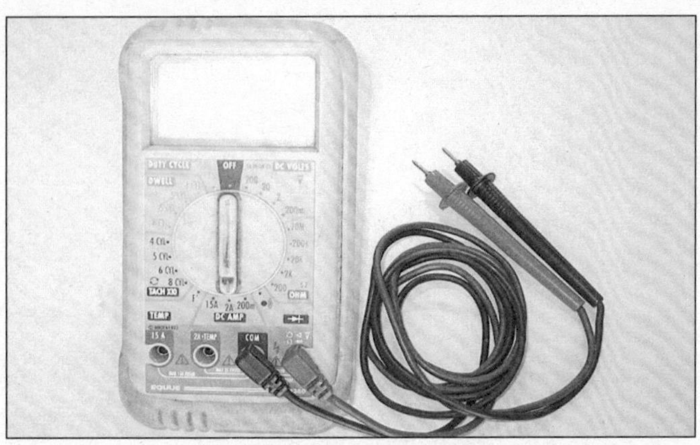

2.5a The most useful tool for electrical troubleshooting is a digital multimeter that can check volts, amps, and test continuity

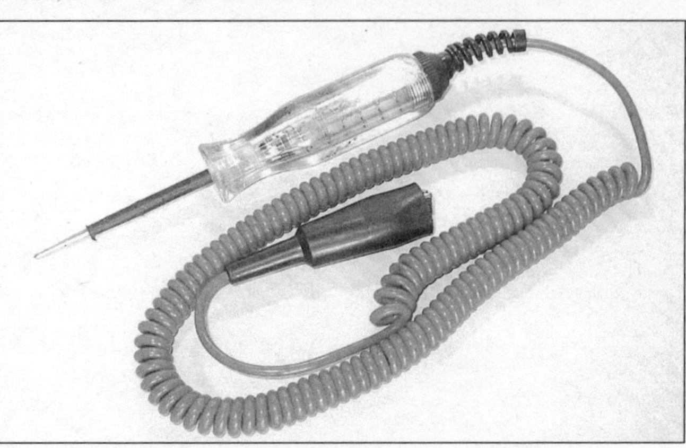

2.5b A test light is a very handy tool for checking voltage

5 The basic tools needed for electrical troubleshooting include a circuit tester or voltmeter (a 12-volt bulb with a set of test leads can also be used), a continuity tester, which includes a bulb, battery and set of test leads, and a jumper wire, preferably with a circuit breaker incorporated, which can be used to bypass electrical components (see illustrations). Before attempting to locate a problem with test instruments, use the wiring diagram(s) to decide where to make the connections.

Voltage checks

6 Voltage checks should be performed if a circuit is not functioning properly. Connect one lead of a circuit tester to either the negative battery terminal or a known good ground. Connect the other lead to a connector in the circuit being tested, preferably nearest to the battery or fuse (see illustration). If the bulb of the tester lights, voltage is present, which means that the part of the circuit between the connector and the battery is problem free. Continue checking the rest of the circuit in the same fashion. When you reach a point at which no voltage is present, the problem lies between that point and the last test point with voltage. Most of the time the problem can be traced to a loose connection.

Note: *Keep in mind that some circuits receive voltage only when the ignition key is in the Accessory or Run position.*

Finding a short

7 One method of finding shorts in a circuit is to remove the fuse and connect a test light or voltmeter in place of the fuse terminals. There should be no voltage present in the circuit. Move the wiring harness from side-to-side while watching the test light. If the bulb goes on, there is a short to ground somewhere in that area, probably where the insulation has rubbed through. The same test can be performed on each component in the circuit, even a switch.

8 If the short isn't obvious or you're having trouble locating it, seek professional help from an electrical repair shop or dealership.

Ground check

9 Perform a ground test to check whether a component is properly grounded. Disconnect the battery and connect one lead of a continuity tester or multimeter (set to the ohms scale), to a known good ground. Connect the other lead to the wire or ground connection being tested. If the resistance is low (less than 5 ohms), the ground is good. If the bulb on a self-powered test light does not go on, the ground is not good.

Continuity check

10 A continuity check is done to determine if there are any breaks in a circuit - if it is passing electricity properly. With the circuit off (no power in the circuit), a self-powered continuity tester or multimeter can be used to check the circuit. Connect the test leads to both ends of the circuit (or to the power end and a good ground), and if the test light comes on the circuit is passing current properly (see illustration). If the resistance is low (less than 5 ohms), there is continuity; if the reading is 10,000 ohms or higher, there is a break somewhere in the circuit. The same procedure can be used to test a switch, by connecting the continuity tester to the switch terminals. With the switch turned On, the test light should come on (or low resistance should be indicated on a meter).

Finding an open circuit

11 When diagnosing for possible open circuits, it is often difficult to locate them by sight because the connectors hide oxidation or terminal misalignment. Merely wiggling a connector on a sensor or in the wiring harness may correct the open circuit condition. Remember this when an open circuit is indicated when troubleshooting a circuit. Intermittent problems may also be caused by oxidized or loose connections.

12 Electrical troubleshooting is simple if you keep in mind that all electrical circuits are basically electricity running from the battery, through the wires, switches, relays, fuses and fusible links to each electrical component (light bulb, motor, etc.) and to ground, from which it is passed back to the battery. Any electrical problem is an interruption in the flow of electricity to and from the battery.

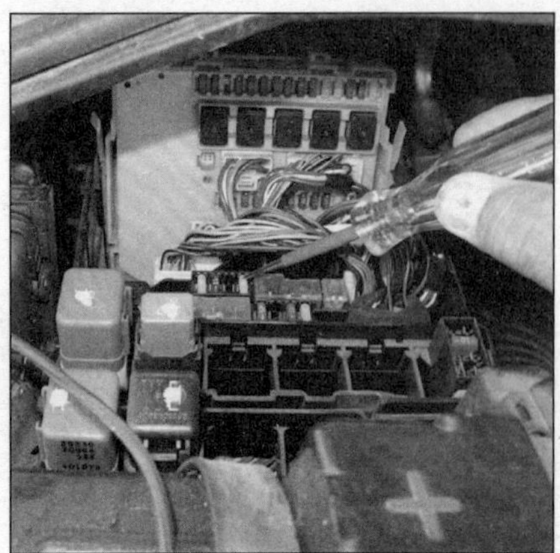

2.6 In use, a basic test light's lead is clipped to a known good ground, then the pointed probe can test connectors, wires or electrical sockets - if the bulb lights, the part being tested has battery voltage

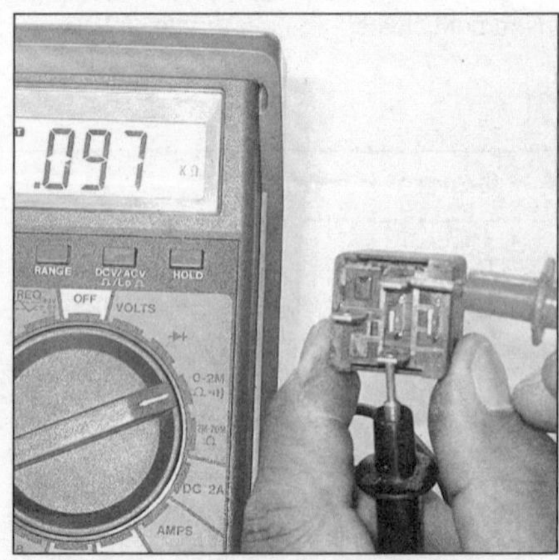

2.10 With a multimeter set to the ohms scale, resistance can be checked across two terminals - when checking for continuity, a low reading indicates continuity, a high reading indicates lack of continuity

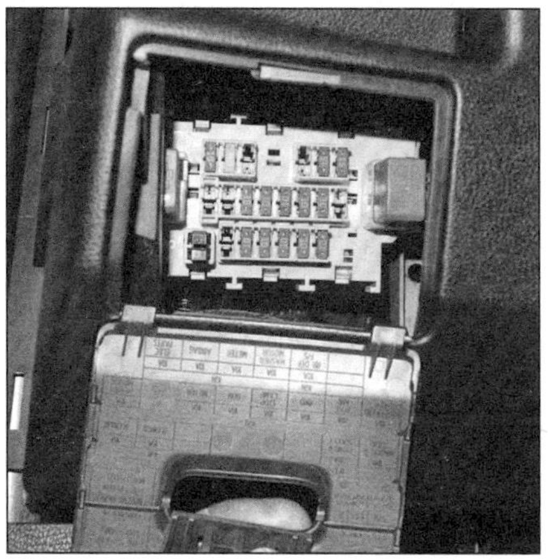

4.1a The interior fuse box is located at the left side of the instrument panel, behind the fuse panel cover

4.1b The fuse box chart is on the back side of the cover

4.1c The Intelligent Power Distribution Module Engine Room (IPDM E/R) is located along the left side of the engine compartment next to the engine compartment fuse/relay box. To release the cover, depress the tabs and lift upwards.

4.1d The engine compartment fuse/relay box is located along the left side of the engine compartment

4.1e The fuse and relay chart can be found on the underside of the cover

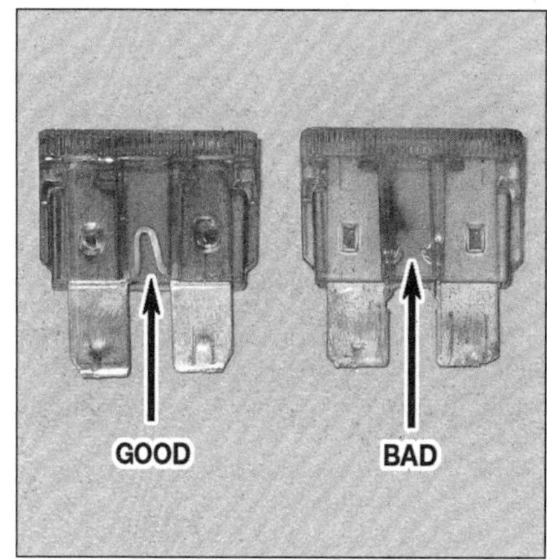

4.3 When a fuse blows, the element between the terminals melts

13 Start by reading the wiring diagram. Knowing where the lead starts and ends will be important in tracing out an open circuit. Always check either side of any connector (when possible) to make sure the open isn't in the connection. Pick a point in the circuit that you can easily access and test backward in both directions. Once you have found which half the open is in, do the same thing to that half, so on and so on, until you've found it.

3 Parasitic battery drain

1 Parasitic drain (sometimes referred to as a parasitic load) is the tendency of the electrical system to drain down the battery's usable energy over a certain amount of time when the ignition is turned off. The small amount of current draw is described in milliamps (mA). 30 milliamps (0.030 amps) is the allowable amount of current draw. An amp meter placed between the post and the battery clamp is used to obtain the readings. Each model, and each model type (depending on which accessories have been added, or were factory equipped) will have a slightly different acceptable parasitic drain.

2 Parasitic battery drain is different from an open or a short in the system; this parasitic load is supposed to be there to allow certain modules, computers, and other devices to gain the necessary voltage to maintain internal requirements. Some modules will power down after a few minutes, some can take up to 45 minutes or more to completely power down (commonly called "going to sleep" or "sleep mode"). Checking for a battery drain on these models takes a highly skilled technician with the proper equipment. It is not advisable to attempt this without proper training.

4 Fuses, fusible links and circuit breakers - general information

Fuses

1 The electrical circuits of the vehicle are protected by a combination of fuses, circuit breakers and fusible links. The main fuse/relay panel and the Intelligent Power Distribution Module Engine Room (IPDM E/R) is in the engine compartment on the driver's (left) side, next to the battery.The interior fuse/relay panel is located inside the passenger compartment on the driver's (left) side of the dash (see illustrations). Each of the fuses is designed to protect a specific circuit, and the various circuits are identified on the fuse panel itself.

2 Several sizes of fuses are employed in the fuse blocks. There are small, medium and large sizes of the same design, all with the same blade terminal design. The medium and large fuses can be removed with your fingers, but the small fuses require the use of pliers or the small plastic fuse-puller tool found in most fuse boxes.

3 If an electrical component fails, always check the fuse first. The best way to check the fuses is with a test light. Check for power at the exposed terminal tips of each fuse. If power is present at one side of the fuse but not the other, the fuse is blown. A blown fuse can also be identified by visually inspecting it (see illustration).

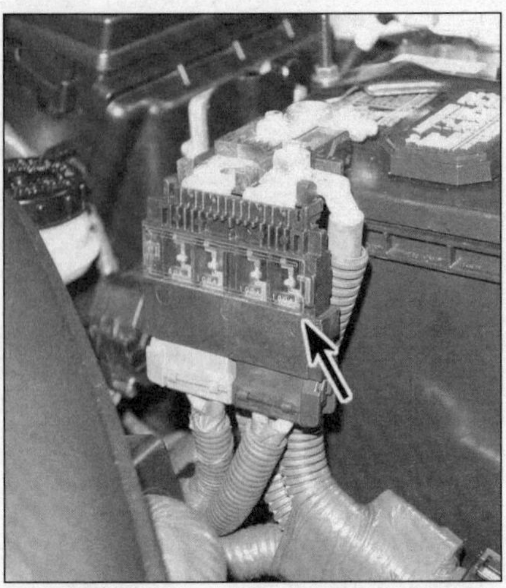
4.6 Location of the fusible links in the fusible link box

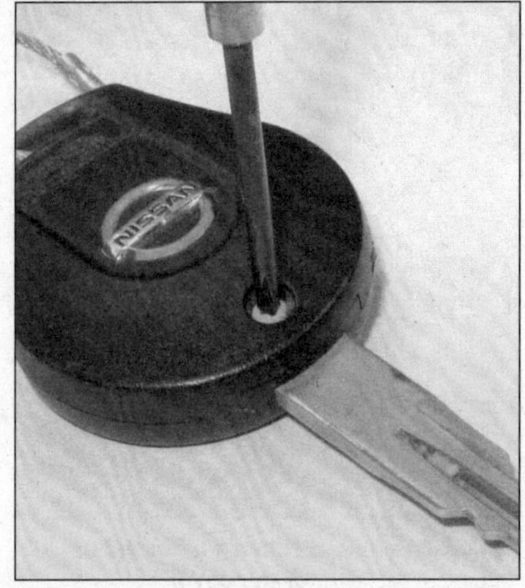

7.1 Remove the screw retaining the key fob body halves

7.2 Pry the key fob apart

4 Be sure to replace blown fuses with the correct type. Fuses (of the same physical size) of different ratings may be physically interchangeable, but only fuses of the proper rating should be used. Replacing a fuse with one of a higher or lower value than specified is not recommended. Each electrical circuit needs a specific amount of protection. The amperage value of each fuse is molded into the top of the fuse body.

5 If the replacement fuse immediately fails, don't replace it again until the cause of the problem is isolated and corrected. In most cases, this will be a short circuit in the wiring caused by a broken or deteriorated wire.

Fusible links

6 Some circuits are protected by fusible links. The links are used in circuits which are not ordinarily fused, or which carry high current, such as the circuit between the alternator and the starter motor. The fusible links are located in the fusible link box, which is part of the positive battery cable terminal (see illustration). After disconnecting the negative battery cable, remove the positive cable terminal and disconnect the electrical connectors from the bottom (the fusible link box must be replaced as a unit).

Caution: *Be sure to troubleshoot the circuit in which the fusible link melted BEFORE installing a replacement fusible link box.*

Circuit breakers

7 Circuit breakers protect certain circuits, such as the power windows or heated seats. Depending on the vehicle's accessories, there may be one or two circuit breakers, located in the fuse/relay box in the engine compartment.

8 Because the circuit breakers reset automatically, an electrical overload in a circuit breaker-protected system will cause the circuit to fail momentarily, then come back on. If the circuit does not come back on, check it immediately.

9 For a basic check, pull the circuit breaker up out of its socket on the fuse panel, but just far enough to probe with a voltmeter. The breaker should still contact the sockets. With the voltmeter negative lead on a good chassis ground, touch each end prong of the circuit breaker with the positive meter probe. There should be battery voltage at each end. If there is battery voltage only at one end, the circuit breaker must be replaced.

10 Some circuit breakers must be reset manually.

5 Relays - general information

1 Several electrical accessories in the vehicle, such as the fuel injection system, horns, starter, and fog lamps use relays to transmit the electrical signal to the component. Relays use a low-current circuit (the control circuit) to open and close a high-current circuit (the power circuit). If the relay is defective, that component will not operate properly. Most relays are mounted in the engine compartment and interior fuse/relay boxes (see illustrations 4.1a, 4.1b, 4.1c, 4.1d and 4.1e).

6 Electrical connectors - general information

1 Most electrical connections on these vehicles are made with multiwire plastic connectors. The mating halves of many connectors are secured with locking clips molded into the plastic connector shells. The mating halves of some large connectors, such as some of those under the instrument panel, are held together by a bolt through the center of the connector.

2 To separate a connector with locking clips, use a small screwdriver to pry the clips apart carefully, then separate the connector halves. Pull only on the shell, never pull on the wiring harness as you may damage the individual wires and terminals inside the connectors. Look at the connector closely before trying to separate the halves. Often the locking clips are engaged in a way that is not immediately clear. Additionally, many connectors have more than one set of clips.

3 Each pair of connector terminals has a male half and a female half. When you look at the end view of a connector in a diagram, be sure to understand whether the view shows the harness side or the component side of the connector. Connector halves are mirror images of each other, and a terminal shown on the right side end-view of one half will be on the left side end-view of the other half.

4 It is often necessary to take circuit voltage measurements with a connector connected. Whenever possible, carefully insert a small straight pin (not your meter probe) into the rear of the connector shell to contact the terminal inside, then clip your meter lead to the pin. This kind of connection is called "backprobing." When inserting a test probe into a terminal, be careful not to distort the terminal opening. Doing so can lead to a poor connection and corrosion at that terminal later. Using the small straight pin instead of a meter probe results in less chance of deforming the terminal connector.

7 Remote keyless entry fob - battery replacement

1 Remove the key fob unit retaining screw (see illustration).

2 Remove the key half from the transmitter half of the key fob, by inserting a small screwdriver into the notch in the body of the transmitter (see illustration).

3 Carefully pry out the old battery with a small screwdriver or a coin (see illustration).

Caution: *Do not touch the circuit board or battery terminal contacts inside the key fob.*

4 Install the new battery, making sure the positive (+) terminal faces the bottom of the case, then reassemble the two halves.

Caution: *Handle the battery by its edges only; holding it like a coin (touching the top and bottom flat surfaces) can reduce the battery's life by partially discharging it.*

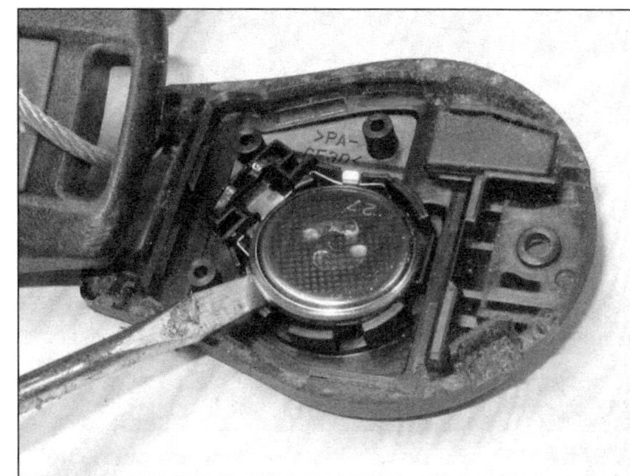

7.3 Carefully remove the battery without touching any other components

Electrical connectors

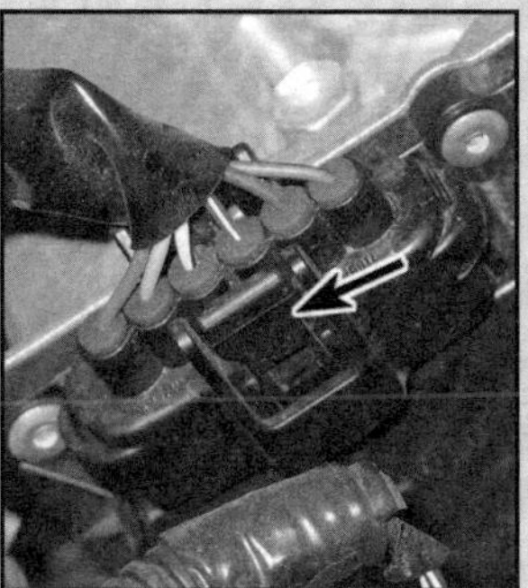

Most electrical connectors have a single release tab that you depress to release the connector

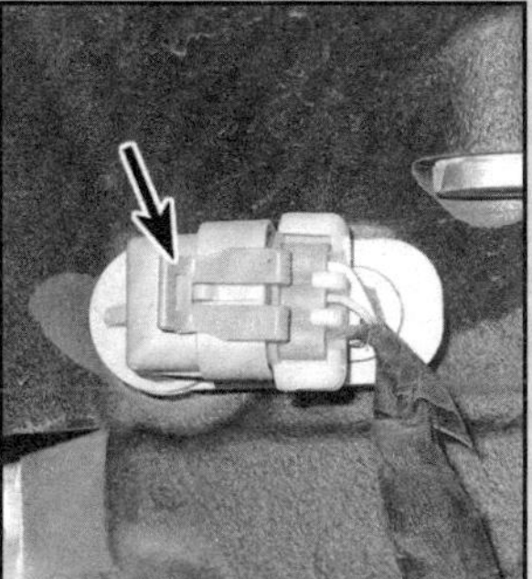

Some electrical connectors have a retaining tab which must be pried up to free the connector

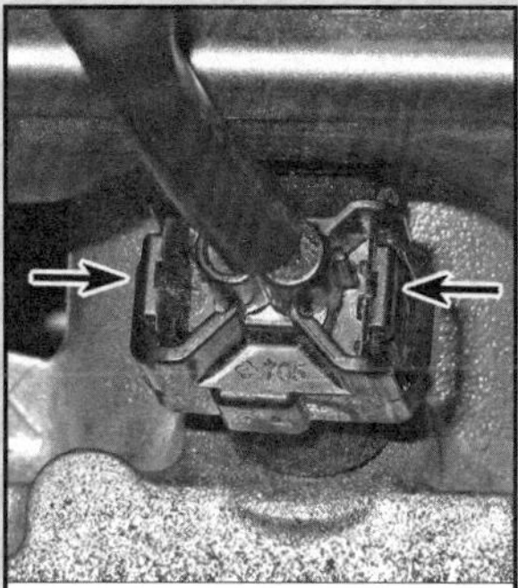

Some connectors have two release tabs that you must squeeze to release the connector

Some connectors use wire retainers that you squeeze to release the connector

Critical connectors often employ a sliding lock (1) that you must pull out before you can depress the release tab (2)

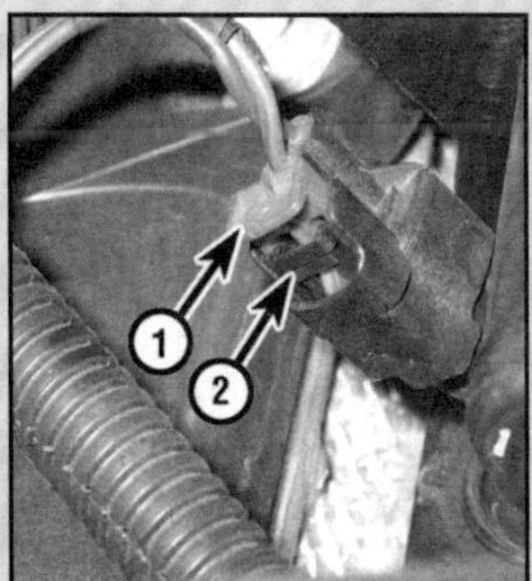

Here's another sliding-lock style connector, with the lock (1) and the release tab (2) on the side of the connector

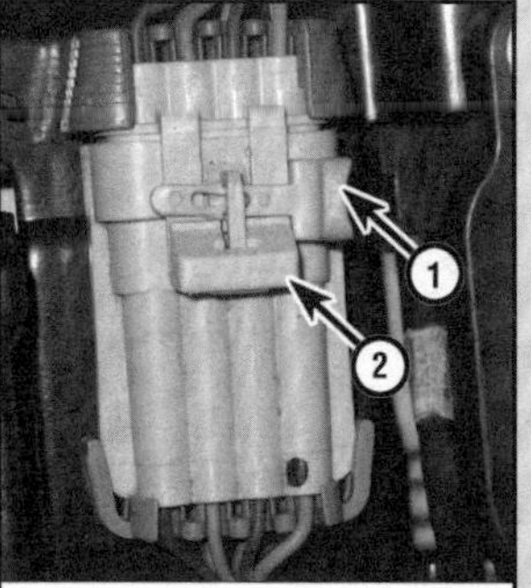

On some connectors the lock (1) must be pulled out to the side and removed before you can lift the release tab (2)

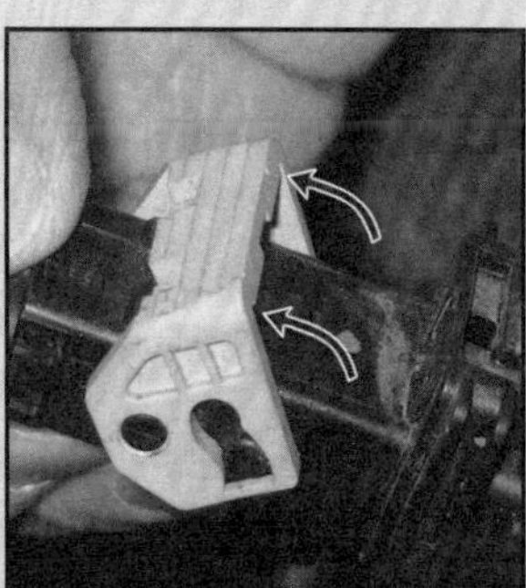

Some critical connectors, like the multi-pin connectors at the Powertrain Control Module employ pivoting locks that must be flipped open

8.3 On 2013 and earlier models, the Body Control Module is mounted under the passenger's side of the instrument panel, behind the glove box

9.6 Press the top and bottom pawl tabs at the same time while pulling the switch outwards

8 Body Control Module (BCM) - general information

1 The Body Control Module (BCM) receives inputs from various switches and sensors and sends commands, some in the form of multiplex voltage signals, to corresponding components to operate them. Some circuits are controlled by the BCM in conjunction with the IPDM (see Section 28) and/or the Powertrain Control Module (PCM) (see Chapter 6). It also receives signals from the air conditioning system and sends those signals to the ECM using CAN communication. Some of the various systems controlled by the BCM are:

Combination switch system
Signal buffer system
Power consumption control system
Auto light system
Turn signal and hazard warning light system
Headlight system
Fog light system
Daytime running lights system
Interior illumination system
Interior illumination battery saver system
Windshield wiper/washer system
Warning chime system

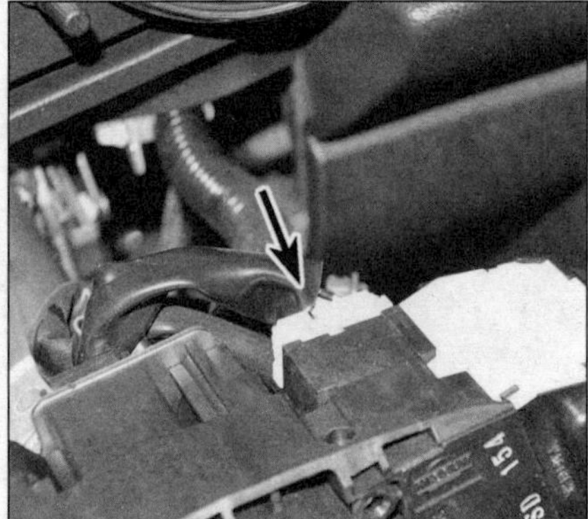

9.3 Disconnect the electrical connector to the wiper switch

Power door lock system
Power window system
Air conditioning compressor clutch
Nissan Anti-Theft System (NATS)
Vehicle security system
Rear window defogger system
Remote keyless entry system
Trunk release system
Intelligent Key system
Ignition push switch system
Electronic steering column lock
Tire pressure monitor system
Retained accessory power (RAP) system

CAN Communication

2 CAN communication is what the BCM and other various control systems use to communicate with each other. These CAN lines allow a high rate of two way communication lines between them. CAN-L and CAN-H connect the various control units. Each control unit transmits/receives data, but selectively reads required data that pertains to that particular module. These lines should not be tampered with or a severe loss or erratic information can occur which will cause different systems not to function properly.

3 On 2013 and earlier models, the BCM is located under the passenger's side of the instrument panel, behind the glove box (see illustration) and under the driver's side of the instrument panel on 2014 and later models. Removal and installation of the BCM is not covered in this manual because special equipment is required to diagnose it and the systems it controls. Additionally, if the BCM requires replacement, it must be programmed with the same special equipment before it will work. Diagnosis and replacement of the BCM must be performed at a dealer service department or a qualified independent repair shop equipped with the necessary tool.

9 Steering column switches - replacement

Warning: *The models covered by this manual are equipped with Supplemental Restraint Systems (SRS), more commonly known as airbags. Always disable the airbag system before working in the vicinity of any airbag system components to avoid the possibility of accidental deployment of the airbags, which could cause personal injury (see Section 27).*

1 Disconnect the cable from the negative terminal of the battery (see Chapter 5).

2 Remove the steering column covers (see Chapter 11).

9.4 Press the top and bottom pawl tabs at the same time while pulling the switch outwards

Wiper/washer switch

2014 and earlier models

Note: *On 2015 and later models, the combination switches (lights and windshield wipers) can't be removed separately - the combination switch must be replaced as an assembly (see Steps 9 through 11).*

3 Disconnect the wiper/washer switch electrical connectors (see illustration).

4 Pull the wiper/washer switch towards the passenger's side of the vehicle while pressing in on the pawls (top and bottom), and remove the switch (see illustration).

5 Installation is the reverse of removal.

Turn signal/headlight switch

Note: *The lighting and turn signal switch is also know as the combination switch.*

2014 and earlier models

6 Pull the switch outward towards the driver's side of the vehicle while pressing in on the pawl tabs (top and bottom) (see illustration).

7 Disconnect the electrical connector from the switch, and remove the switch.

8 Installation is the reverse of removal.

2015 and later models

Note: *On 2015 and later models, the combination switches (lights and windshield wipers) can't be removed separately - the combination switch must be replaced as an assembly if there is a problem.*

9 Remove the steering wheel and clock-spring (see Chapter 10).

10 Disconnect the electrical connectors from the combination switch.

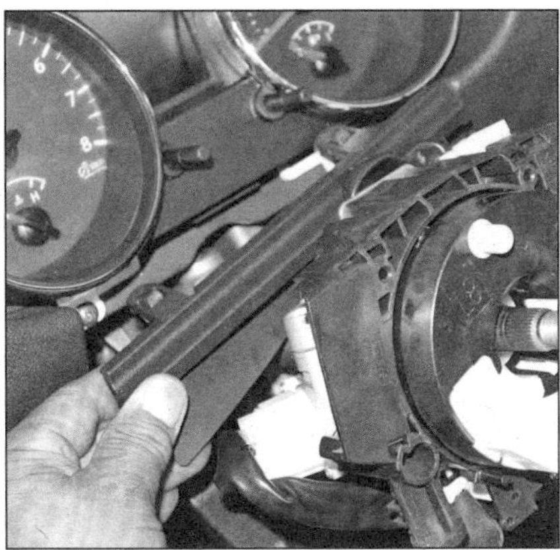
10.3 Carefully pry off the trim panel and flap

11.3 Remove the screws from each side securing the radio to the center instrument panel trim - early models shown, later models similar

11 Remove the retaining screw at the bottom of the combination switch, then slide the switch off of the steering column.
12 Installation is the same as removal.

Hazard Switch

13 Carefully pry out the instrument panel center vent assembly.
14 Disconnect the electrical connector from the hazard switch.
15 Disengage the retaining tabs and push the switch out from behind.
16 Installation is the reverse of removal.

10 Instrument cluster - removal and installation

Warning: *The models covered by this manual are equipped with Supplemental Restraint Systems (SRS), more commonly known as airbags. Always disable the airbag system before working in the vicinity of any airbag system components to avoid the possibility of accidental deployment of the airbags, which could cause personal injury (see Section 27).*

10.5a Instrument cluster retaining screws

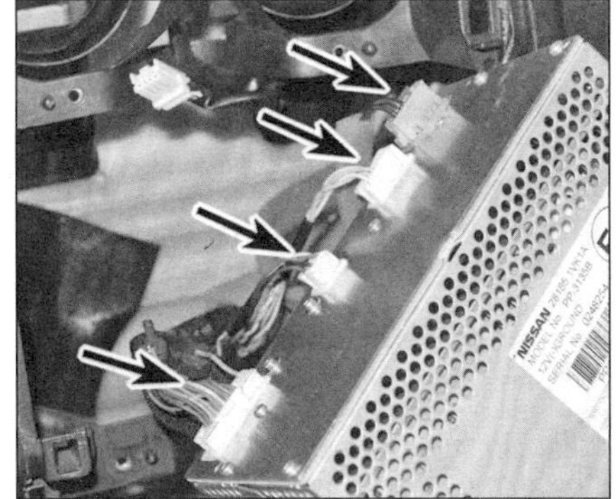
11.4 Disconnect the electrical connectors from the radio

1 Disconnect the cable from the negative terminal of the battery (see Chapter 5).
2 Remove the center instrument panel trim assembly (see Chapter 11) and, on 2015 and later models, the right-side center trim panel above the glovebox and the left-side side trim panel (see Chapter 11).
3 Use a trim tool to remove the trim panel and flap below the instrument cluster (see illustration).
4 Remove the instrument cluster bezel/hood (see Chapter 11).
5 Remove the instrument cluster retaining screws. Pull the cluster out far enough to gain access to the electrical connector and disconnect it (see illustrations).
6 Installation is the reverse of removal. Reconnect the battery and perform the necessary re-learn procedures (see Chapter 5).

11 Radio, speakers and Bluetooth - removal and installation

Warning: *The models covered by this manual are equipped with Supplemental Restraint Systems (SRS), more commonly known as airbags. Always disable the airbag system before working in the vicinity of any airbag system components to avoid the possibility of accidental deployment of the airbags, which could cause personal injury (see Section 27).*

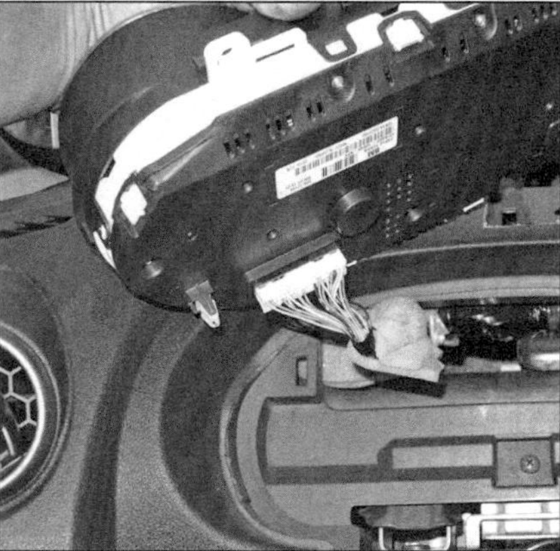
10.5b Disconnect the instrument cluster electrical connector

11.7 Carefully pry off the speaker grille

Radio

1 Disconnect the cable from the negative terminal of the battery (see Chapter 5).
2 Remove the center instrument panel trim assembly (see Chapter 11) and, on 2015 and later models, the right-side center trim panel above the glovebox and the left-side side trim panel (see Chapter 11)
3 Remove the screws securing the radio (see illustration).
4 Disconnect the electrical connectors (see illustration) from the radio and remove the radio.
5 Installation is the reverse of removal. Reconnect the battery and perform the necessary re-learn procedures (see Chapter 5).

Speakers

6 Disconnect the cable from the negative terminal of the battery (see Chapter 5).

Dash-mounted speakers

Tweeters

7 Pry off the speaker grille (see illustration).
8 Remove the speaker mounting screws, then remove the speaker and disconnect the electrical connector.
9 Installation is the reverse of removal. Reconnect the battery and perform the necessary re-learn procedures (see Chapter 5).

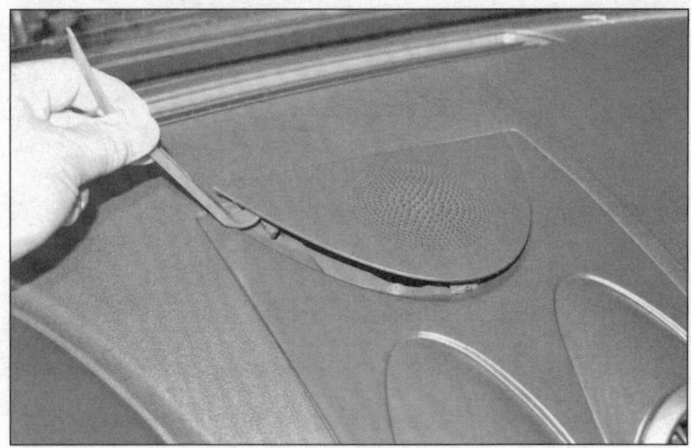

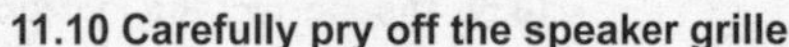

11.10 Carefully pry off the speaker grille

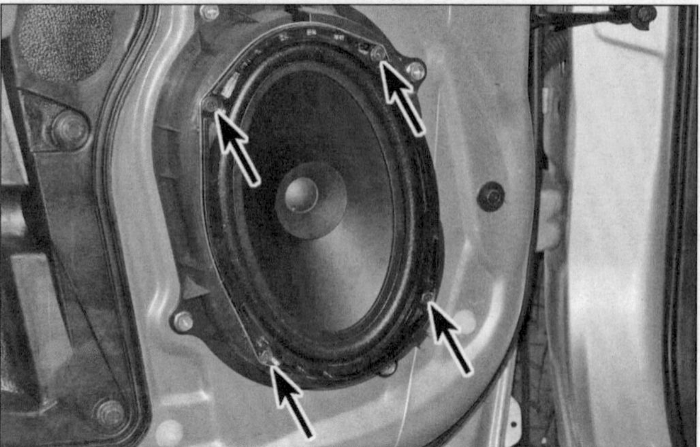

11.14 Door speaker mounting screws

Center speaker

10 Pry off the speaker grille (see illustration).

11 Remove the speaker mounting screws, then remove the speaker and disconnect the electrical connector.

12 Installation is the reverse of removal. Reconnect the battery and perform the necessary re-learn procedures (see Chapter 5).

Door speakers

13 Remove the door trim panels (see Chapter 11).

14 Remove the speaker mounting screws (see illustration), disconnect the electrical connector and remove the speaker.

15 Installation is the reverse of removal.

Rear speakers

16 Remove the rear seat backs (see Chapter 11) and the rear parcel shelf.

17 Remove the speaker mounting screws and pull out the speakers.

18 Disconnect the electrical connectors and remove the speakers.

19 Installation is the reverse of removal.

Subwoofer

20 Open the liftgate and lift out the flooring over the spare tire.

21 Locate the spare tire tightening knob in the center of the spare tire, then loosen the knob by turning it counterclockwise until it can be removed.

22 Disconnect the electrical connector and remove the subwoofer.

23 Installation is the reverse of removal.

Amplifier

24 Slide the passenger's seat fully forward.

25 Using a plastic trim tool, carefully pry up the amplifier cover.

26 Remove the amplifier mounting bolts.

27 Disconnect the electrical connectors and remove the amplifier and mounting bracket as a unit.

28 Remove the amplifier bracket fasteners and separate the bracket from the amplifier.

29 Installation is the reverse of removal.

Steering wheel audio controls

30 Remove the airbag from the steering wheel (see Chapter 10).

31 Remove the audio control mounting screws, disconnect the electrical connectors, and remove the controls.

32 Installation is the reverse of removal.

Bluetooth system

33 The Bluetooth telephone system incorporated in these vehicles allows the use of a Bluetooth cellular phone to make wireless connection between your cellular phone and the Bluetooth controller. This hands-free cellular telephone system allows calls to be sent and received. Personal memos can be created using the Nissan Voice Recognition system as well. Some Bluetooth phones are not compatible with the controller. When a different cellular phone is used or the Bluetooth control is replaced, the phone must be paired up with the controller. Different manufacturers of cellular phones may have different procedures to pair up the phone to the controller. Refer to the cellular phone operating manual for those instructions. The Bluetooth control is built into the radio unit.

Diagnosis

34 The Bluetooth system is diagnosed two different ways: the unit performs a self diagnostic test every time the ignition is turned on; the system can also be diagnosed by a technician using the audio controls on the steering wheel. Seek a qualified repair facility for service and diagnostics.

35 The "ON" indicator is located in the roof console assembly. The indicator will flash while the controller is initializing at power up. This may take 10 seconds or more. If a paired up cellular phone is present in the vehicle the indicator will remain on to indicate that the system is ready for voice commands.

Microphone removal and installation

36 Remove the map light in the overhead console.

37 Disconnect the microphone from its electrical connector and remove the microphone.

38 Installation is the reverse of removal.

12 Antenna - removal and installation

Radio antenna

1 Remove the left side rear seat assist grip.

2 Remove the three clips on the rear left side of the headliner.

3 Pull down the rear section of the headliner just enough to gain working room between the headliner and the roof.

4 Remove the retaining nut and clips, then remove antenna.

5 Installation is the reverse of removal.

Bluetooth antenna

Note: *The antenna is mounted in the rear luggage compartment on the right side under the rear quarter panel.*

6 Remove the right side rear quarter trim panel (see Chapter 11).

7 Disconnect the electrical connectors to the antenna.

8 Remove the Bluetooth unit mounting screws and unit.

9 Installation is the reverse of removal.

13 Rear window defogger - check and repair

1 The rear window defogger consists of a number of horizontal heating elements baked onto the inside surface of the glass. Power is supplied through two fuses and a relay in the IPDM relay box in the engine compartment. A defogger switch on the instrument panel controls the defogger grid.

2 Small breaks in the element can be repaired without removing the rear window.

Check

3 Turn the ignition switch and defogger system switches to the ON position. Using a voltmeter, place the positive probe against the defogger grid positive side and the negative probe against the ground side. If battery voltage is not indicated, check that the ignition switch is On and that the feed

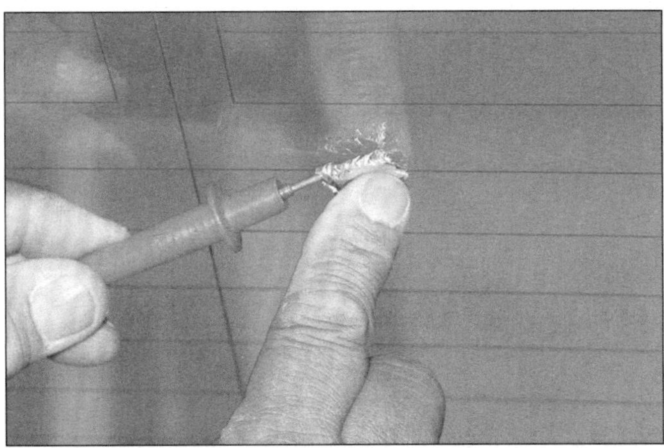

13.4 When measuring the voltage at the rear window defogger grid, wrap a piece of aluminum foil around the negative probe of the voltmeter and press the foil against the wire with your finger

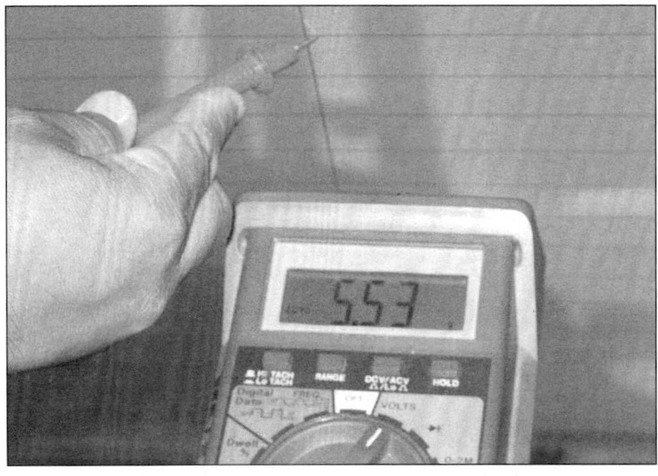

13.5 To determine if a heating element has broken, check the voltage at the center of each element - if the voltage is approximately 6 volts, the element is unbroken; if the voltage is 10 or 12 volts, the element is broken between the center and the ground side; if there is no voltage, the element is broken between the center and the positvive side

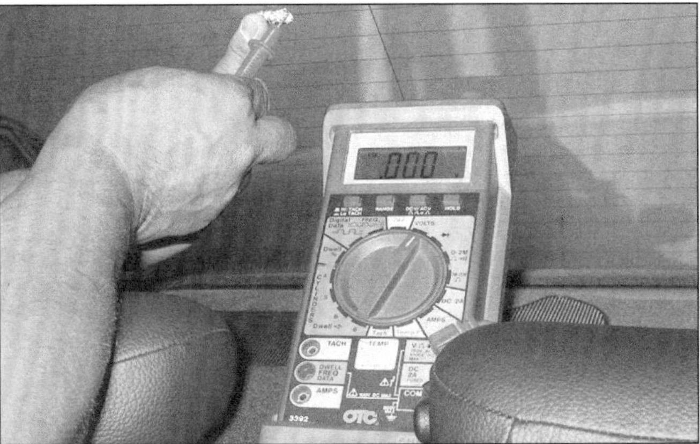

13.7 To find the break, place the voltmeter negative lead against the defogger ground terminal, place the voltmeter positive lead with the foil strip against the heat wire at the positive terminal end and slide it toward the negative terminal end. The point at which the voltmeter deflects from several volts to zero volts is the point at which the wire is broken

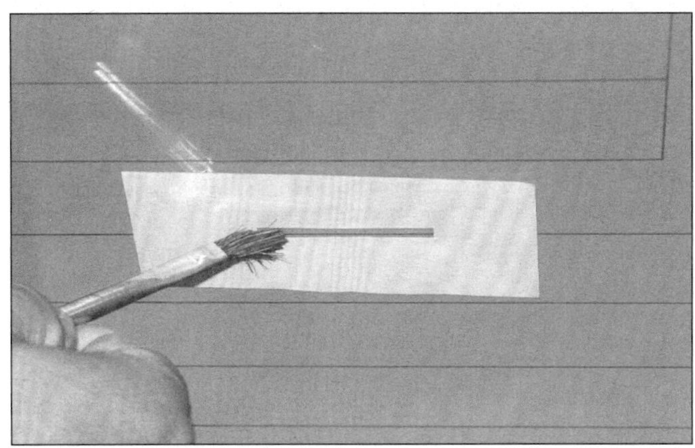

13.13 To use a defogger repair kit, apply masking tape to the inside of the window at the damaged area, then brush on the special conductive coating

and ground wires are properly connected. Check the two fuses, defogger switch, defogger relay and related wiring. A dealer can scan the body control module if necessary. If voltage is indicated, but all or part of the defogger doesn't heat, proceed with the following tests.

4 When measuring voltage during the next two tests, wrap a piece of aluminum foil around the tip of the voltmeter positive probe and press the foil against the heating element with your finger (see illustration). Place the negative probe on the defogger grid ground terminal.

5 Check the voltage at the center of each heating element (see illustration). If the voltage is 5 to 6 volts, the element is okay (there is no break). If the voltage is 0 volts, the element is broken between the center of the element and the positive end. If the voltage is 10 to 12 volts, the element is broken between the center of the element and the ground side. Check each heating element.

6 If none of the elements are broken, connect the negative probe to a good chassis ground. The voltage reading should stay the same; if it doesn't, the ground connection is bad.

7 To find the break, place the voltmeter negative probe against the defogger ground terminal. Place the voltmeter positive probe with the foil strip against the heating element at the positive side and slide it toward the negative side. The point at which the voltmeter deflects from several volts to zero is the point where the heating element is broken (see illustration).

Repair

8 Repair the break in the element using a repair kit specifically recommended for this purpose, available at most auto parts stores. Included in this kit is a plastic conductive epoxy.

9 Before repairing a break, turn off the system and allow it to cool for a few minutes.

10 Lightly buff the element area with fine steel wool, then clean it thoroughly with rubbing alcohol.

11 Use masking tape to mask off the area being repaired.

12 Thoroughly mix the epoxy, following the kit instructions.

13 Apply the epoxy material to the slit in the masking tape, overlapping the undamaged area about 3/4-inch on either end (see illustration).

14 Allow the repair to cure for 24 hours before removing the tape and using the system.

14.3a Headlight housing upper bolts - 2013 and earlier models/2014 and later Rogue Select models shown

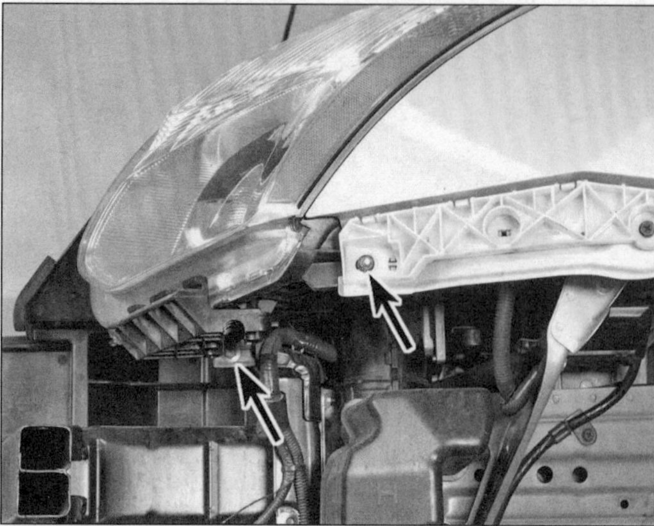

14.3b Headlight housing lower bolts - 2013 and earlier models/2014 and later Rogue Select models shown

15.3 Disconnect and unplug the electrical connector

15.4 Turn the bulb counterclockwise to remove it from the housing

14 Headlight housing - removal and installation

Warning: *The models covered by this manual are equipped with Supplemental Restraint Systems (SRS), more commonly known as airbags. Always disable the airbag system before working in the vicinity of any airbag system components to avoid the possibility of accidental deployment of the airbags, which could cause personal injury (see Section 27).*

1 Disconnect the cable from the negative terminal of the battery (see Chapter 5).

2 Remove the front bumper cover (see Chapter 11).

3 Remove the headlight housing retaining bolts (see illustrations).

4 Pull out the headlight, disconnect the wiring and remove the housing.

5 Installation is the reverse of removal.

15 Headlight bulb - replacement

Halogen bulbs

Warning: *Halogen gas-filled bulbs, which are under pressure, may shatter if the surface is scratched or the bulb is dropped. Wear eye protection and handle the bulbs carefully, grasping only the base whenever possible. Do not touch the surface of the bulb with your fingers because the oil from your skin could cause it to overheat and fail prematurely. If you do touch the bulb surface, clean it with rubbing alcohol.*

Note: *It is not necessary to remove the headlight housing to replace the bulbs.*

1 Ensure the headlight switch is in the off position. Disconnect the cable from the negative terminal of the battery (see Chapter 5).

2 On 2013 and earlier models and 2014 Rogue Select models, remove the air intake duct to access the left-side headlight bulbs.

3 Disconnect the electrical connector from the headlight bulb holder (see illustration).

4 Twist the bulb counterclockwise (see illustration) and remove it from the headlight housing.

Caution: *Don't touch the bulb surface with your fingers, because the oil from your skin could cause it to overhead and fail prematurely. If you accidentally touch the bulb surface, clean it with rubbing alcohol.*

5 Installation is the reverse of removal.

Xenon (HID) headlights

Warning: *Some models use xenon bulbs (also known as High Intensity Discharge [HID] bulbs) instead of halogen bulbs. These can be identified by the high-voltage warning sticker on the headlight housing or under the hood. According to the manufacturer,*

16.1a Insert a Phillips screwdriver through the opening between the radiator support and the headlight housing . . .

16.1b . . . until the screwdriver contacts the headlight housing adjustment screw

the high voltages produced by this system can be fatal in the event of a shock. Also, the voltage can remain in the circuit even after the headlight switch has been turned to OFF and the ignition key has been removed. Therefore, for your safety, we don't recommend that you try to replace one of these bulbs yourself. Instead, have this service performed by a dealer service department or other qualified repair shop.

LED headlights

6 On 2014 and later models (except Rogue Select models), a LED headlight system is available. The headlight low beam, high beam and side marker (parking light) are LEDs and are not separately replaceable. If one fails, replace the headlight housing assembly (see Section 14).

16 Headlights - adjustment

Note: *It is important that the headlights are aimed correctly. If adjusted incorrectly they could blind the driver of an oncoming vehicle and cause a serious accident or seriously reduce your ability to see the road. The headlights should be checked for proper aim every 12 months and any time a new headlight is installed or front end body work is performed. It should be emphasized that the following procedure is only an interim step that will provide temporary adjustment until the headlights can be adjusted by a properly equipped shop.*

1 All models are equipped with one adjustment screw in each headlight housing (see illustrations). The headlights are only adjustable vertically.

2 There are several methods of adjusting the headlights. The simplest method requires a blank wall 25 feet in front of the vehicle and a level floor.

3 Position masking tape vertically on the wall in reference to the vehicle centerline and the centerlines of both headlights.

4 Position a horizontal tape line in reference to the centerline of all the headlights. **Note:** *It may be easier to position the tape on the wall with the vehicle parked only a few inches away.*

5 Adjustment should be made with the vehicle sitting level, the gas tank half-full and no unusually heavy load in the vehicle (see illustration).

6 Starting with the low beam adjustment, position the high intensity zone so it is two inches below the horizontal line.

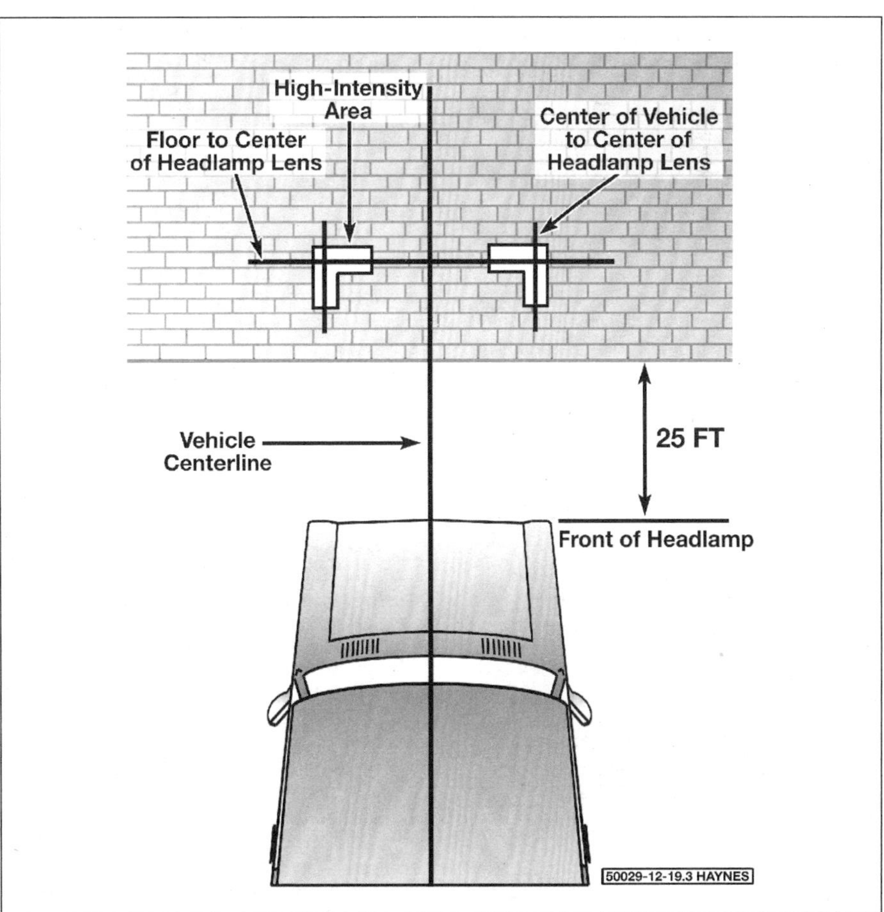

16.5 Headlight adjustment details

Bulb removal

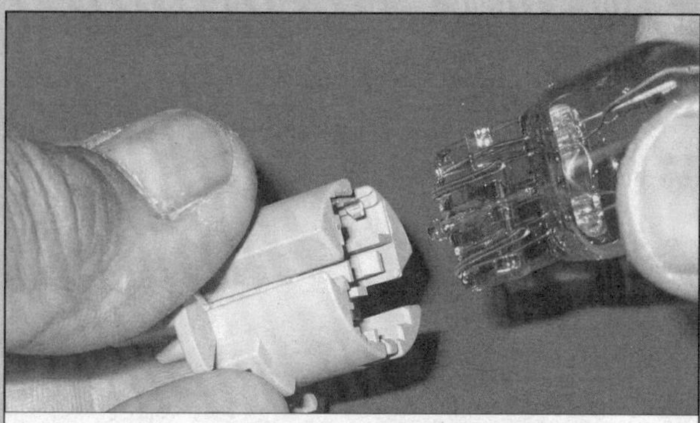
To remove many modern exterior bulbs from their holders, simply pull them out

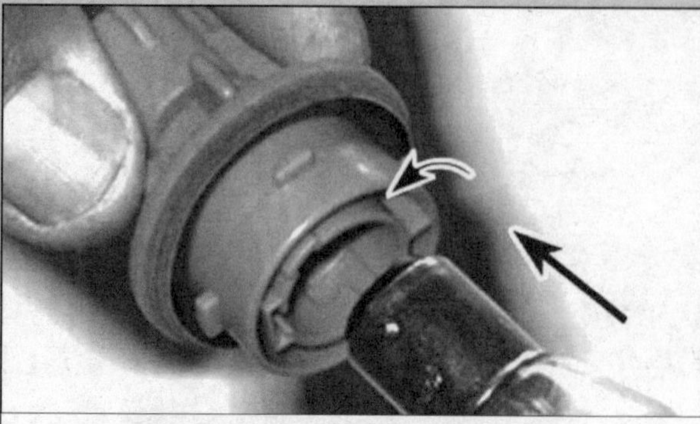
On bulbs with a cylindrical base ("bayonet" bulbs), the socket is spring-loaded; a pair of small posts on the side of the base hold the bulb in place against spring pressure. To remove this type of bulb, push it into the holder, rotate it 1/4-turn counterclockwise, then pull it out

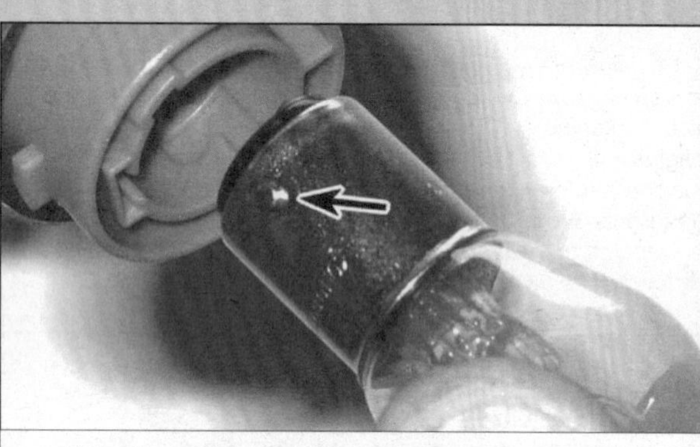
If a bayonet bulb has dual filaments, the posts are staggered, so the bulb can only be installed one way

To remove most overhead interior light bulbs, simply unclip them

7 With the high beams on, the high intensity zone should be vertically centered with the exact center just below the horizontal line. **Note:** *It may not be possible to position the headlight aim exactly for both high and low beams. If a compromise must be made, keep in mind that the low beams are the most used and have the greatest effect on safety.*

8 Have the headlights adjusted by a dealer service department or service station at the earliest opportunity.

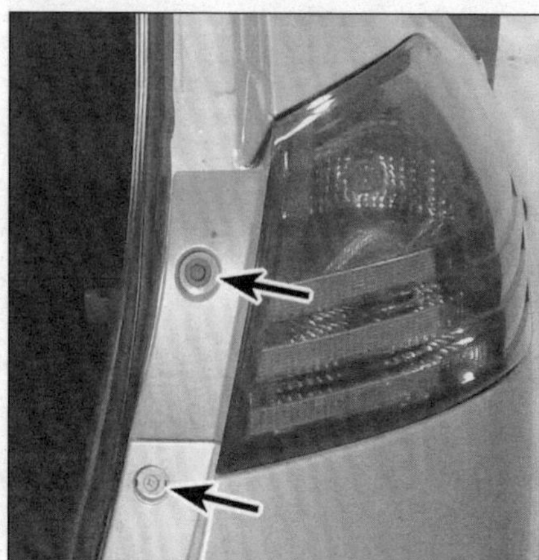
17.8 Remove the taillight housing bolts

17 Bulb replacement

Exterior lights

Front parking/turn signal and side marker lights

Note: *It is not necessary to remove the headlight housing to access these bulbs*

1 From the engine compartment, locate the bulb sockets in the headlight housing. If you're working on 2013 and earlier models, remove the air filter resonator for access to the left side bulbs.

2 Turn the bulb sockets counterclockwise and pull them out of the housing.

3 Remove the bulb from the bulb holder (see Bulb removal at the end of this Section).

4 Installation is the reverse of removal.

Rear turn signal/brake/tail/side marker lights

5 Open the liftgate.

6 On 2013 and earlier models/2014 and later Rogue Select models, remove the liftgate inner trim access panel(s) and reach into the access opening and disconnect the electrical connectors from taillight housing.

7 On 2014 and later non-Select models, remove the side spoiler bolts, then disengage the clips and remove the spoiler(s).

8 Remove the taillight housing assembly bolts (see illustration).

9 Pull the housing toward the rear of the vehicle and, on 2014 and later non-Select models, disconnect the electrical connectors from the taillight housing.

10 Turn the bulb holder counterclockwise to remove it from the housing (see illustration), then remove the bulb.

11 Installation is the reverse of removal.

Back-up lights

12 Open the liftgate.

13 Remove the liftgate trim panel (see Chapter 11).

17.10 Turn the bulb holder counterclockwise to remove it from the housing

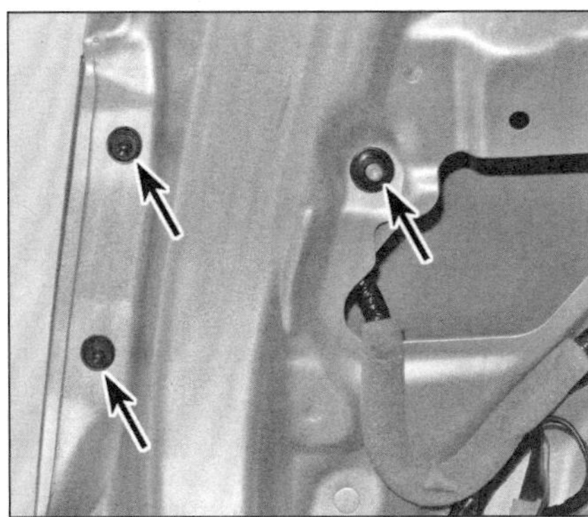
17.14 Back-up light housing fasteners

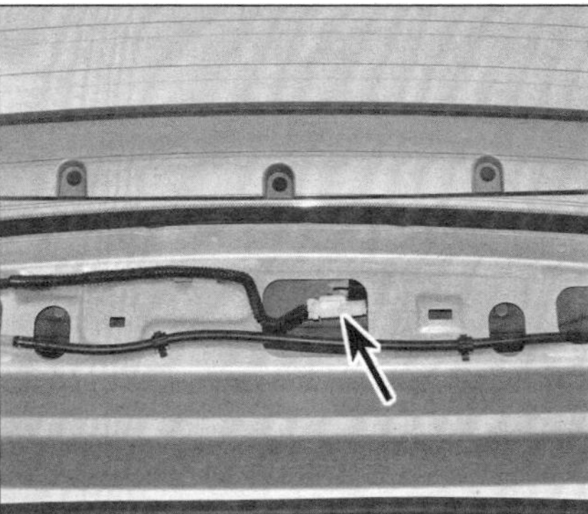
17.33 Disconnect the electrical connector from the high-mounted brake light

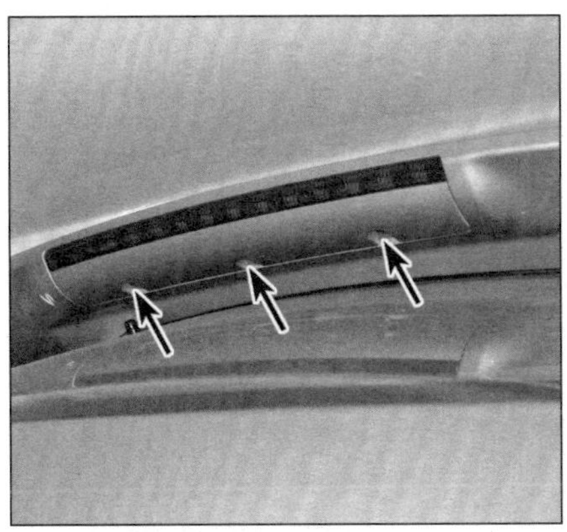
17.34 High-mounted brake light screws

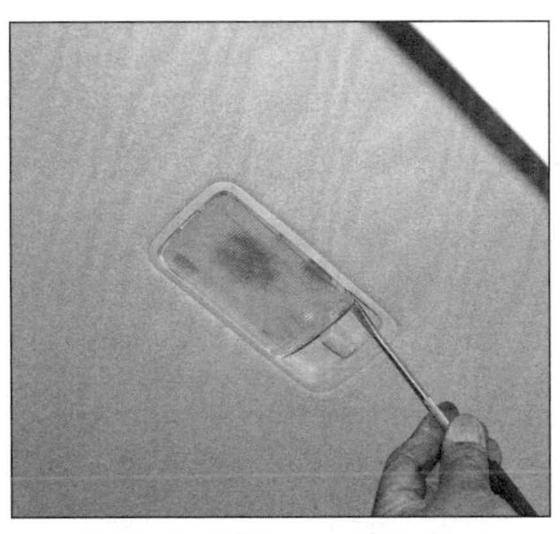
17.36a Carefully pry off the lens

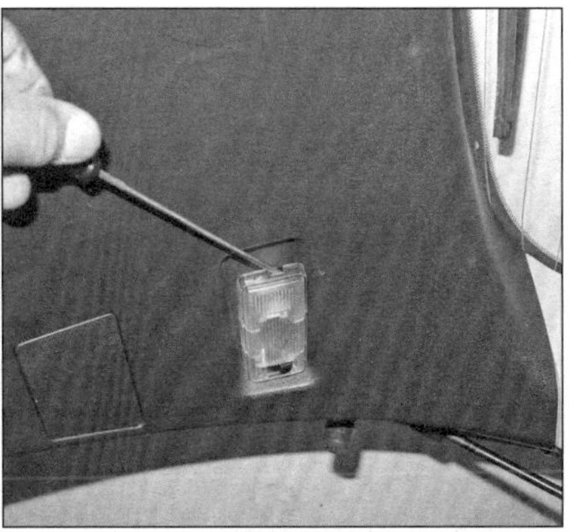
17.36b Release the tab, then pry off the rear liftgate light bulb lens

14 Remove the back-up light housing fasteners (see illustration).
15 Pull the housing toward the rear of the vehicle and disconnect the electrical connector to the back-up light housing.
16 Turn the bulb holder counterclockwise to remove it from the housing, then remove the bulb.
17 Installation is the reverse of removal.

Fog lights

Warning: *Wear eye protection and handle the bulbs carefully, grasping only the base whenever possible. Do not touch the surface of the bulb with your fingers because the oil from your skin could cause it to overheat and fail prematurely. If you do touch the bulb surface, clean it with rubbing alcohol.*

18 The fog lights are controlled by lighting switch inputs to the Body Control Module (BCM). The lighting switch must be in the 1st or 2nd position with the high beams Off before the BCM will request the Intelligent Power Distribution Module (IPDM) to turn the fog lights on. Do not try to bypass this system or internal failure of the BCM, IPDM, or the CPU could occur.

Bulb replacement

19 Remove the fasteners at the front of the inner fender splash shield (see Chapter 11) and reposition the shield for access to the bulb.
20 Disconnect the fog light electrical connector.
21 Turn the bulb holder counterclockwise and pull it out of the housing.
22 Installation is the reverse of removal.

Fog light aiming

23 Ensure all tires are inflated to the correct pressure. Set the vehicle on a level surface, with no load in vehicle other than the driver (or equivalent weight placed in driver's position), and with a full fuel tank.
24 Adjust aiming in the vertical direction by turning the adjusting screw, which is accessed from a small hole on the lower corner of the bumper.
25 Follow the aiming procedure in Section 16, but use these measurements:

- a) *Position a horizontal tape line level with the top of the fog lights.*
- b) *The highest intensity of the beam should fall 4 inches below the horizontal tape line.*

License plate light

26 Carefully pry out the license exterior trim panel from the liftgate.
27 On 2014 and later non-Select models, remove the license plate housing mounting screws.
28 Push the license plate light housing to the right while pulling the end of the housing outwards.
29 Disconnect the electrical connector.
30 Remove the bulb.
31 Installation is the reverse of removal.

High-mounted brake light assembly

Note: *The LEDs in the high-mounted brake light assembly are not separately replaceable. If one fails, replace the assembly.*

32 Open the liftgate and remove the liftgate trim panel (see Chapter 11).
33 Disconnect the electrical connector from the light (see illustration).
34 On 2013 and earlier models/2014 and later Rogue Select models, remove the screws securing the assembly to the spoiler and detach it (see illustration).
35 On 2014 and later non-Select models, the high-mount brake light fasteners are accessed from inside the liftgate.

Interior lights

36 All interior light bulbs are replaced in the same general way. Use a small screwdriver or trim tool to carefully pry off the lens (see illustrations).
37 Push the interior lamp metal tabs at each end and remove the bulb (see Bulb removal at the end of this Section).
38 Installation is the reverse of removal.

18.2 Horn bracket mounting bolt

19.3a Pry open the cap . . .

19.3b . . . then remove the wiper arm nut and mark the arm to the linkage so it can be installed in the correct position

19.7 Wiper assembly mounting bolts

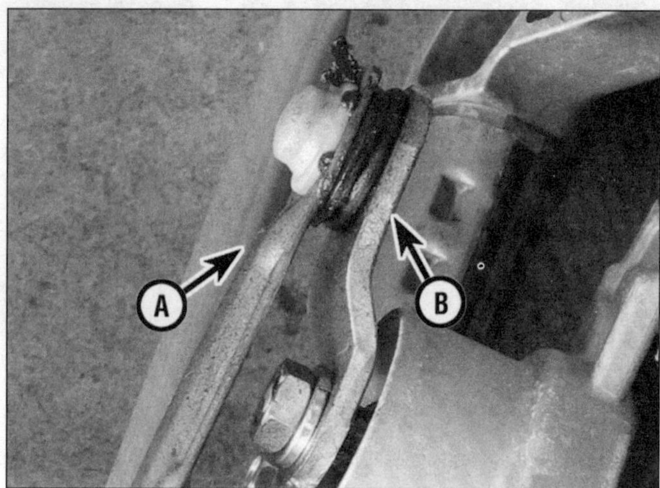

19.8 Pry off the drive arm (A), then remove the crank arm nut (B)

Instrument cluster illumination

39 Instrument cluster illumination is contained within the cluster. Replace the cluster (see Section 10) as a complete unit if there is a problem with any of its individual components.

Bulb removal

40 Typical bulb removal procedures:

18 Horn - replacement

1 On 2014 and earlier models, remove the front bumper cover (see Chapter 11)

2 On 2015 and later models, to remove the low-note horn, remove the grille (see Chapter 11). To remove the high-note horn, raise the front of the vehicle support it securely on jackstand, then remove the driver's side front corner inner fender splash shield fasteners and pull the shield back (see Chapter 11, Section 19).

3 Disconnect the horn electrical connector and remove the bracket bolt (see illustration). Remove the horn.

4 Installation is the reverse of removal.

19 Wiper motor - replacement

Front wiper motor

1 Mark the positions of the blades on the windshield with tape so they can be installed in the same alignment. If the motor has malfunctioned and the blades are not in the park position, mark the blades to their shafts after Step 3 is performed.

2 Disconnect cable from the negative terminal of the battery (see Chapter 5).

3 Pry off the wiper arm pivot caps, then remove the nuts (see illustrations).

4 Remove the wiper arms from the drive studs - lock the wiper arm and use its leverage to wiggle the arm from the stud.

5 Remove the cowl cover (see Chapter 11).

6 Disconnect the electrical connector from the wiper motor.

7 Remove the mounting bolts and remove the wiper motor and drive assembly (see illustration).

8 Pry the drive arm off the crank, then remove the crank nut and separate the crank from the shaft (see illustration).

9 Remove the screws and detach the motor from the drive assembly.

10 Installation is the reverse of removal. When installing the wiper motor assembly, turn it ON and then OFF to place the unit in the PARK position before attaching the wiper arms.

11 Reconnect the battery and perform the necessary re-learn procedures (see Chapter 5).

Rear wiper motor

12 Mark the position of the blade on the liftgate glass with tape so it can be installed in the same alignment.

13 Disconnect cable from the negative terminal of the battery (see Chapter 5).

14 Pull up the wiper arm pivot caps, then remove the nut (see illustration).

15 Remove the wiper arm from the drive stud - if necessary, lock the wiper arm and use its leverage to wiggle the arm from the stud.

16 Remove the liftgate trim panel (see Chapter 11).

19.14 Pry open the cap then remove the wiper arm nut

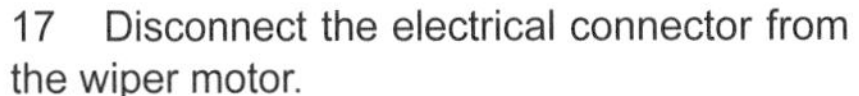

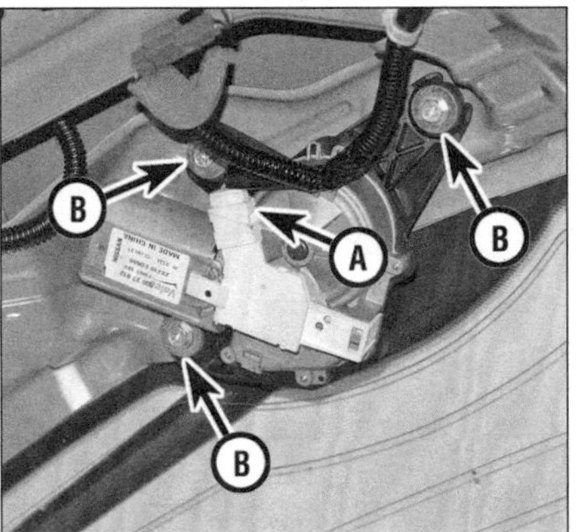

19.18 Disconnect the electrical connector (A) then remove the wiper motor mounting bolts (B)

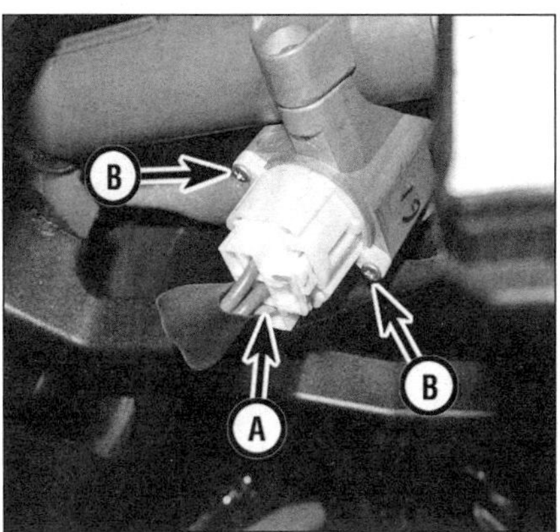

20.4 Depress the tab and disconnect the electrical connector (A) then remove the ignition switch retaining screws (B)

17 Disconnect the electrical connector from the wiper motor.
18 Remove the mounting bolts and remove the wiper motor (see illustration).
19 If necessary remove the pivot seal from the liftgate.
20 Installation is the reverse of removal.
21 Reconnect the battery and perform the necessary re-learn procedures (see Chapter 5).

20 Ignition switch and key lock cylinder

Warning: *The models covered by this manual are equipped with Supplemental Restraint Systems (SRS), more commonly known as airbags. Always disable the airbag system before working in the vicinity of any airbag system components to avoid the possibility of accidental deployment of the airbags, which could cause personal injury (see Section 27).*
1 Disconnect the cable from the negative terminal of the battery (see Chapter 5).

Ignition switch

2 Remove the steering column covers (see Chapter 11).
3 Disconnect the electrical connector from the ignition switch.
4 Remove the screws and pull the switch from the lock cylinder housing (see illustration).
5 Before installing the new switch, make sure the hub of the switch is aligned with the blade on the ignition lock cylinder.
6 The remainder of installation is the reverse of removal. Reconnect the battery and perform the necessary re-learn procedures (see Chapter 5).

Ignition lock cylinder housing

7 Remove the ignition switch (see Steps 1 through 3).
8 Detach the shift interlock cable from the lock cylinder housing (see Chapter 7).
9 Remove the shear-head bolts and detach the lock cylinder from the steering column (see illustration).
10 Installation is the reverse of removal. Tighten the new shear-head bolts until the heads break off.
11 Reconnect the battery and perform the necessary re-learn procedures (see Chapter 5).

Push-button ignition switch

12 Remove the heating and air conditioning control assembly (see Chapter 3).
13 Using a plastic trim tool, disengage the clips on the side panel and remove the side panel from the instrument panel.
14 With the panel removed, disconnect the electrical connector from the push-button ignition switch.
15 Use a small screwdriver to disengage the clips on the NATS antenna amp and pull the switch out of the NATS antenna amp ring
Note: *To remove the NATS antenna amp ring from the panel, depress the two locking tabs and pull the ring off from the front side of the panel.*
16 Installation is the reverse of removal.

21 Cruise control system - description and check

1 All models have an electronically controlled throttle body - there is no accelerator cable (or cruise control cable). When you select the speed that you want to maintain, the PCM controls vehicle speed by opening and closing the throttle plate by means of a computer-controlled solenoid (motor) inside the throttle body.
2 The diagnostic procedures for troubleshooting the cruise control system are beyond the scope of this manual, but if the system can't be set, or the set speed doesn't cancel when the brake pedal is depressed, check the fuses. Start with the fuses in the engine compartment fuse and relay box, then check the fuses in the under-dash fuse and relay box. If the set speed doesn't cancel when the CANCEL button is depressed, check the fuse for that circuit. Also check the operation and adjustment of the brake light switch, ASCD switch or brake pedal position sensor (see Chapter 9).

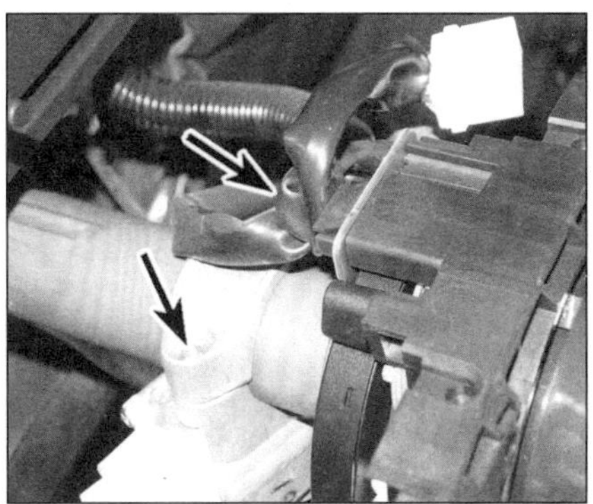

20.9 Drill through the center of the shear-head bolts and use a screw extractor to unscrew them

22 Power window system - general information

1 The power window system operates electric motors, mounted on the doors, which lower and raise the windows. The system consists of the control switches, the motors, regulators, glass mechanisms, the Body Control Module (BCM) and associated wiring.
2 The power windows can be lowered and raised from the master control switch by the driver or by the switch located at the passenger window. Each window has a separate motor that is reversible. The position of the control switch determines the polarity and therefore the direction of operation.
3 The circuit is protected by fuses and a circuit breaker. Check the fuses in the fuse panel. There is a motor for each window in each door. Each motor is equipped with an internal circuit breaker; this prevents one stuck window from disabling the whole system. Refer to the wiring diagrams at the end of this Chapter. Problems within this system can only be diagnosed with a factory scan tool. If you have eliminated the obvious causes of a problem, have the vehicle checked at a dealership service department or other properly equipped repair shop.

24.6 The keyless entry receiver module is located on a bracket behind the glove box

23 Power door lock system - general information

1 The power door lock system operates the power door motors, which are integral components of the door latch units in each door. The system consists of a fuse (in the engine compartment fuse and relay box), the Body Control Module (BCM), the control switches (in each of the front doors), the power door motors and the electrical wiring harnesses connecting all of these components.

2 The lock mechanisms in the door latch units are actuated by a reversible electric motor in each door. When you push the door lock switch to LOCK, the motor operates one way and locks the latch mechanism. When you push the door lock switch the other way, to the UNLOCK position, the motor operates in the other direction, unlocking the latch mechanism. Because the motors and lock mechanisms are an integral part of the door latch units, they cannot be repaired. If a door lock motor or lock mechanism fails, replace the door latch unit (see Chapter 11).

3 Some vehicles have an optional Intelligent Key system that allows you to lock and unlock the doors from outside the vehicle. The intelligent key system consists of the transmitter (the electronic push-button "key") and a remote keyless entry receiver mounted behind the glove box.

4 Some features of the door lock system on these vehicles rely on resources that they share with other electronic modules through the Programmable Communications Interface (PCI) data bus network. Professional diagnosis of these modules and the PCI data bus network requires the use of a CONSULT-III (proprietary factory) scan tool and factory diagnostic information. At-home repairs are therefore limited to inspecting the wiring for bad connections and for minor faults that can be easily repaired. If you are unable to locate the trouble using the following general steps, consult your dealer service department.

5 Always check the circuit fuses first. Refer to the wiring diagrams at the end of this Chapter. Problems within this system can only be diagnosed with a factory scan tool. If you have eliminated the obvious causes of a problem, have the vehicle checked at a dealership service department or other properly equipped repair shop.

Note: *It is not uncommon for wires to break in the harness between the body and the door because repeatedly opening and closing the door fatigues and eventually breaks the wires.*

24 Remote keyless entry system

Description

1 Remote keyless entry is a radio frequency signal sent from a matching key fob to the Body Control Module (BCM). The keyless entry system allows the driver to control interior lights illumination, the horn and the trunk release with the key fob.

2 Up to five key fob ID codes can be stored in one vehicle. Each key fob has to be registered to the vehicle with a scanner. See a dealer repair center, locksmith, or qualified independent repair facility for replacement of the key fobs or diagnostic work for the keyless entry system.

3 When the BCM receives a LOCK signal from the key fob, the BCM locks all the doors. When the BCM receives an UNLOCK signal from the key fob, the BCM unlocks the driver's door first; a second UNLOCK signal from key fob unlocks the remaining doors. Repair procedures require the use of a scanner and schematics. No coverage is offered in this manual for any of the diagnostic procedures.

Module (receiver) replacement

4 Disconnect the cable from the negative terminal of the battery (see Chapter 5).

5 Remove the glove box (see Chapter 11).

6 Remove the mounting screw and remove the remote keyless entry receiver (see illustration).

7 Installation is in the reverse of removal. Programming by a dealer service department is required.

25 Intelligent key system

1 The Intelligent Key system makes it possible to lock and unlock the door locks, open the trunk, and start the engine by carrying around the Intelligent Key. It operates based on the results of electronic ID verification using two-way communications between the Intelligent Key and the vehicle.

2 The system uses an outside antenna to detect the presence of the matching intelligent key in the range of approximately 2.5 feet surrounding the driver and passenger door handles.

3 This function can operate when the Intelligent Key is inside the vehicle. However, there may be times when the Intelligent Key cannot be detected, and will not operate when the Intelligent Key is on the instrument panel, rear parcel shelf, or in the glove box. Also, sometimes it will not operate if the Intelligent Key is in the door pocket of an open door.

4 The Intelligent key battery is replaced the same way as the key fob battery (see Section 7). Before replacing the battery it's always a good idea to have the strength of the battery checked to avoid replacing a good battery if the problem is actually with another part of the system. This can be done at most repair shops that have the necessary equipment, such as a TPM sensor tester. Most quality tire shops and independent repair facilities will have these scanners.

5 When doors are locked or unlocked the Intelligent Key unit sends a signal to BCM via CAN communication line to flash the hazard warning lamps as a reminder. It also sends a chirp signal to the Intelligent Key warning buzzer (front of vehicle) as a reminder.

6 Some functions of the hazard/horn reminder and the auto lock features can be modified. These procedures are in the owners manual of the vehicle if they are available for your car.

7 The Intelligent Key has the same functions as the remote control entry system. Therefore, it can be used in the same manner as the keyfob by operating the door lock/ unlock button and trunk open button.

26 Sunroof - general information, removal and installation

General information

1 The sunroof is powered by a single motor located in the roof.

2 The sunroof switch (tilt and slide) sends an operation signal to the sunroof motor CPU encoder when the switches are pressed. Power is supplied to the motor from the Body Control Module (BCM) located under the instrument panel. The front door switch detects the open/close condition and sends an operating signal to the BCM. The sunroof will retain power for 45 seconds after the

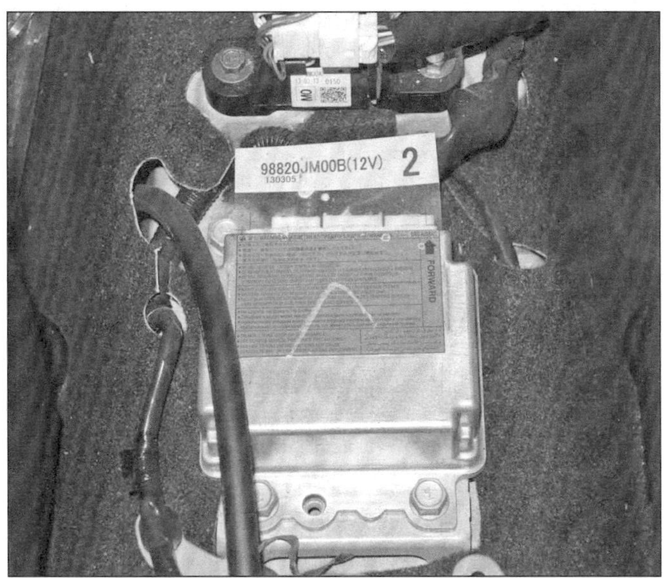

27.3a The airbag diagnosis/sensor unit is mounted under the center console

27.3b The front crash zone sensor is mounted on the radiator support

key has been turned off to operate the system. The retained power can be cancelled by opening the front door, turning the ignition switch to ON again or allowing the 45 seconds to elapse.

3 With the ignition On but the engine Off, operate the sunroof control switch through the tilt and slide functions.

4 Listen carefully for the sound of the motor running.

5 If the motor can be heard but the sunroof glass doesn't move, there's probably a problem with the drive mechanism.

6 If the sunroof does not operate and no sound comes from the motor, check the fuses (in the interior fuse panel and in the engine compartment power distribution center).

7 If there's voltage at the switch, disconnect it. Check the switch for continuity in all its operating positions. If the switch does not have continuity, replace it. If you have eliminated the obvious causes of a problem, have the vehicle checked at a dealership service department or other properly equipped repair shop.

Removal and installation

Sunroof

8 Sunroof removal is beyond the scope of this manual. See a qualified repair facility if any repairs are needed on the sunroof tracks or glass.

Motor assembly

9 Close the sunroof fully.

10 Remove the headliner.

11 Remove the sunroof motor assembly screws and disconnect the wiring harness.

12 Remove the motor assembly by pulling it down.

13 Installation is the reverse of removal.

27 Airbag system - general information

1 These models are equipped with a Supplemental Restraint System (SRS), more commonly known as airbags, designed to protect the driver and the passenger from serious injury in the event of a head-on collision. Some models are also equipped with side impact airbags in the front seats and along the roof rail. All models have a diagnostic control unit, located on the floor under the center console.

Warning: *If your vehicle is ever involved in a flood, or the interior carpeting is soaked for any reason, disconnect the battery and do not start the vehicle until the airbag system can be checked by a dealer service department or other repair facility equipped with the proper tool. If the SRS system is subjected to flooding, the airbags could go off upon starting the vehicle, even without an accident taking place.*

Airbag modules

2 The airbag modules consist of a housing incorporating the cushion (airbag) and inflator unit. The inflator assembly is mounted on the back of the housing over a hole through which gas is expelled, inflating the bag almost instantaneously when an electrical signal is sent from the system. The specially wound wire on the driver's side that carries this signal to the module is called a spiral cable. The spiral cable is a flat, ribbon-like electrically conductive tape that is wound many times so that it can transmit an electrical signal regardless of steering wheel position. Airbag modules are located in the steering wheel, on the passenger's side above the glove box and, on some models, in the seat backs and along the roof rails (side curtain airbags).

Control unit and sensors

3 The diagnosis/sensor unit contains an on-board microprocessor which monitors the operation of the system, and also contains a crash sensor. It checks this system every time the vehicle is started, causing the "AIRBAG" light to go on then off, if the system is operating properly. If there is a fault in the system, the light will go on and stay on and the unit will store fault codes indicating the nature of the fault. If the AIRBAG light goes on and stays on, the vehicle should be taken to your dealer immediately for service. The diagnosis/sensor unit is located under the center console (see illustration). The crash zone sensor is located on the radiator support (see illustration), and the side airbag sensors (satellite crash sensor) are in each door "B" pillar.

Operation

4 For the airbag(s) to deploy, the impact sensor(s) must be activated. When this condition occurs, the circuit to the airbag inflator is closed and the airbag inflates.

Self-diagnosis system

5 A self-diagnosis circuit in the SRS unit displays a light on the instrument panel when the ignition switch is turned to the On position. If the system is operating normally, the light should go out after about five seconds. If the light doesn't come on, or doesn't go out after a short time, or if it comes on while you're driving the vehicle, or if it blinks at any time, there's a malfunction in the SRS system. Have it inspected and repaired as soon as possible. Do not attempt to troubleshoot or service the SRS system yourself. Even a small mistake could cause the SRS system to malfunction when you need it.

Servicing components near the SRS system

6 If you will be working around components and wire harnesses for the SRS system, you must disable the system before beginning any work.

Warning: *Do not use electrical test equipment on airbag system wires; it could cause the airbag(s) to deploy.ALWAYS DISABLE THE SRS SYSTEM BEFORE WORKING NEAR THE SRS SYSTEM COMPONENTS OR RELATED WIRING.*

Disabling the SRS system

Warning: *Any time you are working in the vicinity of airbag wiring or components, DISABLE THE SRS SYSTEM.*

Warning: *An auxiliary voltage input device (memory saver) must not be used when working near airbag system components.*

7 To disable the airbag system, perform the following steps:

a) *Turn the steering wheel to the straight-ahead position and turn the ignition switch to the LOCK position, then remove the key.*
b) *Disconnect the battery negative and positive cables, then wait ten minutes before proceeding with any work.*
c) *Before touching any airbag system component, ground yourself to a metal part of the vehicle to discharge any static electricity built up in your body.*

Enabling the system

8 After you've disabled the airbag and performed the necessary service, reconnect the two-pin airbag connector into the two-pin spiral cable connector (driver's side), the SRS main harness (passenger's side) or the side-impact airbag. Reinstall the lid to the underside of the steering wheel or reinstall the glove box/trim panel or upper trim panels.

9 To enable the airbag system, perform the following steps:

a) *Turn the ignition switch to the On position.*
b) *Make sure nobody is inside the vehicle.*
c) *Make sure the ignition is in the Off position, then connect the battery cables (positive first, negative last).*
d) *With your body out of the path of the airbag(s), turn the ignition switch to the*
e) *On position. Confirm that the airbag warning light is functioning properly.*
f) *Perform the necessary re-learn procedures (see Chapter 5).*
g) *Take the vehicle to a dealer service department or other qualified repair facility and have the airbag system checked and the warning light canceled if it remains lit.*

Removal and installation

Warning: *The bolts used throughout the airbag system to mount the airbag modules, diagnosis sensor unit, crash zone sensor and satellite sensors have a special coating. These bolts are designed to be used once. Replace them with new factory bolts, and never use a substitute fastener.*

Driver's side airbag and spiral cable

10 Refer to Chapter 10, Section 15 for removal and installation of the driver's side airbag and steering wheel (which will give you access to the spiral cable).

Warning: *When installing the spiral cable, be sure to follow the centering instructions carefully.*

Passenger's side airbag and other airbag modules

11 Even if you remove the instrument panel, it's not necessary to remove the passenger's airbag module to do so; it can simply remain installed in the instrument panel. We don't recommend removing any of the other airbag modules either. These jobs are best left to a professional.

Impact seat belt retractors

12 All models are equipped with pyrotechnic (explosive) units in the front seat belt retracting mechanisms for both the lap and shoulder belts. During an impact that would trigger the airbag system, the airbag control unit also triggers the seat belt retractors. When the pyrotechnic charges go off, they accelerate the retractors to instantly take up any slack in the seat belt system to more fully prepare the driver and front seat passenger for impact. The airbag system should be disabled any time work is done to or around the seats.

Warning: *Never strike the pillars or floor pan with a hammer or use an impact-driver tool in these areas unless the system is disabled.*

28 Intelligent Power Distribution Module Engine Room (IPDM E/R) - description, check and replacement

Description

1 The Intelligent Power Distribution Module Engine Room (IPDM E/R) is a solid state device that controls various relays and circuits when commands are received from the Powertrain Control Module (PCM) and/or the Body Control Module (BCM). The circuits under its control are:

Headlights
Parking and side marker lights
Taillights/license plate lights
Fog lights
Windshield wipers
Electronic steering column lock
Air conditioning compressor clutch
Starter relay
Fuel pump relay
Cooling fan relay
Horn relay
Rear window defogger relay

Check

2 The IPDM E/R integrates the relay box and fuse block in the engine compartment fuse block.

3 Although the IPDM E/R is usually very reliable, but it must always be factored in to any diagnosis of the circuits under its control. Thorough testing of the unit requires a proprietary Nissan scan tool, but a simple test, called the Auto Active Test, can help you determine the possible source of a problem with some of the circuits under its control. The circuits checked in this test include the:

Windshield wiper circuit
Tail/parking/license plate light circuits
Fog light circuit
Headlight circuit
Air conditioning compressor clutch circuit
Engine cooling fan circuit
Oil pressure warning light
Starter control
Horn control
Daytime Running Lights (DRL) (Canada Only)
Rear window defogger relay

Auto active test

4 In auto active test mode, then IPDM E/R sends a drive signal to the following systems: rear window defogger, front wipers, tail/license/parking lights, DRL (Canada only), fog lights (if equipped), headlights (High and Low beams), A/C compressor, and the cooling fan.

Warning: *Check all fuses and grounds prior to performing the test.*

5 Lift the windshield wipers from the windshield and close the right front door and hood. Make sure the ignition switch is in the Off position.

6 To initiate the Auto Active Test, turn the ignition switch to the On position and depress the left front door switch 20 times within 20 seconds, then turn the ignition switch to the Off position.

7 Within 10 seconds, turn the ignition switch back to the On position. The horn should beep once, signifying the start of the test.

8 When the test begins, the following sequence of events should happen (and the sequence of events should repeat three times):

a) *The oil pressure light should blink continuously for the duration of the test.*
b) *The windshield wiper should operate on low speed for 5 seconds, then high speed for 5 seconds*
c) *The parking/tail/license plate/fog lights should come on for 10 seconds*
d) *The headlights should turn on and switch from low-beam to high-beam five times*
e) *The air conditioning compressor clutch should engage (click on and off) 5 times*
f) *The engine cooling fan should come on for 10 seconds (mid-speed for five seconds, high-speed for five seconds)*

Diagnosis

Wipers, parking lights/daytime running lights/tail lights/license plate lights/fog lights

9 If any of these systems do not operate during the Auto Active Test, the problem could be caused by:

a) *Wiper motor or the circuit between the IPDM E/R and wiper motor faulty*
b) *Wiper motor ground problem*
c) *Light bulb or the circuit between IPDM E/R and light faulty*
d) *Light bulb/housing ground problem*
e) *Faulty IPDM E/R*

10 If the system in question does operate during the Auto Active Test but doesn't operate under normal conditions, the problem could be a faulty switch, a faulty Body Control Module (BCM), or the circuit between the two.

Air conditioning compressor clutch

11 If the compressor clutch doesn't operate during the Auto Active Test, the problem could be caused by:

a) *Compressor clutch or the circuit between the IPDM E/R and compressor clutch faulty*
b) *Faulty IPDM E/R*

12 If the compressor clutch does operate during the Auto Active Test but doesn't operate under normal conditions, the problem could be a faulty switch, a faulty Body Control Module (BCM), a faulty PCM, a fault in the circuit between the PCM and the BCM, or a fault in the circuit between the PCM and the IPDM.

Electric engine cooling fan

13 If the engine cooling fan doesn't operate during the Auto Active Test, the problem could be caused by:

a) *Cooling fan motor or the circuit between the cooling fan motor and the IPDM E/R faulty*
b) *Faulty IPDME/R*

28.20 Intelligent Power Distribution Module Engine Room (IPDM E/R)

14 If the engine cooling fan does operate during the Auto Active Test but doesn't operate under normal conditions, the problem could be a faulty PCM, a faulty coolant temperature sensor, the circuit between the coolant temperature sensor and the PCM, or the circuit between the PCM and the IPDM.

Oil pressure warning light

15 If the oil pressure warning light doesn't blink during the Auto Active Test, the problem could be caused by:

a) *Problem in the CAN communication circuit between the BCM and the IPDM E/R*
b) *Problem in the CAN communication circuit between the BCM and the instrument cluster*
c) *Faulty instrument cluster*

16 If the oil pressure warning light does blink during the Auto Active Test but doesn't operate when it should (during the bulb check when the ignition is turned On), the problem could be a faulty oil pressure sending unit, a faulty IPDM, or the circuit between the two.

Replacement

Note: *The IPDM E/R is located under the hood next to the battery. Replacing the IPDM E/R requires programming which is not covered in this manual. See a dealer service department or other qualified repair shop for service.*

17 The IPDM E/R can be removed and reinstalled if access to other parts is needed. It cannot be replaced without being programmed.

18 Disconnect the cable from the negative terminal of the battery (see Chapter 5).

19 Remove the cover from the IPDM E/R.

20 Free the IPDM from its release tabs (see illustration), pull the IPDM up and disconnect the electrical connectors, then remove it from the vehicle.

21 Installation is the reverse of removal.

29 Wiring diagrams - general information

1 Since it isn't possible to include all wiring diagrams for every year covered by this manual, the following diagrams are those that are typical and most commonly needed.

2 Prior to troubleshooting any circuits, check the fuse and circuit breakers (if equipped) to make sure they're in good condition. Make sure the battery is properly charged and check the cable connections (see Chapter 1).

3 When checking a circuit, make sure that all connectors are clean, with no broken or loose terminals. When unplugging a connector, do not pull on the wires. Pull only on the connector housings.

Wiring Diagrams List

1. Starting and charging systems
2. Air conditioning and heating systems
3. Engine cooling fan system
4. Power window system
5. Power door lock system (without intelligent key)
6. Power door lock system (with intelligent key)
7. Wiper and washer systems
8. Exterior lighting system (daytime running lights/brake lights)
9. Exterior lighting system (turn signal/hazard warning/back-up lights/headlight aiming motors)
10. Headlight system
11. Interior lighting system
12. Audio system (Bose, satellite radio and telephone adapter) - 2013 and earlier models/2014 and later Rogue Select models
13. Audio system (Bose, amplifier unit) - 2013 and earlier models/2014 and later Rogue Select models
14. Audio system (base) - 2013 and earlier models/2014 and later Rogue Select model
15. Audio system (base) - 2014 and earlier models (except Rogue Select)
16. Audio system (display unit) - 2014 and later models (except Rogue Select)
17. Fuel pump circuit

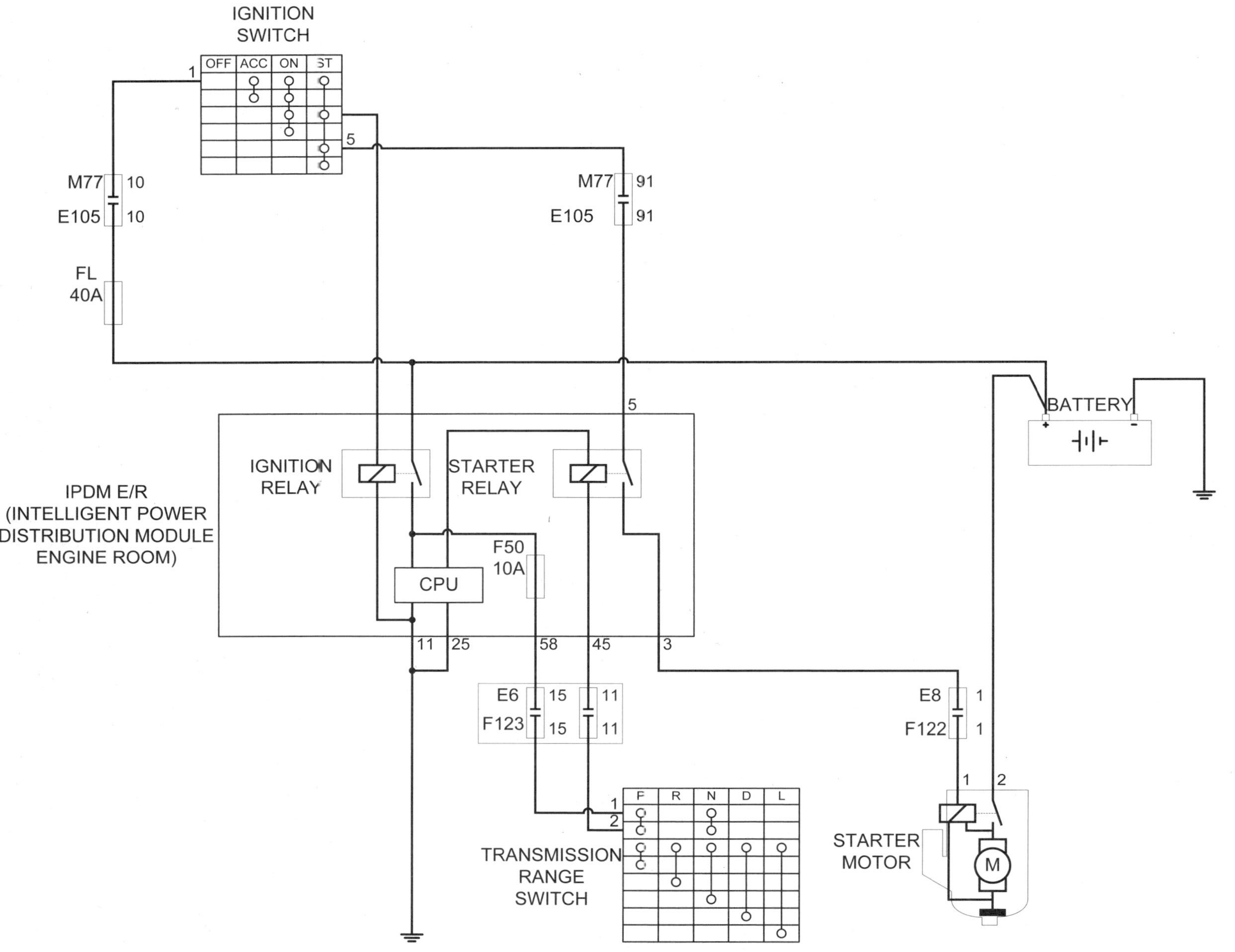

1. Starting and charging systems

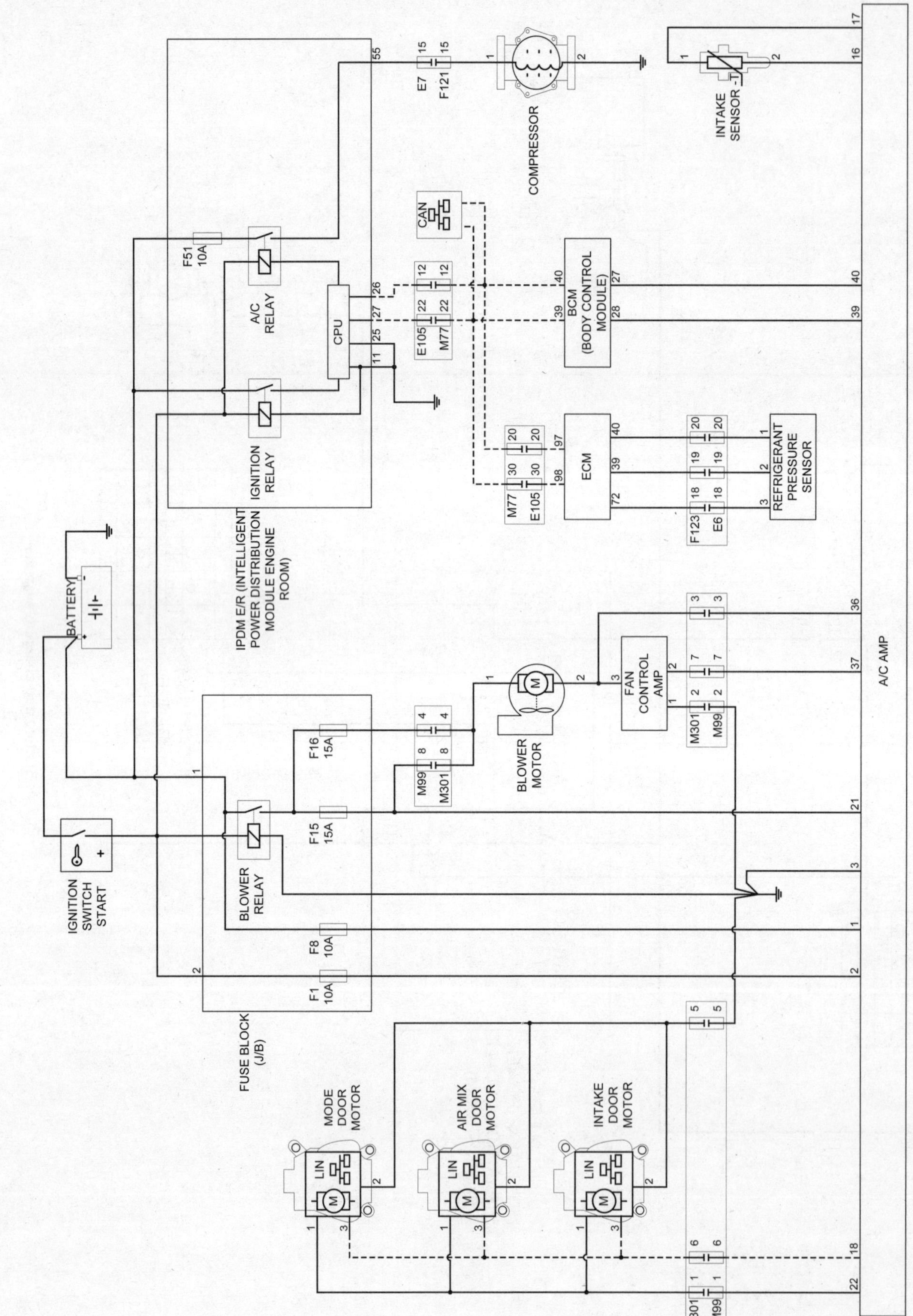

2. Air conditioning and heating systems

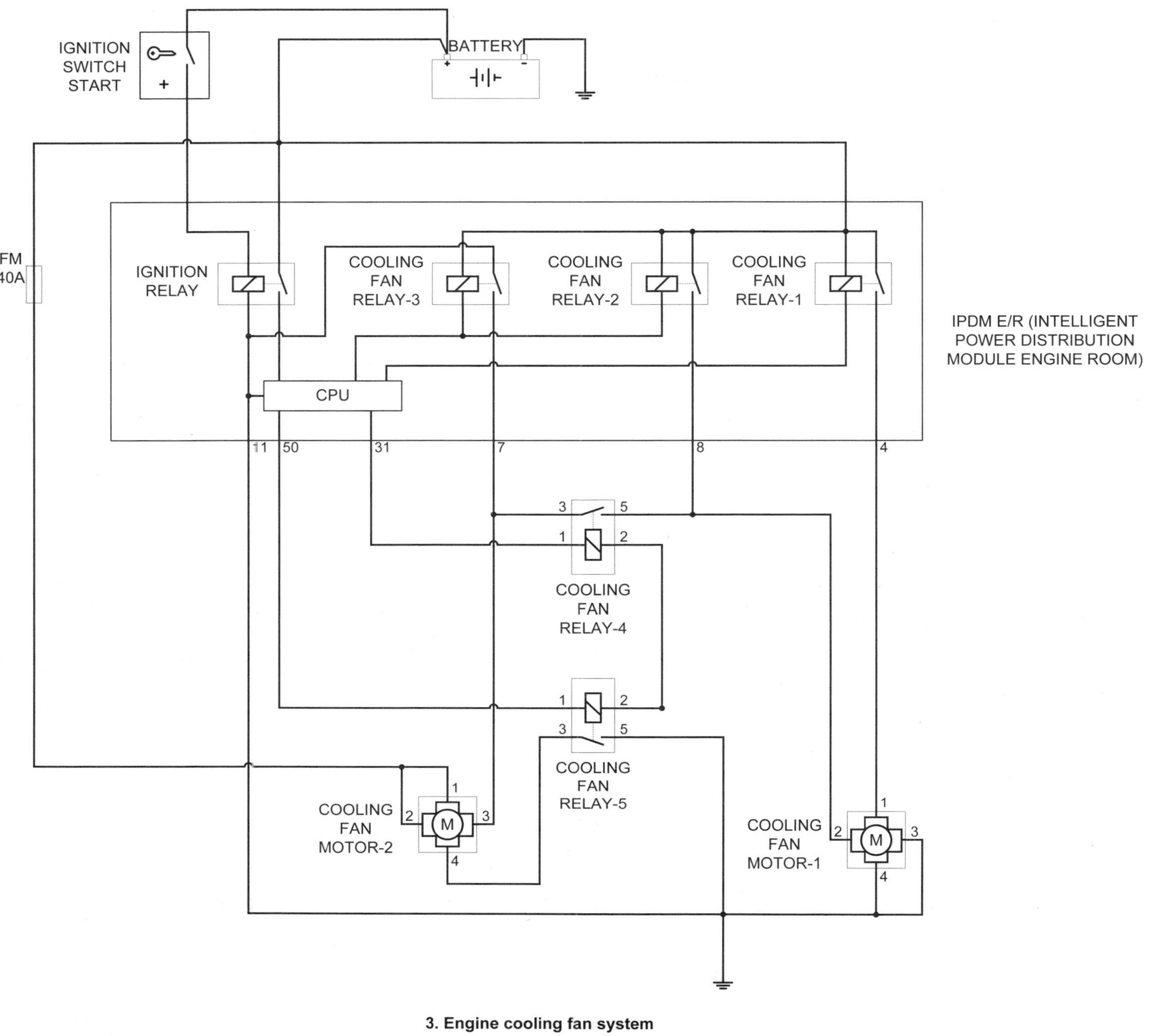

3. Engine cooling fan system

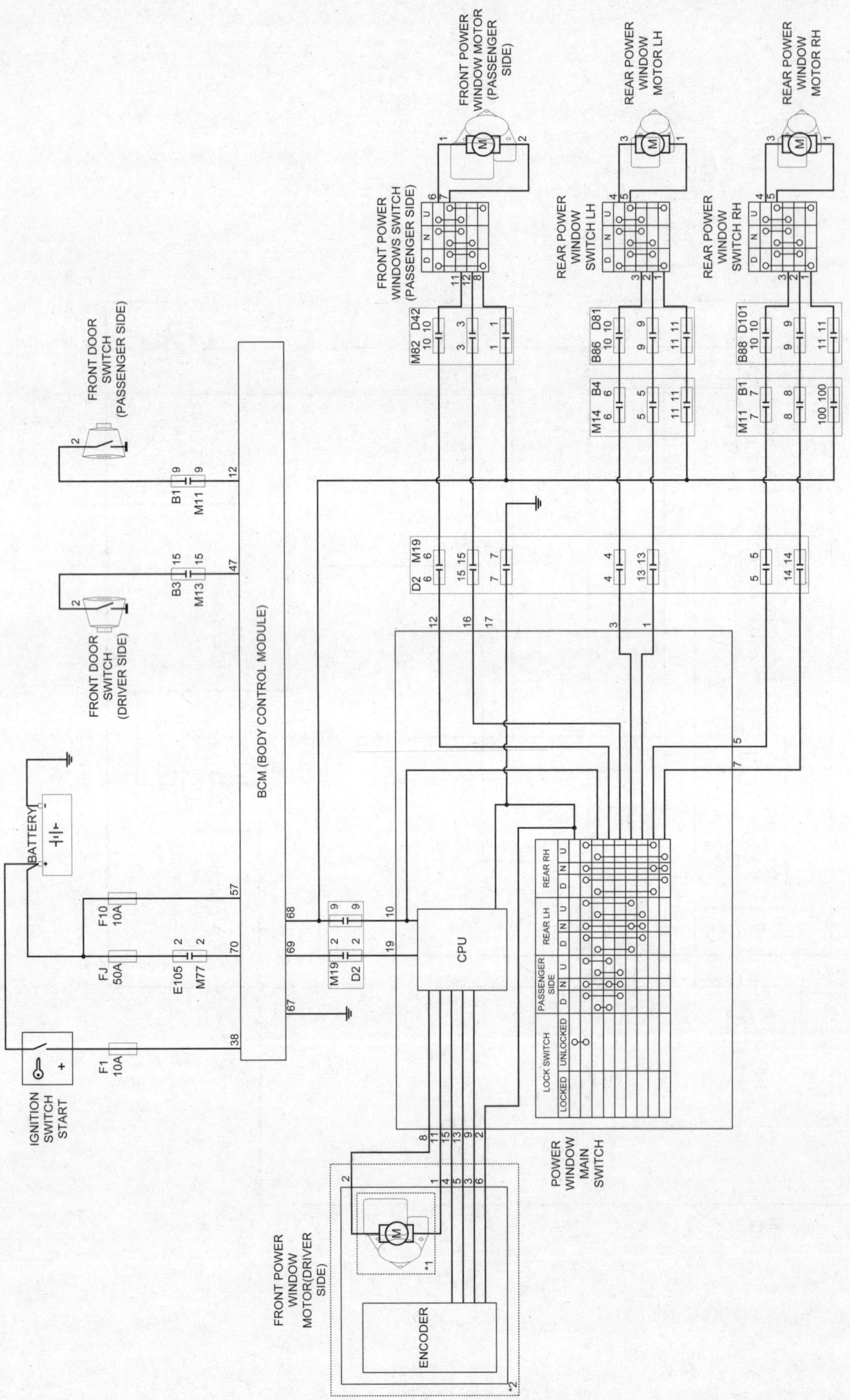

IGNITION SWITCH START

BATTERY

F1 10A

FJ 50A

F10 10A

E105 M77

FRONT DOOR SWITCH (DRIVER SIDE)

FRONT DOOR SWITCH (PASSENGER SIDE)

BCM (BODY CONTROL MODULE)

CPU

POWER WINDOW MAIN SWITCH

LOCK SWITCH: LOCKED, UNLOCKED

PASSENGER SIDE: D N U

REAR LH: D N U

REAR RH: D N U

FRONT POWER WINDOW MOTOR(DRIVER SIDE)

ENCODER

FRONT POWER WINDOWS SWITCH (PASSENGER SIDE)

FRONT POWER WINDOW MOTOR (PASSENGER SIDE)

REAR POWER WINDOW SWITCH LH

REAR POWER WINDOW MOTOR LH

REAR POWER WINDOW SWITCH RH

REAR POWER WINDOW MOTOR RH

*1 Without power window anti-pinch system

*2 With power window anti-pinch system

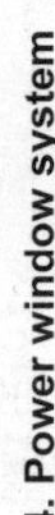

4. Power window system

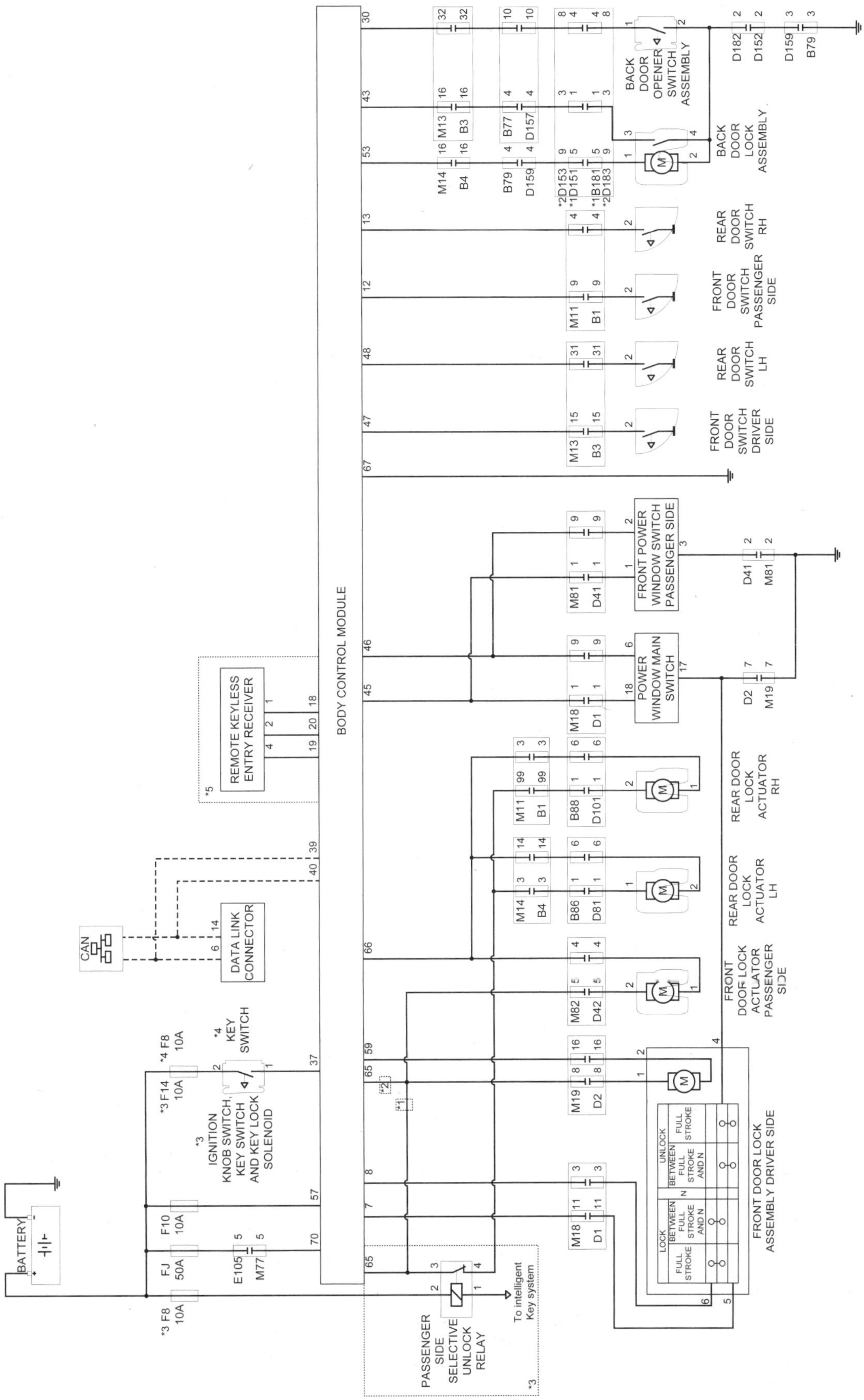

5. Power door lock system (without intelligent key)

*1 Up to 2013
*2 As of 2014
*3 For vehicles with intelligent key
*4 For vehicles without intelligent key
*5 For vehicles with remote keyless entry control system

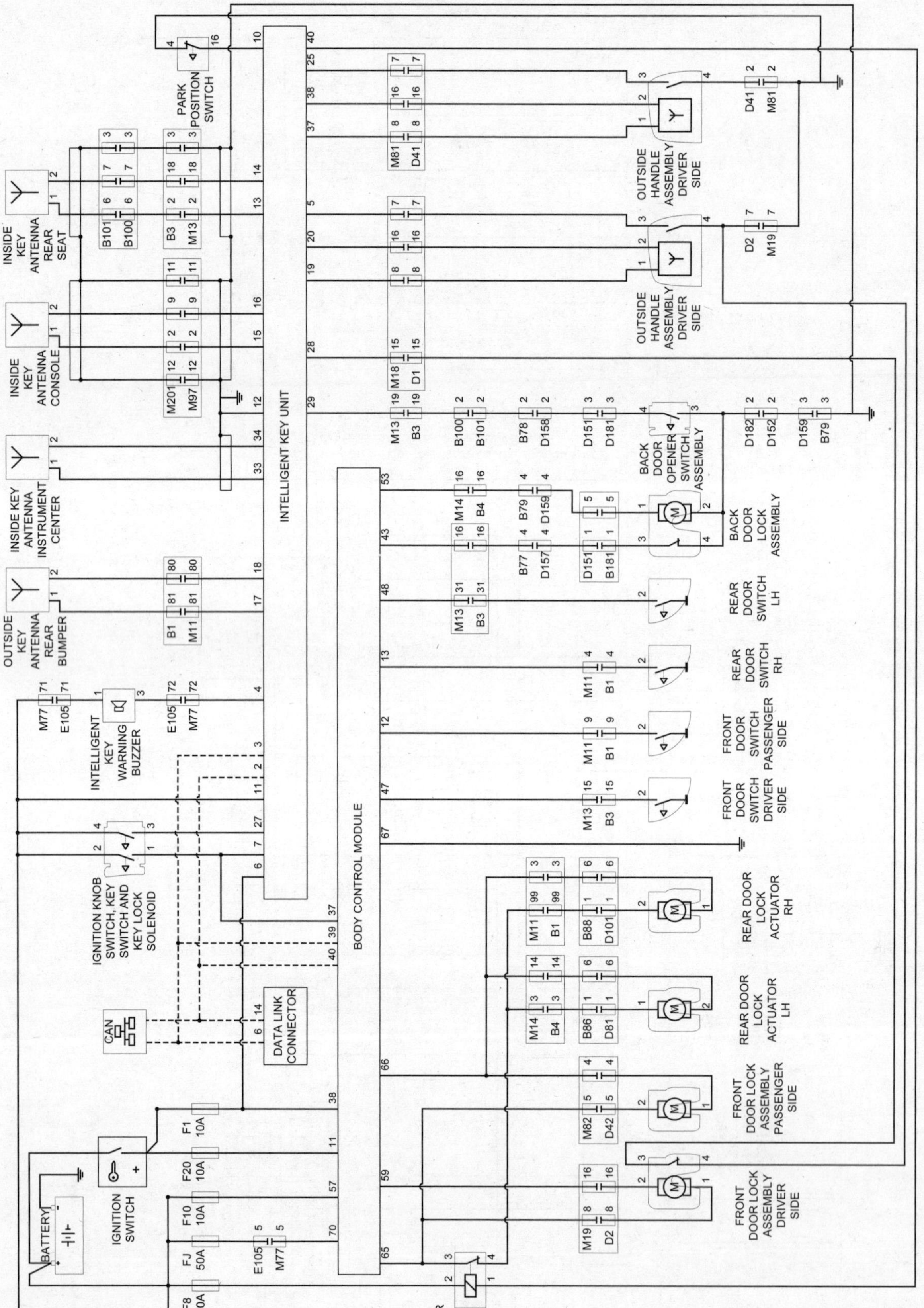

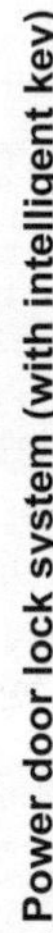

6. Power door lock system (with intelligent key)

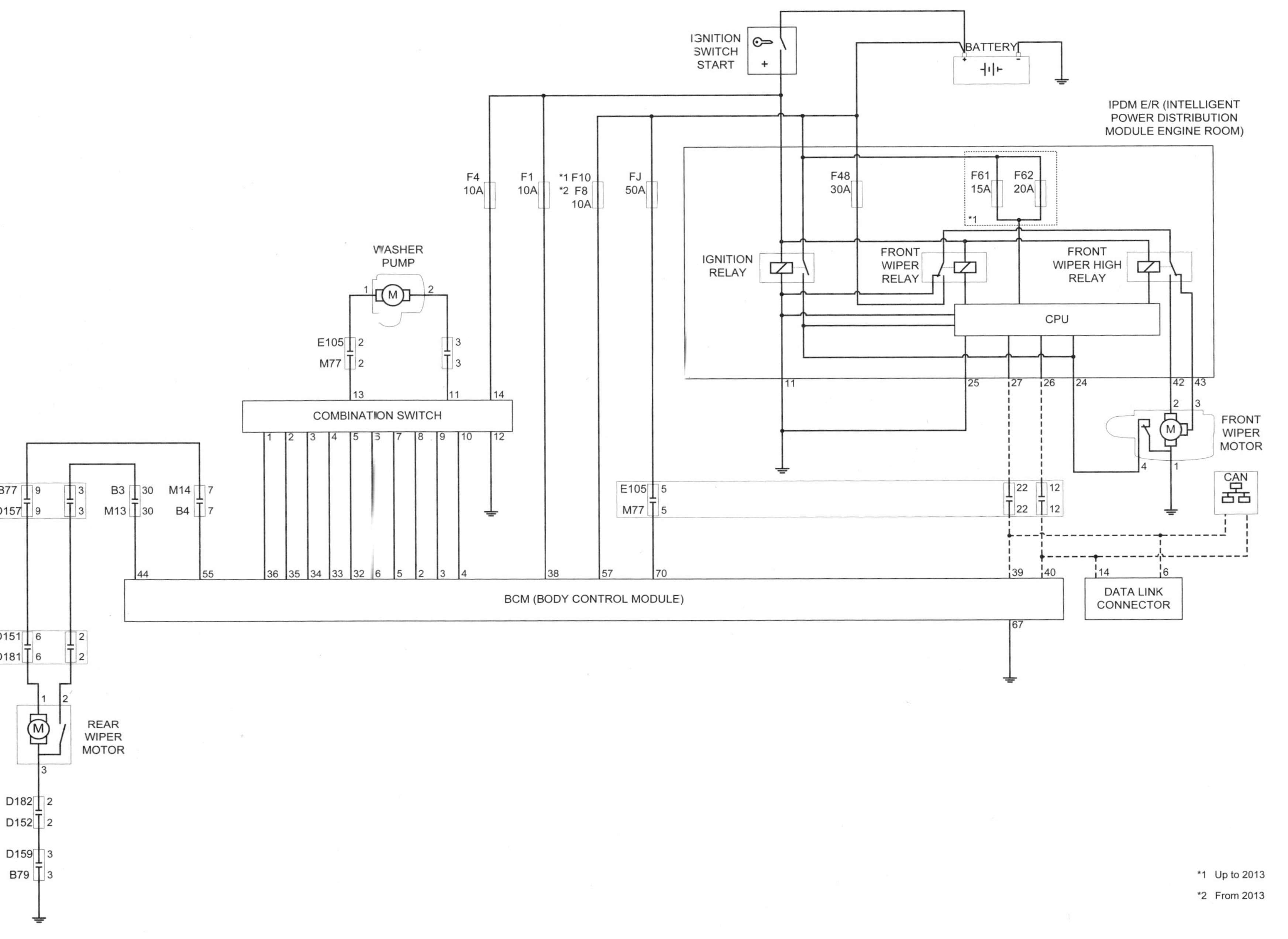

7. Wiper and washer systems

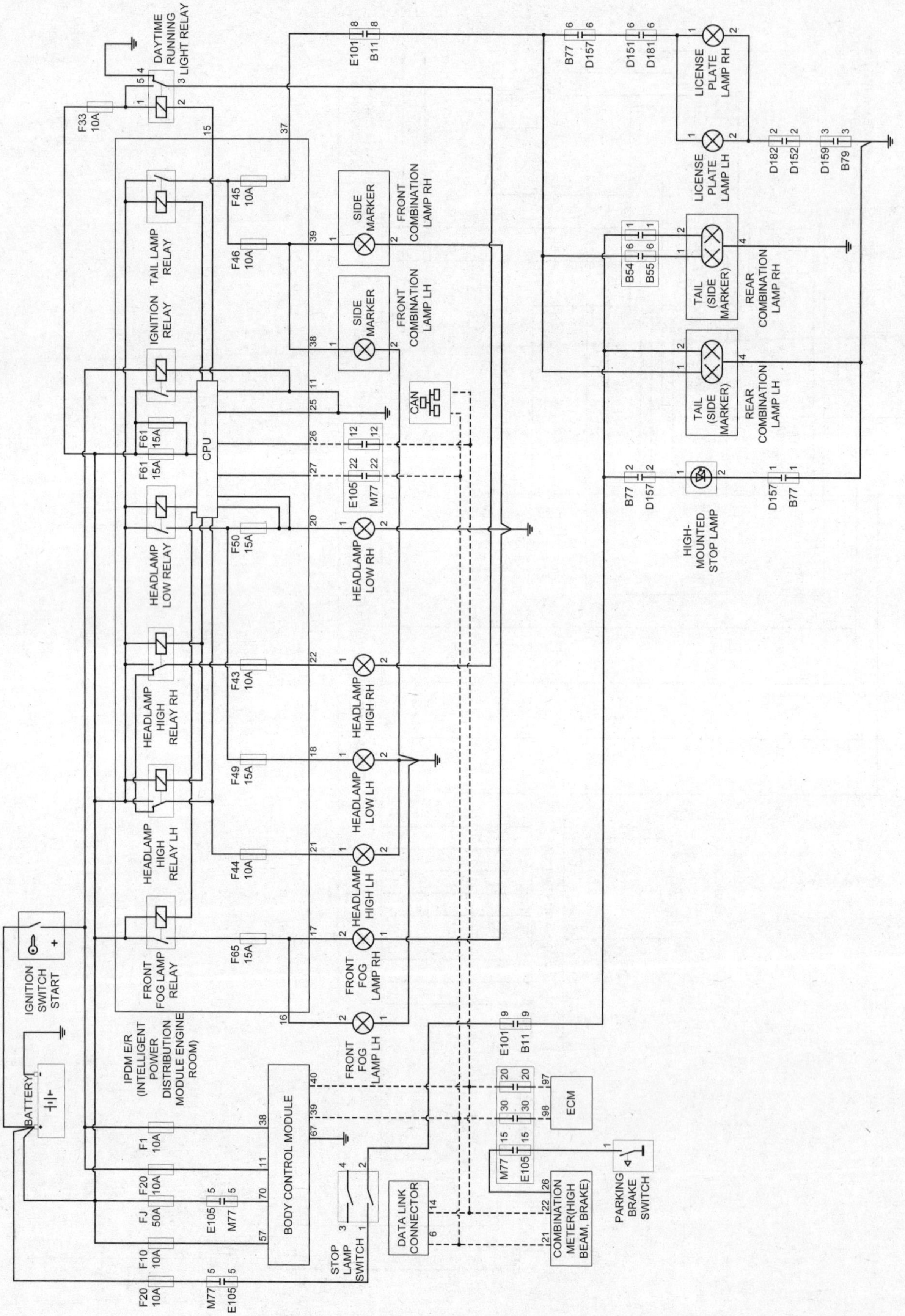

8. Exterior lighting system (daytime running lights/brake lights)

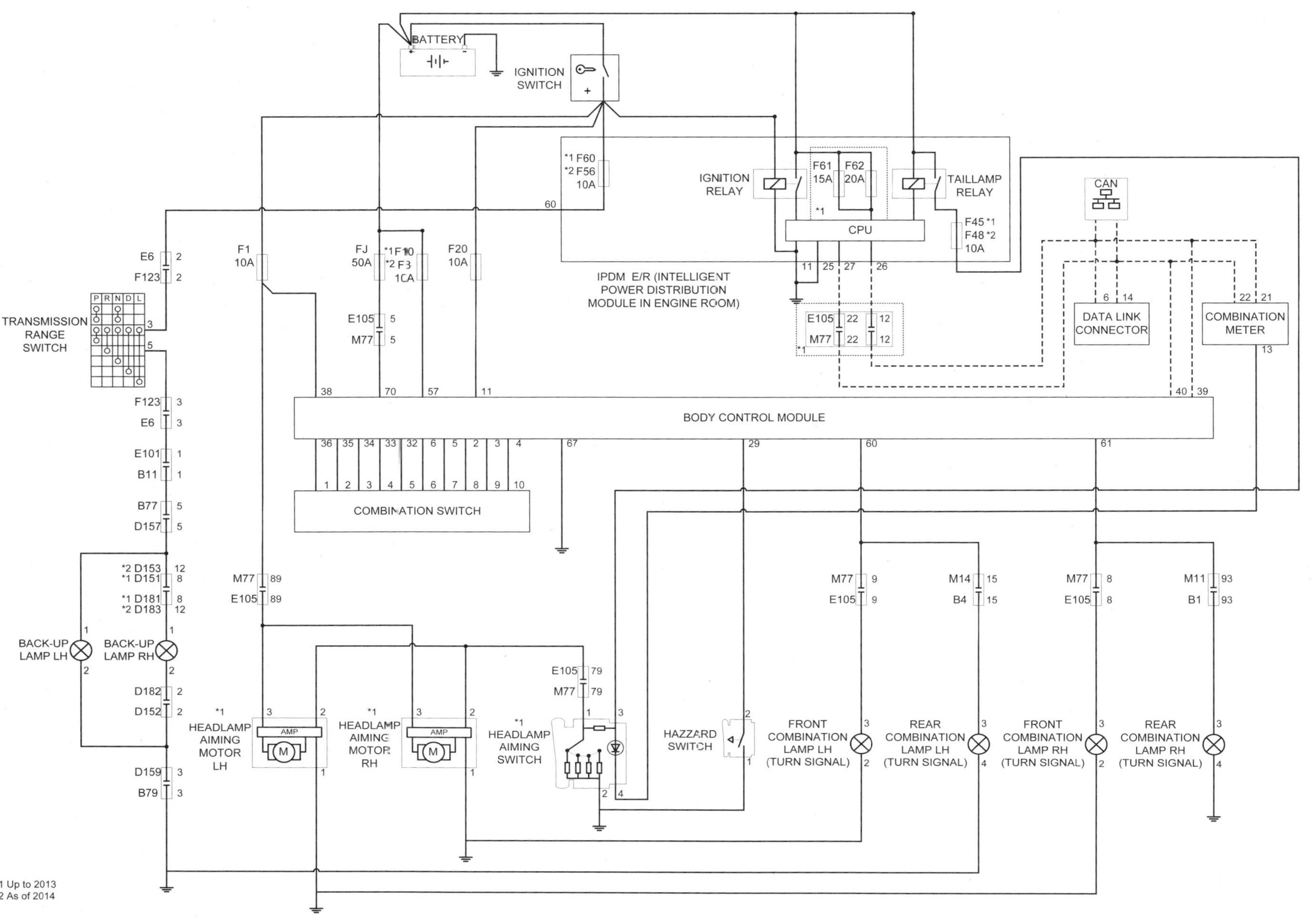

9. Exterior lighting system (turn signal/hazard warning/back-up lights/headlight aiming motors)

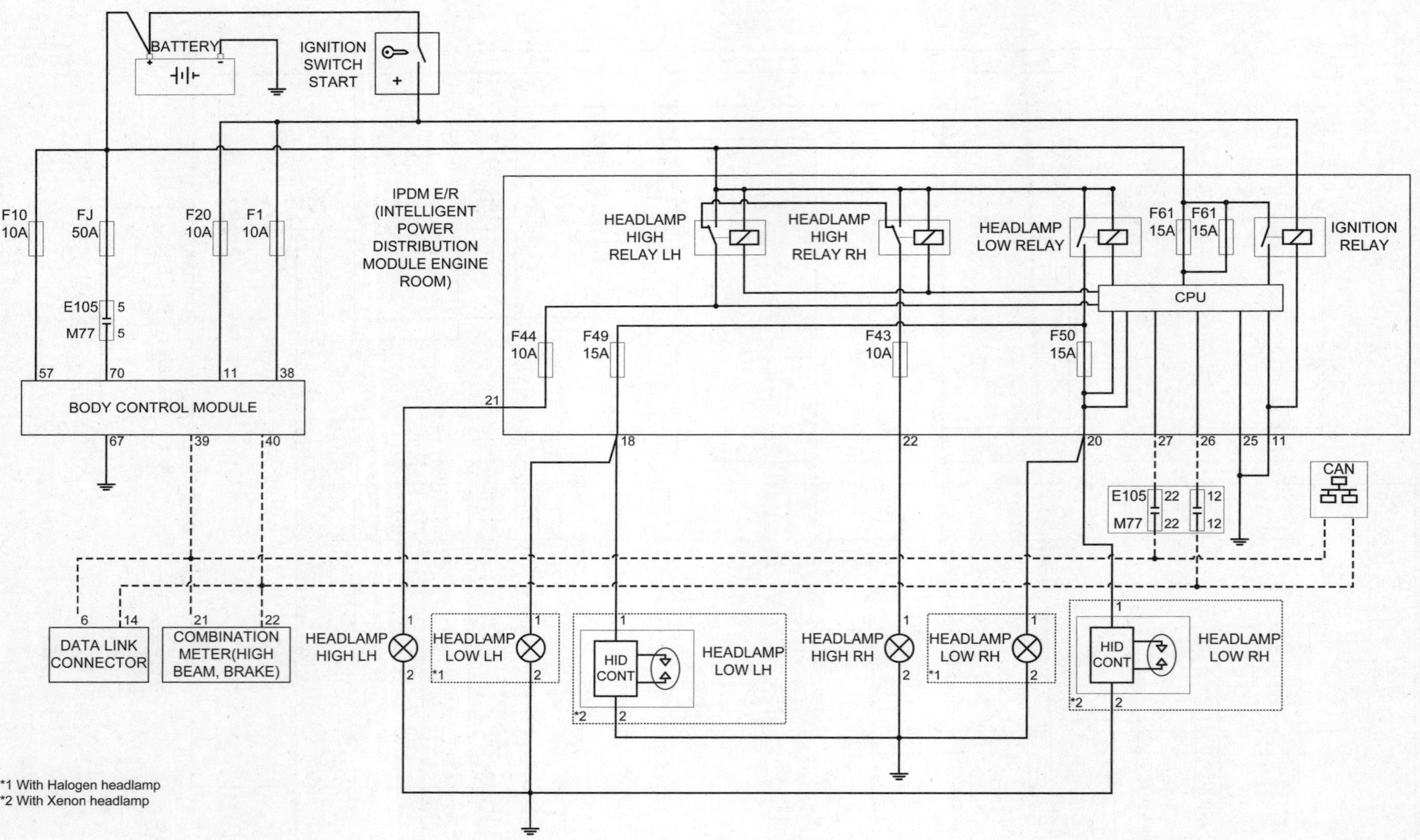

10 Headlight system

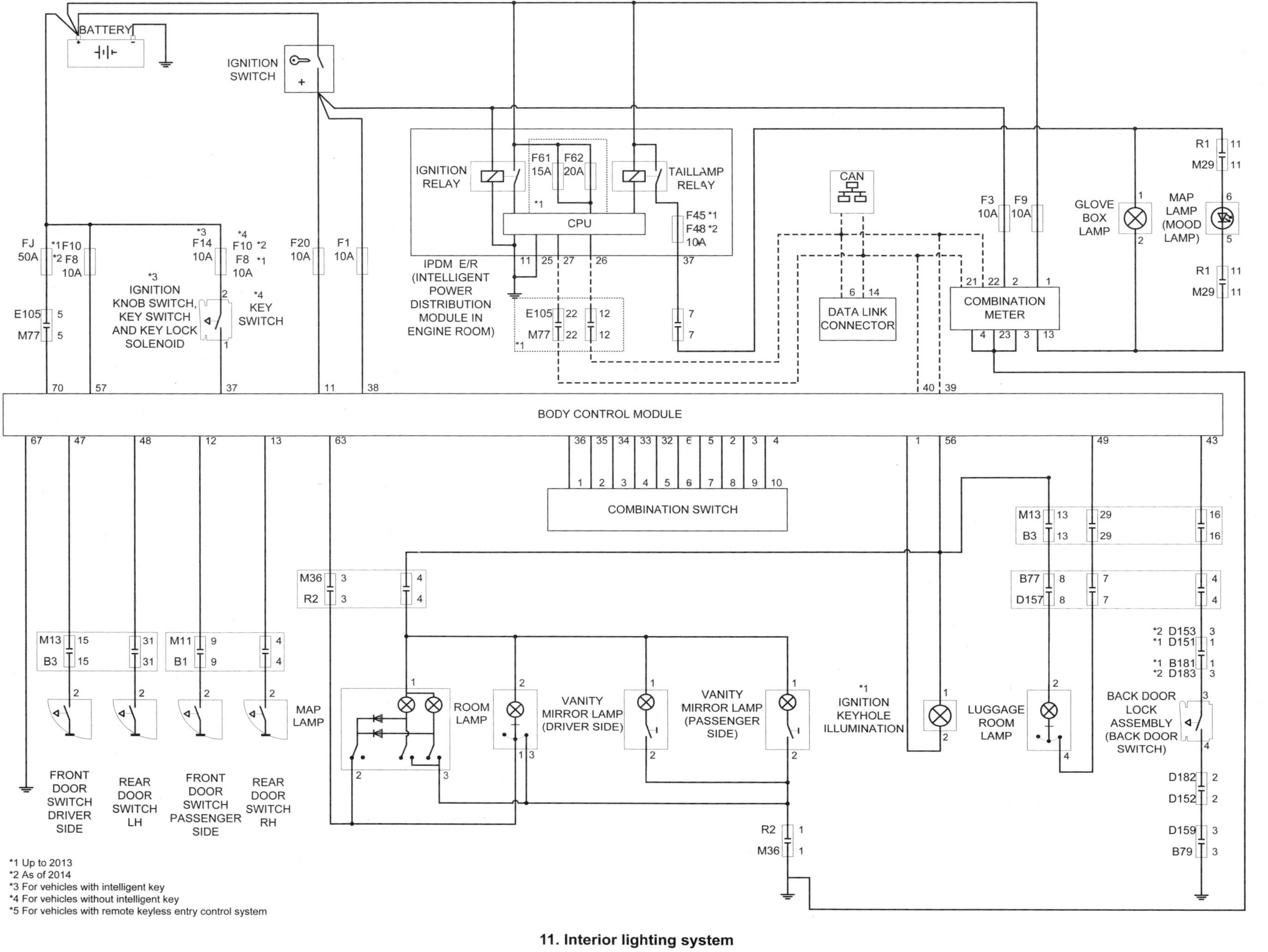

*1 Up to 2013
*2 As of 2014
*3 For vehicles with intelligent key
*4 For vehicles without intelligent key
*5 For vehicles with remote keyless entry control system

11. Interior lighting system

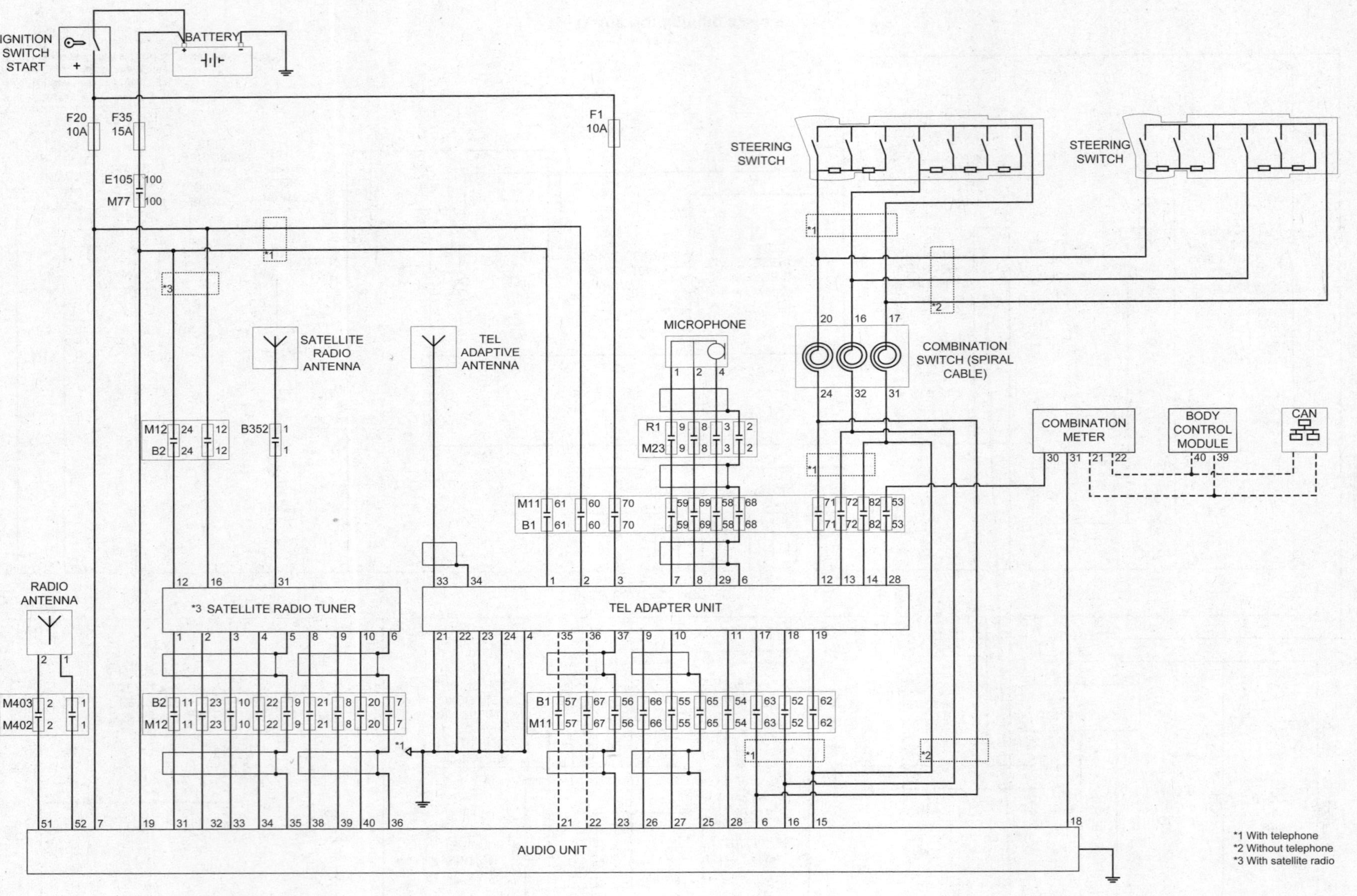

12. Audio system (Bose, satellite radio and telephone adapter - 2013 and earlier models/2014 and later Rogue Select models

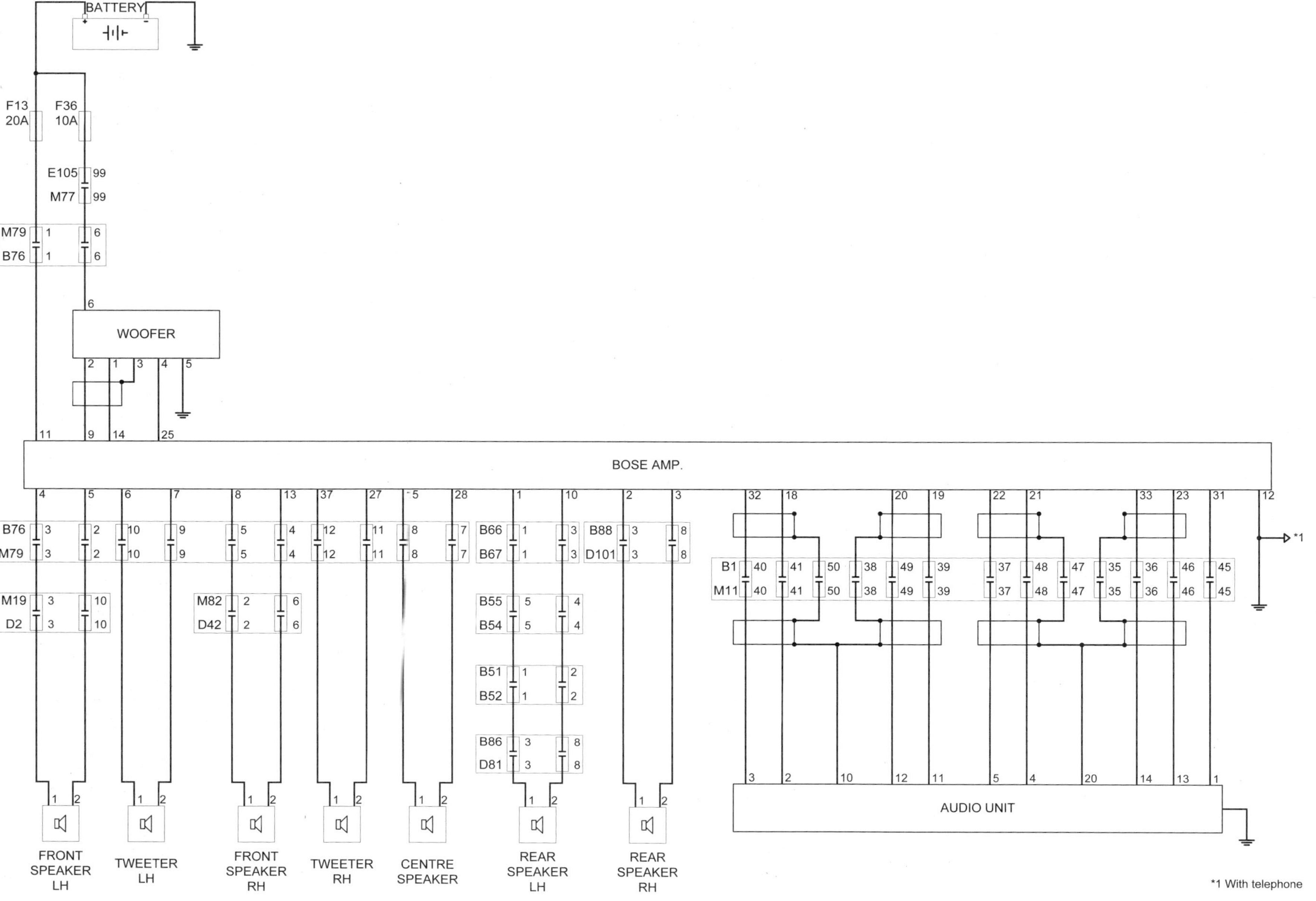

13. Audio system (Bose, amplifier unit) - 2013 and earlier models/2014 and later Rogue Select models

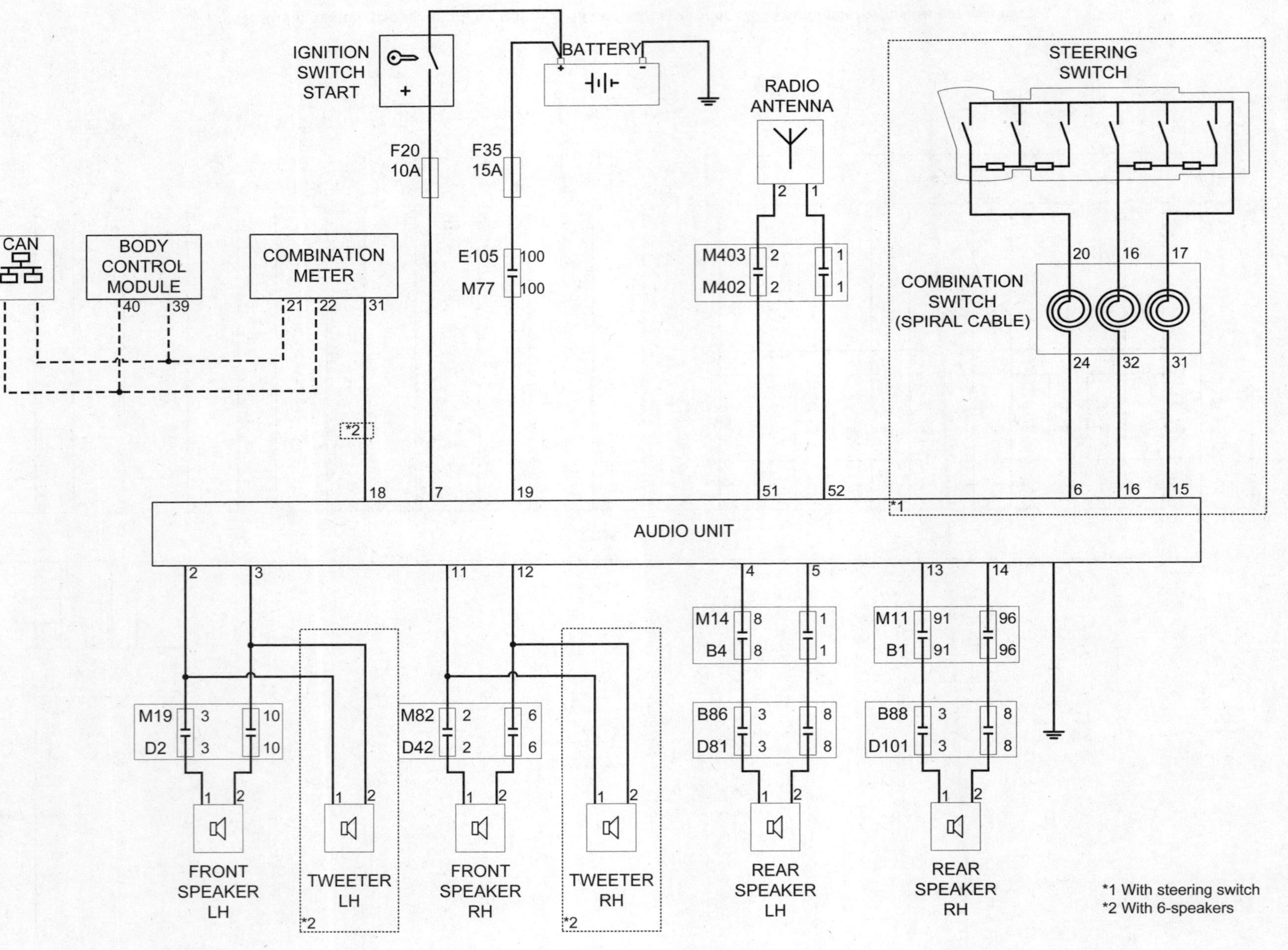

14. Audio system (base) - 2013 and earlier models/2014 and later Rogue Select models

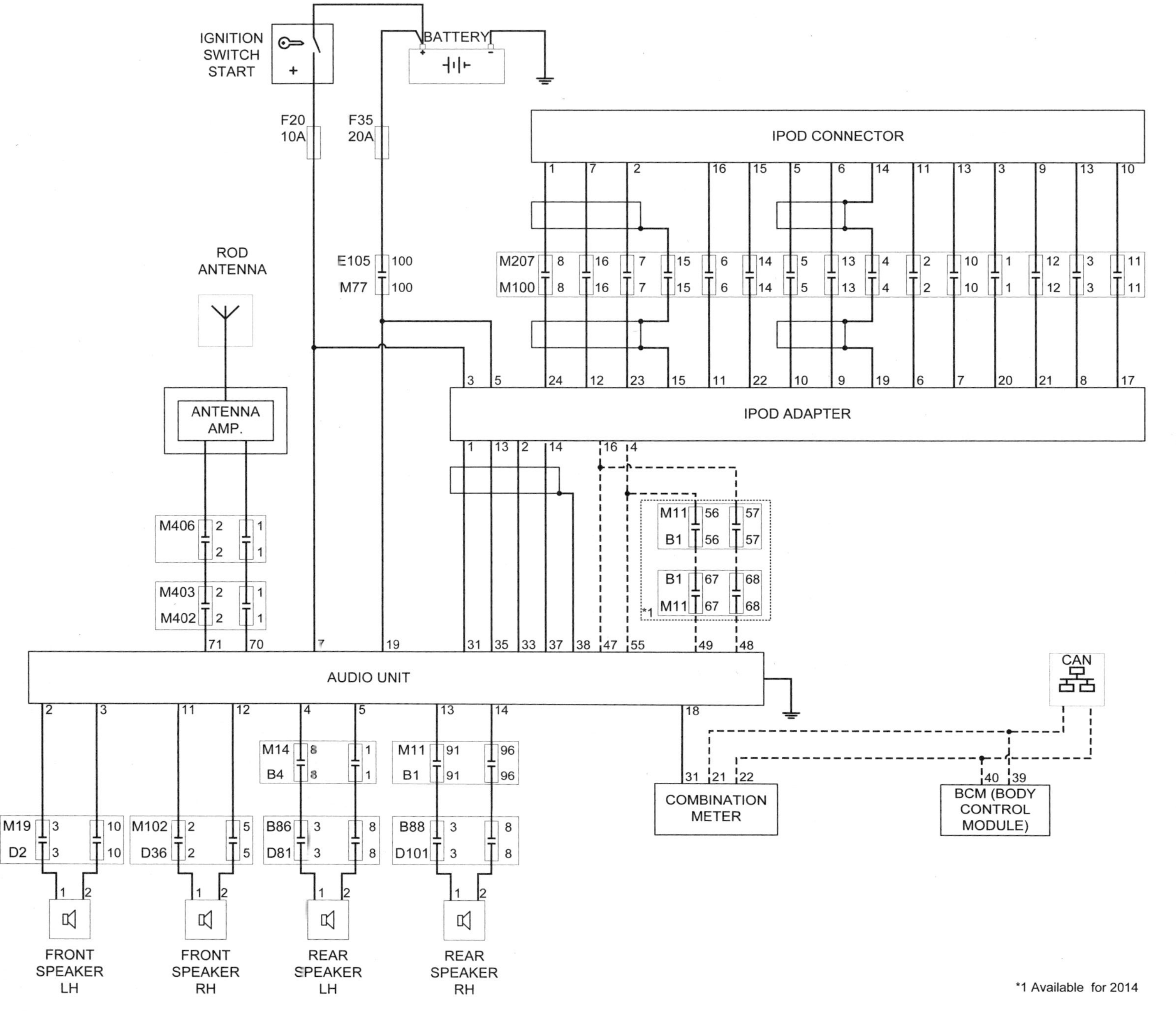

15. Audio system (base) - 2014 and later models (except Rogue Select)

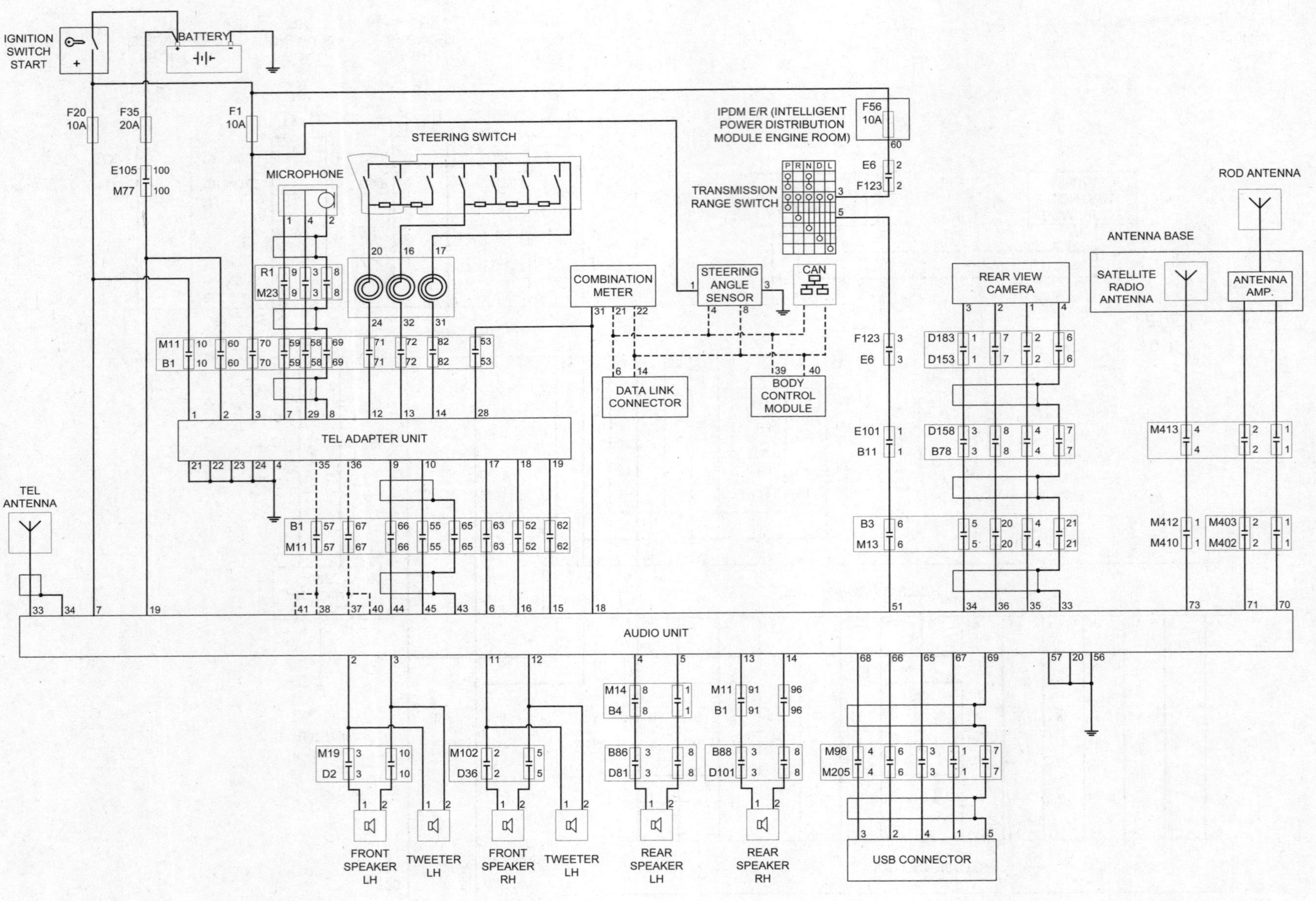

16. Audio system (display unit) - 2014 and later models (except Rogue Select)

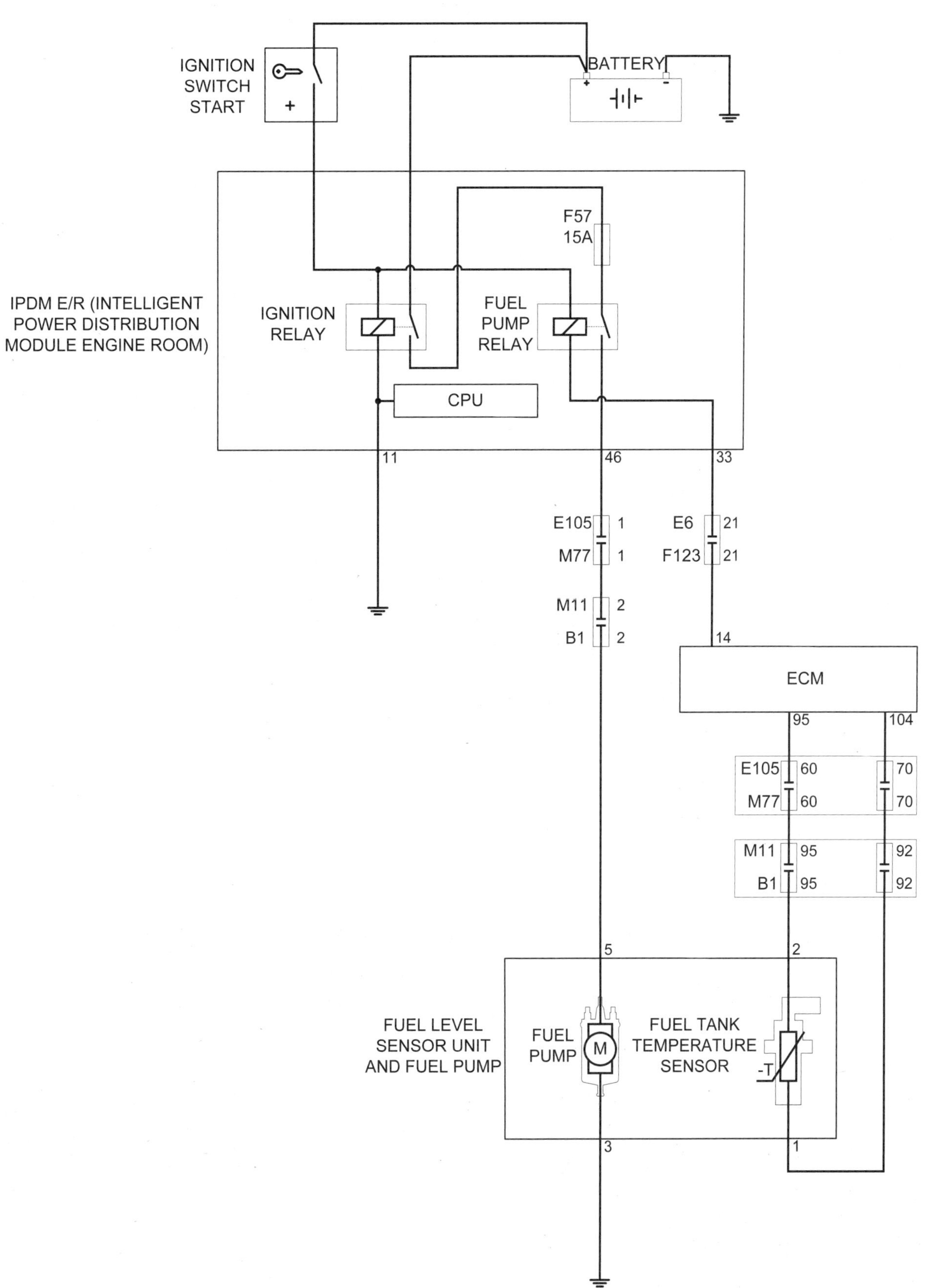

17. Fuel pump circuit

Notes

Index

C

D

E

F

G

H

I

T

U

V

W

Notes

Haynes Automotive Manuals

NOTE: *If you do not see a listing for your vehicle, please visit* **haynes.com** *for the latest product information and check out our* ***Online Manuals!***

ACURA

12020 **Integra** '86 thru '89 **& Legend** '86 thru '90
12021 **Integra** '90 thru '93 **& Legend** '91 thru '95
Integra '94 thru '00 - *see HONDA Civic (42025)*
MDX '01 thru '07 - *see HONDA Pilot (42037)*
12050 **Acura TL** all models '99 thru '08

AMC

14020 **Mid-size models** '70 thru '83
14025 **(Renault) Alliance & Encore** '83 thru '87

AUDI

15020 **4000** all models '80 thru '87
15025 **5000** all models '77 thru '83
15026 **5000** all models '84 thru '88
Audi A4 '96 thru '01 - *see VW Passat (96023)*
15030 **Audi A4** '02 thru '08

AUSTIN-HEALEY

Sprite - *see MG Midget (66015)*

BMW

18020 **3/5 Series** '82 thru '92
18021 **3-Series** incl. Z3 models '92 thru '98
18022 **3-Series** incl. Z4 models '99 thru '05
18023 **3-Series** '06 thru '14
18025 **320i all 4-cylinder models** '75 thru '83
18050 **1500 thru 2002** except Turbo '59 thru '77

BUICK

19010 **Buick Century** '97 thru '05
Century (front-wheel drive) - *see GM (38005)*
19020 **Buick, Oldsmobile & Pontiac Full-size (Front-wheel drive)** '85 thru '05
Buick Electra, LeSabre and Park Avenue; **Oldsmobile** Delta 88 Royale, Ninety Eight and Regency; **Pontiac** Bonneville
19025 **Buick, Oldsmobile & Pontiac Full-size (Rear wheel drive)** '70 thru '90
Buick Estate, Electra, LeSabre, Limited, **Oldsmobile** Custom Cruiser, Delta 88, Ninety-eight, **Pontiac** Bonneville, Catalina, Grandville, Parisienne
19027 **Buick LaCrosse** '05 thru '13
Enclave - *see GENERAL MOTORS (38001)*
Rainier - *see CHEVROLET (24072)*
Regal - *see GENERAL MOTORS (38010)*
Riviera - *see GENERAL MOTORS (38030, 38031)*
Roadmaster - *see CHEVROLET (24046)*
Skyhawk - *see GENERAL MOTORS (38015)*
Skylark - *see GENERAL MOTORS (38020, 38025)*
Somerset - *see GENERAL MOTORS (38025)*

CADILLAC

21015 **CTS & CTS-V** '03 thru '14
21030 **Cadillac Rear Wheel Drive** '70 thru '93
Cimarron - *see GENERAL MOTORS (38015)*
DeVille - *see GENERAL MOTORS (38031 & 38032)*
Eldorado - *see GENERAL MOTORS (38030)*
Fleetwood - *see GENERAL MOTORS (38031)*
Seville - *see GM (38030, 38031 & 38032)*

CHEVROLET

10305 **Chevrolet Engine Overhaul Manual**
24010 **Astro & GMC Safari Mini-vans** '85 thru '05
24013 **Aveo** '04 thru '11
24015 **Camaro V8** all models '70 thru '81
24016 **Camaro** all models '82 thru '92
24017 **Camaro & Firebird** '93 thru '02
Cavalier - *see GENERAL MOTORS (38016)*
Celebrity - *see GENERAL MOTORS (38005)*
24018 **Camaro** '10 thru '15
24020 **Chevelle, Malibu & El Camino** '69 thru '87
Cobalt - *see GENERAL MOTORS (38017)*
24024 **Chevette & Pontiac T1000** '76 thru '87
Citation - *see GENERAL MOTORS (38020)*
24027 **Colorado & GMC Canyon** '04 thru '12
24032 **Corsica & Beretta** all models '87 thru '96
24040 **Corvette** all V8 models '68 thru '82
24041 **Corvette** all models '84 thru '96
24042 **Corvette** all models '97 thru '13
24044 **Cruze** '11 thru '19
24045 **Full-size Sedans** Caprice, Impala, Biscayne, Bel Air & Wagons '69 thru '90
24046 **Impala SS & Caprice and Buick Roadmaster** '91 thru '96
Impala '00 thru '05 - *see LUMINA (24048)*
24047 **Impala & Monte Carlo** all models '06 thru '11
Lumina '90 thru '94 - *see GM (38010)*
24048 **Lumina & Monte Carlo** '95 thru '05
Lumina APV - *see GM (38035)*
24050 **Luv Pick-up** all 2WD & 4WD '72 thru '82
24051 **Malibu** '13 thru '19
24055 **Monte Carlo** all models '70 thru '88
Monte Carlo '95 thru '01 - *see LUMINA (24048)*
24059 **Nova** all V8 models '69 thru '79
24060 **Nova and Geo Prizm** '85 thru '92
24064 **Pick-ups** '67 thru '87 - Chevrolet & GMC
24065 **Pick-ups** '88 thru '98 - Chevrolet & GMC
24066 **Pick-ups** '99 thru '06 - Chevrolet & GMC
24067 **Chevrolet Silverado & GMC Sierra** '07 thru '14
24068 **Chevrolet Silverado & GMC Sierra** '14 thru '19
24070 **S-10 & S-15 Pick-ups** '82 thru '93, **Blazer & Jimmy** '83 thru '94,
24071 **S-10 & Sonoma Pick-ups** '94 thru '04, including **Blazer, Jimmy & Hombre**
24072 **Chevrolet TrailBlazer, GMC Envoy & Oldsmobile Bravada** '02 thru '09
24075 **Sprint** '85 thru '88 **& Geo Metro** '89 thru '01
24080 **Vans - Chevrolet & GMC** '68 thru '96
24081 **Chevrolet Express & GMC Savana** Full-size Vans '96 thru '19

CHRYSLER

10310 **Chrysler Engine Overhaul Manual**
25015 **Chrysler Cirrus, Dodge Stratus, Plymouth Breeze** '95 thru '00
25020 **Full-size Front-Wheel Drive** '88 thru '93
K-Cars - *see DODGE Aries (30008)*
Laser - *see DODGE Daytona (30030)*
25025 **Chrysler LHS, Concorde, New Yorker, Dodge** Intrepid, **Eagle** Vision, '93 thru '97
25026 **Chrysler LHS, Concorde, 300M, Dodge** Intrepid, '98 thru '04
25027 **Chrysler 300** '05 thru '18, **Dodge Charger** '06 thru '18, **Magnum** '05 thru '08 **& Challenger** '08 thru '18
25030 **Chrysler & Plymouth Mid-size** front wheel drive '82 thru '95
Rear-wheel Drive - *see Dodge (30050)*
25035 **PT Cruiser** all models '01 thru '10
25040 **Chrysler Sebring** '95 thru '06, **Dodge Stratus** '01 thru '06 **& Dodge Avenger** '95 thru '00
25041 **Chrysler Sebring** '07 thru '10, **200** '11 thru '17 **Dodge Avenger** '08 thru '14

DATSUN

28005 **200SX** all models '80 thru '83
28012 **240Z, 260Z & 280Z** Coupe '70 thru '78
28014 **280ZX** Coupe & 2+2 '79 thru '83
300ZX - *see NISSAN (72010)*
28018 **510 & PL521 Pick-up** '68 thru '73
28020 **510** all models '78 thru '81
28022 **620 Series Pick-up** all models '73 thru '79
720 Series Pick-up - *see NISSAN (72030)*

DODGE

400 & 600 - *see CHRYSLER (25030)*
30008 **Aries & Plymouth Reliant** '81 thru '89
30010 **Caravan & Plymouth Voyager** '84 thru '95
30011 **Caravan & Plymouth Voyager** '96 thru '02
30012 **Challenger & Plymouth Sapporro** '78 thru '83
30013 **Caravan, Chrysler Voyager & Town & Country** '03 thru '07
30014 **Grand Caravan & Chrysler Town & Country** '08 thru '18
30016 **Colt & Plymouth Champ** '78 thru '87
30020 **Dakota Pick-ups** all models '87 thru '96
30021 **Durango** '98 & '99 **& Dakota** '97 thru '99
30022 **Durango** '00 thru '03 **& Dakota** '00 thru '04
30023 **Durango** '04 thru '09 **& Dakota** '05 thru '11
30025 **Dart, Demon, Plymouth Barracuda, Duster & Valiant** 6-cylinder models '67 thru '76
30030 **Daytona & Chrysler Laser** '84 thru '89
Intrepid - *see CHRYSLER (25025, 25026)*
30034 **Neon** all models '95 thru '99
30035 **Omni & Plymouth Horizon** '78 thru '90
30036 **Dodge & Plymouth Neon** '00 thru '05
30040 **Pick-ups** full-size models '74 thru '93
30042 **Pick-ups** full-size models '94 thru '08
30043 **Pick-ups** full-size models '09 thru '18
30045 **Ram 50/D50 Pick-ups & Raider and Plymouth Arrow Pick-ups** '79 thru '93
30050 **Dodge/Plymouth/Chrysler** RWD '71 thru '89
30055 **Shadow & Plymouth Sundance** '87 thru '94
30060 **Spirit & Plymouth Acclaim** '89 thru '95
30065 **Vans - Dodge & Plymouth** '71 thru '03

EAGLE

Talon - *see MITSUBISHI (68030, 68031)*
Vision - *see CHRYSLER (25025)*

FIAT

34010 **124 Sport Coupe & Spider** '68 thru '78
34025 **X1/9** all models '74 thru '80

FORD

10320 **Ford Engine Overhaul Manual**
10355 **Ford Automatic Transmission Overhaul**
11500 **Mustang '64-1/2 thru '70 Restoration Guide**
36004 **Aerostar Mini-vans** all models '86 thru '97
36006 **Contour & Mercury Mystique** '95 thru '00
36008 **Courier Pick-up** all models '72 thru '82
36012 **Crown Victoria & Mercury Grand Marquis** '88 thru '11
36014 **Edge** '07 thru '19 **& Lincoln MKX** '07 thru '18
36016 **Escort & Mercury Lynx** all models '81 thru '90
36020 **Escort & Mercury Tracer** '91 thru '02
36022 **Escape** '01 thru '17, **Mazda Tribute** '01 thru '11, **& Mercury Mariner** '05 thru '11
36024 **Explorer & Mazda Navajo** '91 thru '01
36025 **Explorer & Mercury Mountaineer** '02 thru '10
36026 **Explorer** '11 thru '17
36028 **Fairmont & Mercury Zephyr** '78 thru '83
36030 **Festiva & Aspire** '88 thru '97
36032 **Fiesta** all models '77 thru '80
36034 **Focus** all models '00 thru '11
36035 **Focus** '12 thru '14
36045 **Fusion** '06 thru '14 **& Mercury Milan** '06 thru '11
36048 **Mustang V8** all models '64-1/2 thru '73
36049 **Mustang II** 4-cylinder, V6 & V8 models '74 thru '78
36050 **Mustang & Mercury Capri** '79 thru '93
36051 **Mustang** all models '94 thru '04
36052 **Mustang** '05 thru '14
36054 **Pick-ups & Bronco** '73 thru '79
36058 **Pick-ups & Bronco** '80 thru '96
36059 **F-150** '97 thru '03, **Expedition** '97 thru '17, **F-250** '97 thru '99, **F-150 Heritage** '04 **& Lincoln Navigator** '98 thru '17
36060 **Super Duty Pick-ups & Excursion** '99 thru '10
36061 **F-150** full-size '04 thru '14
36062 **Pinto & Mercury Bobcat** '75 thru '80
36063 **F-150** full-size '15 thru '17
36064 **Super Duty Pick-ups** '11 thru '16
36066 **Probe** all models '89 thru '92
Probe '93 thru '97 - *see MAZDA 626 (61042)*
36070 **Ranger & Bronco II** gas models '83 thru '92
36071 **Ranger** '93 thru '11 **& Mazda Pick-ups** '94 thru '09
36074 **Taurus & Mercury Sable** '86 thru '95
36075 **Taurus & Mercury Sable** '96 thru '07
36076 **Taurus** '08 thru '14, **Five Hundred** '05 thru '07, **Mercury Montego** '05 thru '07 **& Sable** '08 thru '09
36078 **Tempo & Mercury Topaz** '84 thru '94
36082 **Thunderbird & Mercury Cougar** '83 thru '88
36086 **Thunderbird & Mercury Cougar** '89 thru '97
36090 **Vans** all V8 Econoline models '69 thru '91
36094 **Vans** full size '92 thru '14
36097 **Windstar** '95 thru '03, **Freestar & Mercury Monterey Mini-van** '04 thru '07

GENERAL MOTORS

10360 **GM Automatic Transmission Overhaul**
38001 **GMC Acadia** '07 thru '16, **Buick Enclave** '08 thru '17, **Saturn Outlook** '07 thru '10 **& Chevrolet Traverse** '09 thru '17
38005 **Buick Century, Chevrolet Celebrity, Oldsmobile Cutlass Ciera & Pontiac 6000** all models '82 thru '96
38010 **Buick Regal** '88 thru '04, **Chevrolet Lumina** '88 thru '04, **Oldsmobile Cutlass Supreme** '88 thru '97 **& Pontiac Grand Prix** '88 thru '07
38015 **Buick Skyhawk, Cadillac Cimarron, Chevrolet Cavalier, Oldsmobile Firenza, Pontiac J-2000 & Sunbird** '82 thru '94
38016 **Chevrolet Cavalier & Pontiac Sunfire** '95 thru '05
38017 **Chevrolet Cobalt** '05 thru '10, **HHR** '06 thru '11, **Pontiac G5** '07 thru '09, **Pursuit** '05 thru '06 **& Saturn ION** '03 thru '07
38020 **Buick Skylark, Chevrolet Citation, Oldsmobile Omega, Pontiac Phoenix** '80 thru '85
38025 **Buick Skylark** '86 thru '98, **Somerset** '85 thru '87, **Oldsmobile Achieva** '92 thru '98, **Calais** '85 thru '91, **& Pontiac Grand Am** all models '85 thru '98
38026 **Chevrolet Malibu** '97 thru '03, **Classic** '04 thru '05, **Oldsmobile Alero** '99 thru '03, **Cutlass** '97 thru '00, **& Pontiac Grand Am** '99 thru '03
38027 **Chevrolet Malibu** '04 thru '12, **Pontiac G6** '05 thru '10 **& Saturn Aura** '07 thru '10
38030 **Cadillac Eldorado, Seville, Oldsmobile Toronado & Buick Riviera** '71 thru '85
38031 **Cadillac Eldorado, Seville, DeVille, Fleetwood, Oldsmobile Toronado & Buick Riviera** '86 thru '93
38032 **Cadillac DeVille** '94 thru '05, **Seville** '92 thru '04 **& Cadillac DTS** '06 thru '10
38035 **Chevrolet Lumina APV, Oldsmobile Silhouette & Pontiac Trans Sport** all models '90 thru '96
38036 **Chevrolet Venture** '97 thru '05, **Oldsmobile Silhouette** '97 thru '04, **Pontiac Trans Sport** '97 thru '98 **& Montana** '99 thru '05
38040 **Chevrolet Equinox** '05 thru '17, **GMC Terrain** '10 thru '17 **& Pontiac Torrent** '06 thru '09

GEO

Metro - *see CHEVROLET Sprint (24075)*
Prizm - *'85 thru '92 see CHEVY (24060), '93 thru '02 see TOYOTA Corolla (92036)*
40030 **Storm** all models '90 thru '93
Tracker - *see SUZUKI Samurai (90010)*

(Continued on other side)

Haynes Automotive Manuals (continued)

NOTE: If you do not see a listing for your vehicle, please visit ***haynes.com*** *for the latest product information and check out our* ***Online Manuals!***

GMC

Acadia - *see GENERAL MOTORS (38001)*
Pick-ups - *see CHEVROLET (24027, 24068)*
Vans - *see CHEVROLET (24081)*

HONDA

42010 **Accord CVCC** all models '76 thru '83
42011 **Accord** all models '84 thru '89
42012 **Accord** all models '90 thru '93
42013 **Accord** all models '94 thru '97
42014 **Accord** all models '98 thru '02
42015 **Accord** '03 thru '12 **& Crosstour** '10 thru '14
42016 **Accord** '13 thru '17
42020 **Civic 1200** all models '73 thru '79
42021 **Civic 1300 & 1500 CVCC** '80 thru '83
42022 **Civic 1500 CVCC** all models '75 thru '79
42023 **Civic** all models '84 thru '91
42024 **Civic & del Sol** '92 thru '95
42025 **Civic** '96 thru '00, **CR-V** '97 thru '01
& Acura Integra '94 thru '00
42026 **Civic** '01 thru '11 **& CR-V** '02 thru '11
42027 **Civic** '12 thru '15 **& CR-V** '12 thru '16
42030 **Fit** '07 thru '13
42035 **Odyssey** all models '99 thru '10
Passport - *see ISUZU Rodeo (47017)*
42037 **Honda Pilot** '03 thru '08, **Ridgeline** '06 thru '14
& Acura MDX '01 thru '07
42040 **Prelude CVCC** all models '79 thru '89

HYUNDAI

43010 **Elantra** all models '96 thru '19
43015 **Excel & Accent** all models '86 thru '13
43050 **Santa Fe** all models '01 thru '12
43055 **Sonata** all models '99 thru '14

INFINITI

G35 '03 thru '08 - *see NISSAN 350Z (72011)*

ISUZU

Hombre - *see CHEVROLET S-10 (24071)*
47017 **Rodeo** '91 thru '02, **Amigo** '89 thru '94 & '98 thru '02
& Honda Passport '95 thru '02
47020 **Trooper** '84 thru '91 **& Pick-up** '81 thru '93

JAGUAR

49010 **XJ6** all 6-cylinder models '68 thru '86
49011 **XJ6** all models '88 thru '94
49015 **XJ12 & XJS** all 12-cylinder models '72 thru '85

JEEP

50010 **Cherokee, Comanche & Wagoneer Limited**
all models '84 thru '01
50011 **Cherokee** '14 thru '19
50020 **CJ** all models '49 thru '86
50025 **Grand Cherokee** all models '93 thru '04
50026 **Grand Cherokee** '05 thru '19
& Dodge Durango '11 thru '19
50029 **Grand Wagoneer & Pick-up** '72 thru '91
Grand Wagoneer '84 thru '91, Cherokee &
Wagoneer '72 thru '83, Pick-up '72 thru '88
50030 **Wrangler** all models '87 thru '17
50035 **Liberty** '02 thru '12 **& Dodge Nitro** '07 thru '11
50050 **Patriot & Compass** '07 thru '17

KIA

54050 **Optima** '01 thru '10
54060 **Sedona** '02 thru '14
54070 **Sephia** '94 thru '01, **Spectra** '00 thru '09,
Sportage '05 thru '20
54077 **Sorento** '03 thru '13

LEXUS

ES 300/330 - *see TOYOTA Camry (92007, 92008)*
ES 350 - *see TOYOTA Camry (92009)*
RX 300/330/350 - *see TOYOTA Highlander (92095)*

LINCOLN

MKX - *see FORD (36014)*
Navigator - *see FORD Pick-up (36059)*
59010 **Rear-Wheel Drive Continental** '70 thru '87,
Mark Series '70 thru '92 **& Town Car** '81 thru '10

MAZDA

61010 **GLC (rear-wheel drive)** '77 thru '83
61011 **GLC (front-wheel drive)** '81 thru '85
61012 **Mazda3** '04 thru '11
61015 **323 & Protogé** '90 thru '03
61016 **MX-5 Miata** '90 thru '14
61020 **MPV** all models '89 thru '98
Navajo - *see Ford Explorer (36024)*
61030 **Pick-ups** '72 thru '93
Pick-ups '94 thru '09 - *see Ford Ranger (36071)*
61035 **RX-7** all models '79 thru '85
61036 **RX-7** all models '86 thru '91
61040 **626 (rear-wheel drive)** all models '79 thru '82
61041 **626 & MX-6 (front-wheel drive)** '83 thru '92
61042 **626** '93 thru '01 **& MX-6/Ford Probe** '93 thru '02
61043 **Mazda6** '03 thru '13

MERCEDES-BENZ

63012 **123 Series Diesel** '76 thru '85
63015 **190 Series** 4-cylinder gas models '84 thru '88
63020 **230/250/280** 6-cylinder SOHC models '68 thru '72
63025 **280 123 Series** gas models '77 thru '81
63030 **350 & 450** all models '71 thru '80
63040 **C-Class:** C230/C240/C280/C320/C350 '01 thru '07

MERCURY

64200 **Villager & Nissan Quest** '93 thru '01
All other titles, see FORD Listing.

MG

66010 **MGB** Roadster & GT Coupe '62 thru '80
66015 **MG Midget, Austin Healey Sprite** '58 thru '80

MINI

67020 **Mini** '02 thru '13

MITSUBISHI

68020 **Cordia, Tredia, Galant, Precis & Mirage** '83 thru '93
68030 **Eclipse, Eagle Talon & Plymouth Laser** '90 thru '94
68031 **Eclipse** '95 thru '05 **& Eagle Talon** '95 thru '98
68035 **Galant** '94 thru '12
68040 **Pick-up** '83 thru '96 **& Montero** '83 thru '93

NISSAN

72010 **300ZX** all models including Turbo '84 thru '89
72011 **350Z & Infiniti G35** all models '03 thru '08
72015 **Altima** all models '93 thru '06
72016 **Altima** '07 thru '12
72020 **Maxima** all models '85 thru '92
72021 **Maxima** all models '93 thru '08
72025 **Murano** '03 thru '14
72030 **Pick-ups** '80 thru '97 **& Pathfinder** '87 thru '95
72031 **Frontier** '98 thru '04, **Xterra** '00 thru '04,
& Pathfinder '96 thru '04
72032 **Frontier & Xterra** '05 thru '14
72037 **Pathfinder** '05 thru '14
72040 **Pulsar** all models '83 thru '86
72042 **Roque** all models '08 thru '20
72050 **Sentra** all models '82 thru '94
72051 **Sentra & 200SX** all models '95 thru '06
72060 **Stanza** all models '82 thru '90
72070 **Titan pick-ups** '04 thru '10, **Armada** '05 thru '10
& Pathfinder Armada '04
72080 **Versa** all models '07 thru '19

OLDSMOBILE

73015 **Cutlass** V6 & V8 gas models '74 thru '88
For other OLDSMOBILE titles, see BUICK, CHEVROLET or GENERAL MOTORS listings.

PLYMOUTH

For PLYMOUTH titles, see DODGE listing.

PONTIAC

79008 **Fiero** all models '84 thru '88
79018 **Firebird** V8 models except Turbo '70 thru '81
79019 **Firebird** all models '82 thru '92
79025 **G6** all models '05 thru '09
79040 **Mid-size Rear-wheel Drive** '70 thru '87
Vibe '03 thru '10 - *see TOYOTA Corolla (92037)*
For other PONTIAC titles, see BUICK, CHEVROLET or GENERAL MOTORS listings.

PORSCHE

80020 **911** Coupe & Targa models '65 thru '89
80025 **914** all 4-cylinder models '69 thru '76
80030 **924** all models including Turbo '76 thru '82
80035 **944** all models including Turbo '83 thru '89

RENAULT

Alliance & Encore - *see AMC (14025)*

SAAB

84010 **900** all models including Turbo '79 thru '88

SATURN

87010 **Saturn** all S-series models '91 thru '02
Saturn Ion '03 thru '07- *see GM (38017)*
Saturn Outlook - *see GM (38001)*
87020 **Saturn L-series** all models '00 thru '04
87040 **Saturn VUE** '02 thru '09

SUBARU

89002 **1100, 1300, 1400 & 1600** '71 thru '79
89003 **1600 & 1800** 2WD & 4WD '80 thru '94
89080 **Impreza** '02 thru '11, **WRX** '02 thru '14,
& WRX STI '04 thru '14
89100 **Legacy** all models '90 thru '99
89101 **Legacy & Forester** '00 thru '09
89102 **Legacy** '10 thru '16 **& Forester** '12 thru '16

SUZUKI

90010 **Samurai/Sidekick & Geo Tracker** '86 thru '01

TOYOTA

92005 **Camry** all models '83 thru '91
92006 **Camry** '92 thru '96 **& Avalon** '95 thru '96
92007 **Camry, Avalon, Solara, Lexus ES 300** '97 thru '01
92008 **Camry, Avalon, Lexus ES 300/330** '02 thru '06
& Solara '02 thru '08
92009 **Camry, Avalon & Lexus ES 350** '07 thru '17
92015 **Celica Rear-wheel Drive** '71 thru '85
92020 **Celica Front-wheel Drive** '86 thru '99
92025 **Celica Supra** all models '79 thru '92
92030 **Corolla** all models '75 thru '79
92032 **Corolla** all rear-wheel drive models '80 thru '87
92035 **Corolla** all front-wheel drive models '84 thru '92
92036 **Corolla & Geo/Chevrolet Prizm** '93 thru '02
92037 **Corolla** '03 thru '19, **Matrix** '03 thru '14,
& Pontiac Vibe '03 thru '10
92040 **Corolla Tercel** all models '80 thru '82
92045 **Corona** all models '74 thru '82
92050 **Cressida** all models '78 thru '82
92055 **Land Cruiser** FJ40, 43, 45, 55 '68 thru '82
92056 **Land Cruiser** FJ60, 62, 80, FZJ80 '80 thru '96
92060 **Matrix** '03 thru '11 **& Pontiac Vibe** '03 thru '10
92065 **MR2** all models '85 thru '87
92070 **Pick-up** all models '69 thru '78
92075 **Pick-up** all models '79 thru '95
92076 **Tacoma** '95 thru '04, **4Runner** '96 thru '02
& T100 '93 thru '08
92077 **Tacoma** all models '05 thru '18
92078 **Tundra** '00 thru '06 **& Sequoia** '01 thru '07
92079 **4Runner** all models '03 thru '09
92080 **Previa** all models '91 thru '95
92081 **Prius** all models '01 thru '12
92082 **RAV4** all models '96 thru '12
92085 **Tercel** all models '87 thru '94
92090 **Sienna** all models '98 thru '10
92095 **Highlander** '01 thru '19
& Lexus RX330/330/350 '99 thru '19
92179 **Tundra** '07 thru '19 **& Sequoia** '08 thru '19

TRIUMPH

94007 **Spitfire** all models '62 thru '81
94010 **TR7** all models '75 thru '81

VW

96008 **Beetle & Karmann Ghia** '54 thru '79
96009 **New Beetle** '98 thru '10
96016 **Rabbit, Jetta, Scirocco & Pick-up**
gas models '75 thru '92 & Convertible '80 thru '92
96017 **Golf, GTI & Jetta** '93 thru '98, **Cabrio** '95 thru '02
96018 **Golf, GTI, Jetta** '99 thru '05
96019 **Jetta, Rabbit, GLI, GTI & Golf** '05 thru '11
96020 **Rabbit, Jetta & Pick-up** diesel '77 thru '84
96021 **Jetta** '11 thru '18 **& Golf** '15 thru '19
96023 **Passat** '98 thru '05 **& Audi A4** '96 thru '01
96030 **Transporter 1600** all models '68 thru '79
96035 **Transporter 1700, 1800 & 2000** '72 thru '79
96040 **Type 3 1500 & 1600** all models '63 thru '73
96045 **Vanagon Air-Cooled** all models '80 thru '83

VOLVO

97010 **120, 130 Series & 1800 Sports** '61 thru '73
97015 **140 Series** all models '66 thru '74
97020 **240 Series** all models '76 thru '93
97040 **740 & 760 Series** all models '82 thru '88
97050 **850 Series** all models '93 thru '97

TECHBOOK MANUALS

10205 **Automotive Computer Codes**
10206 **OBD-II & Electronic Engine Management**
10210 **Automotive Emissions Control Manual**
10215 **Fuel Injection Manual** '78 thru '85
10225 **Holley Carburetor Manual**
10230 **Rochester Carburetor Manual**
10305 **Chevrolet Engine Overhaul Manual**
10320 **Ford Engine Overhaul Manual**
10330 **GM and Ford Diesel Engine Repair Manual**
10331 **Duramax Diesel Engines** '01 thru '19
10332 **Cummins Diesel Engine Performance Manual**
10333 **GM, Ford & Chrysler Engine Performance Manual**
10334 **GM Engine Performance Manual**
10340 **Small Engine Repair Manual,** 5 HP & Less
10341 **Small Engine Repair Manual,** 5.5 thru 20 HP
10345 **Suspension, Steering & Driveline Manual**
10355 **Ford Automatic Transmission Overhaul**
10360 **GM Automatic Transmission Overhaul**
10405 **Automotive Body Repair & Painting**
10410 **Automotive Brake Manual**
10411 **Automotive Anti-lock Brake (ABS) Systems**
10420 **Automotive Electrical Manual**
10425 **Automotive Heating & Air Conditioning**
10435 **Automotive Tools Manual**
10445 **Welding Manual**
10450 **ATV Basics**

Over a 100 Haynes motorcycle manuals also available

10/22